D0719321

MARGARET THATCHER

MARGARET THATCHER

Volume One

THE GROCER'S DAUGHTER

John Campbell

JONATHAN CAPE
LONDON

Published by Jonathan Cape 2000

2 4 6 8 10 9 7 5 3 1

Copyright © John Campbell 2000

John Campbell has asserted his right under the
Copyright, Designs and Patents Act 1988 to be identified
as the author of this work

First published in Great Britain in 2000 by
Jonathan Cape
Random House, 20 Vauxhall Bridge Road,
London SW1V 2SA

Random House Australia (Pty) Limited
20 Alfred Street, Milsons Point, Sydney,
New South Wales 2061, Australia

Random House New Zealand Limited
18 Poland Road, Glenfield,
Auckland 10, New Zealand

Random House (Pty) Limited
Endulini, 5A Jubilee Road, Parktown 2193, South Africa

The Random House Group Limited Reg. No. 954009

A CIP catalogue record for this book
is available from the British Library

ISBN 0–224–04097–9

Papers used by The Random House Group Limited are natural,
recyclable products made from wood grown in sustainable forests;
the manufacturing processes conform to the environmental
regulations of the country of origin

Typeset by Deltatype Ltd, Birkenhead, Merseyside
Printed and bound in Great Britain by
Clays Ltd, St Ives PLC

For Alison, Robin and Paddy

Contents

Illustrations

CREDITS

The author and publishers are grateful to the following sources for permission to reproduce illustrations: Camera Press, plates 2, 3, 14, 15, 29, 30, 31; Hulton Getty, plates 4, 5, 9, 11, 18, 20, 21, 22, 26, 28, 32; Mirror Syndication, plate 19; PA News, plates 23, 24, 27, 33; Popperfoto, plates 17, 25; Topham Picturepoint, plates 6, 7, 8, 10, 12, 13, 16.

Acknowledgements

I never meant to write two volumes on Margaret Thatcher. The original intention was a single volume. But as the work progressed the scale of the undertaking became clear. Mrs Thatcher was not only Prime Minister for longer than any other holder of the office this century: she was a hyperactive and interventionist Prime Minister who was closely involved in practically everything that happened in Britain – and much that happened throughout the world – during the 1980s. Even where she was not directly responsible she nevertheless personified the decade, so that biography merges with contemporary history in the widest sense. The years 1979 to 1990 will always be the Thatcher years, and so far-reaching was the transformation of British politics and society that she wrought – or presided over – that we are still coming to terms with it today. Tony Blair is her legatee. Her premiership has already spawned an enormous literature – not only an unprecedented weight of ministerial and other memoirs, but whole books on every aspect of her government: monetarism and privatisation, the miners' strike and the poll tax, the Falklands, Westland and *Spycatcher*. All this and much more lies beyond the scope of the present volume, which attempts only to cover in greater detail than any previous biography Margaret Thatcher's astonishing yet determined rise to power. I still do not intend that the second volume should be too much longer than this one: that is, in total not much longer than my single-volume *Edward Heath*. But the sheer quantity of material to be absorbed by a single writer with no research assistance of any kind meant that the project was simply taking too long with nothing to show. I am very grateful to Dan Franklin of Jonathan Cape, first for keeping faith with the book over a very long haul and encouraging me when my stamina began to fail, and secondly for agreeing to split the work into two so that we could bring the first part out this year.

In the event I believe that this first volume stands very well on its own. The early career of any outstanding individual – including aspects which are in themselves quite trivial or mundane – offers a special fascination which can often be swamped by the great events which necessarily dominate the latter part of major biographies. I hope that my account of the formation of Margaret Thatcher's personality will gain from not being so swamped. Ideally one would have made the break in Mrs Thatcher's career in February 1975, when she suddenly and unexpectedly emerged into the spotlight as Prime Minister in waiting. That was the moment when her life and her prospects really changed: the next four years were essentially a period of preparation for the challenge that faced her in 1979. But such a split would have left this book too short, with too much ground to cover in the next. There was no practical option but to make the same division that Lady Thatcher herself made between her own two volumes of memoirs, *The Path to Power* and *The Downing Street Years*, though my perspective on the story is naturally a little different.

This is not an authorised biography: I have had no direct help or co-operation from Lady Thatcher, nor did I look for any. But neither is it altogether unauthorised: she has known from the beginning that I was writing it and has placed no obstacles in my way. Her office has responded helpfully to requests for information or the text of recent speeches; and she has not discouraged any of her friends, aides or former associates from talking to me. Above all, I am grateful for her permission to quote substantially, and without charge, from her memoirs. HarperCollins also allowed me to quote from Carol Thatcher's life of her father. I do regret, however, that neither Carol nor Lady Thatcher's sister, Muriel Cullen, was prepared to talk to me. Mrs Cullen in particular is the only person other than Margaret Thatcher herself who could tell more of the dynamics of the Roberts household than has been revealed to previous biographers and profile-writers. But she has never talked about her parents or her sister since 1975, and I quite understand that she was not going to make an exception for me.

I am grateful to a very large number of people who did agree to talk to me about their memories of Margaret Roberts at school, at Oxford, in Colchester and Dartford, or of their experience of working with the young Margaret Thatcher in Finchley, at Westminster, in the Ministry of Pensions and the Department of Education and as Leader of the Opposition. Most of these interviews were face to face, but a few were conducted by telephone. Sadly a number of those who spoke to me died before I could complete the book, but I am grateful to them all for their help. The following list includes only those whose testimony has contributed to Volume One; many more will be thanked in due course in Volume Two. For the moment I should like to record my gratitude to Lord Alport, Sir Kenneth Berrill, Sir Clive Bossom, Lord Carlisle, Lord Boyd-Carpenter, Sir Leon Brittan, Miss Sheila Browne, Miss Judy Campbell, Campbell Chambers, Paul Channon, Lord Cockfield, Lord Crickhowell, Dorothy Cooke, Clifford Dack, Mrs Jean Darmon, Eric Deakins, Lord Deedes, Mrs Sheila Diss, Peter Dodson, Sir Edward du Cann, Bill Elliott, Cllr Mrs Mary Fairhead, Philip Fell, Phyllis Fell, Sir George Gardiner, Prof. Sir Douglas Hague, Philip Halsey, Lord Harris of High Cross, Mrs Madeline Hellaby, Lord Holderness, Sir Michael Holt, John Hudson, Henry James, Lord Jenkin of Roding, Simon Jenkins, Rev. Nigel Jilson, Lord Joseph, Tom King MP, Mrs Marie Joliffe, Michael Kinchin-Smith, Lady Polly Lansdowne, Lord Marsh, Lord McAlpine, Peter Merriam, Brian MacArthur, Stuart McClure, Norris McWhirter, Sir Ronald Millar, Lord Moore of Lower Marsh, Sir John Nott, Mrs Joyce Parr, Sir Michael Partridge, Chris Patten, Sir William Pile, Mary Pratt, Mrs Christine Rathbone, Stephen Sherbourne, Dr Donald Southgate, Sir Kenneth Stowe, David Tanner, Cllr Victor Usher, Sir Douglas Wass, Sir Toby Weaver, Mrs Margaret Wickstead, Lord Wyatt, Lady Young and Lord Younger. If I have inadvertently omitted anyone from this list, I beg their forgiveness.

In addition, I am grateful to a number of other people who have written to me about various aspects of Mrs Thatcher's career, most notably Peter Carpenter, Bernard Crick, Harry French, John Julius Norwich, John Pardoe, Mrs Marjorie Sansbury and Clare Woodage.

I am also indebted to a large number of fellow-historians, journalists and friends, some for substantial help, others for casual but suggestive conversations. The following list is far from exhaustive, but I should particularly like to thank Dr Paul Addison, John Barnes, Janet Betts, Dr David Butler, Michael Cockerell, Dr Richard Cockett, Christopher Collins, Dr Alistair Cooke, Dr Philip Cowley, Michael Crick, Leslie Du Cane, Prof. Peter Hennessy, Mark Hollingsworth, Dr Rodney Lowe, Dr Martin Maw, Prof. John Ramsden, Tim Rayment, Dr Anthony Seldon, Phillip Whitehead and not least Hugo Young, the author of the best previous biography of Lady Thatcher, who was particularly helpful with regard to Margaret Roberts' school reports. I must also emphasise a special debt to Christopher Collins for his immense labour in editing OUP's recently-published CD-Rom of Margaret Thatcher's complete public statements. These, with accompanying material, run to fourteen million words. The CD-Rom, including transcripts of previously inaccessible material like radio broadcasts and TV interviews, appeared only just in time for me to use it for this volume – though the reader will see that I have made good use of Mrs Thatcher's frequent appearances on *Any Questions?* in the 1960s. But it will save an enormous amount of time and legwork in writing the second volume. Not only biographers but all historians of the 1980s will be indebted to Oxford University Press for putting this wonderful resource on disc.

I am grateful to James Walsh, director of the Conservative Policy Forum, for permission to quote from documents in the Conservative Party archive; and to Phillip Whitehead of Brook Associates Ltd. for permission to quote from interviews conducted for the television series *The Seventies* and *The Thatcher Factor*. I am particularly grateful to Dr David Butler for allowing me to see the interviews which he and Dennis Kavanagh conducted for the Nuffield studies of the 1974 and 1979 elections; and to Lord Walker and Chris Patten for allowing me to quote from Dr Butler's interviews with them. (Some other interviewees preferred to remain anonymous.) I should like to thank HarperCollins for allowing me to make a substantial number of quotations from Carol Thatcher's biography of her father Denis, *Below the Parapet*; and David Higham Associates for permission to quote from Barbara Castle's diary. If I have not thanked every author and publisher by name for a smaller number of shorter quotations I hope they will forgive me.

I owe a very special debt to Michael Honeybone for sharing with me his unrivalled knowledge of the history of Grantham in general and his research into Alfred Roberts' career in particular; for walking me around the town of Grantham, showing me the impressive interior of Finkin Street Methodist church, and introducing me to a number of local people who remember Alfred Roberts and his daughter. I have to thank both Michael and his wife Diana for reading early drafts of my first two chapters and saving me from several errors of geography and local history. At a late stage Michael also helped trace photographs for me at very short notice.

The fact that most women change their name on marriage makes the business of tracking down the contemporaries of a female subject much more difficult than it is when writing about a man. I am very grateful to Mrs Amanda Taylor, secretary of the KGGS Old Girls' society, for help in tracing school contemporaries of Margaret Roberts; and likewise to Liz Cooke for her help in tracing some of those who were at Somerville with her. I should like to thank John Whittingdale MP, at that time one of the two Conservative MPs for Colchester, for putting me in touch with current members of the Colchester Conservative Association who still remember Margaret Roberts' time as a Young Conservative in the town in 1948–9. Perhaps by the same token I can offer a small brickbat to Hartley Booth, the former MP for Finchley, and one or two others in the Finchley Conservative Association who did their best to prevent me talking to any of their older members whose memories went back to Mrs Thatcher's early years as their Member of Parliament, which they seemed to consider classified information. I am happy to say that they were not wholly successful, and that theirs was the only obstruction I encountered in writing this book. Perhaps they will reconsider in time for the second volume.

I should like to thank Tony Colwell, formerly of Jonathan Cape, for his searching but sensitive criticism of my typescript – particularly the later chapters – at times when I was losing faith in it; Howard Davies for his meticulous copy-editing of the text; and Lily Richards for her brilliant picture research. I am as always indebted to my agent, Bruce Hunter of David Higham Associates for his long-term support and encouragement. I am grateful to Jean Ross-Russell and Mary Zimmern for allowing me to use their houses last summer when I needed temporarily to escape the claustrophobic confines of my own study, and to Margaret Campbell for extending to me the peace and quiet of her house in Wiltshire. Above all I am grateful to my longsuffering wife Alison, who makes it all possible, my daughter Robin and my son Paddy for putting up with me for the last few years. If I suspect that Margaret Roberts cannot always have been the dutiful and submissive daughter she would have us believe she was, it is partly because I have strongminded teenagers of my own. Anyway, it is to them, my patient family, that this book is dedicated, in love and gratitude.

John Campbell
February 2000

1

Dutiful Daughter

THE iconography of Grantham is almost as familiar as the manger in Bethlehem: Alfred Roberts' famous corner shop, with the Great North Road thundering past the window; the sides of bacon hanging in the back, the smell of baking bread, young Margaret weighing out the sugar; the saintly father, the homely mother, Victorian values – thrift, temperance, good housekeeping, patriotism and duty.

It is all perfectly true, so far as it goes. But it is not the whole truth. It is in fact a supremely successful exercise in image management. When, in February 1975, the former Secretary of State for Education sprang from under the noses of the party establishment to snatch the Conservative leadership from Edward Heath, remarkably little was known about her origins. Since getting into Parliament in 1959 she had been happy to present herself as the archetypal Tory lady in a hat and pearls, quintessentially southern and suburban. She had a rich businessman husband, sent her children to the most expensive public schools, lived in Chelsea and represented Finchley. To be a candidate for national leadership in the supposedly classless 1970s, however, it was urgently necessary to discover some less privileged roots: Heath, after all, was the son of a carpenter.

Unlike the Old Etonian Douglas Hurd in 1990 – whose efforts to claim that his father was merely a tenant farmer brought him only ridicule – Mrs Thatcher was genuinely able to do so. 'You can forget all that nonsense about "defence of privilege",' she announced. 'I had precious little "privilege" in my early years.'[1] The journalists who descended on Grantham to investigate were surprised to find that it was true. Within weeks of her defeating Heath, Alfred Roberts' grocery had become a British equivalent of Lincoln's log cabin; and by the time she became Prime Minister four years later

Alderman Roberts himself was mythologised as a sort of small-town Socrates.

Before the end of 1975 there were already three biographies – by George Gardiner, Ernle Money and Russell Lewis (respectively a Tory MP, a recently defeated MP and the former director of the Conservative Political Centre). Each did his bit to establish and elaborate the legend. What began as a simple effort to correct her southern image quickly became an inspired parable for spreading her political message: the corner shop a model for the prudent management of the national economy, Alfred Roberts' pious individualism the foundation of Britain's political regeneration. 'I owe almost everything to my father,' she insisted.[2] At the height of her power in the mid-1980s the historian Peter Hennessy remarked that the country was ruled by Alderman Roberts from beyond the grave.

The problem with this filial iconography is that it originates with Mrs Thatcher herself. From those early interviews with her first biographers through later television confessionals to the final authorised version in her memoirs, she has successfully controlled the presentation of her life story as an improving morality play, illustrating the rewards – personal and national – of hard work, self-reliance, family values and practical Christianity. The first drafts by Gardiner, Lewis and Money were followed over the next fifteen years by a dozen more biographies and hundreds of essays, articles and features. They range from the adulatory through the gossipy to the satirical and the defamatory; but they have all, admiring and hostile alike, essentially accepted the outline of the story as she has told it.

Of course Margaret Thatcher, like everyone else, was formed by her early experience: by her parents, by her childhood and by her education, in and out of school. The influence of her father – and her mother and grandmother – was unquestionably real and lasting. Like most people, however, she also outgrew her family, escaped and transcended it. From the moment she left home Margaret Roberts shook off her family more thoroughly and determinedly than most young people. She got as far away from Grantham as possible and made a new life for herself in the softer south. It was only thirty years later – when both her parents were dead – that she revisited her childhood and recreated it in glowing colours as the foundation of everything she believed in and the source of her political success.

Her picture is too idealised to be wholly true. No child – certainly not one as clever and strong-willed as the young Margaret Roberts –

could possibly have been as dutiful, submissive and receptive to her
father's teaching as she portrays herself. Her account of the strict but
happy childhood above the shop may explain some of her formative
attitudes and mature convictions. It may explain her addiction to
work, her conscientiousness, her interest in politics. But it does not
explain the exceptional single-mindedness that took her to Downing
Street. It does not explain her aggression; or her anger.

A former town clerk once described Grantham as 'a narrow town,
built on a narrow street and inhabited by narrow people'.[3] It is a
plain, no-frills sort of place, brick-built and low-lying: at first sight a
typical East Midlands town, once dubbed by the *Sun* 'the most
boring town in Britain'.[4] Yet Grantham was once more than this.
Look closer and it is a palimpsest of English history. Incorporated in
1463, it was a mediaeval market town, serving a wide and fertile
hinterland between Nottingham twenty miles to the west, Newark
and Sleaford to the north, Stamford and Melton Mowbray to the
south. Kings stopped there on their journeys north: Richard III
signed Buckingham's death warrant in the Angel Hotel, which still
dominates the bottleneck in the middle of the High Street. St
Wulfram's church boasts one of the tallest spires in England: the
Victorian critic John Ruskin used to doff his hat to it when he passed
through by train, and invited his fellow-travellers to do the same.
England's greatest scientist, Isaac Newton, was born seven miles
south of the town in 1642, and educated at the grammar school. His
statue stands outside the town hall, and nowadays a faceless concrete
shopping centre bears his name. But that is all. 'Newton's Grantham'
entirely lacks the tourist appeal of Shakespeare's Stratford, Hardy's
Dorchester or Dr Johnson's Lichfield.

The reason is that industrialisation overlaid the market town with
new layers of economic evolution. There are still some fine houses,
away from the main street; but in the 1840s Grantham became a
railway town. Just too close to London, it lost out to Darlington as
the main locomotive works on the east coast line, but compensated
by becoming a major engineering centre. By the beginning of the
twentieth century, three large iron works were established at the
southern end of the town, around Spittlegate, making steam engines,
agricultural machinery (including the first caterpillar-track vehicles)
and later armaments. In the Second World War Grantham's
munitions factories made the town a target for German bombers.
Today all the heavy industry has gone. Some of the deserted works
stood until 1998, empty brick catacombs mocked by the tacky

prefabs of modern development: a memorial to the decline of British manufacturing. Now they too are gone.

Before the M1 motorway was built, Grantham commanded the central artery of the nation's economic life. As late as the 1950s heavy lorries using the old A1 still crawled through the heart of the town, stopping at the traffic lights where the road narrows outside the Angel and again at the kinked crossroads where the Nottingham road turns off, right outside Alfred Roberts' shop. Yet even then it was an introverted, parochial sort of place. East Midlanders are not as a rule demonstrative, but even by the standards of Newark and Peterborough, Grantham people are peculiarly self-contained and wary: the local word is 'clunch'. It is typical of the town that it makes so little fuss of its most distinguished son: Grantham folk today are equally unimpressed by Margaret Thatcher. For a few years in the 1980s her childhood home was dinkily remodelled as the Premier Restaurant, a shrine for visiting Americans who could not under- stand why the Thatcher birthplace was not a focus of national pilgrimage; it soon closed for lack of local interest and is now a chiropractice, the rooms partitioned into consulting cubicles. There is a plaque on the wall, and a small display of memorabilia in the town museum; but that is all. 'A narrow town . . . inhabited by narrow people.'

Beatrice Stephenson – Margaret Thatcher's mother – was Grantham born and bred. She was born on 24 August 1888 at no. 10 (now no. 55) South Parade, a bare but substantial three-storey semi five minutes from the station, on the southern edge of the town. Her father, Daniel Stephenson, is euphemistically described as a railway- man: he was actually for thirty-five years a cloakroom attendant.[5] He married, in 1876, Phoebe Crust, described as a farmer's daughter (which might mean anything) from the village of Fishtoft Fen, near Boston, who had found work in Grantham as a factory machinist. Beatrice, one of several children, lived at home in South Parade until she was twenty-eight, working as a seamstress. Her daughter says she had her own business; but whether she worked alone or employed other girls there is no record. In December 1916 Daniel died. Five months later, on 28 May 1917, Beatrice married an ambitious young shop assistant – four years younger than herself – whom she had met at chapel: Alfred Roberts.

Years later, when the cult of Margaret Thatcher was at its height, some of her more romantic admirers persuaded themselves that a phenomenon of such transcendant brains and beauty could not possibly be the daughter of a mere provincial shopkeeper and his homely wife. Alan Clark in his diary records Julian Amery assuring him, 'There's blood there, no doubt about it', and goes on:

> The upper classes at one point (before the cause became hopeless) tried to appropriate the rumour that her mother had dallied with Christopher Cust, a notorious *coureur* on the northern Great House circuit, or more bizarrely with the 10th Duke of Grafton.[6]

Cust is the surname of the Brownlow family, Grantham's local magnates who lived at Belton House, three miles to the north, and who took a seigneurial interest in the town. The 5th Lord Brownlow served as Mayor in 1924–5 and his son followed him ten years later, when Alfred Roberts was a leading councillor. In her memoirs Lady Thatcher prints two photographs of the 6th Baron attending local functions: one shows him standing next to her father at a Rotary dinner, the other at a children's Christmas party with herself, aged about ten, bright-eyed beside Lady Brownlow. As her political career developed she cultivated this helpful connection; four decades later she exploited it to borrow some silver from Belton to supplement what she found in Downing Street and considered inadequate. ('There was very little here,' she told Laurens van der Post in 1983.)[7] Was she then borrowing her own family silver? Defeated by her mother, the most fanciful genealogists have tried to pin an aristocratic dalliance on her grandmother, who is said to have been a housemaid at Belton and is supposed to have been seduced by Harry Cust, a Tory MP and famous womaniser. It amused Lady Diana Cooper, who almost certainly was the illegitimate daughter of Harry Cust, to refer to Mrs Thatcher as her niece; others claim to see a striking resemblance to Mrs Thatcher in a portrait of the young Diana Cooper at Haddon Hall.[8] The surname Crust is tantalisingly close to Cust. Was Crust perhaps the name the Brownlows gave their bastards?

It is nonsense. There is no evidence that Phoebe ever worked at Belton. Crust was and is a common Lincolnshire name: in the single year 1849, Phoebe was one of ten Crusts born in the Lincolnshire registration district.[9] Moreover it is snobbish nonsense. The idea that unusual ability suggests an aristocratic bloodline is bizarre, to say the least. But the fact that such a Cinderella fantasy could be peddled – and eagerly believed – in defiance of the plain facts of her perfectly mundane ancestry, is an extraordinary manifestation of the hold Margaret Thatcher exerted on the Conservative imagination in the 1980s.

An even more desperate theory makes Alfred an illegitimate son of the 4th Lord Brownlow – even though his origins are perfectly well documented. He was not a Grantham man, but was born at Ringstead, near Oundle in Northamptonshire, on 18 April 1892, the eldest of seven children of Benjamin Roberts and Ellen Smith. The Roberts side of his family came originally from Wales – few thoroughly 'English' people do not have some Celtic blood in them – but had been settled in Northamptonshire as boot and shoe manufacturers for four generations. Whether it was a purely family enterprise, or employed other hands, we do not know. We do know that Benjamin's younger brother John Roberts branched out into piano and organ building; his great-niece remembers visiting him as a girl and being 'thrilled' to be allowed to play one of two organs in a barn in his garden.[10] She was also impressed by the contrast between his big house and the humble cottage in which her grandmother lived.[11] Benjamin Roberts died before Margaret was born, but Ellen lived to a good age – 'a bustling, active little old lady who kept a fine garden'.[12] But though Ringstead was only forty miles from Grantham and not inaccessible by train Margaret saw her only twice.

Alfred also broke away from shoemaking. A bookish boy, he would have liked to train to be a teacher, but was forced to leave school at twelve to supplement the family income (which suggests that the business was modest). He spent the rest of his life reading determinedly to make up for the education he had missed. He went into the grocery trade and after a number of odd jobs over the next ten years – including a spell in the tuck shop at Oundle school – came to Grantham in 1913 to take up a position as an assistant manager with Clifford's on London Road. It was while working for Alderman Clifford that he met Beatrice Stephenson. They are said to have met in chapel; but she may very well have been a customer as well – London Road runs into South Parade. However they met, Alfred soon began a lengthy courtship.

Mrs Thatcher in later years spoke famously little about her mother; the picture she presented was of a careworn housewife entirely subservient to her dominant husband. So it was something of a revelation when she printed in her memoirs a photograph of Beatrice as a young woman, plump but decidedly pretty, with glossy dark hair (already tied back, but not so severely as later), full lips and an expression of amused intelligence. Posed over a softbound book, she looks like a thoroughly self-possessed young teacher. Whatever motherhood and domesticity did to her in the years to come it is easy to see why Alfred might have admired her.

As a young man born in 1892 Alf was lucky to survive the Great War. He was tall, upright and good-looking, with very blond –

almost albino – curly hair and exceptionally pale blue eyes; but his eyes were seriously short-sighted. All his life he wore thick pebble glasses. He tried to enlist, but was rejected – six times according to his daughter, fifteen times if you believe the local paper[13] – on grounds of defective eyesight. Spared the fate of so many of his contemporaries, he was free to pursue his chosen trade. He worked hard and saved hard, and by 1917 he and Beatrice – he called her Beatie – had saved enough to marry. At first Alf moved in with Beatie and her mother in South Parade. But within two years they were able, with a mortgage, to buy their own small shop at the other end of town in North Parade. Phoebe came to live with them over the shop. Their first child, christened Muriel, was born in May 1921. Beatrice was then thirty-three – old for a first-time mother at that time (though this was not unusual for small tradespeople who needed to build up the business for some years before starting a family). Their second, another daughter, did not come for another four years, by which time Beatrice was thirty-seven. Margaret Hilda Roberts – the choice of names has never been explained – was born over the shop on 13 October 1925.

No. 1 North Parade was already a grocer's when Alfred bought it from Thomas Parker in 1919. It then comprised just the corner shop, with a yard at the back and two floors of cramped living quarters above. Nos. 2–3 were a newsagent's shop owned by Joseph Cross; no. 4 was a greengrocer. Not for another six years – around the time Margaret was born – did Alfred expand his tiny premises by buying out Joseph Cross next door. A year or two earlier he had spread his wings by opening a second shop half a mile away in Huntingtower Road, on the western side of town beyond the station. There is no question that Alfred was ambitious. By 1925 he was advertising in the *Grantham Almanack*, alongside the best shops in Grantham:

A. ROBERTS
Family Grocer & Provision Merchant
If you get it from ROBERTS'S . . . you get – THE BEST
1 North Parade and Huntingtower Road, Grantham

The following year he was able to amend his principal address to 1–3 North Parade; and in 1927 he changed his slogan to *The Quality of Our Provisions Stands Supreme*.[14] Thereafter he stopped advertising: as a town councillor perhaps he thought it improper, or perhaps he no longer needed to.

Lady Thatcher describes her father as a 'specialist grocer'.

> He always aimed to supply the best-quality produce, and the shop
> itself suggested this. Behind the counter there were three rows of
> splendid mahogany spice drawers with sparkling brass handles, and
> on top of these stood large, black, lacquered tea canisters . . .
> Wonderful aromas of spices, coffee and smoked hams would waft
> through the house.[15]

Yet one or two things need to be said about this. First, though
Alfred may well have aimed at quality, he was a general provision
merchant, not a specialist: certainly after he expanded to take in nos.
2–3 he sold cigarettes, tobacco, confectionery and (despite the
existing greengrocer at no. 4) fruit and vegetables. The shop was a
general store.

Second, North Parade was not strictly in Grantham at all. It was in
Little Gonerby; and 'Grantham people traded in Grantham, not in
Little Gonerby'.[16] The *Sunday Express* profile-writer who described
the shop in 1975 as 'the best grocery in the town. All the local
bigwigs had accounts there'[17] – was gilding the lily. The smart grocer
in the High Street was Catlin's; Alfred's original employer, Charles
Clifford, had his main shop in Market Place. Alfred was not in
competition with these two. North Parade was on the very edge of
town; moreover, though itself a handsome Georgian terrace, it was
closely surrounded by some very rough housing – now demolished –
which pressed right up against the Roberts' back yard. While the
heavy engineering was concentrated on Spittlegate to the south,
Little Gonerby was a centre of the malting industry: an extensive area
of small factories and narrow streets of workers' cottages. Alfred
Roberts' shop was on the edge of this social morass: poverty was not
far away.

The maltings workers might not have been Roberts' natural
customers – except for the third point: his shop was also a post office.
This is a fact which the iconography of Thatcherism tends to
overlook. Mrs Thatcher herself never mentions it and few of her
early biographers dwell on it. Yet it subtly changes the picture of
Alfred as the archetypal small businessman and champion of private
enterprise. He was that; but as a sub-postmaster he was also an agent
of central government, a sort of minor civil servant. The post office
franchise was an important part of his business. The post office
between the wars administered nothing like the range of public
services it handles today. Passports and driving licences touched only
a tiny fraction of the population. But the Post Office Savings Bank

was the only bank most people knew; and old age pensions had been paid through the post office since their introduction in 1908. The elderly of north Grantham and Little Gonerby collected their weekly ten shillings from North Parade. To this extent Alfred – even in the 1920s and much more so after 1945 – was an agent of the nascent welfare state; and Margaret was brought up with first-hand knowledge of its delivery system.

The post office was open from 8 a.m. to 7 p.m., Monday to Saturday, with Thursday early closing.[18] During these hours either Alfred or Beatie was always in the shop – Alfred normally at his corner by the bacon slicer – but they also employed two or three assistants, plus another permanently in the post office. In the early years Grandmother Stephenson served in the shop too; later, as they grew up, the girls helped out when they were not at school. 'One of the tasks I sometimes shared', Margaret wrote in her memoirs, 'was the weighing out of sugar, tea and biscuits from the sacks and boxes in which they arrived into 1lb and 2lb bags.'[19] 'The same', she told George Gardiner, 'had to be done with dried fruit and other dried commodities, such as lentils, pearl barley and peas.' Butter and margarine had to be shaped into pound and halfpound pats; even treacle had to be decanted. 'So much was delivered in bulk in those days, you had to have quite a bit of warehousing space.' Looking at the tiny building today you wonder how there was ever room; but to a child it seemed large.

At the back was a great big bake-house; we didn't use it for baking, but all the great sides of bacon were hung there, and the sugar and flour stored in big sacks . . . There was a separate room in which we stored all the soap and soap flakes. A small passage way led from the shop to a sort of dining room, to which people like travellers were shown if they wanted to see my father . . . The whole place was spotless, and we had a cat to keep the mice away.[20]

Growing up in a shop is a very particular upbringing. Obviously the children of shopkeepers do not all go into politics, still less become Prime Minister. Nevertheless there are at least three aspects of the experience which may have influenced the sort of person – and the sort of politician – Margaret Roberts became. First of all, as she herself put it, 'you are always on duty'. A shop is a sort of public house, even when it is closed. 'People would knock on the door at any hour of the night or weekend if they ran out of bacon, butter or eggs. Everyone knew that we lived by serving the customer; it was pointless to complain – and so nobody did.'[21] During shop hours the shopkeeper and his family are in direct contact with the public, on whose continuing goodwill they are dependent; they are bound to offer 'service with a smile' to everyone who comes in. The first words to every customer are 'Can I help you?' This undifferentiated, slightly impersonal eagerness to please is not unlike canvassing for votes.

Second, the shopkeeper makes his living very visibly: there is no mystery or reticence about it. Every penny is taken over the counter, and reckoned up the same evening. He buys wholesale and sells retail, with an appropriate margin; he knows exactly what sells well and what does not, and how variations in price affect sales. A small shop thus displays the working of the market in its purest form. Just as farm children gain early familiarity with reproduction, the child of a shopkeeper cannot grow up ignorant of the facts of economic life, or embarrassed by the need for profit. The daughter of a busy local grocer might, on the contrary, be particularly alert to the possibility of combining public service with private profit.

Third, a grocer above all other tradesmen depends on international trade. A passage in G. K. Chesterton's *The Napoleon of Notting Hill* romantically evokes an old-fashioned grocer standing behind his counter 'surrounded with wares from all the ends of the earth':

> No Eastern king ever had such argosies or such cargoes coming from the sunrise to the sunset . . . India is at your elbow . . . China is before you, Demerara is behind you, America is above your head and, at this very moment, like some old Spanish admiral, you hold Tunis [a box of dates] in your hands.[22]

There is little indication that Margaret Roberts was moved by this romance; more likely she took it for granted that the produce of the world – the tea and coffee, rice, sugar and treacle – all finished up in North Parade. Nevertheless those sacks and polished canisters gave her an early awareness of the reach of international trade – wider than either Europe or the British Empire. It is not surprising that she grew up a passionate believer in global free trade, impatient of protectionist tariffs and political cartels.

Alfred's move into politics was a natural extension of his business. In a place like Grantham most members of the town council – like Alderman Clifford – were tradesmen of one sort or another, effectively representing the Chamber of Trade. It happened that in

April 1927 the council was expanded from twelve members to eighteen. Alfred was one of six candidates put up by the Chamber of Trade to fill the additional vacancies. Since the convention was still that party labels were not used in local government, they stood as Independents. In practice, however, reality was breaking in. All over the country the Labour party was increasingly putting up candidates. Alfred faced a Labour opponent in St Wulfram's ward. In 1927, however, the Independents swept the board. Alfred represented St Wulfram's for sixteen years until he was elected an alderman in 1943.

His political affiliation at this time has been a matter of some speculation. He has been variously described as a Gladstonian Liberal, a closet Conservative or even by inclination 'moderate Labour'.[23] The last can be dismissed. It is based on a misunderstanding of his Methodism, and his positive attitude to postwar reconstruction. The whole purpose of the Chamber of Trade in the 1920s was to be anti-Labour, or specifically anti-Co-op. As a private grocer Alfred was in direct competition with the Co-op. The Independent group on the council was an anti-socialist coalition whose members were spared the need to declare themselves either Conservative or Liberal. There is some evidence that Alfred thought of himself, at least initially, as a Liberal. Twenty-three years later, when Margaret stood for Parliament for the first time as a Conservative in Dartford, Alfred came to support her and was paraded explicitly as a former Liberal who held that the Tories now stood for what the Liberals had stood for in his youth. This was a Tory theme in 1950, when Churchill was particularly keen to woo the Liberal vote. It must have been at least half true if Alfred was prepared to go along with it. His elder daughter Muriel recalled in 1975 her impression that 'he was always a Liberal at heart'.[24] Yet in practice he had been a Conservative for years. He was certainly an active supporter of the Tory candidate at the 1935 General Election, because this was the election at which the ten-year-old Margaret gained her first political experience, running messages between polling stations and the Conservative committee rooms. Ten years later he was equally strongly in the Tory camp against the genuine Independent who had captured Grantham at a by-election during the war. Meanwhile his daughter was already a committed Conservative when she went up to Oxford in 1943. It is difficult not to conclude that long before the war Alfred's Liberalism was as distant a memory as Churchill's.

His overriding purpose in local politics was keeping the rates down. He very quickly became chairman of the Finance and Rating Committee, and retained that position for more than twenty years.

Styled 'Grantham's Chancellor of the Exchequer' by the *Grantham Journal*, he established a formidable reputation for guarding the ratepayers' pennies as carefully as his own. One need seek no further for the origin of Mrs Thatcher's visceral hostility to public spending. In 1936 he successfully opposed a proposal that the council should employ its own direct labour force to maintain the town's newly-built stock of public housing. 'I do not believe', he argued, 'that there is an instance where jobs done by direct labour save money over jobs done by contract.'[25] Another time he objected to the council lending its motor mower to the Boys' Central School one day a week, saying that the local education authority should get its own.[26] He faced his greatest embarrassment in 1937 when he was obliged to ask for a swingeing seven pence rate increase to fourteen shillings in the pound. Characteristically he blamed his colleagues for having approved excessive commitments; his job, he protested, was merely to find the money. 'It is just brought to your notice now', he told them, 'what exactly you have been approving.' He hoped there would be cuts next year. Meanwhile he was sorry to have to ask for an increase 'and more sorry than ever to be one of the men who will have to pay it'. He called for a more efficient collection procedure, since 'the people who don't pay the rates are sponging on those who do, and the people who do pay have to pay higher because some won't pay rates which are due.'[27] It took his daughter half a century to come up with a radical alternative to the rating system which Alfred was worrying about when she was twelve.

On top of his seat on the council and chairmanship of the Finance Committee, Alfred was active in many other areas of Grantham life. At various times he was President of the Chamber of Trade, President of Rotary, a director of the Grantham Building Society and the Trustee Savings Bank, chairman of the local National Savings Movement, a governor of both the boys' and girls' grammar schools and chairman of the Workers' Educational Association. During the war he was Chief Welfare Officer in charge of civil defence and the moving force behind Grantham's two Government-sponsored 'British Restaurants'. In 1943 he was elected the town's youngest alderman and in 1945–6 served as mayor. He was a good mayor in a particularly testing year, presiding not only over victory celebrations and Remembrance Day parades but also the rebuilding necessitated by Grantham's extensive bomb damage. His inaugural speech was hailed by the *Grantham Journal* as the best for years. He was a much-admired public speaker with an ability to strike a note of high-minded idealism well suited to the postwar mood. 'A new era is born', he declared, 'conceived in trial, trouble and affliction . . . brought forth by courage and devotion.'

> Again and again in our human life we learn that without the shedding of blood there is no remission, and the battle for our emancipation has been costly. Because of that cost there is a very serious obligation placed on us to render up service in memory of those by whose sacrifice we stand in perfect liberty today.

Rising above his reputation for rigorous economy, he acknowledged a formidable agenda of reconstruction to inaugurate the new era – better roads and public transport; lighting and sewerage; improved health and welfare services; nursery schools. Above all, like the Labour Government, he accepted that 'the number one priority is housing our people': 'Never can we have a happy town without happy family life, and we cannot have happy family life without proper places in which to live.' Significantly, however, he echoed Conservative impatience with 'malignant' socialist controls, believing that free enterprise would get the houses built faster than Nye Bevan's policy of giving priority to council housing. Roberts' first concern was always to protect the long-suffering ratepayers. But he ended with a high-minded appeal for co-operation: 'Together – and for all.'[28]

So ubiquitous was Roberts' influence by this time that when he gave up the mayor's tricorne the cartoonist on a local paper depicted him choosing from a variety of alternative hats – among them a halo.[29] Nevertheless it is a mistake to exaggerate his position. Some writers have made him out to be a sort of all-powerful city boss, running Grantham virtually single-handed. In truth he was just one long-serving councillor among others, who took his turn at being mayor like all the rest. At least equally powerful was Councillor Stanley Foster – a tobacconist with a men's hairdressing business in the High Street, who was chairman of the Development and General Purposes Committee, chairman of the Wartime Emergency Committee and twice mayor, in 1939 and 1952.

An even more colourful character was Denis Kendall, a flamboyant motor manufacturer who brought the B.MARC armaments factory to Grantham in 1938, bringing much-needed employment to the town. Such was Kendall's popularity that he won a famous wartime by-election against the Government in 1942, retained the seat with a huge majority as an Independent in 1945 and then became a councillor. He founded his own local newspaper, the *Grantham Guardian*, to mock the majority group's pretence that they were not Conservatives in all but name. (Another cartoon showed a giraffe-necked Alderman Roberts addressing the Independent group meeting: 'And in conclusion, ladies and gentlemen, I must congratulate you on your independent spirit which you have shown by agreeing to every proposition I have put before you.' In the background a Kilroy figure is scrawled on the blackboard saying, 'Wot no Tories?')[30] Despite Kendall's lively intrusion, however, if anyone ran the town it was still the Chamber of Trade, under the ever-present patronage of Lord Brownlow. Roberts was conspicuous partly because his unusual height, pale colouring and upright bearing made him distinctive. In truth he was an energetic and public-spirited local worthy, but by no means the exceptional figure his daughter's mythologists have made him out to be.

The most celebrated episode in Alfred's political career was its ending. By 1950 the pretence of keeping party labels out of local government was on its last legs. That year Labour won a majority on Grantham council for the first time; they naturally installed one of their own councillors as chairman of the Finance Committee. Two years later they used their majority, quite legitimately, to elect their own aldermen, thereby displacing Roberts from the council after twenty-seven years. He accepted the decision with dignity but not without self-dramatisation:

> It is almost nine years since I took up these robes in honour, and now I trust in honour they are laid down . . . No medals, no honours, but an inward sense of satisfaction. May God bless Grantham for ever.[31]

His removal was widely deplored as an act of petty ingratitude to an outstanding servant of the local community. Even Denis Kendall called it 'a mucky trick', while Labour councillors themselves were embarrassed: one paid tribute to 'the passing of a good man'.[32] In fact it was a perfectly natural consequence of a swing of the political pendulum. Roberts had had a good innings – he was now sixty – and had no ground for complaint. Nevertheless he nursed a grievance for the rest of his life. Thirty-three years later his daughter famously shed tears when she recalled his deposition in a television interview. Why she should have been so affected so long afterwards goes to the heart of her relationship with her father. It is unlikely that she was so deeply affected at the time. In 1952 she had long ago left home, was married and embarked on her own career. By 1985, on the other hand, six years into her premiership, she may have seen in the ingratitude of politics a chilling premonition of her own demise.

At the heart of all Alfred's community activity was his religion. As a devout Methodist, he made no distinction between commercial, political and religious values. Simultaneously shopkeeper, local politician and lay preacher, he conducted his business on ethical principles and preached business principles in politics. In all three spheres he prided himself on hard work, high standards and integrity. He was indeed a proud man, with a powerful sense of his own worth – tempered by proper Christian humility. Inevitably there have been attempts to portray him as an old hypocrite. But if he had a moralising tendency he does seem to have practised personally what he preached. He was not inflexible: after long opposing the opening of cinemas on Sunday, for instance, he bowed to changed times during the war. He could also be forgiving towards others' weakness: he was not a bigot. His worst fault was parsimony: he was reputed to pay his shop assistants as little as he could get away with. But stories that female assistants were not safe from his wandering hands are unsubstantiated and dismissed by those who knew him. If he did pat the odd bottom it was almost certainly patronising, in the manner of the times, rather than predatory.* He was not a man for hanky-panky. He did not have much sense of humour, or many friends. Long after his death one of his old preaching colleagues – thinking both of his height and of his manner – summed him up in the single word 'lofty'.[34]

He was not just a Methodist, but specifically a Wesleyan: an important distinction. In the middle of the nineteenth century Methodism had split. The Methodist Free Churches, which rejected authority and tended to be politically progressive, seceded from the main body. The Wesleyans, by contrast, adhered to what they held

---

* The origin of the wandering hands story may well be a satirical novel, *Rotten Borough*, which created a local scandal when it was published in 1937. Written pseudonymously by a local vicar's son, it was transparently set in Grantham and mocked recognisable local figures. Part of the plot concerns 'a Naughty Town Councillor', a grocer, who is caught having 'a Bit of Fun' with one of his assistants after hours. The book was rediscovered by the *Guardian* in 1988 and subsequently republished, with the hopeful implication that it was an exposé of Alfred Roberts. In fact it is perfectly clear that the erring dignitary, Councillor Sam Nurture, is a punning send-up of Councillor Stan Foster; and among the whole cast of equally thinly disguised caricatures none resembles Roberts – an indication that in 1937 he was not yet worth satirising. The book was sufficiently libellous for Lord Brownlow to succeed in having it suppressed – it pokes particular fun at Lady Brownlow's amateur theatricals in aid of the local hospital. But it has interest today only as a dated and juvenile lampoon of small town life.[33]

to be the tradition of John Wesley – who never wholly abandoned the Church of England – and became increasingly conservative, both theologically and socially: in nonconformist terms almost 'High Church'.[35] In Grantham these differences were sharply marked. There was a Primitive Methodist chapel immediately behind North Parade, and a Free Methodist chapel just across the way; but Alf and Beatie Roberts attended Finkin Street Wesleyan Church in the centre of town. The different denominations reflected different social castes. The Roberts' membership of Finkin Street was the badge of a certain position in the town: if not the social equals of the Anglicans who worshipped at St Wulfram's, they were a cut above other Methodists, Baptists and other nonconformists. In 1932 the two main streams of Methodism reunited; but not in Grantham. The Grantham Wesleyans – Alf Roberts by then prominent among them – resisted reunion and maintained their separate identity until after the war. This is the explanation of something that has puzzled many observers of Mrs Thatcher's career. In British politics nonconformity has usually been associated with the left. Harold Wilson was fond of quoting the aphorism that the Labour party owed more to Methodism than to Marx. But the Wesleyan Methodism in which Margaret Thatcher was brought up belonged to a different tradition.

Alfred Roberts' Methodism was a religion of personal salvation. His preaching, by all accounts, was fundamentalist, Bible-based, concerned with the individual's responsibility to God for his own behaviour. It was not a social gospel, but an uncompromisingly individualistic moral code which underpinned an individualistic approach to politics and commerce. A man's duty was to keep his own soul clean, mind his own business and care for his own family. At its best it was a philosophy which instilled a further obligation to look after neighbours in need and thence, by extension, to wider community service and private charity: Lady Thatcher has told how her mother always baked extra loaves to give away to neighbours or acquaintances who were temporarily unemployed or otherwise in difficulty. At the same time, however, it carried a strong undercurrent of self-righteousness and moral superiority. The journalist Peter Jenkins, recalling his own upbringing in East Anglia in the 1940s, wrote acutely that 'Wesleyan enthusiasm had given way to a smug nonconformity. Methodism was the religion of prosperous shopkeepers and farmers, a pious celebration of the work ethic and discharge of the religious duty which accompanied the ownership of property.'[36] One group to whom Alfred's charity definitely did not extend were the Jarrow marchers who passed through Grantham in 1936 on their way to London to draw attention to the plight of the unemployed. 'He did not think that what they were doing was right,' his elder daughter remembered.[37]

There is in Mrs Thatcher's descriptions of her parents' good works a strong sense of moral condescension, the Christian duty owed by the virtuous and hard-working to those less fortunate. 'We were always encouraged', she told George Gardiner, 'to think in terms of *practical* help and to think very little of people who thought that their duty to the less well-off started and finished by getting up and protesting in the market place.'[38] From this starting point she developed the philosophy that private charity – an individual voluntarily spending his own money – was morally better than collectivised welfare financed by taxation. From quite early in her political career one of her favourite texts was the parable of the Good Samaritan – who could help the robbed traveller only because he had his own money. There is no record that this was one of Alfred's texts, but it seems very likely.

Finkin Street church – not chapel – is an appropriately imposing building, dating from 1840. The outside is fortress-like, with twin towers flanking a rose window; but inside it is a perfect example of nonconformist church design – a semicircular arena with polished mahogany pews facing a commanding pulpit reached by symmetrical steps on either side, so high that the preacher is nearly level with the gallery. In shape quite unlike an Anglican church, it is essentially a preaching theatre which seems to bind preacher and congregation in an intimate unity. Alf Roberts preached regularly from this pulpit – as well as others in surrounding villages – for nearly half a century. His daughters – sitting in the family pew in the fourth row back – listened to him and others twice every Sunday throughout their childhood. Quite apart from the spiritual message, this was an intensive education in the power of the spoken word. Moreover children were encouraged to participate in services, and there are local memories of young Margaret herself reading from the high pulpit.

Margaret's childhood was dominated by her parents' faith. Sundays – the only day in the week the shop was closed – were almost wholly taken up with church attendance. Sunday school at ten was followed by morning service at eleven. There was just time to get home for lunch before afternoon Sunday school at 2.30 at which Margaret, from the age of about twelve, played the piano for the younger ones; then it was back again for evening service at six. During the week, too, the family's social life was almost entirely church-based. Beatie attended a sewing circle on Tuesdays, often taking Margaret with her; Muriel and Margaret attended the

Methodist Guild on Fridays. Life at home was austere, teetotal, governed by strict rules, particularly while Beatie's mother was still alive. Grandmother Stephenson, Margaret told Patricia Murray, was 'very, very Victorian and very, very strict', a great believer in improving proverbs: 'Cleanliness is next to godliness'; 'If a thing's worth doing it's worth doing well'.

> We were taught what was right and wrong in very considerable detail. There were certain things you just didn't do and that was that. Duty was very, very strongly engrained into us. Duties to the church, duties to your neighbour and conscientiousness were continually emphasised.[39]

The greatest sin of all was wasting time. Every minute of the day was to be filled with useful occupation. 'There was a great sense of effort,' Margaret told Kenneth Harris, 'of always doing something – not necessarily work – talk, discussion, playing the piano, but always something . . . Idleness was a waste . . . It was very important to use your life to some purpose.'[40] Never was a childhood lesson more thoroughly taken to heart. Likewise in this heavily moral context thrift was not just the prudent management of limited resources, but a positive virtue, any hint of extravagance a vice. In her memoirs Lady Thatcher recalls a friend telling her mother proudly that she reused all her tacking cottons in dress-making: 'I consider it my duty.' Even Beatie had not previously taken cheese-paring that far, but she was not to be outdone. 'After that, so did we. We were not Methodists for nothing.'[41]

Margaret's relationship with her mother has been the subject of much speculation, provoked by her seeming reluctance to speak of her while making a hero of her father. Great significance has been attached to the fact that she omits to mention Beatrice in *Who's Who*, describing herself simply as 'd. of Alfred Roberts, Grantham, Lincs', as though she was sprung parthenogenically from the loins of the alderman. In fact this is not unusual: the entries for other prominent women of Lady Thatcher's generation show that about half exclude their mothers. It is most likely that when first invited to submit her entry in 1960, after her election to Parliament, she simply copied the format used by her Oxford tutor, Dorothy Hodgkin, or Florence Horsburgh, the first woman to sit in a Conservative Cabinet, both of whom named only their fathers.[42] Nevertheless in Mrs Thatcher's case the omission does seem symptomatic: she never rectified it when it was pointed out.* When pressed by early interviewers, she remembered her mother only as an overburdened housewife. 'My mother was a good woman who was always intensely practical,' she told Patricia Murray. 'I learned a lot of practical stuff from her. She taught me how to cook and bake bread, how to make my own clothes and how to decorate.'[44] 'I loved her dearly,' she told Godfrey Winn in 1961, then added, 'but after I was fifteen we had nothing more to say to each other. It wasn't her fault. She was weighed down by the home, always being in the home.'[45]

It was a television interview with Miriam Stoppard in 1985 which drew attention to Mrs Thatcher's unwillingness to talk about her mother. This was the occasion when she wept as she described her father being voted off the council. When Miriam Stoppard asked about Beatrice, she replied briefly, 'Mother was marvellous – yes, go on', and turned the conversation back to Alfred. When Stoppard tried again, asking what she thought she had inherited from her *mother*, her answer made it clear that she saw Beatie's role simply as seconding her husband:

Oh, Mummy backed up Daddy in everything, as far as you do what is right. She was terribly proud. I mean she would just say to me sometimes, 'Your father had a very difficult day in council, standing up for his principles.'

When Stoppard tried a third time, asking about Beatie's part in family discussion about politics and current affairs, the response was the same. 'No . . . mummy didn't get involved in the arguments. She had probably gone out to the kitchen to get the supper ready.'[46]

Many years later, in her memoirs, Lady Thatcher tried to set the record straight by devoting more space to her mother. But still she remembered only her domestic efficiency:

I . . . learned from my mother just what it meant to cope with a household so that everything worked like clockwork, even though she had to spend so many hours serving behind the counter . . . She showed me how to iron a man's shirt in the correct way and to press embroidery without damaging it . . . My mother was an excellent cook and a highly organised one.[47]

---

* Much odder is the fact that her daughter Carol, in her biography of Denis Thatcher, repeats the same omission, describing her mother simply as 'the second daughter of Alfred Roberts, a grocer from Grantham in Lincolnshire'. Carol too seems content to write her grandmother out of history. [43]

There is absolutely no recollection of Beatrice as a mother, or as a person with interests or qualities of her own. There is gratitude for the skills her mother taught her; but there is no love in her memory.

In 1989, when she was still Prime Minister, the Labour MP and amateur psychoanalyst Leo Abse published a mischievous, highly tendentious book entitled *Margaret, Daughter of Beatrice*, which attempted a Freudian explanation of Mrs Thatcher's personality and politics by examining her relationship with her mother. On the basis of no evidence at all beyond her published interviews and his observation of her in the House of Commons, Abse first speculated and then − supposition hardening to fact within a few pages − asserted that Margaret was starved of her mother's love when she was a baby. He suggested that Beatrice − the 'affectless mother' − rejected her second daughter because she had wanted a son; and was herself dominated by her own harsh and unloving mother, the 'martinet grandmother' who ruled Margaret's childhood. The infant Margaret was, he believed, denied her mother's breast. The frustration and anger caused by 'her ungenerous suckling and, probably, her early weaning' led to the Education Secretary's vengeful 'snatching' of milk from schoolchildren in 1970, and the Prime Minister's supposed hatred of the NHS and all the nurturing services in the 1980s. Her obsession with tidiness and cleanliness derived from over-rigid potty-training; her love of money from being denied the sight of her own faeces − defecation being equated by Freudians with filthy lucre. This is all entertaining stuff ('Thatcher's deprivation of her defeca-tory pleasures made her an easy lay for Milton Friedman'), but risible; the book was savaged in the psychoanalytic press when it appeared. It is pure speculation, prurient tattle dressed up as the crudest sort of pseudo-science.[48]

And yet, unsourced though his speculations are, Abse does address a real problem. His cod-Freudianism at least attempts an explanation of aspects of Margaret Thatcher's personality which are not explained by her own somewhat cosy portrayal of her childhood. Her inability to summon up a warm word about her mother, even when she is obviously trying to do her justice, is very striking. Most daughters, even when they grow away from their mothers, retain a strong instinctive bond even across the gulf of exasperation and mutual incomprehension. The absence of such a bond does suggest a deprivation of normal mother love. Likewise Margaret's extreme competitiveness in later life suggests a need to fight for attention as a child; her aggression (on the one hand) and almost obsessive conscientiousness (on the other) surely betray a basic insecurity at odds with the comfortable picture she presents of her childhood.

Rejected – or at any rate feeling rejected – by her mother, it is credible that she should have looked for praise and encouragement to her father instead. He was a demanding taskmaster. But by hard work and dedication equal to his own she became his favourite: a surrogate son. By precept and example Alfred showed Margaret the way to escape her mother's sphere of stifling domesticity by competing in a man's world. So she blotted out her mother and idealised her father; in due course she eerily repeated the pattern by neglecting her own daughter while spoiling her son.

She has always presented the Roberts household as a happy and self-contained unit. 'We were a very close family', she told Patricia Murray, 'and most of the things we did we tended to do together.'[49] 'Living over the shop', she wrote in *The Path to Power*, 'children see far more of their parents than in most other walks of life. I saw my father at breakfast, lunch, high tea and supper. We had much more time to talk than some other families, for which I have always been grateful.'[50] This is clearly true, up to a point. At the same time, shopkeeping is notoriously inimical to family life. During shop hours the four of them could never sit down to meals at the same time, since either Alf or Beatie was always in the shop. Even outside opening hours customers or tradesmen were always liable to call. The family could never go on holiday together, either. Beatie used to take the two girls to Skegness for a week – self-catering; Alf would then take another week by himself to play bowls while Beatie minded the shop. On top of this the range of Alf's activities outside the home must have meant that he was out more evenings than he was in. Between the demands of the shop, council business, preaching, school governing and Rotary he can have had little time over for his family.

Margaret claims that he used to take her 'everywhere' with him, to political meetings and council business, thus taking her out of her mother's sphere and into his; but this cannot have been before her teens. In her early years she must have been brought up predominantly by her mother, with help – when Beatie was busy in the shop – from her grandmother and her elder sister. Once again Lady Thatcher was at pains in her memoirs to correct the image she had previously given of her grandmother as a forbidding termagant. 'Not at all,' she now wrote.

She was a warm presence in the life of myself and my sister. Dressed in the grandmotherly style of those days – long black sateen beaded dress – she would come up to our bedrooms on

warm summer evenings and tell us stories of her life as a young girl
... With time on her hands, she had plenty of time for us.[51]

Though this is all, it is still a warmer memory than anything she
writes of her mother.

Despite the four and a half year age gap, Margaret also claimed
that she and Muriel were 'very, very close'.[52] Again the evidence is
unconvincing. The sisters were very different – Muriel much less
academic, less serious, closer to her mother than to her father. She
left school at seventeen in 1938 and left home at the same time –
when Margaret was thirteen – to train as a physiotherapist in
Birmingham. She returned to work in Grantham in 1943 – by which
time Margaret was at Oxford – then in 1950 married a pig farmer
and settled in Essex, where she still lives. From the moment Margaret
exploded on to the nation's consciousness in the 1970s Muriel has
scarcely spoken to the press. She gave one interview to the *Daily
Telegraph* in February 1975 in which she expressed pride in her
sister's success and loyally insisted that Margaret was not at all cold
and aloof but 'a warm and very generous person'. She claimed that
they were good friends and spoke on the telephone 'at least once a
week', but added that this was a fairly recent development. As a
schoolgirl she regarded Margaret as a 'nuisance' who was always
being held up to her by teachers as an example. 'It was not till we got
older that the gap narrowed.'[53]

Muriel also helped Ernle Money with his biography of Margaret
the same year. Since then she has steadfastly refused all requests for
interviews. 'Do as Denis does – don't,' Margaret allegedly told her).[54]
Her silence has not prevented, but rather encouraged, a widespread
belief that the sisters do not get on. It is said that Muriel and her
mother thought Margaret's obsession with politics 'mad'. The story
is even told that Muriel stole her husband, Willie Cullen, from
Margaret – it was Margaret who introduced them at a dance in
Colchester in 1949 – and that this caused a coolness for some years.[55]
It may have been to counteract such gossip that Margaret printed in
her memoirs pictures of the two of them on the beach at Frinton
with their respective children about 1957. Whatever the truth the
only certainty is that Muriel is an utterly different personality from
Margaret – a jolly, direct and easy-going farmer's wife who has
followed Margaret's career from a distance with bemused amazement; she is said to be saddened by Margaret's inability to let go since
1990 and enjoy her retirement. Muriel Cullen is today the only
person who could, if she wished, shed more light on the family
dynamics of the Roberts household in the 1930s. But unless she

chooses to break her silence the historian can only extrapolate from scattered remarks that contradict the idealised image.*

'I had the most marvellous upbringing,' Mrs Thatcher insisted in 1982. 'It stayed with me the rest of my life . . . My goodness it was hard as a young person; it was hard, but it was right.'[57] She insists repeatedly that it was not dull. 'Our pleasure was really confined to church socials,' she admitted to Patricia Murray, 'but don't forget a tremendous social life does revolve around the church. There were supper evenings, singing evenings, spelling bees and that's what our social life really consisted of.'[58] These, she asserts in her memoirs, 'gave me plenty of opportunities to enjoy life, even if it was in what might seem rather a solemn way'.[59] To a radio interviewer in 1982 she struck a defiant note. 'I had the richest upbringing possible. Not rich in money, we hadn't very much money, but rich in the right values.'[60] 'It may not have suited all girls,' she told Kenneth Harris, 'but it suited me.'[61]

Yet she protests too much. There are clear admissions scattered through her interviews with biographers, in stray reminiscences to colleagues, and even in her memoirs, that she did not always appreciate the rigours of her childhood at the time. She once hinted delicately to Ronald Millar, for instance, that church four times on Sundays was too much: 'I think it would have been a little bit better to have been a little bit less'[62]; and in *The Path to Power* she admits that 'on a few occasions I remember trying to get out of going'.[63] She resented being expected to put all her pocket money, and birthday money, into savings stamps.[64] And although she now claims that her mother's dress-making skills kept Muriel and herself 'by Grantham standards rather fashionable'[65], earlier interviews told a rather different story. 'My mother was a very good dressmaker', she told Patricia Murray, 'but my sister and I often felt that our things were different from others.' It was a revelation when Muriel left home and discovered the big shops in Birmingham. 'For us it was an unbelievable luxury to go out and buy something off the peg.'[66]

Constrained by Methodist sobriety and her parents' thrift, Margaret envied the girls she saw attending the Roman Catholic church on the other side of North Parade, 'dressed in white party dresses and pink ribbons . . . The Methodist style was much

---

* 'The closer the family is', Mrs Thatcher once remarked, 'the more virulent the quarrels.'[56] She was actually talking about the European Community; but she may have let slip more than she intended.

plainer.'[67] Most graphically, she described to Miriam Stoppard the agony of shopping with her mother.

> You never buy anything you can't afford to buy, never, but you live according to your means . . . Many's the time I can remember my mother saying, when I said, oh my friends have got more, 'Well, we're not situated like that' . . .
>
> Or when you went out to buy something, and you were actually going to have new covers for the settee, that was . . . a great expenditure and a great event. So you went out to choose them, and you chose something that looked really rather lovely, something light with flowers on. My mother: 'That's not serviceable.' And how I longed for the time when I could buy things that were not serviceable.

'One kicked against it,' she admitted. 'Of course one kicked against it. They had more things than we did.' Later in the interview she explained what it was – apart from pretty clothes – that the unnamed 'they' had more of. 'Home really was very small and we had no mod cons . . . The one thing I really wanted was a nice house, you know, a house with more things than we had.'[68]

Alf Roberts was not poor. As a successful shopkeeper he belonged by the 1930s to the middle middle class; he could scarcely have devoted so much of his time to politics had his business not been securely profitable. At a time when quite ordinary middle-class families up and down the country were discovering the liberation of vacuum cleaners, washing machines and even cars, he could certainly have afforded his family the luxury of a few mod cons; at the very least hot water. They did in fact have a maid before the war, and later a cleaning lady two days a week. It was for religious and temperamental reasons – puritanism and parsimony – not economic necessity, that Alfred kept his family in such austerity. The flashes of rebellion that illuminate Mrs Thatcher's recollections fifty years later betray a sense that she felt the parsimony, like the churchgoing, was taken too far. Ironically Alf and Beatie did move to a larger house with more home comforts the moment Margaret left to go to Oxford.

For all her insistence on the social liveliness of Finkin Street she was well aware that she was missing out on other sides of life. 'For us', she told Miriam Stoppard, 'it was rather a sin to enjoy yourself by entertainment . . . Life wasn't to enjoy yourself; life was to work and do things.'

I would have liked some things to be different. For instance, on Saturday nights some of the girls at my school would go to dances or parties. It sounded very nice. But my sister and I didn't go dancing.[69]

Her schoolfriends, she told Patricia Murray rather sadly, 'would all do far more of those things – out with other people where there was laughter and fun. We always went to serious things, or our laughter and fun was at the church social. It wasn't at the village hall where everyone had a dance.'[70]

The family did get a wireless set after Grandmother Stephenson died in 1935 (when Margaret was ten). This was such an event that she remembers running all the way back from school that day. The wireless was the one form of popular entertainment that was allowed: as well as a lot of serious talk Margaret says they listened to big band music – 'We all loved big band music' – Ambrose, Harry Roy, Henry Hall and Mantovani – and even comedy programmes: Arthur Askey, Richard Murdoch and *ITMA*.[71] Muriel's memory, however, is rather different: to Ernle Money she remembered her parents' musical taste as strictly classical and recalled the relief of being able to listen to dance music when Alf and Beatie, unusually, were both out.[72]

Whatever the truth, Margaret unquestionably longed for a bit more glamour. The highlight of her whole childhood was a visit to London, without her parents, when she was twelve. She was sent to stay with friends – a Wesleyan minister and his wife – in Hampstead. 'I stayed for a whole week', she told Patricia Murray, 'and was given a life of enjoyment and entertainment that I had never seen.' As well as all the usual sights – the Tower of London, the Changing of the Guard, the Houses of Parliament and the zoo – she recalled, 'we were actually taken to the theatre'. The show was the musical *The Desert Song* at the Catford Theatre. 'We saw the crowds and the bright lights and I was so excited and thrilled by it that I've never forgotten that week.'[73] Even in the more polished recollection of her memoirs the revelation of a world beyond Grantham and a life beyond Methodism is unmistakable:

I could hardly drag myself away from London or from the Skinners who had been such indulgent hosts. Their kindness had given me a glimpse of, in Talleyrand's words, '*la douceur de la vie*' – how sweet life could be.[74]

In her memoirs Lady Thatcher writes that her life was further brightened by 'the coming of the cinema to Grantham'. She devotes a whole page to her adolescent immersion in 'the romantic world of Hollywood', discoursing knowledgeably on her favourite films.[75] But apart from the fact that there were already three picture-houses in Grantham before she was born, her account of this previously unsuspected passion contradicts everything she told her first biographers. To George Gardiner in 1975 and Patricia Murray in 1980 she spoke only of occasional Bank Holiday treats to Nottingham:

> I can remember one Bank Holiday going there to see a Ginger Rogers and Fred Astaire film . . . I loved every minute of that day, which is probably why I can remember it so well . . . Going out was something which was viewed as a great treat in your life.[76]

The earlier version is more convincing than the later. Apart from her *tendresse* for Ronald Reagan, Mrs Thatcher as Prime Minister was never known to take the slightest interest in the products of Hollywood – or of the British film industry. Her daughter Carol has written of 'carting her off' to see *Those Magnificent Men in their Flying Machines* on one of her half-terms, 'which was something of a novelty for her because she was never a cinema-goer'.[77] And she once gave her opinion that *Gone With the Wind* was the best film ever made – largely because it contained no sex or violence.[78] What is interesting about her recollection of youthful cinema-going is, first, that it is part of her conscious effort to portray her childhood as less constricted than it really was; and second, that it simultaneously confirms her suppressed ambition to escape. 'Grantham was a small town', she writes, 'but on my visits to the cinema I roamed to the most fabulous realms of the imagination. It gave me the determination to roam in reality one day.'[79] There is no doubt that this is true.

She had a role-model in Grantham itself. Three of Grantham's four cinemas in the 1930s were owned by an energetic former actor, producer and theatre manager, J. A. Campbell, who had successfully diversified into picture-theatres all over the East Midlands. He failed to be elected to the council before the war, but was co-opted in 1941; he was also an active Rotarian, and thus came into contact with Alfred Roberts. His wife, herself active in all sorts of charitable concerns around the town, also got to know the Roberts family and took a particular interest in their precocious younger daughter, whom she used to invite home to listen to gramophone records. The Campbells also had a daughter, Judy, who became a successful actress. Lady Thatcher in her memoirs claims to have 'got to know' Judy, as if they were contemporaries. In fact Judy was nine years older. She had already got away from Grantham and was making her name on the stage by the time Margaret was twelve; she achieved national fame in 1941 singing 'A Nightingale Sang in Berkeley Square', and toured the country as Noël Coward's leading lady in *Present Laughter* when Margaret was seventeen. Margaret may well have met Judy fleetingly on one of her visits to the Campbell house; but Judy has only one memory of seeing Margaret. Her mother once sent her to buy a cauliflower at Roberts' shop – it was not where they normally shopped – as an excuse to take a look at his 'remarkable little girl', whom Mrs Campbell had already spotted as a prodigy. Judy remembers seeing the blonde, blue-eyed Margaret – aged about ten – behind the counter. She also remembers her mother telling her, 'Mark my words, that girl will go far.' Forty years later she raised her eyes to heaven and murmured, 'Mother, you were right.'[80]

But though Judy was in no way a friend of the young Margaret, she was certainly an inspiration at an impressionable age when her adolescent imagination was being fired by visits to the cinema – however rare – and dreams of London. Judy had got away: her picture was in the *Grantham Journal* every other week. Judy was glamorous: as an actress she got to wear pretty clothes. Yet as the daughter of Mr and Mrs Campbell she was also respectable: a local girl of whom Grantham could properly be proud. It may well be, as Lady Thatcher suggests, that knowing the Campbells to be respectable people softened her parents' initial suspicion of the cinema as a den of immorality, so that she was allowed to go more frequently as she got older.[81]

In 1980 Mrs Thatcher told Patricia Murray that she herself did 'quite a lot of amateur acting at school which I enjoyed . . . At one stage I really would have liked to have been an actress.'[82] Coming from her background, with her strong sense of social duty and growing interest in politics, the teenage Margaret was never likely to go on the stage, unless she had really kicked over the traces. ('We were not allowed to go to the theatre very much,' she told Miriam Stoppard. 'That was one's upbringing.')[83] There is in fact no record of her having acted seriously at school; she took part in a couple of pageants, but none of her contemporaries remembers her acting, nor does the school magazine mention her name in any school production.[84] It is just conceivable that she appeared in one of Lady Brownlow's productions, but there is no record of it and it is unlikely that her parents would have approved. Her recollection seems to be a retrospective fantasy. Yet the fact that she could believe that it was so confirms an exhibitionist streak in her outwardly staid character. Inside the serious girl there was an actress waiting to emerge. In her fifties Mrs Thatcher unexpectedly discovered an instinct for the limelight which made her a star on a bigger stage than Judy Campbell ever dreamed of.

What she did do during her childhood was read precociously. This was probably the medium of her father's most direct and lasting influence. Alfred was a voracious autodidact, reputed to be 'the best-read man in Grantham' (though one has to wonder when he found the time).[85] 'Each week my father would take two books out of the library – a "serious" book for himself (and me) and a novel for my mother.'[86] It is a telling distinction: serious books – current affairs and politics – are dry, factual and masculine; fiction is frivolous and feminine. From an early age Margaret shared her father's taste. Reading was a means of self-improvement and advancement in the world; he encouraged the young Margaret to read influential books of the moment like John Strachey's *The Coming Struggle for Power* and discussed them with her. He was of course a member of the library committee, so he got the first pick of these topical books. The family also took a daily newspaper – the *Daily Telegraph* – though naturally not a Sunday one; and, according to her memoirs, several weeklies – the *Methodist Recorder, John o'London's Weekly* and – rather adventurously – the pioneering news magazine *Picture Post*, which started in 1938. But it was all reading with a purpose, not for pleasure. Of course she read some classic fiction; but she confesses that her favourite Dickens novel was *A Tale of Two Cities*, because it was about politics.[87]

The exception to this diet of fact would appear to be poetry. Lady Thatcher claims to have been 'fascinated' by poetry from an early age, and it is true that years later she could still quote large chunks from memory. But the bits she quotes in her memoirs are invariably gems of improving doggerel by the likes of Ella Wheeler Wilcox and Longfellow, encapsulating moral lessons which she took to heart:

> The heights by great men reached and kept
> Were not attained by sudden flight
> But they, while their companions slept,
> Were toiling upward in the night.

Poetry was something to be learned and recited in elocution competitions. Her favourite adult poet was Kipling – she later collected editions of his verse and frequently quoted him; but here again her taste seems to have been confined to the well-known patriotic verses. There is no suggestion that she ever experienced poetry as an expression of emotion or sensitivity of feeling.

This utilitarian attitude to literature was reinforced by her formal education. At school she specialised in science, went on to read chemistry at Oxford, and then took up law. From Oxford onwards she devoted most of her spare time to politics. As a result she never had much time to enlarge on her youthful reading. What she read and learned in her first eighteen years, under her father's influence, remained the bedrock of her literary education. In this sense it is literally true that she learned 'almost everything' from her father.

She always insisted that the most important lesson he taught her was to follow her own convictions. 'Never do things just because other people do them,' he told her when she wanted to go dancing.[88] 'Make up your own mind what you are going to do and persuade people to go *your* way.'[89] 'Never go with the crowd,' she paraphrased his advice in 1982. 'Never, never, never.'[90] The paradox, of course, is that she went on, with no sense of contradiction, to pride herself on taking all her ideas from him. 'He brought me up to believe all the things I do believe and they are the values on which I fought the election.'[91] 'It's the sincere approach', she declared on another occasion, 'born of the conviction which I learned in a small town from a father who had a conviction approach.'[92]

It is a curious thing for a strong-minded woman to proclaim in this way her debt to her father, as if she was no more than his echo. In fact she exaggerated the extent of her fidelity to Alfred's teaching – presumably to divert attention from the important respects in which she had abandoned it. Once she had got away from Grantham and embarked upon her own career she quickly adopted a style of life and political values a world away from his spartan ethic. Symbolically, she abandoned her parents' church and gravitated to the Church of England – the Conservative party (as it used to be) at prayer: so much for Methodism. Discovering in London and suburban Kent the *douceur de la vie* lacking in her childhood, she gave her own children an upbringing as different as possible from the puritanical austerity she claimed had been so good for her. Mark and Carol were not made to go to church, she told Patricia Murray, 'because I'd had so much insistence myself'.[93] 'There was not a lot of fun and sparkle in my life,' she told an audience of children in 1980. 'I tried to give my children a little bit more.'[94] An alternative interpretation is that Mark and Carol were smothered in material comforts in guilty compensation for their mother's absence, for most of their childhood, in pursuit of her political career.

Politically she embraced – and at the zenith of her premiership enthusiastically promoted – materialistic values and an ideology of consumption, based on the easy availability of credit, which would have made Alderman Roberts blench. To Brian Walden in 1981 she admitted that her father disapproved of the Stock Market, which he considered 'a form of gambling'.[95] She explicitly abandoned his dedication to serving the whole community ('Together – and for all') in favour of a blatant policy of rewarding her favoured supporters, the home-owning middle class. She devoted much of the energy of her administration to destroying the independence and vitality of local government, to which Alfred had given his life. One could even see her loathing of railways as a rejection of Grantham. All the while, however, she continued to hymn the homely values of the corner shop, lauding the neighbourly virtues of the 'small town' and the 'close family' in which she had been brought up, as a smokescreen for the increasingly fractured society her policies were deliberately creating. Alf Roberts would have been appalled by 'Thatcherism'.

Yet clearly much that Alfred taught his daughter did go into the forging of her creed. The political personality that Margaret Thatcher became was moulded by her upbringing. But the lessons were surely more generalised and less specific than her account suggests. Essentially she took three things from her father's example. First, it was Alfred who instilled in her the habit of hard work, as something both virtuous in itself and the route to self-advancement. Throughout her life, it was her inexhaustible willingness to work longer hours than anyone else, her refusal to go to bed before she had read every last paper, which enabled her repeatedly to beat down colleagues and opponents by sheer mastery of detail. She once confessed to a recurring nightmare that 'I'm going to take my final degree exam tomorrow and I haven't done a stroke of revision and I'm always terribly glad to wake up.'[96] As Prime Minister, Mrs Thatcher still prepared for parliamentary questions or international summits like a schoolgirl swotting for an exam. She was contemptuous of opponents, colleagues or fellow heads of government who had stinted their homework. But however much they had done, she always expected to have done more.

Second, it was the example of Alfred's tireless community activity which bred in his daughter a powerful impulse towards public service. In his case it was expressed as Christian duty: 'duties to the church, duties to your neighbour'. But this almost missionary vocation to give others – less fortunate, less capable and probably less hard-working – the benefit of his advice was combined with a shrewd understanding of the rewards to be gained from public life.

In other words, 'duty' was a cover – or euphemism – for ambition. Alfred encouraged Margaret to take an interest in public affairs and took her with him to meetings and council business; he showed her a masculine world beyond her mother's narrow domestic sphere. His political ambition was limited to his home town; but within Grantham he involved himself in everything. Margaret's horizon was wider, extending via Oxford to national politics and eventually the whole world. But her restless belief in her duty to put the world to rights was only a projection on a wider stage of the same missionary impulse which took Alfred from the pulpit of Finkin Street church to the council chamber.

Related to this was the third, and perhaps most important, legacy which Alfred gave his daughter: an exceptionally powerful moral sense. More than anything else in her political make-up, it was her fierce confidence that she knew right from wrong – even if what was right was not always immediately attainable – which marked Margaret Thatcher out from contemporary politicians. She believed absolutely in her own integrity and habitually disparaged the motives of those who disagreed with her. This rare moral certainty and unreflective self-righteousness was her greatest political strength in the muddy world of political expediency and compromise; it was also in the end her greatest weakness.

Her moralism, however, was much more aggressive than her father's. Alf Roberts was ambitious, hard-working, outspoken in defence of his beliefs; but his manner was quiet, his style clear but conciliatory. His Christianity was stern, a touch self-satisfied but by all accounts – including his daughter's – surprisingly tolerant and non-judgemental. He always maintained good relations with his opponents in the council chamber. Margaret's temperament was much more combative, more divisive. Both politically and socially she saw the world in black and white and divided people, institutions and countries ruthlessly into sheep and goats: 'us' to be encouraged and rewarded, 'them' to be defeated and destroyed. This crusading quality she did not learn at her father's knee.

So the question remains: where did this aggression come from? Why was she so driven? In spite of everything she would have us believe about her happy family home, her obsessive conscientiousness and extreme combativeness suggest a deep-seated insecurity which must go back to childhood. As the second child did the young Margaret have to compete with her elder sister to win approval from her busy mother and her demanding father? Could there be something in the suggestion that Alfred and Beatie had hoped for a son, so that Alfred in particular invested masculine expectations in her that he had not placed on Muriel? Clearly Margaret had above-average ability for him to work with, and an exceptional willingness to apply herself. But there does not seem to have been much spontaneous curiosity in her reading. It was all work, directed by Alfred, with no moment wasted, no time for the imagination, dreaming or self-discovery. All her life she was pathologically unable to relax, for fear that she would lose ground, be caught out and somehow be punished for it. It is impossible that this pressure was not implanted in childhood.

She did feel stirrings of rebellion, but they were usually suppressed. 'If you were rude or naughty', she once recalled, 'you were sent to your room and you stayed there until you came down and apologised. But this didn't seem to happen all that often.'[97] Of course, the 1930s were a more obedient and deferential age; but even so, it is not natural for a clever girl to have been so dominated by her father as she suggests – even boasts – she was. She conformed, repressed her instinct to rebel; but later, much later, her pent-up rebellion burst with extraordinary energy on the political stage. Her whole career, in fact, is marked by this tension between conformity and rebellion. For twenty years she made her way unnoticed through the consensual, paternalistic Tory party of Churchill, Macmillan and Heath; when she finally broke cover in 1974 to smash the consensus, her radicalism was still couched in the outward forms and language of Conservatism. She continued to dress and speak like a Home Counties lady, even as she detonated a bomb under the British establishment. Is it far-fetched to see this genteel revolution as a form of delayed and displaced revenge upon her father? The very unnatural emphasis with which she insisted on her father's teaching suggests a guilty – perhaps unconscious – compensation for the fact that she was actually striking at much that he held dear.

The most extraordinary thing about Mrs Thatcher's mythologisation of her father is that it was entirely retrospective. Having once escaped from Alfred at the age of eighteen she saw very little of him for the remainder of his life. In 1951 she took her fiancé to meet his prospective in-laws. Denis later described his reception as 'lukewarm . . . I swear her father had to blow the dust off the sherry bottle.'[98] It was only since he had been mayor, in fact, that Alfred had kept any drink in the house at all. Alfred and his son-in-law had nothing in common. Once they were married, Margaret and Denis went back to Grantham rarely. When Beatie died in 1960, Alf remarried – a local farmer's widow called Cissie Hubbard, with grown-up children. 'I suppose that's a good thing,' Margaret witheringly confided. 'She's a nice homely little woman.'[99] He lived until

February 1970. He was proud of his daughter being a Member of Parliament, and was said to have been listening to her on a radio discussion programme just before he died. But he did not live quite long enough to see her in the Cabinet – though, curiously, she believed he did.[100] Perhaps she was thinking of the Shadow Cabinet; but her mistake suggests that he did not share very closely in her triumphs. He had only a graduation photograph of her in his house: nothing more recent, and no pictures of his grandchildren.[101] Mark and Carol were sixteen when Alfred died, yet appear to have little memory of him. The impression is inescapable that Margaret was very much less devoted to her wonderful father while he was alive than she became to his sanctified image after he was dead.

2

Serious Schoolgirl

THE key to Margaret Roberts' escape from Grantham was education. For her, as for other bright boys and girls from relatively humble provincial homes in that interwar generation, the two vital rungs on the ladder which set them on the way to careers in politics were grammar school followed by Oxford – or more rarely Cambridge. Ted Heath the carpenter's son from Broadstairs, Harold Wilson from Huddersfield, Barbara Castle from Bradford, Roy Jenkins from Pontypool were all a little older, but all blazed the same trail a few years before her. Each of them, like her, bore the stamp of their own particular background and parentage. But for all of them, winning a place at Oxford was the critical leap which enabled them to transcend their background and compete on equal terms with the private school educated elite.

Margaret's formal education began a few weeks before her fifth birthday, on 3 September 1930, at Huntingtower Road County Elementary School. A good mile from North Parade – but in the same street where Alfred had his second shop – Huntingtower Road was reputed to be the best council school in Grantham. According to Lady Thatcher's own account she could already read by the time she went there, and she quickly moved up a year. She was already formidably diligent and competitive. At the age of nine she won a poetry recital competition at the local festival – curiously called an *eisteddfod*. When the head congratulated her, saying she was lucky, she denied it indignantly: 'I wasn't lucky. I deserved it.'[1] She would always believe that if she worked hard she would deserve to win. The following year, when still only ten, she won a scholarship to the fee-paying girls' grammar school, Kesteven and Grantham Girls' School, where her sister Muriel had already gone before her. In fact Alfred paid Margaret's fees too, since the scholarship was means-tested; it was nevertheless a useful insurance, and a considerable achievement – though she was still placed initially in the 'B' stream.

KGGS (as it is known) was only founded in 1910, and the first headmistress and several of the original teachers were still there in 1936. It had a mixed intake of around 350 girls, including some boarders. About a quarter paid no fees; conversely a substantial number came from 'good families' from outside Grantham. Though Miss Williams and her staff were all high-minded spinsters, dedicated to their profession, the school's educational horizons were limited: only a handful of girls each year went on to university. From the moment she arrived Margaret Roberts did conspicuously well: but though she was top of her class in her first year she still had to wait another year before she was moved up to the 'A' stream. Her reports give a clear picture of her character. At Christmas 1936 she was said to have 'worked steadily and well throughout the term. She has definite ability, and her cheeriness makes her a very pleasant member of her form. Her behaviour is excellent.' The following July she won praise for 'neat and careful work'. The next year she was 'a very helpful member of her form' and 'achieved a high standard in every subject'.

Once promoted to the 'A' stream she continued to come top every year (except once, when she was second) and the school began to appreciate her potential. By her fourth year her work was showing 'more than usual depth of understanding'; she was 'showing the makings of a real student. She thinks clearly and logically, and expresses herself well in writing.' She was particularly commended for 'the care and thoroughness with which she works always'.[2] In her fifth year (the summer of 1941) she sat her School Certificate: she passed well in all subjects, but her methodical approach naturally directed her towards specialising in the sciences in the Lower Sixth.

In her memoirs Lady Thatcher claims to have had a particularly inspiring history teacher – Miss Ophelia Harding – 'who gave me a taste for the subject which, unfortunately, I never developed'.[3] In earlier recollections, however, she somehow failed to mention Miss Harding. Contemporaries remember her as 'a dear person' – she was one of those who had been at the school since 1910 – but very anecdotal and not at all inspiring. 'The subject was taught as a series of events.'[4] The truth is that by the time she wrote *The Path to Power* Lady Thatcher had developed a bee in her bonnet about history teaching in the national curriculum and was exaggerating Miss Harding's influence retrospectively.

The teacher who did influence her was the chemistry teacher,

Miss Kay. An interest in chemistry was not something she derived from her father, nor was it the most obvious subject for a girl precociously consumed by current affairs; later, when she had set her sights on a political career, she regretted having been sidetracked into science. At the age of sixteen, however, chemistry was her best subject. It suited the practical bent of her mind, and – most important at that age – she liked her teacher. It was a sensible subject, leading to good employment prospects. At the same time science was also glamorous in 1941, a horizon of infinite possibility. 'That was a period', she told George Gardiner in 1975, 'when we were dazzled by what it could achieve. We thought there were no problems that could not ultimately be answered by science.'[5]

Though remembered as an unusually serious girl, Margaret was not unpopular at school. She was not resented, one contemporary told Patricia Murray, 'because she wasn't an exhibitionist, nor was she the bossy type. In fact she was a rather quiet unassuming girl who was generally well-liked.'[6] She was friendly, helpful and generous in sharing sweets and other goodies from her father's shop. Others have an abiding memory of her briefcase always bulging with books, and the fact that it was invariably Margaret Roberts who asked the first question of visiting speakers, in studiously correct parliamentary language.[7] She already commanded a certain authority among her peers: more than sixty years later a contemporary vividly recalled a country walk with friends near Grantham, discussing the facts of life. One girl was confident she knew it all; the others – they were all about eleven – were incredulous. 'Oh yes,' the first girl insisted, 'I got it from Margaret Roberts, and she's always right.'[8]

The only schoolfriend mentioned by name in Lady Thatcher's memoirs was a builder's daughter from ten miles outside Grantham called Jean Farmer.[9] More important to the course of her life, however – the one contemporary she still kept up with until quite recently – was Margaret Goodrich, the daughter of the vicar of Corby Glen, a few miles south of Grantham. A year older than Margaret Roberts, from a more comfortable and educated home, Margaret Goodrich always expected to go on to Oxford; her father took an interest in Margaret Roberts, lent her books, helped her with her Latin and encouraged the grocer's daughter to nurse the same ambition. She used to go to tea at Corby Glen – taking with her, during the war, a string bag full of rationed goods. The vicarage thus furnished her first bolt-hole from the claustrophobia of her own family, while Canon Goodrich was an intellectual mentor very different from her autodidact father. When she took Denis Thatcher to Grantham before they were married, she made a point of going to

Corby Glen to show him what she called 'the library', though the family only thought of it as a room with a lot of books.[10] By contrast Margaret Goodrich never visited the flat above the shop in North Parade.*

Despite her solid academic record, neither her peers nor her teachers regarded the young Margaret Roberts as anything remarkable. Even Margaret Goodrich (now Wickstead) believes that she was 'not outstanding in any way'.[11] Marjorie Sansbury, who taught English at KGGS for many years, barely recalled her: 'She was not distinguished in English . . . Moreover she was a "good" girl. I fear that one tends to remember those who are rebellious.'[12] Her early biographers exaggerated her extra-curricular accomplishments – claiming, for instance, that she was the star, or even the captain, of an exceptionally successful hockey team. In fact, as she admitted in 1971, 'I wasn't really very good at games, although I think I was in the hockey team for some time, but I didn't really enjoy it very much.'[13] In her memoirs she describes herself as 'a somewhat erratic player'.[14] She sang in the school choir, and also played the piano to a good standard – though not at school. She was taught at home, initially by her mother, later by a teacher who came from Lincoln. At the 1937 eisteddfod she and another girl won the prize for the under-14 piano duet. The *Grantham Journal* commended their 'very nice style and technique', but looked for 'a little more vitality and spring in their playing'. (The paper was more complimentary about Margaret Roberts' solo playing, which displayed 'a great deal of ease and facility . . . and had imagination', though it was 'a little uncontrolled in tone'.[15] Perhaps she was better playing by herself than in a team.)

The same year she also won a silver medal for elocution; but though the school dramatic society was active (performing abridged versions of Shakespeare, Sheridan and Shaw's *Saint Joan*), contemporaries are adamant that she was not a member. Nor did she debate at school – as Hugo Young asserted – for the good reason that the debating club was not formed until 1944, a year after she had left. (Lady Thatcher herself does not claim that she did.) In fact it is striking that her name appears not at all in the school magazine, whose recurrent stars – regularly winning prizes and contributing essays and poems – are Margaret Goodrich and Madeline Edwards.[16] It would appear that Margaret Roberts got on quietly with her work and made little wider impact on the school.

---

* In 1982, as Prime Minister, Mrs Thatcher was able to repay some of the kindness she received from the Goodrich family by appointing Margaret's younger brother, Philip, Bishop of Worcester.

She had only been at KGGS three years when the Second World War started; so the bulk of her school life was severely disrupted by the threat of air raids, the fitting of gas masks, the routines of blackout and fire-watching. The hockey pitch was given up to growing hay. Girls' schools suffered less than boys' schools, which lost most of their younger staff. But for five terms the Camden School for Girls was evacuated from North London to double up in the already cramped KGGS building (bringing with them the bust of their founder, the famous Miss Buss): KGGS used the classrooms in the mornings, the Camden girls in the afternoons.[17] From September 1940, however, Grantham came under heavy bombing: the school was never hit, but in March 1941 the Camden girls moved again to a safer haven in Uppingham.

During this period, the *Grantham Journal* boasted after the war, 'Grantham borough suffered more from bomb damage and casualties than any other of Great Britain'. The claim is questionable, but the best figures seem to be 21 raids (from 386 alerts), resulting in 80 houses demolished, 70 people killed and about 200 injured.[18] The heaviest raid, on 24 October 1942, killed 32 people, not far from KGGS. Two bombs fell close to North Parade in February and March 1941. Margaret did much of her work for her School Certificate under the kitchen table. In their spare time KGGS girls did voluntary war work, serving in WVS and Toc H canteens. Life at home was also affected: Alfred was busier than ever in his public role as Chief Welfare Officer, while the shop had to handle the complexities of rationing. Customers had to register with a particular butcher or grocer, who was then responsible for taking their coupons and enforcing fair shares.

Margaret was not quite fourteen when the war began, nearly twenty when it ended; it overshadowed her entire adolescence and was overwhelmingly the formative influence on her political development and specifically her approach to international relations. She came to political awareness in the mid-1930s at just the moment when international crises – in Abyssinia, the Rhineland, Spain and Czechoslovakia – began to dominate the news. Her first political memory was the so-called 'Peace Ballot' organised by the League of Nations Union in 1934. At a time when most Methodists inclined towards pacifism, Alfred appears to have been exceptionally aware of the threatening European situation, convinced of the need for rearmament to resist Nazism, and also – more unusually – concerned about the plight of the Jews. In 1938 the Roberts family briefly gave sanctuary to a seventeen-year-old Austrian girl – the penfriend of Margaret's sister Muriel – sent to England by her parents to escape the *Anschluss*. She did not stay long – Alfred persuaded other Rotary families to take her in turn – but she brought the reality of what was happening in central Europe home to North Parade.[*]

Among the popular books of the moment which Alfred read – and encouraged Margaret to read – were Douglas Reed's *Insanity Fair*, which described the Nazi persecution of the Jews, and Robert Bruce Lockhart's *Guns or Butter?*, one of the most influential early critiques of appeasement. Yet Lady Thatcher's account in her memoirs of the whole Roberts family's robust clear-sightedness – 'We had a deep distrust of dictators . . . I knew just what I thought of Hitler' – is perhaps just a bit self-serving.[20] To Anthony King in 1974 she remembered rather more ambiguously that at first 'one was undecided whether Hitler was doing a superb job of organisation or a terrifying job of tyranny'.[21] It may be relevant that when J. A. Campbell visited Germany on behalf of Grantham Rotary in 1934 – admittedly when Margaret was only nine – his report in the *Grantham Journal* was headlined 'The Great Hitler'.[22]

By the time she came to write her memoirs the Iron Lady was keen to emphasise her lifelong credentials as an enemy of appeasement. As Prime Minister she went to Prague in 1990 to apologise in person for Britain's betrayal of Czechoslovakia at Munich: 'We failed you in 1938 . . . We still remember it with shame.'[23] But the only surviving record of Alfred's view at the time is rather more ambivalent. Speaking as chairman of Grantham Rotary Club's International Service Committee at a dinner in January 1939 – that is four months after Munich – he asserted that Rotary's central principles of 'justice, truth and liberty' were absolute, not relative, warned that might was not always right and insisted that 'weak nations have sacred rights too, and . . . they must be respected'. But he went on:

> It did not matter to them whether people were strongly armed or whether they were almost unarmed. They had seen, quite recently, what one man could do, armed only with a neatly rolled umbrella, with his mind made up and his will intent on peace.

---

[*] Edith Muhlbauer also brought a touch of middle-European sophistication to Grantham: she wore lipstick, smoked Sobranie cigarettes and flirted with the boys. Alfred is said to have worried that she was going to turn into 'one of those girls in Amsterdam'. She remembers him gratefully, however, as 'a serious and lovely man', and the thirteen-year-old Margaret as 'a reserved child with beautiful hair'. After staying with eighteen different families in less than two years she moved on in 1940 to live with relatives in South America.[19]

The next speaker spoke gratefully of Munich as 'a modern miracle' which had prevented apparently certain war.[24]

Roberts certainly condemned appeasement retrospectively. In November 1945, just after his election as mayor, he told a Rotary lunch of the lessons to be learned from the prewar experience.

> We were becoming a race of sentimentalists. We thought we could save the world by being ultra-kind to people who did not understand kindness . . . We cannot and must not keep giving way and compromising in trying to appease an aggressive people. They have got to be made to understand quite firmly and definitely that what they ask for is wrong.[25]

By 1945, of course, that was the conventional wisdom. But there are grounds for thinking that he was not quite so clear-sighted in 1938.

The war itself was a formative influence for Margaret Thatcher's whole generation. Yet it affected her in a crucially different way from her male contemporaries. She was not only just too young to fight: she was the wrong sex. She could have joined one of the women's services when she left school, which would have got her into uniform and closer to the action; but still she could never have gained that first-hand experience of combat which left such a deep and lasting impression on practically all the young men who became her rivals and colleagues in the years ahead. Most of them came out of the forces with a powerful awareness of the barbarity of war, a strong sense of comradeship with the men of all ranks with whom they had served, and a deep-seated if unformed belief that Europe must somehow unite to make another war impossible. Mrs Thatcher's experience on the home front – listening to Churchill in the blackout, following the campaigns with little flags on maps – taught her different lessons. On the one hand, emotionally but not physically involved in the conflict, she was able to preserve a more idealised view of war than those who fought in it. She experienced it – inevitably – at second hand through romanticising books like Richard Hillary's *The Last Enemy*; Barbara Cartland's biography of her brother Ronald, who was killed in the Battle of Britain; and Herbert Agar's *A Time for Greatness*, published in 1944, all of which emphasised the moral uplift of war. On the other hand the war stoked up her patriotism and bred an unshakeable belief in British superiority.

Unlike those who served during or after the war in France, Germany, the Mediterranean or the Far East, Mrs Thatcher never set foot out of England before her honeymoon in 1952. Seen from

Grantham, the peoples of the continent were either odious enemies to be defeated, or useless allies who had to be saved from the consequences of their own feebleness by the British and Americans. By contrast the Americans were cousins, partners, friends: powerful and generous, the saviours of democracy, champions of freedom, prosperity and progress. Nor was this a merely abstract admiration: from 1942 onwards there was a large presence of American airmen stationed at bases around Grantham. Though they excited considerable interest among the local girls, there is no record that any of them tried to take up with Margaret Roberts. She never had much time for that sort of thing. But she saw the Americans around the town, noted the spending power they brought to the local economy, and could hear them flying out each day to bomb Germany – the British boys flew the night missions.[26] RAF Cranwell was just ten miles north of Grantham, and she later claimed to have known some of the British pilots who never came back.[27]

We are dealing with simplistic stereotypes here. But there can be no doubt that Mrs Thatcher's instinctive and lifelong belief in the Atlantic alliance as the first principle of British foreign policy, and her equally instinctive contempt for the continental Europeans, derived from her particular experience of the Second World War – an experience unique among British politicians of the postwar era. The only comparable woman, Barbara Castle (who was fourteen years older), spent most of the war working in the Ministry of Food. Among the men, Harold Wilson was also a desk warrior. But of Mrs Thatcher's future colleagues in Conservative Cabinets, the generation slightly older than her (including Edward Heath, Willie Whitelaw, Keith Joseph, Peter Carrington and Francis Pym) had all fought through the war. Those of her own age (James Prior, Ian Gilmour, Geoffrey Howe) either saw action at the end of it or served in the forces for two or three years after it. The next group, up to fifteen years younger (people like Michael Heseltine, Nigel Lawson and Kenneth Baker), all did National Service; while the generation which increasingly comprised her last Cabinet (John Major, Chris Patten, William Waldegrave, Malcolm Rifkind) were too young to remember the war at all. It is impossible to overemphasise the significance of this gulf of perception. It was not just her sex which made Mrs Thatcher different: the most important consequence of her sex was her lack of military experience.

Whether on account of the war or her extra-curricular interests, Margaret's school work seems to have suffered slightly in the Lower

Sixth. For the first and only time her overall mark slipped below 70 per cent and her grade from D ('exceptionally good') to G (merely 'very good'). While she got her usual Ds in chemistry, biology, zoology and geography, she was pulled down by managing no more than F ('fair to weak') in English and French. (She appears to have dropped history and maths altogether.) 'M. has tackled a new syllabus capably,' her report stated at the end of 1941, commending her 'general intelligence and determination'. At Easter 1942: 'She applies herself steadily and should do very well in her main subjects, but must try to give more attention to French and English.' The next term she duly improved her French and English, but at the expense of her sciences, and got no D grades at all. Her end of year report was guarded – 'Margaret learns her work carefully and has made good progress' – and casts an intriguing doubt on her self-portrayal as a precocious and voracious reader. 'Wider reading', it recommended, 'should develop both her style and her powers of understanding and independent judgment.'[28] Perhaps from the school's point of view she was reading the wrong things.

The problem may have been that she did not get on with the new headmistress. In April 1939 the widely beloved Miss Williams had retired, to be replaced – just in time for the outbreak of war – by Miss Dorothy Gillies, a very different character. Miss Gillies was an Edinburgh Scot, 'a perfectionist and a disciplinarian [who] would not tolerate inefficiency at any level'[29] – just the type, one might have thought, to appreciate Margaret Roberts. For some reason, however, she seems not to have shared Miss Roberts' view of her own potential. First she tried to discourage her from applying to Oxford. ('You're thwarting my ambition,' Margaret told her.) Then she discouraged her from sitting the Indian Civil Service exam, since so few women ever passed it. ('All the more reason to try,' Margaret is said to have retorted.) Miss Gillies refused to teach her Latin, which she would need for Oxford, though she did teach it privately to Margaret Goodrich. (This may be why Harold Goodrich came to the rescue.) Eventually Alfred had to pay for her to have special tuition from a master at the boys' grammar school.

Miss Gillies' obstructiveness is odd, since Alfred had been a governor of the school since 1931 and was soon to become chairman of the governors: but perhaps that is why Miss Gillies wished to take his daughter down a peg. Whatever the reason, Mrs Thatcher nursed a lifelong resentment of Miss Gillies. In 1960, now a newly-elected MP, she paid her first return visit to the school as a distinguished old girl: she caused extreme offence by snubbing Miss Gillies and

gratuitously correcting her Latin.[30]* In 1982 she returned as Prime
Minister to unveil a plaque of herself: this time she fulsomely
remembered Miss Williams and failed to mention Miss Gillies at all.[32]

Though she did not sit her Higher School Certificate until 1943,
she had already received offers from both Nottingham ('our local
university') and Bedford College, London, before the end of 1942.
Despite Miss Gillies, however, she was determined, with Alfred's
support, to try for Oxford, where Margaret Goodrich had already
preceded her. ('I regarded it as being quite simply the best, and if I
was serious about getting on in life that is what I should always strive
for . . . I was never tempted to opt for Nottingham.')[33] So she sat the
Somerville scholarship in December 1942. She narrowly missed a
scholarship (she was, as she points out in her memoirs, only
seventeen); but she was offered a place for October 1944. The lost
year was important since, under wartime regulations, unless she went
up in 1943 she would only be allowed to take a two-year degree
before being called up for National Service. Still it was a considerable
achievement to have won a place. Miss Gillies managed to be quite
extraordinarily grudging:

Margaret is to be congratulated . . . on the very successful
achievement of gaining a place at Somerville College, Oxford. I
hope that she will show wisdom in the allotting of both time and
energy to her work during the coming months, in order that she
may do herself full justice.

At the end of the summer term Miss Gillies was still plainly trying
to defend her original doubts:

A good report: we hope that the past two years of very diligent
work will bring their own reward of a really good Higher School
Certificate, and a successful university career to follow.
  Margaret is ambitious and deserves to do well. She has shown
herself capable of a very thorough mastery of facts and is, I
consider, now ready for the experience of wider scholarship
which a University education has to offer.[34]

With a university place secured, but a year to fill before she could
expect to take it up, the natural thing for a patriotic eighteen year old
in the middle of the war might have been to do as many of her

* 'I always enjoy coming back to Grantham,' Madeline Hellaby (née Edwards)
said to her on this occasion. 'Do you?' Mrs Thatcher replied with astonishment.[31]

contemporaries had already done and join one of the women's services; or, if that would have committed her for too long a period, at least found some other form of war work while she waited to go to Oxford. It is a little odd that she chose instead to go back to school for another year. The autumn term began in August, three weeks early to allow an October break for potato picking.

On their first day back, Miss Gillies called Margaret and Madeline Edwards in to tell them that they had passed their Higher Certificate. (They were in fact the only two who had taken it.) They were then appointed joint Head Girl. That term a new young French teacher, Christine Goodison, joined the school. One of her first assignments was to give Margaret Roberts extra tuition. After her first lesson, other teachers were keen to hear how she had got on, as though she might have found her pupil – only slightly younger than herself – too formidable to handle; in fact she found her 'very biddable, very attentive, very eager to learn'. Correcting one loose piece of translation, she remembers telling Margaret that she must be more accurate or one day she might cause an international incident. It was no secret that Miss Roberts had already set her sights on politics, or at least the Foreign Office.[35]

Just three weeks into the term there came a telephone call from Somerville: a vacancy had arisen – another girl had presumably decided that she had more compelling priorities – so Miss Roberts was offered the chance to take up her place immediately. She therefore left KGGS in the middle of the term, left home and Grantham and went up to Oxford in October 1943, with the opportunity after all to enjoy a full three years.

3

Oxford Tory

GOING to Oxford was the great opportunity which changed Margaret Roberts' life, opened doors to her and set her on the way to a political career. Yet Oxford was not for her, as it was for so many others, a golden period of youthful experiment and self-discovery. In the four years she eventually spent there she made no lasting friendships, underwent no intellectual awakening. She did not light up the university in any way: none of her contemporaries saw her as anything remarkable, still less picked her as a future Prime Minister. In this she somewhat resembled Harold Wilson – another hard-working, conscientious northern grammar school product who made little impression on his clever contemporaries. Unlike Wilson, however, she was already more than half-determined to go into politics and used her time at Oxford quite deliberately to make connections which would be useful to her in years to come. The fact that no one noticed her was largely a function of her sex: Oxford in the 1940s was still a predominantly male society, and the Union in particular – the playground where generations of aspiring politicians strutted, trying out on one another the *mots* and mannerisms they would later take to Westminster – was barred to women, who were obliged to confine their political activity to the less glamorous back rooms of the Conservative Association and the Labour Club. But even within the Conservative Association (OUCA) Margaret Roberts seemed no more than diligent. The most remarkable thing about her Oxford career, in fact, was how little the experience seemed to change her. Though she later claimed that 'my ideas took form at Oxford',[1] her time at university was a much less formative period for her than for most young people. She had unusually fixed convictions when she went up, and she developed them remarkably little while she was there.

45

Admittedly, Oxford in wartime was a shadow of its normal self. There were more women than usual, and fewer men; rather than giving the women more opportunity to shine, however, the men's absence seemed to drain the place of much of its energy. Those that remained tended be either old or in some other way unfit for military service, or else young and waiting to be called up. Though the war was past its crisis by 1943 they were still constrained from throwing themselves into normal undergraduate pleasures by the knowledge that others were in uniform. They compensated by helping in forces canteens and other voluntary war work; and by concentrating diligently on their studies. Only with the end of the war did the atmosphere lighten. The Oxford to which Margaret Roberts returned for her third year in October 1945 was transformed – the blackout lifted, the colleges and clubs suddenly full of young men demobilised from the forces, older, more experienced and more confident than the usual gauche schoolboys, keen both to enoy themselves and change the world. She responded, and in her last two years began cautiously to join in the greater frivolity.

When she first went up, however, she was overawed. Apart from her one memorable trip to London when she was twelve, and going to Oxford for the scholarship exam the previous December, she had scarcely been further afield than shopping trips to Nottingham with Muriel or her mother. The bleak opening of the Oxford chapter of her memoirs is still eloquent after fifty years:

> Oxford does not set out to please. Freshmen arrive there for the Michaelmas term in the misty gloom of October. Monumental buildings impress initially by their size rather than their exquisite architecture. Everything is cold and strangely forbidding. Or so it seemed to me.[2]

She was given rooms in college, but was slow to make friends. 'I kept myself to myself', she wrote in her memoirs, 'for I felt shy and ill at ease in this quite new environment.' She used to take 'long walks on my own . . . enjoying my own company and thoughts'.[3] This, if true, is a serious indication of loneliness, since in later life she abominated walking and would never walk anywhere in town or country if she could avoid it. Some weeks after the beginning of term Margaret Goodrich's parents came to visit their daughter: they called on Margaret Roberts and found her disconsolately toasting crumpets, very glad to see them.[4] 'Yes, I was homesick,' she admitted to Patricia Murray. 'I think there would be something very wrong with your home life if you weren't just a little.'[5] She gradually

filled her rooms with familiar pictures and bits of furniture brought
from home; but at the same time, faced by an alarming preponderance of self-confident public school girls, she felt ashamed of her
unglamorous background. She once asked Margaret Goodrich:
'Don't you wish you could say you had been to Cheltenham or
somewhere, instead of KGGS?'[6]

Her principal antidote to loneliness was work; but in some ways
this only increased it. Chemistry is an unsociable course of study,
involving long hours alone in the laboratory: years later she recalled
that science was 'impersonal', compared with arts subjects which
gave more opportunity for discussion and debate.[7] She was probably
already beginning to regret having chosen chemistry; but she stuck at
it conscientiously – it was her 'duty' – and she was more than
competent at it, combining as she did a clear mind with an infinite
capacity for taking pains. Years later, when she had become Prime
Minister, her former tutors were inclined to disparage her ability.
Dame Janet Vaughan – not herself a chemist but a clinical pathologist
– who became Principal of Somerville in 1945, was frankly
dismissive: 'She was a perfectly adequate chemist. I mean nobody
thought anything of her. She was a perfectly good second-class
chemist, a beta chemist.'[8] Dorothy Hodgkin, the Nobel prizewin-
ning crystallographer, was kinder, but still damned her memory with
faint praise: 'I came to rate her as good. One could always rely on
her producing a sensible, well-read essay and yet there was
something that some people had that she hadn't quite got.'[9]

What she lacked, evidently, was imagination: a faculty she lacked,
as it happens, not just in chemistry. But then, as Dorothy Hodgkin
also noted, 'she was not absolutely devoted to it'.[10] Why should she
be? She had no intention of becoming a chemist, except in the short
term. With a good deal of retrospective malice – since they
thoroughly disliked what she had become – these world-class
academics judged her by the highest academic standards, which were
not appropriate. In her third year she devoted more of her time to
politics and less to work. Had she dedicated herself single-mindedly
to getting a First she might – by sheer application – have succeeded.
As it was she won a university essay prize, shared with another
Somerville girl. But she was not so single-minded. Moreover she was
ill during her final exams. 'I had a rather tough time during schools',
she wrote to an OUCA colleague, 'and had to do some of my papers
in bed feeling thoroughly lousy and incapable of thinking.'[11] In the
circumstances she did pretty well to take a solid Second. It was good
enough to allow her to come back for a fourth year to do a BSc.

Outside her work, her most active commitment in her first two years was the John Wesley Society. This was a natural refuge for a shy provincial girl of Methodist upbringing, an opportunity to meet people like herself with similar habits and assumptions. She attended the Wesley Memorial Church on Sundays, and her social life revolved around the Methodist Study Group and tea parties run by the Students' Fellowship. It would be easy to conclude that the reassuring familiarity of Methodism was simply a comfort blanket while she found her feet: 'a sober but cheerful social life', as she put it, 'which I found the more valuable in my initially somewhat strange surroundings'.[12] But she took it more seriously than that. The Wesley Society used to send its members out in pairs to preach in the surrounding villages – exactly as Alfred preached in the villages around Grantham. Margaret readily joined in this activity. Fifty years later, a Somerville contemporary and fellow-Methodist, Jean Southerst, clearly remembered a sermon she preached on the text 'Seek ye first the Kingdom of God; and all these things shall be added unto you', which was regarded by all who heard it as 'outstanding'.[13] No doubt it owed a lot to Alfred; but it should not be forgotten that when, much later, she was invited to expound her faith from a number of famous pulpits, she had done it before. She was a preacher before she was a politician.

Jean Southerst recalls, as one might expect, that Margaret's commitment to the John Wesley Society was 'gradually overshadowed by her growing involvement with the OUCA' – the university Conservative Association.[14] But the idea that her Methodist identity was something she quickly left behind as she began moving in more worldly circles is contradicted by Nigel Jilson, who was her group leader in the Wesley Society in her third year. Jilson, later a Methodist minister, remembers her as an active and regular member of the group, attending discussions and prayer meetings and 'exploring the faith together as questioning young people'. Whereas Jean Southerst recalls Margaret's Methodism as practical and uncomplicated, Jilson suggests a more spiritual side to her. He remembers a young woman of strong views, open, sincere and – an unusual epithet – 'effervescent'.[15] She kept her politics separate from her faith. Both contemporaries knew that she was a Conservative – which was 'unusual' in 1946 – but she never talked politics with them. Neither – more surprisingly in this context – did she talk much about her father; they knew he was a lay preacher and mayor of Grantham that year, but she did not go on about him.

Her other social activity was singing. This was another link with home: she had sung in the Finkin Street church choir, which had a strong tradition of performing the great choral works with visiting professional soloists. She now joined the Oxford Bach Choir – like Edward Heath a few years earlier – and sang first alto under the baton of Thomas Armstrong, the father of her future Cabinet Secretary, Robert Armstrong. She also sang occasionally in the Balliol/Somerville choir. As well as the *St Matthew Passion* and Brahms' *German Requiem* they sang more contemporary works such as Holst's *Hymn of Jesus* and Constant Lambert's *Rio Grande*. Music, however, was something that found little place in her life after Oxford. She had given up the piano in order to do Latin for her Oxford entrance; and she never went back to it.

By far the most important thing she did in her first term was to join the Conservative Association. There was no question of her joining any other party, or all the political clubs as some new undergraduates did. She had no doubt of her allegiance; she already worshipped Winston Churchill. Another Somerville contemporary, the novelist Nina Bawden, recorded a vivid memory of Margaret Roberts' early political commitment. Recalling 'a plump, neat, solemn girl with rosy cheeks and fairish hair curled flat to her head who spoke as if she had just emerged from an elocution lesson', she remembers being 'genuinely shocked to hear that Margaret had joined the Conservatives'. While fire-watching one night towards the end of their first year she told Margaret that girls from lower middle-class backgrounds like theirs should be trying to build a new and better world, not joining the ranks of the privileged; she added that all the lively people at Oxford were in the Labour Club, while 'all the people in the Conservative Club were as dull as ditchwater'.

> Margaret smiled, her pretty china doll smile. Of course, she admitted, the Labour Club was just at the moment more *fashionable* . . . but that in a way unintentionally suited her purposes. Unlike me she was not 'playing' at politics. She meant to get into Parliament and there was more chance of being 'noticed' in the Conservative Club just because some of the members were a bit stodgy.[16]

This reply disingenuously understates her commitment: she was already a Conservative by conviction, not calculation. At the same time calculation was never absent from her make-up, and Nina Bawden's snapshot is early evidence of the sort of shrewd opportunism which Mrs Thatcher displayed throughout her career.

Miss Bawden's memory also contradicts Mrs Thatcher's insistence that she never thought of a political career until much later.

Another contemporary, Ann Dally, also remembered Margaret Roberts' Conservatism as the only remarkable thing about her.

> In wartime Oxford, most students were left-wing, especially at Somerville . . . We used to laugh at Margaret Roberts when she knocked on our doors and tried to sell us tickets for the Conservative Club ball or a similar event. She seemed so solemn and assured about it and we were intolerant of other people's certainties.
>
> If I had been told that the first woman Prime Minister would be one of us, I would not have put Margaret among my first six guesses. This was because most of us found her boring and I think it did not occur to any of us in those heady days that anyone who was boring could possibly reach high places.[17]

To Janet Vaughan, proud of Somerville's left-wing reputation, Miss Roberts was an embarrassment, a cuckoo in her progressive nest.

> She fascinated me. I used to talk to her a great deal; she was an oddity. Why? She was a Conservative. She stood out. Somerville had always been a radical establishment and there weren't many Conservatives about then. We used to argue about politics; she was so set in steel as a Conservative. She just had this one line . . .
> We used to entertain a good deal at weekends, but she didn't get invited. She had nothing to contribute, you see.[18]

It would be hard to overestimate the effect of this sort of snobbish condescension on the formation of Margaret Thatcher's character. The discovery that all the trendy people were against her only confirmed her certainty that they were all wrong and reinforced her righteous sense of persecution. She encountered the same patronising attitude when she first became Leader of the Opposition in 1975. She had probably met it already at school, where she was used to being a loner who was not allowed to go to dances: it was precisely the attitude Alfred had tried to arm her against by urging her to follow her own – or his – convictions and ignore the crowd. But nowhere can it have been more brutal than at Oxford, where she went up naively expecting to find rational inquiry but met only arrogant superiority. This was her first encounter with the liberal establishment and she did not like it. It hardened her heart: one day she would get even. Janet Vaughan, like Dorothy Gillies, gets no warm words in her memoirs. The experience forged her lifelong view of herself as an outsider, part of a persecuted minority, which never left her – as the journalist Patrick Cosgrave noted in 1978: 'When today she insists – as she does practically every day . . . – that it is vital for her side to win the argument as well as the votes, she is prone to refer to having had exactly the same problem at Oxford.'[19]

Lady Thatcher has always maintained that she had no thought of going into politics until near the end of her time at Oxford. To Patricia Murray she dated the possibility from the moment the Labour Government increased MPs' pay from £600 to £1,000 a year in 1946.[20] Before that, she told Kenneth Harris, 'I just didn't think of being a Member of Parliament.'[21] To all her early biographers she claimed that the idea first struck her at Margaret Goodrich's twenty-first birthday party at Corby Glen.

> At the end of the evening we all finished up in the kitchen and somebody who happened to be talking to me said, 'I feel that what you would really like to do is to be a Member of Parliament', and that was the very first time that it had occurred to me that perhaps one day I could, if the chance ever came. However I was still at university and I knew that my first priority when I came down was to earn my own living and get established.[22]

As early as 1961, however, she had given a racier version to the journalist Godfrey Winn:

> A crowd of us had been to a village hop and come back to make midnight cups of coffee. I was . . . having a fierce argument with one of the boys in the crowd when someone else interrupted to say, 'Of course, Margaret, you will go in for politics, won't you?' I stopped dead. Suddenly it was crystallised for me. I knew.[23]

As time went on the story continued to improve. She told *Woman's Hour* in 1968 that there were 'a number of pilots' at the party, and it was 'one of the young pilots' who spoke to her.[24] By the time she wrote her memoirs she had dropped that detail but given the episode its final polish. The birthday party was now 'a dance', the date specified as 'shortly before my university days came to an end' (which suggests the spring or early summer of 1947), and the person who spoke to her in the kitchen was 'one of the men'. To the suggestion that what she really wanted was to become an MP, she says she replied 'almost without thinking . . . "Yes, that really *is* what I want to do." I had never said it before – not even to myself. When I went to bed that night I found that I had a lot on my mind.'[25]

But this is not at all how Margaret Wickstead remembers the occasion. For one thing her twenty-first birthday was just before Christmas 1944 – nearer the beginning of Margaret Roberts' time at Oxford than the end. Then it was not a dance, but 'a very unsophisticated party', with no alcohol and 'nearly all girls'. As they sat round the kitchen table drinking cocoa, it was not a man but Mrs Goodrich, Margaret's mother, who asked Margaret Roberts what she was going to do. Without hesitation she answered, 'I want to become an MP.' It was not the inspiration of the moment, but a considered reply.[26]

This is not in the least surprising. It is confirmed by Nina Bawden's recollection that she was not 'playing at politics' in her first year; and it is consistent with her purposeful involvement in OUCA. Of course it does not mean that she was not well aware of the difficulties in her way or the necessity to earn a living until she could get a foot on the political ladder. But it does dispose of the romantic and disingenuous story that the idea never crossed her mind until late in her university career; and it usefully illustrates a tendency to embroider her memoirs.

Another Oxford contemporary who was at that party in Corby Glen – and actually shared a bed with her that night – was Sheila Browne. Many years later Miss Browne was Chief Inspector of Schools when Mrs Thatcher became Secretary of State for Education. She remembers Margaret Roberts at Oxford as 'a very unmemorable person' who seemed to take no pleasure in the opportunities of Oxford life. She seemed to be out of her element, always striving dutifully to meet her obligations while the rest of them were bent on enjoying themselves. The party at Corby Glen was the only time Sheila Browne ever saw Margaret on 'home territory'. It was the only time she glimpsed the 'bossy loquacious person' she met again some twenty-five years later; and even then she was more anxious about her clothes and the flower in her corsage than anything else. Miss Browne formed the impression, which she never revised, of a deeply insecure young woman concerned above all to do the right thing.[27]

It was six months after this party – that is at the end of her second year – that Miss Roberts made her first recorded political speech, during the 1945 General Election. At the start of the campaign she was still in Oxford: with other OUCA members she canvassed for Quintin Hogg, who was fighting to retain the seat he had won at a

famous by-election shortly after Munich. (He succeeded, defeating
Frank Pakenham, the future Lord Longford, by nearly 3,000 votes.)
But as soon as the term ended she went back to Grantham to work
for the Conservative who was trying to regain the seat from Denis
Kendall. The new candidate was Squadron Leader Worth, son-in-
law of Sir Arthur Longmore who had lost the by-election. The twin
themes of his campaign were encapsulated in an advertisement in the
Grantham Journal: 'Worth stands for Agriculture and Churchill'.[28]
Margaret Roberts – still only nineteen – acted as warm-up speaker at
meetings before the Squadron Leader arrived. At Sleaford on 25
June, the *Sleaford Gazette* reported, 'the very youthful Miss M. H.
Roberts, daughter of Alderman A. Roberts of Grantham', did not
talk about agriculture, but she did talk about Churchill. She began by
making a virtue of her youth:

> I speak as a very young Tory, and we are entitled to speak, for it is
> the people of my generation who will bear the brunt of the
> change from the trials of the past into calmer channels.

Boldly for one who had never been abroad, she spoke mainly on
foreign policy, taking a line on the restoration of Europe which
skilfully balanced morality with practicality. Germany, she insisted,
'must be disarmed and brought to justice'. She did not mean that the
Germans should be deprived of everything, but 'just punishment
must be meted out'. At the same time, she argued, it was in Britain's
interest that the whole of Europe be restored:

> It was not possible to be prosperous in this country while there
> was a shortage elsewhere [or] to be prosperous and happy in this
> land until we had helped to put other European countries back on
> a wholesome footing. Only when we could trade with other
> countries could we get back to prosperity.

It is fascinating to see in Mrs Thatcher's very first recorded speech
the obligation of internationalism firmly expressed in terms of
increased trade; note also the moralistic force of the word
'wholesome'. She went on to be surprisingly even-handed in
supporting continued co-operation with both the Soviet Union and
the United States. The Cold War had not yet begun. Her emphasis
reflects the universal assumption of the time that Britain was still the
third Great Power, the head of a global empire:

> Miss Roberts was very fervent in her determination to stand by

the Empire. It was the most important community of peoples the world had ever known. It was so bound with loyalty that it brought peoples half way across the world to help each other in times of stress. The Empire must never be liquidated.

Her main point, predictably, was the importance of supporting Churchill. She actually spoke as though she thought his defeat a possibility. Having lost Roosevelt, she urged, the world could not afford to lose Churchill too: Attlee had nothing like the same reputation, and no one knew who a Labour Foreign Secretary might be. She finished, characteristically, by attacking Kendall as an Independent for not knowing where he stood, complaining that he had voted nineteen times against the Government: she never did like people who were not clearly one thing or the other.[29]

If she expected Kendall to lose and Churchill to be returned, she was wrong on both counts. Kendall held Grantham by a huge majority – the only wartime by-election victor to do so – while the Conservative Government was swept from office by a totally unanticipated Labour landslide. Miss Roberts was shocked by the result. 'I simply could not understand how the electorate could do this to Churchill,' she wrote.[30] She was still more shocked to find that others whom she had assumed to be right-thinking Conservatives were not equally dismayed but elated by the election of a Labour Government. She always had difficulty believing that otherwise decent people could genuinely hold opposite opinions to her own. Looking back over half a century she portrayed the 1945 election as the start of the rot which did not begin to be set right until she herself was elected in 1979.

She may have been unmemorable in Oxford, but her contribution to the Tory campaign did not go unremarked in Grantham. Noting that she had inherited 'her father's gift for oratory', the *Grantham Journal* judged that 'the presence of a young woman of the age of 19 with such decided convictions has been no small factor in influencing the women's vote in the division'.[31] Plainly she was, as Sheila Browne noted, a different person on 'home territory'.

Returning to Oxford for her third year she found a university transformed by returning servicemen, older than normal peacetime undergraduates, keen both to build a new world and to celebrate their own survival. Lady Thatcher claims to have enjoyed the seriousness of the new influx; but she also allowed herself to unbend slightly and enjoy a little of the new hedonism. She moved out of college to live in digs, first with two other Somerville chemists, Pauline Cowan and Peggy Lapham, at 12 Richmond Road; later (in her fourth year) with two postgraduates, Mary Mallinson and Mary Foss, at 18 Walton Street. None of these, however, became lasting friends. 'It was at this time', she wrote in *The Path to Power*, 'that I first went out to dances and even on occasion drank a little wine.' She tried smoking, did not like it and decided to spend her money buying *The Times* every day instead. She went to the theatre: she saw Shakespeare, Chekhov, Christopher Fry and 'a wonderful OUDS production which was performed in a college garden and featured Kenneth Tynan, Oxford's latest dandy'.[32] But she was not, so far as we know, tempted to act: nor did she develop any lasting interest in the theatre. What she did discover was a love of ballroom dancing – a taste which stayed with her, though rarely indulged, all her life. Years later, as Prime Minister, she was delighted when the British Ambassador, Nico Henderson, asked her to dance after a dinner for Ronald Reagan at the Washington Embassy. It was something, she confessed, that she had been longing to do all evening but no one dared to ask her. She danced, Henderson recalled, 'extremely well'.[33]

But who did she dance with? Who did she go to the theatre with? There is no record that she had any male friends at Oxford, let alone anyone who could be called a boyfriend. 'Margaret was not one of the "consorts" who often sat in the Union gallery and then joined the men for a drink,' an OUCA contemporary remembers. 'I do not recall ever seeing her with a man except in the course of business.'[34] One of her more fanciful biographers has claimed that she fell in love with the son of an earl who later became a leading Tory.[35] The only candidate who comes near to answering this description is Edward Boyle, who inherited a baronetcy in 1945 and was one of very few OUCA colleagues who genuinely became a friend. A wealthy, gentle, clever and cultivated man, two years older than Margaret, he had interrupted his degree during the war to spend three years in the Foreign Office. Boyle would certainly have been a catch if she had set her cap at him; unfortunately he was a lifelong bachelor. She admired and was fond of him, but nothing more.

The fact is that her social life was wholly subordinated to politics. By her third year, despite competition from the returning service-men, she was senior enough to stand for office within the OUCA. A mark of the progress that women had made during the war was the election, that Michaelmas term, of the Association's first woman President, Rachel Willink (daughter of Churchill's Minister of Health, Henry Willink). That autumn, immediately after the

Conservative debacle at the General Election, Margaret collaborated with Stanley Moss (the next term's OUCA President) and another of the returning warriors, Michael Kinchin-Smith, who had been President of the Union in 1941, to write a policy paper. Her reward was to be elected Secretary, in which capacity she attended a Conservative student conference in London; then Treasurer in the summer term; and finally President in Michaelmas 1946, when she went back to Oxford for a fourth year to take her BSc.

She made her way in the OUCA more by diligence than by any outstanding political gifts. She did not in truth have much alternative. 'Politics was very difficult for Oxford women,' a male contemporary concedes: 'Margaret was excluded not only from the Union but from the select Canning Club. So she had no opportunity to clash swords and measure herself against political opponents, and no occasion to debate politics with her colleagues, except privately.'[36]

One or two women did have the personality to break through this barrier. Rachel Willink 'had an impressive presence and was a leading light of the 198 Club'; Gitta Blumenthal, secretary of the Liberal Club, was 'a glittering extrovert who was one of the few undergraduate women invited to address the Union'.[37] By contrast Rachel Willink remembers Margaret Roberts 'rather as a brown girl': 'She had an attractive brown head of hair, was quiet, nicely dressed and very pleasant to be with, but definitely other than the way one sees her today.'[38]

Another OUCA colleague, Donald Southgate (later a distinguished historian) explicitly seconds this impression, remembering 'a brown dress that was not becoming' and 'traces of puppy fat'. 'I did not find her particularly attractive, apart from the hair and the eyes.' 'No one', he adds, 'ever thought of suggesting that Margaret should address the Union.' Indeed she was rarely heard to speak at all.

> The only occasion on which I heard her make a political speech was at the spring conference of the Federation of University Conservative Associations ... The matter was admirable, the manner unimpressive. She had not learned how to modulate her voice.[39]

One of her later biographers, Kenneth Harris, was an Oxford contemporary of Margaret Roberts in her final year – though he was a Liberal, not a Conservative. Within OUCA, he wrote, she became known as 'an earnest, open, articulate though not charismatic exponent of sound traditional Conservative principles'.

Nobody expected to convert her, nor did anybody expect to be converted by her; but she was honest, consistent, good-natured, and when there was hard work to be done she could be relied upon to get it done.[40]

As her self-confidence grew she made a reputation for organising social events. 'You might think she was a bit bossy', one former member told Harris, 'but on the other hand you didn't see anyone standing around without anybody to talk to, which you did see at many other people's parties.'[41] 'You could always be certain that the food and drink would last out,' another OUCA officer recalled – which was not always the case just after the war – 'and you could also be certain that you would probably meet somebody you had never met before.'[42] While the men made speeches, the principal political skill Margaret Roberts learned at Oxford was the ability to give good parties.

So far as anyone remembers, her views were entirely conventional. Oxford Conservatism in the wake of the 1945 defeat was determinedly forward-looking, anxious to identify itself with the modern, liberal, progressive Toryism associated with Rab Butler, Quintin Hogg and Lord Hinchinbrooke, who were trying to exorcise the hard-faced image of the prewar party. The last policy paper published by the OUCA just before the election gave confident expression to this mood. It was written by three Union stars of the previous generation, two of whom – Hugh Fraser and Julian Amery – later became prominent on the right of the Tory party. At this time, however, they were happy to pronounce that 'Liberal Capitalism is as dead as Aristocratic Feudalism'. They looked forward to 'a state without privilege where each shall enrich himself through the enrichment of all'.[43]

This was precisely the opposite of Tory orthodoxy in Mrs Thatcher's heyday forty years later, when all were supposed to benefit from the enrichment of the few. In 1945, however, ambitious Young Conservatives subscribed unquestioningly to collectivist assumptions. To all appearances Margaret Roberts was no exception. 'There was no sign then of the things which mark her out now,' one contemporary recalled in 1983. 'We were all thoroughly middle of the road liberal kinds of Conservatives. That was the style of those days.'[44] Though conceding that 'there were some highly vocal right-wing Conservatives in those days', another maintained, 'I thought of Margaret as a humane and moderate supporter of Rab Butler and his Industrial Charter.'[45] A third agreed:

One doesn't associate her with ideas . . . She was very nice but an absolutely hard-boiled Conservative Association officer with no particular spark of independent thought. She took Conservatism as it was handed out. She was very determined to make a political career for herself.[46]

The policy paper she wrote with Moss and Kinchin-Smith largely supports this assessment; but perhaps not quite. Kinchin-Smith's recollection is that Moss wrote most of it; but since it is the first statement of political philosophy to which she put her name it is irresistible to scan it for sentences which contain a germ of latent 'Thatcherism'. It began with a windy disquisition on 'the basis of Conservatism', asserting a preference for instinct, tradition and common sense over 'reason' and 'dogma'. So far, so conventional. From this, however, were derived a number of 'principles', mainly relating to the individual's relations to the state.

The individual's capacity for leading a good life shall be the ultimate criterion for any policy.

The individual is more important than the system.

Individual enterprise is the mainspring of all progress.

This is a rather different emphasis from the earlier paper. But then comes a grand assertion:

There is no empirical evidence at all for the existence, either as a real entity or as a true conception, of the mystic community, state or nation that figures in all systems opposed to this principle, such as the Nazi.

What are we to make of this? British Tories – including Mrs Thatcher – have never been shy of quasi-mystical rhetoric about the nation. Or is it an early formulation of the statement that 'there is no such thing as society'? Progressive young Conservatives in 1945 conceded a leading role to the state:

Society is composed of a number of interlocking associations of which the State is the chief.

At the same time the authors were also concerned to limit it, somewhat hopefully proposing that 'the power of the State and state-controlled organisations shall not be greater than the sum of the powers of other associations'.

Along with the rule of law, the private ownership of property was of course a basic Conservative principle. But it was quite severely qualified:

> Private property is only desirable . . . provided it is distributed as widely as possible.

This could imply no more than Eden's vision of a 'property-owning democracy', which Mrs Thatcher's Government claimed to have realised by the sale of council houses and shares in British Gas. But in the context of 1945 it had a distinctly egalitarian ring, an impression confirmed when the authors turned from generalities to the question of how the Tory party should respond to its recent defeat. It would be 'highly dangerous', they warned, 'to consider this defeat solely as a normal swing of the pendulum'. It should be recognised as a historical turning point comparable to 1832.

> A reorientation of conservatism within the framework of the 20th century state such as that carried out by Peel will be necessary if the party is to avoid annihilation.

What precisely this 'reorientation' should involve was unfortunately not spelled out. It would seem to imply an accommodation with the advance of socialism such as Butler and the Conservative Research Department did in fact carry out over the next few years. Yet at the same time there is a distinctly Thatcherite insistence that the party must be 'much clearer than in the past as to what its basic principles are'.

> Conservative policy has come to mean in the eyes of the public little more than a series of administrative solutions to particular problems, correlated in certain fields by a few unreasoning prejudices and the selfish interest of the monied classes.

The first part of this, at least, was precisely Mrs Thatcher's platform when she challenged Heath for the party leadership in 1975, as was the insistence that electoral defeat – though a 'disaster' for the country – nevertheless constituted 'a unique opportunity for "house-cleaning" within the party itself'. Surely Miss Roberts must have written this section?[47]

Altogether the document is too vague to carry much weight of interpretation. Its joint authorship precludes any certain attribution of any of its views to Margaret Roberts. Yet in its insistence on individualism in the face of the collectivist ethos of the time it is more 'Thatcherite' than might have been expected – far more so than the Fraser–Amery paper published under the same aegis less than six months earlier.

In her memoirs Lady Thatcher describes her time at Oxford as an important period of intellectual foundation-building. Yet the only books she specifically mentions having read are Friedrich Hayek's *The Road to Serfdom*, which was first published in 1944, and *Who are 'The People'?* by the anti-socialist journalist Colm Brogan, published in 1943. Reading chemistry for her degree, rather than history or PPE (politics, philosophy and economics) like most aspiring politicians, she was not exposed to the discipline of sampling the whole spectrum of political thought; she was free to read only what she was likely to agree with. It is easy to see why Brogan would appeal to her: he was a vigorous polemicist with a good line in exposing the pretensions of the left. How carefully she read Hayek in 1944 must be more doubtful: Alfred Sherman had the impression in 1975 that she had never read him before.[48] She herself admits that though her instincts were always anti-socialist, 'I had not yet fully digested the strong intellectual case against collectivism' in 1946.[49] But if she did read *The Road to Serfdom* at this time, she also read Keynes' seminal White Paper on Full Employment, published the same year. Many years later she produced a heavily annotated copy from her handbag to berate the young Tony Blair in the House of Commons.[50] She made very little acknowledgement of Hayek's influence over the next thirty years. But this is not surprising: she was always a gut politician, to whom intellectual arguments were no more than useful reinforcement. It is only retrospectively that she would like to claim an intellectual pedigree that was no part of her essential motivation.

Margaret Roberts' one recorded speech of this period, at the Federation of University Conservative Associations conference in London in March 1946, was mainly about the necessary modernisation of the party and specifically the need to widen its class base by attracting more working-class members. This was a common theme of the time, reflected in Lord Woolton's reforms which put a stop to constituency associations expecting candidates to pay their own expenses. But one reported remark jarred with the prevailing mood of democratic egalitarianism. 'We have heard all about this being the age of the common man,' she told her fellow-delegates, 'but do not forget the need for the uncommon man.'[51] Congratulating herself for this line in her memoirs, she only regrets that she did not have the foresight to add 'or woman'.[52]

Then in early October she attended her first party conference, at Blackpool. She loved it. One of the sources of Mrs Thatcher's strength in the 1980s was that – almost uniquely among Tory leaders – she was in tune with ordinary party members. That love affair began at Blackpool in 1946. Though she had worked for the Tory candidate in Grantham in 1945, she had never been a member of the local party since Alfred was officially an Independent, while Oxford Conservatives were a privileged caste. Now she met for the first time the Tory rank and file *en masse* gathered for their first conference since the election defeat, far from chastened but already reacting defiantly to the outrageous impositions of socialism. She was impressed by the sheer number of the representatives, disproving any idea that Conservatism was an extinct creed. She also claims to have been heartened by the strong reaction from the floor against the defeatism of the platform. 'The delegates would have nothing to do with the proposal to change the Party's name,' Churchill's friend Brendan Bracken reported to Lord Beaverbrook. 'They demanded a real Conservative policy instead of a synthetic Socialist one so dear to the heart of the Macmillans and Butlers, and gave Churchill one of the greatest receptions of his life.'[53] 'My instincts', Lady Thatcher wrote in 1995, 'were with the rank and file.'[54] More than any Tory leader before or since, Mrs Thatcher always identified with the ordinary members in the hall: at the most difficult moments of her premiership (in 1980–1 and in 1989) she appealed – invariably successfully – for their support against her faint-hearted colleagues and the carping press. Blackpool 1946 was a revelation.

She returned to Oxford as the OUCA's second woman President. She had spent the summer in Grantham trying to set up a programme of events for her presidential term. This occasioned some correspondence with her secretary of discussion groups, Donald Southgate, which has survived. Her tone is deferential, as though she were the secretary reporting to him and seeking his advice. He was older, more experienced and a man. Though she complained that potential speakers were 'taking the deuce of a time to reply',[55] and some big names – Harold Macmillan, Brendan Bracken, Lord Beaverbrook and Lord Halifax – turned her down, she eventually assembled an impressive list of MPs, mainly from the progressive wing of the party. The main Friday meetings kicked off with Robert Boothby, followed by the former Attorney-General, Sir

David Maxwell-Fyfe; then she arranged a debate on the nationalisation of transport in which the Labour MP Ray Gunter was set up to be 'slain' by Peter Thorneycroft. ('No one was ever more surprised than I', she wrote to Southgate, when Thorneycroft accepted. She did not think there would be much point having a vote, 'unless our members are so slack that they don't turn up. We shall have to have a very efficient whip for the occasion.')[56] Then came Viscountess Davidson (one of the handful of Tory women MPs), Sir Ronald Nugent, Lord Hinchinbrooke of the Tory Reform Committee, and finally the former Cabinet Minister 'Shakes' Morrison.

But this was by no means all. Southgate also established several study groups. There was one on 'The Reconstruction of Europe' which met on Mondays, launched by Lord Dunglass (the future Earl of Home) but thereafter carried on by undergraduates speaking on different countries. A second, on Tuesdays, discussed different aspects of 'The State of the Nation' – including trade unions, the distressed areas, nationalisation, local government and taxation. (The one on the distressed areas was led by C. A. R. Crosland from the Socialist Society.) Southgate himself led a third on 'Constitutional Reform'. ('I like the idea,' she wrote to him in July.) On top of all this the term's programme lists three debates (one on the House of Lords, one with the Socialists and another with the Liberals), a Brains Trust, two or three social events and a discussion on 'The Functions of an MP' (no speaker named). This was an exceptionally full programme.[57]

With the end of the war and under the provocation of a Labour Government, Oxford Toryism was resurgent by 1946. Of course the visible focus of this revival was the Union, where Southgate, Boyle and William Rees-Mogg led the Tory 'front bench' and began to win debates against the dominant Liberals. On 21 November, with Anthony Eden as the star guest, a motion that the Tory party offered 'no constructive alternative' was defeated by 615 votes to 397 – at that time the largest Tory majority in the Union's history. Margaret Roberts learned of these triumphs only at second hand: the Union style – self-consciously clever, witty and flippant – was not hers and she did not attend to listen from the gallery. The voting figures nevertheless reflected considerable credit on her hard work. The OUCA was enjoying a postwar boom, *Isis* acknowledged, 'under the queenly sway of Margaret Roberts' – the first time that adjective was ever applied to her.[58] That term membership topped a thousand for the first time since the 1920s. Clearly it was a good moment to be President, but much of the growth was clearly due to her organizing enthusiasm and efficiency.

The fact remains that she made remarkably little impact on her contemporaries. In her memoirs, and in earlier interviews, Lady Thatcher liked to portray her Oxford years in the approved tradition as a time of intellectual jousting with her peers. 'When I was up at Oxford', she told the *Daily Telegraph* in 1970, 'there was Edward Boyle, Wedgwood Benn, Ludovic Kennedy and Kenneth Tynan. It was talk, talk, talk.'[59] In *The Path to Power* she adds Robin Day, William Rees-Mogg, Kenneth Harris and Tony Crosland to the list of her sparring partners. But this is more embroidery. The only one of these she knew at all well was Boyle, who was Treasurer of the OUCA in her presidential term and then succeeded her as President in Hilary 1947. But even Boyle she misremembers as 'a classical liberal whose views chimed in pretty well with my own provincial middle-class conservatism',[60] whereas others thought of him even then as 'very left-wing . . . a Keynesian and Butskellite before his time', troubled by 'deep anxiety about his privileged background'.[61] She admits that she was 'never as close to William [Rees-Mogg] as I was to Edward', though she 'sensed that there was something formidable behind his somewhat formal exterior' which 'marked [him] out for higher things'.[62] It is unlikely that she even met Tynan or Ludovic Kennedy, who moved in very different circles, literary and dramatic, not political: she certainly does not figure in Kennedy's memories of Oxford.[63] Robin Day went back to Oxford after his war service only in 1947 − after she had gone down. Anthony Benn (as he was then known) she did know slightly. She recalls that he invited her to a party − strictly teetotal − to mark his winning the Presidency of the Union in her final term. He was then campaigning for the admission of women to the Union, so there was an obvious point in inviting her. She comments tartly that Tony Crosland 'even in those days could condescend to a Duchess';[64] but Crosland was a very mature student of nearly thirty who had come back to Oxford after serving in North Africa and Italy since 1943, to whom the likes of Margaret Roberts must have seemed callow indeed. All those mentioned except Tynan had served in the war. Only Boyle was then or later in any sense a friend.

From the point of view of her career, however, her contemporaries mattered much less than the established figures of the Tory party who came to speak for her. The value of this sort of networking cannot be overstated. As she wrote herself, 'It was there [at Oxford] that I first rubbed shoulders with the great figures of the Tory party − and in fact I kept in touch with many of them over the years.'[65] It was not so much that they positively remembered her − it is unlikely that Lord Home, when he next encountered her in Ted Heath's

Shadow Cabinet, recalled having spoken to her European discussion group twenty years before – rather that she was able to claim acquaintance and feel that she had a foot on the party ladder. She probably formed a fairly dim view of some of them, but seeing them at close quarters encouraged her to believe that she could hold her own with them, in due course maybe beat them. At any rate she could feel that she was on the inside track. No one she met at Oxford ever directly helped her or advanced her career; but simply having been President of the OUCA gave her a standing at Central Office which helped her on to the candidates' list.

What Oxford did not give her was a liberal education. In *The Path to Power* she writes that 'I gained a great deal from the fact that Oxford at the end of the war was a place of such mixed views and experience'.[66] Of course she gained something, but less than most of her contemporaries. She did not in fact mix very widely or open herself to new views or experiences. She arrived in Oxford with her political views already settled and spent four years diligently confirming them. She claims that being a scientist gave her 'a somewhat different insight' from the preponderance of arts people with whom she mixed: specifically she grasped Karl Popper's demolition of 'the (alleged) theoretical basis of Marxism'.[67] Undoubtedly her scientific training did give her a clarity and practicality of thought very different from the wishful woolliness of much arts and social science thinking. At the same time she read little or no history at university; and neither then nor later did she read much literature.

This amounted to more than a gap in cultural knowledge. More important, she did not receive the sort of education that delights in the diversity of different perspectives or might have exposed her to the wisdom of philosophic doubt. Her mind dealt in facts and moral certainties. She left Oxford, as she went up, devoid of a sense of either irony or humour, intolerant of ambiguity and equivocation. Of course there are plenty of liberal scientists whose education leaves them humbled by the realisation of the infinite unknowability of things. But Margaret Roberts was never of this type. Her study of science at school and university chimed with her strict moral and religious upbringing and reinforced it, where a more liberal education in the arts or humanities might have encouraged her to question or qualify it. This rigid cast of mind was a source of unusual strength in Mrs Thatcher's political career. But it was also a severe limitation, exacerbating a lack of imaginative sympathy with other views and life-experiences which ultimately restricted her ability to command support.

She left Oxford in the summer of 1947, a qualified research

chemist. For the past year she had been working under Dorothy Hodgkin, in collaboration with a PhD student – a German refugee named Gerhard Schmidt – trying to discover the protein structure of an antibiotic called Gramicidin B, using the same technique of passing X-rays through crystals that Professor Hodgkin had successfully applied to penicillin. As it happened Gramicidin B was more complicated than penicillin, and they failed to crack it. There was no discredit in this: success was not finally achieved until 1980. She was still awarded her degree. But it was not the degree she wanted. In the short run she knew it was the only qualification she had: it was as a chemist that she must start her working life. But she had already set her mind on going into politics. Margaret Wickstead vividly remembers walking with her down Parks Road in Oxford, past Rhodes House, and Margaret Roberts telling her: 'Of course this degree is not much use to me as an MP. I must now try to read Law.'[68] She had got what she wanted from Oxford; but it was not enough.

4

Young Conservative

THERE was no question of reading for the Bar immediately: she could not afford it, neither could Alfred pay her way. Nor, despite the useful contacts she had made, was there any quick way into politics. Both her sex and her age were against her. There was a whole generation of ambitious young men ahead of her, their careers already held back by the war, jostling for the available openings. A lucky few like Major Iain Macleod and Brigadier Enoch Powell found berths in the Conservative Research Department from which they were able to win adoption as parliamentary candidates; more, like Lieutenant-Colonel Teddy Heath, had to take what jobs they could find while they hawked themselves around. Margaret Roberts, only twenty-one and fresh down from university, at least had a marketable qualification. In her final term at Oxford she had signed on with the University Appointments Board. She attended a number of interviews with prospective employers on what is now called the 'milk round' before being taken on by a firm called BX Plastics, based at Manningtree in Essex.

BX Plastics, originally known as British Xylonite, was a well-established company which developed new materials for such products as spectacle frames, raincoats and electrical insulation. During the war it had been taken over by Distillers; later it was swallowed by the American Union Carbide Corporation, and finally by BP. In 1947 its headquarters were at Manningtree on the Stour estuary, twelve miles inland from Harwich, not far from Constable's Flatford Mill and Dedham Vale. But most of the workforce lived in Colchester, ten miles to the south, from where they travelled to work each day on the company bus.

BX employed about seventy researchers. Margaret Roberts was one of ten graduates taken on that summer – three of them women, who were paid £50 a year less than the men. (The men got £400, the women £350 – that is less than £7 a week.) She had understood that she was going to be Personal Assistant to the Research and Development Director, but was disappointed to find herself just another laboratory researcher, working on surface tensions to develop an adhesive for sticking polyvinyl chloride (PVC) to wood or metal. She does not disguise that, as at Oxford, she had a difficult time at first. She did not mix easily with her colleagues, who thought her prim and stuck-up, allegedly referring to her as 'Duchess', 'Aunty Margaret' and 'Snobby Roberts'.[1] The two other new girls, Eileen Rutherford and Audrey Powell, shared a flat in Colchester; Margaret Roberts lived in digs and joined them on the bus, conspicuous in her Burberry coat and gloves.

But what she called her 'teething troubles' eased by Christmas 1947, when the Research and Development section moved to a separate site a couple of miles away in Lawford.[2] Her work caught the eye of the section director, Stanley Booth, who remembered her years later as 'very conscientious, very thorough, hard working'.[3] She also made an impression on the chairman's son, Peter Marrian, who worked briefly in the company at this time: he recalled Miss Roberts as not merely 'the only good-looking woman in the research laboratory' but also as an excellent chemist – 'very go-ahead'. She always seemed to get her way, particularly in securing equipment and materials she needed to conduct her experiments.[4] It is no wonder her colleagues disliked her.

As at Oxford she made no secret of her politics, nor of her ambition. The clerical staff used to tease her, saying 'There goes the future Prime Minister' – never for a moment believing it. But she was impervious to ridicule. 'She used to get so involved when talking about politics', one secretary told Ernle Money, 'that she would get very red with exertion . . . There seemed to be a sort of inner light about her which animated her entirely when she spoke.'[5] Booth was less impressed by her evangelical certainty:

> Most of us tended to be if anything on the left side in those days. I was a bit older and had seen the thirties at close quarters . . . Her views seemed rather simplistic . . . She believed then, as she believes now [1983] that people should stand on their own two feet. I'd come up the hard way and didn't quite see things like that.[6]

Later Booth became a great admirer of his former employee: he converted to the Conservatives when she became leader, with the shrewdly backhanded assessment that 'she didn't possess sufficient imagination to be a good research chemist, which is the best qualification you can have for a politician'.[7] Booth was a remarkable man in his own right. He wrote a thesis on the painter Alfred Munnings, set up a trust to preserve Munnings's house in Dedham as a museum, and devoted thirty years to painstakingly restoring a group of fifteenth-century Flemish weavers' cottages in Dedham. By the 1990s he had evidently grown tired of being asked about his one-time researcher, and had become distinctly jaundiced with her again.[8]

During the eighteen months that Margaret Roberts worked at BX Plastics she lived in digs in Colchester. She lodged with a young widow, Enid Macaulay, at 168 Maldon Road, a street of neat two-storey semis, bigger than they look from the outside. Mrs Macaulay's husband had died only recently, leaving her with two young children, so she filled the house with lodgers, both male and female. In 1978 the Colchester *Evening Gazette* traced one of the men, an accountant named Stewart Heywood-Smith who firmly quashed the angle the paper tried to suggest by insisting that he and Miss Roberts were 'just good friends'.[9] Another lodger, probably not by coincidence, was the secretary of the local Young Conservatives, a young woman named Addi (short for Addison) Neal. The likelihood must be that the first thing Margaret did before coming to Colchester was to approach the YCs for help with finding accommodation. Mrs Macaulay, interviewed in the early eighties, remembered two things about Miss Roberts: first that she was always very smartly turned out – 'nice suits, nice blouses, nice gloves'; and second, her determination to be a politician. She was always busy with political activity of one kind or another, either with the YCs in Colchester or away at weekend conferences.[10]*

When she was not away on Sundays, however, she kept up her religious observance. She attended the Culver Street Methodist Church and, as she had done at Oxford, joined other young people on missions to the surrounding villages. She may have preached: she is certainly remembered reading the lesson, with her too-perfect elocution. To her fellow-Methodists in Colchester she appeared very grown-up and sophisticated. One, Mary Pratt, once asked her home to tea with her parents: she seemed more at ease with older people than with her own contemporaries. She was always so serious, Mary

* When she visited Colchester for the first time as Conservative leader nearly thirty years later Mrs Thatcher spoke to the local Soroptimists, whose then President was Mrs Macaulay.

Pratt felt, that she was 'never a girl'.[11] She would never cycle anywhere like the rest of them – though she had ridden a bicycle at Oxford.

Even among the Young Conservatives she stood out. Colchester had a very active YC branch, set up in 1945 to help revive the local party after the shock of losing the constituency to Labour. By 1949 they boasted 350 members and had their own club with premises in Museum Street. With a good young candidate in Cuthbert ('Cub') Alport, the constituency Association as a whole was flourishing. During 1948 they held seventy indoor and twenty outdoor meetings, regained four council seats from Labour and one from the Liberals and increased their membership to more than 8,500 (of whom 400 were said to be active between elections). In 1950 Alport comfortably recaptured the seat, which he held until 1961.

The Young Conservatives played an important part in this success, as the Conservative Area Agent reported to Central Office in 1949: 'The YCs are active, strong and efficient, although at times a little impetuous . . . [They] provide an excellent flying squad for canvassing in difficult areas.'[12] With her experience in both Oxford and Grantham in 1945, Margaret Roberts threw herself into these tasks energetically. But she had no interest in the social side of activities, which to most members was what the organisation was all about. The Young Conservatives were notoriously used by middle-class young people in the 1940s and 1950s as a dating agency and marriage bureau. She had no time for that sort of thing, as the chairman of the Colchester Young Conservatives, Philip Fell, remembers: 'Margaret tended to think that YC social activities were a waste of time that would have been far better used for direct political activities.'[13]

Another member, Mary Fairland – who nearly half a century later became Mayor of Colchester – remembers Margaret running a bookstall at a summer fête; but generally she was 'not one of us'. She kept herself to herself, dressed in a carefully old-fashioned style that seemed 'dowdy' to other bright young twenty-somethings, and had her own agenda. Unlike the rest of them she was clearly set on a political career.[14*]

What she was interested in was debating. 'In particular', Lady Thatcher writes in her memoirs, 'I thoroughly enjoyed what was called the "39–45" discussion group, where Conservatives of the war

---

* There was in fact another future MP among the Colchester Young Conservatives. Brian Harrison, secretary of the club in 1947–8, was MP for Maldon from 1955 to February 1974. He subsequently emigrated to Australia.

generation met to exchange views and argue about political topics of the day.'[15] The fact that she had not herself served in the war did not hold her back. She was also the principal speaker in a team of four – including Philip Fell – which won through to the final of a national debating competition against much more experienced teams of local politicians. (They were placed something like fifth.) The fact that Fell was several years older, had been to Oxford, fought in the war, was married and was qualifying as a solicitor did not prevent Miss Roberts taking the lead. A photograph in the local paper shows her standing behind a table, looking formidably solemn in a wide-brimmed hat, with her three male colleagues seated around her: the first, but by no means the last image of her dominating a group of men.

'That Margaret was main speaker is self-evident,' Fell comments.[16] 'She and I worked closely together in preparing her speeches' – her material was very well organised but tended to need cutting – 'and keeping the other three team members (I was one) in step.'[17] But he did not warm to her. He felt that she had no human interest in anyone different from herself – which grated on those like himself who had come out of the army believing that officers were responsible for the welfare of their men. 'She was much harder than we were,' he remembers. Unfortunately he cannot recall the content of any of her speeches. So far as he remembers, she supported Rab Butler's Industrial Charter and toed the party line. Colchester was a left of centre local party, strongly influenced by Butler (MP for neighbouring Saffron Walden) and Alport (who became one of the founders of the One Nation group as soon as he got to Westminster in 1950). 'Furthermore we had a seat to win from a moderate and popular Labour member and the most likely way to succeed was to win over the greater part of the 1945 Liberal vote. All this', Fell remembers, 'made me somewhat to the left of Margaret's position.'[18]

Fell's recollection thus confirms Lady Thatcher's account that her instincts were already to the right of the party line which prudence and ambition obliged her to follow. '*The Industrial Charter* represented a compromise between corporatism and free enterprise,' she wrote in *The Path to Power*. 'This tension continued in the Conservative Party throughout the 1950s and sixties. *The Industrial Charter* gave us all something to say, and it kept the party united. But such documents hardly made the pulse beat faster.'[19]

The cool memories of Philip Fell and Mary Fairland need to be balanced, however, by the testimony of others who remember Margaret Roberts' brief time in Colchester much more warmly. Given that she was there for only eighteen months, she made a remarkable impact which bears witness to a growing self-confidence since leaving Oxford. Colchester was the first place where she made friends – disciples even – who remain devoted to her fifty years later. Bill Joliffe, for instance, was chairman of the '39–45 Club'. He and his wife Marie were the core of a group of loyal supporters with whom Mrs Thatcher kept in touch for the rest of her life. Marie still treasures a photograph of Margaret dancing with Bill, looking at that time very plump, double-chinned and blonde. Whenever she came to Colchester, even as Prime Minister, she still knew all the older members by name, asked after others and seemed to them quite unaffected: 'just the same as ever, the same Margaret'.[20] When she revived the granting of honours for political services in 1979, one of the first recipients was a faithful old warhorse of the Colchester party, Sheila Diss, who got an MBE. And when Bill Joliffe died in 1993 Lady Thatcher wrote Marie a letter of sympathy which touched her deeply. Colchester was an important stage in her maturing as a politician.

So far as one can tell she took no active steps to advance her political career. Though she attended weekend conferences, cultivated her contacts and practised her speaking, it was too soon to start looking for a constituency. She did not even apply to go on the Central Office list of prospective candidates. One would like to know what her imagined timetable was, how long she intended staying with BX Plastics before starting to read for the Bar. As it was she had a lucky break. She attended the 1948 party conference at Llandudno – not as a representative from Colchester, but representing the Oxford University Graduates Association. (Philip Fell attended for the Colchester YCs, though he does not remember seeing Margaret Roberts there.) She had hoped to make her maiden conference speech, seconding a motion condemning the Labour Government's abolition of University seats, but was disappointed when a City man was chosen instead. (The City seats were to be scrapped as well.) An Oxford acquaintance, however, introduced her to the chairman of the Dartford Conservative Association, John Miller, who happened to be looking for a candidate. This introduction changed her life.

Dartford had been seeking a new candidate for a year already, since the previous one – a Major Grubb – withdrew. For twelve months Central Office had been sending lists of possible contenders, but Miller and his committee did not think much of any of them. Dartford admittedly was not an enticing prospect – though it was a good place for a first-time candidate to cut his teeth. It was a rock-solid Labour seat with a majority in 1945 of more than 20,000, and one of the largest electorates in the country, covering the three North Kent estuary towns of Dartford, Erith and Crayford. The local Association was run down, following 'a succession of mediocre agents'.[21] Miller, an energetic local builder, was determined to pull it round. He was initially doubtful about the idea of a woman candidate, taking the conventional view that a tough industrial constituency was no place for a woman. But he introduced Miss Roberts to other members of his delegation over lunch on Llandudno pier, and they were impressed. Miller could see that the novelty of a forceful young woman might be the shot in the arm his Association needed. She was invited to put her name forward. Meanwhile Miller wrote again to Central Office mentioning her, but also requesting more names for consideration. They sent him another eleven, but agreed to see Miss Roberts if she would like to come in to the office. She did, and 'created an excellent impression'.[22]

Miller still tried to persuade a number of local businessmen to stand – among them a paint manufacturer named Denis Thatcher who had recently stood as a Ratepayers' candidate for Kent County Council. 'He came to my office in Erith and asked me to think about it,' Denis recalled. 'I said no without hesitating.'[23] Instead a slate of Central Office-approved hopefuls was interviewed in London in late December, from whom five were shortlisted for a run-off in Dartford at the end of January 1949. On 14 January the deputy Area Agent wrote to the deputy party chairman, J. P. L. Thomas:

> Although Dartford is not a good constituency for a woman candidate there is a possibility that Miss Margaret Roberts will be selected; her political knowledge and her speaking ability are far above those of the other candidates.[24]

Her four male rivals included Anthony Kershaw, an Old Etonian barrister and Westminster City Councillor who subsequently became MP for Stroud, 1955–87, serving as a junior minister in 1970–4 and chairman of the Foreign Affairs Select Committee, 1979–87. But the Dartford Executive agreed with the area agent. Miss Roberts was selected and recommended for adoption by the full Association four weeks later. There were mutterings from some members who had missed the meeting. Sir Waldron Smithers, MP for the adjoining seat of Orpington, reported raised eyebrows at the selection of 'a young girl of 23, Miss Margaret Robertson [*sic*] . . . Could they not have got some prominent businessman?'[25] Thomas told him that the party was keen to have more women candidates and assured him that Dartford had made an excellent choice.[26]

The same area agent attended the formal adoption meeting on 28 February and reported enthusiastically to Central Office:

> There were 380 members present and it was a first-class show; quite the best meeting of any type that the Dartford constituency has held for many a long day.
>
> Miss Roberts made a brilliant speech, and the decision to adopt her was unanimous.[27]

Introducing her to the members, Miller described her as 'sincere about her faith' and 'blessed with the gift of eloquence'. The 'brilliance' of her speech evidently owed more to its blazing sincerity than to its content. What is remarkable is the transformation of the earnest but unregarded Oxford undergraduate into a star performer at the first hint of the political limelight. Her speech as reported in the *Erith Observer* was a conventional Conservative attack on the Labour Government's high taxes and stifling controls which discouraged enterprise, created unnecessary shortages and would cause unemployment. It is interesting only for two things. Despite her presentation of herself to the selection committee as a scientist and – more questionably – an expert on industrial problems, she now played to the expectations of her audience by giving them a good dose of housewife economics:

> The Government should do what any good housewife would do if money was short – look at their accounts and see what was wrong.

Secondly she once again made great play with the importance of the Empire. Imperial preference, she declared, was 'still the cornerstone of Conservatism'. Britain should stand with the Dominions and the colonies 'to fight the economic war and follow the road to recovery together'.

The meeting was also notable for Alfred's presence on the platform – the first time that father and daughter had ever spoken from the same platform. It was on this occasion that Alfred claimed to be a Liberal by family tradition, but that the Tories now 'stood for very much the same things as the Liberal party did in his young days'. This was plausible up to a point, and was certainly a claim the

Tories were keen to make in 1950; but it ignored the fact that if there was one thing the Liberals passionately opposed in Alfred's youth it was Imperial Preference.[28]

There is a piquant symbolism in Alfred's presence at this meeting; because also present that evening was Denis Thatcher. He was there as an ordinary member of the Association; but he was invited to supper afterwards to meet the candidate. Denis was then aged thirty-three, general manager of Atlas Preservatives, the family paint and chemicals business founded by his grandfather. During the war he had married a girl named Margaret (known as Margot) Kempson; but she was unfaithful while he was away fighting in Italy, and the marriage did not survive. He was now divorced, and openly looking to remarry. It seems that he was immediately struck by Margaret Roberts, who bore a startling resemblance to Margot. After supper he drove her back to London to catch the last train home to Colchester. This was the start of the relationship that became the anchor of her life. It developed gradually over the next two years; but it began that evening of her adoption meeting, which therefore marks the critical watershed of her career. She arrived, as it were, on her father's arm: she left with her future husband. Her adoption for Dartford was thus the moment when she turned her back on Grantham. Oxford was an escape route. Colchester was no more than an interlude: she had no time to put down roots there and did not become an Essex woman. But though she did not go on to win Dartford she did put down roots, both political and personal, in suburban Kent. By marrying Denis Thatcher she embraced a Home Counties lifestyle. Of course Grantham remained in her blood; but for the next twenty-five years she steadily suppressed it.

Once adopted, Margaret threw herself into the constituency with total commitment. Though she could not seriously hope to win, she had been given an unexpected chance to make her name. She had at most fifteen months before the election to make an impact. First of all, though, she had to move nearer the constituency. So long as she was living and working in Essex she had a very awkward journey into London and out again in order to get to Dartford. But she could not afford to give up her job with BX Plastics until she had found a more convenient replacement; and this was not easy. She had several interviews, but found employers understandably reluctant to take on someone who made no secret of her political ambitions. Eventually she was taken on by the food manufacturers J. Lyons as a research chemist, working in Hammersmith. The job has usually been described as testing ice cream and pie-fillings; but Lady Thatcher writes in her memoirs that 'there was a stronger theoretical side to my work there, which made it more satisfying than my position at BX had been'.[29] Be that as it may – she was never very interested in theory – she stayed in pie-fillings scarcely longer than she had in plastics: less than two and a half years. The *Erith Observer* was impressed that she had 'switched to an entirely different branch of her profession';[30] but the Lyons job was no more than a pay-packet while she pursued the real business of her life.

Three months after her adoption she was able to move to Dartford. Hitherto, while she could stay over only at weekends, John Miller and his wife had put her up. Now she found herself lodgings for a time, until another local Tory couple, Mr and Mrs Woolcott, took her in. For the next few months her routine was punishing. Commuting to London every day meant getting up before six to catch a bus to the station, a train to Charing Cross, then another bus to Hammersmith; the same in reverse in the evening, followed by an evening of canvassing or meetings, chauffeured around the large constituency by a rota of members; and finally speechwriting or other political homework late into the night. It was at this time in her life that she discovered, or developed, the ability to manage on only four hours' sleep. Mrs Woolcott thought her energy phenomenal: 'However tired she was, things never seemed to get her down. She was always cheerful and I can honestly say I never heard her grumble even though there was very little time for fun in her life.'[31]

What Mrs Woolcott did not realise was that Margaret Roberts was having more fun than she had ever had in her life before. She was in her element. She was busy, she had a mountain to climb, and she was the leader. She led from the front, by exhortation and tireless example, and she was the centre of attention: not only local attention, but the first stirrings of national attention, drawn by the still-novel spectacle of a young woman hurling herself into politics.

'She was like someone who has made a vow to take up a religious life, she was so dedicated,' one awed Young Conservative recalled.[32] By sheer energy and enthusiasm Margaret Roberts pulled a moribund constituency party up by its bootstraps. The agent, R. W. Mills, though 'keen and hard-working', was 'not an outstanding organiser', and had been ill. The organisation was said to be 'patchy', with 'a great dearth of really good active workers'.[33] Yet by the end of 1949 the Association was reported to have recruited five hundred new members in Erith alone.[34] This does not quite tally with Central Office figures, which show an increase over the whole constituency of 860 (from 2,300 to 3,160) between July 1949 and August 1951. But this – an increase of 37 per cent – is still impressive. The extent to which it was directly attributable to the candidate may be measured by the fact that two years after her departure membership had fallen back again to 2,500.[35]

The deputy Area Agent was delighted, as he reported to Central Office in August:

Miss Roberts, although young and comparatively inexperienced, has made considerable progress and is putting new life into the Association.

She is a good speaker, devotes a good deal of time to the constituency, and is extremely popular.[36]

She was popular because, as well as speaking and doorstepping, she was prepared to do anything to get herself known. She debated with her opponent, the sitting Labour MP Norman Dodds, before a packed audience in Dartford Grammar School; she danced with him, to the photographers' delight, in Crayford Town Hall. Though the only woman at one branch dinner, she shed her inhibitions by 'leading all the members, septuagenarians and youngsters alike, in a particularly virile version of the Conga'.[37]

The *Daily Mail* caught up with her pulling pints in a working men's club.

The young woman pictured with the glass of mild in her hand and the silver head of Winston Churchill . . . on the lapel of her jacket . . . is Margaret Roberts.

Explaining that she had been chosen to fight Dartford 'over the heads of 26 male competitors', and after tracing her career from Grantham via Somerville to Joe Lyons, the writer came to the pints:

Women rally to hear her speak, but she couldn't get to the men at first. Women aren't allowed in the only men's club in Dartford. So Miss Roberts signed on as a barmaid (the only woman who *can* get in) in order to meet up with her constituents and serves out mild and bitter on appointed evenings. She does the same thing over at Erith . . .

For the picture she removed a pretty hat. She is easy to look at, soft-voiced, feminine, charming and clear-headed. She is also 23, and very fashion-conscious.[38]

Already she knew all about photo-opportunities.

'Easy to look at' or not, the accompanying photograph shows her looking plump-cheeked and distinctly frumpy, her hair (now fair) braided on top of her head. (Perhaps she had not intended to remove her hat.) Two months later, however, another picture in the *Erith Observer* showing her opening a Conservative fête is instantly recognisable as the commanding Prime Minister of forty years later.[39]

Much of the language and many of the ideas which Margaret Roberts voiced in this campaign are equally familiar. Once she had got her foot on the ministerial ladder in the early 1960s, Mrs Thatcher kept many of her instinctive attitudes prudently concealed while she made her way up the party. In Dartford in 1949–50, however, aged twenty-four and with nothing to lose, she spoke more freely in public of her core beliefs than she was to do again for twenty-five years. Of course her speeches were only very briefly reported in the local press: we cannot know whether the snippets quoted were picked out because they were representative of her message or, more likely, because they stood out as unusually frank. Trying to recover her characteristic themes one is putting together a jigsaw from very few pieces. But through the mostly standard-issue Conservative attacks on the extravagance and incompetence of the Labour Government, combined with promises to cut taxes and scrap controls in order to restore incentives and encourage enterprise, some more personal beliefs ring out with a conviction which was undiminished when they were unveiled again after 1975.

In her first big speech after her adoption, for example, to the Association AGM at the Bull Hotel, Dartford, on 31 March, she was careful not to disown Labour's new universal welfare structure – indeed she claimed for the Tories credit for setting up the Beveridge Committee and accepting his main proposals; but she made clear that she would prefer to encourage private provision:

> Miss Roberts stressed that the security a family could have by saving its own money, buying its own house and investing, was far better than the ordinary security one would get from any national scheme.[40]

Then in August Anthony Eden came to Dartford for an open-air rally in the football stadium. It was a big occasion, with the candidates for all the other North Kent seats sitting on the platform – including Edward Heath, adopted two years earlier for the neighbouring marginal seat of Bexley – and the MP for Maidstone, Alfred Bossom, in the chair. Margaret Roberts was chosen to propose the vote of thanks to Eden. She seized the opportunity, capping Eden's cautious promise of no further nationalisation with a ringing defence of individual enterprise. A nationalised economy, she declared, stifled initiative: 'You cannot have the dream of building up your own fortune by your own hopes, your own hands and your own British guts.'[41]

She was always superpatriotic. She condemned the Government's devaluation of sterling in September as a national humiliation, promising that a Tory Government would restore confidence, 'so that the pound can look the dollar in the face and not in the bootlaces'.[42] At the same time, while deploring the Government's dependence on American loans and Marshall Aid, she was extravagantly grateful for 'the extreme generosity of our American friends' and stressed the centrality of the Atlantic alliance.[43] In September, too, she played the housewife card again, speaking to Ted Heath's members in the Bexley Conservative Ladies' Luncheon Club, and demonstrating her remarkable capacity to bring complex matters down to everyday experience. 'Don't be scared of the high-flown language of economists and cabinet ministers', she told the ladies, 'but think of politics at our own household level.'

After all, women live in contact with food supplies, housing shortages and the ever-decreasing opportunities for children [what did she mean by that?] and we must therefore face up to the position, remembering that as more power is taken away from the people, so there is less responsibility for us to assume.[44]

At the very outset of her political career she combined an unusual determination to argue from first principles with an ability to relate them to everyday concerns. Most politicians can talk in high-flown abstractions; even more can prime the parish pump with anecdotal grievances. Margaret Thatcher's unique quality in the 1980s was her ability to marry theoretical principles successfully to populist detail. Margaret Roberts demonstrated the beginnings of the same ability in 1949.

Attlee called the General Election, exceptionally, in the middle of winter. Polling day was 23 February; the campaign was fought in miserably cold, wet weather. Miss Roberts' energy, tackling a solid Labour stronghold in these conditions, won universal admiration. Whether or not she really believed it, she managed to persuade her supporters that she had a real chance of winning. 'Our own people's enthusiasm knows no doubts,' the Area Agent, Miss Beryl Cook, reported to Central Office at the start of the campaign. 'Miss Roberts is a wonderful candidate from every point of view, and they think they have a chance – I do not like to disillusion them.'[45] Nine days later Miss Cook filed a further report:

> I am sending you a note about Dartford because the candidate, Miss Margaret Roberts' performance is so outstanding. Every meeting she has had has been packed, and people turned away.

The previous night, at Erith, she had an audience of 400, with another fifty in the foyer; while Labour drew only seventy.

> She excels at questions, and always gives a straight and convincing answer. She is never heckled; they have too much respect for her. When the meeting ends people crowd round her – generally Socialists – to ask more questions, really genuine ones.
> Her success is equally outstanding in her own personal canvassing. She is out under her own steam as much as the weather will allow, and when really wet with the loudspeaker car. Everywhere she goes she is well received.[46]

In her determination to reach the whole electorate she visited factories to talk to the workers on the shop floor. Tory candidates did not normally do such things; when Labour objected she told them they were welcome to do the same. It was her courage in tackling the enemy head on which impressed the writer Robert Muller, covering the British election for the German magazine *Heute*, as he recalled years later:

> I thought she was incredibly plucky in that safe Labour seat, not to say off her rocker. She seemed absolutely convinced that she was going to get it . . .
> She was a young starlet . . . She was fearless at meetings and pleasant but cool to meet: blinkered, determined, ambitious.[47]

Evidently she saw no need to charm Muller. She charmed practically everyone else, including her opponent, Norman Dodds, who tried at first to patronise her, but quickly formed a high regard for her. When the Sunday *People* – further demonstrating her national impact – wrote her up satirically as 'the election Glamour Girl' – 'She's young – only 24 – and she is beautiful. Lovely fair hair and beautiful blue eyes . . . By the way she's got brains as well' – suggesting that Dodds thought more of her beauty than her brains, he was quick to issue a correction.[48] She reciprocated his regard. Dodds was an old Labour stalwart of the type she approved and respected. Another was Charles Pannell, at that time chairman of the Dartford Labour party and leader of Erith council: when she finally reached Westminster in 1959 Pannell – by then MP for Leeds West – took her under his protective wing and was for many years her pair. She later formed a similarly surprising bond of mutual appreciation with Eric Heffer.

She fought the election on the slogan, unveiled at her formal adoption meeting on 3 February, 'Vote Right to Keep What's Left' – six words which brilliantly encapsulated her message, simultaneously identifying the Conservatives with morality and Labour with ruin and decline. Of course she sounded the same themes as other Tory candidates up and down the country, urging lower taxes, lower public spending and incentives to enterprise in place of rationing and controls. But she expressed these routine prescriptions with an unusual fundamentalism. Hayek may have been in her mind as she painted the election as a choice between two ways of life – 'one which leads inevitably to slavery and the other to freedom'. While other Conservatives – particularly those who had been in the war – were anxious to blur such sharp distinctions, accepting that 1945 had shifted the political argument permanently to the left, Margaret Roberts made no such concession:

> In 1940 it was not the cry of nationalisation that made this country rise up and fight totalitarianism. It was the cry of freedom and liberty.[49]

She did assert, conventionally, that 'the first tenet of Conservatism . . . is . . . national unity. We say one nation, not one class against another.'[50] But that was mainly because she fiercely rejected the notion of the Tories as the party of privilege. 'I did not go to university because my father could pay,' she told a heckler. 'I won my way there. Never let me hear anyone say they could not go to university because they could not pay.'[51] Her idea of national unity excluded class struggle, but extolled individual competition leading quite properly to inequality. It was a perversion of the tax system, she argued, to use it to give equal shares to all: those who worked hardest should not be penalised. Labour's universal welfare policies, she asserted, were 'pernicious and nibble into our national character far further than one would be aware at first glance'. The human spirit under socialism, she said – quoting her father – was like a caged bird:

> It has social security. It has food and it has warmth and so on. But what is the good of all that if it has not the freedom to fly out and live its own life.[52]

How many other young Tory candidates were talking this sort of language in 1950? Some, possibly: Churchill's election theme was 'Set the People Free'. But most, following the lead of Butler and Eden, called only for a marginal shift of emphasis within a broad acceptance of the mixed economy welfare state as an accomplished and irreversible fact. This was certainly the stance of Edward Heath next door in Bexley, Cuthbert Alport in Colchester and Iain Macleod in Enfield. Enoch Powell in Wolverhampton was more thoroughgoing in urging denationalisation wherever possible; but he was eccentric even then, and he too explicitly accepted the welfare state. These were the men, the Tory 'class of 1950', who formed the 'One Nation' group when they got to Westminster and shaped the Tory party's thinking over the next twenty-five years.

For most of that period, as she made her way – ten years behind them – up the party, Margaret Thatcher too accepted the postwar compromise. Even in 1950 she was careful to stress the party's commitment to full employment; she promised that the Tories would not cut family allowances or food subsidies until taxation could be cut commensurately; and she emphasised the need for new housing – to be built by private enterprise. ('For heaven's sake let the private builder get on with it.') In one respect she clearly suppressed her own instinct. In her memoirs she repudiates the 1950 manifesto's 'positively cloying reference to the trade union "movement"'.[53] But she echoed it at the time, endorsing the need for strong trade unions.* Nevertheless for a first-time candidate she had placed her personal beliefs on record with extraordinary candour. They did not change.

The fullest exposition of the issues as she saw them in 1950 is not to be found in reports of her meetings but in an article she wrote for the *Gravesend Reporter*. This is valuable for giving her words in full, not merely the soundbites extracted from a speech. She identified four key issues, ending her presentation of each with the refrain: 'YOU will decide.'

The first, headed 'Britain amongst the Nations', seized on the recent Chinese detention of the frigate HMS *Amethyst* in the Yangtse river to allege that the British flag was now treated with contempt:

No nation stood higher in the eyes of the world in 1945. We had the greatest opportunities for leadership a nation ever possessed, but we didn't take them.

---

* She was actually a trade unionist herself at this time, having joined the Association of Scientific Workers while at BX Plastics.

A prophetic voice [Churchill, of course] urged us to co-operate more closely with Western Europe and America in order to combine against Communism. But for two years his words fell on deaf ears until the initial opportunity was lost . . .

Britain must be restored to her premier position as a nation and as the centre of an Empire. The world needs her . . . YOU will decide.

No credit here for the creation of NATO, but a near-perfect expression of the postwar fallacy that saw Britain uniquely placed at the intersection of Europe, America and the Empire, with an unquestioning but already anachronistic assumption that Britain should naturally lead the world.

Second, 'Britain's Economic Independence' rejects the national humiliation of dependence on American generosity with a long homely parable about a man accepting a loan from a neighbour, quickly exhausting it and then selling his wife's jewellery to pay the grocer.

Are YOU going to let this proud island race, who at one time would never accept charity, drift on from crisis to crisis under a further spell of shaky Socialist finance?

Or do you believe in sound finance and economical spending of public money, such as the Conservatives will adopt?

YOU will decide.

Sound money, lower spending, no borrowing: the prescription was identical in 1979.

Her third issue, Labour's plans for further nationalisation, she opposed not on ideological grounds, but strictly on price: 'Are you going to let the manufacturers whittle down the prices under the stimulus of Private Enterprise, or meekly pay more for nationalised goods?' For her fourth, however, she returned to fundamentalism. Under the heading 'Frustration of Freedom?', she quoted a letter she claimed to have received from a young engineer from the Dominions who was horrified at the docile way the British, since the war, 'were letting ourselves be ordered about by a *system*'. Individual enterprise, she said, had made Britain great.

Do you want it to perish for a soulless Socialist system or to live to recreate a glorious Britain?

YOU WILL DECIDE.[54]

The simple certainty of this dichotomy between soulless socialism and glorious patriotic freedom was, in Margaret Roberts' case, more than just the rhetoric of the hustings. It was the passion of her life. Her election address, too – the leaflet that went through every letterbox – struck an exceptionally personal note. Besides the policy points, it included an extraordinarily immodest account of how she came to be selected as the Tory candidate, stressing her precocity – elementary school at four, secondary school at ten, scholarship to Somerville at seventeen (which was not true) – and her own doubts that she was perhaps too young, until reminded that Pitt the Younger was Prime Minister at twenty-four. 'If ability is present, it is there at any age. After much persuasion, she decided to let her name go forward . . .' Her personal message emphasised her maturity and independence, and promised total dedication:

> The long training I have received has taught me to shape my own opinions judging on the evidence alone . . .
> In Parliament I should vote as my conscience and not the party line dictates.
> I should carry out my task to the utmost of my ability, allowing myself no rest until the duties which fell to my lot were complete.[55]

How many other candidates would have promised so much – and meant it?

Of course she did not win. Such was the enthusiasm of her campaign that her agent persuaded himself that she had an even chance. But the experienced Beryl Cook reported more realistically to Central Office: 'I do not think there is a hundredth chance of winning the seat, but I am quite sure the majority will be down with a bump. This will be an entirely personal triumph for Miss Roberts.'[56] Mrs Thatcher herself told George Gardiner in 1975 that she only hoped to cut Dodds' majority to about 9,000. Five years later she admitted to Patricia Murray that 'we really thought that we might conceivably do it' – that is win. 'We didn't, of course, it came down to about 12,000, but there's nothing like being an optimist when you're young.'[57]

The actual majority was slightly bigger than she remembered:

N. Dodds (Labour)	38,128
M. Roberts (Conservative)	24,490
A. Giles (Liberal)	5,011
Labour majority	13,638

Miss Roberts had cut Dodds' majority by a third and won herself golden opinions. After such a successful blooding there could be little doubt that she would get a winnable constituency before long. The problem was that nationally the Conservatives had almost, but not quite, overturned Labour's 1945 majority. Attlee survived with an overall majority of just five. This meant that there was likely to be another election very soon, making it difficult for candidates like Margaret Roberts to seek greener pastures. She made the best of the situation, telling her supporters at the count, 'You sign on for next time tomorrow morning', and promising an even bigger effort to win the seat at the second attempt.[58] She was enthusiastically readopted at the end of March, announcing 'operation doorstep' and insisting, 'I believe it can be won.'[59] At a dance to mark the anniversary of her original adoption she was presented with a cake, a handbag and a scroll signed by 991 helpers.

Meanwhile she attended a victory ball for the other Kentish candidates who had won their seats: Ted Heath had just scraped Bexley by 133 votes, and Patricia Hornsby-Smith – another formidably dynamic young woman, though she was actually eleven years older than Margaret Roberts – had captured Chiselhurst by a similar margin. Central Office considered these three, plus Robert Carr in Mitcham, the outstanding new candidates in the South-East area.[60] In this company Miss Roberts was not seen as a loser. On the contrary, she was made to feel very much part of a successful team: Central Office judged that the energy of her campaign, keeping Labour workers in Dartford who might otherwise have gone to Bexley, was a crucial factor in securing Heath's success.* The chairman of the Kent MPs, Alfred Bossom, adopted her as a protégée, invited her to his lavish eve-of-session parties at his house in Carlton Gardens as though she were an MP, and tried to help her to a better seat.[62] She in turn fulsomely embraced Kent as her adopted county – not least, as she told the Association of Men of Kent and Kentish Men, because 'it harbours Winston at Westerham'.[63] She already made a habit of referring to her revered leader by his Christian name.

Some of her own language was already astonishingly Churchillian.

---

* It is unlikely that he was grateful. It is a piquant coincidence that these two, whose destinies became so entwined twenty-five years later, should have been constituency neighbours in 1950–1. She wrote in her memoirs that she found him 'crisp and logical' but even at his most affable 'somewhat aloof and alone'.[61]

It was the custom for all the candidates to give New Year messages to the local paper. Most were bland and platitudinous. Margaret Roberts' 1949 message was no exception, offering the sententious hope that 'each of us [may] play our part in the Grand Design with that unselfish courage which alone can make for happier human and world relationships in the years that are to come'.[64] In December 1950, however, while Dodds, Heath and others stuck to the same pious generalities, Miss Roberts issued a clarion call to the West to stand firm against Communism. The outbreak of the Korean War that summer, she declared, represented 'a crisis in world history . . . which demands swift and certain action'.

> We believe in the freedom of the democratic way of life. *If we serve the idea faithfully, with tenacity of purpose, we have nothing to fear from Russian Communism.*
>
> We must firstly *believe* in the Western way of life and serve it steadfastly. Secondly we must build up our fighting strength to be prepared to defend our ideals, for aggressive nations understand only the threat of force.
>
> The situation is already grave, but much is possible for a nation with clear intentions and the ability to carry them into action.[65]

This is an amazing statement from a 25-year-old female prospective candidate in an unwinnable seat. The Iron Lady was already fully forged in 1950.

Margaret Roberts' first parliamentary campaign must have done wonders for her self-confidence. She knew now that she was on her way. With her course firmly set, she could begin to equip herself professionally for the career that lay within her grasp. Testing pie-fillings was no preparation for the House of Commons. As soon as the 1950 election was out of the way she applied to the Inns of Court to start reading for the Bar. She gave up her digs in Dartford and rented a flat in St George's Square Mews in Pimlico. Instead of commuting daily to Hammersmith and returning to Dartford every evening to canvass, she could now devote her evenings to the law, visiting the constituency only when required. She did not really believe that one more push would win it. Yet she was still more visible than most candidates in hopeless seats. Her faithful champion in Central Office, Beryl Cook, worried in 1951 that 'she has taken on rather much, but seems to be coping . . . She is a most able young woman and worthy of a better seat.'[66]

Living in London also enabled her to see more of Denis Thatcher, who did not live in Erith but drove down to Atlas Preservatives each day from Chelsea. Since their first meeting on the night of her adoption their relationship had developed slowly. Margaret had little time for social life in the eleven months up to the election; moreover they were commuting every day in opposite directions. It was 'certainly not', she once insisted, a case of love at first sight.[67] Nevertheless, she wrote in her memoirs, 'It was clear to me at once that Denis was an exceptional man.' In addition to a shared professional interest in applied science – paint and plastics – and compatible politics ('I discovered that his views were no-nonsense Conservatism') she claims that they quickly found cultural tastes in common:

Denis is an avid reader, especially of history, biography and detective novels. He seemed to have read every article in *The Economist* and *The Banker*, and we found that we both enjoyed music – Denis with his love of opera, and me with mine of choral music.[68]

This surely is another of Lady Thatcher's improvements on the truth. Paint and plastics possibly, economics up to a point, but Denis was never a great reader, still less an opera lover; while her own reading since leaving school was largely confined to politics and she never showed any interest in music, choral or otherwise, after leaving Oxford. (As Prime Minister she used to go occasionally to Glyndebourne; but that was as much a political statement of support for privately funded opera as an expression of musical enthusiasm.) It is absurd to pretend that she and Denis were drawn together by shared cultural interests. The great love of Denis's life was sport – above all rugby – in which she had no interest whatever.

Margaret and Denis were not an obviously well-matched couple. Yet at the time they met each of them was what the other was looking for. Denis was thirty-three in February 1949. He had been deeply hurt by the failure of his first marriage. He wanted to marry again before he got too old, but was wary of making another mistake. What he liked about Margaret Roberts, on top of her looks, her energy and her youthful optimism, was her formidable practicality. She was not a girl who was going to make a mess of her life, or complicate his with feminine demands. Dedicated to her own career, she would leave him space to get on with his.

She too was ready to get married, on her own terms. Hitherto she had never had much time for boyfriends. She had men friends –

indeed she preferred the company of men to women – but they were political associates with whom she talked and argued, rather than kissed. She preferred men older than herself: throughout her life she had a series of older mentors – father figures to whom she would quite surprisingly defer, almost visibly suppressing her instinct to challenge and rebut. Keith Joseph, Willie Whitelaw, Airey Neave, Peter Thorneycroft and Ronald Reagan all filled this role in different ways and at different times: beyond the strictly political sphere Laurens van der Post and Immanuel Jakobovitz were others whom she placed on a pedestal of exaggerated reverence. Obviously Alfred Roberts was the archetype, the idealised father whom she had by now outgrown but psychologically needed to replace. When she married she was always likely to choose an older man.

Though she had made a great impact in Dartford as a young single woman, Alfred Bossom – and doubtless others – advised her that to advance her career she really needed to be married. Moreover in sheer practical terms, marriage would enable her to give up her unrewarding job and concentrate fully on law and politics. Yet she had also a strong domestic streak. She may have rebelled against her mother's enslavement to the home, but she was proud of the domestic skills she had learned at her mother's knee; and she had a deep need of security. For six years in Oxford, Colchester and Dartford she had lived first in college, then in a succession of digs. For someone who was already voicing in her speeches an almost visceral belief in home-ownership as the basis of civic virtue, social stability and family life, the urge for a home of her own was exceptionally powerful. With all the demands of her subsequent career she always found time to be an assiduous home-maker.

At the same time her practicality disguised a romantic side to her nature. At the height of her political power Mrs Thatcher was notoriously susceptible to a certain sort of raffish charm and displayed a surprising weakness for matinee-idol looks. Denis did not have these exactly, but he was tall (which she liked), upright and bespectacled (like her father, though Denis was more owlish). He had served in the war and retained a military manner, at once slangy, blunt and self-deprecating. As managing director of his family firm he was comfortably off, drove a fast car – a Jaguar – and had his own flat in Chelsea. In the still grey and rationed world of 1950 he had, as she writes in her memoirs, 'a certain style and dash . . . and, being ten years older, he simply knew more of the world than I did'.[69] But she would not have fallen for a playboy. It was his work that took Denis round the world, and she admired that. She was a great believer in business, and export business in particular. Atlas

Preservatives was just the sort of company on which British economic recovery depended. Beneath his bluff manner, Denis was a serious businessman of old-fashioned views and a moral code as rigorous as her own. He was much more relaxed about politics than she was, but he shared her principles and embodied them in practice. It was not an accident that politics brought them together.

Thus they complemented one another perfectly. While each answered the other's need for security and support, each also appreciated the other's self-sufficiency. Both were dedicated to their own careers, which neither ever curtailed for the other – not Margaret when their children were young, nor Denis when she became a Cabinet Minister. When she was first elected to Parliament she presented her career as an 'outside interest' which helped to keep their marriage happy: 'A wife has to keep pace with her husband,' she told the *Sunday Dispatch* in 1960. 'If she has no outside interest then she has nothing to contribute to a conversation with him.'[70] As their daughter Carol later wrote, their marriage was more a partnership of mutual convenience than a romance:

> If marriage is either a takeover or a merger, then my parents enjoyed the latter. There was a great deal of common ground and a tacit *laissez-faire* agreement that they would get on with their own interests and activities. There was no possessiveness, nor any expectation that one partner's career should take precedence.[71]

Only once, around 1964, did Margaret's growing political prominence strain Denis's tolerance near to breaking point. For the most part he accepted, in a way truly remarkable for a man of conservative views born in 1915, the equality – and ultimately far more than equality – of his wife's career with his own. In this he was indeed 'an exceptional man'. Needing a husband, Margaret chose shrewdly and exceedingly well. The sentence in her memoirs that her decision to marry Denis was 'one of the best I ever made' is a curious understatement.[72] Marriage to Denis was the rock of her career.

He actually proposed in September 1951. After she moved to London, he took her to dinner or 'the occasional play' – she does not mention concerts – and then to the Paint and Varnish Manufacturers' annual dance. She says she first realised he was serious when he gave her a silver and crystal powder bowl for Christmas 1950. He was also – perhaps a surer way to her heart – 'an immense help in the constituency – problems were solved in a trice and all the logistics taken care of'.[73] (This was never the case again, once she moved on from Dartford; but Dartford, or rather Erith, was Denis's patch.) He says he made up his mind to propose while on holiday in France with a male friend. 'During the tour I suddenly thought to myself "That's the girl" . . . I think I was intelligent enough to see that this was a remarkable young woman.'[74] She claims that she 'thought long and hard about it. I had so much set my heart on politics that I hadn't figured marriage in my plans.'[75] Be that as it may, she accepted. But the 1951 General Election came first. Attlee went to the country again in October. Miss Roberts – for the last time under that name – threw herself back into electioneering. It can have done her no harm that Central Office leaked the news of her engagement the day before polling. But of course the seat was still impregnable. She took another thousand votes off Dodds' majority. More important the Tories were narrowly returned to power (on a minority of the national poll). Just seven weeks later Miss Roberts became the second Mrs Thatcher.

During the eighteen-month twilight of the Labour Government, from March 1950 to October 1951, she had continued to nurse the constituency assiduously; but she also continued with efforts to get herself more widely known. She attended weekend courses at the Tory party's training college, Swinton College, and got herself invited to speak in other constituencies. She also attended meetings of the Conservative Candidates' Association where she rubbed shoulders and crossed swords for the first time with rivals of her own generation, who would all be jostling for the same few winnable seats over the next few years. They were almost all men, so she was instantly conspicuous, as Edward du Cann, then candidate for West Walthamstow, recalled:

> She was strikingly attractive, obviously intelligent, a goer. She was often the first in any meeting to get to her feet to ask a question. Most of her fellow-candidates found this habit off-putting: they thought her too keen by far, too pushy.[76]

Among the contacts she made at these gatherings was Airey Neave, then candidate for Ealing North, who was secretary of the Association. She gained a little experience of the party's central organisation by serving as representative of the Conservative Graduates Association on the National Executive. But her proudest moment was seconding the vote of thanks to Churchill at a Conservative women's rally at the Albert Hall on 7 June. This, she has written, was 'a great occasion for me – to meet in the flesh and talk to the leader whose words had so inspired me as I sat with my family around our table in Grantham'.[77] Unfortunately she does not relate what the great man said to her.

Along with the need for enterprise at home, her staple theme continued to be the Churchillian one of resistance to Communist aggression. Though the initial panic over the Korean War had eased as the conflict settled into stalemate, she still devoted an unusual amount of attention to foreign affairs. In July 1951 she treated a ward meeting to a classic statement of the domino theory. The true nature of Communism, she declared, was being revealed in China, where a million people had already been executed without trial since the Communist takeover in 1949. 'No democratic country', she asserted, 'can stand by and watch this going on.' France was already having trouble in Indo-China.

> If that country falls, Siam will go and then Singapore and Malaya. Our naval base would be lost and Australia and New Zealand would be cut off. Communism would spread through Malaya into Burma and India, which borders Russia. It is vital we hold what we have in the Far East.

In the Middle East, too, she condemned the Government's weakness in the face of Persia's nationalisation of British oil assets. 'Eastern people', she asserted with the assurance of one who had never been east of Harwich, 'are very quick to sense vacillation.'[78]

She launched her second Dartford campaign on 10 October with what the *Gravesend Reporter* called 'one of the finest speeches of her political career . . . a slashing attack on the Socialists' which brought together all her favourite themes. 'Under the Socialists', she insisted, 'this country will never really pay its way. It will go from one crisis to another and eventually come to such an enormous crash that Britain will go out of existence as Great Britain once and for all.' The answer, she still believed, lay in the Empire:

> The hope of this nation as a future trading nation stands on co-operation and trading with our own dominions and colonies. We shall shortly be facing some Japanese and German competition, and we must seek our first markets in the colonies and also be the first markets as far as they are concerned.

One moment she proclaimed that Labour had brought the country to the brink of ruin; the next she took it for granted that Britain was still a global superpower. 'If we can co-operate on matters of defence through the Empire and the United States, and so to greater things, we can defend the world on a world basis.'[79]

This undiminished faith in Britain's 'greatness' recurs repeatedly in her campaign speeches – even in the context of a homily on individual rights and responsibilities:

> Everyone, at any and every level, who is prepared to say 'I have a right to this or that', must also say 'I have a responsibility towards myself, my neighbours and my country'; and that responsibility, whoever I may be, is to do all in my power to see that Britain achieves the maximum greatness of which she is capable.[80]

There is something almost totalitarian in this mystical insistence that the individual owes his overriding duty to advancing the 'greatness' of the nation. It sits oddly with her otherwise classical liberal belief in the individual's freedom to pursue his own economic interest. This tension between liberalism and nationalism persisted throughout her career, coming to a head in her schizophrenic approach to Europe in the latter days of her premiership. Both strands were present in her political make-up from the beginning. But when they pulled different ways her most fundamental political allegiance was always to the nation and her quasi-religious belief in British 'greatness'.

With no Liberal standing this time she had a straight fight with Dodds. Once again her meetings were packed; once again her star speakers, such as they were – Sir Herbert Williams, the former MP for Croydon, and Melford Stevenson KC, the future High Court judge – were heckled while she was heard with rapt attention. The press still loved her, and she loved a photo-opportunity. The *Daily Graphic* posed her in Attlee Drive, beside a 30 mph speed limit sign. She was smartly dressed, as always, in black with a black feathery hat and a large handbag: but for the rosette on her right shoulder she might have been going to a funeral. 'Miss Roberts,' the accompanying text burbled, 'tall, slim and brown-haired, loves a fight.' She had 'fought her way' from elementary school to Oxford; she loved canvassing on the strongest Labour estates; she was 'happiest in the middle of her political enemies'. She actually wished that she was heckled more: 'When hecklers get up at my meetings', she claimed, 'I get a mental jump for joy . . . It gives me something to get my teeth into – and the audiences love it.'[81]

Both halves of this statement are revealing. She loved demolishing opponents; increasingly she also loved playing to the gallery. Once again one gets a strong sense of the dominating personality of the 1980s fully formed. Yet already she was beginning to rein in her individuality. Her 1951 election address is much more bland and conventional than the strikingly personal appeal she put out in 1950. For the next twenty-five years, in fact, she rarely let either the public or her colleagues glimpse the fundamentalist views or the fighting mettle she had displayed so vividly in Dartford in 1949–51.

In a two-horse race, with an almost identical turnout, Miss Roberts took slightly more of the Liberal vote than Dodds did, so knocking another thousand off his majority:

N. Dodds (Labour)	40,094
M. H. Roberts (Conservative)	27,760
Labour majority	12,334

But it was clear that she would never win the seat. In the few weeks between the election and her wedding, the constituency paid her its farewells and thanks. 'With her energy, ability and wonderful qualities', the vice-chairman declared, 'she has raised the Association from a mediocre affair to something which is alive.' Her candidacy had 'put Dartford on the map'. They gave the new Mr and Mrs Thatcher an inscribed silver salver as a wedding present.[82]

The wedding, on 13 December, emphasised the bride's new life in the Home Counties rather than her Midland roots. She did not go back to Grantham to be married – it was, she writes, 'more convenient for all concerned that the ceremony take place in London'[83] – nor did she invite any of her schoolfriends. She was married in the Wesleyan Chapel, City Road – described by one writer as 'the Westminster Abbey of the Methodist Church';[84] but this was mainly because Denis, as a divorced man, could not remarry in an Anglican church. From now on Margaret increasingly identified herself with the Established Church. There are indications that Alfred was not very happy with his daughter's choice of husband. The Rev. Skinner, the family friend with whom Margaret had stayed on her first visit to London at the age of twelve, assisted at the service; but Denis told Carol years later that Alfred thought the ceremony 'half-way to Rome'.[85] The bride did not even wear white, but a brilliant blue velvet dress with a matching hat decorated spectacularly with ostrich feathers: a replica of the dress worn by Georgiana, Duchess of Devonshire, no less, in Gainsborough's painting. Finally the reception was hosted not by her father but by her Kentish Conservative mentor, Alfred Bossom, at his house in Carlton Gardens. The largest contingent of the fifty guests came from the Dartford Conservative Association. John Miller proposed the couple's health. It was very much a Kent Conservative affair.

Typically, the honeymoon combined holiday with work – a few days in Madeira sandwiched between business trips to Portugal and Paris. It was Margaret's first experience of foreign travel, but she never had much time for holidays; she was almost certainly impatient to get back to start homemaking, passing her Bar exams and looking for another seat. On their return she moved into Denis's flat in Swan Court, Flood Street, Chelsea – just off the King's Road – and began life as Margaret Thatcher. With marriage accomplished, she told Miriam Stoppard many years later, 'this was the biggest thing in one's life now sorted out'.[86]

5

Superwoman

AFTER the precocious triumphs of her two Dartford candidacies, Margaret Thatcher's career was stalled for the next six years. Just when she had made such a spectacular beginning, marriage and then motherhood took her abruptly out of the political reckoning. In the long run, marriage set her up, both emotionally and financially: Denis's money gave her the security and independence to dedicate her life to politics. But in the short run it set her back five years.

Not that she became a housewife: far from it. But she was obliged to concentrate her energies on her secondary ambition – to become a lawyer – while putting her primary political goal temporarily on hold. She was forced – reluctantly – to sit out the 1955 General Election. Not until 1958 was she able to secure a winnable constituency from which to resume her march on Westminster. Frustrating though it was at the time, this enforced period of retrenchment did her no harm. In 1950 she was young, conspicuous and headstrong: had she got into Parliament at that age she would inevitably have attracted a lot of attention and probably identified herself irreparably as a naively vigorous right-winger. As it was, six years of marriage, motherhood and law both matured her and made her much less visible, enabling her to slip easily into a career path of rapid but inconspicuous promotion, without weakening her fundamental instincts and convictions. Those who make their move too soon in British politics seldom make it to the top.

At first she simply enjoyed transforming Denis's bachelor flat into a married home. Lady Thatcher is intensely proud of her practical skills as painter, wallpaperer and seamstress. They could easily have afforded to have the Swan Court flat redecorated; but Mrs Thatcher the young housewife was as reluctant to delegate as Mrs Thatcher the Prime Minister: she rarely trusts anyone to do anything better than she can do it herself. She also learned to shop in the King's Road; to cook – more ambitiously than she learned at home – and to keep house for her husband. Denis continued to reverse-commute, driving to Erith every morning against the rush hour traffic and back for dinner every evening. Her memory of this domestic interlude is idyllic:

> To be a young married woman in comfortable circumstances must always be a delight if the marriage is a happy one, as mine was. But to be a young married woman in those circumstances in the 1950s was very heaven.[1]

Her marriage coincided neatly with the end of the Labour Government, which she equates simplistically with 'the reawakening of normal happy life after the trials of wartime and the petty indignities of postwar austerity'.[2] Rationing was gradually ended, living standards rose: life *was* better under the Conservatives – as she had assured the electors of Dartford it would be. She relished having a home of her own, for the first time in her life, with all that that represented to her both personally – in terms of her private identity and security – and ideologically. The fact that it was rented, at a controlled rent of just £7 a week, did not worry her. The British middle-class fetish for home ownership, which she did so much to encourage and reward, had not yet taken hold.

For the first time in her life she had money and could begin fully to enjoy *la douceur de la vie*. She could at last surround herself with all those enviable mod cons she did not have in Grantham or in any of her cheerless digs. In Swan Court she could afford to entertain and quickly turned herself into a formidable hostess. Although in her memoirs she concedes that 'I may have been perhaps rather more serious than my contemporaries, Denis and I enjoyed ourselves quite as much as most ... We went to the theatre, we took holidays in Rome and Paris (albeit in very modest hotels), we gave parties and we went to them, we had a wonderful time.'[3]

But of course she also worked. Along with the cooking and the housework, she now had time to pursue her legal studies. She had already, before her marriage, enrolled to eat her dinners in the Inner Temple: she now attended courses at the Council for Legal Education, working towards her intermediate Bar exams in the summer of 1953. If he did not know it already, Denis discovered that he had married a workaholic who would stay up long after he had gone to bed, or get up early, to finish whatever she had to do. He supported and encouraged her; but he put his foot down when she proposed studying accountancy as well.[4]

In the wake of her Dartford exposure she was still seen as a rising political star. She was scarcely back from her honeymoon before she was invited to write an article for the *Sunday Graphic* on the role of women in the 'New Elizabethan Era'. King George VI had just died: the paper, with remarkable prescience, picked out the newly-married Mrs Thatcher as a young woman almost exactly the same age as the new Queen (she was actually six months older) who might have a part to play in the new reign. The result, headlined 'Wake Up, Women!', was the most explicitly feminist clarion call to her own sex that Margaret Thatcher ever made.

'Women', she wrote, 'can – AND MUST – play a leading part in the creation of a glorious Elizabethan era.' She deplored the convention that expected women to give up careers in order to have children. She insisted that they *could* be combined. 'The idea that the family suffers is, I believe, quite mistaken.' She cited the Principal of Somerville, Janet Vaughan, as a woman who had successfully combined a professional career with bringing up two daughters. Then she specifically applied the same principle to the field of her own ambitions and called on more women to go into politics. Not only that, but there should be no glass ceiling on their advancement:

> Should a woman arise equal to the task, I say let her have an equal chance with the men for the leading Cabinet posts. Why not a woman Chancellor – or a woman Foreign Secretary?[5]

This was a startlingly radical thought in 1952. (Half a century later it still is: no woman has yet held either post.) At that time only one woman had ever sat in a British Cabinet – Margaret Bondfield as Minister of Labour back in 1929–31. Florence Horsbrugh became the second in 1953. But Miss Horsbrugh, like Miss Bondfield, was unmarried; she was also sixty-four years old and unlikely to rise higher than the Ministry of Education. There can be no doubt that in throwing down this challenge Mrs Thatcher was declaring the reach of her own ambition. She did not accept that marriage should close her political options, nor did she accept any limit on her potential. It was surely only tact that prevented her including the premiership itself within the legitimate range of 'a woman . . . equal to the task'. Her pretended modesty and amazement when she seized the right to challenge for the top job in 1975 is belied by this explicit declaration of her long-term ambition in 1952.

So long as she had no children, marriage itself was no bar to looking for a better seat. Her memoirs suggest that she initially decided to suspend her ambitions for a time; but 'try as I would my fascination for politics got the better of all contrary resolutions'.[6] So she went to see Beryl Cook at Central Office and put her name back on the candidates' list, specifying that she was only interested in seats within a thirty-mile radius of London. John Hare, the party vice-chairman in charge of candidates, promptly sent her name to Holborn and St Pancras, a central London marginal held by Labour with a majority of less than 2,000. 'Miss Beryl Cook', he told the local Association, 'has the highest opinion of her ability, intelligence and charm', adding – since the constituency particularly wanted a candidate with a trade union background – that 'she was at one time a member of the Association of Chemical and Scientific Workers'.[7] Hare kept pressing her claims and succeeded in getting her included on the shortlist of eight. At the beginning of September, however, she wrote to the chairman withdrawing her name:

> I have been round the constituency very thoroughly in the last few days and have come to the conclusion that at present I would rather not tackle an area so close to Central London, as it has no community life of its own.[8]

The rough community life of Holborn and St Pancras – with no certainty of winning – was not what she was looking for.* After Dartford she thought she could do better. In January 1953 the Tory MP for Canterbury resigned. Though well beyond her thirty-mile limit, Canterbury was a blue-chip seat and the capital of her adopted county. She put her name forward. But she was not even shortlisted.

Central Office was so keen to give her a leg up that it put her name forward in glowing terms to the BBC as a possible panellist on the controversial television discussion programme *In the News* – the programme that made household names of Michael Foot, Bob Boothby and A. J. P. Taylor. She was 'a very bright girl, young, under thirty, very good-looking with a first at Oxford'.[9] (The last was, of course, not true.) The producers, however, were not persuaded. Her participation would certainly have changed the chummy masculine ethos of the programme. But the BBC was probably right to reject her. Out of her element she could still be very gauche. The previous summer she had gone back to Somerville for a gaudy. In recognition of her emerging prominence

---

* Holborn and St Pancras eventually adopted a local councillor who failed to win the seat in 1955. Geoffrey Johnson-Smith captured it for the Conservatives in 1959, but lost it again in 1964.

Janet Vaughan invited her to speak for her generation (immediately following Iris Murdoch, who spoke for the slightly older cohort). Her contemporaries, as Ann Dally remembers, 'feared the worst, and so it was'.

> She had lost the Midlands accent that her fellow students had known. Now she sounded more like Princess Elizabeth, who was not yet Queen . . .
>
> Princess Elizabeth used to talk of 'May Husband and Ay', which was quite a joke among our . . . generation. To our surprise Margaret, newly married, now said just that and we, her contemporaries, felt ashamed that one of us could be so embarrassing. She then gave us her views on marriage and home life expressed in such sanctimonious platitudes that we were even more embarrassed to be associated with her. She didn't talk of children because at that stage she had none, though most of us were already mothers.

'She seemed not unpleasant or bossy', Ann Dally reflected from the perspective of 1990, 'but alien and uncongenial.' After dinner she found Janet Vaughan glum and angry: 'That was *dreadful*. I'll *never* invite her to speak again.' But she did, because Mrs Thatcher remained inescapably the most distinguished Somerville woman of her generation – precisely, as Ann Dally concedes, because she was not 'one of us'.[10]

Almost certainly Margaret Thatcher wanted to have children – she would have regarded it as part of her duty, one of those social expectations she was programmed to observe – even though she must have known it would make finding a seat more difficult. She was confident of her own ability to handle the competing demands on her time; but local Conservative Associations were a different matter. Whatever her calculations, they were knocked sideways in August 1953 when she surprised herself and her doctors by producing twins. This was a wonderful piece of Thatcherite efficiency – two babies for the price of one, a boy and a girl, in a single economy pack, an object lesson in productivity. 'How typical of Margaret!' Ann Dally remembers one of her jaundiced contemporaries exclaiming. 'She *would* have twins!'[11] She had been expecting a single child in late September, but her labour pains started six weeks early. She went into Queen Charlotte's Hospital on Thursday 13 August, was X-rayed next day and found to be carrying twins; they were delivered by Caesarean section on Saturday the 15th, weighing 4lbs each. The story told in numerous interviews and repeated in her memoirs is that Denis could not be contacted for several hours because he had 'very sensibly' gone to watch the final Test Match against the Australians at the Oval. Eventually 'he received two pieces of good but equally surprising news. England won the Ashes, and he found himself the proud father of twins.'[12]

There are two things wrong with this family legend, which was repeated yet again by Carol in her biography of Denis. The first is that England did not win the Ashes on the day the twins were born. The Test Match actually started, unusually, on that Saturday: it did not finish until the following Wednesday, when England's first Ashes victory on home soil since 1926 was celebrated with scenes reminiscent of the relief of Mafeking. Denis may well have been there – Margaret stayed in hospital for a fortnight. He may also have gone to the cricket on the Saturday, and on to the pub afterwards while she was giving birth: but memory has conflated the two events. Unlike the conquest of Everest by Hillary and Tenzing on Coronation Day two months earlier, Margaret Thatcher did not contrive to give birth on a day of national rejoicing.

The second oddity is the suggestion that Denis did not know that Margaret was expecting twins before he left for the Oval on Saturday morning. If, as she says, she was X-rayed on the Friday, and the decision made then to deliver them by Caesarean the following day, he would surely have been told on the Friday. (Incidentally why did it take an X-ray to discover that she was carrying two babies? Even in 1953 a stethoscope could surely have picked up two heartbeats.) The whole story appears to be a romantic embroidery. Either that or Denis was an exceptionally detached father, even by the standards of the time. Of course no father dreamed of attending his child's birth at that date. It is just possible that he neglected to telephone the hospital at the end of the day's play to hear how the operation had gone, especially since bad light ended play early with Australia 275 all out, England 1 for nought. But the idea that he was not informed the day before that Margaret was expecting twins, and would need a Caesarean, stretches credulity.

Whatever the truth, giving birth to twins with the minimum disruption of her career became part of the Thatcher legend. She did not enjoy her pregnancy, which made her feel uncharacteristically unwell, so getting two children for the labour of one suited her admirably. 'As she now had one of each sex', Carol has written, 'that was the end of it as far as she was concerned – she needn't repeat the process.'[13] She could get on with what was more important to her.

There and then, in her hospital bed, she committed herself to taking her final Bar exams in December. She had passed her intermediates in May and, twins or no twins, she was not going to postpone her finals. In fact their arrival six weeks early gave her more time. 'If I fill in the entrance form now,' she recalled thinking, 'pride will not let me fail. And so I did.'[14]

Juggling career and family, she believed, was simply a matter of good organisation. To John Hare, who wrote congratulating her and asking if he should stop sending her name to constituencies, she replied that having unexpectedly produced twins, 'I had better not consider a candidature for at least six months. The household needs considerable reorganisation and a reliable nurse must be found before I can feel free to pursue such other activities with the necessary fervour.'[15]

On coming out of hospital she first hired an Australian nurse for six weeks while she found a permanent Barnardo's-trained nanny, called Barbara, who stayed for five years. To give themselves more space, she and Denis rented the adjoining flat, knocking through a connecting door: this arrangement, with Denis and Margaret in one flat and Barbara and the twins next door, ensured undisturbed nights and maximum peace and quiet in the daytime for Margaret to work. She duly passed her final exams, was called to the Bar and joined her first chambers in January 1954. Meanwhile, contrary to her later accounts, she did not stop looking for a winnable seat.

'I did not try for the 1955 election,' she told *Woman's Hour* in 1986. 'I really just felt the twins were . . . only two, I really felt that it was too soon. I couldn't do that and so I didn't try for a candidature then.'[16] In fact, as she subsequently acknowledged in *The Path to Power*, she did try for Orpington when Sir Waldron Smithers died at the end of 1954. It is not surprising that she was tempted: it was the perfect constituency for her, practically next door to Dartford but an absolutely safe – in normal circumstances – Tory seat full of just the sort of suburban homeowners whom she would later call 'her' people. Unfortunately it fell vacant just a couple of years too soon for her. Though she was shortlisted – twins notwithstanding – the Association chose its own chairman, Donald Sumner, who sold himself as the local man 'who really knows the state of the roads in Lock's Bottom'.[17] Two years later Margaret and Denis moved to Orpington and bought a house in Lock's Bottom. Had the Association chosen her in 1955, of course, they would not have faced the famous by-election seven years later when Sumner left politics to become a judge and the seat was sensationally snatched by Eric Lubbock for the Liberals.

Swallowing her disappointment, she recognised that she was unlikely to find a constituency before the next election and resolved to make the best of it, telling Hare that she would now 'continue at the Bar with no further thought of a parliamentary career for many years'.[18] When Eden – finally succeeding Churchill in April 1955 – immediately went to the country, she spoke for Tory candidates in a number of Kent and Essex seats, including Ted Heath's Bexleyheath. But she hated being a supporting player: 'Once you have been a candidate everything else palls.'[19] She did not mean to stay on the sidelines for very long. In February 1956 she put her name back on the Central Office candidates' list and attended a course in television skills for Tory hopefuls.[20] And as soon as the selection cycle began again, two years into the new Parliament, with sitting Members declaring their intention to stand down, she was quickly back on the constituency trail – though Mark and Carol were still only three.

'I should vegetate if I were left at the kitchen sink all day,' she told the London *Evening News* in 1959. 'I don't think the family suffers at all through my political ambitions.' It was all a matter of good management, she went on. 'The key to the whole plan' was 'a first-class nanny-housekeeper to look after things in the wife's absence'.[21] This, she admitted, cost money; but in these early interviews she made no bones about her dependence on nanny.

When the children were very young I always had an English nanny. I never had an *au pair* because I couldn't really have gone out and left them with an easy mind. I wouldn't have been quite certain whether the *au pair* could speak English or knew how to ring the hospital if anything happened.[22]

Later, when she was Prime Minister, she somewhat changed her tune. Though she always admitted, when pressed, that she had been lucky to have help, the image of privilege had to be downplayed. She was now keen to present herself to Middle England as having been an ordinary working mum, coping with crises single-handed: 'There is no point in complaining about it. You just have to get on and do it . . . because in most cases it's your job because Dad has gone to work and Mum is left to cope. So you do cope.'[23]

While she was practising at the Bar, in Mark and Carol's pre-school years, she told Patricia Murray, 'I was never very far away – my chambers were only about twenty minutes from home, so I knew I could be back very quickly if I were needed.'[24] That was true – though perhaps optimistic – so long as the family was living in Chelsea. 'I was there with them quite a lot during the early stages,' she claimed in 1979.[25] But in 1957, when the twins were four, the hitherto very low rent on their two flats in Swan Court was steeply increased as a result of the Conservative Government's abolition of rent controls – an act which the Thatchers in principle thoroughly approved. Rather than pay the new commercial rent they moved out of London to a large suburban house in Lock's Bottom, Farnborough.* This gave Denis a much shorter daily drive to Erith. But it meant Margaret commuting every day – either by car through Bromley, Lewisham, New Cross and Southwark to Waterloo Bridge, or by train from Orpington to Charing Cross. She could not now be home in twenty minutes. Then when she got into Parliament in 1959 she was not at home in the evenings either. The nannies had to cope – first Barbara, later another, much older, known as Abby. 'They kept the children in order and I always telephoned from the House shortly before six each evening to see that all was well.'[27]

Years later, when she had become a role model for career women the world over, but also wished to be seen as the guardian and champion of family values, Mrs Thatcher tried to square the circle by emphasising that she had been exceptionally lucky. Thanks to Denis's income she could afford help with the children; finding a London constituency allowed her to pursue her career without neglecting the family. 'I was dead lucky,' she told Miriam Stoppard. 'Everything in my life happened to go right.'[28] Or as she told another interviewer: 'Everything bounced right.'[29] Contrary to her encouragement to married women in 1952 to follow her example, she now saw herself as a fortunate exception. 'It was only this unusual combination of circumstances', she wrote in her memoirs, 'which enabled me to consider becoming an MP while I had young children.'[30] Most mothers in less fortunate circumstances, she now believed, should put their children first: 'I do passionately believe', she insisted in 1979, 'that many women take the view, and quite rightly, that when their children are young their first duty is to look after the children and keep the family together.'[31]

As Prime Minister she came increasingly to blame social problems, crime and educational failure on working mothers neglecting their children: the basic unit of society was the family, and the heart of the family was the mother. 'Thatcher to Women', *Today* summarised an interview she gave in 1988: 'Always Put Your Family First'.[32] She now talked up the 'vocation' of motherhood and deplored the

---

* She described the house somewhat disingenuously in 1960 as 'medium-sized'. It had five bedrooms, three reception rooms and a one-and-a-half acre garden.[26]

number of 'latchkey kids' left to come home from school to an empty house because mother was working. Insensitively flaunting her own good fortune in being able both to work from choice and afford first-class child care, she seemed unaware that most women worked from economic necessity and could not afford child care.

She would always vigorously deny that she neglected her children. 'I spend lots of time with the children,' she assured the *Sunday Dispatch* in February 1960.[33] A year later she told Godfrey Winn that staying at home all day did not necessarily make a good mother. 'You can stay at home all day and still bring up your children appallingly.'[34] And it is true that she was with them as much as the demands of her career allowed and made excellent provision for them when she was not there. She was exceptional in her power of organisation and her ability to juggle several balls at once. She was undoubtedly stimulating when she was with them: she would certainly have been overpowering if forced to be with them the whole time. It is impossible to imagine her not working. At the same time it cannot truly be said that she put her family first. She put her career first and organised the family around it. This was the understanding at the heart of the Thatcher marriage – she and Denis both put their jobs first, quite independently of one another – and Mark and Carol were slotted into the same arrangement. As she expressed it explicitly to George Gardiner in 1975: 'Work is the most important thing, and it comes first.'[35]

It is clear from Carol's biography of her father that Margaret was a remote and often preoccupied mother, always rushing in and dashing out again. The children's needs were just one set of demands to be fitted into her days. When she commuted to London from Kent, Carol writes, 'I remember her leaving home each day and coming back in the evening, when she would sit in the living room with a pile of papers on her knee.' Denis, of course, was of the type and generation of fathers who took no part in the business of parenting at all. Even so, he had more time for little human touches, as the nanny Barbara noted: 'He was very good at remembering to wave up at the nursery window as he left for work' – this was when they were still living in Swan Court – 'whereas Mrs Thatcher, whose mind was already on her job, would forget.'[36] Margaret was an early believer in what a later generation of working mothers called 'quality time'. It's not so much the actual time you're with them', she told Patricia Murray, 'but how much attention you devote to them during that time.'[37] As with politics, so with child care, she threw all her energy into whatever she was doing at any particular time. Because she was out so much, when she was being mother she tried to compensate by doing everything. She did not like delegating and believed, as a matter of principle, that there was nothing she could not do if she only made the time. 'She made the twins royal blue jersey-style jackets,' Barbara recalled. 'Because I could knit and she was so competitive she couldn't bear the thought that anyone might say "I can do this, you can't".'[38] Another time she allegedly spent two days making elaborate cakes for their fourth or fifth birthdays, in the shape of a fort for Mark and a car for Carol.[39] The fact that such feats were remembered so vividly suggests that they were exceptional. (In any case the twins' birthday fell conveniently in August, when both the courts and Parliament were in recess.)

She tried to compensate for her frequent absence by using intensively the time she was with them. She was not, by all accounts, a strict parent. One mother who knew the family in Farnborough in the early sixties complained that, while in Parliament Margaret advocated corporal punishment for young offenders, 'she never raised a finger to the twins' even when Mark was poking his sister's eye with a stick. 'Instead she used that hypnotic voice of hers at times when I'd have belted my kids.'[40] Her own sister Muriel, in a very rare recollection given to George Gardiner, confirms this:

> She never shouted at them. It was all sweet reason. I could have screamed at her sometimes for being so reasonable. And her attitude all the time was to *teach* the twins interesting things . . . They arrived at our farm once when we were in the middle of lifting potatoes, and straight away she said 'Oh good, we can *teach* the twins how the machine works'. Again, one holiday I can remember us all going out in a boat, but Margaret immediately said to the twins, 'Now you'll be able to *learn* how to crew.' She was always so imaginative with them, so stimulating.[41]

Mark and Carol were not exactly spoiled, but they were certainly indulged. They did not lack for clothes or expensive toys: their childhood was very different from the constricted existence Margaret had endured in Grantham. 'You tend to try to give your children things you hadn't had,' she admitted to Patricia Murray. 'I did encourage them to go to most things.'[42] They had family holidays – traditional English seaside holidays, first at Bognor, then at Seaview on the Isle of Wight where they rented the same house for six years running from 1959. But Carol notes bleakly: 'Family holidays didn't appeal to Denis or Margaret.' Denis frequently managed to be in Africa for the whole of August, 'making sure that he was back for the start of the rugby season'.[43] It is hard to believe that Margaret did not occupy her time on the beach with serious reading while the twins entertained themselves with other families. There is not a lot of educational sightseeing on the Isle of Wight. More adventurously they also went skiing as a family every Christmas from 1962 – quite an unusual thing to do in the early sixties. Carol describes her mother as 'a cautious skier' who worked hard on perfecting her technique but eschewed speed: 'she had no intention of returning with a leg in plaster.'[44]

In its own way Mark and Carol's privileged childhood was as deprived as Margaret's own. What the young Thatchers missed was 'normal' family life in the sense of the continuous presence of one or both parents. The pattern was one of fairly long absences punctuated by periods of strictly timetabled attention. For all Margaret's talk of giving them more 'fun' than she had as a child, there was not much spontaneity or warmth in their upbringing. She was always very formal and correct with the children, and expected them to be so too. She dressed them in inappropriately smart clothes. Her old schoolfriend Margaret Goodrich (by now Wickstead and living in Lincoln) remembers Margaret bringing the twins to visit when they were about seven: Mark was dressed like Little Lord Fauntleroy in a satin shirt and velvet shorts, and refused to shake hands with her son, dressed more sensibly for the sandpit, because he was 'too scruffy'.[45]

One of the most telling paragraphs in Carol's book recalls her Thatcher grandmother, Denis's mother, who lived in Notting Hill Gate with her divorced daughter, both of them doting on Denis. 'My grandmother's high spirits', Carol writes, 'had not toned down with age. She remained outrageous and full of fun – completely different to my mother, which is why they never really got on. Margaret never even had a meal in her mother-in-law's house, but Mark and I used to see our aunt Joy and grandmother several times a year.'[46] By contrast Carol does not mention that she ever saw her Roberts grandparents at all.

'When I look back', Carol goes on, 'I have no doubt that my mother's political ambitions – and the single-mindedness with which she pursued them – eclipsed our family and social life.' She does not blame Margaret. 'No woman gets to the top by going on family picnics and cooking roast beef and Yorkshire pudding for Sunday lunch with friends.'[47] As a working woman bringing a second full-time income into an already prosperous home (and then spending a good deal of it on child care and private school fees) Mrs Thatcher was blazing a trail which became commonplace in her daughter's generation. Moreover she was not just working for her own fulfilment, or for money: she had a mission, and ultimately she achieved it. Plenty of prominent men – political leaders, businessmen and artists – have followed their calling at the expense of their families. History will not blame Margaret Thatcher for having done the same. But she deceives herself if she thinks her family did not suffer for her single-mindedness. It is an enduring problem to which there is no easy answer. The present generation of high-flying career women – and their husbands – have certainly not solved it. Where Lady Thatcher is open to criticism is in the inconsistency between her own practice and the 'family first' line which she began to preach once her own family was grown up. The feminist pioneer of the New Elizabethan age courageously anticipated the pattern of lifestyle which became common in the 1980s, achieving in her own career an apotheosis scarcely dreamed of in 1952, and becoming in the process a role model for the generation behind her; only to turn around and condemn her emulators, preaching to other women the very values she had defied thirty years before.

Mark and Carol reacted in opposite ways to their upbringing. Mark's response was to seek attention, and he generally got it. Margaret lavished all the time she could spare on her son, who was not bright and needed special tuition to get into Harrow. He was 'the extrovert of the family and ... lacked concentration', she explained to Godfrey Winn in 1961.[48] The result of her indulgence was that he grew into a mother's boy, a spoiled prig with an inflated sense of his own importance which swelled grotesquely with his mother's fame. Carol, by contrast, was largely left to fend for herself: though much the cleverer of the two – she got seven O levels to Mark's three – she was sent to a less prestigious school and only by her own initiative managed to transfer to St Paul's Girls' School in the Sixth Form. She grew up with a low sense of her own worth, but consequently unpretentious, cheerfully self-deprecating and much more independent than her brother. Few pairs of twins can ever have turned out so differently. Each seems to have been formed by a different aspect of their childhood experience – Carol by the long periods of neglect and Mark by the compensating bursts of over-protective mother-love.

Margaret Thatcher's legal career was brief and undistinguished, but nevertheless an important stage in her political apprenticeship. Less than six years elapsed between her being called to the Bar in January 1954 and her entering the House of Commons in October 1959. For those six years, however, her commitment to the law was characteristically thorough and purposeful, and it achieved its purpose. She had recognised before she even went to Oxford that law would be a much better profession than chemistry from which to launch into politics, first as a means of gaining practical experience of legislation in action, and second as a profession whose short terms and flexible hours would allow her both to nurse a constituency – supposing she could find one – and feel that she could always get home in an emergency if required. So it proved.

Through a series of six-month pupillages she gained a rapid introduction to the different branches of the Bar: criminal with Frederick Lawton in King's Bench Walk, Chancery with John Brightman in New Square, and finally tax law in the chambers of Sir John Senter. She had already decided, following a meeting with Senter at the House of Commons a couple of years earlier, to specialise in tax law, rather than using her science degree, as she had originally intended, to apply for the highly specialist Patent Bar. Tax – the very stuff of politics – was a far more promising area for an aspiring politician. Moreover the technical detail of tax law, involving painstaking accuracy in researching precedents and arguing principles, but little call for imagination or humanity and very little court work, suited her admirably. She had hoped to join Sir John Senter's chambers on completing her pupillage; but when the time came he suddenly decided to contract his chambers, so there was no room for her. This was a blow, though she took it philosophically. She joined another tax specialist, C. A. J. Bonner at 5 New Square, Lincoln's Inn, instead.

It has been suggested that Senter – or possibly his clerk – did not want a woman in his chambers. Certainly women were still conspicuous by their rarity in the Inns of Court: the few exceptions tended to stick to 'feminine' specialisms like divorce and family law, rather than challenge hard masculine preserves like tax. Undoubtedly Mrs Thatcher did meet some prejudice at the Bar. On the other hand it was Sir John Senter who had encouraged her to take up tax law in the first place, and took her on as a pupil; his change of mind did not affect her alone, but also another pupil, Patrick Jenkin, so her sex cannot have been the only reason. Wherever she did encounter prejudice, her technique was simply to ignore it while giving it nothing to feed on. She worked at least as hard as any man. She arrived promptly in the morning, wasted no time on gossiping or long lunches, went home at 5.30 and usually took work home with her. As a woman she was different because she did not mix socially with other barristers and pupils: she did not go to the pub at the end of the day. But she pulled her weight professionally: she relished showing the men that she expected no concessions. If anything, Patrick Jenkin remembers, her reputation with her peers was the more formidable because they knew that she had passed her exams while nursing twins, and that she went home every evening to look after her husband and children.[49]

She did not always go home, however, since she still devoted many of her evenings to politics. The Bar was a nursery for ambitious Tory politicians – some of them already in the House. In Frederick Lawton's chambers she re-encountered Airey Neave (MP for Abingdon since 1953) and also met Michael Havers; in Sir John Senter's she worked with Tony Barber (MP for Doncaster since 1951) as well as Patrick Jenkin. She quickly joined the Inns of Court Conservative Association and served on its executive – the first woman to do so – from 1955 to 1957. This was an important forum not only for networking and getting noticed but for serious policy-making. In 1958 the Association published a famous report, titled *A Giant's Strength*, which advocated ending the legal privileges of the trade unions. Too provocative for the Macmillan Government, this was an early premonition of a shift in Tory thinking which led, over the next twenty-five years, first to Ted Heath's abortive Industrial Relations Act in 1971 and ultimately to the progressive emasculation of the unions by Mrs Thatcher's successive Employment Secretaries in the 1980s. One of the authors of *A Giant's Strength* was Geoffrey Howe, already as chairman of the Bow Group one of the most prolific pamphleteers of radical Conservatism. Margaret Thatcher may have joined in some of the discussions which led to the report; but she had no hand in writing it.

Unlike Howe, she was never a great formulator of policy. Her only publication before she sprang to prominence in 1975 was a single speech delivered in 1968, and that was a very broad statement of principles. But her convictions were already clear. Patrick Jenkin remembers arguing with her about the nationalised industries some time around 1957. He, as a conventionally progressive young Tory, was all for introducing more industrial democracy. Mrs Thatcher had no patience with that sort of tinkering: she already wanted to sell the nationalised industries back into the private sector.[50]

She was not a brilliant lawyer. In the two years she practised under her own name she impressed everyone who worked with her as highly competent, thorough and meticulous; but as soon as she got into Parliament she was happy to give it up. 'You can do two things,' she explained to Miriam Stoppard in 1985. 'You cannot do three things.'[51] Her name was formally taken down in 1961. Thus she was never truly a lawyer-politician in the same way as Jenkin or Howe. The law, like chemistry, was part of her apprenticeship: its discipline shaped her mental equipment, but she never joined the legal tribe. She retained an elevated, almost mystical, reverence for the rule of law as the foundation of English liberty. Indeed she was fond of remarking that the rule of law was a more fundamental condition of democracy than the relatively recent innovation of universal suffrage.[52] But she had seen enough of the profession from the inside not to be in awe of its pretensions. As Prime Minister she treated lawyers as just another professional conspiracy to be brought to heel in the public interest; appeals to her professional solidarity fell on deaf ears. Her experience between 1953 and 1959 valuably inoculated her against the claims of legal protectionism.

In 1957, when the twins were three, Mrs Thatcher began again actively seeking selection for a winnable constituency. Despite her record at Dartford and glowing references from Central Office, she did not find it easy. Conservative Associations, frequently dominated by women, are notoriously reluctant, even today, to select women candidates; that they were reluctant in the mid-1950s to adopt a young mother of twins is scarcely surprising. In truth it is more remarkable that she did, before the end of 1958, manage to persuade a safe London constituency that she could handle the double burden. The party archives reveal a vivid picture of the difficulties she had to overcome.

The first seat she tried for was Beckenham, another in the north Kent suburban patch which she had made her particular stamping ground. The vacancy arose from the elevation of Patrick Buchan-Hepburn, the former Government Chief Whip, to the House of Lords in the New Year's Honours List. Her name was not included on the initial Central Office list of those thought to be interested: she was presumably believed to be still in 'cold storage'. But she quickly indicated that she was interested and was included on a shortlist of eight to be interviewed on 28 January. Her rivals included Major Ian Fraser MC; the journalist and historian Ian Colvin; and a *Daily Telegraph* journalist, Philip Goodhart, who had fought Consett in 1950. One of Mrs Thatcher's disadvantages was that her male rivals tended to have had a 'good war' – a very important credential in the 1950s which she could not match. At the final run-off some dissatisfaction was voiced with the choice on offer: some members wanted a local man – 'Either a local business man or someone who has an outstanding amount of parliamentary experience. One has to face it, Beckenham is a plum seat.'[53] A few months later, when she had moved to Farnborough, Mrs Thatcher could have claimed a local connection. Unluckily, however, the by-election came too early for her. The Association chose Goodhart, who held the seat until 1992, but never rose higher than a junior defence job in Mrs Thatcher's first administration.

Towards the end of 1957 Lady Davidson announced her intention to stand down from the Hemel Hempstead seat which she had taken over from her husband, the former party chairman, J. C. C. Davidson, in 1937. Mrs Thatcher immediately expressed her interest; but she was not included on the initial shortlist of six – all men. It was said that after twenty years of Lady Davidson the Association could not face another woman. The list included three who eventually made it to Westminster (James Allason, William Clark and Andrew Bowden); but the executive told Central Office they were not impressed by any of them and asked for more names. In January 1958 they interviewed fourteen more hopefuls, including Margaret Thatcher, but rejected most of them as either too academic, too inexperienced or simply the wrong type for the constituency. Mrs Thatcher was rejected not – ostensibly at least – because of her sex or her young family, but with the brief, damning verdict: 'Limited outlook'. They probably found her uncomfortably intense. Lieuten-ant-Colonel Allason was selected; he went on to serve until October 1974, but came no closer to office than PPS to John Profumo in the early sixties.[54]

If this was discouraging, Mrs Thatcher must have fancied her chances at Maidstone, where her old Kentish mentor Alfred Bossom (now Sir Alfred) was finally pressured into retiring at the age of seventy-six. He encouraged her to apply, and made every effort to press her claim; but since he had been on bad terms with the Association for some time his support was probably counterproduc-tive. Nevertheless she made it on to the final shortlist of three: the others were the local chairman, Captain Litchfield, and John Wells – Eton and Oxford, served in submarines during the war, contested Smethwick in 1955. The decisive meeting was on 14 March. Wells spoke first, mainly about how he would nurse the constituency, with very little politics. He came across as 'very pleasant, ebullient, quick, keen and energetic', with a good sense of humour. Mrs Thatcher took the opposite approach and – as the Area Agent reported to

Central Office – coped badly with questions about her family commitments:

> Mrs Thatcher spoke next, and went straight into politics, leaving only a very short time at the end of her talk for her tactics in nursing the seat. She was asked about her ability to cope as a Member, having in mind the fact that she had a husband and a small family, and I do not think her reply did her a lot of good. She spoke of having an excellent nanny and [said] that as a member she would have the mornings free (quite ignoring the fact that Members have committees in the mornings). She also spoke of having the weekends free, and made no reference to spending time in Maidstone at the weekends. She did say she would have to give up the Bar.

Naturally the fact that Wells had four children under ten was not an issue.

Captain Litchfield spoke last, and poorly. The result of the first ballot gave Wells 31 votes, Mrs Thatcher 23 and Litchfield 17. She was not yet out of it if she could pick up most of Litchfield's support; but in fact she only put on another four votes, while Wells took nine to lead by 40–27. The acting chairman still thought it was close enough to propose putting both candidates forward for the full Association to choose; but the majority was 'adamant' that it wanted Wells and got its way. Even so, a dozen dissidents declined to make the choice formally unanimous.[55]

Sir John Wells, as he became – on Mrs Thatcher's recommendation – in 1984, was another blameless backbencher who represented Maidstone for twenty-eight years without achieving office or making any national mark at all. He served on various horticultural committees and the parliamentary waterways group. It is a measure of the difficulty Mrs Thatcher had in getting into Parliament that she kept losing out to good chaps – public schoolboys all – like Goodhart, Allason and Wells. This was the type of Member that Conservative Associations in safe seats in the south of England wanted in the 1950s – not the sort of crusading anti-socialism that had gone down so well in a Labour stronghold like Dartford. Despite his criticism of her handling of the family question, there is just a suggestion in the Area Agent's summing-up of the Maidstone selection that Mrs Thatcher had tried to moderate her militancy to fit the constituency:

> Very pleasant personality – good speaker – calm yet forceful

delivery and very much to the point. Has a thorough grasp of politics – tendency to the right of centre. A fine brain – great 'appeal'.

'This lady', he concluded, 'should surely be in Parliament soon.'[56]

But how was she to get there? By good fortune the next safe seat where the sitting Member announced his intention to stand down was Finchley, a prosperous slice of North London stretching from Hampstead Garden Suburb in the south to Totteridge and Whetstone in the north. (It included five underground stations at the top of the Northern Line.) A suburban constituency was always going to suit Mrs Thatcher better than a county town like Maidstone: Finchley eventually turned out to be ideal for her. But here again she had a struggle to secure it in the face of powerful prejudice. She was helped by the fact that the local Association was in bad shape. Despite a comfortable Conservative majority of nearly 13,000 in 1955, the Liberals had been making a big effort – specifically targeting the large Jewish vote – and had captured several council seats. The Area Agent was alarmed and asked Central Office to reclassify Finchley as a marginal. The request was seriously considered:

> This is a difficult one. The agent is idle and the organisation nothing like potential. The MP has been there too long for the good of the constituency. The whole place needs a shake up. Nevertheless I don't regard it as a supermarginal . . .
>
> We shall no doubt be getting changes in Finchley soon? Frankly if we lost Finchley we lose Gaul as well.[57]

Sir John Crowder announced that he was stepping down in March 1958 (just four days before the Maidstone decision). By 15 May Central Office had sent the Association the names of some eighty hopefuls to consider, among them Margaret Thatcher plus at least a dozen more who would eventually join her in the House – most prominently Neil Marten, Peter Tapsell, Dennis Walters and Monty Woodhouse – and also the blind journalist T. E. Utley. The selection committee had specifically ruled Jewish applicants out of consideration, since the Liberals had already selected one and there was no point competing for the Jewish vote while alienating anti-Semitic Conservatives. Then the deputy Area Agent – herself a woman – reported that a local woman councillor had been added to the list: 'For your information I gather that Finchley are determined to see some women so that they may be seen to have gone through the motions, but I should be very surprised indeed if they selected one.'[58]*

In June the long list was reduced to twenty, including two more women: Margaret Thatcher and Lady Huggins (widow of Sir Godfrey Huggins, colonial governor and briefly Prime Minister of the ill-fated Central African Federation). At this point the seventeen members of the executive voted for a shortlist of three: Mrs Thatcher was on everyone's list, coming top with seventeen votes, ahead of a local businessman (and holder of the Military Cross) Thomas Langton, with nine, and the soldier-scholar, hero of the Greek resistance, now director of Chatham House, Monty Woodhouse, who got eight. Lady Huggins and the other woman got no votes at all. 'It will be interesting', the deputy Area Agent minuted, 'to see whether the 100 per cent vote for Mrs Thatcher contained some people who were willing merely to include one woman in the list of four, but there is no doubt that she completely outshone everyone we interviewed.'[60]

Almost immediately, however, Woodhouse withdrew on being selected for Oxford (another seat in which Mrs Thatcher had expressed interest, even though it was beyond her area). Rather than go ahead with only two, the executive decided to add the two next-placed candidates – Ian Fraser again, with whom she had contested Beckenham the year before, and Francis Richardson – to make a shortlist of four, for a final run-off on 14 July.

The other three were all in their forties, all public school educated and all accompanied at the decisive meeting by their wives. Mrs Thatcher was thirty-two, blonde, bright-eyed and bursting with energy but not accompanied by her husband. This was for the very good reason that he was abroad, in South Africa, 'going out after orders', as she put it at the meeting.[61] Just as he had been when the twins were born, Denis was effectively incommunicado. He must have known that Margaret was in the running for Finchley before he left on his month's tour. But the interval between shortlisting and selection was only two weeks; the first he knew of her success was

---

* These anti-feminist and anti-Semitic mutterings lend colour to Sir Dennis Walters' recollection of Sir John Crowder storming at Lord Hailsham, then party chairman, that Central Office was trying to give Finchley a choice between 'a bloody Jew and a bloody woman' – meaning Peter Goldman, director of the Conservative Research Department, and Margaret Thatcher.[59] In fact, though Smith Square was undoubtedly keen to get Goldman into the House, he did not even make the shortlist at Finchley. His unlucky fate was to be the loser in the Orpington by-election.

from a discarded newspaper which he picked up on a flight from Johannesburg to Lagos.

The selection was a close-run thing. Unfortunately Miss Harris's report to Central Office says more about the losers than the winner. She was disappointed that Fraser, who 'really put up the best show on the standards of sincerity, ability and political knowledge' came third behind the more youthful and vigorous but less knowledgeable Langton. Mrs Thatcher pipped Langton by one vote on the first ballot – 35 to 34 – with Fraser trailing with 21 and Richardson nowhere with just one.* On the second ballot Mrs Thatcher squeezed home by 46 votes to 43.

She had won the vote, but she had still to win the acceptance of the whole Association. 'Woman Chosen as Conservative Prospective Candidate', the *Finchley Press* reported. 'Barrister, Housewife, Mother of Twins'.[62] The London *Evening Standard* featured the same angle. 'Tories Choose Beauty', ran its headline. 'The woman many Tories reckon their most beautiful member has been chosen candidate for Finchley.'[63] Her sex remained a contentious issue. Sir John Crowder made no secret of his disgust at the idea of being succeeded by a woman; and Central Office feared trouble at the formal adoption meeting on 31 July. In the event she had a triumph:

> We had anticipated that there might have been some volume of opposition to Mrs Thatcher as a clique in the constituency were known to be opposed to a woman candidate.
>
> In fact the Chairman handled the meeting extremely well and Mrs Thatcher gave a most excellent speech and altogether went down splendidly.
>
> When the resolution proposing her adoption was put, it was carried with about five descensions [*sic*] who looked extremely red-faced and stupid.[64]

Under the headline 'Mrs Thatcher Captures Tories', the *Finchley Press* report was ecstatic – though still unable to resist harping on her sex:

> Speaking without notes, stabbing home points with expressive hands, Mrs Thatcher launched fluently into a clear-cut appraisal of the Middle East situation, weighed up Russia's propagandist moves with the skill of a housewife measuring the ingredients in a

---

* Fraser was more successful at Plymouth, Sutton a few months later and duly won the seat in 1959. He was a Government whip from 1962 to 1964, but lost to Dr David Owen in 1966 and never got back.

familiar recipe, pinpointed Nasser as the fly in the mixing bowl, switched swiftly to Britain's domestic problems (showing a keen grasp of wage and Trade Union issues), then swept her breathless audience into a confident preview of Conservatism's dazzling future . . .

Willy nilly her spellbound audience felt the exhilaration of Conservatism planing through the spray of a lifting wave . . . The Conservatives came to see – and went away conquered. If any had come to oppose, they went away converted.

At the end of her speech she faced only three questions. First she was asked, inevitably, how she would reconcile being an MP with her family responsibilities: she evidently dealt with this more successfully than she had done at Maidstone. Second she was asked how she would win back the voters lost to the Liberals: her answer was hard work: 'Success is what you put into it.' Finally, 'another man asked Mrs Thatcher's views on a new "anti-Socialist" organisation [in other words a Conservative-Liberal alliance against Labour] and the candidate shredded it before his eyes'. She spoke warmly of her twins, saying that she wanted to meet everyone in the constituency 'family to family'. But the *Finchley Press* reporter did not think that she exploited her sex: quite the contrary:

> Once in her stride as a speaker she has the ability – if not the determination – to restrain femininity: no one could accuse her of throwing her womanhood at the audience.
>
> Moreover she is an original speaker. Her phraseology is not a cliché-ridden discourse like that of many women politicians. Of course she is a practised speaker in the most critical of theatres: the Courts of Law. But by the same reasoning she is also a practised thinker.
>
> The Conservatives of Finchley and Friern Barnet have armed themselves with a new weapon – a clever woman.[65]

Over the next fifteen months she threw herself into the task of getting to know the constituency with her usual thoroughness, holding meetings in each of the ward branches, leading canvassing parties and conducting 'an intensive campaign to meet as many of the electors as possible'.[66] Her pace was perhaps not quite so hectic as it had been in Dartford nine years earlier. There she had been a single woman with no obligations outside her work; now she was married with children and a home to run. Moreover, though she took nothing for granted and treated it as a marginal, Finchley was in fact a safe seat. She had not the urgent sense of being a missionary in enemy territory; she was among friends – once she had overcome initial reservations – securing her base for a long parliamentary career. For that purpose Finchley suited her admirably. The only drawback was that she had just gone to live in Kent, and the constituency was the wrong side of London. In every other respect it was ideal. An analysis of the constituency for the Nuffield study of the 1964 General Election identified its defining characteristics as 'prosperity, femininity and intellect'.

> In 1964 over a third of Finchley adults were in the managerial, executive and professional middle class (grade A/B), compared with a national average of only 14 per cent. The proportion educated beyond the age of 15 was twice as high as in the country at large. More than half of Finchley families owned their own homes, and women outnumbered men by nearly three to two. A further feature was the large Jewish community, widely but perhaps exaggeratedly estimated at one fifth of the electorate.[67]

Prosperous middle-class homeowners, relatively highly educated and concerned for the education of their children, with a strong Jewish element – this was to be Mrs Thatcher's personal electorate: these were 'her people', who embodied her cultural values and whose instincts and aspirations she in turn reflected and promoted for the next thirty years. One can only speculate about how differently her politics might have evolved had she become Member for Maidstone, Oxford or Grantham; as it was she became perfectly typecast as Mrs Finchley.

In years to come the Jewish community would form one of the strongest pillars of her local support, and she developed a warm admiration for the Jewish traditions of self-reliance, entrepreneurship and family values which increasingly represented everything she wanted to promote in the British people as a whole. In the short run, however, the Jewish vote was a potential problem. The Liberals' recent advance in the constituency was achieved largely by exploiting allegations of anti-Semitism at Finchley Golf Club involving a number of prominent Conservatives. Soon after her adoption Mrs Thatcher set out the position in a handwritten letter to Central Office. 'The electorate of Finchley', she began, accepting the highest estimate, 'is nearly 25 per cent Jewish.'

For reasons with which I need not bother you, the Jewish faith have allied themselves to Liberalism and at the last local election won five seats from the Conservatives on our council. We are now finding great difficulty in making headway in these particular areas, particularly in Hampstead Garden Suburb. As Finchley has had a Liberal MP in the past[*] we are naturally apprehensive and are now making great efforts to further the Conservative cause. I fear the division as a whole has not been very dynamic in the past.[68]

Her solution was to concentrate on the younger voters by setting up a new branch of the Young Conservatives in the Garden Suburb. Doubtless she was remembering her Colchester experience. She requested a message from the deputy chairman, Oliver Poole, to launch the new branch. Poole obliged – not precisely in the terms she had suggested – and a week later she wrote again to thank him: the inaugural meeting was packed and enthusiastic and eighty new members had been recruited. By such means the Liberal tide was halted: at the council elections in May 1959 they gained no more seats.

Mrs Thatcher's hyperactivity in a previously somnolent seat irritated Sir John Crowder – still of course the sitting Member – who complained to Central Office that she was inviting speakers to the constituency without his knowledge.[69] In February she specifically targeted the Jewish vote by bringing Keith Joseph to Hampstead Garden Suburb. The *Finchley Press* flagged him rather surprisingly as a 'cricketing MP' and stressed his experience of social work;[70] but the single sentence of his speech that it reported was impeccably libertarian. 'Life', he told the meeting, 'is a private affair. It is the government's job to remove some of the obstacles – not to force the individual to conform to a pattern.'[71] Joseph was not yet a member of the Government; but others whom she invited – through the good offices of the Chief Whip, her old Dartford neighbour, Ted Heath – included the Minister of Labour, Iain Macleod; the recently resigned Chancellor, Peter Thorneycroft; and the Pensions Minister, John Boyd-Carpenter – all future colleagues with whom her fortunes would be closely entwined. She was already making useful connections.

But what sort of things was she saying at her own meetings? So far as one can judge from the local press her speeches were a mixture of the sort of simple Conservative low-tax free-enterprise philosophy

---

[*] The seat was briefly held by a Liberal between December 1923 and October 1924.

she had preached at Dartford with a good dash of the 'Never had it so good . . . Don't let Labour ruin it' party line coming from the Macmillan Government and Central Office. Lady Thatcher writes in her memoirs that she was already 'uneasy' with Macmillan's increasing interventionism;[72] and she certainly did continue in 1958–9 to sound some distinctly free-market notes which could be characterised as proto-Thatcherite. She harped repeatedly on the importance of keeping taxes low as an incentive to wealth creation:

Someone has to make the money in order that others may spend it . . . Who makes the money? It is made all the time by individual effort, and unless you give incentives to individual effort all the time, there is nothing to tax and no benefits for the Welfare State.[73]

Or again:

It is no use to decry surtax payers and drive them abroad – out of their industry comes revenue.[74]

She warned that the Government could not create jobs for all by propping up declining industries: 'It would be quite wrong to put an enormous subsidy on horses and carts when tractors were coming in.'[75] But at the same time she was happy to demonstrate that life was better under the Conservatives by boasting of increased public spending on schools, hospitals, housing, roads and sewers, all of which created employment. Even after a dozen years of peacetime full employment, the Tories were still sensitive to the charge that they were the party of unemployment. Mrs Thatcher explicitly endorsed the Government's policy of encouraging industry to locate in areas of unemployment.[76] In this respect she was in no way out of the mainstream of Tory candidates happy to be carried into Parliament on Macmillan's expansionist tide.

The Thatcher family was on holiday on the Isle of Wight in early September 1959 when Macmillan called the election. She hurried back to throw herself into what the *Finchley Press* hyperbolically dubbed 'the political struggle of all time'.[77] Despite their setback in May it was the Liberals – represented by a 6'7" barrister called Ivan Spence, a war hero with a colourful career as a globetrotting adventurer – who made the running, talking up their chances by trying to present the election as a two-horse race between themselves and the new Conservative candidate, whom they portrayed as 'perhaps a little too clever'. One Liberal councillor even angled for the support of disgruntled Tories who did not want a woman MP.[78*] Mrs Thatcher's characteristic response was to ignore the Liberals: she fought Finchley as a local microcosm of the national contest to choose a Conservative or a Labour Government, Macmillan or Gaitskell as Prime Minister. 'Those who are not with us', she declared simply, 'are against us.'[79] She never had any time for third parties confusing the clear choice between good and evil. At the same time, facing no serious threat from Labour, she could afford the same courteous relations with the young Labour candidate, Eric Deakins, that she had enjoyed in reverse with Norman Dodds.

Deakins, then a Tottenham councillor, eventually got into Parliament in 1970 as MP for Walthamstow, held junior office in the 1974–9 Labour Government, but lost his seat at the high tide of Thatcherism in 1987. His recollection of fighting Mrs Thatcher in Finchley is ambivalent. On the one hand he found her an impressive opponent – very determined, a superb debater, always thoroughly well briefed: when the three candidates were questioned about the atrocity at Hola camp in Nyasaland, she alone had a copy of the report of the committee of inquiry, had read it and was able to read out selected extracts to rebut criticism of the Government. On the other hand, he felt she lacked humanity and was impervious to criticism: she was punctiliously correct in all her dealings with him, but 'absolutely cold through and through'. He never felt he made any contact with her; and when he finally got to the Commons in 1970 she never acknowledged him.[81]

Her election address spelled out in conventional terms how eight years of Conservative Government had made life better for the voters of Finchley. Under the headings 'Your Money', 'Your Home', 'Your Job', 'Your Children' and 'Your Retirement' (with just a nod to foreign affairs, 'Your Defence'), it summed up the Tory record succinctly as 'Taxes Down, Benefits Up, Earnings Up, Standard of Living Up, Building Up'. There is no suggestion that it might not be the Government's job to provide houses, benefits and employment in ever-increasing abundance. Only a personal declaration at the end has the ring of Mrs Thatcher's own voice. 'A vote for

---

* Her sex does not appear to have been a serious issue, but it helped attract the attention of the national press. There were still only 81 women candidates across the whole country. The *Daily Mirror* named Mrs Thatcher, equal with Pat Llewellyn-Davies (contesting Wandsworth Central for Labour and ten years older than Mrs Thatcher), as 'the prettiest in the election stakes', while acknowledging that 'as well as being beautiful' she was also a barrister, MA and BSc.[80]

any other person', she asserted, 'is a vote for a Socialist Government.
Do not shirk this issue.'

> I believe that it is by emphasis on home life, greater educational
> opportunities and liberty under the law that National character
> can be strengthened and moral standards upheld.
>
> As your Member of Parliament I may not always be right; but
> you may be sure that I will be honest and fearless: I shall do my
> best to serve my Country and my Constituency.

It was signed, unusually, 'Margaret H. Thatcher'.[82]

Two debates bringing the three candidates together on the same
platform yielded one or two more personal positions. At the first she
declared her support for the return of corporal punishment for
violent criminals, announcing herself 'one of those who thought that
a sharp short birching might be carried out'. And in reply to a
question on nuclear disarmament she distanced herself firmly from
the conventional pieties of her own address by asserting her
passionate belief in strong defence as a guarantee of national security.
She would not disarm before others had done so.[83] She took a more
surprising line at a meeting organised by the United Nations
Association. She had gone into the campaign robustly defending the
British-French invasion of Suez in 1956, presenting it simultaneously
as an act of self-defence and a pre-emptive strike against an ambitious
dictator who was threatening regional stability: 'We went in to
protect British lives and property,' she argued. 'Most people agree it
was right to go in, and Nasser would not have got where he now is if
we had gone on.'[84]

In *The Path to Power* Lady Thatcher suggests that while loyally
supporting British action against Egypt she was worried by its
questionable legality.[85] This may explain her unexpected advocacy of
a strengthened UN, with no veto – in other words, majority voting
on the Security Council – and a permanent international force to
enforce its decisions. This, she declared, 'would solve the whole
problem of the United Nations'.[86] This was no doubt what a UN
Association meeting in 1959 wanted to hear; but it is not an idea she
would have countenanced for a moment as Prime Minister.

The result in Finchley was never in doubt. The Liberals' efforts
were enough to gain them some 4,000 votes from Labour but not
quite enough to put them into second place: they made almost no
impact on the Tory vote. Mrs Thatcher thus increased the Tory
majority from 12,825 to 16,260.

Mrs Margaret Thatcher (Conservative)	29,697
Eric Deakins (Labour)	13,437
Ivan Spence (Liberal)	12,260
Conservative majority	16,260

Though she held the seat without serious alarm through various boundary changes for the next thirty-two years, her majority was never so large again. The lowest it ever fell was in October 1974, when it dipped below 4,000; but even in her years of dominating the national stage her majority in Finchley never again hit five figures.

Finchley was indeed a microcosm of the national result. With the Liberals doubling their previously tiny share of the vote – to 6 per cent – at the expense of Labour, while the Tory share held almost solid (slipping from 49.7 per cent to 49.4 per cent), Gaitskell's hopes were dashed and Macmillan increased his overall majority to exactly 100. This was the high point of Tory fortunes in the postwar period, a zenith of confidence not to be touched again until Mrs Thatcher's own unprecedented run of three consecutive victories in the 1980s. The party she joined at Westminster in October 1959 was riding high; political analysts wondered if Labour would ever hold office again. Within a few years the pendulum had swung, and the first fifteen years of Margaret Thatcher's parliamentary career were served against a background of increasing uncertainty and loss of confidence within the party – from which it fell to her, eventually, to lead an astonishing recovery.

All this lay in the future. Nevertheless the *Finchley Press*'s 'political observer' had no doubt in October 1959 that a new star had been born. In support of 'a fine candidate of apparently limitless stamina', the Tory organisation in Finchley had excelled itself: few constituencies could have enjoyed 'candidates who gave them such a lead, addressed so many meetings or held such crowds in their expressive hands'. 'Even before the election she attracted vast national publicity as a woman who was "going places", appeared on TV, was heard on the radio, filled columns in the national press.' Margaret Thatcher, the writer concluded, 'will put Finchley on the map'.[87]

In fact Finchley had put Margaret Thatcher on the map. She was on her way.

6

Backbencher

THE Tory class of '59 were an undistinguished lot. With the Conservatives winning a three-figure majority, there were 64 new Tory members elected for the first time. Inevitably some of these lost their seats again in the Labour victories of 1964 and 1966, so were unable to sustain a long career. But only five of the new intake had won promotion to junior ministerial office before 1964, and only four eventually made it to the Cabinet. The four were Margaret Thatcher and Jim Prior (in 1970), Peter Rees and Nicholas Ridley (in 1983); of these only Mrs Thatcher got her first taste of office before 1964. She was, in fact, with Monty Woodhouse, the first of the new intake to win promotion after just two years in the House. The rest of the class comprised one or two who certainly should have been given an opportunity, like Peter Tapsell; a handful of mavericks like Humphrey Berkeley and Julian Critchley; but above all a solid preponderance of nature's backbenchers, men like Timothy Kitson, Kenneth Lewis, Fergus Montgomery and John Wells – all of whom stayed the course long enough to see the only filly in their number romp away with the race.

Being a woman was simultaneously an advantage and a handicap. As one of only twelve women Members on the Conservative side of the House (Labour had thirteen) Mrs Thatcher was immediately conspicuous – the more so since she was younger, prettier and better-dressed than any of the others – but also for this very reason patronised and disregarded. In her memoirs she insists that 'everyone in those early days was immensely kind' to her.[1] But in the clubby masculine world of the Palace of Westminster she could not be one of the boys. 'With a majority of 100', Jim Prior recalled, 'we took life fairly light-heartedly . . . She wasn't really one of our set.'

I heard her make the occasional speech and knew roughly what her views were, but at that time the few women in the Parliamentary party tended not to be accepted so easily by their male colleagues.[2]

Peter Rawlinson (Member for Epsom since 1955) remembered Mrs Thatcher specifically as a woman striving to make an impact in a male environment, 'earning male admiration which she seemed to enjoy while at the same time making efforts to show that such tribute by itself was not enough'. Her male colleagues frankly patronised her earnest enthusiasm:

She appeared rather over-bright and shiny . . . She rarely smiled and never laughed . . . We all smiled benignly as we looked into those blue eyes and at the tilt of the golden head. We, and all the world, had no idea what we were in for.[3]

She was always combative, Edward du Cann remembers, but in those early days she would generally back down gracefully when she had made her point.[4] The alternative was to be written off as strident and bossy. Julian Critchley, in one of his many satirical memoirs, recalls Mrs Thatcher joining himself and a couple of colleagues at lunch. 'My God,' one of the others exclaimed when she had gone, 'she is like the chairman of my women's committee in High Peak – but writ hideously large.'[5]* She had to be careful to keep this side of her character out of sight for the next twenty years while she climbed the ladder: not until she was Prime Minister did Tory MPs come to enjoy being hectored by a strong-minded woman. To a considerable extent she succeeded. The columnist Hannen Swaffer, predicting 'a brilliant future' for her just a fortnight after the election, listed among her many qualities 'a friendly tolerance towards opponents'.[6]

She was possibly better appreciated by her opponents, certainly by the one Labour member who had most to do with her. Charles Pannell had been leader of Erith Council when Margaret Roberts had been adopted to fight Dartford in 1949: he had admired her then and now took her under his protective wing and suggested that she become his 'pair'. This was a shrewd move on his part, since she was both an exceptionally fastidious pair ('By fastidious I mean that she would never have thought of breaking a pair. She always stood by her word') and one who had more need than most MPs to get back

---

* This must have been the former Minister of Works, Hugh Molson, MP for High Peak since 1939 (and for Doncaster before that), a Tory of the old school.

to her family.[7] They became good friends, and the arrangement lasted until Pannell retired in 1974. 'He was exactly the kind of good-humoured decent Labour man I liked,' she wrote in her memoirs.[8] For his part Pannell told his fellow Leeds Member, Denis Healey, very early on, to watch her, 'saying that she was exceptionally able, and also a very nice woman'. Healey thought this was 'quite a compliment, coming from a Cockney engineer who was famous for his rough tongue'.[9]*

From the start she was happy to exploit whatever advantage her sex gave her. Producing twins may have delayed her finding a seat, but now that she was in the House a young mother made good copy. The very day after the election, the London *Evening News* ran a piece headlined 'Mark's Mummy Is An MP Now', with a picture of Mrs Thatcher wearing a dark suit and pearls (but unusually no hat) supposedly window shopping in Oxford Street, playing at being 'a very ordinary housewife': 'It's the first chance I've had to look at the shops since the campaign started.'[11] In fact she was on her way to Portland Place to record a BBC interview – not an opportunity given to many of her sixty-three new male colleagues. Nor did her instant exposure end there: she was almost immediately invited to be a guest on *Any Questions?*, where she gave 'clear replies' (according to the *Finchley Press*) on subjects ranging from road safety to exports – mentioning that her husband was an exporter – and German neo-Nazis, and firmly slapping down Woodrow Wyatt, who had been a Labour MP on and off since 1945.[12] One questioner, Wyatt recalled, asked what the panel had discussed at dinner.

> I answered first and, as I was finishing, Mrs Thatcher broke in with her best putting-down voice and withering smile. 'May I make one thing quite clear, Mr Chairman. We weren't discussing very much at dinner. We were mostly listening to Mr Woodrow Wyatt.' In the laughter I thought to myself 'Ho, to that brassy blonde.'[13]

The press continued to be fascinated by her ability to combine the demands of Parliament and her constituency with those of her family. In February 1960 the *Evening News*, billing her as 'Britain's most talked-about, hard-hitting new woman MP', signed her up for

---

* She had other favourites among Labour Members. Showing Margaret Wickstead round the Houses of Parliament soon after she got there, they passed Geoffrey de Freitas (Member for Lincoln, and hence Mrs Wickstead's MP) in a corridor. '*What* a nice man,' she said. '*What* a pity he's not one of us' – perhaps her first recorded use of the expression.[10]

a series of articles. 'The timetable of being a Member of Parliament fits quite well with family duties,' she wrote, emphasising that the recesses conveniently coincided with school holidays. When the House was sitting she always telephoned the twins just before six o'clock. Denis was not neglected because he was away so much himself. 'Family life is centred around the weekends when we are at home together and devote most of the time to the children.'[14] This was 'very true', Carol concedes, until Mark, at the age of eight, and she at nine, went off to boarding school. After that, 'we were together as a family only at half-terms, summer holidays, Easter and Christmas'.[15] Even then her mother always had piles of work to get through.

Her assertion that with good organisation it was possible for a woman to do two jobs drew furious letters from several less affluent working women who objected that she did not do two jobs at all, but paid others to look after her children for her. Thousands of poor mothers, they pointed out, went out to work and looked after their kids as well.[16]

She prided herself on always being there when the children needed her. In March 1960 she apologised to a constituency meeting for her quiet voice: she had been 'reading stories to a sick child'. The *Finchley Press* duly reported that Mark had had his appendix out: 'Mrs Thatcher's Son: An Operation'.[17] Most of the time she did keep family and politics apart. But she paraded Denis in Finchley as often as he was available. 'One did come to spend an awful lot of time in the damned constituency,' he told Carol years later. 'I always did the annual dinner and dance of the Conservative Association and was certainly up there a couple of times a month at dinners . . . and that sort of thing.'[18] In July 1960 the Thatchers entertained fifty Finchley Young Conservatives at their house in Kent: Margaret was reported to have done all the catering herself.[19]

She was an exceptionally conscientious constituency Member. She held an evening surgery once or twice a month from 6.30 to 9.00, and reckoned to have written nearly two thousand letters to constituents alone in her first ten months. Unlike many MPs at that time, she employed a full-time secretary, Paddi Victor-Smith, to help her with this formidable correspondence. This, as she admitted, was another advantage afforded her by Denis's money, an essential element in managing her life as she did. MPs pay – £1,250 per annum in 1959 – included no secretarial allowance until 1969.

Mrs Thatcher's parliamentary career received a tremendous boost within a few weeks of arriving at Westminster when she came third in the ballot for Private Members' Bills. This threw her in at the deep end, but also gave her the opportunity to make a conspicuous splash: instead of the usual uncontroversial debut delivered in the dinner hour to empty benches, she made her maiden speech introducing a controversial Bill. Though by no means unprecedented, such a high-profile debut is normally reserved for established figures parachuted straight into the Cabinet from business or the trade unions, like Ernest Bevin or John Davies, not to green young neophytes. Inevitably Margaret Thatcher seized her chance and made certain of a triumph. She brought herself emphatically to the attention of the whips, demonstrated her competence and duly saw her Bill – the Public Bodies (Admission to Meetings) Bill – on to the Statute Book with the Government's blessing. Behind the scenes, however, neither the origin nor the passage of the Bill were as straightforward as they appeared. The newly-elected 34-year-old endured some bruising battles, both in the House of Commons and in Whitehall; and the Bill that emerged was neither the one she originally intended nor the one she introduced. It was a tough baptism.

An MP who wins a high place in the Private Members' ballot is swamped with proposals for Bills which he or she might like to introduce. Mrs Thatcher's first preference was for a Bill to change the law in relation to contempt of court; but this, she wrote in her memoirs, 'seemed rather dry and I could not summon up much enthusiasm for it. So I thought again.'[20] In fact she had got some way with drafting a Bill on this subject before she was warned by the Attorney-General, Sir Reginald Manningham-Buller, that it was too complex for a Private Member's Bill: the Government would deal with the matter.[21] Next, she claims that she proposed to introduce a Bill to curb the power of the trade union closed shop, as advocated by the Inns of Court Conservative Association pamphlet, *A Giant's Strength*, published the previous year. This would indeed have made a sensational start to her career. In the event, she writes, 'the Whips made it clear to me that I would not have the Party's support . . . Although younger Tories and many backbenchers were restive on the issue, the prevailing ethos in the upper ranks of the Conservative Party was still one of accommodating and appeasing the unions.'[22] There is probably an element of hindsight in this recollection. Be that as it may, she did not push her luck; instead she picked up a more manageable example of union abuse to do something about.

The issue was the right of the press to cover local government. This was thought to have been enshrined in an Act of 1908.

Recently, however, some councils had been getting round the requirement of open meetings by barring the press from committees and going into a committee of the whole council when they wanted to exclude reporters. (This was not a new trick. The *Grantham Journal* complained about Alfred Roberts using it in 1937 to conceal the extent of the council's overspending.)[23] More provocatively Nottingham and some other Labour councils had denied access to 'blackleg' reporters who continued working during a newspaper dispute. It was this which had drawn Conservative anger. The 1959 manifesto contained a pledge to 'make quite sure that the press have proper facilities for reporting the proceedings of local authorities'.[24] But it turned out that the Government proposed to achieve this by a new code of conduct rather than by legislation. It is not known who encouraged Mrs Thatcher to force the issue. 'No one persuaded me,' she told George Gardiner in 1975. 'The decision was my own.'[25] In her memoirs, too, she describes it as her own spontaneous response to what she considered an 'extremely feeble' cop-out by the Government.[26] But on this question she evidently found enough support – or was giving voice to a sufficiently widespread backbench demand – to risk going ahead against the expressed preference of the Minister of Housing and Local Government, Henry Brooke, and his officials.

Mrs Thatcher has written that Brooke was 'consistently sympathetic' to her proposed Bill: she blames his officials for the obstruction she encountered.[27] The files in the Public Record Office confirm that she crossed swords with Brooke's Permanent Secretary, the redoubtable Evelyn Sharp (immortalised as 'the Dame' in Richard Crossman's diaries). Her problem was that she needed the Department's help to draft her Bill; but the Department would only countenance a minimal Bill falling well short of her objective. Mrs Thatcher proposed to go ahead with her own much tougher measure. 'I warned her flatly', Dame Evelyn minuted, 'that if she did I thought the Government would be bound to advise the House to vote against it.' Mrs Thatcher compromised very reluctantly. Dame Evelyn recorded 'an extremely unsatisfactory discussion' at which Mrs Thatcher seemed to go back on 'the clear understanding which I thought we had reached with her, and on the understanding she gave to the minister'. Eventually Mrs Thatcher settled for half a loaf: 'She said that provided the Bill made *some* advance – which I said it would – she would be content . . . She would be most grateful for a Government-drafted Bill on the lines I had outlined.'[28]

There were two catches. First, she was not allowed to reveal her sympathy with Tory MPs who might try to strengthen the agreed

Bill, but must defend it as though it was her own; second, as Brooke's Parliamentary Secretary – Keith Joseph, in his first ministerial job – spelled out to her, she was not permitted to acknowledge the help of Government draftsmen in framing her Bill. So she was caught both ways, while the Government kept its options open over whether or not to support the Bill if it ran into opposition. The Bill eventually published on 24 January 1960 was judged by *The Times* 'to have kept nicely in line with Conservative thinking'.[29] In fact it was a fairly toothless measure which increased the number of bodies – water boards and police committees as well as local authorities – whose meetings should normally be open to the press; required that agendas and relevant papers be made available to the press in advance; and defined more tightly the circumstances in which reporters might be excluded – but still left loopholes through which, as Dame Evelyn happily expressed it, 'an ill-disposed local authority could drive a coach-and-horses'.[30] It was still open to a majority to declare any meeting closed on grounds of confidentiality.

The Bill quickly met opposition from two directions. On the one hand was the quietist view supported by the local authority organisations and a number of Labour MPs with roots in local government – including Mrs Thatcher's friend Charles Pannell – that unnecessary legislation could only 'disrupt satisfactory arrangements which already exist in many parts of the country'.[31] This was essentially Henry Brooke's position. On the other hand came the argument that it was wrong to open council meetings merely to the press: they should as a matter of principle be open to the public too. When Mrs Thatcher tried to widen her measure to meet this objection, however, she discovered that she was boxed in by the long title she had initially announced – the Public Bodies (Admission of the Press to Meetings) Bill – which could not be altered without a Government motion. She was now more than ever dependent on the Government to get her Bill through.

The Second Reading was set down for 5 February. To ensure a good attendance on a Friday morning, Mrs Thatcher sat down and wrote 250 handwritten letters to Tory backbenchers requesting their support. She was rewarded with a turnout of about a hundred. She immediately ignored the convention by which maiden speakers begin with some modest expression of humility, a tribute to their predecessor and a guidebook tour of their constituency. Margaret Thatcher wasted no time on such courtesies:

> This is a maiden speech, but I know that the constituency of Finchley which I have the honour to represent would not wish

me to do other than come straight to the point and address myself to the matter before the House. I cannot do better than begin by stating the object of the Bill . . .

She spoke for twenty-seven minutes with fluency and perfect clarity, as the *Finchley Press*, reporting her 'brilliant debut', admiringly recorded:

Parliament . . . saw the expressive play of her hands as she hammered home her points, but the notes she held in her left hand were not referred to as she spoke. They dropped, leaf by leaf, on the bench as she strode through her speech.[32]

With characteristic thoroughness she began by tracing the legislative background from the 1908 Act and various previous attempts to revise it – a Bill introduced by the Labour Government in 1930 which had fallen 'due to a rather precipitate change of Government, which I do not think even the most optimistic hon. Member opposite would believe was imminent at the moment' (a typically triumphalist gibe) – and two Private Members' Bills in 1949 and 1950, before setting out the key points of her own measure. The interest of the speech is her emphasis not on the freedom of the press as a good thing in itself, but on the importance of controlling local government expenditure. If one looks in a maiden speech for the exposition of themes which will recur at the height of the speaker's career, here is the first expression of a concern which led ultimately to the poll tax. Local authorities in England and Wales, Mrs Thatcher told the Commons in February 1960, spent £1,400 million a year (another £200 million in Scotland). Less than half of this 'not insignificant' amount was raised by the rates – the rest came from the taxpayer. 'The first purpose in admitting the press is that we may know how these moneys are being spent.' She quoted from Lord Franks' recent report on Tribunals of Inquiry: 'Publicity is the greatest and most effective check against arbitrary action.' There is no recognition whatsoever of the positive value of local government, no mention that her own father had been a councillor and alderman for twenty-five years. She admitted that many councils already guaranteed the press more access to their proceedings than her Bill required: she was only trying to establish 'a minimum legislative code of practice'. In other words, like the ratecapping legislation of the 1980s, her 1960 Bill was a general measure directed at all councils in order to control the abuses of a few. In truth it had no teeth: she confessed that she had hoped to lay down a specific schedule of circumstances defining when councils might invoke confidentiality to exclude the press, but that this had proved impracticable. It is nevertheless striking that her first essay in legislation as a young backbencher should have been an attempt to limit the autonomy of local government.

Only near the end of her speech did she refer to the trade union 'blacking' which had led to the demand for a new code of conduct – statutory or otherwise – in the first place. It was the abuse of the 1908 law the previous summer, she concluded, which required action to protect the rights of the citizen. 'The paramount function of this distinguished House is to safeguard civil liberties rather than to think that administrative convenience should take first place in law': not a principle she always remembered twenty-five years later. Only at the very end did she thank Brooke and his department for their help – she did not mention drafting – and the House for its indulgence to a new Member.[33]

Her seconder, Frederick Corfield, Member for Gloucestershire South, immediately congratulated her on 'an outstanding maiden speech . . . delivered with very considerable clarity and charm'. She had introduced her Bill 'in a manner that would do credit to the Front Benches on either side of the Chamber'.[34] Later speakers in the debate reiterated the same compliments. It was practically compulsory in 1960 to praise a lady speaker's 'charm'; but the tributes to her front bench quality were more significant and probably more sincere. Her friend Charles Pannell – an opponent of the Bill – congratulated his protégée on 'rather a beautiful maiden speech' and went on to call it 'almost a model to the occupants of the Government Front Bench on how to deliver a speech in favour of a Bill, instead of having a dreary essay read to us in a turgid monotone'.[35] Barbara Castle – as a journalist a supporter of the Bill – recognised 'an outstanding maiden speech';[36] another future Labour Cabinet Minister, Michael Stewart, praised 'a most striking, impressive and skilful performance'.[37] The former Attorney-General, Sir Lionel Heald, one of her sponsors who had helped her draft the Bill and knew something of the 'troubles and difficulties' she had faced, commended her bravery in taking on such a challenge within a few weeks of entering the House.[38] Even Henry Brooke was fulsome:

> No words of mine can be too high praise for the brilliance of the speech with which my hon. Friend . . . opened the debate. She spoke with charm, as we all expected, she spoke with a fluency which most of us would envy, and she achieved the rare feat of making a Parliamentary reputation on a Friday.[39]

Tributes completed, however, Brooke firmly distanced the Government from her measure. He acknowledged that it had been his intention to honour the Government's manifesto pledge by means of a code of conduct, had she not 'quite independently' produced her Bill. He gave backhanded credit to 'my hon. Friend and her supporters' for 'a genuine and sincere endeavour to remedy a situation which is at present unsatisfactory'; but warned that it was 'not exactly the method I should have chosen . . . It may need a considerable amount of improvement.' In any case, whether the Bill fell or carried, he proposed to proceed with his voluntary code.[40]

In fact it passed its Second Reading – on a free vote, with many Labour Members supporting and some Tories opposing – by 152 votes to 39, a margin which persuaded Brooke to lend his support to the procedural problem of changing the Bill's title to extend its application to the public, against the obstruction of Labour opponents. Eventually the retitled Bill went into committee in mid-March. At the first session in Standing Committee C, Mrs Thatcher, opposing a Labour amendment to substitute a voluntary code, delivered a remarkable statement of her philosophy of legislation:

> I oppose the Amendment on one main ground. Rightly or wrongly I came to the House of Commons believing that it was the task of Parliament to make laws and that it was not part of its task to delegate that responsibility to a Minister, except where strictly necessary. If we increase the amount of delegated legislation, we do not fulfil our function. It is the task of Members of Parliament clearly to indicate the minimum standards which they wish to be laid down. Anything above those minimum standards can then be covered by a voluntary code . . . but that is in no sense a substitute for law made by Parliament.[41]

She claimed that she had always intended the Bill to admit the public as well as the press. Then who, Michael Stewart asked, drafted the long title? 'I am afraid that I drafted the Long Title,' she replied disarmingly, 'having been here about a fortnight.'[42] Over the next few weeks she had to battle hard for her Bill. She suffered a serious defeat when she failed to carry a clause giving public access to all committees exercising delegated functions; she had to settle for committees of the full council only. *The Times* regretted that this reduced the Bill to a 'half-measure': 'As it now stands the Bill requires less of local authorities than they should be prepared voluntarily to concede in order to keep the public properly informed of their affairs.'[43] After this, however, the committee quickly concluded its proceedings amid more congratulations. Charles Pannell expressed sympathy for the ordeal Mrs Thatcher had gone through:

> If one considers . . . the remarkable change in the Bill that there has been, one realises that the hon. Lady has had a terrible experience with her Bill in her first Session. Now that we have agreement, we must express sympathy with her and hope that she will have fewer sleepless nights than she has had hitherto.[44]

Back on the floor of the House the emasculated Bill carried its Third Reading on 13 May, without a vote. For the Government Keith Joseph paid another compliment to Mrs Thatcher's 'most cogent, charming, lucid and composed manner', which had contributed to the passage of 'a delicate and contentious measure perhaps not ideally suited for a first venture into legislation'.[45] In the Lords the Bill earned another historical footnote when Baroness Elliot of Harwood became the first peeress to move a Bill in the Upper House, before it finally received the Royal Assent in October. After exactly a year it was an achievement of sorts, but rather more of an education. As a piece of legislation it was ineffective. Two years later *The Times* complained that some councils were still ignoring the spirit of the Act;[46] and in the late 1960s Mrs Thatcher's own Tory-controlled local council in Barnet still made a practice of delegating executive powers to committees in order to exclude the press.[47] A further weakness was exposed, ironically, in the 1980s when it was found that the Act did not apply to the new quangos which took over many of the functions of local government and the nationalised industries following privatisation and the abolition of the GLC.

Nevertheless Mrs Thatcher had learned in a few months more about the ways of Whitehall – and specifically about the ability of officials and the Tory establishment together to stifle reform – than most backbenchers learn in a lifetime. The files in the Public Record Office show that the combative instinct which drove her to fight back, and eventually prevail, was already well-developed. 'Her technique', Brooke noted after one encounter, 'is to say that she must have much more than she really expects to get . . . We have to hold her to what she agreed.' Likewise the parliamentary draftsman warned that it would be counterproductive if Mrs Thatcher attended a meeting with Commons officials: 'She probably has very little idea of the point at issue . . . and if she treats them as she treated us, she may well put their backs up. This is not a thing you can say to her.'[48]

Another civil servant shrewdly noted the hostility not only to trade unions but also to local government which underlay her Bill:

> Mrs Thatcher is obsessed with the minority of councils who might act irresponsibly, whereas we have had in mind the great majority of local authorities whose relations with the press are basically satisfactory.
>
> I could not help thinking that it was a pity that a Bill of such importance to local authorities should be in the hands of a private member, whose knowledge of local government is limited, and who clearly holds a low opinion of local authorities, their members and officials.[49]

Did this official know that Mrs Thatcher was brought up in a household dominated by local government? Probably not: at this period of her career she never talked publicly about her father. Instead she projected an extreme antipathy to local government. Was this hostility, as has been suggested, a reaction to the Grantham Labour group's ungrateful dismissal of Alfred in 1952, prompting a filial desire for revenge on all Labour councils and by extension on local government in general? Or was it rather a much deeper reaction against Alfred himself and the repression of her childhood? One would love to know what Alfred thought of his daughter's Bill. Most probably, like most people of all political persuasions involved in local government – including Finchley council – he would have regarded it as a clumsy interference with the right of local authorities to conduct their own affairs. Did he tell his daughter so? We know that he paid a rare visit to Margaret and Denis in Farnborough for a few days after Beatrice died that autumn. They must have discussed her Bill. Lady Thatcher does not say. But the curious absence of her father from her adult life, until her rediscovery and posthumous canonisation of him after 1975, is nowhere more striking than during her sponsorship of this Bill, attacking the autonomy of local government, at a time when he was still very much alive.

Mrs Thatcher's conduct of the Public Bodies Bill, as a novice backbencher taking on a senior Cabinet minister of her own party, his Permanent Secretary and the parliamentary draftsmen, in the belief that they were all being either feeble or obstructive, displayed a degree of political aggression to which Whitehall was unaccustomed. Officials did not know how to handle a forceful woman who did not play by bureaucratic rules or accept their departmental wisdom. Their successors were to have the same problem twenty years later, multiplied tenfold by her authority as Prime Minister. No one in

1960 imagined that a woman could ever be Prime Minister. But her luck in winning a high place in the Private Members' ballot, and her plucky exploitation of the opportunity, had certainly put her in line for early promotion. The *Daily Telegraph*'s Peterborough column noted that her maiden speech 'has not been, and probably is unlikely to be, excelled by any of her contemporaries'. In the gallant style of the day, the writer (probably Bill Deedes, then Member for Ashford) went on: 'To her intellectual and forensic abilities she added yesterday a new frock and not merely charm but an uncanny instinct for the mood of the House, which some Members take years to acquire – and many never achieve at all.'[50]

The popular papers loved her too. 'Fame and Margaret Thatcher made friends yesterday,' the *Sunday Dispatch* declared; but this was no surprise since 'the pretty ash-blonde from Farnborough, Kent, has had success as a hobby since she started walking and talking'. The subject of all this attention tried to inject a little realism into the dizzy projection of her prospects, insisting that she 'couldn't even consider a Cabinet post until my twins are older'.[51] This after less than four months in the House! But the combination of ruthlessness and charm – aggression cloaked by femininity – which she had so quickly demonstrated was eventually to prove unstoppable.

Mrs Thatcher did not speak again on the floor of the House for more than a year. But she did put her head above the parapet a second time by voting in committee for the reintroduction of corporal punishment for young offenders, which had been abolished by the Labour Government in 1948. Possibly unaware of her views, the whips put her on the Standing Committee to consider Rab Butler's Criminal Justice Bill – a measure designed, in Butler's own words, 'in line with the best modern thought' to deal with an upsurge in juvenile crime by means of 'constructive short-term training' in detention centres. In his memoirs Butler recalled with distaste the trouble he had with 'Colonel Blimps of both sexes – and the female of the species is deadlier than the male' – who demanded the return of the birch.[52] He was given a particularly rough ride at the Conservative Women's Conference in April 1961. Two months earlier the young female Member for Finchley had joined with five other Tories on the Standing Committee in support of an amendment to restore flogging moved by the 74-year-old Member for Ayr, Sir Thomas Moore. (The other five were all much older than Mrs Thatcher, three of them military or naval men.) Explaining her vote, she showed herself profoundly at odds with Butler's 'best modern thought'.

> In our desire for the humanitarian reform of offenders we seem to have lost sight of the purpose of criminal courts and the true aims of punishment.

Rehabilitation was fine where it worked, but it was not always suitable:

> Some cases which come before the courts concern persons who are so hardened, vicious and amoral that a much more curative element is needed in the sentence.

Some offenders might be mental cases, but she did not agree that all were:

> If, instead of giving him a short, sharp lesson, we encourage in him a feeling of self-justification, we may completely blot out all feeling of guilt or shame.

She had no faith in Butler's detention centres:

> The method of a short, sharp shock . . . no longer seems to be the aim of detention centres. It seems, almost imperceptibly, to have been modified. If detention centres offered a severe alternative . . . there would be no demand for corporal punishment.

She was at pains to stress that her support for 'a modified form of corporal punishment, caning and in very serious cases birching', was not based on emotion or a desire for vengeance but was a practical response to 'a new young type of criminal, who uses violence not for the purposes of robbery, but for the sake of violence, and who takes pleasure in inflicting violence'. She did not believe that violent punishment would only breed more violence. Caning was 'an unhappy alternative, but I think it is the only alternative readily available to beat the crime wave in the coming years'.

She ended with a disingenuous disclaimer, directed at the whips. 'I do not in any way seek either publicity or promotion by way of rebellion, but I do not think that can stop one from holding sincere views in this matter when I consider that it is necessary.'[53] Her rebellion certainly brought her publicity; but it did nothing to retard her promotion, just seven months later. Moore's amendment was easily defeated in committee by 26 votes to 6 (Paul Channon and Julian Critchley among the majority). At Report stage in April the floggers mustered 69 votes – nearly a quarter of all Tory backbenchers, the biggest Tory revolt since 1951.* But the Government was unmoved. In her memoirs Lady Thatcher wrote that this was 'the only occasion in my entire time in the House of Commons when I voted against the party line'. This is not surprising, since she was in Government or on the front bench for almost the whole of that time, down to November 1990. The whips probably felt that an articulate young right-winger was less dangerous inside the Government, where she was muzzled, than outside. As a result, the strength of her populist convictions remained largely unsuspected for the next fifteen years.

She made one more backbench speech, in the Budget debate in April. Since her maiden speech had introduced a Bill, and she was soon afterwards given office, this was the only speech in her entire career, until after she had ceased to be Prime Minister, which was not based on a tight brief: uniquely she was speaking for no one but herself. She even began with a joke. Referring, daringly, to the current prosecution of D. H. Lawrence's *Lady Chatterley's Lover* for obscenity, she remarked that she was being asked to follow 'a man who has described his friendship with his gamekeeper, particularly as he described it in such graphic terms, using four and five letter words'. It was true that the previous speaker, the Labour Member for Ashton-under-Lyne, had referred in his speech to a friend who was a gamekeeper; but he had said nothing remotely improper, so it is a puzzle to know what she meant. However it demonstrates an attempt to show her lighter side.† She quickly got down to brass tacks, with a specialised point about the Inland Revenue's powers in relation to speculators which might have been piquantly quoted back to her in the mid-1980s:

---

* Despite Butler's recollection of female Blimps, the rebels included, among the expected military men and knights of the shire, just two of the twelve Conservative women MPs – Margaret Thatcher and Irene Ward. The tabloids loved the idea of Mrs Thatcher in this company: the *Sunday Pictorial* called her 'the most beautiful Tory flogger'.[54]

† Not that she approved of *Lady Chatterley*. Thorough as ever, she obtained a copy before appearing on *Any Questions?* the previous November and said that she got through it in three hours and twenty minutes. 'That was because I was not anxious to linger on it at all.' She did not think the book should have been prosecuted, however, even though it clearly offended 'the ordinary standards of public taste', since prosecution only gave it a boost.[55]

It is the speculator in shares we want to get at – the person who is making a business of buying and selling shares, not to hold them for their income-producing properties, but to live on the profit which he makes from the transactions. That is the person most of us would like to get at.

The central point of her speech was more familiar: the need to cut public expenditure in order to reduce and simplify company taxation. She feared that the overall figure could not be cut, 'if only because the welfare services are expanding', but it was vital to control it as a proportion of GNP. She looked forward to the report of the Plowden Committee, due in June.

At present the system of control of Government expenditure is very dangerous in that it gives all the appearance of control without the reality, and that is about the worst situation which one can possibly have.[56]

This was as far as she went in criticising the Government's economic management, though she claims in *The Path to Power* that she was already 'uneasy about the general direction in which we seemed to be going'.[57] There is perhaps just a hint of this unease – as well as of her already rooted distrust of officials – in her final words. Looking forward to Selwyn Lloyd's next budget, she wished him well 'throughout the many battles that he will have in the process with his Treasury advisers'.[58] She already suspected, before she had even got into government, that the Treasury, like the rest of Whitehall, was dedicated to thwarting sound Tory policies.

Did she already have a sense that it might fall to her, in due course, to sort them out? It is difficult to believe that she did not, though she knew that she would have invited ridicule if she had voiced her ambition openly. She dropped a revealing hint in the autumn of 1960 when she was invited to be one of six guests at the Woman of the Year lunch at the Savoy. They were all asked who they would like to be, if not themselves. Three of the six – Lady Pakenham (now Lady Longford), Lady Reading and the actress Evelyn Laye – chose conventional real-life heroines: Florence Nightingale, Marie Curie and the Latin scholar and poet, Helen Waddell. The editor of *Vogue* would have liked to be Eve; the director of the WRNS went for Helen of Troy. Margaret Thatcher's extraordinary choice was Anna Leonowens, the nineteenth-century English governess at the court of the King of Siam, whose story had recently been made into the musical *The King and I*. 'She translated democracy into the country she visited,' Mrs Thatcher told the lunching ladies. 'I envy Anna the way she went to Siam, not merely as a job but with a sense of destiny.'[59] This is an artlessly candid statement of how she saw her purpose in life: she was a missionary, a teacher, an evangelist who would bring enlightenment to her benighted country.

Further evidence that some, at least, of her parliamentary colleagues perceived her quality is a book published in 1962 by the veteran Scottish Labour MP, Jean Mann. Once again, Labour opponents seem to have appreciated her more than her own side, to whom she was perhaps a too familiar type. *Woman in Parliament* is part history, part memoir of the first generation of women MPs, with a final chapter casting an eye over the newest recruits. On Margaret Thatcher, Miss Mann was spot on, recognising that her sheer stamina and determination would take her very near the top:

> A maiden speech and a private member's Bill in one go! Mrs Thatcher does not believe in taking two bites at a cherry. She takes two cherries in one bite. 'Twins', for instance, qualified chemist and barrister, another . . . . 'A speech of front-bench quality'. At this pace Margaret Thatcher is quite capable of quads and the Foreign Office.[60]

Like Mrs Thatcher herself in 1952, Jean Mann stopped short of naming the top job as coming within a woman's grasp. She died in 1964, so did not live to see her estimate of Mrs Thatcher's potential not only fulfilled but surpassed.

In the summer of 1961, after months of cautious soundings, the Macmillan Government finally announced Britain's application to join the European Economic Community – the Common Market, as it was then universally known. Ted Heath was appointed to lead the negotiations. This was the biggest decision in postwar politics, which determined – even though it was another decade before Britain's third application was successful – the gradual redirection of British policy towards ever-closer involvement with the continent. In time Mrs Thatcher as Prime Minister came to feel that this involvement had gone too far, and set herself to slow or even to reverse it. She felt no such doubts in 1961. She writes in her memoirs that she saw the EEC at this time as 'essentially a trading framework – a Common Market – and neither shared nor took very seriously the idealistic rhetoric with which "Europe" was already being dressed in some quarters.'[61] This may be so; but she certainly understood perfectly well that the Treaty of Rome had long-term implications for national sovereignty, and accepted them. In a characteristically thorough speech in her constituency on 14 August, lasting nearly two hours and packed with 'facts, figures and political logic', she tackled the question of sovereignty head on.

First she denied that Britain faced a choice between Europe and the Commonwealth, as many older Tories feared. The Commonwealth would only benefit from Britain being strong and prosperous; there should be no problem safeguarding Commonwealth food exports. Besides, she frankly admitted, the Commonwealth was not the same as twenty or thirty years earlier: 'Many of us do not feel quite the same allegiance to Archbishop Makarios or Doctor Nkrumah or to people like Jomo Kenyatta as we do towards Mr Menzies of Australia.' Seldom has that point been more squarely put.

Second, she warned that it was important to join the Community quickly in order to be able to help shape the Common Agricultural Policy. In fact it was already too late for that: the Six were pressing on deliberately to settle the CAP before Britain was admitted. But the principle she enunciated – that Britain needed to be in at the beginning of future developments – was an important one whose truth did not diminish.

Third and most crucially, Mrs Thatcher faced up to fears of loss of sovereignty and national identity and dismissed them as groundless. Britain already belonged to alliances – principally NATO – which limited her sovereignty: these were an *exercise* of national sovereignty, not a derogation of it. As a member of NATO, Britain helped formulate common obligations.

> Sovereignty and independence are not ends in themselves. It is no good being independent in isolation if it involves running down our economy and watching other nations outstrip us both in trade and influence.
>
> We should be failing in our duty to future generations if by refusing to negotiate now we committed this country to isolation from Europe for many years to come . . . France and Germany have attempted to sink their political differences and work for a united Europe. If France can do this so can we.[62]

What is remarkable about this statement, in retrospect, is its unblinking acceptance of the political dimension of a united Europe and Britain's proper place within it. Mrs Thatcher dismisses the Commonwealth: by this time, with new African countries gaining independence every year, she had outgrown the youthful enthusiasm for the Empire on which she had still laid so much stress at Dartford. But she makes no mention of the rival pull of America, which in later years she was to champion so strongly as an alternative to absorption in Europe. Though she was always grateful for Lend-Lease and Marshall Aid, she had not yet fully discovered America as her model society: she had not yet been there. She had scarcely been to continental Europe either, for that matter. Yet her speeches at this time were full of quite natural references to Britain's place in Europe. Calling for the independent taxation of women in her speech in the budget debate, for instance, she deplored the fact that Britain treated married working women worse than anyone else in Europe.[63] And visiting Friern Hospital in her constituency she claimed that, following the 1959 Mental Health Act, 'we lead Europe in our approach to mental health'.[64] Of course the key to her view of Europe lay in the word *lead*; it was the common assumption of British politicians applying to join the Community in the early 1960s – and still in the early 1970s – that Britain would be going in to lead Europe, or at least to share in the joint leadership. It was the confidence that Britain would still be a great power within Europe – indeed a greater power as part of Europe – which allowed them to contemplate with equanimity the loss, or pooling, of formal sovereignty. It is a striking illustration of this confidence that even so ardent a nationalist as Margaret Thatcher felt no qualms in 1961 on the subject which exercised her so furiously thirty years later.

Seven weeks after making this speech she joined the Government.

7

Junior Minister

To her first biographers Mrs Thatcher maintained that her invitation to join the Government in October 1961 was entirely unexpected. George Gardiner relates that she was lunching with her sister Muriel when she was called to see the Prime Minister. She went expecting only that she might be asked to move or second the formal reply to the Queen's Speech, an honour often given to a promising backbencher. Instead she returned to Muriel having been offered the job of joint Parliamentary Secretary at the Ministry of Pensions and National Insurance. The offer had come a little sooner than she would have liked, when the twins were only eight; but she knew that in politics, 'when you're offered a job you either accept it or you're out'.[1] So she accepted.

But this was disingenuous: in her memoirs she was more honest. There she admits that 'I . . . had more than an inkling of what my future post might be'. She knew there was a vacancy at Pensions since Patricia Hornsby-Smith had resigned for personal reasons at the end of August. It made obvious sense for Macmillan to maintain the quota of women in the Government – three – by appointing another woman in her place.* There was rumoured to be another vacancy in the Ministry of Aviation; but 'much as I would have liked it, I could not see them giving Aviation in those days to a young woman'. It is not clear how she could have known about this second vacancy, which arose only as the last link in the very minor reshuffle which Macmillan carried out that day. Be that as it may, Monty Woodhouse got the Aviation job, and Mrs Thatcher was offered 'the expected appointment' at Pensions, which she 'enthusiastically accepted'.[2] Years later she liked to tell the story that when she asked

---

* The other two were Edith Pitt, Parliamentary Secretary at the Ministry of Health, and Mervyn Pike, Assistant Postmaster-General. Both were unmarried.

Macmillan what the job involved, he told her cheerfully that she would only be expected to look in to the Department around eleven each morning and sign a few letters.

In a shrewd profile two days later, *The Times* noted that 'a woman Minister who has a young family to look after is something new to the Commons'. (Only one previous woman minister had had children at all: that was Edith Summerskill, whose children were grown up before she took office in 1945.) Despite the obligatory reference to her getting 'her trim feet on the first rung of the ministerial ladder', the writer went on to recognise that Mrs Thatcher was not just a pretty face:

> Her undoubted intellectual gifts, her charm, her youthful appear-
> ance and her debating ability have impressed Ministers whenever
> she has spoken. Those who know her well detect a strong will,
> some might say almost a ruthlessness, behind her smiling
> appearance.[3]

While *The Times* saw her appointment as an advance for married women, the *Guardian* saw it as merely one woman replacing another in a 'woman's' job. 'After the time Dame Patricia spent in the job without getting promotion' – ten years as Parliamentary Secretary in three departments – 'it seems clear that to Mr Macmillan's mind women politicians should stick to good works.' Of the possible alternative women, the *Guardian* would have preferred to see Joan Vickers promoted – an opponent of capital punishment from the left of the Tory party. Mrs Thatcher, the writer noted, had also rebelled, 'but in a way more popular with the bulk of the party. She was in favour of corporal punishment.'[4] Probably Macmillan and his Chief Whip, Martin Redmayne, did simply want another woman. Neither paper picked up the fact that Mrs Thatcher was not only the youngest woman ever appointed to ministerial office but also (with Woodhouse) the first of the 1959 intake to win promotion.

She stayed in the Ministry of Pensions and National Insurance (MPNI) for three years, longer than she might have wished in one department; but it was a good department in which to serve her ministerial apprenticeship. The nature of the work suited her perfectly. Though she knew next to nothing about social security when she arrived, she quickly set herself to master both the principles of the system and the immensely complex detail. ('It is nice to have something to get your teeth into,' she told the *Daily Mail*.)[5] With her tidy mind – honed by both chemistry and law – and her inexhaustible appetite for paperwork, she rapidly achieved a rare command of both aspects which enabled her to handle individual cases confidently within a clear framework of policy. The MPNI was not a department where a minister – certainly not a junior minister – had large executive decisions to take, rather a mass of tiny decisions investigating grievances and correcting anomalies across the whole range of benefits and human circumstances. Three years of this gave Mrs Thatcher a close working knowledge of the intricacies of the welfare system which – since she never forgot anything once she had learned it – became a formidable part of her armoury twenty years later (though much of her detailed knowledge by then was out of date).

The MPNI also offered a thorough training in the ways of Whitehall: since its clients spanned the whole population – widows and pensioners, workers and unemployed, farmers and fishermen, the disabled and mentally ill – the work of the department touched practically every other domestic department in the Whitehall village – Health, Housing, Labour, Trade, Agriculture, the Scottish Office and of course the Treasury – requiring frequent meetings and joint committees to resolve difficulties. Though unglamorous, few ministries offer a wider grounding in the web of government.[6] (By contrast Education, her next ministerial posting in the 1970s – and her only other experience of office before becoming Prime Minister – is one of the most isolated departments.) Mrs Thatcher was always grateful for the training she received at the MPNI. She frequently referred to it in later years (whereas she rarely mentioned her time at Education) and claims in her memoirs that it was part of her grooming of John Major as a potential successor that she appointed him to the equivalent job in 1985, adding the characteristic gloss: 'If that did not alert him to the realities of social security and the dependency culture, nothing would.'[7] She later sent Edwina Currie, Michael Portillo and Stephen Dorrell to the same first posting (and Major did the same with William Hague).

The drawback to the MPNI was that the subject matter itself was narrow and often nitpicking, requiring no broad strategic overview or much political sensitivity beyond the capacity to say 'no' as sympathetically as possible. Mrs Thatcher's femininity was a help here, when she chose to deploy it; but the fact was that once she had mastered the technical complexity, the welfare system did not arouse her sympathy. She could be moved by an individual situation – for instance she wanted to scrap the earnings rule for widowed mothers, because she still recalled 'the heartbreaking sight of a recently widowed mother eking out her tiny income by buying bruised fruit at my father's shop in Grantham'[8] – but claimants in the mass she instinctively regarded as spongers who should have made provision for themselves. Her job, as she saw it, was to apply the rules as tightly as possible in order to protect her real object of concern, the hard-pressed taxpayer. In public, of course, she had to defend the system; but at least once she vented her true feelings to an old friend, telling a shocked Margaret Wickstead about her 'awful job', besieged by 'dreadful people' demanding 'our money'.[9] Her stint at the MPNI did not teach her to love the welfare state. On the contrary, it gave her a powerful sense of a potentially limitless demand on the public purse which must at some future date be capped.

Her first minister was John Boyd-Carpenter, a pugnacious character whom Macmillan had left at the MPNI since 1955. 'He was a marvellous teacher,' she later recalled, 'fantastic man, total command of his department.'[10] He won her undying gratitude by coming down to meet her at the door the first morning she turned up bright and early at the department (situated in John Adam Street, just off the Strand). This gallantry made such an impression on her that she made a point of extending the same courtesy to her own juniors at the Department of Education ten years later. In his memoirs Boyd-Carpenter confessed that he took the trouble only because she was a lady: his initial expectations of her were low.

> Knowing that she had two young children, a husband in Burmah Oil,* a house in Kent and like the rest of us a constituency to look after, I must admit that I wondered whether I or the Department would get much help out of her.
>
> Was the appointment of this charming and good-looking lady just one of Macmillan's gimmicks?

His doubts were rapidly dissolved:

> Despite the fact that to the male eye she always looked as though she had spent the morning with the coiffeur and the afternoon with the couturier, she worked long and productive hours in the Ministry.

Boyd-Carpenter came to admire both her hard work in the Department and her combativeness in the House of Commons: 'Such spirit, competence and courage in a newly-appointed Parliamentary Secretary are so rare that I then came to the conclusion that she would go very high in public life.'[11]

* This was an anachronism. Atlas Preservatives was not taken over by Burmah until some years later.

This of course was written in 1980. Nineteen years earlier, at the end of his first meeting with his new Parliamentary Secretary, Boyd-Carpenter's first words to his Permanent Secretary, Sir Eric Bowyer, were 'She's trouble'.[12] To keep her busy, they set her to make a major study of women in the National Insurance system. Nothing came of it, no public statement was ever made; but Mrs Thatcher took it very seriously and worked very hard at it. It was important for her to feel that she was dealing with policy, not just with the delivery of benefits. Bowyer was a Permanent Secretary of the old school, a gruff Glaswegian who worked long hours, rarely set foot outside the Department but saw every piece of paper that went to ministers: he too was initially sceptical but came to have a high regard for a junior minister whose work-rate matched his own. Officials lower down the Ministry were more ambivalent. Mrs Thatcher exasperated them by the meticulousness with which she corrected and redrafted every letter they put up for her to sign, sending them back to be rewritten if she was not satisfied; sometimes even ripping them up, like a schoolmistress with a bad essay.[13] She could be witheringly abrasive. Sir Kenneth Stowe, many years later her first Principal Private Secretary in Downing Street, remembers a meeting between ministers and officials which began quietly with Boyd-Carpenter questioning this and agreeing that, until he brought Mrs Thatcher in; the atmosphere changed abruptly as she began interrogating some luckless official. 'What does this mean?' she demanded. The official explained. 'You could have fooled me.'[14]

In her memoirs she concedes that generally 'the calibre of officials I met impressed me'.[15] Yet the lesson she took from the MPNI, and never forgot, was that civil servants had their own agenda. She has frequently told how she caught them out offering advice to Boyd-Carpenter's successors which they would not have dared to offer him because they knew he would not take it. 'I decided then and there that when I was in charge of a department I would insist on an absolutely frank assessment of all the options from any civil servants who would report to me.'[16] Whether this always happened in Downing Street in the 1980s is debatable; but Mrs Thatcher never had any doubt of the need to show her officials very quickly who was boss. Even as a junior minister she always wanted the fullest possible briefing. On one occasion she found herself unable to answer a series of deliberately arcane questions put by her Labour shadow, Douglas Houghton, to catch her out. She was furious and told her officials that it must never happen again. It never did.[17]

Her view of the Department's function was heavily moralistic.

Another future Permanent Secretary, Sir Michael Partridge, remembers her getting very worked up about reports that retired bank managers were claiming unemployment benefit. She thought this was disgraceful – the middle class behaving like the working class, abusing the system. Not at all, an Assistant Secretary told her, it was just the middle class treating the benefit system in the same way that they did the tax system. 'That's not funny,' she retorted. Years later Partridge dared to remind her of this incident. Lady Thatcher was unrepentant: 'But I was right,' she insisted. In the early 1960s she was told she could not stop this loophole without provoking a Tory revolt. But it rankled: she never forgot, and at the first opportunity after she became Prime Minister she leaned on her Social Security Secretary, Patrick Jenkin, to close it.[18]

In July 1962, when Macmillan sacked a third of his Cabinet in an ill-judged effort to revive his faltering Government, Boyd-Carpenter was finally promoted. His successor at the MPNI was Niall Macpherson; he in turn was replaced the following year by Richard Wood. Both were much milder personalities than Boyd-Carpenter; neither was destined for higher office, though Wood served as Minister for Overseas Development under Heath. The result was that Mrs Thatcher, though still only joint Parliamentary Secretary in charge of National Insurance and National Assistance, was allowed to assume a much more dominant role within the Department than is usual for a junior minister. Lord Holderness (as Wood became in 1979) naturally denies this. He admits that she was 'very abrasive' and always knew what he should do, but maintains that as a junior she 'carried no guns': he was the minister. They could not have been more different personalities. Wood, the third son of the Earl of Halifax, was an aristocrat, an Old Etonian and a war hero with a tin leg: the embodiment of *noblesse oblige*. He found Mrs Thatcher's tough approach to social security unsympathetic. She applied firm principles to individual cases and once she had taken up a position she stuck to it.[19]

She did not have much time for either of her fellow Parliamentary Secretaries who dealt with the war pensions and industrial injuries side of the Department's work. Up to July 1962 this was Richard Sharples (later appointed Governor of Bermuda by Ted Heath, and assassinated in 1973). Sharples was then replaced by Commander Stephen Maydon – a former submarine officer, tall and distinguished-looking 'with a conning-tower voice', but not very bright. The day Wood took over from Macpherson he called in his two juniors to brief him about their work. Mrs Thatcher spoke fluently for fifteen minutes about National Insurance; but as soon as Maydon started on war pensions she began interrupting and correcting him, till finally he objected: 'Margaret, you are very annoying.'[20] She had no patience with anyone who did not do his homework. Maydon never held another ministerial job: he left politics in 1970 and died the next year.

Pensions and National Insurance was not a high-profile department in 1961: its Minister was not a member of the Cabinet until it merged with the Department of Health (to create the DHSS) in 1968. It offered a joint Parliamentary Secretary few opportunities to shine in the House of Commons – little more in fact than resisting Labour pleas for higher benefits or more generous treatment of specific categories. But from her first appearance at the dispatch box Mrs Thatcher did not lack self-confidence. Pressed by Richard Crossman, Barbara Castle, Douglas Houghton and others, she quickly became adept at playing variations on what she called (in February 1963) 'my usual theme of "No"'.[21] At first friends and opponents alike continued to patronise her, complimenting her on 'the very charming argument which she is putting with great ability',[22] or 'the very charming way in which she revealed to the House her vital statistics'.[23] Sometimes she played up to this sort of coy banter. In January 1964 she announced, in response to criticism that some of her figures had been out of date, 'I have got a really red-hot figure . . .' 'The House', she has written, 'dissolved into laughter, and it took a moment for me to realise my *double entendre*.'[24] Sir Michael Partridge thinks she knew very well what she was doing: using her femininity to disguise a weak argument.[25] 'I am very glad that I am not wearing a red dress today,' she rallied flirtatiously. 'To continue, I have a bang up-to-the-minute figure . . .' Then she resumed her speech.[26]

It was not long, however, before Labour MPs started complaining that 'charming speeches do not fill the bellies of pensioners, widows and others who are in need'.[27] Nor was she always charming. Her put-downs of opponents, though usually courteous, could be distinctly crisp – 'I am glad that the hon. Member comprehends the basis of the scheme. But I must say that at certain times he seems to do his best to conceal the fact'[28] – not to say, as Barbara Castle charged on one occasion, 'rather tart'. (Mrs Thatcher retorted – tartly – that she must have picked it up from Mrs Castle.)[29] Another time she demonstrated familiarity with the dance craze of the moment by calling Michael Foot – then a left-wing backbencher – a 'master of the twist'.[30] Boyd-Carpenter admired her combative spirit:

The only trouble was that when she really got going on an opponent you had to almost pull her off the opposition front bench when she started to chase them about. The Chief Whip used to tell me to hurry her on with the legislation in hand. I think she thought it a little bit unsporting when I did, because she was enjoying herself so much.[31]

In the cold print of *Hansard*, these exchanges can seem fairly tame; but she evidently raised Labour hackles by her tendency to lecture. 'The hon. Lady ought not to chide us', Peggy Herbison objected, 'about what we should consider to be our priorities and what we should not.'[32] An exchange with Douglas Houghton in February 1963 is typical both of her relish for an argument and of the difficulty old-fashioned Labour gentlemen like Houghton had in dealing with it. He had the temerity to suggest that she was being ruled by her officials. 'Nonsense,' she retorted, then half-apologised:

Mrs Thatcher: The hon. Member will forgive me if occasionally I say 'Nonsense' to him . . . I am sure he will take it in the right spirit. Nevertheless I meant it . . .
Houghton: The hon. Lady is much too attractive to become a school ma'am type. She must use the word 'Nonsense' with great restraint when referring to interjections that I make.[33]

Mrs Thatcher was always very keen to spell out to woolly-minded Labour Members the principles behind the insurance system or the earnings rule;[34] to insist that 'we do not think it right to pay more to a person when he is out of work than he could possibly earn when he is employed';[35] or to remind them of 'the slight matter of £.s.d.'[36] She was firmly against both cold weather payments and a Christmas bonus for pensioners.[37] They in turn complained of her 'logical argument and lawyer-like explanation';[38] or that she made only an 'administrative, bureaucratic, actuarial case' for her decisions.[39]

She revealed her underlying approach most clearly in her first big speech from the dispatch box in March 1962, when Boyd-Carpenter showed his confidence in her by putting her up, rather than himself, to reply to a Labour motion condemning the failure of benefits to keep up with inflation. She led off, characteristically, with a barrage of comparative statistics. 'She left MPs stunned with statistics . . . For 40 minutes she scarcely stopped to draw a breath.'[40] But in the middle of it she let slip one of those unguarded words which

Oppositions pounce on. 'It is a pity', she told Houghton, 'that his party has chosen to adopt the line that those who get on and make extra earnings by their own efforts' – she meant surtax payers – 'must be publicly decried and milked as often as possible.'[41] The insensitive word 'milked' was never forgotten; it was regularly thrown back at her much as one or two later indiscretions were quoted against her when she became Prime Minister.

The Labour left-winger John Mendelson criticised this speech in terms which are worth quoting at length because they epitomise the impression Mrs Thatcher made on the Commons at this stage of her career:

> The hon. Lady made a technically highly competent speech. To that extent I join in the congratulations which have been offered her. It was a very fine piece of work, speaking for the first time in a major debate of this kind and showing the mastery of the facts that she did. However I warn her that with that technical competence she is in danger of doing what she referred to when she said that she had academically gone very thoroughly through the report that she was discussing.
>
> My impression at the end of the hon. Lady's speech was that all she had given us was a purely academic performance. It was remarkable that she was capable of making a long speech on the tragic position of many of our old people without making any reference whatsoever to her real experience of how they live. All the time I felt that I was back in the university seminar and that we were having a purely academic exercise.[42]

The young minister's finest moment in the 1959 Parliament, however, came four months later on the day following Macmillan's culling of his Cabinet. The House met in a state of shock. By chance the first business was questions to the Minister of Pensions; but Boyd-Carpenter had been promoted to the Cabinet as Chief Secretary to the Treasury. His successor at the MPNI had not yet been named. Into the breach stepped the joint Parliamentary secretaries. Of fifteen questions tabled, Mrs Thatcher answered fourteen; Sharples – her senior both in age and in length of service – answered just one. It was not simply the fact that Mrs Thatcher answered, but the way she did it, that made an impact. 'Amid the gloom and depression of the Government benches', one observer wrote, 'she alone radiated confidence, cheerfulness and charm.'[43] For once she displayed a light touch – even a sense of humour – which lifted Tory spirits. Amid gleeful Labour jeers about the temporary nature of ministerial appointments and suggestions that Macmillan would soon be drawing his own pension, she promised modestly to pass on various comments to her right hon. Friend the Minister 'when I have one'.[44] 'The only question in some minds', the *Guardian* sketch-writer Norman Shrapnel wrote, 'must have been, did she really need a right honourable Friend? Already . . . she looked perfectly capable of pensioning them all off and running the whole works herself.'[45] It was a performance of exceptional composure under pressure.

As a junior minister – the most junior minister in the Government – Mrs Thatcher was generally debarred from giving her views on the wider issues of politics. Twenty years later, she and her most ardent supporters portrayed the latter years of the Macmillan Government as the period when the Tory party lost faith in free enterprise and sold out to feather-bedding corporatism. In her memoirs she is forgiving, recognising that Macmillan was 'much affected by the experience of two world wars' and 'reacting against the unemployment and deflation of the 1930s which he had seen as MP for Stockton-on-Tees'. But she implies that her own views were already divergent. 'Things looked different from the perspective of Grantham than from that of Stockton.'[46]

There is naturally very little evidence of dissent from Government orthodoxy in these years: she was an ambitious politician with a career to make. Nevertheless there are hints, in two speeches in her constituency during 1962, of independent thinking. At her local party AGM in March she was happy to celebrate the 'affluent society': 'Marx today', she declared, 'would have to say "Workers, you have nothing to lose but your refrigerators, your car, your TV and all your other luxuries".' At the same time, however, she warned that the country was paying itself more than it earned and must compete in world markets to maintain its standard of living. Rather unusually she circulated a questionnaire to two hundred members of the local party asking them: 'What steps do you think the Government should now take for the benefit of the country?', promising to pass the answers on to ministers.[47] The Central Office agent, Miss Harris, commented wearily: 'I would hazard a guess that she will find herself the happy possessor of about a hundred different solutions.'[48] But was she looking for solutions, or counting on her electors to endorse her own instincts – an early exercise in populism, appealing over the heads of the party establishment to the rank and file?

That summer she loyally defended Selwyn Lloyd's 'pay pause' – the Conservatives' first attempt at an incomes policy; but in the same speech she clearly identified herself with mounting backbench pressure for action to curb unofficial strikes and the trade union closed shop. 'We are approaching the time when Trade Union laws ought to be revised.' With Ted Heath's negotiations entering their critical phase, she also once again endorsed the Government's application to join the Common Market – though rather as a matter of necessity than with enthusiasm. 'We cannot go on as we are,' she argued. 'We must have expanded markets. The end of the world has not come if we don't go into it, but it would be far better if we did.' She already identified Germany rather than France as the dominant power in Europe. By retreating into political isolation, she warned, 'we leave the ascendancy to Germany. We must accept the role of being a powerful partner in European affairs.'[49] Five months later, however, General de Gaulle's veto condemned Britain to another decade on the outside.

The collapse of his European policy holed Macmillan's Government very near the waterline: by the summer of 1963 it was listing badly and beginning to sink. The restructuring of the Cabinet had failed to rejuvenate the Government, which now faced a dynamic new Leader of the Opposition, Harold Wilson, twenty-two years younger than the Prime Minister. Macmillan was made to look even more out of touch by the titillating revelations of the Profumo scandal, which engulfed the administration in a slurry of sexual rumour and suspected sleaze. There were stirrings in the party that it was time for the old conjuror to retire. In private Mrs Thatcher made no secret of her support for this view. Betty Harvie-Anderson (MP for East Renfrewshire) recalled her arguing strongly for a change of leader;[50] and Macmillan's PPS listed her as one of four junior ministers 'not in full support' of his carrying on.[51] In public she shrugged off the Profumo embarrassment as a purely individual misfortune. But her insistence that the party was bigger than any single individual had an unspoken implication for Macmillan too:

No one person, however great, can win an election for a political party. Equally, no one disaster affecting one person can lose an election for a great party . . .

We have made too much of one or two people, and we think that they can win or lose elections for us. Don't be depressed if one particular person transgresses. It doesn't lose an election unless the Party loses faith in itself.[52]

Macmillan considered stepping down; but then, as Prime Ministers do, determined to soldier on – until, three months later, on the
eve of the party conference, ill health suddenly compelled him to
retire after all. In the famous fiasco which followed, Mrs Thatcher's
first preference was for Rab Butler – 'a statesman', as she later
condescendingly described him, 'of vast experience and some vision'
– rather than Lord Hailsham, whom she knew better but who had 'a
reputation at that time for erratic judgement'. She does not appear to
have considered skipping a generation to go for Maudling or Heath.
When asked by the whips' office her view of Alec Home, she says
she questioned whether it was 'constitutionally possible';[53] though if
it was possible for Hailsham to renounce his peerage it must equally
have been possible for Home to do the same. Her characteristically
practical concern was that neither Hailsham nor Home could return
to the House of Commons without a by-election which in the wake
of Orpington they could not be sure of winning.

She admired Home, however, and quickly rallied to his Macmil-
lan-inspired bandwagon. Behind his diffident aristocratic manner she
had recognised in his performance as Foreign Secretary a steely Cold
Warrior after her own heart: he was, she told a ward meeting in her
constituency, 'an Iron Man in resolve' who had the virtue,
'unfortunately rare among politicians', of saying exactly what he
meant without wasting words.[54] Her memoirs make the same point
with a waspish flash forward to an unspecified but unmistakable
comparison: 'He exhibited none of those tendencies, so characteristic
of those who aspire to be Foreign Secretary, towards regarding the
processes of negotiation as an end in themselves.'[55]

If she was pleased by the substitution of the clear-sighted Home
for the increasingly misty-eyed Macmillan, however, she was
disappointed that the new Prime Minister did not undertake a wider
reshuffle than was forced on him by the refusal of Iain Macleod and
Enoch Powell to serve under him. When Richard Wood arrived at
the MPNI to replace Niall Macpherson he found his Parliamentary
Secretary in 'some turmoil', on tenterhooks to see what her own
future might be.[56] She evidently felt that two years of Pensions and
National Insurance was enough. She could hardly have hoped for
promotion, but she might have looked for a sideways move to
another department to widen her experience. It is not surprising that
Wood found her a difficult subordinate over the last year of the
Government's life.

As the election which seemed certain to end the Tories' thirteen-year rule approached, Mrs Thatcher could not be absolutely confident of retaining Finchley. The Liberals were making a big push to try to win the seat, building on the presence they had already established on Finchley and Friern Barnet councils. With an energetic young candidate in John Pardoe, and boosted by their sensational by-election victory at Orpington, they had made Finchley one of their top twenty target seats, declaring it the 'Orpington of North London'.[57] In the May 1962 council elections they won every seat contested in Finchley (taking five from the Tories, one from Labour and holding two) and three in Friern Barnet. The Conservatives retained control in Finchley only through their unelected aldermen. The following year the Liberals made another clean sweep, giving them control with a 19–5 majority. Friern Barnet remained hung, with no party gaining overall control. Unluckily for the Liberals, however, these were the last local elections before the creation of the Greater London Council. Finchley and Friern Barnet were submerged in the Borough of Barnet, giving the battered Tories a chance to regroup.

In January 1962 the constituency agent, Major Nevard, died and the Association appointed a new man, Roy Langstone, with a successful track record in other London seats. Langstone quickly improved the organisation to beat off the Liberal challenge; he subsequently stayed in Finchley for nearly twenty years, adapting successfully to the rather different challenge of holding the seat for Mrs Thatcher when she was able to spend less time on her own patch. In 1963–4, of course, she continued to work the constituency tirelessly, not so much because she was seriously afraid of losing – though she never took any election for granted – as because that was her nature. The *Finchley Press* loved her:

> A lady makes you feel when you speak to her that YOU matter more than anything.
> Margaret Thatcher does just that. Crowded though her day inevitably is, she has the inborn grace of a priority consideration for individuals. For people as a whole, too. Because, when she makes a speech, she does not 'orate'. She talks naturally and spontaneously, giving much thought to her words, but also keeping straight to the matter in hand.

Combining her duties as housewife and mother with her heavy workload as minister and MP, the writer concluded, Mrs Thatcher made women feel 'very proud of our sex. She inspires our platforms and gives heart to our undertakings ... She is ... every inch a lady.'[58]

There is no doubt that she was capable of arousing great enthusiasm. Yet there were always some who found her cold. Miss Harris of Conservative Central Office attended her constituency AGM in March 1962 and reported devastatingly to Smith Square: 'Mrs Thatcher made her usual competent speech. It is a pity that with such a good endowment of brains and beauty she has so little humanity.'[59]

Spring 1964 pricked the Liberal bubble. First they failed to win any of Barnet's four seats on the new GLC in April, trailing in third place behind Labour while the Tories comfortably took all four; then in May they won only six of Finchley's twelve seats on Barnet council, and none in Friern Barnet, reducing them abruptly to irrelevance in the new local government structure.[60] Come the General Election in October, Pardoe still fought an energetic campaign, swamping the constituency with orange posters and talking up his chances extravagantly, presenting himself as the radical alternative to two conservatives. (The Labour candidate this time was Albert Tomlinson, a decent but undynamic local councillor described on his own election address as 'a likeable and kindly man'.)[61] But fighting Mrs Thatcher, Pardoe faced two problems. First, she was an exceptionally visible Member who in five years had won herself a strong personal vote. Despite her family and ministerial commitments, the *Finchley Press* reckoned on 18 September, 'there can be few Members who have spent more time among their constituents than Mrs Thatcher'.

> She is personally well known to and genuinely loved by the people for her friendliness and the sympathetic way in which she handles each and every problem ...
> No Member in fact could have more clearly proved herself . . . a true representative of her constituents' interests.[62]

This frankly partisan view was confirmed by a survey carried out for the Nuffield study of the 1964 General Election which found that almost half of her constituents could name Mrs Thatcher as their MP, 'compared to only one in fourteen who could name the Liberal candidate and one in thirty who could name the Socialist'.[63]

Second, while Pardoe tried to stir up local issues, Mrs Thatcher studiously ignored him and concentrated her fire on Labour, the national opponent. 'Those who are not for us are against us,' she declared at her adoption meeting: the election was about choosing a

Conservative or a Labour Government.[64] In her election address and her campaign speeches she rehearsed the achievements of the Conservative Government; warned of higher taxes under Labour; promised a faster rate of housebuilding – a target of 400,000 a year – with encouragement for owner occupation; and called for an inquiry into trade union law; but otherwise said nothing remotely personal or unconventional. Recalling the election thirty years later, Pardoe was struck by the absence, at this stage of Mrs Thatcher's career, 'of any very pronounced views about anything apart from capital punishment'. He concluded that she became a 'conviction politician' only later.[65]

On the platform she was formidable, rebutting criticism of the Government with volleys of statistics. She held ten meetings during the campaign, attracting audiences of 150–180 in the last few days – far more than Pardoe or Tomlinson. The author of the Nuffield study was impressed by the 'articulateness and serious interest shown by Finchley audiences'.

Almost the only light relief came at a large Tory gathering where the first question was from a lady who wanted to know 'why had the Conservative Government done nothing about the lavatories which won't flush? . . . It is not a laughing matter, it is happening all over the country.' Mrs Thatcher negotiated this one with great skill and turned eagerly to the next hand raised, only to be asked, 'What is the purpose of life?' She later remarked [presumably to a Swiss TV crew who were filming her campaign], 'You mustn't get the wrong impression of us; after all this is Hampstead Garden Suburb.'[66]*

To the end, Pardoe insisted that the result would be close, with no more than 2,000 votes in it either way. Mrs Thatcher, unusually, predicted a majority of 10,000.[67] She was the more nearly right.

Margaret Thatcher (Conservative)	24,591
John Pardoe (Liberal)	15,789
Albert Tomlinson (Labour)	12,408
Conservative majority	8,802

---

* The author was Bernard Donoughue, at that time a young lecturer at LSE, later head of James Callaghan's Downing Street Policy Unit, and later still – as Lord Donoughue – a minister in Tony Blair's Government.

Her vote was down by 4,000, her majority nearly halved; the Liberals had succeeded in pushing Labour into third place. But the Labour vote had not been seriously squeezed. It was an exaggeration for Pardoe to claim, at the count: 'We are treading hard on your heels, Madam.'[68] Finchley was still a comfortably safe Tory seat. More significant was the impact of the Liberal advance on the national result. By nearly doubling their share of the vote (to 11 per cent) largely at the Conservatives' expense, they helped Labour back into government with a wafer-thin majority of four. After thirteen years of Tory rule and the shambles of 1963, Alec Douglas-Home came astonishingly close to winning re-election. But he failed, narrowly, and his failure ended Mrs Thatcher's first experience of government. 'I never went back to collect anything after the election,' she told George Gardiner. 'A Department is always interested in the incoming Minister, not the outgoing one. Once you're out, you're out. And I didn't want to embarrass anyone by saying goodbye.'[69]

Margaret Thatcher was not just disappointed by the Conservative defeat: for virtually the only time in her life – at least until 1990 – she was actually depressed by it. She did not like losing. She had never been the sort of politician who can see any virtue in opposition, or any benefit to the country in giving the other side a turn. She quite genuinely believed a Labour Government to be a bad thing, and blamed her own party for having allowed it to happen. She remembered Rab Butler telling the newly-elected Tory Members in 1959 that if they played their cards well they should be in office for twenty-five years. Instead, she told Carol, 'we didn't play our cards well, a lot went wrong and we were out of office in 1964'. This was a lesson she never forgot.[70]

More seriously, she also suffered a personal reaction. Carol suggests that she was exhausted after a particularly strenuous campaign in Finchley on top of her ministerial work, and driving back to Farnborough late every night. In one respect her family life was eased, since both Mark and Carol were now at boarding school – Mark at a prep school in North London, Carol in Hertfordshire – so neither was at home in mid-October; but she was having problems with Denis, who seems to have undergone some sort of mid-life crisis in 1964. This was first disclosed in Carol's biography of her father, published in 1996, and we only know what little she reveals. It appears that he was working too hard; partly because Atlas Preservatives was undercapitalised and struggling to survive, and he worried that not only his own family but the life savings of his mother, sister and two aunts depended on its continuing success; but partly also because Margaret was out so much that he had no one to go home to. 'Often he wouldn't leave till half past nine,' a colleague recalled. 'He stayed at work because she was busy working as well.' Eventually his doctor ordered him to take a break. So he did. 'I got myself on a boat – it shook Margaret – and took myself off to South Africa.' An unnamed friend remembers it as more than simple physical exhaustion:

> He was terribly depressed and decided to go to South Africa to sort himself out. I knew he was unhappy because he discussed it with me. He had his mother and Joy, who doted on him, and a wife who was totally absorbed in her political career.[71]

The last person he would have discussed it with was Margaret. They lived their lives on separate tracks, each pursuing their own career with little reference to the other. He did not bother her with his business problems, and she did not bother him with politics, beyond an occasional constituency function. No wonder she was shaken when he suddenly took himself off for a long sabbatical. He was often abroad on business, usually in Africa, with no more contact than an occasional postcard; but this was different. If his mother and aunts depended financially on Denis, so did her career. To someone as robust as Margaret, the idea of Denis having a nervous breakdown must have been alarming. Denis was not the type to whinge: he was more likely to keep up a good front and then crack. What would she do then? She must have worried about the implications for herself and the twins if he were seriously ill. Not that he did not thoroughly support her ambition. On the contrary, the decision he took, after pondering the direction of his life on safari in southern Africa, to sell the family firm was not only intended to secure his family's future but represented a deliberate subordination of his career to hers. He was nearly fifty; she was not yet forty. He had done as much as he could with Atlas; he had been warned that he needed to slow down if he was not to kill himself. She was well launched on a trajectory which, win or lose in 1964, might reasonably be expected to lead to the Cabinet within ten years. So he made his decision. But he did not discuss it with Margaret until it was a *fait accompli*.

In fact the sale of Atlas to Castrol turned out very well for Denis. According to Carol, it realised £530,000, of which his personal share was £10,000. But other accounts suggest that it was worth very much more than that. In practice the sale of his family firm made Denis a millionaire. Secondly, instead of narrowing his responsibilities it widened them. Denis had expected to carry on running Atlas for Castrol, but now as an employee without the stress of ultimate responsibility. To his surprise Castrol offered him a place on the board, with salary and car to match. (The car was a Daimler with a personalised number plate DT3.) When just a few years later, Castrol in turn merged with Burmah, Denis did very well in terms of share options and once again was invited on to the board. From being the overworked chairman of a successful but insecure paint and fertiliser business, Denis spent the last decade of his working life as a highly paid executive in the oil industry; which in turn left him well placed to pick up lucrative non-executive directorships after his retirement.[72]

But all this was in the future. In October 1964 Denis's health and state of mind cast an additional shadow over Margaret's life just at the moment when her party had lost the General Election and been thrown out of office. Alec Home reappointed her to the same portfolio in opposition, junior Pensions spokesman, still under Richard Wood, shadowing Labour ministers who before the election had been shadowing her. Politically and personally, this was the lowest point of her life. Uncharacteristically she fell ill herself at the end of the year.

Yet it worked out for her, as it did for Denis. In opposition, in a parliamentary party reduced by fifty, promotion came faster than it would have done in office. In three years she was in the Shadow Cabinet: she would not have made the real Cabinet so soon if Home had won. She had served a thorough apprenticeship at the MPNI: when the Conservatives returned to power she would have a department of her own. In terms of her personal career, 1964 was a timely setback – almost a blessing in disguise.

8

Opposition

FOR the next six years Margaret Thatcher was the Conservative Opposition's maid of all work. Between 1964 and 1970 she held six different portfolios – three as a junior spokeswoman, successively on pensions, housing and economic policy, and three as a member of the Shadow Cabinet, shadowing Power, Transport and finally Education. In principle Ted Heath – who replaced Alec Douglas-Home as Tory leader in July 1965 – did not like shuffling his colleagues around so frequently: this was one of his criticisms of Harold Wilson's management style. He believed in treating opposition as a period of preparation for government; his preference was for giving his shadow ministers time to master their subjects. In practice this was not always possible; but no one was shifted around so much as Mrs Thatcher. This reflected both recognition of her ability to get on top of any brief very quickly and – less flatteringly – an assumption that she was a useful odd-job woman who could be shoved into any vacancy but was not being groomed for any particular department.

In fact, when the Conservatives returned to power in 1970 she was confirmed in the last department she had been shadowing, Education. But in the meantime she had been given an unusually wide experience of shadow responsibilities which stood her in excellent stead as Prime Minister two decades later, going some way to compensate for her relatively narrow ministerial experience. Though her average tenure of each portfolio was less than a year she did nothing by halves, but always thoroughly mastered each one before moving on. She recognised the value of her wide apprenticeship, as she told the Commons on her first appearance as shadow Education Secretary: 'When one has held six portfolios in seven years one can wind up on almost any subject.'[1] Of course her experience was all on the domestic side: she was given no opportunity to learn about either foreign policy or defence. And even on the home front she had no chance to cover crime and punishment, agriculture or health. Even so it was an unusually broad training. Above all, she was not confined to traditionally 'feminine' subjects: this was perhaps her biggest breakthrough.

Initially Douglas-Home sent her back to shadowing National Insurance, still nominally under Richard Wood, though Wood recalls that she immediately took charge of their review of policy.[2] But watching Labour ministers administering the same system which she had been answerable for just a few weeks earlier was a dispiriting business. On her first appearance at the Opposition dispatch box she tried to make a joke of her unfamiliarity with the role, hoping 'never to attain such skill in opposition' as Houghton had done, and drew on her three years' experience to patronise Peggy Herbison and her incoming colleagues who were now learning the constraints of responsibility.[3] She harried the new Joint Parliamentary Secretaries – Harold Davies and Norman Pentland, both much older than her – either for having failed to do their homework or for tamely trotting out their departmental briefs. On 3 December she twitted Davies, a nice old Welsh left-winger, who was dutifully resisting extending the period for claiming certain benefits:

> He gave the same arguments which I know backwards, although he sounded as if he actually believed them. I do not think that I ever sounded as if I believed them. Indeed I do not think that I ever gave them from the Dispatch Box.[4]

Free of office, she continued her campaign to abolish the earnings rule for widows, and was generously delighted when Miss Herbison finally succeeded where she had failed. Ever concerned for widows, she would even have liked to compel husbands to make provision for their wives in the event of their death:

> I am speaking entirely personally from this Box, because I have not yet converted my party, any more than the right hon. Lady has converted hers, but I think that widowhood as such should be entitled to certain benefits.[5]

At the turn of the year, however, the loss of office combined with worry about Denis made her uncharacteristically ill. At Christmas the family went to Switzerland for their now regular skiing holiday – Denis had flown out early to continue his convalescence. But the alpine air, as Carol tells it, 'couldn't restore Margaret's deteriorating health: she came down with pneumonia in January 1965.' She was 'very surprised'.

> I've enjoyed very good health [although] I haven't looked after it in particular. Denis hadn't been well and Mark had pneumonia. After having tried to cope with absolutely everything, I came down with it. I remember it so very well because Winston Churchill died in January 1965 and I couldn't go to the lying in state in Westminster Hall. I had to watch the funeral on television.[6]

To the *Finchley Press* she contributed a predictable tribute to her first great political hero, 'the greatest of them all'. It is interesting only for its stress on the ups and downs of Churchill's career before his 'hour of destiny'. She quoted his axiom, 'In war, resolution; in defeat, defiance; in victory, magnanimity; in peace, goodwill' – the first half of which at least she inscribed on her own political standard.[7]

She was out of action for ten days, missing among other things an appearance on *Any Questions?* But she was back at work in February, her normal energy restored. With another General Election likely as soon as Wilson saw an opportunity to increase his wafer-thin majority, Sir Alec had put Heath in charge of a rapid policy rethink. Mrs Thatcher's contribution was to collaborate with Keith Joseph – now shadowing Social Security – on two reports. The first, on 'Pensions and the Care of the Elderly', was their own work; the second represented the conclusions of the National Insurance policy group, made up of MPs, industrialists and academics, which they jointly chaired. The former, building on work begun in office, aimed to promote 'almost universal financial self-sufficiency in retirement . . . by about the end of the century', while retaining the basic state pension in the meantime.[8]* This was in contrast to Labour's ambitious and expensive plan for universal graduated state pensions, introduced after the 1966 election by Dick Crossman. The group report expressed the same objective – 'to bring about a big shift in pensions from State to private provision' – in more forthright terms designed to go straight into the next Conservative manifesto.[10] It also proposed to cut the link between pensions and earnings, tying them instead only to the cost of living – a crucial shift only achieved

---

* Rab Butler – still, for another few months, chairman of the Conservative Research Department – judged the Joseph–Thatcher pensions paper the best – 'for sheer quality and presentation' – of all the policy reports.[9]

by Mrs Thatcher's first Chancellor, Geoffrey Howe, in 1979. More generously, it committed the party to ending the anomaly whereby some very old people who were too old for the state scheme when it began in 1948 were still denied pensions. This was a cause which Airey Neave had taken up strongly. Mrs Thatcher knew Neave from their days in the Candidates' Association in the early fifties. Joseph had helped her with her Private Member's Bill in 1960. Working closely with both of them on these reports forged links which would be of the profoundest significance for her career in 1974–5.

Back in the Commons Mrs Thatcher was not a core member of Heath's fourteen-man team fighting Jim Callaghan's Finance Bill – a *tour de force* of parliamentary opposition which did more than anything else to make Heath leader; but she made occasional closely argued contributions, mainly in her self-appointed role as the widows' champion. In May she gave the Financial Secretary to the Treasury, Niall McDermott, a hard time on the assessment of Estate Duty on widows' houses, citing legal chapter and verse to claim that it should be based on the occupational not the development value, and threatening to take him apart 'molecule by molecule' – a neat reminder of her scientific background – till a very late hour if he did not concede. McDermott nevertheless refused, maintaining gallantly that 'the hon. Lady . . . has such grace and charm that even the prospect of being taken apart molecule by molecule by her has its attractions'.[11] She enjoyed, in fact a mutually flirtatious relationship with McDermott – the type of tall, smooth-tongued barrister for whom she always had a weakness. Moving another amendment in July to relieve working widows she complained that when the Government wanted to say 'no' 'they always put up the handsomest man to do so'. He responded that when the Opposition had no case 'they put up their most attractive representative to try to beat the brow of Treasury Ministers'.[12]

Two weeks after this exchange Alec Douglas-Home announced his resignation of the Tory leadership. Mrs Thatcher was 'stunned and upset'. It is a measure of her isolation from Westminster gossip that she claims to have had no inkling that Sir Alec was coming under pressure to step down, allegedly orchestrated by supporters of Ted Heath. 'I never ventured into the Smoking Room so I was unaware of these mysterious cabals until it was too late.'[13] Her exclusion was partly a function of her sex, but also reflected her compartmentalised life and her nose-to-the-grindstone view of politics. Harder to explain is why she was so upset. Much as she admired Sir Alec, he was clearly not cut out to be Leader of the

Opposition; the party needed a more aggressive and modern style of leadership to wrest the political initiative back from Labour and rethink its policies. Given her declared 'unease' with the trend of the party since the early sixties one might have expected Mrs Thatcher to be one of those younger Tories impatient for a new beginning.

In fact, once the contest for the succession was joined she was persuaded to back the more aggressive of the contenders. Her first inclination was for Reggie Maudling. She had known Heath longer, since their time as candidates in adjacent Kentish seats in 1949–51. They had spoken on one another's platforms, but they had not become close and their acquaintance, as she curiously puts it, 'had never risked developing into friendship'.[14] They were in truth very similar people – from similar social backgrounds, both humourless, single-minded and ambitious. But Mrs Thatcher disguised her ambition with a cloak of femininity: her manners were impeccable and she responded to a certain style of masculine gallantry. Heath had a curt manner and made no pretence at gallantry; long before he had any special cause to dislike Margaret Thatcher he was uncomfortable with her type of Tory lady, with her immaculate clothes, pearls, hats and gushing manner. So until she forced herself on his attention he barely noticed her. Maudling, by contrast, was the sort of man she liked – though her regard was not reciprocated. She had got to know him as MP for Barnet, the neighbouring constituency to Finchley and part of the same Borough. 'I liked his combination of laid-back charm and acute intellect.'[15] Ten years later, when she won the leadership, she still had a sufficiently soft spot for Reggie to make him Shadow Foreign Secretary – a choice she quickly regretted. In 1965 he was her initial preference for leader.

It was Keith Joseph who changed her mind. Whereas Maudling, the front runner, complacently did very little canvassing, Heath's supporters mounted a highly professional campaign, run by Peter Walker, targeting each Member through the colleague thought most likely to influence him or her. Joseph was detailed to telephone Mrs Thatcher and persuade her that Heath's chilly determination was a better bet than Maudling's easy-going charm. 'Ted', he told her, 'has a passion to get Britain right.'[16] She was persuaded, and immediately set about persuading others.

It is significant that neither of them thought seriously of voting for Enoch Powell, though he threw his hat into the ring with the backing of a handful of future Thatcherites like Nicholas Ridley and John Biffen. Both Joseph and Mrs Thatcher were increasingly influenced by Powell's advocacy of free-market ideas over the next few years. But in 1965 Powell was seen as an eccentric maverick and they were practical politicians. Insofar as Powell's free-market agenda was an issue in the leadership contest – which was presented almost entirely as a choice between contrasting personalities – Heath's abrasive energy seemed likely to embrace as much of it as was politically realistic. It was Heath, after all, who had abolished Resale Price Maintenance in 1964. What attracted Mrs Thatcher to Heath's standard – and kept her loyal for nine years, despite a personal relationship that never became warm – was respect for his seriousness of purpose, which matched her own. In that sense he was a strong leader. It was only when she came to reject the direction in which he was leading that she turned against him.

Heath won only narrowly – 150 votes to 133, with fifteen for Powell – so every switched vote counted. Writing in the *Finchley Press* a few days later Mrs Thatcher was judiciously even-handed. First she paid tribute to Home's integrity and selflessness: 'He knew nothing of cynicism nor of artifice.' Then she praised both Heath and Maudling: 'The decision was a difficult one to make, for both are good.' Doubtless remembering that the *Finchley Press* circulated in Maudling's constituency as well as her own, she did not say how she had resolved it; but she concluded by endorsing the victor, in the tones of a housemistress welcoming a new head: 'We are all now working hard and happily under Edward Heath. He will be a hard taskmaster, but will only drive others as hard as he drives himself.'[17]

Though elected as a new broom, Heath initially felt obliged, with an election possible at any moment, to retain all his predecessor's Shadow Cabinet. But in October he did reshuffle his front bench. Margaret Thatcher was delighted to be switched at last from Pensions and National Insurance (which she had been doing in and out of office for four years) to Housing and Land. First, it was an *attacking* brief, with a juicy target in Labour's new Land Commission, ripe for her forensic attention. Second, it reunited her with Boyd-Carpenter, who was now shadowing Housing. Third, the brief included a subject with which she was to be closely – and ultimately fatally – involved for the rest of her career: the rates. Her first task, before Parliament even returned that autumn, was to reply to a debate on the reform of the rating system at the party conference in Brighton.

Typically she began by refuting the idea that rating was a dry subject: 'In fact it is one full of controversy and feeling.' She could have said that again twenty-five years later. Already the rates were deeply unpopular among the Tory rank and file. Earlier in the year she wrote in the *Finchley Press* that she received more letters on this than on any other subject.[18] In her Conference speech she gave her backing to some kind of rebate scheme to relieve individual hardship. Significantly, however, she resisted calls to shift more of the burden of local spending on to general taxation. 'The taxpayer', she reminded representatives, 'already foots a far larger proportion of the bill for local expenditure than does the ratepayer.' It was important to keep a sufficient proportion of local expenditure with the local authorities, 'otherwise the whole basis of local government is undermined for good and all'.

The task of a local councillor who was not responsible for rating would be absolutely marvellous. He could demand everything, the sky would be the limit, and he could blame the Government always if he did not get it. It would cease to be local government. It would cease to have any semblance of responsibility whatever.

Specifically she rejected the idea of transferring the whole cost of education to the Exchequer, though she thought some properly national services like teacher training might be transferred. She announced plans to limit the rate burden to 3.5 per cent of GNP, but rejected alternative methods of raising local revenue, including local income tax, as impractical. 'It is very easy', she warned prophetically, 'to put down a motion criticising a system and calling for reform. It is very difficult to find a method of reform which would result in less hardship than the system we already have. We must not fall into the error of having change for the sake of change.'[19] This was exactly the conclusion successive Environment Secretaries came to after repeated re-examinations of the problem – until 1985.

Any rate rebate scheme, she later insisted in the Commons, should be simple, comprehensible and *fair*. Labour's, she maintained, was none of these.[20] In the same vein she attacked Labour's proposed 'betterment levy' on increased land values: 'It used to be said that a tax should be certain in its incidence, cheap to collect and simple.' Critics of the Community Charge might have reminded her of these principles twenty years later. Back in the autumn of 1965, however, the junior Opposition spokeswoman on housing and land was on the warpath. In the debate on the Address on 11 November she laid into Fred Willey's ill-conceived Land Commission – intended to control the price of development land – in her best schoolmistress style. After twelve months in office, she declared, she would have been ashamed to publish a White Paper so lacking in essential detail.

This is the kind of thing which I would have gone into thoroughly before I dared to come to this House, and I would have expected anyone who comes here with a proposal to put on a tax to have gone into it thoroughly. If the right hon. Gentleman has not, he does not know his job. I feel very strongly about this.[21]

Crossman defended Willey on the ground that he had been ill; but his diaries admit that Mrs Thatcher's criticism of the whole botched project was fully justified.[22] By the time the Land Commission was finally established in January 1967 she had moved on to another brief. But she wrote a characteristic article in the *Daily Express* condemning its impact on ordinary homeowners. The article itself was an over-detailed series of hypothetical examples. But the *Express* headline – 'Devastating: This Tax on Home and Garden', over a picture of suburban semis allegedly threatened by socialism – transformed it into an early example of the sort of middle-class populism she was in due course to make her own.[23]

Mrs Thatcher shadowed housing and land for less than six months. Much as she relished demolishing Labour incompetence, she still found this 'a depressing time'. [24] Like other Conservative spokesmen, she railed at Labour's broken promises, higher taxes ('The first lesson of socialism is increased taxation . . . and it is the middle income group who have to pay most') and slippery 'doubletalk'.[25] But Wilson was only biding his time before calling a second election which the Tories, even with a new leader, had no hope of winning. In Finchley Mrs Thatcher did her best to project enthusiasm for Heath in the terms Keith Joseph had used to her. He was, she told her adoption meeting on 10 March, 'a man of decision and used to command – a man who has a passion to get Britain right, a fitting leader for Britain now'.[26] But privately she was critical of the Tory manifesto, a list of 131 detailed promises culled from the various policy groups which had been beavering away since 1964, not connected to a single theme. Indeed she was publicly critical. 'I dislike making promises at election time,' she told a constituency meeting. 'It is the negation of democracy if we have to bribe the electorate.'[27] She believed in offering the electorate a clear choice between opposed ideologies. Her own election address led on the fundamental theme that every action of the Labour Government increased the power of the state over the citizen. Conservative philosophy was the opposite: 'The State was made for Man, not Man for the State.'[28]

Such fundamentalist flourishes apart, however, the greatest interest of her 1966 campaign is the emphasis she laid on Europe. 'Europe', she declared on 18 March, 'is the cornerstone of our campaign.' It was only three years since de Gaulle's veto, and the General was still in power in France. Nevertheless, she wrote in the *Finchley Press*:

A Conservative Government would like to enter Europe at the first favourable opportunity. Many of the obstacles which were present in 1963 have now been mitigated or have disappeared. Whatever we do Europe will be strong economically and influential politically. We should be taking a lead in fashioning her policies, and we should enable our exports to benefit from her vast markets.[29]

'Together', she ventured, 'I believe we could form a block with as much power as the USA or Russia.'[30]

She had not yet visited the United States, and was not yet in thrall to the Special Relationship. Like her leader, she still saw the restoration of British 'greatness' in a European, not an Atlantic, context. 'We should take the *initiative* in foreign affairs', she declared in her address, 'and not merely follow our American friends.'[31] This is a somewhat mysterious statement. As a good Cold Warrior, Mrs Thatcher surely cannot have been echoing left-wing criticism of Wilson's inability to distance Britain from the Vietnam War? Yet it is hard to see what else she could have been referring to. Perhaps she had been listening to Enoch Powell.

For the rest she followed the party line by promising reform of industrial relations law, the preservation of good grammar schools and the encouragement of home-ownership – the last with a hint of Thatcherite bravado: 'These are fresh fields to conquer.'[32] She was of course now perfectly safe in Finchley, even in a Labour year. The Liberal tide had ebbed, though their new candidate, Frank Davis, was the former leader of Finchley council who had won local fame by running a fleet of private buses in competition with London Transport. (John Pardoe had gone off to fight, and win, North Cornwall.) Labour's candidate, Yvonne Sieve, was a part-time economics lecturer (and young mother) who concentrated her campaign on social issues. Mrs Thatcher's election address stressed her growing national profile, but added:

It is in Finchley and Friern Barnet that Mrs Thatcher is best known, where her energy, charm and sympathy have won her popular acclaim. Her work on behalf of constituents who have needed her has been enormous. She has fought injustice, smoothed the way through officialdom and assisted all who have approached her by interview and correspondence.[33]

The result was never in doubt. Though her vote actually fell slightly, Mrs Thatcher was one of only three Tories to increase her majority, with Labour pushing the Liberals back into third place:

Mrs M. Thatcher (Conservative)	23,968
Mrs Y. Sieve (Labour)	14,504
F. Davis (Liberal)	13,070
Conservative majority	9,464

Nationally Labour won a landslide, with a majority of nearly a hundred. The Tories were condemned to another five years of opposition. With the certainty of a long haul ahead, Heath reshuffled his team, taking the chance to drop several of the older hands, like Boyd-Carpenter, Duncan Sandys and Selwyn Lloyd, whom he had inherited from Home. There was some discussion of putting Mrs Thatcher in the Shadow Cabinet. Jim Prior, then Heath's PPS, remembers suggesting her as the statutory woman.

> There was a long silence. 'Yes,' he said. 'Willie [Whitelaw, the Chief Whip] agrees she's much the most able, but he says once she's there we'll never be able to get rid of her. So we both think it's got to be Mervyn Pike.'[34]

Actually the idea of a statutory woman was a new one. There had not been a woman in a Tory Cabinet since Florence Horsburgh in 1954, nor in the Shadow Cabinet since the party went into opposition. But Wilson had included Barbara Castle in his first Cabinet in 1964 and promoted her the following year. If the Tories had to be seen to follow suit, Margaret Thatcher was a more obvious counterpart to Mrs Castle than the much gentler Mervyn Pike. Whitelaw's preference for keeping Mrs Thatcher down for a little longer suggests that she was already seen as an uncomfortable colleague. Iain Macleod, however, now Shadow Chancellor, had spotted her potential and, it is said, specifically asked for her in his shadow Treasury team. 'This one is different,' he is reported to have told Nigel Fisher. 'Quite exceptionally able, a first-class brain.'[35]

Some doubt is cast on this story by the fact that Fisher failed to mention Mrs Thatcher in his 1973 biography of Macleod, while listing five other members of his team who became ministers in 1970.[36] Robert Shepherd's more recent biography, however, cites Barney Hayhoe (then a member of the Research Department) recalling Macleod telling Heath: 'Let me have Margaret Thatcher in my team.'[37] Heath agreed. She became Treasury and Economic Affairs spokeswoman, outside the Shadow Cabinet but in some respects better placed to make a mark than she would have been inside it.

It is not surprising that Macleod should have wanted her. Though politically very different, they had in common a zest for debate and a talent for destructive opposition. Mrs Thatcher admired Macleod's uncompromising aggression, his gift for the withering phrase and – perhaps more surprisingly – his political sense. 'Iain always got the politics of any problem right,' she recalled many years later.

He had an instinct for how the ordinary person would react to situations and proposals. He would look at a budget in political terms first and establish what the consequences would be of a certain course of action. He believed you had to bring human nature into your calculations. If you did not get it right politically, the economics would then turn out to be wrong.[38]

Macleod was both a deeply humane and a deeply cynical politician – not an obvious hero for a crusading moralist like Margaret Thatcher. But Macleod's ambivalence has exerted an extraordinary posthumous fascination over Tories of all shades, from One Nation liberals like Ian Gilmour and Chris Patten to free-marketeers like Norman Tebbit and John Redwood. Though the content of her politics increasingly diverged from his, Mrs Thatcher learned a lot from Macleod's tactical opportunism: with all her strong convictions she became by the 1980s an extremely skilful politician – a rare combination which accounts for much of her success. Like Macleod, she understood the importance of getting the politics of any situation right.

She also learned some of the skills of leadership from the way Macleod ran his Treasury team, fighting Callaghan's 1966 and 1967 Finance Bills line by line on the floor of the House.

We met every morning, we looked at the days following and we decided who was in charge of amendments, who was going to move them, what advice we needed. And it was exciting, and you were happy to be totally dedicated to this immediate task.

This was one of the very few periods in Mrs Thatcher's career when she operated as a team player, contributing her own particular expertise as a tax lawyer to a delegated effort. She clearly found it a liberating experience. When her own time came to lead she was not so good at delegating; yet she copied much of Macleod's method of working.

> He worked very much by discussing [his ideas] with a group of people who discussed freely, and then he would gather up the views and draw conclusions from them . . . He did it far more that way than by sitting down with a damp towel round his head . . . I have a good deal of sympathy with that and maybe I learned a lot from him, being one of the younger members in that group. I did learn that you frequently get the ideas from the interplay of an idea with the personality and not just by reading in a personless atmosphere . . . That was one of my very vivid impressions of Iain, this clarity of expression and being able therefore to pick out the wheat from the chaff . . . You have got the basic idea and you eliminated the irrelevant matter.[39]

Mrs Thatcher certainly enjoyed testing arguments by uninhibited discussion; but she also burned a lot of midnight oil. She reckoned to win arguments by the thoroughness of her homework; and never was this more awesomely demonstrated than in her first speech on Treasury matters on the third day of the Budget debate in May 1966, when she stunned the House by announcing that she had read every Budget speech since 1946. No one doubted that she had.[40] She ran rings round the Chief Secretary to the Treasury, Jack Diamond, suggesting that he did not understand his own speech and worsting him decisively when he failed to grasp the impact of Selective Employment Tax on working women like herself who paid for child care. 'The hon. Lady must know', he protested, 'that this is a tax on employers.' 'Precisely,' she shot back. 'These women are employers. Clearly the Front Bench have not even thought of this.'

The heart of her speech was a wholesale demolition of the philosophy and practice of Selective Employment Tax (SET), which she ridiculed as an administrative absurdity worthy of Gilbert and Sullivan. The idea was to penalise service industries in order to favour manufacturing; all businesses paid it, then those deemed 'productive' could apply for a refund. 'This is absolute nonsense,' she scoffed. 'I really think the right hon. Gentleman needs a woman at the Treasury. This is just sheer stupidity. If my chief had come to me and put up a cock-eyed scheme like that, I should have asked him if he was feeling all right.'[41]

It was a sign of her growing confidence that she was willing to use her femininity in this way as a stick to beat the Government with. *The Times* developed the picture of a battling woman lambasting male stupidity:

> With her blonde curls a constant bobbing reminder of the prospective increase in hairdressing charges she attacked the whole structure of the tax with incisive feminine logic. Mr Diamond and Mr Callaghan at his side soon found themselves assaulted with every female weapon short of the rolling pin . . .
>
> By this time she was in full stride, her impeccable accent beginning to hammer on Labour ears like some devilish Roedean water torture.[42]

The point is that such reports no longer merely patronised her femininity but presented it – even if still in sexist terms (the blonde curls, feminine logic and the rolling pin) – as a source of strength. No more did every succeeding speaker refer routinely to her 'charm'. On the contrary Niall McDermott, replying to this speech, acknowledged that 'we have learned to respect the hon. Lady's ability and calibre'.[43] And it must have been after this performance that Macleod 'adjourned to the bar with Angus Maude . . . and over a drink confided: "After listening to Margaret's speech tonight it no longer seems absurd to think that there might one day be a woman Prime Minister." '[44] 'I have heard many excellent speeches from women Ministers and Members from the front and back benches of the House of Commons,' he wrote in the *Daily Mail*, 'but cannot recall another in a major debate that was described as a triumph.'[45]

Mrs Thatcher's contributions to the Tories' guerrilla war against the 1966 Finance Bill, as recorded by *Hansard*, convey the strong impression of a woman in full command of her brief and of the House, flexing her parliamentary muscles with increasing assurance and evident enjoyment, at home equally with the detail and the principle of taxation, ticking off Labour ministers for their failures of homework or deriding their lack of understanding. Of course Macleod's thirteen-strong team – which also included Patrick Jenkin, Terence Higgins and John Nott – could make little headway in the face of Labour's huge majority; but Macleod was a great believer in keeping ministers on the hop, dividing the House frequently to keep up Conservative morale, and here again Mrs Thatcher was an apt pupil, unwilling to let any expenditure of public money go unscrutinised. It is worth remembering that twenty years before she herself enjoyed a three-figure majority in the 1980s she had experienced being on the wrong side of such a majority in the 1960s. Unfortunately for parliamentary democracy, the demoralised Labour party of the eighties did not give her Government anything like the rough ride she and Macleod gave Callaghan in the sixties.

In the end, contrary to normal practice, they even divided against the Third Reading at the end of July. Mrs Thatcher took a final swipe at SET. Under 'this particular poll tax', as she had earlier called it[46] (deeming it a poll tax because it used the National Insurance system as the basis of collection, ignoring equity and differing social circumstances), £1,130 million was to be collected and £890 returned. 'As a means of collecting about £240 million of revenue', she mocked, 'with no contribution to greater productivity, this is an idiotic way of proceeding.' The Budget as a whole was 'a disastrous Budget', combining 'financial misjudgement and administrative lunacy . . . a fitting monument to an incompetent Government'.[47]

The Government's management of the economy was by now an easy target. Ever since taking office Wilson had set his face against devaluation. That month continuing pressure on the pound, exacerbated by a seamen's strike, forced Callaghan to impose a draconian package of deflationary measures including a 10 per cent increase in purchase tax, a £50 holiday travel allowance and a wage freeze. Labour's honeymoon – so overwhelmingly renewed just four months earlier – was over: the Government plumbed depths of unpopularity previously unimagined. Mrs Thatcher was in the right job at the right time. In view of her subsequent duel with Callaghan ten years later, when he was Prime Minister and she Leader of the Opposition, there is interest in what she wrote about him in an end of session round-up for the *Finchley Press*. She was contemptuous of George Brown, rewarded for the shambles of the Department of Economic Affairs by promotion to the Foreign Office. She had only marginally more respect for Callaghan:

> James Callaghan is a good talker. He usually makes a competent debating speech, but for too long people have confused the ability to make a good speech with the ability to take the right decisions and carry them out. Mr Callaghan can put it across, but in my view, and events have borne this out, his ability falls far short of what is needed to be Chancellor of the Exchequer.

'You can't say he has lost control of the situation,' she concluded scornfully. 'He never had it.'[48]*

At the party conference in Blackpool in October Mrs Thatcher had the opportunity of replying to a debate on taxation. She spent nine hours preparing her speech, and was rewarded with her 'first real conference success'.[50] Not since the unknown Patricia Hornsby-Smith in 1946, in Peterborough's memory, had a woman scored such a triumph: 'Mrs Thatcher is not unknown, but her qualities surprised the delegates yesterday. Thoroughly relaxed, she banged out sentences with the elusive rhythm some of her peers find it so hard to achieve.'[51] Macleod, writing a few days later in the *Daily Mail*, judged her speech (following her Finance Bill success in May) 'the second half of a magnificent double';[52] while the still pre-Murdoch, Labour-supporting *Sun* hailed a new star under the headline, 'A Fiery Blonde Warns of the Road to Ruin': 'Mrs Margaret Thatcher, the pretty blonde MP for Finchley, got a standing ovation for one of those magnificent fire-in-the-belly speeches which are heard too seldom.'[53]

In truth most of her speech was pretty dull, displaying her technical mastery of tax law. But she had learned how to please a Tory audience, claiming with what even she admits was 'more than a touch of hyperbole' that SET constituted 'a step not merely towards Socialism but towards Communism'. (Bernard Levin wrote scornfully in the *Daily Mail* that such rhetoric debased 'politics and language alike', revealing 'only the peculiar process that passes for thinking in the minds of people like Mrs Thatcher and those who applauded her'.)[54] The high point of the speech, however, came when she was berating Callaghan for his record of increasing taxes in every budget since 1964, climaxing in the ringing cry: 'This chap Callaghan must go!'[55] Patrick Jenkin – who had known her in chambers in the 1950s – remembers this vividly as the first time he heard the authentic Thatcher voice and style. Thirty years later he recalled her words with the same *frisson* he felt at the time.[56]

Having put down this marker for the future, however, Mrs Thatcher had a fairly quiet next twelve months, illumined by occasional flashes which reveal the hardening of her convictions. Back in the Commons in October she condemned the Government's prices and incomes policy in fundamentalist terms as both

---

* The only senior Labour minister she had any time for was the unflashy Michael Stewart, whom she judged 'steady and reliable . . . the sort of person who would do well at any job he was given' – rather like herself. She thought shuffling him from the Foreign Office to make way for Brown 'an absurd way to run a Government'.[49]

bureaucratic and economically futile: she was quite clear that it was impossible to fix prices, and the attempt to do so was 'the first step on the journey to coercion'. At the same time she had fun teasing Crossman, now Leader of the House, for his cheerful self-contradictions.[57] Crossman in his diary gave her full marks for 'a good, tough professional speech'.[58] She spent much of the following session pointing out anomalies and injustices in the application of the legislation. Fighting another Finance Bill over the spring and summer of 1967, her main fire was as usual directed to taxation, and particularly surtax, several times enunciating what became known two decades later as the 'trickledown' theory. 'If the Government were more concerned to further the remarkable people', she declared in the Budget debate, 'the ordinary people would do very much better.'[59] Replying in June to the Labour left-winger Eric Heffer, who told her that in worrying about the 'brain drain' of talent to the USA she was talking about very few individuals, she agreed, but added:

> I say that the future of people in industry depends tremendously on the small group of people who can create more wealth, and they are far more valuable to the ordinary working person than those of us who work here, including the right hon. Gentleman, who cannot.[60]

That year she herself paid her first visit to the United States. It was a revelation to her. In her forty-two years she had scarcely been out of Britain before, apart from her honeymoon and, since 1962, her annual skiing holiday. Ever since the war she had been well disposed towards America as the arsenal of democracy and Britain's great English-speaking ally in the cause of Freedom. But the potential love affair had not been consummated until now. In the spring of 1967 she went on an American government 'leadership programme' designed to show rising young British politicians the American way of life; for six weeks she was whisked all round the country. 'The excitement which I felt', she wrote in her memoirs, 'has never really subsided. At each stopover I was met and accommodated by friendly, open, generous people who took me into their homes and lives and showed me their cities and townships with evident pride.' Typically her theoretical awareness of the 'brain drain' was brought into focus by meeting a former constituent from Finchley who had fled 'over-regulated, high-taxed Britain' to become a space scientist with NASA.[61] Two years later she went back for a four-week speaking tour under the auspices of the English Speaking Union. Henceforth

America became for her the model of an enterprise economy and a free society: not only American business practice, but American private health care, American penal policy and American business sponsorship of the arts were the examples she encouraged her ministers to study in the eighties.

After eighteen months working with Macleod she got her reward in October 1967. By her performances in the House Mrs Thatcher had certainly earned promotion to the Shadow Cabinet; but still she only gained it when she did because Mervyn Pike stepped down on grounds of health. She now had no rival as the statutory woman. Significantly, however, Heath did not simply give her Miss Pike's social services portfolio – which would have been a traditionally 'feminine' responsibility. He brought in Robin Balniel to do that job and set Mrs Thatcher to shadow the Ministry of Power, replacing Keith Joseph who switched to Trade. Power – comprising coal, nuclear energy, electricity and the new prospect of North Sea gas – was an unmistakably 'masculine' brief. More important than the portfolio, however, admission to the Shadow Cabinet marked Mrs Thatcher's arrival at the top table, just eight years after entering Parliament. As Whitelaw had foreseen, she would not easily be got rid of now. In less than another eight years, in fact, she had toppled Heath and leapfrogged over Whitelaw to seize the leadership.

Such an outcome was unimaginable in 1967. Of course this was mainly because she was a woman, and the notion of a woman Prime Minister still belonged to the realms of futuristic fantasy. In March the *Sunday Times* ran a book on future leaders. Mrs Thatcher – 'Not so dumb blonde. Exceptionally able but particularly on questions of cash. Wins hearts of Conference delegates as well as MPs' – was priced at 1000–1, the back marker in a field led by Peter Walker (10–1) and Jim Prior (33–1). On the Labour side Shirley Williams was 500–1 behind people like Richard Marsh (5–1), Bill Rodgers and Roy Hattersley (10–1).[62] Both Mrs Thatcher and Mrs Williams were clearly excluded from serious consideration; but the fact that Mrs Thatcher was reckoned even more improbable than Mrs Williams reflects the fact that while she was admired – after a fashion – she was assumed to be limited. She was alarmingly industrious, a good tax lawyer who could get up a technical brief, but essentially she was a swot. Edward du Cann told her constituency Association in 1969 that she worked harder than anyone else in the Shadow Cabinet.[63] Paul Channon accompanied her on a trip to Moscow the same year and remembers her rushing around ceaselessly looking at nuclear power stations and the metro system, never drawing breath.[64] Chris Patten, then in the Research Department, recalls 'an intense blonde' with a voice 'like a friendly dentist's drill' who was always demanding detailed and specific briefing about aspects of National Insurance or the precise powers given by this or that Government circular.[65] Peter Rawlinson, who was not strictly a member of the Shadow Cabinet before 1970 but attended many of its meetings as shadow Attorney-General, claims to have found her 'rather agreeable and in those days unspoilt, even if demonstrably ambitious and strangely insensitive'. She talked too much. 'How she talked! . . . I believe that she honestly did not realise how irritating she was.'[66] A hint of this irritation broke surface in 1968, when the *Sunday Express* Crossbencher column reported colleagues coming away from meetings complaining that she *never* stopped arguing.[67]

Her uncomfortableness as a colleague was vividly captured by Woodrow Wyatt, writing in the *Sunday Mirror* in December 1969. Wyatt was still a Labour MP, but he had a lot of Tory friends.

> She is more of a niggler than a debater. Anti-feminists may feel that she is the sort of thing that happens if you allow women to go into politics. Her air of bossiness, her aptitude for interfering, can be very tiresome and irritating to easy-going men who do not always want to be kept up to scratch, particularly by a female. It confirms their suspicion that women prefer petty points to the broad view . . . It is hard to imagine anyone daring to say anything frivolous to her.[68]

What it came down to was that she was not a member of the club. In British public life it is not done to be seen to work too hard: 'effortless superiority' was the ideal which men like du Cann, Channon, Patten and Rawlinson admired. Mrs Thatcher, despite having been to Oxford, was not a gentleman: she took the business of politics altogether too seriously, and she did not always know how to behave. A senior Treasury official serving in Washington when she visited the United States in 1967 was horrified by the way she lectured the Director of the IMF, Pierre-Paul Schweitzer – a languid, cigarette-smoking French intellectual of a type she had probably never encountered before – on subjects he knew far more about than she did – and altogether behaved 'like a bull in a china shop'.[69] A foretaste of her performance as Prime Minister, perhaps, but not the style expected of a junior Opposition spokeswoman.

Lady Thatcher herself has written that she felt marginalised as a member of Heath's Shadow Cabinet. 'For Ted and perhaps others

1. Alfred Roberts soon after his election as Councillor, 1927.
2. Margaret, aged four, and Muriel, aged eight, in 1929.
3. Alfred Roberts' shop fallen on hard times after his retirement.

4. Alfred in his mayoral robes, 1945. with Muriel (*left*), Beatrice and Margaret.

5. Margaret Roberts soon after coming down from Oxford.

6. Research chemist, 1951.

7. At a
Conservative
fête in Dartford
(Note the mono-
grammed hand-
bag).

8. Conviction
politician, 1951.

9, 10, 11. Canvassing in Dartford, 1951.

12. Homework (with Churchill to hand).

13. Three Kent candidates: Patricia Hornsby-Smith (Chislehurst), Edward Heath (Bexley) and Margaret Roberts (Dartford).

14. Denis and Margaret on their wedding day, December 1951.

15. Mother of twins, August 1953.

16. With Carol and Mark soon after her election to Parliament in 1959.

17. The new Parliamentary Secretary for Pensions, 1961.

I was principally there as the "statutory woman" whose main task was to explain what "women" . . . were likely to think and want on troublesome issues.' It was not only that she had no rapport with Heath. She felt that she had 'only three real friends around the table' – Keith Joseph, already an important ally; her old Oxford contemporary Edward Boyle; and Peter Thomas.[70] Her memory betrays her here, since Thomas was not a member of the Shadow Cabinet, having lost his seat in 1966. (He came back as Welsh Secretary and party chairman in 1970.) She also forgets Macleod, who was still Shadow Chancellor. Nevertheless it is clear that she no longer felt – as she had done as Treasury spokesman – part of a team. If initially she talked too much she soon learned to shut up and bide her time. It is striking that she contributed no papers to Shadow Cabinet during the two and a half years she served in it. The Conservative party archive lists papers by most other members, but none from her. Another telling indication of her isolation is that though she attended every working session of the famous Shadow Cabinet weekend at Selsdon Park in January 1970 she was absent from dinner both evenings.[71]

Meanwhile shadowing Power gave her the chance to master another important area of policy. Interviewed by the *Sunday Telegraph* just after her appointment she said it was 'a great surprise'; she was now 'busy genning up on the subject for all she was worth'.[72] It was still the era of cheap imported oil. North Sea gas had recently been discovered, but not yet oil. The Labour Government was running down the coal industry, a policy the Conservatives broadly supported against a good deal of traditional Labour anguish. Altogether Power was another excellent portfolio for her, using her scientific training in handling technical questions of nuclear energy and mineral deposits, but also facing her directly for the first time with the political problem of the nationalised industries. As an extra bonus the Minister she found herself shadowing was Richard Marsh, whom she had known years before when he was an active Young Socialist in Dartford. Marsh, she told the *Sunday Telegraph*, was 'nice, clever – and good-looking'.[73] At the time he was a high-flyer – the *Sunday Times*' favourite for Prime Minister. In the event Wilson moved him sideways to Transport in 1968 and dropped him the following year. He finished up running British Rail.

Just as with Housing and Land two years earlier, Mrs Thatcher's first responsibility after being appointed to Power was to wind up a debate at the party conference. Once again her speech has a prophetic piquancy, since the subject was privatisation – or, as it was then called, denationalisation. She had to answer a succession of grass-roots calls for the next Conservative Government to change the balance between the private and public sectors by denationalising wherever possible. Even from the floor of the Tory conference, however, ideas of what was possible were strictly limited in 1967. The future right-wing MP John Gorst, for instance, who spoke immediately before Mrs Thatcher, dismissed privatising the telephone service as 'impracticable. The price would be astronomical.' While strong on the principle of private enterprise over public he had only general exhortations to offer in place of practical proposals. From the platform, Mrs Thatcher took exactly the same line, stressing the Tories' philosophical objection to nationalisation as an infringement of economic freedom, but proposing no specific candidates for denationalisation, talking only of injecting 'as much competition as possible' into the public sector, before returning to the high ground of individual liberty and ending with a quotation from Churchill. Of course she was speaking for the Shadow Cabinet: her hands were tied by Heath's (and Macleod's) hostility to serious privatisation. In that light one can read her admission that 'we cannot immediately denationalise everything' as a coded hint that she would indeed like to privatise everything in due course. But her short-term emphasis was on the need to stop Labour nationalising any more.[74]

Back at Westminster she was thrown in the deep end again. Her first duty when Parliament returned was to lead the Conservative response to Lord Justice Edmund Davies's report on the Aberfan disaster a year before, when a slag heap engulfed a Welsh village, killing 116 children and 28 adults. The report seriously criticised the National Coal Board and its chairman, the former Labour Cabinet Minister, Lord Robens. Mrs Thatcher had a tricky path to tread between human sympathy and political point-scoring. She writes in her memoirs that she 'held back' from stating explicitly that Robens should have resigned.[75] But privately she was furious with her old boss Richard Wood – a former Minister of Power – who queered her pitch by declaring publicly that Robens was not to blame.[76] In the Commons she strongly criticised Robens for not visiting the scene of the accident – enunciating a doctrine which she certainly made her own practice as Prime Minister.

When tragedy strikes, the person in command should go to the scene as quickly as possible. This may be as a result of my own background of a family company. [Presumably she meant Atlas Preservatives.] When anything happens, the person who is the head of it goes immediately . . . He is responsible for the whole outfit, and he must go . . . to show people that he is there to see what is going on and to extend sympathy.

More than that: the tribunal exposed 'bungling ineptitude' by the NCB and the responsibility rested at the top. 'I despise any organisation or person who attempts to pass the buck further down the line.' She strongly implied that Robens should have resigned, but noted that this principle 'does not always seem to attach to resignations these days'. In fact she was unfair on both counts. Marsh revealed that Robens had offered his resignation, but that he had refused it. Moreover Robens had deliberately decided not to visit Aberfan until several days after the accident, judging that he would only have been in the way of the emergency services. It remains a moot point whether visits to the scenes of disasters by members of the Royal Family, ministers or, indeed, the Prime Minister are more of a distraction than a comfort.

Finally, though the tragedy was supposed to have nothing to do with party politics, Mrs Thatcher could not resist a political dig at the unaccountability of nationalised industries.

I make this comment. It is a jolly sight easier to exercise control in private industry. For instance it would be easier to tip [Lord Eccles] off Courtaulds than it seems to be to exercise control over the National Coal Board. This, surely, is wrong.[77]

Shadowing Power, in fact, was all about the nationalised industries. Every speech, every utterance, that Mrs Thatcher made during the year that she held this portfolio – and the following year when she was switched to Transport – shows her developing ever more clearly the conviction that public ownership was economically, politically and morally wrong. Though she never cited him, all the signs are that she had been reading – or rereading – Hayek, whose two-volume elaboration of *The Road to Serfdom*, *The Constitution of Liberty*, was published in 1960. She was certainly beginning to come under the influence of the independent free-market think-tank, the Institute of Economic Affairs (IEA), run by Arthur Seldon and Ralph Harris. But already she had the gift of putting their arguments into clear unacademic language of her own. On one hand she delighted in demonstrating that public ownership was inefficient, on the other that it was destructive of individual freedom. In her party conference speech she took the high ground, with her own confident simplification of British history:

It is good to recall how our freedom has been gained in this country – not by great abstract campaigns but through the objections of ordinary men and women to having their money taken from them by the State. In the early days people banded together and said to the Government, 'You shall not take our money before you have redressed our grievances.' It was their money . . . which was the source of their independence against the Government.

Not only public ownership, she asserted, but all public spending reduced freedom. Parliament's historic function was not to spend money, but to stop the Government spending it. 'Once Parliament wants to spend more . . . our liberties are at the same time curtailed.' Nationalisation, far from giving 'power to the people', actually transferred ever more power to the state.[78]

Her other refrain was that Governments were simply not competent to make economic judgements. In her second Commons speech as a member of the Shadow Cabinet, winding up the second day's debate on the Queen's Speech, she made the point with characteristic directness:

Civil servants have not got the expertise at their disposal which a merchant bank has. If they had such expertise they would probably be working very successfully for a merchant bank. If a project is a good one the chances are that some merchant bank or other will support it.

In other words – as she was inclined to tell Permanent Secretaries to their face twenty years later – civil servants if they were any good would not be civil servants at all. Still less did she believe that ministers were competent – though she could not resist contradicting this message with a hubristic little boast. Complex projects, she told Peter Shore, required 'expertise which the Minister has not got and which I have not got – though I am probably nearer to having it, coming from a family of professional managers'. Once again she presumably meant Denis's family, though it was pushing it to claim that she had acquired management skills by marriage.[79]

She was most specific about coal, which fell within her brief. In several speeches on Marsh's Coal Industry Bill she spoke scathingly of the futility of continuing to send men down the pits 'in conditions in which there will certainly be some deaths and much danger, to dig up coal that no one wants to buy'. She accepted that running down the industry involved an obligation on the Government to help redundant miners but shed no tears for the loss of mining jobs. She would not send her son down the pit, and she wondered how many NUM officials would wish to send theirs.[80] Seventeen years before her showdown with Arthur Scargill, Mrs Thatcher dismissed mining as 'a sacred cow'[81] and looked forward to a very different future for coal:

> Morale will be raised and the right people recruited at managerial level only when the industry has finished its contraction and is once again competitive on its own unsubsidised merits. At that point it can expand.[82]

It is sometimes suggested that Mrs Thatcher was a late convert to the counter-revolution that was building on the Tory right in the late 1960s. *Hansard* clearly shows that this was not the case. Her speeches are shot through with assumptions and asides which reveal that her essential philosophy was already fully-formed. She was not widely identified as a ground-breaking ideologue because she was not an intellectual, like Keith Joseph, painfully searching for solutions, nor an eager policy beaver like Geoffrey Howe, a prolific author of radical pamphlets. Mrs Thatcher dealt in simple convictions which most Conservatives and most political commentators regarded as hopelessly unsophisticated. The IEA, however, certainly counted her on their side of the faultline that was beginning to divide the Tory party. Writing in the theoretical *Swinton Journal* in 1968, Arthur Seldon drew attention to the widening gulf between the centrist approach (which he identified with Maudling, Boyle and Boyd-Carpenter) and the very different views of 'Powell, Joseph, Margaret Thatcher, Maude, Macmillan (the Younger), Howe, Biffen, Braine, Jenkin and others who offer a distinctive philosophy and distinctive principles'.[83] Powell, Macmillan and Braine excepted, this list constitutes, as John Ramsden has written, 'a remarkable prefiguring of the post-1975 Party leadership'.[84] It is particularly noteworthy that Mrs Thatcher is placed third after Powell and Joseph, though this may simply reflect her seniority as a member of the Shadow Cabinet. Nevertheless the following year Seldon evidently had doubts about her. In October 1969 he wrote to Howe: 'May we hope for something better from Margaret? She said one day here [at the IEA] that she was one of a small group of Tory politicians like Enoch, Keith and you who saw the value of the market in economic affairs.'[85]

Howe's reply was perceptive, shrewdly discerning – as few others did at this time – the potential that was to transform British politics

over the next two decades. 'I am not at all sure about Margaret,' he
wrote.

> Many of her economic prejudices are certainly sound. But she is
> inclined to be rather too dogmatic for my liking on sensitive
> matters like education [she had just become shadow Education
> Secretary] and might actually retard the case by oversimplification.
> We should certainly be able to hope for something better from
> her – but I suspect that she will need to be exposed to the
> humanising side of your character as much as to the pure welfare
> market monger. There is much scope for her to be influenced
> between triumph and disaster.[86]

Uncertainty over her position arose because while her instincts –
or 'prejudices' as Howe called them – were clear, she took very little
part in policy-making. She writes in her memoirs that while
shadowing Power, 'my main interest was in trying to find a
framework for privatisation of electricity generation'. To this end she
visited power stations 'and sought all the advice I could from
business contacts' – which makes it sound a strangely solitary
initiative. It turned out to be 'a fruitless enterprise . . . I had not
come up with what I considered acceptable answers by the time my
portfolio was changed again' in October 1968.[87]

There *was* a Power policy group, but as she wrote to Edward
Boyle (who was in charge of the policy-making exercise) soon after
taking it over, she was not impressed by its membership. 'Frankly it
is not high-powered enough and having been carefully through all
its deliberations, I feel it has reached a bit of a stalemate.' She wanted
to add one or two new people, including Nicholas Ridley and John
Peyton. 'Our problem is that most of those who know the inside
story are employed by one or other of the Nationalised industries.'[88]
Her frustration is palpable; but she was not yet willing to rock the
boat. Nick Ridley chaired another group on the nationalised
industries which did come up with a recommendation for wholesale
privatisation, as advocated by Powell. But Heath and Macleod
thought the ownership of industry irrelevant and feared that any
whisper of denationalisation would lose votes. Mrs Thatcher was a
member of the Economic Policy committee which considered and
rejected Ridley's report in February 1968. She did not demur.[89]

That autumn she was invited to give the annual Conservative
Political Centre (CPC) lecture at the party conference. This was a

considerable honour: previous lecturers had been recognised party thinkers like Butler, Boyle and Joseph. Mrs Thatcher, the *Times* diarist noted, was being offered 'an opportunity much coveted by the party's intellectuals through the years – and certainly the best chance a high-flying Tory politician ever gets to influence party thinking on a major theme'.

> She is a blonde bluestocking of great charm, and not only Tories in the House think she has a better brain, though less demagogic skill than Barbara Castle, to whom she is the Tory party's answer.[90]

According to the *Daily Mirror*, Mrs Thatcher was originally invited to mark the fiftieth anniversary of women winning the vote. 'But she wouldn't have any of that feminist stuff.'[91] She took instead the broad title 'What's Wrong with Politics?' Because it turned out to be her only general statement of her political philosophy before she unexpectedly became a candidate for the leadership in 1975, her lecture has been closely studied and widely reprinted, read with hindsight as a complete blueprint of Thatcherism. It is true that there is nothing in it which she would have retracted twenty years later, and plenty that shows the consistency of her thinking. Yet at the same time she said little that anyone in 1968 thought in the least remarkable. The Tory party was in a considerable ferment in the summer of 1968, as grass-roots loathing of the Government combined with mounting criticism of Heath's leadership to fuel demand for a sharper, more distinctive Conservatism. Mrs Thatcher's lecture did dimly reflect this rising tide. Instead of nailing her colours boldly to the Powellite mast, however, she offered an uncharacteristically woolly, largely conventional Tory critique of the growth of government. Concern about the size, complexity and facelessness of modern government was a commonplace right across the political spectrum in the sixties. The New Left warned of 'alienation' and demanded more 'participation'. The right blamed socialism and talked vaguely of 'getting government off people's backs' and 'rolling back' the state. Mrs Thatcher's CPC lecture was just another Shadow Cabinet expression of this line – padded with some oddly naive banalities and altogether much less strikingly expressed than many of her Commons speeches. Such press coverage as the lecture received was typified by the *Guardian*'s headline: 'Time to reassert right to privacy'.[92]

The fact is that it would have been imprudent for an ambitious young frontbencher, only recently appointed to the Shadow Cabinet, to have come out openly as a Powellite in October 1968.

Only six months earlier Powell had been sacked from the Shadow Cabinet for making his notorious 'River Tiber' speech calling for a halt to coloured immigration and the assisted repatriation of immigrants. This speech transformed him overnight from a cranky economic theorist into a national figure with a huge popular following, a hate-figure to the left and a looming challenge to Heath's leadership. Mrs Thatcher was never close to Powell in the few months they sat together in the Shadow Cabinet: Powell was an explicitly masculine politician who frankly deplored the intrusion of women into politics. But she was already interested in his economic ideas; she also 'strongly sympathised' with his argument about immigration. When Heath consulted all his colleagues before dismissing Powell her advice was that he should stay his hand; she was unaware that at least three other senior members (Boyle, Macleod and Hailsham) would have resigned if Powell was not sacked. She regretted that Powell's new notoriety henceforth overshadowed his economic ideas, allowing opponents to tar free-market thinking with the same brush as either right-wing extremism or crackpot nostalgia, or both at once.[93]

That autumn, in the run-up to the party conference – just when she was writing her lecture – Heath made a speech in Scotland firmly repudiating those Tories – Edward du Cann was the latest offender – who were attracted by the seductive Powellite prescription of rolling back the state. 'That', he declared, 'though a century out of date, would certainly be a distinctive, different policy.'

> But it would not be a Conservative policy and it would not provide a Conservative alternative. For better or worse the central Government is already responsible, in some way or another, for nearly half the activities of Britain. It is by far the biggest spender and the biggest employer.[94]

That was precisely what Powell, the IEA and, in her heart, Mrs Thatcher, wanted to reverse. Most practical Conservatives, however, though they might pay lip-service to the idea of some marginal denationalisation, took it for granted that a large public sector was a fact of life. *The Times* – edited since 1967 by William Rees-Mogg – applauded Heath's speech as 'plain common sense':

> The crux of the dispute lies between those who believe that modern Conservatism should involve the use of the resources of the State in order to strengthen the opportunities of individual life and those who believe that the Government should in some

almost inconceivable way withdraw itself from a large part of national life.

Heath, this editorial confidently concluded, understood the modern world. 'His critics seem to resent the modern world and refuse therefore to use the most necessary means to solve its problems.'[95]

It was in the context of this overwhelming orthodoxy that Mrs Thatcher spoke at Blackpool. The same week, just up the coast in Morecambe, Powell delivered an alternative budget, dramatising his flimsy hold on modern reality by proposing to halve income tax by denationalising practically the entire public sector. He drew the line only at the railways and the mines. Mrs Thatcher offered no such fireworks. She merely condemned the 'increasing authoritarianism' of Labour's prices and incomes policy as she had done many times before, and as Heath and Macleod did at this time just as unequivocally – calling instead for the 'Conservative way' of keeping prices down by competition. She called for lower taxes, lower public spending and incentives to enterprise; but she made no mention of denationalisation. She did suggest that taxes could be cut by encouraging private provision for health care and pensions: but this was no more than she and Joseph had proposed in 1965. She did, however, strike one distinctive note which with hindsight can be seen to be significant:

> We now put so much emphasis on the control of incomes that we have too little regard for the essential role of government which is the control of the money supply and management of demand.

In their 1983 biography of Mrs Thatcher, Nicholas Wapshott and George Brock pointed out that the next passage closely followed a speech by Powell made at Halifax as long ago as 1957, but recently republished:

> It would mean, of course, that the government had to exercise itself some of the disciplines on expenditure it is so anxious to impose on others. It would mean that expenditure in the vast public sector would not have to be greater than the amount which could be financed out of taxation plus genuine saving. For a number of years some expenditure has been financed by what amounts to printing money.[96]

She was well aware that worrying about the Government printing too much money was dismissed by sophisticated economists as laughably outmoded; but she insisted that they were wrong:

There is nothing *laisser-faire* or old-fashioned about the views I have expressed. It is a modern view of the role the government should play now, arising from the mistakes of the past, the results of which we are experiencing today.

She was careful not to mention Powell in this context. She made coded amends, however, a minute later by quoting him at length on the subject of hospital planning – an example of something which only the Government could do. This surely was indirect acknowledgement of the debt she recognised to Powell's economic thinking.

The most interesting passages in this mainly cautious manifesto are the most personal, where gleams of the mature Thatcher suddenly shine through. Towards the end of her lecture she explicitly anticipated two of the most famous aphorisms of her prime. First she robustly defended high salaries in return for hard work – 'There is nothing wrong with people wanting larger incomes ... What *is* wrong is that people should want more without giving anything in return' – and rejected the accusation of materialism: 'Money is not an end in itself. It enables one to live the kind of life of one's own choosing.' The wealthy might choose to devote their 'hard earned cash' to music, the arts or charity. 'The point is that even the Good Samaritan had to have the money to help, otherwise he too would have had to pass on the other side.' Thus one of the key parables of High Thatcherism was first expounded back in 1968.

Still more significantly, she ended with an unfashionable defence of party politics, rejecting the widespread hankering for 'consensus'. 'We have not yet appreciated or used fully', she suggested, 'the virtues of our party political system.' The essential characteristic of the British system was the concept of the Opposition, which ensured not just an alternative leader but 'an alternative policy and a whole alternative government ready to take office'. Consensus she dismissed as merely 'an attempt to satisfy people holding no particular views about anything'. It was more important to have 'a philosophy and policy which because they are good appeal to sufficient people to secure a majority' – in other words, what she later called 'conviction politics'. She concluded:

No great party can survive except on the basis of firm beliefs about what it wants to do. It is not enough to have reluctant support. We want people's enthusiasm as well.[97]

More than anything else it was this crusading spirit which was Mrs Thatcher's unique contribution to the anti-collectivist counter-revolution which ultimately bore her name. Others expounded the ideas which she seized on and determinedly enacted. The force which transformed British politics over the next twenty years was Mrs Thatcher's belief that politics was an arena of conflict between fundamentally opposed philosophies, her contempt for faint-hearts and her ruthless view that a party with a clear philosophy needed only a 'sufficient' majority – not an inclusive 'consensus' – to drive through its programme. Few who heard the shadow Minister of Power set out this credo in Blackpool in October 1968 paid much attention at the time. Even when she grasped the party leadership seven years later few colleagues or commentators really believed she meant what she said. In fact the essence of Thatcherism was there in her words that day: not in the unremarkable policies so much as in her fierce belief in them.

Someone who evidently did notice the CPC lecture was the editor of the *Daily Telegraph*, Maurice Green. In the spring of 1969 Green invited Mrs Thatcher to expand her ideas before a wider audience by writing two articles for the paper. The first, 'Consensus – or choice?', repeated her contempt for woolly centrism: 'Clash of opinion is the stuff of which democracy is composed.'[98] The second, 'Participation – in what?', developed an idea she had only touched on at Blackpool: that the right answer to the trendy call for popular 'participation' was not more tiers of government but less government participation in people's lives – in other words more individual responsibility, self-reliance and choice and less dependence on the state. Together the two articles form a considerably crisper summation of her ideas than did the lecture.

They also exude a strong concern for practicality. Politics she defined as 'the act of finding solutions to problems. Acceptable solutions'.[99] Tiptoeing on to the minefield of denationalisation she acknowledged that the challenge was to find practical means of gradually shrinking the public sector: she proposed a piecemeal sell-off, recognising that 'before a buyer or buyers could be found, those parts of industries which could be denationalised would have to be reorganised into units that make them attractive and saleable'. At the same time she had no patience with 'administrative impossibility' as an excuse for doing nothing: ' "Administrative impossibility" so often turns out to be possible under another Minister or Government.' More clearly than ever, Mrs Thatcher displays in these articles an exceptionally clear-sighted appreciation of the balance between theory and detail, principle and practicality. Repeating her distrust of mandates and election bribes, she insisted that offering a political alternative must mean 'more than a catalogue of specific promises'. It should mean 'a different conception of ways of life tempered by reality'.[100] The last three words are crucial: but she meant precisely what she said – a different vision *tempered* by reality, not negated or vetoed by it.

Despite these rare excursions into print, the fact remains that Mrs Thatcher was always at her best in the bearpit of debate, rather than on paper. At the beginning of May 1968 – five months before the CPC lecture – she displayed her calibre in an Opposition censure debate on the subject of rising prices. The Government's defence was led by Barbara Castle, appearing for the first time in her new role as Secretary of State for Employment and Productivity and already exhausted. ('Never in my whole life have I been worse prepared,' she confessed in her diary.)[101] By contrast Mrs Thatcher, winding up for the Opposition, was on top form and, as usual, in command of her subject. In cold print her speech is an indigestible mass of figures; in delivery it was another *tour de force*, as Andrew Alexander reported in the *Daily Telegraph*:

> Mrs Thatcher gave a dazzling performance, firing salvo after salvo of devastating statistics into the Labour benches like a cannon firing grapeshot into a crowd.
>
> It is always rash to take on Mrs Thatcher where facts and figures are concerned. Tonight, Labour references to the deficit they had inherited had clearly riled her and she had decided to give the Socialists a statistical bombardment they would not forget in a hurry.
>
> Year by year she took them through the records since 1951 to show that the Tory record on current account deficits and surpluses was far from deplorable and outstandingly better than Labour's had been. Labour MPs looked on with awe and discomfort.[102]

As on the occasion when she went through every Budget speech from 1946 onwards, she remorselessly rehearsed the record over sixteen years to show that while both parties had run up deficits in election years (1951, 1955, 1960 and 1964), the Tory Government had always got quickly back into the black the following year, whereas Labour had incurred three consecutive years in deficit since 1964, rising to a record in 1967. The *Telegraph*'s Peterborough column wondered why no one had defended the Tory record so effectively in the previous three and a half years. 'It has been necessary', she conceded, 'to invoke the help of the library'. 'But the Commons library has been wide open to 240 Tory MPs since 1964', Peterborough pointed out. 'Why has it been left to Mrs Thatcher to do the homework?'[103]

That autumn she was switched again, to Transport. There was disappointment among the commentators that she was moving there just too late to shadow Mrs Castle. 'Their duels', the *Telegraph*'s political editor H. B. Boyne wrote, 'would have made the sparks fly.'[104] Instead she found herself once again shadowing Dick Marsh. ('I look forward', she told the House, 'to the time he shadows me.')[105] The move was not exactly a demotion. Since her replacement covering Power, Sir John Eden, was not in the Shadow Cabinet it could even be construed as a promotion. Boyne, commenting that her range was 'unrivalled in versatility by any Conservative woman MP', thought she was obviously 'booked for an important post' in a Heath Cabinet.[106] Nevertheless she was disappointed; compared to Power, Transport was 'a brief with limited possibilities', since Barbara Castle had already carried through the Government's major legislation before leaving.[107] At least she suffered none of the male condescension which was heaped on Mrs Castle, a non-driver, when she was given Transport. Mrs Thatcher was able to tell the *Telegraph*'s motoring correspondent that she was an experienced cross-London driver: very much 'a Point A to Point B motorist', she admitted, but she took a thrifty pride in the fact that her old Ford Anglia had outlasted several of Denis's more expensive cars.[108]

Interestingly, she did not see her job as simply championing the road lobby. Though famous as Prime Minister for her enthusiasm for 'the great car economy' and a corresponding detestation of the railways, she was strikingly positive – in her first Commons speech on the subject – that the most urgent need was for more capital investment in British Railways. 'If we build bigger and better roads', she warned – thirty years before the argument was widely accepted – 'they would soon be saturated with more vehicles and we would be no nearer solving the problem'.[109]

The following month Marsh brought in the Transport (London) Bill, the main purpose of which was to transfer London Transport to a new Transport Executive under the control of the GLC, writing off in the process 90 per cent of its value. Mrs Thatcher pounced, giving a revealing glimpse of the way her mind was now working:

It may surprise the Minister to know that he is one of the first practical exponents of denationalisation by the Powell principle. If he reads the speeches of my right hon. Friend the Member for Wolverhampton SW he will see that this is one kind of denationalisation which my right hon. Friend was advocating . . .

I warn him that this will be a very useful precedent when hon. Members change sides in the House and we consider denationalisation proposals. We shall remember the action taken by the Minister and consider it possible to denationalise undertakings at less than their book value.[110]

The Labour MP Stan Newens objected that transferring assets from one public authority to another was quite different from privatising them; but Mrs Thatcher disagreed. She was clearly going out on a limb, with no Shadow Cabinet authority. But in her open acknowledgement of Powell, her confidence that the Tories in government would pursue denationalisation, and above all her practical interest in how it might be achieved, this is a remarkable interjection. The realisation that Governments could sell nationalised industries at less than their value was one which stayed with her.

She had another prophetic little exchange with Marsh six months later, on the Report stage of the Bill. Mrs Thatcher believed that the Bill gave too wide powers to the (then Conservative-controlled) GLC. Marsh told her they had been agreed 'with the biggest Conservative authority in the country'. 'Not with me,' she retorted. No, Marsh conceded, not with her; but if ever she were in office and tried to repeal them she would find herself very unpopular across the river. Seventeen years later she not only repealed the powers but abolished the GLC itself; and she was indeed very unpopular across the river.[111]

That summer she paid her first visit to the Soviet Union – the counterpart, as it were, of her visit to the United States two years before. She was invited as Opposition Transport spokeswoman, principally to admire the Moscow metro and other Soviet achievements in the transport field, but she also found time to take in nuclear power stations as well as the usual tourist sights. She travelled with Paul Channon – then Arts spokesman – and his wife, who were left gasping by her determination not to waste a moment.[112] Of course she had no illusions about the moral and material bankruptcy of the Soviet system: her instinctive hostility had been sharpened by her experience of campaigning for the past four years for the release of Gerald Brooke, a British lecturer and one of her constituents, whom the Russians had charged with spying in the hope of swapping him for two of their own spies. (A swap was finally agreed just before her visit.) Her own somewhat self-congratulatory account of the trip tells of embarrassing her guides by asking awkward questions and correcting their propaganda; but while the drab streets and empty shops confirmed her preconceptions she also saw enough of the long-suffering victims of the system to convince her that they must sooner or later reject it. Believing passionately that Communism was contrary to human nature she was confident that it could not endure. She always thought that the Cold War was there to be won.[113]

In October she celebrated ten years in Parliament, marking the anniversary with a ball at the Royal Lancaster Hotel. In her speech she noted how the world had changed in those ten years: in 1959 South Africa had still been a member of the Commonwealth, Eisenhower was President of the United States, Britain had not yet applied to join the Common Market and the first man had not yet gone into space. There were no Beatles, no David Frost, no hippies and no 'permissive society'. But some things, she asserted, did not change: 'Right is still right and wrong is wrong.'[114]

Two months later she elaborated her alarm at the permissive society. The *Finchley Press* marked the turn of the decade by asking a number of local figures what they hoped to see in the 1970s. Mrs Thatcher replied that what she hoped and what she expected were two different things: she would like to see 'a reversal of the permissive society'. It was said that people were freer today than in the past. She disagreed.

> I question whether a person who gives in to his every instinct and whim is free. It seems more likely that he is a slave to his own appetites. Surely an educated society should consist of people capable of self-discipline; capable also of appreciating the necessity for law and order.

She also hoped to see 'the divorce rate fall, greater understanding between the generations, and more emphasis on the family as a unit'. On the material side she hoped to see inflation curbed – but she did not say how.[115]

She could not have guessed that before the new decade was out she would be Prime Minister, inheriting both an inflation rate and a divorce rate more than twice the 1970 level. In office she presided over – and by her economic reforms accelerated – a continued fragmentation of family life more rapid than the sixties ever dreamed of. She regularly blamed the decline in the moral standards of society on the liberalisation of the legal framework promoted by the Labour Government in the sixties – what she called in her memoirs the 'almost complete separation between traditional Christian values and the authority of the State'.[116] Yet at the time she supported much of this agenda. She opposed the 1968 liberalisation of divorce law. But she voted for the legalisation of homosexuality between consenting adults, and also for David Steel's Abortion Bill. In both cases she has written that she was influenced by the individual suffering she had witnessed in her work at the Bar.[117]

On two other social questions which defined left and right in the Conservative party she made her views discreetly clear. Though she had abandoned her support for birching young offenders, she continued to vote at every opportunity for the retention and, after its abolition, the return of capital punishment for murder. The latest occasion was in June 1969, when Duncan Sandys' attempt to bring back hanging was lost by 256 votes to 126. Likewise on immigration, while she privately assured Powell that she was 'strongly sympathetic' to his views[118] and defended his right to free speech, she distanced herself from his lurid populism by suggesting that he should put his case to Parliament. ('I think you should always be willing to take your views to the final test.')[119] She gave no public hint – as she famously did as Leader of the Opposition in 1978 – that she shared his fears. When Sandys did force a vote in Parliament, however, in February 1969, she voted – with 120 others on a free vote – in favour of stricter controls. Heath and most of the Shadow Cabinet abstained; but Mrs Thatcher joined Alec Douglas-Home, Tony Barber and Willie Whitelaw in backing a tougher line.[120] The signals were clear enough for anyone who wished to read them. Nevertheless when she was shifted for the last time before the election to take over the Education portfolio from Edward Boyle she was not generally identified as a fully paid-up right-winger.

With hindsight the appointment of Mrs Thatcher to replace her old Oxford friend Sir Edward Boyle as shadow Education Secretary is a symbolic moment in the transformation of the Tory party. A gentle, liberal, high-minded Old Etonian baronet who had already been Education Secretary in 1962–4, Boyle personified the educational consensus which had promoted comprehensive schools and 'progressive' teaching methods: as a result he was the principal target for the right-wing backlash which was developing in defence of selective schools, discipline and traditional teaching methods. In 1967 his bipartisan approach was unprecedentedly thrown out by the normally docile party conference; the backlash gathered strength with the publication of the first 'Black Paper' on Education in March 1969. Angry Conservatives in the shires and suburbs fighting to preserve their grammar schools regarded Boyle as a traitor – a socialist in all but name. Mrs Thatcher – grammar-school-educated, defiantly middle-class and strenuously anti-socialist – was in every way his opposite. Yet Heath intended no change of policy by appointing her.

Some mystery surrounds Boyle's decision to leave politics in 1969. He always insisted that he was not forced out, but went by his own free choice.[121] But he was clearly unhappy with the rising tide of right-wing sentiment in the party and felt little enthusiasm for another stint at the Department of Education, while he seemed unlikely to be offered any sufficiently tempting alternative. He chose instead to accept an invitation to become Vice-Chancellor of Leeds University.* His friends believed that Heath should not have let him go so easily: another music-loving bachelor, Boyle was supposedly one of Heath's few real friends in politics. Yet Heath failed to offer him another position. His first choice to fill the vacancy was Keith Joseph – another anguished liberal baronet with a serious interest in education. But Reggie Maudling was 'utterly unwilling' to take over Trade and Industry.[123] In these circumstances it was always the dependable Mrs Thatcher who was moved. The appointment was widely applauded as a shrewd piece of party management. There had been speculation that Heath might have taken the opportunity either to signal a shift of emphasis by appointing a right-winger like Angus Maude, or alternatively to reaffirm the Boyle line by appointing Christopher Chataway. By contrast, the *Daily Express* believed, Mrs Thatcher was 'noted for her middle-of-the-road views'.[124] The *Financial Times* agreed:

> The choice of Mrs Thatcher shows that Mr Heath has resisted the pressure from the Right to appoint a dedicated opponent of the comprehensive system. Instead he has picked an uncommitted member of the 'shadow' Cabinet who has won a high reputation for her grasp of complex issues in the fields of finance, social security, power and transport.[125]

---

* Mrs Thatcher clearly found the idea of voluntary withdrawal from politics incomprehensible. 'There is *no one* who can replace you,' she wrote to him – before she knew that she was going to be the one to do so. 'However if this is what you want I am very happy for you.'[122]

The *Daily Telegraph* likewise thought that the appointment 'will appeal to Conservative supporters who considered Sir Edward too far to the Left, without offending the so-called "progressives". It certainly does not indicate any change of policy.'[126] The *Sunday Telegraph* suggested that she had been chosen for presentational reasons – 'not for what she thinks but for what she is and for the mileage to be got out of her. It helps that a woman is to do the job, and it should help particularly on TV.'

The writer of this piece, Ivan Rowan, had no compunction about seeing her first as a female:

> Mrs Thatcher is a very pretty woman in a soft suburban way with a nice mouth and nice teeth and large round dolly eyes, like a candy box tied off with two shiny bows of blue ribbon.

At the same time he observed that people tended to be 'disturbed by the sci-fi contrast between those peaches-and-Ealing [*sic*] good looks and the metallic and transistorised intellect behind them':

> [She has] a slow, attractive smile, but even quite experienced politicians can sometimes find her chilling to cross. Something happens to her eyes, like a cold wind passing over a Norfolk beach.

On the basis of her votes for homosexuality and abortion he too classed her 'a middle-of-the-roader'; but she possessed 'one of the best minds in politics' and intended to go 'as far as the game will carry her'. Pressing her on how far that might be, he cornered her into asserting that 'no woman in my time will be Prime Minister' – nor Chancellor or Foreign Secretary either. 'Anyway', she professed disingenuously, 'I wouldn't want to be P.M.; you have to give yourself to it one hundred per cent.'[127]

In fact of course she did have strong views on education. As Nora Beloff in the *Observer* was almost alone in pointing out, she 'has made no secret of her desire to see the party campaign more aggressively in favour of freedom of choice and against regimentation'.[128] She had sent her own children to the most expensive private schools – Mark was now at Harrow, Carol at St Paul's; but no one in 1969 considered this a disqualification for running the state system. On the specific question of comprehensivisation she had a perfect microcosm of the whole controversy in her own constituency. Since 1965 the Labour Government had required Local Education Authorities to draw up schemes to convert their grammar and secondary modern schools to comprehensives. Conservative-controlled Barnet was split, but nevertheless voted in 1966 to go ahead with comprehensivisation. Without getting too embroiled, Mrs Thatcher gave general support and encouragement to the twenty-odd rebel Tory councillors and the parents of the threatened grammar schools who continued to oppose the scheme. At the 1966 election she promised that a Tory government would withdraw Labour's circular requiring the preparation of plans; she always insisted that the party was not against comprehensivisation where appropriate but she deplored the disappearance of good grammar schools.[129] In May 1969 she went further and specifically supported the campaign to preserve the excellent Christ's College from being merged.[130] So she came to the education job already well versed in the local dimension of the national argument.

Nationally, however, comprehensivisation was proceeding rapidly. By 1970 32 per cent of all secondary school children were in comprehensive schools; under a mixture of moral and financial pressure from the Department of Education and Science only a handful of LEAs had refused to submit conversion schemes.[131] Several big Conservative-controlled councils were among the most enthusiastic pioneers of comprehensives. Progressive opinion took it for granted that the momentum was unstoppable. There were still 'pockets of resistance', Boyle admitted to a sympathetic Birmingham alderman just before he resigned. It was 'a difficult subject for our Party', and the next Conservative Government would have to take 'a number of most uncomfortable decisions when we are returned to power'; but he was sure there were 'absolutely no political dividends to be gained from any attempt to reverse the present trend in secondary education'.[132] Even with Boyle gone, this remained the general view of the Shadow Cabinet. Whatever her own preference might have been, Mrs Thatcher inherited an agreed line which left her very little room for manoeuvre.

The initial press response to her appointment highlights the extent to which experienced commentators heard only what they expected to hear. Of course they did not read the *Finchley Press*, and it is true that she scarcely uttered a word about education outside Finchley before October 1969. It is also possible that her views were ignored because she was a woman. But there is another explanation, which may be read as a kind of compliment. Opponents of comprehensive schools, like supporters of capital punishment and opponents of immigration, were dismissed by most of the liberal press as neanderthal reactionaries. Mrs Thatcher was regarded as too intelligent, and too ambitious, to be seriously right-wing.

Her first interviews, however, immediately revealed her true instincts. She was 'very excited' with her latest job she told the *Daily Mail*, 'and cannot wait to get down to work'.[133] 'After the economy I believe education is the most important thing,' she told the *Finchley Press*, adding – a little pointedly – 'I hope I shall be able to keep this position for some time.'[134] But while she repeated that her appointment represented no change in policy, she struck a very different note from Boyle. 'I have nothing against comprehensive education,' she assured the *Daily Express*. 'Indeed I know many parents who prefer it. I certainly do not propose to unscramble plans that are already in existence.'[135] What she objected to were 'botched-up' schemes yoking together schools that were not designed as comprehensives. This sounded entirely reasonable, in line with Tory support for diversity, parental choice and local option, as opposed to Labour regimentation and centralisation. But of course the whole point of a comprehensive system was that it should be comprehensive. It was disingenuous to talk of parents 'choosing' comprehensives if others could still choose grammar schools. Comprehensives could only be comprehensive if selection was abolished; so long as the grammar schools creamed off the best students 'comprehensives' would only be a new name for secondary moderns.

These artless comments – contrary to her normal practice of saying nothing until she had had time to study her new brief – ensured that the knives were out for Mrs Thatcher even before she faced the Commons in the debate on the Address, barely a week after her appointment.* The *Guardian* derided what it called the 'old familiar song' of Tory hypocrisy: talk of 'botched-up schemes' was just a fig leaf. 'The Thatcher dictum means that until Britain is all Stevenage and spruce estates there will be no truly comprehensive system; and that means never.'[137]

The next day she appeared on *Any Questions?* and was given a hard time by the Labour MP John Mackintosh and the editor of the *New Statesman*, Paul Johnson. 'Will you support the positive policies that Boyle stood for in education?' Mackintosh pressed her. 'Many of

---

* This time she was appointed to her new job just after the party conference, instead of just before, so she did not have to plunge straight in with a speech to the Tory faithful. Her Conference speech that year, still as Transport spokesman, was the platform's reply to a debate on women's issues; it was a careful balancing act, supporting equal pay and equal opportunities while insisting simultaneously on a wife's right to be supported if she chose not to go out to work. 'Let us recognise', she urged, 'that perhaps the most important job of all is the creation of family and family life.'[136] Now that her own children were nearly grown up she was becoming much less keen on encouraging other mothers to follow her example.

them, yes,' she replied. 'Why not all of them?' 'Because I too have ideas.'[138] In the Commons Labour and Liberal speakers queued up to denounce her. The Labour left-winger Willie Hamilton thought Boyle's departure at this moment 'rather sinister'.

> I have much admiration for the hon. Member for Finchley and a great respect for her ability, but we on this side of the House think that she will be the 'skinhead' of the Tory party in educational matters. I hope that we are proved wrong.[139]

Others repeated the charge that opposing 'botched-up' schemes was just a formula for indefinite delay; while her old Liberal opponent John Pardoe put his finger on the logical contradiction inherent in trying to preserve a hybrid system: 'Comprehensive education can be comprehensive only if we eliminate alternative forms of selective schooling. We cannot wait for ever to do this.' Pardoe, interestingly, wanted full comprehensivisation with 'some sort of market place system' to give choice to all: he actually advocated education vouchers, but regretted that he had not yet convinced his party.[140]

Mrs Thatcher's reply was unusually defensive. She denied any sinister intent and explained that in speaking of 'botched-up schemes' she was merely thinking of her own constituency:

> A grammar school in a condemned building is to be amalgamated with a secondary modern school in a condemned building one mile away, across two main arterial roads . . . Both buildings are inadequate.

She blamed the Department of Education and Science for refusing funds for a purpose-built school. She devoted most of her speech, in fact, to the funding crisis she saw ahead in education, quoting figures to show that even projecting current policies at current growth rates would require more than doubling education spending in the next ten years. These figures, she said, were 'very sobering'.[141] Behind the headline-grabbing controversies over comprehensives and school milk, she actually devoted most of her energy over the next four years to battling for a bigger slice of national spending for education.

A couple of weeks later the *Times* education correspondent, Brian MacArthur, had a long interview with her – 'the first since she really took the measure of her new job'. He was left in no doubt that she expected to be Education Secretary within two years and saw 'obtaining sufficient resources as her biggest worry'. Having stirred a hornets' nest she was now clearly anxious to fudge the comprehensive question. ('She is no supporter of the Angus Maude wing of the Tory party.')

> Although her position will not, in fact, be far removed from that of Sir Edward Boyle, the preservation of a top tier of grammar schools within a national system of mostly comprehensive education is emerging as her standpoint.[142]

Looking back in her memoirs, Lady Thatcher wished she could have argued for preserving grammar schools on principle, not just case by case.[143] In fact she did, from these first weeks of her responsibility for education, clearly assert the principle of diversity – the headline over MacArthur's interview was 'No Monopoly in Education'. She lost no time in lending her support to the nine LEAs which were refusing to go comprehensive.[144] But at the same time she clearly accepted that she could save only 'a small top layer' of the most famous grammar schools. She was not proposing to stake her career on fighting the march of comprehensivisation.

> What she will try to inject into the national debate . . . is the argument that schools should provide for the abilities and aptitudes of all children, instead of concentrating on the advantages or disadvantages of any particular system of schooling.[145]*

Mrs Thatcher may have hoped that such a pragmatic compromise would prevent her tenure of Education being dominated by the issue of comprehensivisation. But in practice her hand was forced by Edward Short, Labour's Education Secretary – a former headmaster and a doctrinaire proponent of comprehensives – who blew her compromise apart by introducing a Bill in February 1970 to compel the handful of recalcitrant LEAs to comply. Even Boyle called this 'highly dictatorial';[147] it was in fact unnecessary and counterproductive, since all it did was to provoke resistance to a process which was already proceeding very rapidly. Mrs Thatcher was bound to fight it, and in doing so she could not help revealing her gut instincts. With

---

* MacArthur's memory of this first interview is that Mrs Thatcher frankly admitted that she had much to learn. A few weeks later she showed him a speech she was about to give to a headteachers' conference. It was all about secondary schools, whereas the audience was mainly primary heads. MacArthur was struck both by her initial unawareness of whom she was addressing, and by the professionalism with which she rapidly adapted the same speech to fit a different audience.[146]

unlucky timing her father died just two days before the Second Reading; she did not let that keep her away from the debate, but it must have reduced her normal preparation time and may have lowered her guard. Her speech was a defiant defence of selection. She denied that the eleven-plus exam condemned 80 per cent of children irrevocably as failures by citing the clearly exceptional case of a Finchley boy who won a scholarship to Cambridge after going to a Secondary Modern and transferring later to a Sixth Form college. She likewise denied that comprehensives would promote equality of opportunity, since there would always be differences between schools in different areas:

> If it is in a very good neighbourhood the chances are that . . . the children there will be of wide-ranging ability and it will be a good school with a large sixth form. If it is a school in a twilight area, or a poor area, it may be a poor school with a poor staff.[148]

This passage is very revealing. First, the vagueness of its phrasing ('the chances are', 'it may be') betrays a politician talking from prejudice rather than evidence. Then the rigidity of her social classification – neighbourhoods are either 'good', 'twilight' or 'poor' – highlights her instinctive sense of a moral pecking order. Third, she assumes that the measure of a good school is the size of its sixth form. Good schools are by definition high-achieving schools in 'good' areas which will naturally attract the best staff. When she remembered, she was careful to insist that of course there were good secondary moderns – it was after all Labour which wanted to abolish them. And she always professed that her first criterion for approving comprehensive schemes would be the educational interests of all children. Labour and Liberal MPs who followed her, however, had every excuse for charging that her real concern was with preserving the advantages of the gifted few. Pardoe called her speech 'disgraceful', the debate 'a sad day for education. The hon. Lady has thrown secondary education right back into the cockpit of politics.'[149] Winding up for the Government, Alice Bacon – Short's Minister of State – also condemned the shift in Tory policy since Boyle's departure.[150]

In fact it was the Government which raised the political stakes by forcing the pace unnecessarily on what was hitherto a remarkably consensual policy. Mrs Thatcher was shadow Education Secretary for only eight months. She showed early signs of willingness to go along with the consensus, accepting the formula of local option to avoid taking up a doctrinaire position against comprehensivisation.

The policy staff in the Conservative Research Department congratulated themselves on 'the civilising of Margaret Thatcher's views on education over the last two months'.[151] Short's Bill, by proposing to make it compulsory, flushed out her basic hostility to the principle. But still Conservative policy did not materially change. At the Selsdon Park conference of the Shadow Cabinet at the end of January education was barely mentioned. The Bill fell when Wilson called an early election. All it achieved was to expose Mrs Thatcher's lack of sympathy with the policy she very soon found herself having to pursue in office.

Meanwhile she was coming to terms with the rest of her new brief, getting to know the education world by speaking at a busy round of seaside conferences. The policy she had inherited was confidently expansionist. At a time when the Tories were promising to cut public expenditure overall, they were committed to higher spending on education. They were pledged to implement the raising of the school-leaving age to sixteen (which Labour had postponed in 1968), to maintain spending on secondary education while giving a higher priority to primary schools, and to double the number of students in higher education over ten years. Mrs Thatcher's consistent theme as shadow Education Secretary was the need for more money and the promise that the Tories would find it. She was even sympathetic to the teachers' claim for higher salaries. When they resorted to striking, she deplored Short's failure to condemn their action as typical Labour weakness:

> This must surely be the first time that a Minister, in the middle of negotiations to which he is a party, has condoned strike action which is, in effect, directed at the Government.[152]

But she did not blame the teachers. With the profession some 4,000 under strength, she advocated a restructuring of pay to keep good teachers teaching. In the Commons on 18 February she regretted that Short had not taken a more positive initiative to break the deadlock 'in which a responsible profession finds it is being driven to take action which is alien to its nature'.[153] These must be the most sympathetic words about any group of strikers that Mrs Thatcher ever uttered; they reflect her concern, as Secretary of State in waiting, to keep on good terms with the profession for which she hoped very soon to be responsible.

At the end of January the Shadow Cabinet met for a weekend

conference at the Selsdon Park hotel in Surrey. Within a few years Selsdon became one of the great myths of modern politics. It is supposed to be the moment when the Tory party embraced a New Right free-market programme, a proto-Thatcherite policy which was subsequently betrayed by the Heath Government in a series of abject U-turns, leading in turn to Heath's replacement by a new leader with the resolution to resume the Selsdon policy and carry it into effect. In 1973 some of the dissidents who opposed Heath's U-turn formed the Selsdon Group to defend what they thought had been agreed there; and after the 1974 defeat Mrs Thatcher was happy to proclaim herself 'Selsdon Woman'.[154] In fact 'Selsdon Man' was an invention of Harold Wilson, a public relations stunt which backfired. Wilson seized on Selsdon to portray the Tory party as prehistoric reactionaries who would abolish the mixed economy welfare state and take the country back to the 1930s. The truth was much less dramatic. The Selsdon Park weekend was no more than an attempt to get the Shadow Cabinet under one roof for forty-eight hours to tie up the loose ends of policies already largely agreed over the past four years. There was no strong ideological slant to the proceedings – quite the contrary; and the minutes now available in the Conservative party archive show that the discussion was remarkably scrappy and unfocused.

Mrs Thatcher took a surprisingly active part, however, at least in those sessions – only about half the total – for which minutes survive: these happen to be the subjects outside her current responsibility about which she knew most, pensions and family allowances, both of which were discussed at some length on the Saturday. The rough verbatim note gives a vivid sense of disjointed conversation between colleagues. On pensions she intervened frequently and authoritatively, asking sharp questions with a characteristic concern for cost, especially when Geoffrey Rippon and Robert Carr pressed for disability pensions. She thought 'invalidity' a better word, warning that 'disability can include almost anything' and would involve a 'tremendous increase in outgoing'.

On family allowances there was quite a debate. The shadow spokesman Robin Balniel called the existing system 'wasteful and illogical'; Iain Macleod was keen to scrap it and use the tax system instead. Keith Joseph argued that the present system penalised the poorest, and Mrs Thatcher seemed to agree:

You increase the number of the poor by the method you are using. Mr Houghton [Labour's Social Security overlord, 1964–6] was very anxious that he should not use a method of family allowances which would encourage people to go on having large families which they could not afford.   —

To this Quintin Hogg commented that he did not 'see people procreating just to get these small allowances'. At the same time Mrs Thatcher was very clear on the importance of paying family allowance to the mother. If payment went to the father through the tax system 'it ceases to be a *family* allowance. Views of women voters.' She revealed that she had recently reread the 1945 debate: 'One of the reasons for the Act was that it was a way of paying the *family* more, which couldn't be done by wages.' She was interested in the idea of means-tested grants from the local authorities to help with expenses like school clothes; then went further and suggested tackling poverty through the schools: 'We probably need nursery schools with free food.' Only nine months later she was cutting free school milk.

She saw family allowances specifically as a way of relieving poverty, which was a further argument for paying them to the mother. 'Then if you take the book into a Post Office everyone knows you are below a certain level.' If the shame of claiming led to low take-up of benefit, she evidently saw that as a gain to the Exchequer. She revealed that she herself did not collect her allowance, but then spoiled the effect of this public-spirited sacrifice by saying that she claimed tax relief instead – which Barney Hayhoe from the Research Department pointed out she could only do because she was paying surtax.

Among a large number of subjects rapidly covered on Sunday morning was the control of prices. No one suggested that this meant anything other than the control of wages: money supply was not mentioned. Mrs Thatcher's contribution was pessimistic, even fatalistic. When Heath said that he had come to the conclusion that the Government had responsibility for public sector pay but should leave the private sector to negotiate for itself – 'Throw it back to them. If you don't like wages going up, don't put them up' – she interjected helpfully: 'They will.' She cited the car industry as an example: 'There is competition in the industry, but they all put them up. Will still go on going up.' She agreed with Hogg that they would get nowhere till management could sack workers without facing a ruinous strike; but when Macleod suggested they needed a good public sector dispute to stand firm on she echoed Carr in hoping that they would not choose the nurses or – her own responsibility – the teachers: 'If we do stand pat – please do it on unskilled and not on skilled ... There isn't scope for increasing teachers' productivity unless you're prepared to spend money on mechanical aids.' Heath grumbled gloomily that even the dustmen were popular.

On housing too Mrs Thatcher chipped in very readily, rather surprisingly hoping that they would *not* move towards a system of subsidising the tenant rather than the house (which was precisely the point of the 1971 Housing Finance Act, a means of targeting need in place of universal subsidy). Not for the first time, the minutes suggest that Heath quickly slapped her down. A little later she voiced a clear view of public housing as a strictly limited safety net: 'Surely 30 per cent council houses is enough for people unable to afford accommodation. Ought to give priority in new housing to those who cannot afford it.'

Finally they got to education. But Heath made it bluntly clear at the outset that the party had 'got our education policy'. There was thus no need to discuss comprehensive schools. They had only to decide what to say in the manifesto about the proposed independent university of Buckingham. The rough minutes reveal a clear division between Keith Joseph and Mrs Thatcher, who were broadly sympathetic to the notion on free-market grounds, and Heath, who was emphatically sceptical – not least because he remembered Max Beloff, the moving spirit behind the proposed university, as a left-wing socialist at Oxford.

Heath: If people want to set it up they can do so. But we do not want to be landed with subsidising it. Nothing we can do about it. They can apply for Privy Council approval and Privy Council will decide whether or not to give it.

Joseph: One of the most encouraging things if it could be done.

Heath: Max Beloff.

Mrs Thatcher: Can I make a speech giving it a fair wind?

Heath: Running a modern university is an enormous . . .

Mrs Thatcher: Do you mind if I say we would be delighted to see one provided no public money involved?

Hogg: Might I ask how much money? Where would they get awards from? How much in capital investment?

Mrs Thatcher: £10 million revolving fund, loans to students, and of the same order . . . from same sources as money for hospitals – from business firms.

Barber: I am attracted by it.

Joseph: Didn't need to be in the manifesto as long as Margaret can say something.

Heath: Always said there is nothing to stop them doing it, put their own money in it, keep educational standards – but don't want it to come to State for money to keep it going. Never commit myself to saying whether independent schools are better than state ones or not.

Joseph: First class educational policy.

Macleod: Not opposing it.

Heath: As soon as one says one welcomes this, they say what practical form does your welcome take?

Joseph: Only Royal Charters.

Heath: No.

Mrs Thatcher: Can't get finance until they are sure they will get Royal Charter.

Rippon: Thatcher University Limited.

Mrs Thatcher: That is the Open University for which we are refusing money.

Joseph: Against your normal thesis this.

Heath: No, this is technically the position . . . If you like to say they have right to set up independent university and if they reach standard, Privy Council will approve.

Barber: Suggest we welcome it 'at no cost to the State'.

Heath: So unrealistic.

Mrs Thatcher: If I can do it in a speech – they are desperately anxious to get a Royal Charter.

Heath: Not committing myself to Royal Charter. Wouldn't trust Max Beloff for a minute. Already got too many universities.[155]

Apart from the ideological gulf between Mrs Thatcher's instinctive support for an institution independent of the state and Heath's equally reflex hostility, the most fascinating exchange is the reference to the Open University. Mrs Thatcher's instant response to Geoffrey Rippon's sneer that Buckingham should be known as Thatcher University Ltd is that, on the contrary, her really favoured protégé is not Buckingham but the Open University – a Labour creation, routinely derided by Tories as a Wilsonian gimmick. It had received its Royal Charter in 1968 and was due to take its first students in 1971; but Macleod planned to abort it when the Conservatives returned to power. To her credit, Mrs Thatcher saw its potential as a democratic – and economical – way of extending educational opportunity to thousands of highly motivated people who had missed out on a conventional university. It is clear that she wanted to back the OU, and also clear that her enthusiasm was both a surprise to her friend Keith Joseph and contrary to her normal careful guardianship of public money. She was always liable to make an exception for projects she particularly approved of.

This was admittedly her subject; but the evidence of these minutes supports Peter Rawlinson's recollection that Mrs Thatcher was quite a talkative member of the Shadow Cabinet. She clearly made her views known. At the same time she was not a member of the inner group. Her detachment was emphasised by the fact that she missed dinner on both the Friday and Saturday evenings. The whole Shadow Cabinet attended on Friday with the exception of Peter Carrington, who was abroad. But Mrs Thatcher was booked for another appearance on *Any Questions?*, recorded in Northampton, which she clearly saw as a higher priority, and was not expected to arrive before midnight.* On Saturday she was absent again – at a constituency dinner for, of all people, Enoch Powell. Heath was said to be anxious that all his colleagues should be present, while recognising that some had prior commitments. Curiously, however, it was reported in Finchley that Mrs Thatcher was at Selsdon Park. In her absence Powell told his hosts that he was sure she would not be a silent participant: 'She has never been a yes-woman.'[156] Some local loyalists criticised the invitation to Powell, demanding to know where Mrs Thatcher stood in the smouldering feud between Heath and Powell. At the Association AGM in March Mrs Thatcher defended the invitation on grounds of free speech.[157] The *Finchley Press* in turn defended her:

> The facts that Mrs Thatcher was not at the [Powell] dinner but with Mr Heath and her Shadow Cabinet colleagues, and that she sits with them on the Opposition Front Bench, are surely sufficient indication that she stands in relation to Mr Powell's extreme views as they do.[158]

So was she at Selsdon or at Finchley? She was certainly not at Selsdon; she was clearly not present for the formal part of the Powell dinner either. Yet she turned up, with Denis, before the end – after the press had gone, but in time to pay honour to Enoch without being seen to snub Ted: a subtle piece of political semaphore. By the next morning she was back at Selsdon Park.

For the first three or four months of 1970 the Conservatives were still confident of winning the next election, whenever it was held.

---

* Altogether she appeared on the programme ten times in the four years between June 1966 and May 1970.

Though Heath personally never established much rapport with the electorate, the party had enjoyed huge leads in the opinion polls for the past three years; devaluation, the persistent sense of economic crisis, mounting inflation and the Government's humiliating retreat from trade union reform had left Labour discredited, demoralised and apparently doomed. There was no need, however, for Wilson to go to the country before 1971: the most favoured time was the autumn of 1970. Then in the spring the polls went suddenly into reverse. Better trade figures, Roy Jenkins' conspicuously responsible Budget, the prospect of England defending the football World Cup in Mexico – whatever the reason, the transformation was bewildering. In May Labour did unexpectedly well in the local government elections, regaining control of most of the authorities it had lost since 1966. Despite warnings that it would be wiser to let the recovery mature, Wilson could not resist seizing the moment. With the polls still temptingly favourable and the Tories commensurately rattled he called the election for 18 June.

Once Heath's victory had made nonsense of the polls, many Conservatives claimed to have been confident all along that they would win. More honest, Lady Thatcher admits that she expected to lose.[159] Not personally, of course: she was secure in Finchley, where the local Labour party did not even have a candidate in place when Wilson went to the Palace. They hurriedly selected a young community theatre worker, an anti-apartheid and civil liberties activist who was unlikely to give her much trouble. But this was the first election in which she featured as a national figure, albeit in the second rank. Central Office arranged for her to speak in a number of constituencies beyond her own patch, all over the south and east of England; clearly she did not detect the enthusiasm which others claim to have felt. She was also chosen to appear in one of the Tories' election broadcasts. Despite the television training course she had taken in the fifties and regular appearances on the radio, she was not a success; her planned contribution had to be cut, as Barry Day, a member of the Tories' highly professional publicity team, recalled:

> She was filmed in a park, where she was surrounded by kids going up and down slides screaming. Margaret looked extremely out of touch. She was saying 'I believe you should have a choice for your children' and gave the impression she hoped they wouldn't be sick all over her dress. She was very ill at ease with the camera and with the children.[160]

Characteristically, however, Mrs Thatcher realised that television was a skill that had to be mastered. 'She was clever enough to ask for help,' Day acknowledged. 'Margaret wanted to learn while most of the rest of the senior Tories wished television would just go away.'[161] The man she turned to for coaching, who would eventually get the credit for transforming her image, was Gordon Reece.

Her growing national profile – but also her image problem – was reflected just before the campaign started by her inclusion in a series of articles on 'Tomorrow's Tories' in the new Murdoch-owned *Sun*. She was featured fourth – after Tony Barber, Peter Walker and Geoffrey Rippon – in a piece by Anthony Shrimsley entitled 'Lady in Waiting' and accompanied by a singularly plain and unflattering photograph. 'She is determined. She can be aggressive,' Shrimsley wrote. 'But she also possesses an appearance which can best be described as gracious.' In the interview Mrs Thatcher was at pains to dispel this impression, which went back to Godfrey Winn's 1961 profile in the *Daily Express* likening her to the Queen. She insisted she was just an ordinary girl, a grocer's daughter. 'I would hate people to think I was one of those women who was always worrying about her appearance.'

The rest of the article labelled her more clearly than ever before as a right-winger: the first effort by the new *Sun* to claim her as its own. Her picture was captioned with an unequivocal quotation: 'I am right-wing on law and order'. She was described as 'unhysterically but firmly in the law and order camp'; in favour of the death penalty, but with discretion for judges and liberal use of the Home Secretary's prerogative for mercy; reluctantly resigned to the fact that birching was 'no longer a practical possibility'. The coming battle over comprehensive schools, however, would establish her place in the Tory spectrum as 'comfortably but not extremely to the Right'. Shrimsley concluded with another of those teasing predictions:

> One day someone will achieve the unclimbed height of becoming Britain's first woman Chancellor of the Exchequer. It might not be too outrageous for Mrs Thatcher to wonder whether she could be the one who does it.[162]

Law and order figured prominently in her 1970 campaign. As if anticipating defeat she concentrated – judging from the *Finchley Press* – less on what a Conservative Government would do than on deploring the decline in national morals under Labour. 'We want to teach young people to lead responsible lives,' she declared at her adoption meeting. 'We thought it was about time we put that in. Education must mean more than taking "A" and "O" Levels.'[163] At

Whetstone on 8 June she linked moral decline with the growth of pornography: 'I fought the Divorce Bill, and was against any revision of the Obscene Publications Bill. In fact I think this should be strengthened.'

She said that she had supported the Abortion Act and the Sexual Offences Act, but she was already becoming alarmed at the sort of homosexual material now being sent through the post and thought it should be investigated.[164] Her election address likewise emphasised the moral dimension of politics: the title of the Tory manifesto, *A Better Tomorrow*, meant not merely prosperity but integrity, tolerance, personal responsibility, the rejection of violence and respect for law. 'Our British character is worth conserving and I believe it has much to contribute to the problems of this troubled world.' So far as practical proposals went, she mentioned only tax cuts, pensions for the over-80s and trade union reform, plus priority for primary education and no rush to comprehensives. She condemned Labour for building only 366,000 houses in the past year when they had promised half a million.[165]

There was not much Selsdon Woman in any of this. It is by far the woolliest address she ever fought on – scarcely the personal manifesto one might expect of an aspiring Cabinet minister in an incoming radical Government. The most interesting speech she made during the campaign, in fact, was not on the hustings at all, but at a dinner of the National Association of Head Teachers in Scarborough on 25 May, in which she set out what she regarded as the fundamental aims of education. These were, first, to develop the talents of every child; second, to develop sufficient skilled manpower for society's needs; third, to teach young people to lead responsible lives; fourth, to develop the capacity for informed judgement; and fifth, to advance knowledge. Unexceptionable though these objectives were – if somewhat prescriptive – she got into trouble by seeming to suggest that some children were unteachable:

> There are those who wish only to read the comic strip and the headline, whose problems, stemming sometimes from home backgrounds, cannot be overcome, however dedicated the teacher.
>
> One of our most difficult tasks as politicians is to decide how we can help these children.
>
> Better nursery provision in areas of social handicap will help, as will better school buildings, but we would delude ourselves if we expected quick solutions.
>
> Our ultimate hope is that these children will be good parents

and will provide for their own children the birthright of understanding and affection which they themselves perhaps lacked.[166]

She was quoted as estimating that perhaps a third of children were ineducable. Whether or not she really suggested such a high figure, Ted Short was quick to pounce.

This stupid comment really lets the cat out of the bag on Tory education policy. They are only concerned with the bright children and are content for the rest to become hewers of wood and drawers of water.[167]

Her opponent in Finchley, Michael Freeman, echoed Short's condemnation in his own style, calling Tory policy a form of apartheid – 'separate development for a privileged few and second class status for the masses'.[168] This was inescapably the image she was stuck with as she went to the Department of Education.

In her memoirs Lady Thatcher describes attending her own count in Hendon Town Hall, then going on to the *Daily Telegraph* party at the Savoy where it became clear that the Conservatives had won.[169] In fact Finchley did not count until the Friday morning. Carol's memory of that night is more accurate:

We were on our way to Lamberhurst* when the news of the early exit polls came over the car radio.
'If that result is right, we've won,' exclaimed Margaret, obviously surprised. Denis turned the car round and we went to the *Daily Telegraph* party at the Savoy.[170]

That first exit poll, from Gravesend, was announced by the BBC at 10.30; the first results were declared soon after 11.00. For both Labour, who had thought themselves to be cruising towards re-election, and for the Tories, resigned to defeat and just waiting to turn on their leader, the reversal of expectations was hard to grasp. For Mrs Thatcher the result meant the likelihood of Cabinet office. She returned to Finchley after an hour and a half's sleep to learn that she had increased her own majority by nearly two thousand:

---

* In 1965, soon after the sale of Atlas to Castrol, Denis and Margaret had sold their house in Farnborough and bought an even larger one – a half-timbered mock Elizabethan mansion called The Mount – in Lamberhurst, near Tunbridge Wells.

Mrs M. Thatcher (Conservative)	25,480
M. Freeman (Labour)	14,295
G. Mitchell (Liberal)	7,614

| Conservative majority | 11,185 |

She complimented her supporters on 'one of the nicest and smoothest campaigns ever' and managed to sound as though she had never doubted the national result: 'The Conservative party has tremendous inner strength and loyalty which carries on whatever happens and always brings us back to government.'[171]

She was not in the first batch of Cabinet ministers named that day, but was summoned to Downing Street on Saturday morning to be offered, as expected, the Department of Education and Science. (Most shadow ministers got the Department they had been shadowing: the principal exceptions were Reggie Maudling, who went to the Home Office so as to let Alec Douglas-Home go back to the Foreign Office, and Keith Joseph, who was switched from Trade and Industry to Health and Social Security). She was immediately asked if she would like to be the first woman Prime Minister. Her reply was categoric – but also barbed: ' "No," she answered emphatically, "there will never be a woman Prime Minister in my lifetime – the male population is too prejudiced." '[172] She preferred to get on with the job in hand. She went home to read her first boxes, before turning up at the Department bright and early on Monday morning.

9

Education Secretary

MARGARET Thatcher was Secretary of State for Education and Science for three years and eight months. This made her one of the longest serving ministers in the education department since the war – surpassed in the postwar period only by George Tomlinson (1947–51) under Attlee, by David Eccles' two stints (1954–7 and 1959–62) under Churchill, Eden and Macmillan, and by Keith Joseph (1981–6) in her own Government. The outgoing Labour Government had got through four Secretaries of State in six years. Mrs Thatcher's time at the DES formed a crucial period of her political development, if only because it constituted her only experience of heading a government department before she became Prime Minister, responsible for running the entire Whitehall machine, just five years later. Unfortunately it was an unhappy experience; or at least that was how she came to remember it. When she sent Joseph, and later Kenneth Baker, to Education in the 1980s she warned them that it was 'an awful Department'. She left Baker in no doubt that she had 'had a searing time dealing with officials there'.[1] Yet there was an element of hindsight in her recollection. In truth her time at the DES was a good deal less embattled – and a good deal more successful – than she later suggested.

Heath sent her to Education mainly because he had to send her somewhere, and after all her switches of the previous six years that was the portfolio she happened to be shadowing when the music stopped in June 1970. Education was not high on the Government's agenda; no major policy initiatives were planned. Moreover it was a conventionally suitable department for a woman: the only previous woman to sit in a Tory Cabinet, Florence Horsburgh, had been Minister of Education – for thirteen months – in 1953–4. When Iain Macleod died suddenly just four weeks after the Government took office, Mrs Thatcher's name was canvassed in some quarters as a possible replacement Chancellor. Though inexperienced she had proven expertise. 'She is a very formidable Tory,' the *Guardian* suggested. 'A tax specialist, a barrister and as tough as old boots. Unlike Sir Keith Joseph, she does not dither over decisions. She will act instinctively.'[2] But it is most unlikely that Heath ever considered her before choosing the more amenable Tony Barber. In his view Education was about her ceiling. Yet it was in some ways the worst possible department for her.

It was a department with an entrenched culture and a settled agenda of its own which it pursued with little reference to ministers or the rest of Whitehall. The convention was that education was above politics: government's job was to provide the money but otherwise leave the running of the education system to the professionals. Political control, such as it was, was exercised not by the DES but by the local educational authorities up and down the country; the real power lay with the professional community of teachers, administrators and educational academics, all of whom expected to be consulted – and listened to – before any change in the organisation or delivery of education was contemplated. Political interference in the content of education was absolutely taboo. The Secretary of State, in fact, had very few executive powers at all. One of Mrs Thatcher's Labour successors complained that his only power seemed to be to order the demolition of an air raid shelter in a school playground;[3] while a former Permanent Secretary compared trying to manage education through the DES to 'steering a ship with a rubber tiller'.[4] It was not a department for an ambitious minister keen to make her mark.

Politically as well as temperamentally, Mrs Thatcher was antipathetic to the DES. She instinctively disliked its central project, the spread of comprehensive schools, and the whole self-consciously 'progressive' ideology that lay behind it. She disliked the shared egalitarian and collectivist philosophy of the educational establishment, and resented the fact that they all knew each other extremely well. Attending her first teachers' union dinner soon after coming into office she was disturbed to discover that her senior officials were 'on the closest of terms' with the NUT leaders. She particularly disliked the assumption that her views were immaterial and her only function, as the elected minister, was to get the money to carry out the predetermined policy. In addition she correctly sensed that the educational mafia frankly disliked her. 'It was soon clear to me', she wrote in her memoirs, 'that I was not among friends.'[5] She came to the Department, the *Sunday Times* reported, with the image and reputation of 'the ultimate Tory lady': 'The blonde permed hair, sharp blue eyes, bright blue coats, rightish convictions and Home Counties voice which have helped to make her a darling of Conservative Party conferences . . . have made many educationalists wary of [her].'[6]

The DES traditionally looked for two qualities in its Secretary of State. On the one hand, the Department's self-esteem required a leader of high intellectual calibre and broad liberal culture. In recent years Rab Butler, Edward Boyle, Lord Eccles, Lord Hailsham and Tony Crosland had all approximated to this ideal; Mrs Thatcher emphatically did not. Senior officials were sniffy about her science degree and her lack of cultural interests. They thought her 'not in the top flight intellectually'; her chemistry was 'only a first degree' and she was not a distinguished lawyer; she was 'at a loss' with philosophy and 'contemptuous' of broad ideas, 'totally circumscribed by her background' and thoroughly insular.[7]

She was the absolute stereotype of the clever sixth-form girl who reads chemistry; she was a marvellous examination candidate because she could read and remember almost anything. She sorted all the information out into drawers in her mind. But . . . she lacked that other vital dimension: imagination. She had a totally unoriginal mind.[8]

In addition she was pedantically meticulous and worked unnecessarily hard, insisted on reading and correcting every document and would not delegate or trust anyone to do anything for her. Her manner of working was not calculated to endear her to officials who looked back fondly to the relaxed academic style of Butler, Boyle and Eccles.

At the same time, however, the DES – always potentially a Cinderella department – wanted a minister who would fight its corner in competition with Cabinet colleagues and against the Treasury; and in that respect Mrs Thatcher quickly proved her mettle. She was not a heavyweight but she was a fighter. The stubbornness which exasperated her officials within the department delighted them when it was deployed against the rest of Whitehall. She could be 'brutal' and 'a bully'; but the obverse was that she was 'strong, determined and bloody-minded enough to wear down the Treasury'. She was 'absolutely maddening', one of her most senior mandarins recalled. 'We liked that.'[9] Despite her intellectual limitations – perhaps because of them – she turned out to be highly effective at winning the resources to carry out the Department's policies; so that in the end they came reluctantly to regard her as one of the best of recent Secretaries of State. They certainly preferred her to her immediate predecessor, Ted Short, a pernickety former headmaster who was as narrow-minded in his way as she was but much less effective; and even to Shirley Williams (1976–9), who was personally delightful, ideologically congenial but infuriatingly indecisive. In fact, once they had explained to her the constraints of her office, Mrs Thatcher was in some ways the civil servant's ideal minister: hard-working and demanding, but a good advocate for the Department, with – at that time – no educational agenda of her own.

That is not to say that she did not have strong views, only that she had no power to impose them. Her attitude to education was simple, prescriptive and defiantly old-fashioned: she saw it not as a process of awakening or intellectual stimulation but as a body of knowledge, skills and values to be imparted by the teacher to the taught. ('Mrs Gradgrind Thatcher', one profile not unfairly called her.)[10] She deplored the new child-centred teaching which held that everything was relative and value-free. In a characteristic aside in her 1968 CPC lecture she condemned the modern culture of questioning received beliefs without going on either to evolve new ones or reaffirm the old. Commenting wryly on a report of the French student leader Daniel Cohn-Bendit being awarded a degree for posing a series of intelligent questions, she said she 'would have been happier had he also found a series of intelligent answers'.[11] She later quoted with approval a critic who complained that 'We are feeding doubts into our children, not beliefs.'[12]

As Secretary of State she took great pride in her own (very slight) experience of teaching. In her first Oxford summer vacation she had taught maths and science for six weeks at a Grantham boys' school. She used to recall this brief exposure to the chalkface to establish her credentials. 'I enjoyed it,' she told George Gardiner. 'I used to go on until I knew they'd got it, and I wasn't prepared to let them go until they'd got it.'[13] She thought it a dereliction of duty if professional teachers failed to do the same: she once railed to her senior Schools Inspector that 'if *she* had those kids *she* would teach them to read'. But she was thinking of teaching one-to-one, or at least small groups, as she taught her own children – not classes of thirty or forty.[14] In her heart she probably knew this, which is why in her memoirs she admits that she had no 'calling' to be a teacher: 'I do believe that good teachers need a vocation which most people just do not have.'[15] Teachers, of course, regarded such pieties as simply an excuse for underpaying them. In principle she did value good teachers – it was the teaching unions she blamed for protecting bad teachers while imposing a left-wing political orthodoxy of under-achievement. But in 1970 the Secretary of State had very little power to affect either the quality or the content of education.

Her officials also found that she could be personally very considerate – 'cherishing, gentle and kind . . . very sympathetic to individuals', always making cups of coffee for everyone or even cooking supper if they were working late. She actually had a small kitchen installed in the Department, where she would run up scrambled eggs or baked beans; she was very good at remembering who liked what. Her staff were amused by her motherly side – there was a famous occasion when she adjourned an important meeting so that she could nip out before the shops closed to buy the particular sort of bacon that Denis liked for his breakfast. No one else could be trusted to buy the right sort. But nobody ever suggested that she left work early or in any way put her family responsibilities before her ministerial duties. Quite the contrary: she was 'a trouper', who always fulfilled what she promised, punctiliously sat through the whole of education debates, took a close interest in the work of junior officials (including specialist sections of the Department like the school architects), and always came to office parties.[16]

Ironically it was her very success as a departmental minister, winning resources for policies she did not in her heart approve, which retrospectively poisoned her memory of the DES. From the perspective of the 1980s her record as a high spending minister with the reputation of having 'gone native', who had tamely followed the departmental line and failed to halt the spread of comprehensivisation, was an embarrassment to her which never ceased to rankle. Stuart Sexton, a special adviser to successive Education Secretaries in the 1980s, felt that the Prime Minister 'hated the Department of Education, because I think she realised they had taken her for a ride . . . She had this ingrained memory of name after name of officials who had been principals or assistant secretaries or whatever and she obviously hated them because they had imposed their view on her.'[17] The fact is, however, that she did not hate them all at the time; nor did all of them hate her.

She certainly had her difficulties, beginning with the Permanent Secretary, Sir William Pile. Newly appointed in June 1970, Pile was an old DES hand who had spent most of his career in the Department, now coming back as its head after a spell in the Home Office as Director of Prisons. Described by the Whitehall historian Peter Hennessy as 'a genial, quiet, pipe-smoking official who . . .

liked to look on the bright side',[18] he was at the same time 'a doughty defender' of the DES line who 'liked to stick to his guns'.[19] So did Mrs Thatcher. Twenty-five years later Pile recalled her as narrow-minded, emotional, impossible to argue with, driven by passions which he found 'abhorrent', and 'an indifferent decision-maker', always wanting to do things which he had to tell her she could not do. In their three and a half years together, however, he recalled only two 'flaming rows' – both over questions where she wanted to exceed her powers.

One was the highly publicised case of a left-wing teacher sacked by a London school for publishing a book of his pupils' poems. He appealed to the Inner London Education Authority and was reinstated. Mrs Thatcher, siding with the governors, wanted to overturn the appeal, but Pile had to tell her she had no standing in the matter: if she intervened she would only be overruled in the courts. She found it hard to accept that she did not have the power. In the end she gave way very reluctantly, leaving a threatening note in her box: 'Very well. But I will remember this in my memoirs.' (She did not: she barely mentions Pile at all.) Their second row was about an official who had made a sensitive decision affecting her constituency without reference to her. Once again she wanted him dismissed. Pile refused. She could never understand that sacking people was his job, not hers.[20]

At the lowest point of their relationship she actually sought to have Pile himself removed. She tried to persuade Heath to move him, even stooping to suggest that his Russian wife made him a security risk (as though the Russians were interested in the secrets of the British education service). In this case it was the head of the civil service, Sir William Armstrong, who would not have it. It is a central principle of the Whitehall system that ministers cannot change their permanent officials at will.

Generally, however, Mrs Thatcher and Pile got along better than this episode suggests. Other senior officials in the Department saw nothing wrong with their relationship, and feel that reports of their hostility were greatly overdone. One private secretary who saw them together every day judged that they were generally very correct with one another: they did have rows, but they both got on with the job and finished up with considerable mutual respect.[21] They gave each other birthday presents; when Pile suffered a mild heart attack on a visit to India Mrs Thatcher was very solicitous; and when the Government fell, Pile organised a farewell party for her which was by no means automatic. (No similar event was held for Short.) And years later, despite their differences, Pile still paid tribute to her complete integrity.

She had an equally tense relationship with some of her other senior officials. The Senior Chief Inspector of Schools, Bill Elliott, was a donnish character who had admired Eccles and Boyle and found Mrs Thatcher by contrast narrow, humourless and stubborn: her repeated refrain was 'Mr Elliott, you are wrong'. He too recalls that she was always wanting to sack teachers, or otherwise interfere beyond her powers, and having to be told that she could not. She once told him that all the schools in London were incompetent, 'and it's your fault!' On the other hand, while she might tear strips off the inspectorate in private, Elliott knew that when necessary she would fight for 'my HMI' like a lioness defending her cubs.[22]

When Elliott retired in 1972 she was able to replace him, temporarily, with a man much more to her liking, Harry French, a down-to-earth, non-public school type who had come up through the ranks – literally, via the Army Educational Corps. But French was already past the normal retirement age, and at the beginning of 1974, she could not prevent him being succeeded by his deputy, Sheila Browne – another strong personality with whom she did not get on. With the exception of Indira Gandhi, Mrs Thatcher was never comfortable with other powerful women; her relationship with Sheila Browne was complicated by the fact that they had known each other at Oxford – they even shared a bed after Margaret Goodrich's twenty-first birthday party in 1944. Miss Browne always felt that Mrs Thatcher resented her presence in the department as an unwelcome reminder of a past she preferred at that stage in her career to keep under wraps. She denies that she 'loathed' Margaret Thatcher: but their professional relationship was not an easy one.[23] Miss Browne served as Senior Chief Inspector until 1983, when she became Principal of Newnham College, Cambridge.

If senior officials found Mrs Thatcher difficult to deal with, more junior ones found it still harder to stand up to her. One recalled in 1979 that he came out of meetings with her feeling 'like a peeled banana'.[24] Pile, protective of his staff, felt that she was frequently unfair: civil servants were not equipped to deal with her emotional, often highly personal, style of argument. Some were frankly afraid of her:

She's a killer: she kills off ideas, reputations and people in her own mind . . . If you crossed her you would never get a job or a good report . . . She makes up her mind about someone in ten seconds and then very rarely changes it. As soon as you open your mouth you are categorised.[25]

At the same time she could be chillingly impersonal:

> At moments I thought she was nothing but ice; I never felt there was any warmth at all. But her manners were impeccable . . . She could believe you were appalling, but would behave impeccably.[26]

With juniors and seniors alike she was always determined to win arguments, at whatever cost in bruised egos. If she was losing the main point at issue, she would abruptly change tack to pick up a different point in order to win on that. Sir Kenneth Berrill – later Mrs Thatcher's first head of the Whitehall Think-Tank but at this time chairman of the University Grants Commission – never forgot his first exposure to her extraordinary aggression, which was unlike any other minister he ever served: instead of seeking agreement, like most politicians, Mrs Thatcher would always seize on a point of difference and widen it, antagonising those she should have been trying to persuade.[27] Likewise Norman St John Stevas (one of her junior ministers from 1972) reflected that 'her prowess in argument was impressive, but I used sometimes to think that she might gain even more support from those with whom she had discussions by occasionally losing a point'.[28]

Her worst relationship was with the young official who was appointed at the end of 1970 to head her private office. John Banks was an avowed Labour supporter who did not disguise his allegiance. He lasted less than a year before Pile agreed that she was entitled to ask for someone more compatible. But this was a bad appointment in the first place. Nothing is more calculated to make an insecure minister feel threatened than an uncongenial private secretary. Banks left the civil service soon afterwards.

Neither was she altogether happy with her junior ministers. It was a much-reduced team compared with Labour: where Short had three Ministers of State (including Jennie Lee as Arts Minister) plus two under-secretaries, Heath gave Mrs Thatcher just two under-secretaries, plus Lord Eccles as Arts Minister, nominally under her Department but housed in a separate building with the title of Paymaster-General. In her memoirs she ticks them off characteristically as 'one friendly, one hostile and one neutral'.[29] Eccles was friendly, but too grand a figure in his own right to be called a subordinate: as a former holder of her office he was available as a source of experienced advice, while running his independent operation from a mansion in Belgrave Square. Of her two under-secretaries she believed that one, William van Straubenzee – 'a close friend of Ted Heath' – had been sent to keep an eye on her. Remembered in the Department as 'tubby and emollient' but 'a bear of very little brain', van Straubenzee was definitely not her type. The other, Lord Belstead, was even more lightweight. Eton and Christ Church, a Wimbledon tennis player in his day, he was 'a charmer ... very obedient', good at sending deputations away happy but otherwise 'out of his depth'.[30] Youngish hereditary peers capable of representing departments in the Upper House being hard to come by, Belstead resurfaced to hold a succession of junior offices throughout Mrs Thatcher's years in Downing Street, finally replacing Willie Whitelaw as Leader in the Lords. But he never became a heavyweight – still less another Willie.

In due course both van Straubenzee and Belstead were dispatched to Northern Ireland. They were replaced respectively by Norman St John Stevas and Lord Sandford. Stevas was the only one of her juniors Mrs Thatcher had any time for; in general, being pathologically unwilling to delegate, she did not see much point in them. Stevas, however, she had a soft spot for; he was colourful, 'a card', and one of the few people who could make her laugh. Their relations at that time, he has recalled, were 'cordial, friendly and indeed affectionate'. Already, however, he observed the fundamental difference of outlook that was to end his ministerial career in 1981: 'I marvelled that she had an opinion on everything that was clear, definite and concise. I used to wonder that she saw everything in black and white, since the universe I inhabited was made up of many shades of grey.'[31]

Her relationships within the Department were not all bad, however. In particular she struck up a surprising rapport with the Deputy Secretary, Toby Weaver. Weaver was one of those rare civil servants who become conspicuously identified with developing and carrying through a policy in their own right – in his case the promotion of polytechnics alongside the universities, creating the 'binary' system of higher education (largely achieved under Tony Crosland). No one more perfectly embodied the progressive educational establishment which Mrs Thatcher so despised. Brought up by Sir Stafford and Lady Cripps virtually as their adoptive son, Weaver married the daughter of Labour's first education minister, Sir Charles Trevelyan. From Cripps and Trevelyan he inherited an austerely high-minded strain of paternalistic socialism; but at the same time he was a great admirer of able women. To the fascination of their colleagues in the DES, Weaver and Mrs Thatcher somehow 'clicked'; the personal chemistry was right. Despite the gulf in ideology she trusted him, and Weaver became immensely skilled at handling her. He would stay late to have a word in her ear at the end of the day; he always seemed to be a step behind her, whispering what she needed to know about people she was about to meet. He was particularly clever at 'letting her think she was winning' – his own recollection – even as he persuaded her to implement his, or the Department's, policies. In fact he seems to have been a perfect Sir Humphrey Appleby, subtly manipulating his minister against her professed intentions. At the time she was deeply appreciative: she wrote him a letter of profuse thanks on his retirement in 1973 and took trouble to secure him a special knighthood. In time, however, as she began to believe that the department had taken her for a ride, it was above all Weaver whom she came to blame. He was deeply hurt that she omitted any mention of him in her memoirs.[32]

Once she was rid of John Banks she was also well served by his successor, Philip Halsey, a much better choice to head her private office, deliberately picked by Pile to smooth her ruffled feathers. Aged forty-three in 1971, Halsey was only three years younger than Mrs Thatcher herself, a late-entry civil servant who had previously been a headmaster, experienced, emollient and discreet. He became, in Weaver's phrase, her *fidus Achates* – her faithful companion – accompanying her on visits to schools and conferences, someone she trusted completely and with whom she could relax. More than anyone Halsey was responsible for her improved relations with the education world towards the end of her period at the DES. He rose to be Deputy Secretary from 1982 to 1988, when Kenneth Baker appointed him chairman of the Schools Examinations and Assessment Council.[33]

One person she was not close to was her parliamentary private secretary. Many ministers use their PPS as an intimate confidant as well as bag-carrier; it is often the first rung on the ministerial ladder for young hopefuls who later rise to prominence themselves. But twenty years later none of her colleagues or officials could even remember that Mrs Thatcher had a PPS. In fact she had two. The first, who held the post for most of her time at the DES, was Alfred Hall-Davis, a brewer who had been chairman of Charringtons before becoming MP for Morecambe and Lonsdale in 1964. He was appointed a whip in late 1973 but made no further mark in politics and died in 1979. His short-lived replacement, Fergus Montgomery, was not much more distinguished. After serving Mrs Thatcher for just three months, he lost his seat in the February 1974 election. He got back in October 1974, in time to act as one of her campaign managers in the 1975 leadership election, and served again as her PPS for her first year as Leader of the Opposition. But though he stayed in the Commons until 1997 neither she nor her successor ever gave him a job in government.

Mrs Thatcher arrived at the DES on Monday morning 22 June determined to show that she was the boss.* She marched in, with no conversational preliminaries, and presented Pile with a list of points for immediate action written on a page torn out of an exercise book. Number one was the immediate withdrawal of Short's circular requiring local authorities to prepare schemes for comprehensivisation. Neither she nor anyone else seems to remember what any of the others were. This is symptomatic: her fifteen or eighteen points were simply declaratory, intended to assert her activist intentions. She had in fact no positive agenda. She was committed by the Tory manifesto to a number of broad objectives all of which, apart from the slowing down of comprehensivisation and more Government support for direct grant schools, were uncontroversial, even consensual. Her main priority was switching more resources into primary education, with an ambitious new primary school building programme. 'This', she told the party conference revealingly in October, 'is the thing the Government controls.'[35] The Government was committed to raising the school-leaving age to sixteen – a long-planned change postponed by Labour in 1966 – and to continuing the expansion of higher education (specifically the polytechnics). The manifesto also promised an inquiry into teacher training. All this she carried out.

Of course there was a right-wing agenda for education which had been gathering increasingly vocal support in the constituencies over the past few years, evidenced by the hounding of Edward Boyle. It was spelled out, soon after the Government came into office, in an article in the *Spectator* by Dr Rhodes Boyson. Boyson was not yet an MP, but as a prominent secondary school headmaster and contributor to the controversial Black Papers on education which had been appearing since 1969 he was a leading figure in the backlash against progressive education. In his *Spectator* article he set out what the right wanted from the new Secretary of State: in addition to slowing comprehensivisation, she should scrap the proposed raising of the

---

* The Department was then still housed in its 'splendid old quarters in Curzon Street' in Mayfair. But in 1973 it moved to 'a hideous new office block', Elizabeth House in Waterloo Road.[34]

school-leaving age; expand only vocational higher education; introduce student loans instead of grants and promote fee-paying nursery schools. She could also restructure teachers' salaries so that good teachers could be paid more than bad ones.[36]

One must assume that Mrs Thatcher was privately sympathetic to most of this programme; but she was not committed to any of it and was careful to remain uncommitted. Some time after she took office a lunch was arranged for her to meet Professor Brian Cox and the other Black Paper authors. Cox told her that he saw himself as a moderate in the educational debate. A few days later she wrote to Cox: 'I also regard myself as a "moderate", but anyone who believes as we do in excellence in education is liable to be called a right-wing extremist.'[37] At this stage in her career she was unwilling to be so labelled. She implemented none of the right's programme over the next four years. Nevertheless by withdrawing Short's Circular 10/65 within a few days of coming into office, without going through the usual processes of consultation, she seemed to go out of her way to confirm the left's stereotype of a reactionary ideologue bent on stopping educational progress in its tracks.

Short led the outcry, accusing her in the Commons of 'sheer high-handed ideological arrogance' and dubbing her 'Selsdon Woman':

> If she continues along the doctrinaire reactionary path she has taken so far, she will find herself in the middle of utter chaos before many months are past . . . It is almost inconceivable . . . to the whole educational world that anybody could act so stupidly and so irresponsibly.[38]

This was pretty arrogant and doctrinaire in itself. But the haste of Mrs Thatcher's action, and the lack of consultation, laid her open to criticism. 'The bold and beautiful Minister for Education', wrote the Sunday *People*, 'has made a disastrous mistake. Not only because she has undermined a progressive education policy, but because she has done so without taking the time to work out an alternative.'[39] The *Daily Mirror* accused her of turning the education system into 'a confusing lottery'[40]; even *The Times* thought she was creating 'a policy vacuum'.[41] Nor was it only her opponents who were critical. It was reported from Number Ten that the Prime Minister was 'exceedingly annoyed' with his Education Secretary.

She had been quite inept in calling a press conference two days after appointment and against the advice of her officials. It was an example of precisely the 'instant government' that Heath was absolutely determined to avoid.[42]

Mrs Thatcher professed herself surprised by all the fuss. First, she was only implementing the manifesto, fulfilling a pledge made long before by both Heath and Boyle. Secondly, the effect of withdrawal was purely permissive. 'Had I been in fact imposing extra restraints on someone', she told an interviewer a few months later, 'I should have expected an absolute furore, but I was not stopping anyone from doing anything, nor was I changing the law.'[43] All she was doing was relaxing the element of compulsion in Labour's policy, restoring the right of individual local authorities to make their own decisions to suit their local needs. In the Commons she marvelled that Short could 'equate authoritarianism with the enlargement of freedom'. Where the present pattern was working well there would be no change. 'I fail to see what is reactionary or extreme about that.'[44]

Once again her pragmatism sounded quite reasonable; but it offended against the passionately held consensus of the day. 'It is all very well for Mrs Thatcher to say that decisions . . . must be taken at a local level', the *Observer* argued, but 'there must surely be a national framework'.[45] 'One nation', the *Guardian* asserted, 'needs one system.'[46] Even most of the Tory press – for instance the *Sunday Times* – largely followed opinion polls which showed strong support for comprehensive schools. The new tabloid *Sun* expressed some sympathy for Mrs Thatcher's short-term reservations but nevertheless favoured comprehensivisation in principle:

> It is wrong to try to force through comprehensive schemes where there aren't suitable buildings or staffs available – as Labour did.
> But it is wrong to abandon the target of making all state secondary education comprehensive, eventually.
> Mrs Thatcher's idea of leaving everything to local choice – or local chance – won't work.[47]

The truth is that the swift withdrawal of Circular 10/65 was a declaratory gesture of little practical consequence. It enraged the left and briefly encouraged the right; but its only effect was to throw the initiative back to the LEAs, most of which – including many big Tory authorities – were too far down the road to comprehensivisation to want to turn back now. In practice – to her subsequent chagrin – comprehensivisation proceeded faster than ever during

Mrs Thatcher's time at the DES. Under Section 13 of the 1944
Education Act final approval of every local scheme still lay with the
Secretary of State; and Mrs Thatcher took this responsibility very
seriously. She was meticulous in examining every scheme personally,
burdening herself with a 'massive workload'[48] and giving rise to
allegations of deliberate delay; in November 1971 she told the
Commons that she currently had 350 schemes under consideration. [49]
Where she could discover valid grounds for refusing approval she did
so; but in practice she found few schemes that she could reasonably
stop. In very many cases – including, piquantly, her own old KGGS
in Grantham – schools had to merge, on purely practical grounds, to
create Sixth Forms to cope with the raised school-leaving age. The
result was that over the four years of Mrs Thatcher's tenure of the
DES she rejected only 326 out of 3,612 schemes which were
submitted to her; that is about 9 per cent.

Of course it was this small minority which made the headlines.
Wherever she withheld approval from a scheme she laid herself open
to the charge that she was making nonsense of the Government's
professed policy of leaving local decisions to local option. Ironically
the most publicised row was in her own constituency where Barnet
Council, after much coming and going, had finally agreed with
Short what was called Plan C. On taking office Mrs Thatcher
immediately invited the council to think again. To the *Finchley Press*
she explained:

> I continue to be bombarded by ordinary people about the present
> plan, and it seems to me that on ordinary democratic grounds, the
> protests are getting so great that I would hope the local education
> authority would reconsider the plan.

Her difficulty was that the local Conservatives were divided. The
threatened grammar schools were in her part of the Borough, and
their most vocal supporters were members of her Association. 'If
Plan C is submitted', she admitted, 'I cannot say what my position
would be because I would then be in a judicial capacity.'[50] The LEA
postponed a decision until the autumn, sending out a questionnaire
to test local opinion. The 28,000 replies yielded 86 per cent support
for Plan C. [51] The council accordingly voted by 42–20 to go ahead.
Forgetting her judicial capacity, Mrs Thatcher did not hesitate to call
the decision 'unfortunate', implicitly encouraging the rebels to fight
on.[52] The following summer, having taken her time to consider the
various plans, she threw the council's arrangements into disarray by

approving some and rejecting others (after the school allocations for September had already been sent out). The council leader, Victor Usher, in normal times a strong supporter, found her decision 'incomprehensible'.

> I just cannot fathom what is in Mrs Thatcher's mind. We have all given a tremendous amount of time working out the best future for our secondary schools. We have wasted five years on argument and discussion. We might just as well have waited for her to tell us what to do.[53]

The most contentious scheme involved creating a new comprehensive by merging a famous old grammar school, Christ's College, with Alder School across three widely separated sites. Unquestionably Mrs Thatcher had some grounds for thinking this less than ideal. But when the council came back with a new proposal, to split the new school across the three sites by age instead of subject, so that children would now only move to a different building at the age of fourteen, she rejected that too. Usher again accused her of ignoring educational criteria and overriding local wishes to impose her own agenda.[54] In the short term the result was stalemate. But Mrs Thatcher wielded only a temporary veto. The council stuck to its plan, and two years later when a Labour Government returned, the merger went through.

Other places where Mrs Thatcher did her best to stop or modify proposed comprehensivisation schemes included Birmingham, Walsall, Harrow and Surrey – all Conservative-controlled at least up to 1972. In Surrey she was accused of going improperly behind the back of the council to encourage opposition to its plans: she was said to have had a clandestine meeting with grammar school campaigners at a tennis club near Weybridge. In the Commons Short characteristically charged her with waving 'a white sheet at the Dispatch Box, but acting with cloak and dagger in all her liaisons with all the worst elements in the local authorities'.[55] In fact she was quite open about encouraging parents to fight to save historic grammar schools. In January 1972 she told the former *Daily Mirror* magnate Cecil King that she had 'tried to help Surrey County Council to retain their four great grammar schools, but an overwhelmingly Conservative council was bullied into letting them go'.[56] At the party conference later that year she boasted she had upheld objections in favour of ninety-two 'famous grammar schools with supreme reputations' and publicly called on parents to help her to save more: 'I can only express the hope that those who believe intensely in the future of grammar schools ... will be as vocal in their own areas and outside this conference hall as they are today.'[57]

In 1973 Labour's new education spokesman, Roy Hattersley, accused her of 'capricious and arbitrary use of her powers', abusing her judicial function by playing 'ministerial roulette' with councils' plans; he also alleged that she was using spending restrictions to stop schemes she disliked by preventing necessary building.[58] That autumn these charges took more serious form. A pressure group called the Forum for the Discussion of New Trends in Education published an *Indictment of Margaret Thatcher*, a densely argued 35,000-word pamphlet alleging that she had systematically abused her powers for political ends. The radical barrister Louis Blom-Cooper lent his support, calling for the Secretary of State to be prosecuted.[59] Nothing came of it, if only because she was out of office within a few months. In fact, Bill Pile felt that there was no question of her exceeding her powers. While he thought that the amount of time she spent scrutinising schemes for grounds to reject them was disproportionate and certainly politically motivated, the Department's lawyers were clear that in this at least she was within her rights under the 1944 Act.[60]

She was further constrained by the knowledge that Heath and the rest of the Cabinet would not back her in any head-on confrontation with the educational establishment. The spirit of Boyle still determined Tory policy; all she could do was nibble at the edges of the progressive consensus, insisting that she was only trying to preserve an element of diversity and parental choice. 'On the odd occasion when I have had to use my powers under the 1944 Act', she told the 1971 conference, 'I am glad to say it has been on the side of the parents against authority, where that authority has used its powers deliberately to eliminate all choice in respect of a particular group of parents.'[61]

She did what she could – as promised in the manifesto – to help the 176 Direct Grant Schools, calling them 'the bridge between the completely independent system and the State system'.[62] They were under attack 'not because they are bad, but because they are very good. What a terrible philosophy to try to hold back a good school while the others catch up.'[63] She found more money for them – an extra £2 million from the £9 million saved by her notorious cutting of free school milk, a switch condemned by Short as 'a shabby redistribution' from the many to the few;[64] but this only restored what Short had cut two years earlier. She also promised direct

Government support for pupils whose local authorities refused to pay their fees. (This was another exercise of local option she did not approve.) She explicitly defended the survival of private schools not as bastions of privilege but 'a safeguard for all our children against a State monopoly in education'.[65] The private sector, she maintained, acted as a 'pacemaker' for the state system. In a television interview she dealt defensively with the question of her own children attending private schools: Mark was simply following in Denis's footsteps, and Carol naturally must have the same opportunity. She professed, unconvincingly, to 'hope that one or other of them will . . . partake of the state system, to which I am a very considerable contributor by way of tax'.[66] But among friends she was more bullish: 'You name me a Labour member of the Opposition who hasn't sent his own son to independent schools,' she demanded at her annual dinner dance in Finchley in 1972.[67] The *Finchley Press* helpfully described Harrow (whose fees at that time were £759 per annum) as 'Britain's most successful comprehensive school'.[68]

The result of all the sound and fury was that comprehensivisation proceeded faster than ever during Mrs Thatcher's time at the DES. Denounced on the one hand by the progressive lobby for holding it up, praised on the other by the *Daily Telegraph* and the right-wing Monday Club for doing more than any previous Secretary of State to slow it down,[69] she actually made very little difference at all. Between June 1970 and February 1974 the number of secondary pupils in comprehensive schools doubled to 62 per cent.[70] She herself made differing claims to different audiences. To education conferences – for instance, addressing an NUT dinner in 1972 – she tended to stress how few schemes she had stopped; whereas to party audiences she would boast of how many grammar schools she had saved. Unquestionably she did not like what she was powerless to prevent. She squared her conscience by telling herself that she was only bowing to a temporary fashion. She accepted that non-selective education was 'coming with increasing speed', as she told the *Times* education correspondent, Stephen Jessel, in November 1970. But she went on:

I do not accept that it will stop there; that is to say that non-selective education is not the last word in education.

I believe that in many areas it is a stage we shall only go through . . . I fully expect that there will be a system of some selective schools again . . . This is one reason why I am absolutely determined not to impose one system and none other.[71]

In education as in other things, it was as though she knew that the
tide would eventually turn in her favour. But by then it was very
difficult to put the clock back.

Her first serious challenge on coming into office in June 1970 was to
defend the education budget. Just like her own Government nine
years later, the Heath Government took office promising immediate
economies in public spending to pay for tax cuts. Macleod's first act
as Chancellor – virtually his only act before his sudden death – was
to demand a series of savings from the departments. Having
established in opposition that the Tories were committed to
increasing education spending, Mrs Thatcher was in a better position
than most of her colleagues to resist: both she and the Chancellor,
she told the *Today* programme, had made plain that 'education is a
spending area'.[72] Even so, she was required to find some short-term
economies. She did so by raising the price of school meals and
stopping the supply of free milk to children over the age of seven.
These were from her point of view unimportant cuts, falling only on
the welfare benefits which had got loaded on to education while
protecting the essential business of education itself – in particular the
expensive commitment to proceed with the raising of the school-
leaving age, and her promise to improve the standard of primary
school buildings. In 1971 she was able to announce 'a huge
building drive' to replace old primary schools, spending £132
million over three years from the savings on school meals and milk.[73]
She also reprieved the Open University, which Macleod had
earmarked for the axe before it had enrolled its first students. 'With
all our difficulties', she boasted, 'the cuts have not fallen on
education.'[74]

Her department was also responsible for the decision to introduce
admission charges for museums and galleries; but this was Lord
Eccles's policy from which Mrs Thatcher prudently kept her
distance. (She claims in her memoirs that she accepted museum
charges 'reluctantly', but successfully resisted library charges, remembering her father's debt to Grantham public library.)[75] When Tony
Barber announced his package in October, she was generally
thought to have done well: the row over school milk did not blow
up until the following year. As Prime Minister a decade later she was
keen to insist that her ministers owed their first duty to the
Government's collective strategy, not to their departments; but in
1970, like every other departmental minister, her priority was to

fight her own corner. She made a point of telling journalists that she had taken on the Treasury and won.

> Shall we just say I got my own way in the end? I think it is up to every Minister to battle for his or her department.
>
> I was quite determined to keep my pledge, which on the whole was to spend more on the primary school sector. Educationally I had virtually no cuts to offer, and I stuck to that.[76]

Her most remarkable feat was saving the Open University. The Tories in opposition had sneered at the projected 'university of the air' as a typical Wilson gimmick. Not only Macleod but even Boyle had intended to scrap it. The libertarian right, which supported the proposed independent university of Buckingham, regarded the OU as an unnecessary extension of state provision at the expense of existing commercial correspondence courses: far from extending opportunity to able people who had missed out on higher education, Boyson predicted in the *Spectator*, it would simply be filled up by teachers seeking to extend their qualifications.[77] But Mrs Thatcher took a different view. She was persuaded, principally by Walter Perry – the OU's first Vice-Chancellor – that it was a serious and worthwhile enterprise which would genuinely extend opportunity. It was also good value for money, an economical way to produce more graduates. So even though the Department itself was not strongly committed to it, she had already determined to defy the Treasury death sentence and allow it to go ahead.[78] She indicated her intention at the same press conference, two days after taking office, at which she precipitately announced the withdrawal of Circular 10/65. Contrary to the impression he gives in his memoirs, Heath was furious at this exercise of 'instant government', too: she had unilaterally reversed the party's policy before he had even appointed the junior minister – van Straubenzee – who would be responsible for the universities. Within days of appointing her he was already talking 'quite openly' of getting rid of his Education Secretary 'if he could'.[79]

Patrick Jenkin visited Macleod in hospital just before he died and found him very depressed that Mrs Thatcher had saved the Open University. 'It's all slipping away,' he said.[80] It was indeed an astonishingly self-confident assertion of independence by a relatively junior minister in the first days of her first Cabinet job. Thirty years later, when the Open University is established as a great success, the credit for its conception is usually given to Harold Wilson and Jennie Lee; but Margaret Thatcher deserves equal credit for single-handedly allowing it to be born when her senior colleagues were intent on aborting it. It is one of her more surprising and unsung achievements.*

She had to fight off the Treasury to raise the school-leaving age, too. But here at least she had the Prime Minister and Cabinet on her side. It was a manifesto commitment, and one which enabled the Tories to score points off Labour. 'The Labour party reneged on the obligation,' Mrs Thatcher told the party conference in October. 'We shall fulfil it.'[82] There was powerful opposition from the Tory right, and from parts of the educational world as well. The *Daily Telegraph* called the policy 'little short of lunatic'. It was very expensive, the schools could not cope with the sudden expansion of numbers and there was no benefit in compelling unwilling teenagers to stay at school. 'Mrs Thatcher should have the courage to get rid of a piece of doctrinaire nonsense with which she should never have been saddled.'[83] If she felt any sympathy for such views, however, she did not show it. Believing that education was in principle a good thing she was happy that children should have more of it; more cynically, she was content to take the credit for a major social advance. On this issue, Ronald Butt wrote in *The Times*, Mrs Thatcher stood 'unrepentently and without qualification alongside progressive fashion. She is quite sure that it is right to raise the school-leaving age, and doesn't mind if she is called a left-winger for taking this stand.'[84] When Cecil King, over dinner in January 1972, put to her Boyson's argument that truancy would simply rise and schools become unmanageable, she countered strongly:

Mrs Thatcher said the same arguments had been used for not raising the age when she was ten. But there was more to it this time, as raising the age to sixteen fits in with A-levels, O-levels, and all the machinery for providing children with higher education.[85]

Clearly she had been persuaded by the DES administrative agenda as well as by the social vision. Yet within a couple of years she had

---

* More predictably she supported Buckingham as well, which finally opened in 1974. But the whole point of Buckingham was independence of Government funding. Ralph Harris, one of its founders, remembers coming with others to see Mrs Thatcher at the DES. She was delayed, so they were received by van Straubenzee, who was keen to help, anxious to know what the Department could do. When Mrs Thatcher arrived she brushed him aside: she understood immediately that all Buckingham wanted was to be left alone.[81]

come to think that the change had perhaps been pushed through too quickly. A paper in the Conservative party archive shows that before she left the Department she set up a study group to look at the problems the schools were facing, 'as she felt that it had been wrong to go for compulsory schooling as opposed to compulsory education during the extra year'. She now regretted that 'more thought and resources had not been given to the needs of those kept on in school' by the raising of the leaving age.[86] This is a specific instance where she felt that she had allowed the Department to take her for a ride.

She was also inclined to blame her officials for failing to foresee the hornets' nest she would stir up by cutting free school milk. To the Department it seemed an obviously sensible and uncontentious economy. The Government was currently spending more on providing free milk than books for schools; much of the milk was never drunk – partly because the crates of little bottles were not refrigerated, partly because children's taste had simply moved on since Attlee's day. Labour had already stopped the supply to secondary schools, with no public outcry and no ill effect on children. By ending the provision to children aged seven to eleven, Mrs Thatcher was merely continuing a process which Labour had begun: as she pointed out when introducing the necessary legislation in June 1971, milk would still be provided free to those children who were prescribed it on medical grounds, and schools could still sell milk.[87] She later regretted that she had not compelled schools to sell it.[88] Insofar as she was withdrawing a previously universal benefit in accordance with the Tory belief that those who could afford to pay should do so, it could be presented as an ideological measure; but in truth it was a minor administrative rationalisation, ending a wasteful anachronism.

She was unprepared for the furore it aroused. In the Commons, Short indulged his usual vein of hyperbolic outrage. 'Taking the milk away from the nation's young children', he raged, was 'mean, squalid, unworthy of a great country, but it is typical of the philosophy of this astounding pre-Disraeli Government.'[89] When the Bill came back to the House in the autumn, Labour backbenchers competed with one another in crudely personal vituperation. Willie Hamilton lambasted Mrs Thatcher variously as 'Mrs Scrooge with the painted face . . . a reactionary cavewoman . . . a desiccated calculating machine with a head full of figures but . . . no bloody vision';[90] William Price called her 'the most mean and vicious member of a thoroughly discredited Government';[91] and Gerald Kaufman (rather lamely) charged that she was to British education 'what Attila the Hun was to Western civilisation'.[92] Meanwhile the

Sun asked 'Is Mrs Thatcher human?'[93] and dubbed her 'The Most Unpopular Woman in Britain'.[94]

It was the personal nature of the attacks which shook her. For the first time in her political career her sex was being used against her. The fact of a woman, a mother, taking milk from children was portrayed as far more shocking – unnatural even – than a man doing the same thing; and the cruel nickname 'Thatcher – Milk Snatcher' (coined by a speaker at the 1971 Labour party conference) struck a deep and lasting chord in the public mind. It certainly made her name: image recognition was never again a problem for her. An opinion poll in January 1972 – near the nadir of the Government's popularity, with unemployment topping a million, a miners' strike threatening and several other crises for which she was not responsible – found Mrs Thatcher the most unpopular minister. 'She isn't simply unpopular,' the London *Evening Standard* reported; she was 'hated, detested, the constant butt of unpleasant jokes, smirks, and violent verbal attacks', not so much for what she did as for what she *was*.[95] It was her preachy, middle-class manner that irritated. She drew ridicule for suggesting on television that poor children could avoid the stigma of receiving free school meals by bringing in money in a sealed envelope which would be opened and then solemnly returned to them.[96] The public felt that she did not know what she was talking about. Every time she spoke she reinforced the impression that she had no idea of how the poor lived.

Neither had many other Tory ministers, of course: but Mrs Thatcher always seemed blithely unaware of her own ignorance. Coming from a relatively humble home herself, she was happy to extrapolate naively from her own experience with no sense of incongruity. She would recall how she, as a girl, used to take her milk money into school each day: so why could not others do the same? When officials in the Department did raise the possibility that some children would not drink milk at all if they did not get it at school, she knew better. 'Gentlemen,' she told them, 'none of you is a mother. No mother ever neglects her child.'[97] Another story that quickly passed into myth was the occasion, very early in her time at the DES, when she was visiting Rhodes Boyson's Highbury Grove comprehensive in Islington and dropped in on a chemistry class. The teacher was explaining how the sulphur content in food forms silver sulphide. Mrs Thatcher's interruption was captured on television.

Particularly on breakfast spoons, you know, the spoons you use for boiled eggs. You dip in, and if they're silver they go brown and mother has to clean them. So these days we tend to use stainless steel, don't we?[98]

Within a year the *Daily Sketch* had her telling the class that 'these are not made from silver like the ones you have at home'.[99]

She was hurt to find herself presented as an unfeminine monster who stole milk from the mouths of babes and sucklings, especially since – as she claimed unconvincingly in her memoirs – she was 'never happier than in children's company'.[100] There is no question that the sudden storm of public detestation 'shook her to the core'. Toby Weaver says it 'temporarily unhorsed her'; Bill Pile witnessed tears.[101] She was upset because she thought the criticism unfair: 'Why do you go for me, much more than you went for my predecessors?' she demanded of the *Guardian* journalist, Terry Coleman. 'Why, why? Why are you doing it?'[102] The *Daily Express*'s hard-boiled columnist Jean Rook told her bluntly to stop whingeing:

> I do wish Margaret Thatcher would stop behaving like the frail, pale Most Misunderstood Girl in the School . . .
>
> Show some spunk, Margaret. Remember flaming Barbara Castle when she came back at critics like a blow lamp.
>
> You've got it in you. In fact I'd say you'd got it in you to be quite a bit of a snooty, hard-hatted, steel-blue-eyed bitch.
> Show us.[103]*

She did. It was said that Denis was so worried that Margaret could not stand the heat that he advised her to get out of the kitchen: but he has denied it, and it would have been out of character for her to buckle.[105] On the contrary, though she may have wavered, the very viciousness of the assault made her more determined to fight back. The playwright Ronald Millar, who was already writing speeches for Heath and would later become her most trusted speech doctor, met Mrs Thatcher for the first time at the height of the 'milk-snatcher' row. The occasion was a dinner at the Carlton Club during the 1972 miners' strike; there was a power cut, and they were dining by candlelight. 'She looked radiant and ridiculously young,' he wrote later. Under attack for her middle-class image, she had been advised not to wear her pearls when appearing on television.

She fingered them for a moment while she considered this, then suddenly blazed, 'No! I'm damned if I will! They were a wedding

---

* Two years later she told Jean Rook that her gibe had struck home. She misquoted it only slightly, and added: 'I didn't forget that.'[104]

present from my husband and if I want to wear them I'm going to!' Her voice was rather high-pitched and her hair bobbed furiously but there was no mistaking her contempt for such personal attacks or her resolve not to bow to them.[106]

Even before the milk row broke she had faced demonstrations whenever she visited universities and colleges of higher education: the early seventies were the high noon of student militancy. Opening a new building at Enfield College of Technology in March she countered the robotic chants of 'Thatcher out! Revolutionary socialism in!' with characteristic defiance. 'Whether you like it or not', she shouted back, 'Thatcher is here to stay!'[107] The students in 1971 never guessed how right she was: twenty years later most of them were probably good Thatcherites. Later that year she met similarly rough receptions at Liverpool Polytechnic, the Queen Elizabeth Hall on the South Bank, and at the London School of Economics. Philip Halsey remembered the South Bank demo as 'not pleasant', but Weaver says Mrs Thatcher 'never turned a hair'.[108] 'I've never been physically frightened for myself,' she told the *Daily Mail*, 'but it's a bit of a shock when you see mounted police and you know they're all there because you're there.'[109] Years later she said that facing these student demonstrations as Education Secretary was 'just about the very best training a Prime Minister could have'.[110]

She was a target for student protest not simply as a 'fascist' Tory minister, but specifically over muddled proposals to curb the political activity of student unions – on a false analogy with real trade unions – by making membership voluntary: the National Union of Students – led by its then President, Jack Straw – argued that the services it provided for students (including insurance, cheap travel and other benefits) depended on a compulsory subscription. The Vice-Chancellors backed the students' case. At the height of her unpopularity over school milk this was one battle Mrs Thatcher could do without: in January 1972 she backed down and postponed any change in student union funding for further inquiry.

Of course Mrs Thatcher had no love for the universities, regarding them – with some reason – as hotbeds of state-subsidised subversion and intolerance, not to mention idleness, drugtaking and sexual licence. She was stuck with the continuing expansion of higher education already projected into the next decade; but she was privately unenthusiastic, scornful particularly of the fashionable emphasis on sociology and social science (which she considered an oxymoron). Within six months of leaving office she was already suggesting on *Any Questions?* that the growth of higher education should be cut back.[111] Not until she was Prime Minister, however, in a changing intellectual climate, was she in a position to curb what she saw as the universities' privileged self-indulgence: while at the DES, following her retreat on student unions, she largely looked the other way and concentrated on other areas of her responsibility. She did try to encourage more students to live at home while taking their degrees, both as a way of saving money and to keep them under some parental influence. She was 'thankful', she writes in her memoirs, that Carol – then studying law at University College, London – was living at home: not surprisingly, she was getting 'a hard time' from fellow-students.[112] But she resisted, for the moment, calls to replace student grants with loans.

At the beginning of 1972 there was speculation in the press that Heath might sack his Education Secretary. She herself told Cecil King that 'the so-called liberals (the left-wingers, the long-haired and all that group)' were determined to get her out of office, 'and will doubtless succeed'.[113] (One of the most prominent of those liberals, Lady Plowden – author of the influential 1967 report on primary education – had earlier told King that Mrs Thatcher was 'intelligent and able, but so *silly*. She had antagonised so many people quite unnecessarily.')[114] In fact Heath stood by her in her darkest hour. At the end of the month he invited her, with Pile and other of her officials, to Chequers to discuss her future plans. This was a clear signal that she was not about to be removed (though Pile took it as a sign that he was not to be moved either). She 'emerged radiant', the *Daily Mail* reported. 'The comeback has begun.'[115]

Four days later Heath defended her at Prime Minister's Questions in the Commons. First Gerald Kaufman asked if he would dismiss her, following her 'petty-minded and vindictive interference with Manchester Corporation', forbidding them providing hot drinks with free school dinners as a way of getting round the milk restriction. Heath told him it was a purely legal matter: the LEA was obliged to charge for milk. Then Short condemned her 'constant monotonous decisions . . . to reject local authority reorganisation schemes'. Heath replied that it was her statutory duty to judge every scheme: 'At least she has not tried to bully local authorities to accept one scheme.' Finally, after a Tory, William Clark, had praised her for saving a grammar school in Surrey, Harold Wilson took up Kaufman's question. If Mrs Thatcher could introduce a Bill to stop free milk – 'one of the filthiest Bills that we have ever had in this House' – she could equally easily introduce another to allow LEAs to provide free drinks with meals. Heath repeated that he saw no need for a change in the law, and recalled that Labour had cut secondary school milk without any exemptions at all.

Invited by another Conservative to congratulate Mrs Thatcher on her achievements since taking office, he did so generously, mentioning specifically the increased primary school building programme, the continuing expansion of the polytechnics and the raising of the school-leaving age, with the increased staffing that involved.[116] She was grateful for his support. 'I like to think', she wrote in her memoirs, 'that it showed Ted's character at its admirable best . . . However unreliable his adherence to particular policies, he always stood by people who did their best for him and his Government.'[117] Even her tributes were always touched with acid.

From this low point her fortunes sharply improved: the second half of her time at the DES was, at least in terms of public perception, dramatically more successful than the first. This was partly due to the fact that from late 1971 she had a new press officer, Terry Perks, with whom she got on exceptionally well. Formerly at the Home Office under Henry Brooke, now drafted to Education from the Department of Transport, Perks finished up as Bernard Ingham's deputy in Number Ten during the 1980s: he had a lot to do with Mrs Thatcher's more professional presentation of herself from 1972 onwards. The first sign that she had turned the corner actually came before the end of January when she won an unexpectedly good reception from a NUT dinner. She was able to reap the credit for having finally given the go-ahead to raising the school-leaving age. She made 'a splendid speech', *The Times* reported, 'full of warmth, wit and friendly reproach to her critics. Seasoned Thatcher-watchers reckoned it her best public appearance yet.'[118]

From this she went on to an even more unlikely triumph at the NUT conference in April. 'Visibly trembling' when she began her speech,[119] she was helped rather than hurt when a section of her audience walked out – regarded in those more courteous days as 'an unparalleled public snub'[120] – and finally won a standing ovation after expressing her belief in smaller comprehensives – a clever way of excusing her rejection of plans for big ones. The *Sunday Telegraph* hailed this speech as 'The Making of Mrs Thatcher'.[121]

Two months later a *Times* profile described her 'remarkable political rebirth'. She still might not be popular; but in a Cabinet lacking in outstanding personalities, she was now the fourth best-known minister. The paper's education correspondent, Stephen

Jessel, ascribed her success, somewhat backhandedly, to her lack of an overarching vision:

> It is not intended as a criticism of Mrs Thatcher to argue that under her the education scene has entered a period of benign neglect; quite possibly this is what is needed after ten years of sustained change and expansion. Her instinct is in the fullest sense conservative; she is evidently sceptical of many progressive orthodoxies . . . She has shown few educational initiatives, and this again is not necessarily a cause for criticism. Her preference is clearly for the brake rather than the accelerator.

Her early 'disasters', Jessel judged – the over-hasty withdrawal of Circular 10/65, the school milk row and her attempt to curb the student unions – were all matters of style, not content. 'A really sensitive politician would have avoided much of the obloquy created by the way these issues were treated.' But Mrs Thatcher had delivered the Tories' manifesto promises and protected the education budget. Of all her predecessors, the one she most resembled, ironically, was Short: 'Both are widely disliked, both are canny politicians and bonny fighters. Both have a kind of gritty and arguably misdirected sense of purpose.'[122] It is hard to know which of them would have disliked the comparison more.

Mrs Thatcher sealed her rehabilitation in the eyes of the educational establishment with the publication, towards the end of 1972, of her White Paper, *A Framework for Expansion*. This represented the culmination of a whole raft of policies the DES had been working on for twenty years. Her officials are unanimous in affirming that she had remarkably little to do with its conception: she was merely the midwife. It projected a 50 per cent rise in education spending (in real terms) over the next ten years, pushing education's share from 13 to 14 per cent of total government expenditure (overtaking defence for the first time). Within this overall growth there was to be a vast expansion of nursery education, designed to provide free part-time nursery places for 50 per cent of three-year-olds and 90 per cent of four-year-olds by 1981 (concentrated at first in areas of greatest need); a 40 per cent increase in the number of teachers – from 360,000 in 1971 to a projected 510,000 in 1981, which would cut the average teacher–pupil ratio from one to 22.6 to one to 18.5; and the continued expansion of higher education, evenly divided between the universities and polytechnics, to a target of 750,000 students by 1981 (an increase from 15 to 22 per cent of eighteen-year-olds).[123]

This was a hugely ambitious plan, and a triumph for the DES. Pile was afraid that Mrs Thatcher would not swallow it: in fact she took it all on board without demur. At a time when Government spending was expanding on all fronts she was determined to get her share of it. Having had to fight the Treasury hard over her first two years to get the money she wanted for school building and improving teachers' pay, she was taken aback by the ease with which the Cabinet accepted her proposed White Paper. She had expected another battle.[124] Very soon she came to repudiate her own enthusiasm for it. Looking back, she wrote in her memoirs, it was 'all too typical of those over-ambitious, high-spending years . . . 'In retrospect the White Paper marks the high point of the attempts by Government to overcome the problems inherent in Britain's education system by throwing money at them.'[125]

At the time, however, she basked in the almost universal praise her plans attracted. Every minister likes to put his or her name to something big; and she was happy to be seen as less of a reactionary than had been thought. *A Framework for Expansion* was the last throw not only of expansion, but of consensus in education. Apart from failing to abolish the eleven-plus, the *Guardian* suggested, the White Paper showed Mrs Thatcher 'more than half way towards a respectably socialist education policy'.[126] Her principal monument was to be the commitment to free nursery schools. This had been a recommendation of the Plowden Report in 1967, following the efforts over many years of the National Campaign for Nursery Education. It was a long-standing ambition of the department which her officials added to the draft White Paper only when they found her unexpectedly sympathetic. In principle she would have preferred to encourage fee-paying private nursery schools, as the Tory party's education policy group had recommended in opposition: but she seized gratefully on the idea of promoting free local authority schools as a popular move which would divert attention from the storms she had aroused over school milk and comprehensivisation. She was converted to a Plowdenesque belief in equality of early opportunity, as she explained to George Gardiner in 1975:

> You found that by the time children came to school at the age of five a lot of them were already behind because they came from homes where no interest was taken in the children, where the parents didn't talk to them . . .
>   Of course, the State can never take the place of good parents . . . But it can help redress the balance for those born unlucky.[127]

After the age of five she believed that life was a competition which the best should win; but a level starting line was within her philosophy.

The first priority was therefore to provide schools in the most deprived areas. This complemented Keith Joseph's concern (at the DHSS) with breaking what he called the 'cycle of deprivation'. It also accorded with political reality, since Conservative authorities in middle-class areas tended not to want state nursery schools competing with existing private ones, whereas Labour authorities did want them. The result was the only instance in her whole career of Mrs Thatcher deliberately practising positive discrimination. In promoting her policy, however, she was very firm that she was talking about nursery *education*, for no more than three hours a day, 'not child minding as a public service for working mothers'.[128] 'The case for nursery education', she insisted, 'is an *educational* case.'[129] 'I would not like to see a nation of children who know only the day nursery as home,' she told the League of Jewish Women in her constituency.[130] Her stress on education was admirable; but the need for childminding was also real and growing. She was already displaying a lack of concern for the problems of working mothers which was to become more serious when she became Prime Minister. Now that her own children were grown up she seemed increasingly to believe that mothers should not go out to work – certainly not full time – unless they could afford to pay for private child care.

Over-optimistically as it turned out, she denied that her nursery school programme was too ambitious. Unlike 'pie-in-the-sky pronouncements by people whose hearts may be in the right place but who sometimes seem averse to the simplest forms of calculation', she boasted that her plans were strictly costed and affordable.[131] Alas, her optimism was blown away within a year by the quadrupling of oil prices following the Yom Kippur war and the consequent recession which forced cutbacks in Government spending for the next decade. Mrs Thatcher's bold plans were under threat before she had even left office. They were not pursued by her Labour successors after February 1974; and by the time Mrs Thatcher returned to Downing Street as Prime Minister in 1979 her interest in using the state to extend educational opportunity had passed. Not until 1995 did the aspiration to offer nursery places to all pre-school children creep back on to the political agenda. A generous vision which might have been the most far-reaching legacy from Mrs Thatcher's time as Education Secretary was sadly destined to go down as one of the great might-have-beens of recent history.

The expansion of nursery schools and polytechnics, an extra year

of schooling, better buildings, more teachers, secondary reorganisation – Mrs Thatcher's time at the DES was all about the delivery of
education, scarcely at all about the content. Fifteen years later, in her
second term as Prime Minister, she decided that the schools were
failing and determined to challenge the educationists' professional
monopoly; she sent Kenneth Baker to her old department to
introduce a unified national curriculum, and took a close interest in
its content herself. But in 1970–4 she accepted the convention that
politicians had no role inside the schools.

In fact thinking on this question within the DES had been
cautiously shifting ever since Boyle's time.[132] But the notion of a
national curriculum was seen politically as a socialist idea: it was Jim
Callaghan who placed it openly on the agenda in his Ruskin College
speech in 1976, calling for a 'great debate' on education. As a
Conservative, Mrs Thatcher rejected it on libertarian grounds. 'A
minister should not have power over ideas,' she declared firmly soon
after taking office in 1970. 'I would not like to see over here a system
as in France where all schools keep to the same curriculum.'[133] She
did set up an inquiry into literacy standards chaired by the historian
Sir Alan Bullock, as well as the promised committee on teacher
training, chaired by Lord James of Rusholme. She once, at a
headmasters' conference in 1972, flew a kite for the possibility of a
broader curriculum, at least up to O level; and on the same occasion
ventured to advocate a more vocational choice of subjects, alluding
delicately to 'the danger of being over-attracted by the intellectual
and emotional appeal of some of the more modern courses' – by
which she meant the social sciences.[134] In general, however, she held
her tongue and confined her efforts to winning the resources to
expand the existing system.

She managed to avoid the blame for the fiasco of the Government's attempt to impose admission charges for entry to museums
and galleries. It was a surprising policy for Heath to have supported:
even odder that the minister who championed it was Lord Eccles,
one of the most cultured politicians of the postwar period. Apart
from simply raising revenue, their argument was that people only
appreciated what they had to pay for. Defending the charges in the
Commons in 1973 Mrs Thatcher played a straight bat, detailing the
museums' need for more money, denying that charging would
reduce attendance and averting a threatened backbench rebellion by
conceding that the institutions should be allowed to keep their own
takings.[135] Norman St John Stevas, who took over the arts brief from
Eccles in December 1973, claims that he, not Mrs Thatcher,
negotiated this and other concessions with the Treasury. Just a week

after taking office Stevas announced that each gallery would be allowed to offer one free day every week, while pensioners and school parties would still enjoy free entry.[136] Enough Tories – including Jeffrey Archer – did nevertheless rebel to cut the Government's majority to six. But the whole exercise proved a waste of time and money when the incoming Labour Government instantly scrapped the charges in March 1974, two months after they had come into force. The evidence of those two months was that admissions did fall sharply. As Prime Minister Mrs Thatcher squeezed arts budgets, leading some museums to impose voluntary admission charges; but she never tried to reimpose compulsory charges.

She did one service to the arts in the dying days of the Heath Government by strongly supporting the introduction of Public Lending Right, the culmination of a long campaign by the Society of Authors to win a token payment to the author for every book borrowed from a public library. Eccles had opposed this tiny act of justice; but Stevas pushed it through, deploying Mrs Thatcher to browbeat Terence Higgins, the Financial Secretary, who was not even given a chance to present the Treasury case:

> She gave him one of her looks and said:
> 'Terence, why do you *always* look so miserable?' The unfortunate Mr Higgins never fully recovered from this observation, and the authors were the beneficiaries.[137]

In the end, however, even she could not protect her department from the heavy cuts Barber was forced to impose at the end of 1973. Patrick Jenkin, who had replaced Maurice Macmillan as Chief Secretary in 1972, remembers Mrs Thatcher as by far the toughest spending minister he had to deal with: she would not settle with him at all, but insisted on going over his head to Heath and Barber before she would accept the curtailment of her cherished plans.[138] In the Commons she put a brave face on her loss:

> All ministers dislike having to make cuts in their forecast expenditure, and naturally my hon. Friends and I are disappointed that we have had to revise our plans for this year and next; but we recognise, as most people do, that we cannot insulate the education service from the economic situation any more than could the Labour Government.

Excluding Scotland, science and the arts, the DES share of the cuts amounted to £157 million out of a total departmental budget of £3.5 billion. This she described as 'serious but not disastrous': she gave the impression that the cuts would only slow the projected building programme and procurement by LEAs, insisting that the department's essential priorities – including the nursery programme – had been substantially preserved.[139] This was her last speech from the dispatch box as Education Secretary. Just over a week later, when the miners – whose overtime ban had already reduced the country to a three-day week – voted for a full-scale strike, Heath finally gave in to the hawks in his Cabinet and called the fatal General Election which removed him from office.

Mrs Thatcher's wider role as a member of the Heath Government remains a source of embarrassment to her. Not only did she pursue policies in her own department which she later came to repudiate, and fail to promote others which in retrospect she wished she had embraced more vigorously. She also conspicuously failed to dissent from economic policies which she very soon came to regard as disastrously flawed and which, she would have us believe, she instinctively knew to be wrong all along. For someone who would later make so much of being a 'conviction politician' this was a singularly unheroic performance, on which she and her biographers have had to expend much effort in trying to explain or deny.

Part of her explanation is that she was too fully occupied with her own departmental responsibilities to have time for the wider picture. This was the basis of Keith Joseph's subsequent apologia; but it is not really credible in the case of a woman of such tireless energy and stamina as Margaret Thatcher, especially since the economy was the one area of policy outside her own department in which she was keenly interested. She made no secret that her ultimate ambition was to be Chancellor. More to the point is the fact that she was pretty rigorously excluded from any input into economic policy. Of course every modern British Government – her own was certainly no different – has concentrated control of the economy in a tight inner group often extending no further than the Prime Minister and Chancellor. Economic strategy in 1970–4 was very firmly dictated by Heath, with Barber his loyal (though not always convinced) executor. No other minister had much of a role: even John Davies, the Trade and Industry Secretary, was effectively excluded from the decision to reverse the Government's original policy of non-intervention in industry. Mrs Thatcher was more isolated than most, however, partly because Education is by its nature an isolated department with relatively little impact on other departments, which meant that she sat on very few Cabinet committees; but also because her sex and her personality combined to exclude her from the collective camaraderie of what was for the most part an exceptionally harmonious and united Cabinet.

It was already clear in opposition that Heath disliked her. In Government, Jim Prior says that the Prime Minister 'cold-shouldered' her, placing her deliberately at the far right-hand end of the Cabinet table where he could not see her.[140] (But someone has to sit there; and she ranked near the bottom of the Cabinet pecking order.) After she had supplanted him as leader, stories began to circulate about how Heath used to get annoyed with her talking too much in Cabinet. It was said that he would tap his blotter in visible irritation and once actually leaned down the table to tell her to shut up.[141] But he was not alone in finding her trying. Willie Whitelaw told Cecil King early in the Government's life that she was unquestionably able, 'but in her dealings with people she is apt to lecture and bulldoze her way, when more conciliatory methods would be more successful'.[142] Reggie Maudling used to return to the Home Office after Cabinet meetings raging about 'that bloody woman', complaining that she 'never listened'.[143] Even the Cabinet Secretary, Burke Trend, once begged Bill Pile to 'keep that woman's mouth shut' in Cabinet.[144] Clearly she was not shy of expressing her views – at least at first. But by the time the Government was diverging from what she might have believed the right path, she had exhausted her colleagues' patience. She writes in *The Path to Power* that she had 'just one political friend in Cabinet' – Keith Joseph.

> Although I generally had polite and pleasant relations with my other colleagues, I knew that we were not soulmates. Doubtless they knew it too . . . What with the formidable difficulties I faced in Education, I therefore had little incentive to try to win wider strategic points in Cabinet.[145]

The Government notoriously made two major U-turns in economic policy, both in 1972. First, in response to rising unemployment – which in January 1972 passed the symbolic and at that time politically intolerable figure of one million – and an alarming 'work-in' by Glasgow shipworkers against the threatened closure of their yards, Heath reversed the policy of not bailing out 'lame ducks' on which he had fought the 1970 election and started to throw money indiscriminately at industry in a successful (but inflationary) effort to stimulate the economy into rapid growth.

Second, when inflation rocketed – as a result partly of sharp increases in the price of imported commodities (copper, rubber, zinc and other raw materials) even before the 1973 oil price shock, but also, it was almost universally believed, of excessive domestic wage increases – the Government abandoned its apparently principled rejection of incomes policy and introduced, from November 1972, an increasingly complex system of statutory wage and price control. Both policies commanded wide support on the Conservative benches and in the press. A handful of eccentric monetarists – most prominently Enoch Powell, more tentatively people like John Biffen, Jock Bruce-Gardyne, Nicholas Ridley and Ronald Bell – warned that the Government was itself fuelling the very inflation it was attempting to cure; while a rather larger number of more traditional right-wingers were disturbed by the socialistic overtones of the Government's increasing interference in the economy. But in the short term both policies appeared to be working: the economy boomed, unemployment fell and inflation was contained. Until the double blow of the oil crisis and the miners' strike at the end of 1973 the Government seemed to be surmounting its problems with a good chance of re-election in the autumn of 1974 or spring of 1975.

There is little evidence that Mrs Thatcher offered any serious objection to either U-turn. She positively supported what many regarded as the forerunner of the later reversals, the nationalisation of the aircraft division of Rolls-Royce in 1971. She relates in her memoirs that she was alerted by a constituent to the fact that the company was in trouble, and asked Denis to look at the accounts. He spotted an elementary flaw: they were treating research and development costs as capital expenditure. Thus armed, she writes, she was able to go to Cabinet and amaze her colleagues with her knowledge.[146] However this may be, she still defends the nationalisation of Rolls-Royce – politically embarrassing though it was for a Conservative Government – as necessary on defence grounds, to save the aero-engine business, not as industrial intervention to prop up a lame duck. Rolls-Royce was in fact successfully returned to the private sector during her own premiership.

On the other hand she claims to have been 'deeply troubled' by the commercially unjustified rescue of Upper Clyde Shipbuilders in January 1972. She discussed it privately with Bruce-Gardyne, who was 'scathing' about it.[147] But she did nothing. Two months later she was fortuitously absent – owing to 'a long-standing scientific engagement' – when the content of Barber's 1972 Budget, foreshadowing Davies's Industry Bill, was sprung on the Cabinet. But it would have made no difference if she had been there. A report in *The Times* named her as one of a number of Cabinet Ministers who 'frankly confess their uneasiness about the socialist implications' of the Government's new strategy; but that was all.[148] Cabinets did not leak so freely in those days, nor did ministers brief the press with their private views. Mrs Thatcher uttered no public indication of dissent, unless there was a coded message in her speech to the party conference in October, when she declared pointedly that 'I believe it is right for any Government to honour the terms of its manifesto. That is precisely what we are doing in education.'[149] 'Should I have resigned?' she asks in her memoirs.

> Perhaps so. But those of us who disliked what was happening had not yet either fully analysed the situation or worked out an alternative approach. Nor, realistically speaking, would my resignation have made a great deal of difference.[150]

If we allow that she was disturbed by the industrial policy U-turn – if only because it exposed the Government to a good deal of gleeful mockery from Labour – there is no doubt that she fully supported the Government's counter-inflation policy. 'We had no clear theory of inflation or the role of wage settlements within it,' she admits. 'And without such a theory we drifted into the superstition that inflation was the direct result of wage increases.'[151] It was not just a matter of drifting: all her pronouncements from 1970 onwards repeat the conventional orthodoxy of the day: that unjustified wage rises caused inflation.[152] In his memoirs Nicholas Ridley claimed to remember Mrs Thatcher coming up to him and Biffen in the lobby during a division on the Bill:

> 'I wish I could join you in your battle,' she said. 'You could,' we replied, 'if you resigned and joined us.' She didn't. I don't think she realised at that time the gravity of the situation.[153]

But Biffen has no recollection of any such clear statement of dissent. On the contrary he – like Enoch Powell – considered Mrs Thatcher, as a loyal Cabinet minister, fully 'identified with all the Government's economic policies'. So far as he was aware she gave out no coded signals of sympathy with those who were opposing the policy from outside the Government,[154] any more than any of her colleagues remembers her questioning it from within. Peter Walker insists that 'there was no free market voice in the Cabinet . . . Keith Joseph later argued that we should control the money supply, but neither he nor Margaret nor Geoffrey [Howe] did so at the time.'[155]

She does not dispute this judgement: 'There were brave and far-sighted critics who were proved right. But they were an embattled, isolated group. Although my reservations steadily grew, I was not at this stage among them.'[156]

On the contrary, she strongly and specifically defended the Prices and Incomes policy as 'absolutely necessary' at a time when large wage awards were pushing up unemployment. 'The Government had stimulated employment by the expansion of credit,' she told her constituents in February 1973. 'But the only way inflation could be contained was by bringing in a prices and incomes policy.'[157] 'The only thing now which will stabilise this country from inflation is the support of public opinion behind the Government.'[158] At her AGM a few weeks later she insisted that the Government must stand up to 'wreckers' in the unions who were trying to break Stage 2 of the policy.

> We are poised to win the inflation battle if we stand firm when we are challenged. There can be no special cases in Stage 2. It is vital we go on to the next stage with everyone being treated alike. If there are a lot of special cases we have lost the last battle.[159]

The third big issue of the Heath Government on which Mrs Thatcher expressed no contrary view at the time was Britain's entry into the European Community. Heath's achievement in persuading President Pompidou to lift de Gaulle's veto, negotiating acceptable terms, winning a substantial bipartisan majority in the House of Commons and forcing the enabling legislation through against the determined opposition of a section of his own party, finally joining the Community on 1 January 1973, was the one unquestioned success of his ill-fated Government. Mrs Thatcher was firmly and conventionally supportive of the European project, as she had been since Macmillan first launched it in 1961. The Conservative opponents of entry – led by Enoch Powell – included several like John Biffen, Richard Body and Teddy Taylor who were to be among her own strongest supporters in the future when she turned against further integration with Europe. On the other hand many more who followed her lead in the 1980s and 1990s – including Nicholas Ridley, George Gardiner and Norman Lamont – were at that time among the most prominent pro-Europeans. Twenty years later they came to believe that Heath had taken Britain into the Community on a false prospectus, in defiance of his promise to join only with the 'full-hearted consent' of the British people, by presenting the Community as a purely economic enterprise – a common market – and glossing over the long-term political ambition for 'ever-closer union'.

In her memoirs Mrs Thatcher accepted her share of the blame for what she now considered a serious misjudgement. With hindsight she believed that the terms of entry 'should have been considered more carefully'; and called the issue of sovereignty 'the dog that barely barked at the time'. In fact Powell and the other Tory opponents of entry made strenuous play with the sovereignty issue. (Labour opponents tended to concentrate more on the detailed terms.) But no one listened – as she admits:

> It seemed to me then, as it did to my colleagues, that the arguments about sovereignty which were advanced by Enoch Powell and others were theoretical points used as rhetorical devices.[160]

Her own case for joining was admittedly less robust on the question of sovereignty than it had been in 1962. At a special Saturday morning meeting in Finchley, after the conclusion of the negotiations but before the Commons vote, she made the case for entry principally in terms of the enlarged market; but at the same time she linked it to a sense of political belonging:

> We found we weren't able to get into Europe, but Europe got on without us. It is important that we have access to these expanding markets, and not be on the outside looking in.

'We have a great deal to contribute to the development of Europe,' she argued, betraying her view of Europeans as excitable foreigners. 'Our experience, our calm, will add a great deal.' But she did not at this date think that Britain had nothing to learn from the continent. 'Our social services are not better, but in some respects not as good as those in Europe.' Harmonisation, she suggested, would not be easy – an admission that social questions were not seen as being excluded from the Community's future development. She did not believe that foreigners would flock to take advantage of British benefits: the movement of labour was more likely to be the other way, since wages, even for the unskilled, were often higher in Europe. 'We are not such a magnet as you might think . . . I don't believe that the British taxpayer will have to fork out for everyone else.' On the specific question of sinking British identity in a United States of Europe she was unconcerned:

I think we have a tendency in this country to be slightly isolationist in some things, but expect other people to listen to us when it comes to anything else. In the voting we are allowed full status of other major nations. France is no less French, or Holland less Dutch, for joining. We have a very great deal to contribute.[161]

As Education Secretary Mrs Thatcher had less opportunity than almost any other minister to contribute personally to the development of the Community in the first year of British membership. She showed little interest in forging European links where the possibility arose.* But towards the end of 1973 it was reported that Heath was thinking of making her Minister for Europe.[163] This was not the first time he had considered moving her. In November 1972, when Peter Walker replaced John Davies at Trade and Industry, Heath offered him the choice of Geoffrey Howe or Margaret Thatcher as his number two, in charge of Consumer Affairs. The job carried a seat in the Cabinet, so it would not strictly have been a demotion for Mrs Thatcher. Walker, however, understandably thought that she would make an uncomfortable deputy and chose Howe. (He admits in his memoirs that he did not welcome the idea of working with a woman.)[164] It was an extraordinary moment for Heath to have considered moving Mrs Thatcher – just before she produced her major education White Paper. The fact that he did so suggests that he still thought of her as a maid of all work who could be transferred from portfolio to portfolio at will. He probably also thought that price control was a suitable job for a woman. It is a piquant thought that she might have been responsible for operating the Government's prices policy. In fact the experience would almost certainly have convinced her, even more swiftly than it did Howe, of the futility of trying to hold prices down by law. Even so, she was 'thankful' that she was not offered this 'poisoned chalice'.[165]

Nevertheless there are indications that she would have welcomed a move – presumably after she had launched her White Paper. She

---

* For some time the British Council had been working to create an exchange scheme whereby students in EEC countries would be able to spend a year, or a term, at a university in another member country, as part of their course: a precursor of the idea that later became the very successful Erasmus scheme. Having agreed a pioneer scheme with the German Government, the Council assumed that DES approval would be a formality. They were staggered, therefore, when after a long delay Mrs Thatcher vetoed it on the ground that while the Government appreciated the benefit to foreign students studying in Britain she could see no reciprocal advantages to British students going abroad.[162]

had spent three years at the Ministry of Pensions under Macmillan and Home, and by the middle of 1973 she was the longest-serving Education minister since Attlee's time. Ambitious for the top jobs – the Treasury or the Foreign Office – she wanted to broaden her experience beyond the social departments. In November 1973 it was disclosed that for the past year she had been taking French lessons at the Foreign Office.[166] Was this because she had been tipped off to prepare for the European job or just her way of dropping a hint? There is no way of knowing whether Heath seriously thought of sending her to Brussels: it would have been another piquant appointment, with incalculable consequences if it had come off. But any leak of his intentions was usually enough to make Heath change his mind. A few weeks later the *Observer* changed its story: now she was tipped to replace Geoffrey Rippon at the Department of the Environment after Christmas.[167] In fact she stayed where she was – as did both Davies and Rippon – until the General Election removed them all from office.

She had no reservations about supporting the Government in its life or death stand against the miners. In the early days of the combined oil and coal crisis she defended the Government's imposition of a three-day week in industry to save energy and preserve oil stocks. 'Either the Government has got to let things run', she declared in Finchley, 'or take emergency powers to conserve stocks and use them prudently like a frugal housewife.'[168] The action taken, she claimed a few weeks later, had been both necessary and successful. It is an enduring myth that the three-day week was a time of power cuts and candles: those folk memories date from the 1972 miners' strike. The whole purpose of the three-day week in 1973–4 was to prevent a repetition of those scenes. It succeeded, and it was precisely this success, as Mrs Thatcher pointed out on 26 January, which drove the NUM to escalate their action from an overtime ban to a full-scale strike. 'In my opinion', she asserted provocatively, 'the miners' leaders are now trying to force their members to strike because our steps have succeeded and theirs have not.'[169]

At the same time she fought like a tiger to protect her own patch. She was furious when she learned that restrictions on heating public buildings were to be applied to schools, especially when the *Sun* blamed her for letting children shiver. Jim Prior, chairing the relevant committee dealing with the emergency, remembers the three-day week as the first time he fully appreciated 'Margaret Thatcher's absolute determination to fight her corner'.

Margaret was absolutely furious because she had not been properly consulted. She laid down the law to Tom Boardman [Minister of State at the DTI] in a way that I had never heard it laid down before. I was most impressed.[170]

In Finchley she boasted that she had got the proposed ban reversed within twenty-four hours.[171] Though it was not her departmental responsibility, she also took up the case of hairdressers whose business was being damaged by the three-day week: she was always susceptible to claims for special treatment from groups in whom she was personally interested.[172]

In her memoirs Lady Thatcher confirms that she was one of those ministers – among them Prior and Lord Carrington, the party chairman – who wanted Heath to go to the country several weeks before he did.

> Denis and I, our friends and most of my Party workers, felt that we now had to pick up the gauntlet and that the only way to do that was by calling and winning a general election.

She was frustrated by Heath's 'strange lack of urgency'.

> He seemed out of touch with reality. He was still more interested in the future of Stage 3 and in the oil crisis than he was in . . . the survival of the Government.

She still believes the Government would have won – or at least 'scraped in' – at an earlier election fought 'unashamedly' on the issue of union power.[173]

Yet her public stance at the time was not much less conciliatory than Heath's. While she condemned the miners' leaders and attacked Communist influence in the NUM, she insisted that the Government's offer to the miners – in the range of 13–16 per cent – was 'generous' and argued that the Government had 'kept faith with the miners' when it could have switched to other energy sources: 'In the last few years oil has been cheap and we could have diverted much more to the power stations, but we remained loyal to the miners and ordered coal to keep the pits open.' She appealed to the miners in turn to vote against a strike. At the same time she pointed out that North Sea gas and oil would soon give the Government alternatives to both coal and imported oil. 'The prospects are enormous.'[174] In the prevailing mood of almost apocalyptic gloom, this was an unusually optimistic message.

On 4 February, however, the miners voted overwhelmingly to

step up their action; and Heath finally bowed to the clamour for an election, though still seeking a settlement of the dispute by referring the miners' claim to the Pay Board while the election was in progress. He was honourably determined not to fight a confrontational campaign against the miners, even though that would almost certainly have given him his best chance of winning. Mrs Thatcher in all her published and reported statements loyally followed her leader's line. 'Our aim is a Britain united in moderation and not divided in spirit,' she declared at her adoption meeting on 11 February. The Government had sought 'a settlement that is fair and reasonable to everyone concerned . . . I think everyone will agree that the Government has done everything possible to prevent a strike.'[175] Her election address emphasised Moderation and Fairness, and the importance of defeating the militants to preserve 'our traditional way of life'.

> This Is Our Aim. A Britain united in moderation, not divided by extremism. A society in which there is change without revolution. A Government that is strong in order to protect the weak . . . Once the General Election is behind us we must put aside our differences and join in a common determination to establish and maintain a secure, civilised and fair society.

Of course those soft words – like her quoting St Francis of Assisi five years later – were open to a harsher interpretation. But there was no aggression in them: no hint of red-blooded Toryism, or 'clear blue water'. More specifically, there was no sign whatever in February 1974 that Mrs Thatcher was preparing to distance herself from Heath's 'corporatist' strategy of trying to run the economy by agreement with both sides of industry. On the contrary she echoed the Tory manifesto in promising that the Government, if re-elected, would reform the ill-fated Industrial Relations Act 'in the light of experience after consultation with both sides of industry' – the very essence of corporatism. She advocated ballots for union elections, and an end to welfare benefits for strikers. But she envisaged no relaxation of the statutory incomes policy – quite the reverse: 'We shall . . . press ahead with the pay and prices policy, if necessary stiffening it in the light of the developing economic situation.' The next Tory Government, she promised, would strengthen the Price Commission to give it powers to control the price of key foodstuffs directly.[176]

In fact she said nothing remotely out of line with Government policy as pursued for the past two years. Though she was a Cabinet minister with a high profile and a reasonably safe seat, Central Office chose not to deploy her extensively around the country – the risk of student demonstrations was still too great – or at all on television, where she still came over poorly. (She did one radio phone-in with Willie Whitelaw and appeared with Heath and Carrington at one press conference.) Instead she spent most of the campaign in her own constituency, holding what the *Finchley Press* called 'a string of public meetings' in Finchley and Friern Barnet, at which 'she stressed vehemently the case for keeping a Tory government', while attacking Labour's profligate spending plans as 'an exercise in irresponsibility'.[177]

Boundary changes meant that she could no longer take the seat for granted: she had lost part of North Finchley and all of Totteridge to Chipping Barnet, and part of Hampstead Garden Suburb to Hendon South: on paper these changes helped both Labour and the Liberals, who were again mounting a strong challenge. Moreover she had a potential problem with the Jewish vote as a result of Heath's even-handed policy of refusing to supply Israel with military parts, or even allow American planes to supply Israel from British airfields, during the Yom Kippur war. This issue allied Mrs Thatcher once again with Keith Joseph, the only Jewish member of the Cabinet. Together they protested, but Heath and Alec Home were determined to avert an Arab oil embargo by maintaining strict neutrality. She met the Finchley branch of the Anglo-Israel Friendship League to assure them that she opposed the Government's policy.[178] This was the most difficult period in her long and close relationship with her Jewish constituents; but her position was not seriously threatened, as her agent told a journalist:

> I'm not seriously worried, because she has done so much personal work with the Jewish community here. She goes to their functions, she knows the rabbis by their first names, and a lot of Jewish people are active members of our association.[179]

The journalist was the future historian Peter Hennessy, then on the *Times Higher Education Supplement*, who had been assigned to tail the Education Secretary for a day. His report gives a vivid account of the last campaign she was to fight as a primarily local figure. (It is noteworthy that, almost alone in the Cabinet, she is not mentioned once in the Nuffield study of the February election: by October she was a major player.)[180] ' "On the stump" ', Hennessy wrote, 'is too coarse an expression to apply to the electioneering activities of Mrs Margaret Thatcher.'

'On the shimmer' would be a more appropriate description of her queenly progression through the motions of putting the Tory case to the people.

Sensibly for a working minister with a safe seat, she rations her radiance carefully, running the Department of Education and Science by telephone and ministerial box, confining herself to interviews at Conservative Central Office in the mornings and speeches in the evenings, leaving her afternoons free for speech writing and correspondence.

With no candidate to track during the afternoon Hennessy took the chance to talk to Roy Langstone, her agent for the past twelve years, and found him 'eulogistic' about his MP – and prescient too. 'Normally women in politics are a bloody nuisance,' he complained.

But she is the most fantastic person I've ever worked for in 27 years as an agent. She gets more done in a day than most MPs do in a week. The greater proportion of this constituency would be very, very proud to see Mrs Thatcher as the first woman Prime Minister of this country. I know she's got the capabilities. One of these days maybe; one never knows.

That evening two hundred of the party faithful – 'all of whom, no doubt, would like to see her in No. 10' – turned up to hear her speak in a tiny church hall in Whetstone. 'Part of her appeal', Hennessy reckoned, 'must surely be her amazingly wholesome appearance', with 'not a hair out of place' and 'that whiter-than-white smile'. Faced with tricky questions, he wrote, 'Mrs Thatcher adopts an air of intelligent innocence . . . an air of pained surprise when people fail to understand the sweet reasonableness of her position'. One question in particular, about 'the iniquity of high profits accruing to supermarket chains' she dealt with 'in a manner calculated to set the Tory heart athrob':

As someone who had had to work for everything she owned, she would far rather work for a company that made a profit than one that did not, said Mrs Thatcher, shimmering slightly and demonstrating, yet again, that Righteousness can be beautiful.[181]

No doubt it went down well, but the first part of this answer was simply not true. Righteousness can also be self-deceiving.

This was an election the Tories confidently expected to win. Indeed one reason Heath fought such a poor campaign was that he was afraid of winning too heavily: he did not want a majority of 1931 proportions gained by smashing the unions. In the event he failed to polarise the country sufficiently. The continuing power restrictions merely irritated the voters while defusing the sense of crisis on which the Government's case depended. By referring the miners' dispute to the Pay Board the Government seemed to call in question the point of having an election at all. Labour was still in disarray over Europe and beginning to be torn apart by the new hard left: Wilson did not expect to win any more than Heath expected to lose. In these circumstances the electorate called a plague on both their houses and turned in unprecedented numbers to the Liberals.

Mrs Thatcher felt the effect in Finchley, where the Liberals fielded their best candidate since John Pardoe, a young Jewish solicitor named Laurence Brass who made effective play with the Government's 'betrayal' of Israel, claiming as the Liberals always did that it was neck and neck between himself and her, with Labour nowhere.[182] Perhaps a little worried, Mrs Thatcher conducted herself with less courtesy to her opponents than previously: despite spending most of her time in the constituency, she vetoed a joint meeting of the three candidates, and refused to be interviewed on local radio, so that the others could not appear either. (She also pulled out of a television debate with Roy Hattersley when she learned that the BBC wanted to film it in a North London comprehensive.)[183] Unquestionably she wanted the Government to be returned. However disillusioned she may have been by some aspects of Heath's policies, she was shocked by Enoch Powell's disloyalty in giving up his seat and advising the electors to vote Labour. She enjoyed office too much to want to lose it. As she told the *Sunday Telegraph* on one of her rare trips out of London, the election was a bit of a distraction: 'What I really like is taking decisions.'[184] But by polling day, she writes in her memoirs, 'my optimism had been replaced by unease'.[185]

She was still perfectly safe in Finchley. As usual the Liberal hype could achieve only so much. On a reduced poll (and revised boundaries) her vote was 7,000 down, the Liberals nearly 4,000 votes up, but Labour still held on to second place. Her majority was nearly halved but the two opposition parties cancelled each other out.

Margaret Thatcher (Conservative)	18,180
Martin O'Connor (Labour)	12,202
Laurence Brass (Liberal)	11,221
Conservative majority	5,978

Nationally it was a different story. The Liberals won an unprecedented six million votes, nearly 20 per cent of the poll. They were rewarded with just fourteen seats, but their advance fatally damaged the Tories, helping Labour to scrape a narrow majority – 301 seats to 297 – despite winning a slightly lower share of the poll – 37.1 per cent against 37.9 per cent. For a few days Heath clung on, trying to do a deal with the Liberals to keep him in power. But this could only have succeeded had he been able to promise proportional representation. A number of his senior colleagues would have paid that price; Mrs Thatcher was one who certainly would not. Her antagonistic brand of politics was always opposed to any form of compromise or coalition which blurred the sharp choice between competing systems. 'Although I wanted to remain Secretary of State for Education', she wrote in her memoirs, 'I did not want to do so at the expense of the Conservative Party's never forming a majority Government again'.[186] How many others in that Heath-dominated Cabinet would have joined her in defying him can never be known; it was never put to the test, since even if Heath and Jeremy Thorpe had been able to sell a deal to their respective parties, they still did not command a combined majority in the new House. The weekend's haggling simply served to make Heath look like a bad loser. Although no party had clearly won the election, there was no question who had lost it.

Heath held a last Cabinet on Monday afternoon before being driven to the Palace to resign. It was by all accounts a bleak occasion: he was determined that it was not the end of his Government, merely a temporary interruption, so there were no thanks, tributes or recriminations. Only one minister felt she could not let the moment pass without a word of valediction. It was Margaret Thatcher who insisted on speaking 'in emotional terms of the wonderful experience of team loyalty that she felt she had shared since 1970'.[187] Was this hypocrisy or just her idea of good manners? If she really meant what she said, or even if she was simply voicing the conventional sentiments that she thought should be expressed on such an occasion, it would suggest that her repudiation of the late Government and all its works over the next few months was indeed as sudden, unpremeditated and opportunist as it appeared to most of her former colleagues at the time. Insofar as this effusion was exaggerated, however, it is a measure of how well she had learned to dissemble her true views behind a mask of gushing sincerity. Either way it makes an ironic end to her three and a half years' service in Ted Heath's Cabinet.

It is most unlikely that she really hoped to go back to the DES after the election; she was ready for a move. To the director of the Cambridge Institute of Education, one of many people in the educational world who wrote to express their regret at her passing, she replied that she was sad to leave but added intriguingly: 'I shall always retain my interest in education, and I hope that one day I may be able to do something for it once again.'[188] What could she have meant, except that she nursed the possibility that she might one day become Prime Minister? But if she was not sorry to go, the DES was surprisingly sorry to lose her. Pile threw a 'splendid farewell party' for her, described by *The Times* as 'a unique occasion. Never before had an outgoing education secretary been given a parting on this scale.'[189] The education correspondents, who had so loathed and mocked her when she first arrived, now queued up to praise her. Even the *Guardian*, house journal of progressive educationists, paid ironic tribute to a Tory minister:

> In several respects Mrs Thatcher [was] a more egalitarian Minister than her Labour predecessor. Her support for primary schools, polytechnics, the raising of the school–leaving age, and the new nursery programme will all provide more help to working class children than the Labour programme actually did.[190]

The Times offered a more mixed assessment of her style and legacy. 'She has never been a friend of educational journalists, nor of the National Union of Teachers,' Tim Devlin conceded.

> She had the bearing of a school ma'am, an inability to suffer fools and an irritating habit of reducing educational arguments to legalistic principles and cutting deputations short by quoting relevant education acts . . .
>
> But at the end of her reign it was the fashion to consider that she was not as bad as all that.
>
> Historians will probably consider her achievements to have been remarkable during a period when the country was heading towards the verge of economic bankruptcy.

Already she could be seen as the last flourish of a heroic age of educational expansion, now coming to an end. Her Labour successor, Reg Prentice, was taking office in a much harsher climate.

> There is a loss of faith now. Student disquiet, violence and truancy at many city schools have cast doubt on the efficiency of conventional forms of education. We have moved a long way

from the Boyle–Crosland and the Robbins Report era of expansion, particularly in higher education.[191]

Devlin's contemporary verdict is echoed by the historian Rodney Lowe. Looking back from a world transformed – ironically – by Thatcherism, Lowe criticises Mrs Thatcher in her earlier incarnation for failing to anticipate the developments of the next two decades, damning her with backhanded praise as 'a conventionally strong departmental minister, maximising resources for traditional ends', but in no sense radical. While making minor cuts in milk and meals, she ducked the need to find serious savings – by such innovations as student loans and two-year degrees – to finance her planned expansion. She spoke of the need to improve technical and vocational education, and talked about parental choice and giving more power to school governors, but she did little in practice about either. The burgeoning polytechnics were allowed to become indistinguishable from universities. She blocked movement towards developing a national curriculum. It was only Jim Callaghan's Ruskin College speech in 1976 – two years after Mrs Thatcher left the DES – which began to move education forward to the new agenda which her Education Secretaries – Keith Joseph, Kenneth Baker and Ken Clarke – would develop in the 1980s.[192]

From her time at the DES, however, she learned a number of lessons which she would carry back with her into government in 1979. First, as she reflected on her experience, she became convinced of the malign power of officials with their own agenda to block, frustrate and manipulate all but the most determined ministers. The more she reinvented herself over the next five years as a 'conviction politician' with a mission to cut public spending and roll back the state, the more embarrassed she was by her own record as a high-spending minister, the more determined to punish the DES for having led her astray and to ensure that her entire Government from 1979 did not go the same way. Mrs Thatcher came into office with fixed resolve – unlike Harold Wilson and Ted Heath, for instance, both of whom had been civil servants themselves – to take on and subdue the civil service, which she defined as part of Britain's problem. In part this perception was based on a misconception. The DES is not an elite department; generally speaking, it does not attract the best minds in Whitehall. With some exceptions, Mrs Thatcher formed a low opinion of the calibre of her officials at Education; she was therefore unprepared to discover in 1979 just how good the high-flyers who surrounded the Prime Minister could be. She never lost her intense suspicion of the civil service as an institution; but she quickly gained the greatest respect for a large number of individual civil servants whom she came to trust and rely on much more than she trusted her political colleagues.

Secondly, she learned from the failure of the Government as a whole to maintain its sense of direction and purpose in the face of mounting political pressure. At its simplest this expressed itself as a determination not to duplicate Heath's notorious U-turns. But this was not so much an ideological point as a political one. She had not, by her own admission, yet grasped the theoretical monetarist analysis of the Government's failure: like most of the rest of the Tory party she would have been happy to go along with Heath's policies so long as they appeared to work. When the Government's authority was challenged, she was one of those who pressed for an early election, and expected to win it. What dismayed her was the Government's loss of control of events, leading to electoral defeat.

In her memoirs she is surprisingly generous about the unlucky Prime Minister. With hindsight, she writes in *The Path to Power*, 'I can see more clearly how Ted Heath, an honest man whose strength of character made him always formidable . . . took the course he did . . . It is easy to comprehend the pressures on him.'[193] Partly, of course, this is to excuse her own responsibility as a member of his Government; but it also points an implicit contrast with her own resolution in 1980–1. For Heath lost, not because his policy was wrong or even unpopular in itself, but because it led the Government into contradictions and anomalies which it could not resolve, confrontation with the very group it had most sought to appease and an election the Prime Minister patently did not want, which was tantamount to an admission that the Government had lost the ability to govern.

Heath lost the ability to control events, paradoxically, because he tried to control too much: all the complex machinery of prices and incomes control – the Pay Board, the Price Commission and the rest – left the Government still helpless in the face of soaring imported food and commodity prices on the one hand, and the industrial muscle of the miners on the other. Corporatism – the attempt to govern by agreement with the 'social partners' (the TUC and the CBI) – left the Government dependent on the goodwill of powerful interests which it could not command. The lesson Mrs Thatcher took from the Heath Government was not so much monetarism, which she grasped later as a useful technical explanation, but rather a compelling affirmation of an old Tory article of faith – the self-defeating folly of over-ambitious government. Government – she instinctively believed – must be strong, clear, decisive; but the experience of the Heath Government taught that it could only appear strong by holding itself above the economic fray, not taking responsibility upon itself for every rise in unemployment or inflation. It was that lesson, more than any other, which enabled her Government to rise above the economic devastation of the early 1980s.

'I left Downing Street', Lady Thatcher writes, 'sad but with some sense of relief. I had given little thought to the future. But I knew in my heart that it was time not just for a change in government but for a change in the Conservative Party.'[194]

10

The Peasants' Revolt

LESS than a year after losing office in March 1974 Margaret
Thatcher was elected leader of the Conservative party. This was
a stunning transformation which no one would have predicted
twelve months earlier: one of those totally unexpected events –
which in retrospect appear predestined – that constitute the
fascination of politics. One of the most extraordinary things about
Mrs Thatcher's seizure of the Tory leadership is that scarcely anyone
– colleague or commentator – saw her coming. Even after the event
her victory was widely disparaged as a freak of fortune of which she
was merely the lucky beneficiary. Or as Enoch Powell put it, with a
mixture of envy and grudging admiration: 'She didn't rise to power.
She was opposite the spot on the roulette wheel at the right time,
and she didn't funk it.'[1]

But the fact that she did not funk it was crucial, and not at all an
accident. It should have been foreseen by anyone who had worked
closely with her over the previous twenty-five years; for she had
been quietly preparing for the opportunity all her life. When it came
she was ready. It takes extraordinary single-mindedness and stamina
to reach the topmost rung of British politics, an obsessive dedication
to the job to the exclusion of other concerns like money, family,
friendship and the pursuit of pleasure. Like Harold Wilson, like Ted
Heath, but more than any of her Conservative contemporaries,
Margaret Thatcher possessed that quality of single-minded dedication to her career. She never made any secret of her ambition: it was
only because she was a woman that the possibility that she might go
right to the top was not taken seriously. No one who had known her
at Oxford, at Colchester or Dartford should have been surprised that
when the chance offered she left her male rivals at the post.

Of course she was lucky. But as the South African golfer Gary

Player famously remarked: 'The harder I practise the luckier I seem to get.' The nine-year-old Margaret Roberts was making the same point when she indignantly retorted to the headmistress who congratulated her on winning a poetry prize: 'I wasn't lucky. I deserved it.' Throughout her career Mrs Thatcher was often credited with being lucky, above all in the repeated self-destruction of her adversaries. But she made her own luck; she seized chances from which others shrank, and exploited their hesitation with ruthless certainty. This was never more the case than in the twelve months after February 1974.

Yet it was still an unpredictable combination of other factors which created her opportunity. First, she benefited from an intellectual revolution – or counter-revolution – in Tory thinking which had been building over the previous ten years but which was suddenly brought to a head by the shock of electoral defeat, creating the opening for a radical change of direction. This was a development in which she played very little part, yet one which reflected her most deeply held convictions, so that she had no difficulty taking advantage of it. At the same time a fortuitous pattern of personal circumstances ruled out of contention virtually all the other candidates who might, a year earlier, have hoped or been expected to harness this opportunity to their own careers. Ted Heath himself or his closest colleague and heir apparent, Willie Whitelaw; Enoch Powell, the Old Testament prophet, or Keith Joseph, the zealous convert; even Edward du Cann, chairman of the backbenchers' 1922 Committee – all had stronger claims, a larger following and a greater likelihood of success than Margaret Thatcher; but each, one after the other, either rendered himself unelectable or declined to stand, leaving Mrs Thatcher, despite the apparent disqualifications of her sex and relative inexperience, almost by default the only candidate with the nerve to seize the crown.

The revolution in Tory thinking had two strands – economic and political. On the one hand there was a sudden revival of interest in the free-market economic ideas quietly propagated for years on the margins of serious politics by the Institute of Economic Affairs but largely derided by the conventional wisdom in both Whitehall and the universities. Throughout the 1960s the fact that the only prominent politician to preach the beauty of the unfettered market was Enoch Powell was enough to tar the message with the taint of crazed fanaticism. One or two Shadow Ministers – Keith Joseph, Geoffrey Howe and, more tentatively, Mrs Thatcher – did forge links with the IEA while in opposition and made speeches flirting with radical notions like privatisation and the encouragement of private health insurance. None of them, however, persisted with such heresies in government: charged by Arthur Seldon with betraying their principles, both Joseph and Howe pleaded the pressure of political reality. Joseph spent his time at the DHSS adding extra layers of bureaucracy to the Health Service; while in February 1972 Howe (then Solicitor-General) specifically defended Mrs Thatcher's caution in the education field: 'Opinion in favour of the policies you mentioned turns out to carry less weight than militant response (apparently very politically damaging) to even quite modest applications of those policies e.g. on school milk or student union finance.'[2]

From the middle of 1972 onwards, however, the Government's U-turns in economic policy had begun to make converts for the Powellite critique. At Westminster a small but significant band of dissident backbenchers – Ridley, Biffen, Bruce-Gardyne and half a dozen more – formed the Selsdon Group to try to bring the Government back to what they believed had been its 1970 principles. In Whitehall Alan Walters, an academic economist briefly seconded to the Cabinet Office, made no headway at all with a monetarist analysis of the causes of inflation and quickly resigned; at that stage, by their own admission, Treasury mandarins attached little importance to the money supply. But in Fleet Street an influential group of economic journalists led by Samuel Brittan on the *Financial Times* and Peter Jay and William Rees-Mogg on *The Times* took up the cause and began to expound it in their columns. When the Heath Government fell, therefore, there was quite suddenly a fully-fledged monetarist explanation of its failure available for disillusioned Tories – including ex-ministers – to draw upon.

At the same time there was among ordinary Tories in the country a more generalised mood of mounting frustration at the failure of successive Conservative Governments to halt or reverse what seemed a relentless one-way slide to socialism. Not only in the management of the economy but in almost every sphere of domestic and foreign policy – immigration, comprehensive schools, trade unions, Northern Ireland, Rhodesia – Heath had appeared almost deliberately to affront the party's traditional supporters while appeasing their tribal enemies. Strikes, crime, revolting students, pornography, terrorism, inflation eating away at their savings, even decimalisation, all stoked in saloon bars, golf clubs and the columns of the *Daily Telegraph* a rising anger that the country was going to the dogs while the Tory Government was not resisting but rather speeding the process. By the time Heath lost the February 1974 election an ugly mood had built up in the Tory party which lacked only heavyweight leadership to weld together the two elements – the political backlash and the economic analysis – to form a potent combination which ultimately became known as Thatcherism.

The unlikely catalyst was Keith Joseph – hitherto no one's idea of a rebel or a populist, but a former Cabinet Minister of long experience and unimpeachable integrity who was almost uniquely qualified to lend intellectual rigour to political revolt. Up to February 1974 the dissidents were mainly either ivory-tower academics or political mavericks: so long as Heath's senior colleagues remained united in support of the policies they had pursued in government the critics could only snipe from the wings. It needed a member of the Shadow Cabinet to come out against the record of the late Government: Joseph was perfect because he did it with such evident pain and penitence, not from crude ambition or political opportunism. In office he had been – with Mrs Thatcher – the biggest spender in the Cabinet, and accordingly the biggest disappointment to his friends at the IEA who had once entertained high hopes of him. In fact their criticism had already begun to trouble him before the February election. Out of office his conversion was dramatic. He was shocked when Alfred Sherman – a former Communist, now a virulent free-market polemicist – refused to shake his hand.[3] In a series of long conversations during March and April, Sherman and Alan Walters convinced him that everything the Heath Government had done by intervening in industry, subsidising lame duck industries and particularly by letting the money supply rip in pursuit of rapid growth, had simply fuelled the inflation the Government was trying to control. He subsequently described how he had thought he had been a Conservative for the past thirty years, but now realised that he had been a 'statist' all along, bewitched by the delusive power of government.[4] Having seen the light, he set out with a religious fervour rare in high-level politics to atone for his past sins by bringing the Tory party – and ultimately the country – to a realisation of the true faith.

Mrs Thatcher was no more than Joseph's loyal sidekick in this process, and scarcely even that. We have to assume that she underwent a similar Damascene conversion; but we do not really know, because while Joseph was making speeches and working out his ideas in public, frankly confessing his errors, she said and wrote nothing at all. Though she arrived at the same destination – possibly more quickly, certainly with less agonising – and subsequently garnered to herself the political harvest of the ferment which Joseph unleashed, she contributed virtually nothing to the public debate until after she became leader. In interviews – for instance in July 1990 – she has sometimes claimed rather more for her own role:

> All of a sudden a few of us said, 'Look, we didn't get into politics for this.' After the defeat of 1974 Keith Joseph and I asked how did it happen? We went back over the fundamental philosophy.[5]

But this is self-aggrandisement. In her memoirs she was more honest, confessing that 'between the February and October 1974 elections most of my time was taken up with work on housing and the rates' – the new shadow responsibility which Heath had given her.[6] She joined Joseph for some of his conversations with Sherman, but more as a listener than as an active participant. Joseph's recollection confirms that she did not have the same need to work through the arguments:

> It is a characteristic of Margaret Thatcher to have by instinct much that some other people such as I tend to have only by laborious analysis. Of course we exchanged views, yes. But deep intellectual discussions, no, because she was there – she knew that in trying to do good we had done harm.[7]

Mrs Thatcher never pretended to be thinker. She was a politician, and – unlike Joseph – an intensely practical and ambitious one. It is not the job of politicians to have original ideas, or even necessarily to understand them. Professional economists like Peter Jay used to sneer that Mrs Thatcher never really understood monetarism. But she did not have to. It was enough that she saw its importance; she possessed – as Joseph did not – the much more important and rare ability to simplify complex ideas and mobilise support for them. No intellectual herself, she was nevertheless unusual among politicians in acknowledging the importance of ideas. She had always believed that politics should be a battle of ideas between fundamentally opposed philosophies; it was a characteristic of her leadership that she systematically used intellectuals and academics – those whom she thought were on her side – to underpin her policies and furnish her with arguments and intellectual ammunition. As Prime Minister she developed an informal think-tank of her favourite academics to advise her.

The veteran editor of the *Sunday Express*, John Junor, recalls suggesting to her, some time in 1974, that she should follow Joseph's lead by making a speech herself on Tory philosophy: her immediate response was to ask whom she should get to help her with it, Hugh

Trevor-Roper or Robert Blake?[8] She did not have the intellectual self-confidence or training to think theoretically herself: yet she had the humility to value those who could do it for her. She may indeed have grasped instinctively in the spring of 1974 that the economic analysis which Sherman and Walters were laboriously teaching Joseph explained not only the failure of the Heath Government but everything that old-fashioned Tories like Denis and herself felt had been going wrong with the country ever since the war. She quickly came to see that it offered the necessary doctrinal basis for the sort of fresh start the defeated party was crying out for. At the same time she recognised, as an innately cautious politician, that the moment was not yet ripe to break cover.

The result of the February election had left the Tory party in a sort of limbo. With another election certain within a few months – as soon as Wilson saw an opportunity to increase his precarious majority – there was no early possibility of challenging Heath's leadership, even if there had been an obvious challenger in waiting. Nor was there time to undertake a comprehensive policy review. Heath was shocked by his unexpected defeat, unwell – he was already suffering from a thyroid deficiency which was not diagnosed until the following year – but stubbornly determined to admit no error and allow no recrimination over the record of the past four years. The lesson he drew from the debacle of confrontation with the miners was that the Conservatives must try harder than ever to show themselves moderate and consensual in order to unite the country and win back the votes lost to the Liberals – which was the opposite of what his party critics wanted. He made as few changes in his shadow team as possible, promoting only one or two loyal supporters like Nicholas Scott and Paul Channon. But he had one key vacancy to fill: Tony Barber had decided to leave politics, so he needed a new shadow Chancellor.

The bold choice would have been to give the job to Joseph; with hindsight it might have been the wise choice too, a way of containing Joseph's uncomfortable soul-searching within a context of loyalty. Instead he chose the former Home Secretary, Robert Carr, the mildest of 'One Nation' Conservatives who could be relied on not to rock the boat. Joseph declined any other portfolio but opted for a roving brief which left him free to follow the promptings of Sherman and Walters wherever they led him. Ian Gilmour became chairman of the Conservative Research Department, with another young left-winger, Chris Patten, promoted to director.

Some policy committees were established, on the same lines as in 1965–70, with the significant omission of one on economic policy, which would have had to include awkward customers like Nicholas Ridley and John Biffen, chairmen respectively of the backbench Finance and Industry committees. In fact the one area in which Heath saw a need for new policies was housing. He told the Shadow Cabinet that the voters he met wanted 'some radical and drastic changes in policy aimed particularly at the problems of ordinary people' – specifically the cost of mortgages and the burden of the rates – 'which should take priority over rather more abstract principles'.[9] The key job of developing and selling these shiny new policies which would form the centrepiece of the party's appeal at the next election he entrusted to Margaret Thatcher: an indication that he still saw her as an efficient and amenable agent of his will, not as a potential troublemaker.

It was a similar failure of political intelligence which led him to allow Joseph, as part of his roving responsibility, to set up a new policy-making forum distinct from the party's official Research Department. The Centre for Policy Studies was supposed to study the comparative performance of European economies in order to see what lessons could be learned about the social market economy of possible application to Britain. At least that was how Joseph sold the idea to Heath. But if Heath saw it as a harmless way of keeping Joseph out of mischief it was a serious misjudgement. The CPS quickly became the crucible of Joseph's intellectual revolution – a meeting place where those interested in changing the party's thinking could meet to discuss their ideas before separating to write papers and pamphlets. Sherman was soon installed as director, with Nigel Vinson – another ardent free-marketeer, a self-made entrepreneur who had been a trustee of the IEA since 1970 – as Treasurer. Having sanctioned the CPS on the understanding that it should not compete with the CRD for funding from the party's traditional sources of support, Heath felt he had been tricked when Vinson persuaded seventeen members of the CBI to give £1,000 each to launch the Centre.[10] Established in May, the CPS held its first meeting at the House of Commons in June before acquiring permanent premises in Wilfred Street, Westminster, in July. Joseph was chairman. Mrs Thatcher, in her own words, 'jumped at the chance to become Keith's Vice-Chairman'.[11] But once again none of her colleagues seems to have attached much significance to Mrs Thatcher's name on the letterhead.

Joseph did try to have his discordant analysis discussed in Shadow Cabinet. He presented a paper on inflation on 3 May. The minutes record that it was agreed that uncontrolled expansion of the money supply was 'an important factor'; but 'the real difficulty arose over timing and in deciding what the actual increase should be at any particular time'. (This indeed turned out to be the problem after 1979.) In the meantime the Shadow Cabinet believed it was still more important to avert the high social cost of unemployment.[12] In their memoirs Jim Prior and Peter Walker admit that they did not take Joseph's simplistic monetarism seriously. They also insist that he was at this stage a lone voice – though Walker's recollection suggests that both Mrs Thatcher and Geoffrey Howe were reserving their positions.

> Margaret did not side openly with Keith, except to say that we should pay careful attention to what he was saying. Geoffrey Howe said he thought there were two sides to the argument and we should consider both. They were not passionately endorsing Keith's view. And the rest of the Shadow Cabinet were convinced that there was no magic which, with a wave of the wand of a particular indicator of money supply, could make your problems disappear.[13]

From the opposite camp John Ranelagh gives a much more graphic account (from an unnamed source) of another meeting that summer to which various economic experts had been called to give evidence. Heath had so far unbent as to allow Alan Walters to put the monetarist case against the former Chief Economic Adviser in the Treasury, Sir Donald McDougall, an orthodox Keynesian who denied any link between inflation and the money supply. Professor James Ball of the London Business School was then expected to back McDougall; unexpectedly, however, he sided with Walters. This was not what Heath wanted to hear, so he simply disregarded Ball's contribution and concluded the discussion, saying they were all agreed that the policies of the late Government had been right 'but ... we did not persist with them long enough'.

> Sir Keith Joseph's eyebrows shot up; Angus Maude shook his head and looked down; Sir Geoffrey Howe looked astonished; and Margaret Thatcher sat without expression with her back to the wall, away from the centre table. Heath had lost his sense of objective reality.[14]

This is very dubious; apart from anything else Angus Maude was not a member of the Shadow Cabinet. As John Ramsden has written, 'this makes a good story, but seems likely to have conflated more than one meeting and to have over-dramatised the clash of personalities'.[15] It does accurately reflect, however, Joseph's conviction that his arguments would not get a proper hearing in the Shadow Cabinet. The result was that he decided to go public with a series of major speeches, largely written for him by Sherman.

The first, at Upminster on 22 June, condemned the socialistic drift of both parties since 1945. 'The path to Benn', he declared, 'is paved with thirty years of interventions; thirty years of good intentions; thirty years of disappointments.'

> For half of that thirty years Conservative Governments, for understandable reasons, did not consider it practicable to reverse the vast bulk of the accumulating detritus of Socialism which on each occasion they found when they returned to office. So we tried to build on its uncertain foundations instead . . . I must take my share of the blame for following too many of the fashions.[16]

Such an admission of fault by a senior ex-minister four months after losing office was sensational enough; but it stayed just about within party bounds by being phrased as an attack on socialism. A second speech at Leith at the beginning of August attracted less attention. But the third, delivered at Preston on 3 September just days before Wilson was expected to announce the General Election, really set the cat among the pigeons. Later published with the title 'Inflation is Caused by Governments', it constituted the first full-dress exposition of the monetarist case by a front-rank politician since Enoch Powell went out on a limb in 1968. Not only did it all but explicitly blame the Tory Government for creating inflation by stoking up the money supply in pursuit of growth. Most provocatively Joseph argued at Preston that economic policy should no longer be dictated by the goal of full employment. Ever since the thirties, he noted, politicians of all parties had been 'haunted by the fear of long-term mass unemployment, the grim, hopeless dole queues and towns which died'.

> So we talked ourselves into believing that these gaunt, tight-lipped men in caps and mufflers were round the corner, and tailored our policy to match these imaginary conditions. For imaginary they were.[17]

This was positively inflammatory, challenging not merely the conventional economic wisdom on inflation but the central taboo of

British politics, allowing Labour to claim that the Tories, if returned to office, would deliberately create unemployment – the very charge Heath's generation of Tories had spent their whole careers trying to live down. Joseph argued that the published figures exaggerated the extent of real long-term unemployment. He accepted that sound monetary policy – what he called 'monetary continence' – would cost jobs in the short term: but estimated that three or four years should be enough to get back to sustainable full employment. The experience of the 1980s was to show that this was hopelessly unrealistic. But Joseph's Preston speech was a decisive moment in postwar politics, a seminal text of Thatcherism, in which the control of inflation was for the first time accorded higher priority than the maintenance of full employment. The CPS had mounted a successful press operation to prepare the ground: Rees-Mogg cleared two whole pages of *The Times* to print it in full, and even the *Sun* gave it extensive coverage. A fundamental philosophical split in the Tory party was now out in the open.

Not surprisingly Heath and Carr, when they got wind of this bombshell, tried to limit the damage. Casting around for someone who might influence him, they correctly identified Mrs Thatcher as the colleague closer to Joseph than any other; yet they still seem not to have been aware how far she had embraced his views. Jim Prior was deputed to persuade her to try to stop 'this disastrous speech': 'Margaret replied that it was the work of Alfred Sherman: she felt that Keith did not always understand the political impact of arguments, but that she did not have much influence over him.'[18]

Clearly she was still playing her cards close to her chest. Either she had not yet fully committed herself to Joseph's revolt or she still thought it prudent to dissemble the extent of her conversion. By her own admission she did not take much part in CPS discussions until after his Upminster speech in June. By the time of his second speech at Leith in August she was 'more actively involved . . . attending Keith's meetings, commenting on his suggestions and preparing my own notes and papers on the areas of education and social services which I knew best'. She says she saw a draft of the Preston speech, found it 'one of the most powerful and persuasive analyses I have ever read' and declined to suggest any changes.[19] But she does not claim any more positive input into it than that. Others have claimed that she was already attending the Economic Dining Club, a monetarist parliamentary group founded by Nick Ridley after he was sacked (or by his own account resigned) from the Heath Government in 1972. Cecil Parkinson says that she was elected in March 1974 in place of Enoch Powell, and became an 'enthusiastic' member.[20] Ridley, however, did not think she joined until after she had become leader.[21] If she did attend earlier she did not make a great impression. She was still at this stage listening and learning.

The fact is that, as she says in her memoirs, she was very fully immersed in her front-bench job as shadow Environment Secretary. This was a high-profile opportunity in an area of policy she had always been interested in but had not previously covered. It took her all her time to get on top of it. Sheila Browne ran into her soon after she had taken it over and found her uncharacteristically harassed, complaining that the wide-ranging DoE empire – taking in transport as well as housing and local government – was too big to master in her usual detail.[22] 'The thing I most resent about being in opposition,' she told the *Liverpool Daily Post*, 'apart from not being able to take decisions, is that one has no staff. If you want to look up a reference to something, you have to go to a library and do it yourself.'[23] As a conscientious politician with a compulsive need to do her homework, she had little time for thinking about economics.

After nearly five years dealing with education, however, she relished a change: as she had found in 1964–5, it is no fun shadowing someone else doing your old job. Moreover the loss of office released her to express her personal philosophy more freely than she had been able to do while at the DES. Labour's Environment Secretary was Tony Crosland. Never one to shirk the big targets, she took the chance offered by her first Commons speech as his opposite number – a debate on London at the end of April – to denounce the doctrine of equality expounded in his new book, *Socialism Now*, specifically as it applied to education. 'Equality', she declared, 'is death to education.'

> Education is about opportunity, and opportunity is the opportunity to be unequal. If children's only opportunity is to be equal ... it is no opportunity at all ... Opportunity is the opposite of equality.[24]

In the same speech she cheekily berated her successor, Reg Prentice, for failing to get more money for the DES. 'I was a good badgerer of the Treasury', she boasted, 'and I obtained a great deal for education; but the right hon. Gentleman sees money going everywhere but to his Department.'[25] Considering the financial crisis which had decimated her own plans just five months earlier, she was remarkably sanguine about Labour's spending plans. In another speech two months later she positively congratulated the Government on its decision – soon reversed – to go ahead with the Channel Tunnel. 'We are going through a period', she lamented, 'when all the exciting big projects are stopped and politics appears to have become about bread and cheese.' To Labour protests she was forced to concede that of course bread and cheese were important; but she insisted that the nation needed 'visionary ideas' as well.[26]

Parliamentary opposition, however, was just a matter of going through the motions – more than ever this summer when the Conservatives had to hold back for fear of precipitating an election before they were ready for it. Mrs Thatcher's real job was to come up with the bright new housing policies which Heath wanted to put in the forefront of the party's next manifesto to win back the middle-class voters who had cost the Tories the February election by defecting to the Liberals. Frankly what he was seeking was a short-term electoral bribe, but one which could be presented as consistent with the long-standing Conservative philosophy of encouraging home-ownership. The first priority was some form of help for homebuyers. In a number of papers to the Shadow Cabinet over the summer Mrs Thatcher's housing policy committee – a group which included Hugh Rossi, John Stanley (later her PPS) and Nigel Lawson – examined various options, from subsidising the building societies and direct payments to savers to encouraging the sale of council houses. It was a better use of public money, the group argued in an interim report in June, to help people to become owners than to subsidise them indefinitely as tenants. The target should be to increase home-ownership from 50 per cent of the population to 70 per cent.[27]

Mrs Thatcher warmly supported the objective; but she had doubts about some of the means proposed to achieve it. She had to be bullied into accepting policies she did not like; yet accept them she did. At meetings in the Research Department she argued vigorously against the principle of subsidising mortgages.[28] On the other hand, she explained in *The Path to Power*, she was 'acutely aware of how much the middle classes were suffering'.

> Because of the inflation which we and the Labour party had conspired to create, the value of people's savings had been eroded by negative real interest rates . . . House values had slumped. So had the stock market . . . Tax increases were bearing down on businesses and people.

'In such circumstances', she persuaded herself, it could be justifiable

271

to make 'modest temporary provision for the interests of the middle classes . . . on whom future prosperity largely depends'.[29] But she resisted committing herself to a specific figure. She describes how she was summoned to Heath's house in Wilton Street at the beginning of August to be confronted by Heath, Carr, Walker and Gilmour, all insisting that she should promise to hold interest rates 'below 10 per cent'. She reluctantly agreed, only to have Heath ring her on her carphone when she was on her way to record the announcement, pressing her to specify a figure, as low as possible. Again she agreed, but refused to go lower than 9.5 per cent.[30]

She was also suspicious of selling council houses at discount prices, as championed particularly by Peter Walker. It was not that she approved of public sector housing: on the contrary, she announced during the October election that she would have liked to abolish council housing altogether, except for the elderly and other special cases.[31] As part of her self-education in housing matters she asked the journalist Simon Jenkins – then on the *Evening Standard* – to take her to see some of 'these terrible council estates'. He told her there were some good ones too. ' "No," she said, "there are just bad ones." I was given a cup of tea and placed politely beyond the pale.'[32] She held no brief for council housing, then; but she feared the anger of existing homeowners who had saved to buy their houses at the market rate if council tenants were given Government handouts to enable them to buy their houses on the cheap. Twenty years later, when the sale of more than a million council houses was recognised as one of the defining achievements of Thatcherism, she acknowledged that this argument was 'narrow and unimaginative'; but she still felt it made political sense at the time.[33]

The Shadow Cabinet minutes contain no record of her reservations, however; and no word of them reached the press. On the contrary, *The Times* reported in June that her emerging policies were causing 'controversy in the Shadow Cabinet, some of whose members believe that Mrs Thatcher's policy leans towards socialism'.[34] Maybe she herself inspired this story in an attempt to discredit the policies that were being forced on her. Robert Carr was reported to be worried about the cost, and Heath himself was said to have agreed only 'grudgingly' that the money must be found. Lady Thatcher's recollection is the very opposite: it was she who worried about the cost while 'Ted and those around him seemed to entertain no such caution'.[35]

The package she eventually announced at the end of August comprised three different forms of housing subsidy. First she promised to hold mortgages to a maximum interest rate of 9.5 per cent, to be achieved by varying the tax rate on building societies. Second, council tenants would be helped to buy their houses at a 33 per cent discount. Third, first-time buyers would be encouraged to save by a direct Government bribe of £1 for every £2 saved. Most significant for the long term, however, was her fourth commitment: a promise to abolish the rates.

This was another area of dispute with Heath. Defeat had made him more reckless, perhaps more cynical, than he had been before 1970. Desperate for popular policies to reverse February's result, he was determined to promise nothing less than abolition. Mrs Thatcher was once again more cautious. She was happy to look at ways of easing the burden on ratepayers – she was now prepared to support shifting the cost of teachers' pay from local authorities to the Treasury, something she had opposed while at the DES – but she wanted time to study the problem and find a workable alternative before committing herself to outright abolition. In the Shadow Cabinet on 21 June she argued that some form of local property tax was probably unavoidable and proposed a Select Committee to try to find a solution on an all-party basis. Heath insisted that this was no good – the party needed 'something hard on rates for the manifesto'.[36] In other words he – the apostle of national unity – was looking for party advantage while Mrs Thatcher was seeking consensus.

In the Commons during July she stuck to her guns, arguing for a quick inquiry modelled on the James committee into teacher training which she had set up while at the DES, which had reported in a year. She asserted traditional Tory support for the importance of local government ('Local authorities carry out their tasks better than Whitehall could'), and insisted that the local authorities must be fully consulted about any reform ('To do otherwise would be high-handed and arrogant'). These were not sentiments often on her lips in the 1980s. But at the same time she also prefigured ratecapping, insisting that central government must control local spending and advocating a system of block grants which would fix spending limits while protecting local independence in deciding how to spend the money.[37]

Once again, however, she was pressured to go further than she wanted. Another meeting of party heavyweights at Wilton Street (this time Heath was flanked by Carr, Whitelaw, Prior and Michael Wolff from Central Office) 'bludgeoned' her into promising abolition of the rates before they had decided what to put in their place. The August package eventually spoke of replacing the rates with 'taxes more broadly-based and related to people's ability to pay', meanwhile transferring to the Treasury the cost of not only teachers' pay but parts of the police and fire services. 'I felt bruised and resentful', she wrote in her memoirs, 'to be bounced again into policies which had not been properly thought out.' Yet she was still too loyal, or too junior, to refuse. Heath was still the leader, backed by a united core of senior colleagues. She had not yet fully committed herself to Joseph. In the last resort she was still willing to conform to protect her career. 'I thought that if I combined caution on the details with as much presentational bravura as I could muster I could make our rates and housing policies into vote-winners for the Party.'[38]

So she made a virtue of necessity and adopted the objectionable policies as her own, despite the incredulity, verging on contempt, of the very people who in a few months would be her most ardent supporters. *The Times* voiced exactly the distaste she felt herself for selling 'public assets . . . at knockdown prices to a class of citizens who, according to Conservative thinking of the day before yesterday, have been feather-bedded for too long';[39] while the promise of 9.5 per cent mortgages was widely dismissed as economically illiterate, an attempt to thwart the free market as futile as a statutory incomes policy, and precisely the sort of cynical electoral bribery the Tories rightly condemned when practised by Labour. 'Like Mr Shore's promise to make up their losses to the Court Line victims', *The Times* complained – Court Line was a failed travel agency – 'it encourages the belief that groups falling on hard times have only to identify themselves loudly enough and the Government will come to their financial rescue.'[40] So did Mrs Thatcher genuinely persuade herself that her policies were right? Or did she go along with policies she knew to be flawed, expecting to lose the election anyway?

The answer is probably a bit of both. She probably did expect to lose the election, but she was too combative a politician to do so willingly. Whatever her reservations about Heath, she regarded a Labour Government dominated by the left and unions as a greater evil, to be prevented by almost any means available. Moreover she did believe passionately both in helping homeowners and in reforming local government finance. Reluctant though she had been to make it, she felt herself bound for ever after by her promise to abolish the rates – with ultimately fatal results for her career. For some reason she did not feel the same obligation to redeem her patently unrealistic mortgage pledge; yet she always believed that mortgage payers deserved help. As Prime Minister she was unshakeably committed to subsidising homeowners by means of mortgage interest tax relief. 'At last', she proclaimed in Finchley during the October election campaign, 'someone has thought about doing something for the non-militant, non-organised, non-political people who feel they have been forgotten.'[41] These were 'her' people, and she never felt any compunction about rewarding them: as Nigel Lawson found in the 1980s, there was always a tension between her knowledge of what was right in principle and her desire to help groups she regarded as deserving. In truth Heath's sweeteners were not so abhorrent to her as she has sometimes claimed. It was having them forced on her that she did not like.

Mrs Thatcher's performance over the summer and autumn of 1974 – arguing passionately in private against policies which she would then defend equally passionately in public – demonstrated the maturing of a formidable political skill. By her championing of subsidised mortgages she showed that she possessed not only the good lawyer's ability to argue a weak case; any self-respecting politician can do that. She also had a preacher's ability to invest even a poor case with moralistic force: this more than anything else was the secret of her success over the next fifteen years. In the years of her success she boasted of being a 'conviction politician'. But it should never be forgotten that both words carried equal weight, the second as much as the first. She had powerful convictions, certainly; but she could be brilliantly insincere too, when the situation required it, and such was her reputation for burning integrity that few could spot the difference. At a number of critical points in her later career it was only this which enabled her to skate on some very thin ice and get away with it.

One consequence of her commitment to her housing pledges was that, once she had staked her reputation on them, she was not prepared to temper them for the sake of Heath's other electoral strategy, a willingness to form some sort of government of national unity. Opinion polls (and the Tories' private polling) had registered strong public support for some form of coalition to end the confrontational politics of the last few years. There were two problems for the Tories in trying to harness this mood. First, Heath himself was seen as the embodiment of confrontation, an obstacle to coalition who would have to stand aside before even the Liberals, let alone Labour, would consider serving with the Conservatives; which was not at all what Heath had in mind. Second, national unity was not the sort of battle cry to enthuse the party faithful. As a result the Tories fought the election half-heartedly, under a lame duck leader with a muddled message and a lacklustre campaign.

Mrs Thatcher disliked this instinctively and on principle. Her CPC lecture back in 1968 had make clear her contempt for the concept of consensus politics. Having once been persuaded to make firmer commitments than she would have liked on both mortgages and rates, she was not now willing to see them negotiated away as part of an all-party fudge. On the contrary, she made her pledges steadily more categorical as the campaign went on, promising first that mortgages would be cut 'by Christmas' and then that the rates would be abolished within five years, by Christmas 1979.[42] The Nuffield study of the October election notes that neither Mrs Thatcher nor Keith Joseph made much reference to Heath's national unity appeal.[43]

A week before polling day, however, she was summoned to see Heath before going on *Any Questions?* to be told the new coalitionist line she was expected to take. 'I was extremely angry,' she has written. 'For myself I was not going to retreat from the policies which at his insistence I had been advocating.'[44] Nevertheless she put a pretty good face on her brief, accepting – unlike Roy Hattersley – that in the event of no party winning a majority there might have to be some form of coalition. She could never serve in a Cabinet with Michael Foot or Tony Benn, but conceded that 'there are people in other parties, and some in the Labour party . . . who do hold a very similar view to ours, and then we would have to come together, because that was the wish of the people on election day'. But then she spoiled the effect – as Hattersley pointed out – by insisting that the housing promises she had made were 'non-negotiable, happen what may'.[45]

She was in fact the Tories' star performer in the October 1974 campaign. She still made only two trips out of London, to Norfolk and Essex; but largely because her policies were their only new ones, she appeared more than ever before on television and radio, featuring in three of the party's election broadcasts and three of the morning press conferences, including the final one with Heath, Lord Carrington and Geoffrey Howe. (Carrington said very little, the *Times* diary noted, 'which left Mrs Thatcher to speak out for the aggressive right'.)[46] She was coached for her television appearances by Gordon Reece, who began to get her for the first time to relax in front of the camera. With Reece's help she was judged to have done so well in the Tories' first broadcast that she was promoted to introduce the second.[47]

Her promise of cheap mortgages was the liveliest issue of a dull election. The veteran election-watchers David Butler and Dennis Kavanagh recorded that her pledge to implement the cut by

Christmas 'drew very full and sympathetic coverage, probably more than any similar electoral initiative since the war'.[48] Labour was seriously alarmed, but could not make up its mind how best to respond. Crosland alternated between calling it 'a pack of lies' which would never be implemented and 'midsummer madness' which would put 5p on income tax if it was; he finally settled for damning it as 'a moral outrage' which would give disproportionate benefit to the better off at the expense of the poor.[49] Twice the Environment Secretary and his shadow appeared together on television, first on *Weekend World* with Peter Jay and then on the BBC with Robin Day. Crosland tried to patronise Mrs Thatcher, Alan Watkins remembers, 'with that elaborate scorn which [he] reserved for women who thought they were clever'.[50] She retorted in that direct first-person style which would soon become familiar:

My approach is let's help people to help themselves . . . Unless I do that I am going to have to spend vastly more sums . . . building and buying up houses. That is much more expensive than my way.[51]

She left absolutely no doubt that the Tory policy was *her* policy. Harold Wilson jeered that there was 'good old Tory philosophy under that pretty hat'.[52]

In fact Labour need not have worried; polls soon showed that the public did not believe the Tories' promises.[53] Despite this, however, the high-profile exposure did Mrs Thatcher much more good than harm. It temporarily damaged her credentials with the right, who were dismayed to see her once again betraying her professed beliefs, using public money to distort the market in pursuit of votes. But the sheer feistiness of her performance, and indeed her pragmatism, stood her in good stead when she came to appeal to the whole body of middle-of-the-road MPs just three months later. She had valuably shown herself not as a naive right-winger but as a vigorous vote-getter and a seasoned pro.

Of course she was on safe ground in making incredible promises, since there was never much chance of the Tories winning the election. Her real fear was of a Labour landslide: '1966 all over again'.[54] Yet one must wonder whether by polling day she really wanted to win, or thought that Heath deserved to win. On the one hand she might have been embarrassed to find herself Environment Secretary, committed to cut mortgage rates to 9.5 per cent by Christmas; or alternatively obliged to refuse office if Heath tried to ditch her promises in order to form a coalition. On the other, even so partisan a politician as she was cannot have failed to calculate that another defeat was the first prerequisite for the radical redirection of Tory thinking which Keith Joseph had been advocating at Upminster and Preston – just so long as she did not lose her own seat.

This time she had real grounds for anxiety in Finchley. She faced the same two principal opponents as in February, but with the additional unknown quantity of a National Front candidate who might be expected to take votes from her. So long as Labour and the Liberals continued to split the non-Conservative vote fairly evenly she would be all right; but a little tactical voting or a Labour landslide could have unseated her. With the Liberals losing ground in the polls, Labour had serious hopes of defeating her: Harold Wilson paid her the compliment of visiting the constituency, telling the Labour candidate, 'I gather you have dear Margaret on the run.'[55] There was no Conservative frontbencher Labour would rather have unseated; but even her opponents had to acknowledge that she was a diligent and popular MP. The Labour candidate, Martin O'Connor, tried to pin down where she stood in the great Tory ideological divide. 'Is she a follower of Sir Keith Joseph and his ideas which every commentator has explained must lead to enormous unemployment?' Clearly he could not believe it: 'Are we going to see our delightful, intelligent and middle-class MP sit watching while people in her own constituency are thrown out of work? I challenge her to say precisely where she stands.'[56]

This was a challenge she was careful to avoid. Instead she concentrated as usual on the threat to freedom posed by the extreme left – 'They hope that the Socialist society will become total and irreversible . . . Do we become the most state-controlled society in the world outside the Iron Curtain?' – while presenting her own housing package as an example of the principled Tory alternative:

> Conservatives wish to help people towards independence. To run their own lives in their own homes in their own way . . .
> Labour believes in making people dependent on Government. We believe in helping them to be independent from Government.[57]

In the event the expected landslide failed to materialise. With just 39.2 per cent of the vote (against 35.8 per cent), Labour gained only eighteen seats for an overall majority of four: instead of repeating 1966, Wilson had succeeded only in replicating 1964. Mrs Thatcher's majority was cut by 2,000 (on a lower turnout), but it was still sufficient:

Margaret Thatcher (Conservative)	15,498
Martin O'Connor (Labour)	12,587
Laurence Brass (Liberal)	7,384
Janet Godfrey (National Front)	993
Conservative majority	2,911

At the count Mrs Thatcher's voice was 'cracked and strained'; but Roy Langstone told the press he was never worried, except by the strain on her.[58] In fact, as events turned out, the national result was probably the best possible for her. An unexpectedly successful rearguard action was creditable enough to enable Heath to dismiss calls that it was time for him to stand down; yet at the same time it was still a defeat, the party's third in four elections under his leadership, so it only fuelled the gathering consensus that he could not survive much longer. Meanwhile such a tiny majority was unlikely to sustain Labour in office for a full term – thus offering an unusually fruitful prospect of opposition for whoever succeeded in replacing him.

As soon as the October election was out of the way, the struggle for the Tory leadership was unofficially on. Quite apart from the simmering revolt on the right, too many Tory MPs with no quarrel with Heath's policies came back to Westminster convinced that the party could never win under his leadership. Several of his friends advised him to step down immediately to avoid getting hurt. Others urged him to recognise that after two defeats his position was naturally and legitimately in question, but that if he resigned and offered himself again with some show of humility he might still be re-elected. His personal authority among his colleagues was still strong, and his critics could field no credible champion. Fatally, he preferred to listen to those who urged him, in his own words, to 'tough it out'.[59] He felt vindicated by the closer-than-expected election result, believed the country still faced a grave economic crisis in which his experience would be needed and saw no reason to give any ground to his detractors. He wanted to stay on to lead the Tory campaign for a 'Yes' vote in the forthcoming European referendum. Above all, he was determined to block the growing influence of the right. In fact it was precisely his determination to hang on which delivered the party to his opponents. By refusing to submit his leadership to an early test he not only threw away his own best chance of survival; he made it practically impossible for Willie Whitelaw or any other candidate from his own wing of the party to succeed him. By clinging on he allowed time for a dark horse to emerge who would eventually consolidate all the various strands of discontent against him.

It is not quite true to say that Mrs Thatcher came from nowhere. Her name was always included in lists of possible contenders. Back in April, the *Daily Express* had asked: 'Do you fall off your chair laughing at the idea of Mrs Thatcher becoming Tory leader?', claiming (though it did not name them) that 'there are shrewd men in the Tory party . . . who do not'.[60] In September the *Times* diary reported that 'Some right-wing Tories tip Margaret Thatcher as the next leader of the Conservative Party, should they lose the forthcoming election' – but went on to quote Enoch Powell deriding the idea on the grounds that 'They would never put up with those hats or that accent'.[61] More than once Mrs Thatcher was obliged to deny that she had any such ambition. A week after the election the *Sunday Times* ran a rule over a large field of possibilities – Whitelaw, Joseph, Christopher Soames, Peter Walker, Geoffrey Howe, Jim Prior, Margaret Thatcher, Robert Carr – judged them all to be unproven but singled out Mrs Thatcher as possessing 'a clear mind and a growing public'.[62] Ronald Butt in the same paper considered that 'Mrs Thatcher, because of sheer ability, is a real contender, despite the apparent handicap that she is a woman'.[63] But that was the rub. In *The Times* a few days later Bernard Levin, while disclaiming any prejudice himself, nevertheless thought her sex an insuperable disqualification:

> Mrs Thatcher is a gifted and practical politician, whose formidable strength of character belies that Dresden appearance. She would need time to accustom people to the oddity of it, but time is the one thing the Tories do have. And yet I do not think they will do it, and I am not certain that they would be wise to. The male chauvinism of the people of this country, particularly the women, is still dreadful, and her sex would be a severe handicap. Besides there is the too-cool exterior (if only she would burst into tears occasionally); if the voters would not warm to Mr Heath they are unlikely to warm to Mrs Thatcher, and there is no point in the party jumping out of the igloo and onto the glacier.

Levin went on to dismiss all the other contenders – Joseph on ideological grounds ('The Tories would have to be quite sure that they want to change direction sharply, and there is as yet no sign that they do'), Whitelaw, Carr, Soames and Edward du Cann simply because they were not credible personalities – before concluding that the party would do best to stick with Heath.[64] However strongly commentators like Butt and Levin praised Mrs Thatcher's ability, the assumption remained almost universal that she could not in the final analysis be considered a serious candidate. And, publicly at least, she herself seemed to endorse this view. Just before the election, in one of a number of similar disclaimers which would be quoted ironically against her in years to come, she stated firmly that it would be 'years – and not in my time – that a woman will lead the party or become Prime Minister'.[65] On *Any Questions?* she was equally emphatic, yet left just a window of possibility:

> I wouldn't be overjoyed at the prospect of being the leader of a party at the moment . . . Nor do I think somehow that the country is ready to have a woman leader . . . unless there really clearly is no alternative man available. Now I just don't see that there will therefore be a woman Prime Minister in the next ten years. Now let's not think beyond that.[66]

Even with potential supporters she maintained this line. Patrick Cosgrave has written that he and his colleagues on the *Spectator* – all of them desperate to see Heath replaced – would have preferred Mrs Thatcher to Joseph all along, but she rejected their support in October, partly because she would not stand against Joseph, but also because she did not believe at that stage that she could have won.[67]

Joseph was the obvious standard-bearer of the right – not because he possessed any of the qualities of political leadership but because by his speeches over the summer he alone had staked out a clear alternative to Heath's discredited centrism. He was almost bound to stand, even though it is unlikely that he could have gained enough support to win. Mrs Thatcher quickly cast herself as his loyal supporter, explicitly discouraging speculation about her own chances. 'You can cross my name off the list,' she told the London *Evening News* the day after the General Election. 'I just don't think I am right for it.'[68] 'By the weekend', she wrote in *The Path to Power*, 'I had virtually become Keith's informal campaign manager.'[69] This is an exaggeration: she could never have been anyone's campaign manager – her range of contacts was too narrow. If anyone filled that role it was probably Nicholas Ridley – not that he was much better fitted for it. Joseph certainly left his friends in no doubt that he felt it his duty to stand as soon as Heath agreed to submit himself for re-election. But then, just two weeks after the election, he made a speech in Birmingham which spectacularly confirmed the doubts of those who thought he lacked the judgement or the nerve for leadership. Turning from economics to the more sensitive area of social policy he incautiously suggested that 'our human stock' was threatened by the birth of too many children to adolescent mothers 'in social classes four and five'. He was immediately accused of advocating compulsory birth control, even the sterilisation of the lower orders to prevent them breeding, caricatured as 'Sir Sheath' Joseph and vilified as a monster of eugenics. It was an ordeal comparable to that which Mrs Thatcher had endured over the withdrawal of school milk; but to a sensitive, genuinely compassionate man like Joseph it was too much. He apologised, tried to explain; but his anguished explanations only exposed him to further ridicule. Exactly four weeks after the Edgbaston speech, he concluded that he was not the stuff of which leaders are made and decided that he would not be a candidate.

The first person he told – on 21 November – was Mrs Thatcher. We have only her account of the conversation, but if that can be believed she did not hesitate. 'I heard myself saying: "Look, Keith, if you're not going to stand, I will, because someone who represents our viewpoint *has* to stand." '[70] The telling is disingenuous: in practice she was a good deal more cautious than this suggests. Yet there is no reason to doubt that it accurately represents her instinctive reaction. In all her carefully phrased denials of the idea that she could ever aspire to the highest offices, there was always a qualification which suggests that she did not, in her heart, rule them out. As long ago as her *Sunday Graphic* article in 1952 she had insisted that women should aim for the top jobs: and if any woman was in a position to do so it was herself. She was careful to deny that she nursed any such ambition, because it would have been counterproductive to admit it. But she always suggested by way of explanation that she was a 'realist', or that men would not accept a female Prime Minister in her lifetime:[71] she never said that a woman could not do the job. In a television interview in 1973 she declared that she 'would not wish to be Prime Minister. I don't have enough experience for that job'[72] – which clearly implied that she might have the necessary experience at some time in the future. And in September 1974 she was still insisting: 'I don't want to be leader. Being leader means total commitment. But I have a family.'[73] She did not add that her children were now grown up and her husband about to retire.

In one little-noticed interview in the *Sunday Express*, published on 20 October, she specifically denied that she was ruling herself out 'in the long run'. She agreed that she had said that there would not be a woman leader in the next ten years:

Yes, I did feel that at one point. But I'm not sure that I do any longer. The prejudice against women is dropping faster than I expected, and I think a woman may succeed before that time.

She was beginning to realise that it was not, as she had previously maintained, necessary to have held one of the three great offices of state.

I believe that a woman could lead the party one day in this country. If that time comes, and people thought I was that woman, I would accept the challenge and do the job to the utmost of my ability.[74]

Yet her earlier denials show that she was well aware of the weight of the odds against her. Her instant response to Joseph only committed her to see if she had enough support to make it sensible to stand, to represent their viewpoint. It is not certain that even Joseph immediately recognised her as the next best person to carry the banner which he had laid down: some of Joseph's supporters – Norman Fowler for one – certainly did not.[75] Even Denis, according to her own account was incredulous when she told him her intention. ' "You must be out of your mind," he said. "You haven't got a hope." '[76] Carol confirms that Denis was 'shocked' and did not believe that she could win;[77] while Alistair McAlpine – soon to be a close friend of the family – actually has Denis asking vaguely, 'Leader of what, dear?'[78] Consistent with the way they had run their marriage for the past twenty years, however, Margaret took no notice of his advice. Politics was her affair, as business was his, and if she thought she should stand then of course he would support her; he simply hoped she would not be too badly hurt. He probably assumed that she would lose because he could not immediately grasp the upheaval to his own life if she should win.

Her admirers, and indeed Lady Thatcher herself, have subsequently made great play of her courage in sticking her neck out. 'It might have put me on the back benches for life, or out, I did not know,' she told one of her first biographers. 'But the one thing I seemed to have was the power to make a decision when a decision had to be made.'[79] The feminist writer Melanie Phillips doubted that any of the other women then in politics – Shirley Williams or even Barbara Castle – would have shown the same readiness to challenge the male establishment of their party.[80] Years later in her memoirs Lady Thatcher was still claiming that she would have been 'politically finished' if Heath had won.[81]

There is no question that it took nerve to expose herself to the onslaught of publicity she invited by standing. Nevertheless it is difficult to see that she was really staking her career, unless she had been utterly humiliated. Defeated Tory leadership contenders are normally accommodated in the new team: the fact of having demonstrated a certain level of support makes it impossible for the winner to exclude them. Mrs Thatcher's position in Heath's Shadow Cabinet could not have become much more uncomfortable than it was already; yet Heath was obliged to promise before the first ballot that she would keep her place in his team. The alternative outcome was that her candidacy would open the way for someone else to beat Heath; in that case too the new leader would have been bound to give her a prominent position, just as John Major did Michael Heseltine in 1990. This was the expectation of David Wood, the political editor of *The Times*, who wrote at the turn of the year that Mrs Thatcher's candidacy would probably 'succeed only in smoking out into the open a more successful male challenger to Mr Heath', but that by simply standing she had jumped to the front of her political generation and guaranteed herself a leading position in the party for some years to come, making her 'a safe bet' to be the first woman Chancellor.[82] Likewise *The Economist*, still convinced that Heath was invincible, judged Mrs Thatcher 'precisely the sort of candidate who ought to be able to stand, and lose, harmlessly . . . giving her party the cathartic feeling of choice and advancing her position within it, arousing little bitterness, in a way that no other candidate probably could'.[83] It unquestionably took personal courage for Mrs Thatcher to put her head above the parapet; but the strictly political risk was fairly small.

On 25 November Mrs Thatcher thought it right to tell Heath of her purpose in person, though it had already been heavily trailed in the weekend papers. She saw him in the Leader's room at the House of Commons. It was reported at the time – and the story can only have come from her – that he neither stood up nor invited her to sit down, but merely grunted, 'You'll lose.'[84] Lady Thatcher's published version is that 'He looked at me coldly, turned his back, shrugged his shoulders and said, "If you must." '[85] Either way the interview was evidently brief and chilly. But there is no suggestion that Heath was greatly worried by her candidature or thought it uniquely treacherous of her to stand. Having reluctantly agreed that new rules should be drawn up to allow a challenge to a sitting leader, he probably imagined that she would be the first of several hopefuls who might now throw their hats into the ring. This, she writes in her memoirs, was her expectation, too. She thought it 'most unlikely' that she would win.

> But I did think that by entering the race I would draw in other stronger candidates who, even if they did not think like Keith and me, would still be open to persuasion about changing the disastrous course on which the party was set.[86]

There were two ways in which this might have happened. First, once Mrs Thatcher had fired the starting gun, ensuring that there would have to be a contest, others – possibly from within the Shadow Cabinet, more likely from outside – might feel emboldened or obliged to come forward, rather as Anthony Greenwood's announcement of his intention to stand against Hugh Gaitskell for the Labour leadership in 1960 had forced Harold Wilson to take up the challenge (at which point Greenwood withdrew). If Heath was vulnerable, there were surely male candidates better qualified to challenge him than Mrs Thatcher. Alternatively, if none came forward on the first ballot it was possible that Mrs Thatcher's candidacy might reveal sufficient dissatisfaction with Heath to force him to step down, thus freeing Whitelaw and perhaps other senior members of the Shadow Cabinet (Prior? Walker? Pym?) to enter the second ballot. In either of these scenarios, Mrs Thatcher's role would be to act as a stalking horse for the replacement of Heath by a more acceptable leader: she was not generally perceived as leadership material in her own right.

Until the end of the year it was not even certain that she would be a candidate: she had merely declared her intention to force a contest if no one else did. She told the *Daily Mail* that she would stand only if there was 'a certain amount of support';[87] in Finchley Roy Langstone explained that it was 'one of those perhaps and maybe situations'.[88] She would not stand if a better candidate came forward. All sorts of imposing names were canvassed: Christopher Soames, Churchill's son-in-law, who had been Minister of Agriculture under Macmillan and Home, but had lost his seat in 1966, after which Wilson had appointed him Ambassador to France; Julian Amery, another well-connected old imperialist who had served as a middle-ranking minister under Heath; Richard Wood, her former boss at the Ministry of Pensions ten years before; Hugh Fraser, son of the 16th Lord Lovat, a former Secretary of State for Air (and still at that time husband of Lady Antonia). That such little known or superannuated grandees were seriously proposed indicates both the party's desperation and the establishment's abiding snobbery: the

Grantham grocer's daughter was not seen to offer a serious answer to the party's problem.

The strongest candidate to emerge in the weeks after Joseph's withdrawal was Edward du Cann. Indeed for a brief moment the leadership seemed to be his for the asking. Though he had never held Cabinet office and was widely distrusted as an ingratiating flatterer (known to his enemies as 'Uriah'), he occupied a pivotal position as chairman of the 1922 Committee, responsible both for representing the anxieties of backbenchers and for approving the new rules under which any leadership contest would be held. A Treasury minister under Macmillan, he had been appointed party chairman by Alec Douglas-Home in 1965; but he had never got on with Heath, resigned in 1967 and was given no office in 1970. Four years later his lack of Cabinet experience turned out to be his greatest asset, since it meant that – unlike Joseph or Mrs Thatcher – he bore no responsibility for the failures of 1970–4. 'Of those whose records are politically clean', the former editor George Gale wrote in the *Spectator* at the turn of the year, 'Edward du Cann is the likeliest, the ablest and potentially the most successful and powerful.'[89] His candidacy was strongly promoted by senior backbenchers like Airey Neave and Peter Tapsell as the ideal anti-Heath candidate; yet at the same time his chairmanship of the 1922 Committee lent him a sort of neutrality which made him credible as a unity candidate as well. Mrs Thatcher recognised that his credentials were stronger than hers and declared her willingness to step aside if he decided to stand.

Though the newspapers loved to tease their readers with speculation about the possibility of a woman Prime Minister, few commentators really believed it was practical politics. Surveying the twenty-six women MPs just four years earlier, the *Daily Mirror*'s redoubtable columnist Marjorie Proops had concluded scornfully that 'None of them . . . needs waste a second of her time on such an improbable fantasy';[90] and other prominent journalists agreed. John Junor, the veteran editor of the *Sunday Express*, remembered scorning the idea that a woman could even be Chancellor, let alone Prime Minister: 'In my male chauvinist fashion I regarded all women politicians as essentially second-rankers.'[91] The deputy editor of the *Sunday Times*, Frank Giles, was in the United States when the prospect of Mrs Thatcher's candidacy came up. 'I was repeatedly asked whether it was likely that a woman could attain such a position . . . Without hesitation and with total conviction I told audiences to dismiss such an idea from their minds.'[92]

It was not just her sex that told against her, however. She was also seen by many as an inexperienced lightweight who had held only one Cabinet office, and that a welfare department where she was widely thought to have been dominated by her civil servants. She had never made a speech of any importance outside her own front-bench or departmental brief: even to her admirers she still looked more like a natural follower than a potential leader. The left dismissed her as a strident right-winger, but younger right-wingers of the 1970 intake like Norman Tebbit were not impressed by what they had seen of her either. She had been a disappointingly conventional Education Secretary, while her opportunistic advocacy of Heath's mortgage bribe had convinced the free-marketeers that she had no true understanding of their case. 'She wasn't a name that was being bandied around,' Tebbit recalled. 'She was thought of I think by many to be fortunate to get into Ted Heath's Cabinet.'[93]

Above all she was judged to be too narrowly suburban, middle-class and southern in image and appeal – though this caricature was often expressed in thoroughly sexist terms. Derek Marks in the *Daily Express*, for instance, thought her 'totally out of touch with anybody but carefully corseted, middle-class, middle-aged ladies'.[94] Woodrow Wyatt in the *Sunday Mirror* still saw her as 'a limited, bossy, self-righteous and self-complacent woman' who would take the Tory party in 'an extremist, class-conscious, Right wing direction' which would keep it out of office for a decade.[95] 'To anyone north of the Trent', David Watt wrote in the *Financial Times*, 'she might as well come from Mars.'[96] Leading Heathites like Peter Walker and Ian Gilmour, who believed that the Tory party must stay on the middle ground to stand a chance of winning elections, argued their case not in terms of policy but frankly in terms of class stereotype, warning graphically of the danger of retreating into a middle-class suburban bunker: Conservatives, Gilmour wrote in January, must not 'retire behind a privet hedge into a world of narrow class interests and selfish concerns'.[97] John Peyton – the former Minister of Transport who was MP for Yeovil – declared his support for Heath on the eve of the first ballot on the ground that 'Margaret is pure Surbiton in all its glory and that won't do for me'.[98]

It was allegedly Walker who spotted the possibilities for black propaganda in an interview Mrs Thatcher had given just before the election to a magazine called *Pre-Retirement Choice*, in which she advised pensioners to buy tinned food as a hedge against inflation, especially what she called 'the expensive proteins: ham, tongue, salmon, mackerel, sardines'. With her own husband approaching retirement she claimed a special understanding of their fear of rising prices eating away at the value of their fixed incomes.[99] The story, leaked at the beginning of December with the spin that Mrs

Thatcher was advocating 'hoarding', was picked up and duly denounced by Labour MPs and pensioners' spokesmen, the National Housewives' Association and even a former Tory Chief Whip, Lord Redmayne; letters in her own *Finchley Press* accused her of insensitivity to poorer people who could not afford to buy in bulk.[100] A man claiming to be a shopkeeper in the Finchley High Road, who turned out to be entirely fictitious, rang a radio phone-in programme to allege that she used to buy from his shop and used her position to try to get special treatment during a sugar shortage. It was the 'milk snatcher' row over again – a nasty glimpse of what she could expect if she dared to challenge the party establishment.

Once again she was deeply hurt by the unfairness of the allegation. She invited the press to inspect her larder, to demonstrate that she had only a prudent and moderate stock of tins – a single shelf containing a few cans of meat and salmon and six jars each of fruit, jam and honey. [101] For a moment her supporters thought she might crack under the strain: Patrick Cosgrave wrote that 'a combination of fatigue and distress seemed almost to overwhelm her'.[102] Even Cosgrave's own journal, the *Spectator* – her strongest supporter in the Tory Press – believed that she had been 'very foolish indeed' and thought the affair would damage her. 'For the milk-snatcher to become the food-hoarder', it noted in its diary column, 'shows precisely the same political ineptitude as Sir Keith Joseph displayed; and it is likely to have the same political consequence.'[103] In fact, like the milk row, it only stiffened her determination. 'Don't underestimate me,' she told the journal's editor-proprietor Harry Creighton at lunch a few days later: 'I saw how they broke Keith, but they won't break me.'[104]

The 'hoarding' row was a nonsense. All her article really revealed was the old-fashionedness of her assumptions about shopping and thrifty housekeeping: she still thought in her mother's terms of bottling fruit for the winter, of tinned rather than frozen food, of specialist grocers' shops not supermarkets. Though she frequently told interviewers that she regularly did her own shopping for the family ('I'm just an ordinary working wife,' she told the London *Evening News* in September, 'I trot up to the launderette')[105] she never appeared to have caught up with the modern image of the 1970s housewife as portrayed by Shirley Conran's hugely successful *Superwoman*, published in 1974. Yet the pictures of her modest larder did her no harm. The truth is that her frugal ways were probably closer to the real experience of the majority of ordinary voters – north and south of the Trent – than the metropolitan sophisticates and Sunday magazine style gurus realised. And a good many middle-of-the-road Tory MPs were disgusted by the evidence of the depths to which Heath's supporters were prepared to stoop to discredit her.

Back at Westminster where the leadership contest would actually be decided, Heath had inadvertently given his challenger another opportunity which she grasped with both hands. In reshuffling his front bench team at the beginning of November he moved Mrs Thatcher from Environment – which she had only shadowed for nine months – to become deputy Treasury spokesman under Robert Carr. It is not clear whether Heath intended this as a promotion or a snub. 'There is an awful tendency in Britain', she had once complained, 'to think of women as making excellent Number Twos, but not to give them the top job.'[106] After her starring role in the election campaign she had earned another promotion. According to Peter Walker, 'Ted knew that she had been interested in the economic side, she was a good performer and he wanted to recognise her talent.'[107] But then he would have done better to have gone the whole way and made her Shadow Chancellor. Having earlier denied that job to Joseph, he may have seen giving Mrs Thatcher the number two spot as a gesture towards balance; in his memoirs Heath says that he hoped to 'disarm the right' by allowing her 'the opportunity she needed to make runs in the House of Commons'.[108] It has been suggested that he should have known better than to give his rival the very platform from which he had launched his own successful leadership campaign in 1965; but this is hindsight, since at the time he made the appointment Joseph was still the standard-bearer of the right and the possibility of Mrs Thatcher becoming a challenger had probably not occurred to him.

Nevertheless, making her deputy to so bland a performer as Carr was simply inviting her to outshine her nominal superior. Unwittingly, Heath had given her the perfect opportunity to show her paces by taking on Labour's powerful Treasury team – Harold Lever, the millionaire Chancellor of the Duchy of Lancaster, Joel Barnett, the Chief Secretary, and the Chancellor himself, Denis Healey – giving the demoralised Tory MPs something to cheer for the first time in months. Carr was no match for a bruiser like Healey. By her usual combination of hard work and calculated aggression Mrs Thatcher quickly assumed the leadership of the Tories' opposition to Labour's Finance Bill, leading a team of junior spokesmen almost all of whom became members of her own Cabinet a decade later: David Howell, Nigel Lawson, Nicholas Ridley, John MacGregor, Tony Newton, Peter Rees and Norman Lamont (with Cecil Parkinson as whip). Most of the detailed work was done upstairs in Standing Committee A after Christmas. But on 17 December on the Second Reading of Healey's autumn Finance Bill, she effectively launched her campaign with what the Labour MP Brian Sedgemore called 'a fighting leadership speech'.[109] When Healey tried to throw her by crudely taunting her with the hoarding allegation, she defiantly turned it against Labour ministers who bought expensive houses 'in good Tory areas': 'I am not as successful as the Chancellor at hoarding houses. I cannot afford to hoard houses as do the Chancellor and the Prime Minister. If I could, I would.'

This was pretty silly stuff. Healey had recently bought a farm in Sussex, and Wilson a lease on a house in Lord North Street in addition to his holiday home in the Scilly Isles, whereas she and Denis had sold The Mount on moving back to Chelsea in 1972. They bought a small house in Flood Street, just across the road from the block where they had started their married life, though for a time they also retained a weekend flat in Lamberhurst. But it gave her backbenchers some sport. It also marked the beginning of a deliberate attempt to modify her wealthy image. More seriously she declared the Opposition's intention to harry the Government with a mass of amendments: 'Let me warn the Chief Secretary that I am a very good night worker.' The rest of the speech was a characteristically detailed condemnation of the new Capital Transfer Tax as a damaging attack on saving.[110] The Tory benches loved it. Even Labour speakers complimented her: Margaret Jackson (the future Margaret Beckett), who followed her, said that she had never heard Mrs Thatcher before but was 'very much impressed by her fluency and by the logic of many of the arguments she put forward, although I was not convinced by their end result'.[111] Only Enoch Powell – who had returned to the House in October as an Ulster Unionist, bitterly conscious that he had excluded himself from the Tory party at just the moment when the leadership might have been his on a plate – was still sourly unconvinced of the former high-spending Education Secretary's conversion to monetary continence:

> I do not think I have ever heard inflation denounced so convincingly. Satan never rebuked sin with such eloquence as she denounced inflation . . . Then one waited: for surely something ought to have followed . . . Between the end of her denunciation of inflation and her commencement of an examination of the individual clauses of the Bill, there was not a gap large enough to insert the point of a pin.[112]

But Powell was quibbling. This single speech did more than anything yet to encourage sceptical Tories to take Mrs Thatcher seriously. Yet at the end of 1974 she was still a very long shot; Heath had also been performing better, giving notice that he would still be hard to beat. David Wood reported in *The Times* that Tory MPs were 'still at their wits' end to name a plausible candidate to challenge Mr Heath', especially since du Cann was about to rule himself out: 'Mrs Thatcher will probably stand, but the Conservative party does not want a woman leader and has taken a minor gaffe about the number of tins in her larder as an excuse for crossing her off the list.'[113]

In fact du Cann's withdrawal, and the failure of any of the grandees to come forward, left Mrs Thatcher the only candidate on the list. So long as du Cann was in the field she remained bound by her promise to stand aside. But in the second week of January he reluctantly concluded that his business affairs would not stand the close scrutiny he would attract by offering himself. He invited Mrs Thatcher – with Denis, unusually – to his house in Lord North Street to tell her of his decision. He recalls the two of them sitting together on his sofa like a housekeeper and handyman applying for a job. Privately du Cann was 'a bit miffed' that she made no attempt to persuade him to change his mind.[114] His more discreet published account is that she appeared 'surprised but careful not to say so'.[115] He felt her suppressed excitement at the knowledge that his decision cleared the way for her to do what she had wanted to do all along.

The most important consequence of du Cann's withdrawal was that it brought Airey Neave into Mrs Thatcher's camp. Neave is a somewhat shadowy figure, famous for having escaped from Colditz during the war and reputed to have maintained links with the security services: he knew everyone and knew everything about everyone. MP for Abingdon since 1953, he had been a junior minister under Macmillan until forced by ill health to leave the Government at the 1959 election: Heath – then Chief Whip – is said to have told him bluntly that he was 'finished'. Heath strenuously denies it;[116] but he certainly gave Neave no advancement after 1965, nor even the compensatory knighthood which any other MP of comparable standing might have expected. Whatever the reason, Neave was determined by 1974 that Heath must go: he did not greatly care who replaced him. His importance was that he was not a paid-up right-winger. He offered his services first to Willie Whitelaw. When Whitelaw declined he joined those trying to persuade du Cann to run; only when du Cann too finally refused did he switch his efforts – and the support he had gathered for du Cann – to the only candidate prepared to stick her neck out:

Hitherto Mrs Thatcher's campaign had been a makeshift affair run by Fergus Montgomery, her former PPS, and William Shelton, the Member for Streatham. From the moment Neave took over he set up a skilled and professional campaign designed to transform her from a stalking horse into a serious challenger.

Nothing did more to raise her credibility, however, than another blistering encounter with Denis Healey in the House of Commons. On the Committee Stage of the Finance Bill on 21 January she once again condemned the disincentive effect of Capital Transfer Tax, passionately defending the principle of inheritance as a basic human freedom. 'Why does the Chancellor take such objection to such efforts for one's children?' she demanded. 'Some think of it as a duty and a privilege.'[117] Her flaunting of the word 'privilege' was a provocation Healey could not resist. Winding up the debate the next day, in a deliberate effort to stir up Tory divisions, he denounced her speech as 'a defiant reassertion of birth and privilege – of the right of inheritance against the whole current of democratic politics in the twenty century'. Invoking the legendary heroine of the Spanish left in the war against Franco, he dubbed her derisively the 'La Pasionaria of privilege' and alleged that she had 'decided . . . to see her party tagged as the party of the rich few. I believe that she and her party will regret it.'

After a storm of angry points of order, Mrs Thatcher counter-attacked with withering scorn:

> I wish I could say that the Chancellor of the Exchequer had done himself less than justice. Unfortunately, I can only say that I believe he has done himself justice. Some Chancellors are macro-economic. Other Chancellors are fiscal. This one is just plain cheap.

She played her old trick of rebuking his ignorance of the effects of his own policy:

> When he rose to speak yesterday we on this side of the House were amazed how one could possibly get to be Chancellor of the Exchequer and speak for his Government knowing so little about existing taxes and so little about the proposals which were coming before Parliament. If this Chancellor can be Chancellor, anyone in the House of Commons could be Chancellor.

Capital Transfer Tax, she asserted, would affect 'not only the one in a thousand to whom he referred but everyone, including people born like I was with no privilege at all. It will affect us as well as the

Socialist millionaires.' First it would damage the economic structure of the country by its effect on family businesses, farming and woodlands.

> Secondly it damages the very nature of our society by concentrating power and property in the hands of the State and of those politicians whose only ambition is the pursuit of power for its own sake.
>
> We believe that the future of freedom is inseparable from a wide distribution of private property among the people, not concentrating it into the hands of politicians.

The tax, she concluded bluntly, could not be amended. 'It should be withdrawn.'[118]

This was a brilliant parliamentary performance, demolishing Labour's bully, drawing timely attention to her own humble origins and broadening out to a fundamental statement of her political philosophy, all in a single column of *Hansard*. Instead of apologising or denying Healey's allegation, she gloried in it, brazenly affirming the middle-class values of property and inheritance which Healey was hypocritically attacking. Tory MPs, demoralised by the humiliations and retreats of the Heath era, had not heard such fighting talk for years. 'Here was a senior figure', Nicholas Ridley recalled, 'who didn't seem beaten at all; she exuded confidence and certainty. She made a lot of converts.'[119] It was not only her natural supporters on the right who were impressed. 'Amidst the shambles and doubts of that time', Francis Pym acknowledged, 'here was one person who could articulate a point of view with conviction.'[120] As a result of this two-minute speech, *The Times* reported the next day, 'far fewer members . . . are speaking dismissively of a woman's candidature . . . than they did a fortnight ago when she announced her challenge.'[121]

Suddenly she looked like a leader, a fighter who made the rest of the Tory front bench – Whitelaw, Carr, Howe – look like a lot of wimps. But this brief speech also set the tone of her challenge over the next two weeks – a tone and a message quite different from Keith Joseph's over the previous six months. Joseph had pitched his opposition to Heath in terms of economic theory and his discovery that well-intentioned Keynesianism actually destroyed the nation's capacity to create wealth. Mrs Thatcher's appeal was at once more high-flown – unafraid of lofty absolutes like Freedom – and more down-to-earth, defining freedom in the daily concerns of individual taxpayers, homeowners and businessmen. It is often said that Tory MPs did not know what they were doing when they elected Mrs

Thatcher leader. This is true only in that she did not set out a detailed agenda of specific policies – monetarism, tax cuts or privatisation. But it cannot be said that she disguised her beliefs to win the leadership. On the contrary, from this ringing retort to Healey to the first ballot ten days later, she declared her philosophy very clearly: if some who voted for her did so without fully realising where her ideas would lead, the fault was theirs for failing to believe that she meant what she said. In fact what the party responded to was not so much her beliefs themselves as the burning self-belief with which she expounded them: it was not her convictions that they voted for, but her conviction.

As would always be the case from now on, she had a good deal of help with finding the right words to frame her message. Though Joseph kept scrupulously in the background, she received journalistic assistance from Sherman and other writers from the *Telegraph* stable who had worked with him over the past year – Peter Utley, John O'Sullivan, Frank Johnson – and also, most importantly, from Angus Maude, an old ally of Enoch Powell and long-time champion of middle-class values who had been in the wilderness since being sacked from Heath's Shadow Cabinet in 1966. It was Maude who wrote the article with which she effectively launched her campaign on 30 January – the day after nominations closed – in (appropriately) the *Daily Telegraph*. The paper had invited a number of potential leaders – not just the three declared candidates,* but also Joseph, Carr, Prior and Whitelaw – to set out their stalls under the title 'My Kind of Tory Party'. Heath's offering was a self-parody of woolly centrism, full of vague appeals to moderation, balance and national unity. Mrs Thatcher, by contrast, returned unapologetically to the defence of middle-class interests:

> If 'middle-class values' include the encouragement of variety and individual choice, the provision of fair incentives and rewards for skill and hard work, the maintenance of effective barriers against the excessive power of the state and a belief in the wide distribution of individual *private* property, then they are certainly what I am trying to defend . . .
>
> If a Tory does not believe that private property is one of the main bulwarks of individual freedom, then he had better become

---

*Hugh Fraser had come forward as a quixotic alternative for traditionalist right-wingers who could not bring themselves to vote for a woman.

a socialist and have done with it. Indeed one of the reasons for our electoral failure is that people believe too many Conservatives *have* become socialists already ... Why should anyone support a party that seems to have the courage of no convictions?[122]

The next day she set out her reasons for standing in a speech to her constituents in Finchley. This was somewhat more coded, as though she had been warned not to sound too extreme. Yet she still began uncompromisingly by defending her decision to give the party a choice, promising to unite behind Heath if he was re-elected, but insisting that the contest was 'not simply about an individual ... but about the whole nature and style of the party's leadership since 1945': fair warning of the scope of her project. 'It is not a particularly easy time for me,' she confessed.

Some people ... have not hesitated to impugn my motives, to attribute to me political views which I do not hold, and suggest that the idea of a woman aspiring to lead a great party is absurd: a strangely old-fashioned view, I should have thought.

She was at pains to deny both the idea that in defending freedom she was defending privilege – 'I had precious little privilege in my early years' – and the impression that all her supporters were 'reactionary right wingers'. The election, she insisted, was 'not a confrontation between left and right'.

I am trying to represent the deep feelings of those many thousands of rank-and-file Tories in the country – and potential Conservative voters too – who feel let down by our party and find themselves unrepresented in a political vacuum.

She went on to list six 'traditional ideals of Toryism' which the party needed to rediscover 'in the desperate situation of Britain today'. They make an interestingly slippery list. First, 'compassion and concern for the individual and his freedom' – a curious yoking together of two concepts, compassion and freedom, which in political shorthand are usually opposed. Someone had clearly advised her that she should get a reference to compassion in somewhere. Second, 'opposition to excessive state power' – no one could object to that, but the definition of 'excessive' was left open. Third, 'the right of the enterprising, the hard-working and the thrifty to succeed and to reap the rewards of success and pass some of them on to their children' – her now standard refrain, but prudently qualified by the weaselly reservation 'some'. Fourth, 'encouragement of that infinite diversity of choice that is an essential of freedom' – again a fairly standard formula, but this time given limitless possibilities by the word 'infinite'. Fifth, 'the defence of widely distributed private property against the socialist state': she did not spell out what this might mean. Sixth, 'the right of a man to work without oppression by either employer or trade union boss' – a clear signal of intent to try again to tackle the union problem, rendered superficially even-handed by the reference to oppressive employers.

What is interesting about these six points is that they all amount to the same thing: individualism against collectivism, private property (and by implication private health and education) against taxation and state provision. Only the last contains anything like a specific policy commitment. There is nothing about the economy or the money supply, unemployment or inflation, not a word about foreign policy or defence. Yet allowing for the coded expression, this speech, if it meant anything at all, was a clear repudiation of the fundamental assumptions of 'progressive' social policy – Labour and Conservative – since the war. It might have been nothing but a catalogue of Tory buzz-words. But her conclusion once again made her purpose unambiguous:

> There is a widespread feeling in the country that the Conservative party has not defended these ideals explicitly and toughly enough, so that Britain is set on a course towards inevitable socialist mediocrity.
> That course must not only be halted but reversed.[123]

As important as her message, however, was the need to humanise her image, neutralise the gender question and persuade both the public and Tory MPs that she really was a credible leader. Paradoxically she no longer needed to prove that she was tough enough for the job: it was becoming a cliché, as David Wood noted in *The Times*, to say that she was 'the best man among them'.[124] But that raised the alarming spectre of a feminist harridan – the worst sort of woman. What she now had to do was to make a virtue of her femininity. With Gordon Reece's help, therefore, she presented herself to the press and television as an ordinary housewife, old-fashioned, home-loving and non-feminist, thus allaying both male fears and female disapproval. 'What people don't realise about me', she told the *Daily Mirror*, 'is that I am a very ordinary person who leads a very normal life. I enjoy it – seeing that the family have a good breakfast. And shopping keeps me in touch.'[125] Just as she had turned the hoarding allegation to her advantage by parading her thrifty larder, and refused to be cowed by gibes about middle-class values but picked up the intended insult and wore it with pride, so she played along with the pretence that she was 'just' a housewife and milked it for all it was worth. For the benefit of the *Daily Mail* she went shopping with her sister.[126] On the morning of the ballot she was filmed cooking Denis's breakfast and photographed putting out the milk bottles. And for the *Daily Mirror* she staged a pantomime of housework which the paper presented, only half-satirically, as a metaphor for political dynamism:

> Margaret Thatcher had all her chores neatly lined up at the weekend. First there was the kitchen to tidy. Then the bathroom, a dash around with a duster and on to the shopping and the laundry. And after that she had to tidy up the Tory party, polish off Ted Heath and give Britain a good spring cleaning.
>
> With Margaret Thatcher it is sometimes a bit hard to tell whether she wants to be Prime Minister or housewife of the year.[127]

In her book on the marketing of Mrs Thatcher's image some years later Wendy Webster noted the irony that she who had so decisively rejected her mother's housebound domesticity at the outset of her career 'began for a moment to look just like her' – playing the 'little woman' in order to storm the citadel of male power.[128] The irony was that her strategy was so successful that in the second ballot Willie Whitelaw felt he had to try to compete by being photographed in an apron doing the washing-up.

At the time of the 'milk snatcher' row three years earlier she had refused to sacrifice her pearls; but now, on Reece's advice, she virtually gave up wearing hats. She told the *Daily Mail* that she had not bought a new one for two years;[129] from now on she wore a hat only on rare formal occasions like the State Opening of Parliament. Reece's coaching was also evident in a new, softer image on television. In an interview for *World in Action*, the *Daily Telegraph* reported, 'she came alive as never before ... almost diffidently, frequently blushing, passionate but mild in affirming Conservative values'.[130] *The Times* was struck by her 'modesty and charm'.[131] Though combative – 'They know I don't flinch from attack ... I can and do attack when it is needed and attack vigorously' – she was careful not to appear divisive, saying that she would like Heath in her team 'if he wanted it – and I should want him to want it'; but drawing the line at Powell, at least for the moment. ('He deserted his own people.') She could still be sharp, however. On the BBC's *Midweek* she rejected her southern image, pointing out that Heath was more of a southerner than she was. Asked if she could win back votes in the north of England she replied tartly, 'It wasn't I who lost them.' These interviews were a revelation to Tory MPs crowded round television sets at Westminster; one of her team reckoned they were 'worth twenty votes to us; many MPs had never seen her like that before and did not know what she was really like'.[132]

It was partly a function of her sex, partly of her character, that even parliamentary colleagues of long standing barely knew her. An obsessive workaholic with, in her early days, a family to get back to, she had spent scarcely any time on the back benches: she had never had the leisure or the inclination to frequent the bars and smoking rooms of the House. Few Members had ever heard her speak except to a narrow brief. Norman Tebbit 'had only ever exchanged a dozen words with her' before he was drawn into her leadership campaign in January.[133] Norman Fowler had scarcely met her, but retains a vivid image of her queuing alone with her tray in the Commons cafeteria.[134] Mark Carlisle likewise knew nothing about her, except what he had heard at second hand from Reggie Maudling, which was not complimentary.[135] Even Patrick Jenkin, who had known her since they were in chambers together twenty years before, felt that he had no idea either of her views or of her leadership qualities.[136] But the fact that she was a largely unknown quantity actually suited Neave's purpose very well.

Neave arranged for curious backbenchers to meet her singly or in small groups over tea or a glass of wine in Robin Cooke's room in the House of Commons (Cooke was the MP for Bristol West). Mrs Thatcher used these occasions skilfully to project the softer side of her personality, answering their queries and worries, and generally charming them by her unexpected femininity and her willingness to listen to their concerns – in complete contrast both with her fighting style in the chamber and with Heath's chilling lack of social grace. After years of scarcely noticing his backbenchers, Heath's last-minute efforts to ingratiate himself proved embarrassingly counterproductive. In an open letter to her constituency chairman Mrs Thatcher pointedly called for 'a leadership that listens';[137] and this humility was one of her principal attractions. She did not hector or preach, but allowed disgruntled MPs to feel that she understood their grievances and frustration. In this way, though practically the whole of the party establishment was ranged against her, she made herself the champion of the foot soldiers of the parliamentary party who felt slighted and frozen out by Heath's remoteness.

Mrs Thatcher's function was still widely seen as attracting enough support to force Heath to resign, leaving Whitelaw or some other serious candidate to come forward and reunite the party. A few days before nominations for the first ballot closed, the *Sunday Times* reported that the bookmakers made Whitelaw – at 6–4 – the favourite to win on a second or subsequent ballot, with 5–2 on Heath to survive; du Cann was still 5–1, Mrs Thatcher 8–1, Jim Prior and Julian Amery 12–1 and Keith Joseph, Geoffrey Howe and Hugh Fraser the outsiders at 16–1.[138] Four days earlier Barbara Castle – a keen observer from the other side of the political fence – wrote in her diary: 'Despite the fact that Margaret Thatcher is now giving Heath a hard run for his money, mine is still on Heath's victory. You can't find two Tories to agree on an alternative to him.'[139] Right up to the first ballot most of Fleet Street, including the two *Telegraph* titles, agreed with her: only the *Daily Mail* reported a poll of MPs which suggested that Heath might struggle to win the first ballot – and even the *Mail* did not (contrary to its later boasts) support her.[140] The *Daily Telegraph* reflected on the party's problems from a distinctly Thatcherite standpoint, yet merely hoped that Heath when re-elected would take more notice of his critics.[141] *The Times*, equally critical of Heath, nevertheless wanted Whitelaw to succeed him and in an editorial on 1 February scarcely mentioned Mrs Thatcher at all.[142] The paper's political columnist, George Hutchinson – who had once written a biography of Heath – hoped that Whitelaw as leader would unite the party by bringing back Powell, Boyle and Soames, with Heath going to Brussels as an EC Commissioner.[143]

The complacency of Heath's supporters played into Neave's hands. They never really believed it possible for the former Prime Minister to be beaten by an inexperienced woman. He had the public support of the whole Shadow Cabinet, except Keith Joseph. (Norman St John Stevas, who later made much of the fact that he was the only other member of the Shadow Cabinet to vote for Mrs Thatcher, nevertheless supported Heath on the first ballot and only switched to Mrs Thatcher on the second.)[144] Elder statesmen like Alec Home and Reggie Maudling were wheeled out to consolidate support for the status quo. Home stressed Heath's unrivalled international experience; Maudling warned the party not to become 'lost in an arid waste of doctrine'.[145] The attitude of the party's elders was typified by Rab Butler, who visited the Research Department during the campaign and remarked to Chris Patten as they went up in the lift: 'We don't have to take this Thatcher business seriously, do we?'[146] The constituency chairmen came out overwhelmingly for Heath: a Harris poll in the *Daily Express* found that 70 per cent of Tory voters still thought him the best leader.[147] As a result, while Neave and his team were assiduously combing the lists of Tory MPs – as systematically and professionally as Peter Walker had done for Heath in 1965, finding the right colleague to influence each individual – Heath this time had no proper campaign at all. It is still uncertain who if anyone was meant to be in charge: Walker, Kenneth Baker, Timothy Kitson all deny that it was them. (Mrs Thatcher in her turn suffered exactly the same problem in 1990: it seems to be impossible for incumbent leaders to run a decent campaign.) The Heath camp simply took for granted what they read in the newspapers and repeated to one another, that all sensible people were still for Ted and only a small fringe of right-wingers and diehard anti-Marketeers would vote for 'that dreadful woman'.

They underestimated the extent of disillusion with Heath among a significant body of MPs who were neither particularly on the right nor anti-Europe. Recent research – based on confidential interviews with almost all the 276 MPs – has confirmed that on a left–right spectrum, the right did vote almost solidly for Mrs Thatcher and most of the left for Heath. But the largest group, who could not be defined as either left or right, voted primarily on grounds of personal loyalty or lack of it; those to whom Heath had given office in 1970–4, even (perhaps surprisingly) a majority of the newest Members who had entered Parliament only in 1974 under his leadership, tended to stick with him. Members for northern seats, and those who had been to the most prestigious public schools, were also more likely to support him, confirming the social element in the opposition to Mrs Thatcher.

By his remoteness, insensitivity and sheer bad manners, however, Heath had exhausted the loyalty of a large number of backbenchers who had no cause to be grateful to him: this category – which included some distinctly leftish figures like Tony Newton who had experienced the quality of her leadership on the Finance Bill – simply wanted a change of leader. Most of them did not want Mrs Thatcher to become leader, they certainly did not want a lurch to right-wing policies, but they were persuaded to vote for Mrs Thatcher on the first ballot by a combination of the Heath camp's counterproductive assurance that Heath would be comfortably re-elected and Airey Neave's opposite tactic of deliberately playing down Mrs Thatcher's support, so that the only way those who wanted Whitelaw or a wider choice of candidates could get the result they wanted was by supporting Mrs Thatcher on the first ballot.[148] A week before the poll, Neave's canvassing showed around 120 pledges for the challenger; but he let it be known that she had no more than seventy. Privately he told the Labour MP Tam Dalyell, out of the corner of his mouth: 'Put your money on the filly, Tam, if I were you.'[149] But in the bars and smoking rooms where Tories met to consider their vote the message was spread that she was 'doing very well but not quite well enough'.[150]

At least one natural Heathite who was persuaded to vote against his convictions looked back with hindsight on 'one of the greatest mistakes of my political life'. His vote, he reflected, was 'a typical example of Edward Heath losing his basic support' simply by failing to cultivate it. 'If he had taken the trouble to address one sympathetic or personal word to me after my election in February 1974 he could have had me . . . As it was . . . I was courted by the Thatcher campaigning team and fell for it.'[151]

There is a good deal of anecdotal evidence of others who fell for Neave's subtle disinformation though they did not for a moment want his candidate to win. Norman Tebbit has claimed that he and John Nott persuaded Michael Heseltine to vote for Mrs Thatcher. Heseltine has always refused to reveal how he voted, but his very refusal suggests that he did not vote for Heath.[152] The most critical group of tactical voters, however, was a clutch of senior backbenchers from the left of centre – perhaps as many as thirty – led by Sir John Rodgers and Sir Paul Bryan (both old colleagues of Heath from way back who had been alienated by his sheer unfriendliness) – who originally intended to abstain but decided at the last minute to vote for Mrs Thatcher to ensure that Heath did not defeat her by the 15 per cent margin of victory needed to ensure his survival.[153]

The result of all this second-guessing was that the unfancied filly not only gained enough votes to open up a second ballot, but actually topped the poll. Heath mustered only 119 supporters: Mrs Thatcher – for whatever mixture of motives – attracted 130, while sixteen voted for Fraser and another eleven abstained. (Not all of them deliberately: Jim Prior's train was late.) 'The word sensational', the *Mail* reported, 'was barely adequate to describe the shock wave that hit Westminster' when the figures were declared.[154] From the establishment's point of view the figures were not only bad enough to oblige Heath to step down immediately. ('We got it all wrong,' he told his stunned team.)[155] They also made it very difficult for Whitelaw to pick up his banner with any prospect of success.

Fifteen years later Michael Heseltine ran Mrs Thatcher close enough to force her to step down, only for John Major to come in, pick up most of her votes and defeat him in turn. But in 1975, by the normal British understanding of elections, Mrs Thatcher had won already. She had defeated the incumbent and therefore asserted an unanswerable moral claim on the prize. Whitelaw was bound to announce that he would now come forward as the unity candidate who could bind the party's wounds; but it was too late – Mrs Thatcher's stature was hugely increased by her unexpected victory. The fact that three more contenders – Prior, Howe and John Peyton – threw their hats into the ring as well merely underlined that none of them had any chance of catching her. They were simply putting down markers: had they been serious about trying to stop her they should all have backed Whitelaw. Saluting her achievement, the *Daily Telegraph* suggested that it was almost bad form to force a second ballot at all after she had done the dirty work of getting rid of Heath. If four more challengers now came forward, the paper argued, it would seem to the country

> that a whole herd of fainthearts left it to a courageous and able woman to topple a formidable leader and that then, profiting by her success, they ganged up to deny her her just reward.
>   This is not fair to any of the people we are talking about, agreed; no, but it will smell all the same.[156]

In fact, of course, ganging up was just what they did not do. There were rumours that Neave's machiavellian hand was visible here too: it was later revealed that Humphrey Atkins, the Chief Whip, had encouraged both Prior and Howe to stand.[157] It made little difference how many candidates offered themselves. Mrs Thatcher was the woman of the moment, and the force was with her. 'The wider the choice', she told ITN News, 'the stronger the position of the person who is finally chosen.'[158] The *Finchley Press*, delighted that their local heroine was now a national star, had no doubt about the outcome: 'Heath down – now for the rest.'[159] Facing the massed flashbulbs of the press after the declaration of the vote she exuded confidence. 'The hands look so delicate', the *Express* reported, 'but the eyes are steel blue and the smile is certain.'[160] 'I've got a lot to offer,' she declared. She had no doubt that she could handle Harold Wilson. She had 'fantastic stamina, great physical strength'.

> I've had a fiery baptism in politics. If I've not had as much experience as Ted, I've a woman's ability to stick with a job and get on with it when everyone else walks off and leaves it.[161]

The picture editors had a field day. Barbara Castle, equally scornful of the 'brave warriors who have now crept out of hiding . . .

to climb on the second ballot bandwagon', watched with professional admiration the wave of publicity that Mrs Thatcher was now riding:

> The papers are full of Margaret Thatcher. She has lent herself with grace and charm to every piece of photographer's gimmickry, but don't we all when the prize is big enough? What interests me now is how blooming she looks – she has never been prettier . . . She may have been up late on the Finance Bill Committee; she is beset by enemies and has to watch every gesture and word. But she sails through it all looking her best. I understand why. She is in love: in love with power, success – and with herself . . . If we have to have Tories, good luck to her.[162]

Yet so ingrained was the belief that the election of a woman leader was still a fantasy too far that even Mrs Castle was not quite convinced that she would pull it off; nor could all the newspapers which had supported Heath instantly abandon their allegiance to his natural heir. The *Mail* was now decisively for Mrs Thatcher, the *Daily Telegraph* implicitly so; but the *Sunday Telegraph* and the *Financial Times* ('The Choice is Thatchlaw') still sat on the fence.[163] The *Daily Express*, the very day after it had launched a centre-page crusade in support of the beleaguered middle class, bizarrely warned in an editorial that 'the Tories have got to decide now whether they want to be a national movement or a party that represents the aspirations of the middle classes' and hoped Tory MPs would have 'the common sense to elect Willie Whitelaw';[164] the *Sun* too still believed that 'the big money is on Whitelaw'.[165] The *Sunday Times* opted for Whitelaw's greater breadth of appeal, shrewdness and wisdom to unite the party.

> Margaret Thatcher would have to work very hard, and show much more inspiration than she ever has so far, to remove the impression that she represents, by image, by class, by geography and by attitude, all that is narrowest in modern Conservatism.[166]

But Tory MPs were too caught up in the excitement of what they had so unexpectedly done to heed such reservations. In the week between the two ballots the novelty and kudos of being the first major political party in the Western world to elect a woman leader overcame the previous doubts of many who had intended to switch their votes, and of a good many more who had voted for Heath. 'Electing Margaret Thatcher would be the most imaginative thing the party has done for years,' one supporter told the *Daily Mail*; 'The time has come for a change', said another, 'and it would be absolutely right for the Tories to come up with a woman leader, who may even be a woman Prime Minister.'[167]

Philip Cowley's analysis suggests that only about fourteen who had supported Mrs Thatcher on the first ballot abandoned her on the second, while she picked up another thirty votes from those who had previously voted for Heath or Fraser, or had abstained. If he was to win, Whitelaw would have needed to hold practically all Heath's vote as well as taking some of Mrs Thatcher's. In fact he managed to hold barely half of Heath's vote, the rest splitting fairly evenly between Mrs Thatcher on the one hand and Prior, Howe and Peyton (who took hardly any of their combined vote from Mrs Thatcher) on the other. Though she gained only another sixteen votes overall – just seven more than the simple majority required to win on the second ballot – Whitelaw's poor showing and the fragmentation of the vote among the rest made her margin of victory look more decisive than it really was.[168] The figures were

Margaret Thatcher	146
William Whitelaw	79
Geoffrey Howe	19
James Prior	19
John Peyton	11
Abstentions	2

276

Woolly, bumbling and platitudinous, Whitelaw was in fact a very unconvincing candidate to put up against Mrs Thatcher in the full confidence of her first round victory. An admirable deputy – as he proved over the next thirteen years – he never looked like a leader and never looked as if he wanted to be leader. (Fifteen years later he recognised the same reluctance in Douglas Hurd. 'The trouble with Douglas', he confessed to Kenneth Baker, 'was the same with me in 1975. He doesn't really want to be leader.')[169] He went through the motions of giving the party a choice, and even managed to give Mrs Thatcher the impression that he expected to win.[170] But he very plainly did not stand for anything except a soggy 'unity'. 'We can achieve that unity', he told his Penrith constituents, 'only by moderation, breadth of vision and generosity.'[171] 'United for what?' the *Daily Telegraph* quite reasonably asked.[172] He was 'strong on human sympathy', the *Mail* allowed, 'but weak on economics'. Mrs Thatcher by contrast clearly offered 'a more decisive understanding

... of the supreme economic danger now facing Britain', in other words inflation.[173]

The difference was graphically demonstrated on the Saturday between the two ballots when they were both engaged to speak at a Young Conservative conference at Eastbourne. They agreed – absurdly – not to make campaigning speeches. Whitelaw duly restricted himself to answering questions on devolution: he was heard with scant enthusiasm and even a few boos. Mrs Thatcher felt no such inhibition but seized the chance to rouse the conference with a stirring call to 'back the workers and not the shirkers', winning a standing ovation – helpfully captured by the television cameras – from what was in those days a strongly left-of-centre audience. 'Young Tories Hail Mrs Thatcher' ran one Sunday headline.[174] At the subsequent press conference she was noticeably more upbeat than a 'somewhat glum' Whitelaw, and added insult to injury by giving him 'a smacking kiss' which featured on all the next day's front pages. 'That kiss may prove to be Mr Whitelaw's consolation prize,' the *Sunday Telegraph* presciently noted.[175]

The next day Mrs Thatcher withdrew from appearing with the other four candidates on *Panorama*, though this was against her own instinct. She had already agreed to take part, and did not like going back on her word to the producer; but she bowed to Gordon Reece's judgement that she would best underline her status as the front runner by staying above the battle, leaving the also-rans looking grey and irrelevant in her absence.[176] As usual Reece's image-management was spot on. The nadir of Whitelaw's ineptitude was allowing himself to be photographed at the kitchen sink, pretending to wash up, in a vain effort to match Mrs Thatcher's credentials as a housewife. ('As soon catch me on a golf course,' she scornfully remarked.)[177] 'Anyone can do the washing up,' a correspondent wrote to *The Times*. 'What this country needs is someone to lead us.'[178] Tory MPs could see that Whitelaw was not the man.

Her only tricky moment, in fact, came when her opponents spread whispers that she was 'cool' on Europe. With the referendum on Labour's renegotiated terms of entry just four months away, this had the potential to swing a lot of votes away from her. She had to rush out a statement, drafted by George Gardiner – in those days a Euro-enthusiast – stamping on the story. ('I'm for Europe snaps Margaret', was how the *Express* reported it.) Joining the Community, she declared, was Heath's outstanding achievement.

This torch must be picked up and carried by whoever is chosen by the party to succeed him. The commitment to European partnership is one which I fully share.[179]

The day of the second ballot – Tuesday 11 February – offers some telling cameos of the Thatcher household. Denis left for work at 7.00 a.m. as usual, driving down the M4 to Burmah's headquarters in Swindon. Carol was in the middle of her Law Society exams; she had been forced to move out to stay with a friend near by while Flood Street was taken over by political advisers and supporters. She had an exam that afternoon, but dropped in to see her mother in the morning. Margaret, preoccupied with her own date with history, was oblivious. 'You can't be as nervous as I am,' she told her daughter. 'She crossed the fingers on both hands. "We're not sure if we've got the numbers."' There was no champagne on ice: she was afraid that even having her hair done before the ballot might be tempting fate. Carol did not learn the result till she came out of her exam at five o'clock, when she had to leave by a back door to avoid the press. Meanwhile Denis was given the news by his secretary: he received it calmly – though it would utterly transform his life – and drove back to London to join Margaret for a victory celebration at Bill Shelton's house in Pimlico.[180]

The new leader's first engagement on receiving the result had been another press conference in the Grand Committee Room, off Westminster Hall. She began by being suitably gushing and humble, carefully paying tribute to all her predecessors.

> To me it is like a dream that the next name in the lists after Harold Macmillan, Sir Alec Douglas-Home, Edward Heath is Margaret Thatcher. Each has brought his own style of leadership and stamp of greatness to the task. I shall take on the work with humility and dedication.

The only surprise was that she did not go back as far as Churchill – the Tory leader she was really proud to be succeeding; but she made good the omission with a tearful tribute to 'the great Winston' on television that evening.[181] Having got the pieties out of the way with a gracious acknowledgement of her defeated rivals – 'I know they will be disappointed. But I hope we shall soon be back working together as colleagues for the things in which we all believe' – she 'took complete charge' of the conference in a manner that would become very familiar.

The new Tory leader stunned her audience into silence with her rapid, almost brusque replies to questions. She kept calling 'Next question, next question', as she outpaced the flustered press gang.

At one time she called out confidently: 'You chaps don't like short, direct answers. Men like long, rambling, waffling answers.'

Asked if she had won because she was a woman, she replied crisply: 'I like to think I won on merit.' She even had the confidence to risk a joke. Asked about foreign affairs, she replied: 'I am all for them.' She then acknowledged, with 'disarming feminine charm', 'I am the first to understand that I am not expert in every subject.'[182] Swivelling this way and that to give all the photographers a good picture, she announced pointedly, 'I am now going to take a turn to the right, which is very appropriate.'[183] It was an astonishing performance: already she had the press eating out of her hand.

She moved on to stamp her authority on the party organisation, whose every effort up to a few hours before had been devoted to preventing her victory. There was nothing improper in that: Conservative Central Office serves the leader, not the party, for as long as he or she is leader. She would have no choice but to retain most of Heath's Shadow Cabinet; but she was perfectly entitled to purge his officials. 'I have no doubt that there were many anxious thoughts behind the polite smiling faces that evening,' she recalled in her memoirs. 'And not without reason.'[184] She went next to Shelton's party in Pimlico; but she stayed only forty minutes – just long enough to be photographed with Denis and Mark (characteristically Carol kept out of the limelight while Mark courted it) – before going off for a working dinner with the Chief Whip, Humphrey Atkins. Wasting time in celebration was not her style. 'She had the job she wanted', Carol wrote, 'and she couldn't wait to get started.'[185] A bemused Denis was taken off to dinner by Norman Tebbit. The new Leader of the Opposition finished up, characteristically, by going back to the Commons to take her leave of Standing Committee A which was still ploughing through the Finance Bill.

Nothing had impressed Tory MPs more than the way she had stuck to this chore throughout the leadership contest – each Tuesday, Wednesday and Thursday from four o'clock until sometimes well after midnight. On the evening of her first ballot victory she was there as usual, speaking and voting until at least 11.20 p.m. The next night – an all-night sitting – she was present to vote at ten past one, though not later. On the evening of the second ballot, when she had just been elected leader, she appeared in time to vote at about ten o'clock and was formally congratulated by the Labour chairman, Richard Crawshaw. She replied graciously that 'due to circumstances beyond my control I have been called to higher things and, therefore, may not be with the Committee very much longer.' She paid tribute to her Tory colleagues whose 'degree of competence, extent of knowledge and skill in argument . . . must have been most disturbing to those who sit on the other side, as well as very enjoyable to everyone concerned', expressed her regret that she would not be able to see the job through, but remarked tartly that she hoped they would get on with it: progress always seemed very slow in her absence, because 'women are always very economical in their speeches'.[186] The fact that she took the trouble to take leave of the Committee in this way is extraordinary tribute to her dedication to the hard grind – rather than the glamour – of politics.

Before going to bed she called in to see Carol, who had asked to see her.

> I was half-asleep when she knocked on the door and I can't remember exactly what we said to each other. But I do recall that she instantly looked the part: the aura of power about her was almost like a halo.

For all her careful outward modesty, Carol confirms that her mother was not astonished to find herself leader.

> The outside world may have been surprised . . . but she had clearly seen herself in a central role. When the political Polaroid developed into a photograph and confirmed her vision, she was already ahead of the game. I was reminded of the famous scene in the Robert Redford film *The Candidate* where the victorious politician grabs an aide in the loo and barks at him, 'OK, what do we do now?' My mother knew exactly what to do and embraced the leadership as if it had always been her destiny.[187]

The political world had had a week to get used to the idea, but still the reactions ranged from enthusiasm to horrified incredulity on the Tory benches and misplaced glee on the Labour side. The *Daily Mail*, claiming to have backed the winner all along, hailed 'a sensational and historic moment' with the front-page headline 'The Lady is a Champ' and a three-page inside feature, 'The One-Woman Revolution', continued on subsequent days. 'The Tories have chosen a woman of ambition, nerve and brilliance to lead them. They have also chosen to live dangerously.'[188] The *Express* quickly came into line with a typical effusion by Norman St John Stevas

('Magnificent Margaret') and a Cummings cartoon showing Harold Wilson as leader of the Fuddy-Duddy party thinking he should have a sex-change to modernise his image.[189] In fact most Labour MPs believed that the Tories had just handed them the next election on a plate. Marcia Falkender remembers a meeting of senior ministers just after the news broke:

> They were all laughing, joking and slapping each other on the shoulders with remarks to the effect that all was now well. 'That's it, we're home and dry', was the general tenor. 'No need to worry about the next election. It's a foregone conclusion.'

Only Peter Shore, in Lady Falkender's recollection, recognised immediately that Mrs Thatcher would be very hard to beat.[190] In fact Tony Benn realised it too – 'I think we would be foolish to suppose that Mrs Thatcher won't be a formidable leader'[191] – and so did Barbara Castle:

> She is so clearly the best man among them . . . I can't help feeling a thrill, even though I believe her election will make things much more difficult for us. I have been saying for a long time that this country is ready . . . for a woman Prime Minister.[192]

Tony Benn characteristically welcomed Mrs Thatcher's election on the ground that it would give the electorate a clear choice between left-wing socialism and right-wing Toryism.[193] Mrs Castle, by contrast, thought Mrs Thatcher would be good for Labour in the long run, for a rather different reason: she hoped it would feminise politics. 'To me, socialism isn't just militant trade unionism. It is the gentle society, in which every producer remembers he is a consumer too.'[194] This is an interesting anticipation. Mrs Thatcher's competitive view of society could in no way be described as gentle; but she did, in pursuing her crusade against old-style socialism, strongly champion the interests of consumers before producers. In the moment of Mrs Thatcher's victory, Mrs Castle seems almost to be peering beyond Thatcherism to the post-Thatcherite consumerist socialism of Tony Blair's New Labour.

The defeated Heathites were appalled by what their party had done. 'There is no reason in logic, history, philosophy or expediency', Ian Gilmour told his Amersham constituents a few days after the second ballot, 'why the Tory Party should join the Labour Party in moving towards the extremes.'[195] Paul Channon remembers thinking Mrs Thatcher 'a right-wing fanatic who could never win the middle ground'.[196] Forgetting that Heath's only victory – in 1970 – had been gained on a proto-Thatcherite platform, they shared the assumption that the Tories could not win from the right. No one was more dismayed than the younger generation of ambitious, left-inclined, Cambridge-educated Conservatives – Kenneth Clarke, Leon Brittan, Norman Fowler, Peter Temple-Morris – who feared that their mainly northern seats would be jeopardised by Mrs Thatcher's limited southern appeal. 'There was a feeling that this was a pretty strange step to take,' Fowler recalled. 'I suppose that we all felt it was a bit of a throwback . . . It wasn't the modern Conservative Party – it sounded like a different party altogether.'[197] Privately Clarke talked wildly of 'counter-revolution'; publicly he warned that the party under its new leader must do more than voice middle-class grievances if it wanted to be re-elected; it had to show that a prosperous and free society could be run 'with compassion and concern for those who need help'.[198] These self-consciously progressive young Conservatives – who had mainly voted for Geoffrey Howe – feared the worst. Yet at least one old proponent of the Middle Way was cheered by Mrs Thatcher's election. In an otherwise gloomy letter about galloping inflation, Harold Macmillan wrote to a friend that there was 'one delightful feature which has relieved us all':

> The breakthrough of women's lib into the Conservative party from which men have been deposed and a gracious lady has taken the leadership in her stride amid universal acclaim. She is the product of her own strong character and good sense and the pent-up animosity against the regime which in ten years has destroyed the Conservative party.[199]

In fact there was a good deal of uncertainty – even among her supporters – as to what the future might hold. 'When we found ourselves with Margaret as leader', Norman Tebbit recalled, 'there were a lot of people who were frankly incredulous.'[200] Even though he had been involved in her campaign he was not at all sure what he had helped to elect and feared she might be no improvement on Heath. 'There was little point changing the leader if we were going to be stuck with the same policies.'[201] Likewise the *Sun* – still respectfully referring to her as Margaret, not yet Maggie – thought that if she were to move the party 'a little to the right . . . that may be all to the good'; but seemed by no means certain that she would.

No doubt Mrs Thatcher and her colleagues will quickly work out

what Thatcher-type Toryism is really about . . . what Tories really
stand for.

What is important to all of us is that they should once again be
clearly seen to be standing for SOMETHING.[202]

Even the political editor of the *Daily Mail*, Tony Shrimsley – in
due course to become director of communications at Central Office
– did not know what to expect. Mrs Thatcher had 'butchered' her
way to the Tory leadership 'like a Boadicea' (perhaps the first use of
that comparison). But would she turn out to be 'one of England's
great queens' or a Tory equivalent of Barry Goldwater, the right-
wing Republican presidential candidate thrashed by Lyndon Johnson
in 1964? Would she 'succeed brilliantly' or 'crash spectacularly'? No
one could tell, Shrimsley concluded. 'But while she is finding out,
heaven help anyone who stands in her way.'[203]

The best contemporary appreciation of what Mrs Thatcher was
about was found, not surprisingly, in the *Daily Telegraph*. The writer
was clearly very close to her thinking, if not actually a member of her
team. Lady Thatcher herself quotes the editorial in her memoirs; but
it is worth reprinting, since it so precisely expresses her own view of
her hopes and ambitions at the outset of her Long March on
Downing Street.

> What kind of leadership Mrs Thatcher will provide remains to be
> seen . . . But one thing is clear enough at this stage. Mrs Thatcher
> is a bonny fighter. She believes in the ethic of hard work and big
> rewards for success. She has risen from humble origins by effort
> and ability and courage. She owes nothing to inherited wealth or
> privilege. She ought not to suffer, therefore, from that fatal and
> characteristic twentieth-century Tory defect of guilt about wealth.
> All too often this has meant that the Tories have felt themselves to
> be at a moral disadvantage in the defence of capitalism against
> socialism. This is one reason why Britain has travelled so far down
> the collectivist road. What Mrs Thatcher ought to be able to offer
> is the missing *moral* dimension to the Tory attack on socialism.
>
> If she does so her accession to the leadership could mark a sea-
> change in the whole character of the party political debate in this
> country.[204]

It is a remarkable tribute to the consistency of her political purpose
that this editorial could have been reprinted a decade later without
the need to change a word.

11

Leader of the Opposition

MARGARET Thatcher said that it was 'like a dream' to follow in the footsteps of Macmillan, Home and Heath. But none of these predecessors had faced such a daunting prospect on becoming leader. Macmillan and Home had both taken over in government, with all the authority and patronage which the premiership instantly bestows. Ted Heath's inheritance in 1965 was more comparable with Mrs Thatcher's. The first Conservative Leader of the Opposition since Bonar Law to lack the prestige of having already been Prime Minister, he suffered a dispiriting five years up to 1970 while he struggled to impose himself on a party which never learned to love him. Yet at least Heath had won the leadership in a straight fight after the voluntary resignation of Alec Douglas-Home; and his senior colleagues – with the possible exception of Enoch Powell – were solidly behind him. Mrs Thatcher's position was very different. She had seized the leadership as the result of a backbench revolt against the party establishment. Practically the whole of her predecessor's Shadow Cabinet had openly opposed her, and the majority were still unrepentantly identified with Heath's policies. The party was badly split, both personally and ideologically, and she had split it.

Moreover she was seriously inexperienced. Heath had held three Cabinet posts before becoming leader, and had also been Chief Whip. Mrs Thatcher had held just one, and that in a social services department. She had no executive experience of either economic or foreign policy. Today such a lack of form is not unusual – neither Neil Kinnock nor Tony Blair had any government experience before becoming Leader of the Opposition – but in 1975 it was unprecedented. Colleagues who had seen Mrs Thatcher as an industrious but lightweight junior found it hard to adjust to the idea of such a naive and unsophisticated politician in the role of leader.

Even those who had campaigned for her were not sure what they had persuaded the party to elect, and the party in the country did not know her at all. For all these reasons, in addition to the startlingly novel factor of her femininity, she was even more on trial than most new leaders, facing a mixture of scepticism, curiosity and snobbish condescension, shading into latent or outright hostility. Many pundits waited confidently for her to fail. Even her own *Finchley Press* reckoned that she had just eight months, to the party conference in October, to establish herself.[1]

Nevertheless not everything was against her. First, the traditional instinct of the Tory faithful to rally to a new leader was boosted in Mrs Thatcher's case by the party's sense of amazement and self-congratulation at becoming the first major political party in the Western world to elect a woman leader; then the knowledge that the whole party would look foolish if the experiment turned out badly produced an unprecedented upsurge of gallantry and a chivalrous reflex to protect her. Women in Conservative committee rooms who were always said to be most hostile to other women in positions of power found an unexpected pride in suddenly having one of their own in charge, while the crustiest saloon bar chauvinists felt obliged to give the filly a chance. Barbara Castle observed this phenomenon in the House of Commons:

> Margaret's election has stirred up her own side wonderfully; all her backbenchers perform like knights jousting at a tourney for a lady's favours, showing off their paces by making an unholy row at every opportunity over everything the Government does.[2]

More specifically such key elders of the Tory party as Alec Home, Quintin Hailsham and Peter Carrington – all loyal friends of Heath who could easily have made her life impossible had they so wished – determined that the new leader must be supported and set a strong example to that effect. Above all Willie Whitelaw, the principal rival whom she had defeated in the leadership contest, determined to be both a good loser and a loyal deputy. This was by no means easy for him, since he and Mrs Thatcher had little in common, either personally or politically. His wife was said to have advised him to have nothing to do with her, and in all the years of their association they never had a social meal together. Though she immediately named him deputy leader and consulted him about other appointments, Mrs Thatcher was not at first quite sure that she could trust him. Whitelaw felt hurt that she treated him no differently from any other member of the Shadow Cabinet. It took a word from Norman

Tebbit before she began to take him fully into her confidence.[3] Even then she could still be brutal. 'I have never been spoken to that way in my life,' he told friends on one occasion when she tore him off a strip for not knowing his brief;[4] and as late as 1978 Roy Jenkins, seated next to Whitelaw at a dinner, found him complaining gloomily about 'how absolutely ghastly life was with that awful woman' and wondering whether he should resign.[5] Having stood against her and lost, however, Whitelaw felt an almost military sense of duty to subordinate his views to hers. With his deep knowledge of the party he would sometimes warn her what the backbenchers or the constituencies would not wear; but he would not oppose her. Friends who looked to him to represent the tradition of 'One Nation' Conservatism felt that he overdid this self-denial, politically neutering himself instead of boxing his weight. Yet in opposition and later in government, Whitelaw steadfastly refused to lend himself to any appearance of factionalism. His unwavering support over the next thirteen years was indispensable to her survival and her success.

Conversely she was greatly helped by the ungenerous behaviour of Ted Heath. There is always in the Tory party an element of guilt towards a discarded leader. Despite his defeat – perhaps even because of it – Heath still retained immense prestige and his electoral credibility was greatly restored by his personal triumph in the European referendum. Polls consistently showed that the public shared his unwavering belief in the need for a prices and incomes policy to combat inflation, and more than once suggested that the Tories would do better if he were still leader. Mrs Thatcher was fortunate that Heath took his removal from the leadership so badly. She skilfully wrongfooted him at the outset by calling in person at his house in Wilton Street the day after her election so as to be seen to honour her commitment to offer him a place in her Shadow Cabinet, even though he had already announced his intention to return to the backbenches. Like their previous interview when she told him of her decision to stand against him, it was a brief encounter: Heath's faithful PPS, Timothy Kitson, had to detain her in polite conversation for a few minutes before she left so as to prevent the press knowing just how brief.

The two camps subsequently leaked conflicting accounts of the meeting. Heath denied that she had offered him a job; Mrs Thatcher's office insisted that she had but that, anticipating his refusal, she had also invited him to lead the Tory campaign in the European referendum. One of her first biographers, Ernle Money, produced an inventive account – improbable in detail but all too plausible in spirit – of Heath refusing both offers with childish monosyllables, 'Won't' and 'Shan't'.[6] Whatever the truth – and their memoirs do not differ over the substance of what transpired – she was seen to offer an olive branch which he refused. He did it again after the referendum, when she generously praised his contribution in the House of Commons and elicited not a flicker of response; and yet again at the party conference in October when he snubbed an intended reconciliation meeting set up by Willie Whitelaw. For the next four years Heath pointedly failed to render his successor any but the most minimal praise or recognition – to the increasing irritation of party members who were desperate to see the two leaders publicly reconciled and contrasted Heath's prolonged sulk unfavourably with Alec Douglas-Home's gentlemanly self-abnegation in serving under Heath himself. By his graceless performance, Heath threw away a potentially powerful position. Had he only been prepared to offer a degree of subtly qualified support he would have retained an influential voice as an elder statesman and made it impossible for Mrs Thatcher to exclude him from the Government in May 1979. Instead he not only cast himself into a sort of internal exile but made it harder for his former colleagues in the Shadow Cabinet to mount any sort of counter to her leadership. It was his stubborn egotism in 1974 which created Mrs Thatcher's opportunity to seize the helm in the first place; over the next fifteen years Heath's perceived disloyalty did almost as much as Whitelaw's loyalty to make her position impregnable.

She continued to benefit, too, from her novelty. A woman leader was something different in the grey-suited soap opera of British politics. Whatever she did was news, and she was inexhaustibly photogenic. Moreover she played up to her news value, making herself available for interviews and photocalls with a wider range of printed and broadcast media than any previous political leader, with the result that press interest in her lasted far longer than the bubble of exaggerated expectations which briefly surrounded Heath in 1965. Politics apart, there was undisguised admiration for her rise from humble roots and her unflinching seizure of her opportunity. This was the period when the legend of the corner shop suddenly gained currency, with the rapid appearance of three adulatory biographies backed up by picture spreads in all the papers showing the modest building beside the Great North Road, Alfred in his alderman's robes with his homely wife and primly turned-out daughters, the stories of the young Margaret's confident retorts to teachers and awesome determination to overcome all obstacles to her success. It was routinely reported that she had won a scholarship to Oxford and then a First Class degree – or sometimes two. With her wealthy husband, comfortable houses in Kent and Chelsea and two apparently model children, she was the embodiment of Shirley Conran's *Superwoman*, published the previous year. Her curriculum vitae seemed irresistible, with the fantasy of a woman Prime Minister the natural end of the fairy tale.

Above all she was borne up by a growing public mood of disillusion with the left, still in 1975 confined to the margins of the political mainstream but growing all the time and helpfully amplified by a battalion of previously left-leaning columnists in the popular and middle-market press who fell in love – some of them almost literally – with the Tories' combative new leader. While the hard thinking that would overturn an economic orthodoxy was still being done in the relative obscurity of the Institute of Economic Affairs and the Centre for Policy Studies, surfacing in little-noticed pamphlets by backroom policy analysts and anguished lectures by Keith Joseph, the public mood which was gradually forming to support an assault on the ever-leftward assumptions of the previous thirty years was increasingly given voice by a handful of polemical writers who vigorously declared their defection from Labour. Bernard Levin, thrice weekly in *The Times*, lost no opportunity to heap praise on his new heroine. The former editor of the *New Statesman*, Paul Johnson, announced in September 1977 his discovery that Labour was no longer the champion of the oppressed, but had become the party of 'union bureaucrats and bully boys'.[7] The historian Hugh Thomas, who had once edited a famous attack on the establishment, published a similar recantation in the *Daily Mail* in November 1976, while Woodrow Wyatt, the former Labour MP who had so often mocked Mrs Thatcher in the past, now promoted her in his weekly column in the Labour-supporting *Sunday Mirror* as an entirely new sort of Tory leader.

Mrs Thatcher appealed to these life-long anti-Conservatives because, as Wyatt explained, she was not part of the traditional establishment. 'She did not seem much like a Tory, but she had the Tory party to work for her, which was a useful start.'[8] Or as Lord Chalfont, another former Labour minister, put it, she 'struck a chord which was waiting to be struck . . . All those fears of bureaucracy, of too much government, of the erosion of the freedom of the individual, fears of anarchy . . . she just came at a time when all these fears began to coalesce.'[9] Several of these high-profile recantations were published in 1978 under the title *Right Turn*, edited by the Conservative MP, Patrick Cormack, and dedicated to Margaret Thatcher. Perhaps the most startling convert was the former deputy leader of the Labour party, the choleric but popular Lord George-

Brown, who stopped short of going over to the Tories but made no secret of his defection from Labour. The former Education Secretary, Reg Prentice – bloodily deselected by his local Labour party in 1977 – did actually cross the floor to join the Conservatives. All these and others created a sense of movement across the political spectrum which was immensely helpful to Mrs Thatcher's cause.

Yet her position remained insecure for the whole period 1975–9. Though Whitelaw and Carrington made sure there was no overt move against her, a powerful section of the party, including most of Heath's senior colleagues whom she was obliged to retain in the Shadow Cabinet, remained conspicuously uncommitted to her. They believed that she had won the leadership by accident and was likely to prove a short-lived aberration – 'an unfortunate although possibly necessary interlude', as one member of the Tory Reform Group put it, 'which allows the party to get the bile out of its system before – regrettably after another election defeat first – it can settle back into a normal orthodox pattern once more'.[10] They thought she placed far too much faith in Keith Joseph, whose political judgement they derided, and listened too credulously to maverick intellectuals like Alfred Sherman; but they were confident that when it came to the point they had the weight of numbers and experience to control her. They were not greatly worried by her tendency to embrace simplistic panaceas like monetarism since they took it for granted, as experienced politicians, that no one could take such nonsense seriously for long. If she did become Prime Minister, the combination of civil service advice and the realities of office would quickly educate her. All parties, they assured themselves, tend to play to their extremes in opposition, but they return to the centre ground when back in government.

Jim Prior, Ian Gilmour and Norman St John Stevas all confessed after 1979 that they underestimated Mrs Thatcher. 'We did not fully appreciate at first that she was the strong determined leader which she subsequently turned out to be,' Prior admitted.[11] Reviewing Gilmour's book *Inside Right*, which elegantly restated the Tory party's enduring values of moderation, pragmatism and freedom from doctrine, Stevas confidently asserted that Mrs Thatcher would not disagree with a word of it: 'The shift to the right in the party in 1970 under Mr Heath was largely rhetorical and it is the same under his successor . . . today.'[12] As a result they felt no need to organise any sort of factional grouping to restrain her. Publicly and in private, they supported her punctiliously but with a marked lack of enthusiasm. Conducting off-the-record interviews for their study of the 1979 election, David Butler and Dennis Kavanagh noted that whereas Heath's colleagues in similar circumstances between 1966 and 1970 were always anxious to assure them that whatever his shortcomings in opposition he would make an excellent Prime Minister, Mrs Thatcher's shadow ministers made no such claim for her.[13]

She was further handicapped by her inability to shine in the House of Commons. Despite some successes earlier in her career, from her maiden speech to her recent put-down of Denis Healey, Mrs Thatcher was never comfortable in the Commons, particularly in opposition. She could make a good clear speech to a Government brief; but opposition calls for different skills – spontaneity, improv- isation, wit, ridicule and the ability to think quickly on her feet – none of which came naturally to her. Harold Wilson in his prime was the acknowledged master of this style: Mrs Thatcher was more like Ted Heath – dogged, factual, humourless and over-prepared. She briefed herself exhaustively in advance and used mnemonics to remember the points she wanted to make; but she was always inclined to lecture, which the House dislikes. As a junior minister she had benefited from the chivalry of an overwhelmingly male assembly; now that she was leader, chivalry was forgotten and she had to battle to make herself heard above Labour heckling designed to rattle her, becoming shrill and strident as a result. It was said that she could be formidable in the afternoons, but rarely after dinner: 'At night the Commons becomes a more masculine place, and she fades.'[14] She was at her best when she threw away her notes and let her self-belief shine through. But in four years as Leader of the Opposition she had more flops than triumphs in the chamber and never established mastery of it.

More than anything else, however, Leaders of the Opposition are judged from month to month on the opinion polls; and by this all- important measure her record was not impressive. The Tories gained a brief initial boost from her election; but then the two main parties ran roughly neck and neck for eighteen months, neither able to establish a consistent lead. Soon after James Callaghan succeeded Wilson in March 1976 the Government was shaken by a major sterling crisis which forced it to seek emergency credit from the International Monetary Fund. Thereafter, for about a year from October 1976 the Tories chalked up substantial leads of ten, fifteen or even twenty percentage points, while a clutch of by-election losses eliminated Callaghan's tiny majority. Only a deal with the Liberals in March 1977 averted an early election; but from then on the Government began to recover. Callaghan's personal approval rating ran consistently ahead of Mrs Thatcher's, and by the autumn of 1978 Labour had once more drawn ahead. The likelihood is that if Callaghan had seized his moment to go to the country that October he would have won; in which case it is hard to believe that Mrs Thatcher's leadership would have long survived.

In the event Callaghan delayed, the public sector unions conspired to destroy their own Government and a Conservative victory in May 1979 became inevitable. But for most of the previous four years such an outcome was by no means a foregone conclusion. Mrs Thatcher did not lead a triumphant march on Downing Street, armed with a radical blueprint to transform British politics; neither could she simply wait confidently for the prize to drop into her lap. On the contrary, throughout the whole of her period in opposition she was under constant pressure from polls and pundits alike to widen the Tories' appeal by pursuing 'moderate', consensual policies – incomes policy, co-operation with the unions, even proportional representation – in order to unite the party and the country. Yet she still came across as dangerously extreme. Six months before she became Prime Minister those who had warned that she was too suburban, strident, right-wing and inexperienced to win seemed very likely to be vindicated.

Mrs Thatcher was formally elected Leader of the Conservative Party at a meeting of MPs, candidates, peers and party officials on 20 February, her nomination proposed by Lord Carrington and seconded by Lord Hailsham. Before that she had already been rapturously acclaimed by the 1922 Committee and presided rather awkwardly over a meeting of the existing Shadow Cabinet, minus only Heath himself, who had flown to Malaga to lick his wounds. 'I can still remember that first Shadow Cabinet meeting,' one member recalled, 'the long faces and people stumbling into the room . . . There was a desperate feeling that the Conservative party had met a calamitous fate.'[15] Lady Thatcher herself recalled the 'slightly unreal atmosphere since none of those present had yet been formally re-appointed and some would not be'.[16] Owing to the circumstances of her election, however, her room for reshuffling the personnel she had inherited from Heath was very limited; just because they had almost all voted against her, paradoxically, she was bound to keep most of his colleagues in post. In solidarity with the defeated leader, Geoffrey Rippon and Peter Thomas voluntarily stood down; while Robert Carr overplayed his hand by asking for Foreign Affairs or nothing, and so got nothing. But Carr was a herbivore who posed no threat on the backbenches. The same went for Paul Channon and

Nick Scott, two more junior Heath protégés whom she also dropped. In fact the only potentially dangerous heavyweight she sacked was Peter Walker.

Since Walker had been the most outspoken critic of Keith Joseph's Pauline conversion over the past twelve months his removal was no surprise. But it was clumsily done, considering that they had previously got on well as colleagues in the Heath Cabinet: she told him that she needed to bring in younger talent – though Walker at forty-two was one of the youngest members of the Shadow Cabinet. 'There was no personal warmth between us,' she wrote in her memoirs. 'He clearly had to go.'[17] In a press statement Walker called his departure 'the only honest solution and one which I accept and welcome'. Unrepentant, he warned of his 'grave doubts about the extreme monetarist policies currently fashionable within parts of the Conservative party', and hoped that Mrs Thatcher would 'not be persuaded to accept the deceptive temptation of a rigid monetarist policy'.[18] To his mentor Edward Boyle he wrote apprehensively:

> I do rather fear for our party at the moment – the Right have never been in such command in my lifetime. Whilst I will enjoy the new freedom I fear that it will be some time before those of us with more liberal views again have influence.[19]

Walker's apprehension was well-founded; yet in the short term he was the only major casualty. The rest of Heath's senior colleagues were for the moment unassailable. In addition to the deputy leadership, Whitelaw initially took on a roving brief with a special responsibility for devolution before becoming Shadow Home Secretary the following year. Carrington continued as Leader in the Lords. Hailsham took no portfolio, but was effectively shadow Lord Chancellor. Francis Pym retained the Agriculture portfolio and Jim Prior was reappointed to the critical job of shadow Employment Secretary – an important signal that Mrs Thatcher recognised the Tory party's imperative need to be seen to mend its fences with the unions. As chairman of the Conservative Research Department since 1974, Ian Gilmour had been no less contemptuous of monetarism than Walker; but Mrs Thatcher was slightly intimidated by Gilmour, as she often was by very tall men. She regarded him as a serious intellectual, albeit on the wrong wing of the party. She removed him from the Research Department, but compensated by making him first shadow Home Secretary, then shadow Defence Secretary when she needed home affairs for Whitelaw.

Michael Heseltine was too much his own man to be called a

18. The new Conservative Cabinet at the State Opening of Parliament, July 1970.
From the left: Francis Pym, Sir Alec Douglas-Home, Reginald Maudling, Edward Heath,
Iain Macleod, Sir Keith Joseph, Geoffrey Rippon, Margaret Thatcher, Gordon Campbell.

19. Education Secretary and Prime Minister at the Tory Party conference, 1970.

20. Visiting the American School in St John's Wood, London, 1971.

21, 22. The challenger with two of her key supporters,
Keith Joseph (*left*) and Airey Neave.

23. Press conference after defeating Heath on the first ballot.

24, 25, 26. The new leader at home with Denis (*above*) and Mark (*below left*).

27. After her party conference speech, October 1976, with (*from left to right*) Reginald Maudling, Keith Joseph, Willie Whitelaw and Peter Thorneycroft.

28. 'Labour Isn't Working', summer 1978.

29, 30. General Election, spring 1979:
Norfolk (*above*) and Halifax (*below*)

31. Victory celebrations at Conservative Central Office, May 1979, with Peter Thorneycroft, Denis, Carol and Mark

32. The grocer's daughter enters Downing Street, 4 May 1979.

33. 'Where there is discord, may we bring harmony.'

Heathite, but he was another she was bound to keep on, even though – as she wrote in her memoirs – she already distrusted him, both for his undisguised ambition and for his hankering for an interventionist industrial strategy of 'picking winners'.[20] In addition, Airey Neave told David Butler, she was always 'terrified of Michael Heseltine making awful gaffes or commitments every time he got up to speak'.[21] Nevertheless she left him in place shadowing Tony Benn at the Department of Industry, until the famous incident in 1976, when Heseltine picked up the ceremonial mace and brandished it at the Labour front bench, gave her the excuse to move him. Patrick Jenkin likewise retained Energy, Timothy Raison replaced Channon shadowing Environment and Alick Buchanan-Smith kept Scotland. Bound by her promise to keep all her defeated rivals in the leadership contest she even retained John Peyton, initially as shadow Leader of the House, later at Agriculture, though she ultimately dumped him in May 1979. Finally Norman St John Stevas, very much on the left of the party despite his attempt to reinvent himself as a devoted Thatcherite, retained Education and responsibility for the arts.

The biggest surprise was the resurrection of Reggie Maudling to be shadow Foreign Secretary. This was a clear sign of weakness on Mrs Thatcher's part, an admission that her own inexperience in foreign affairs left her needing another heavyweight of the previous generation to compensate for the loss of Heath and Carr. As she explained on radio, Heath and Home had taken care of foreign affairs for so long that no one else in the next generation had much experience in that area.[22] Though widely praised as an imaginative and generous appointment it was a mistake from every point of view. As a former Chancellor of the Exchequer, Maudling was an unrepentant Keynesian and the most authoritative advocate of incomes policy, while his relaxed approach to international affairs was equally out of sympathy with Mrs Thatcher's hawkish stance towards the Soviet Union. If his appointment was intended to signal a more sceptical approach to Europe – Maudling had never shown much enthusiasm for the Community – it was an impression she quickly had to correct before the referendum campaign got under way. Within a year she had appointed Douglas Hurd as an additional front bench spokesman to sound a more positive note towards Europe. Finally Maudling was lazy and past his political prime; he had never liked Mrs Thatcher and made scant pretence of taking her seriously as leader. He was soon heard complaining to friends that 'the woman is impossible'.[23] Jim Prior suggests that he finally sealed his fate by an incautious gibe in November 1976 when Mrs

Thatcher told the Shadow Cabinet that she had not been favourably impressed by the newly-elected US President, Jimmy Carter, but 'sometimes the job could make the man'.

> 'Yes', commented Reggie Maudling. 'I remember Winston's remark – if you feed a grub on royal jelly it will grow into a Queen bee.' Some took it badly, some were hard put to contain their mirth. Margaret was po-faced. I did not fancy Reggie's chances in the next reshuffle.[24]

Sure enough, she sacked him the same month. 'When I told him that he had to go', she wrote, 'he summoned up enough energy to be quite rude.'[25] Maudling's version was that she told him, 'You're getting in my way.'[26] He left the front bench a sick and disappointed man and died in 1979.

The key job, of course, was Shadow Chancellor. The obvious choice would have been Keith Joseph; but Willie Whitelaw persuaded her that Joseph would be a liability in such an exposed role. She chose to retain him as her private economic guru with 'overall responsibility for policy and research', unencumbered by a departmental brief. 'You always need a first-class mind to co-ordinate the thinking out of new policies,' she explained, comparing Joseph's role with Rab Butler's after 1945.[27] Probably her preferred alternative would have been John Biffen, whom she admired as an early champion of free-market solutions when she and Joseph were still compromised by corporatism. But Biffen – like his mentor, Enoch Powell, an ardent opponent of the EEC – declined to join the front bench until after the referendum. He then accepted the Energy portfolio and later replaced Heseltine shadowing Industry until his health gave way. Even then it was still widely believed that Mrs Thatcher intended him for the Treasury when she formed a government.[28] In the meantime she turned to Geoffrey Howe, an appointment she ungenerously describes in her memoirs as 'a calculated gamble'.[29] In fact Howe was an excellent choice – like herself a diligent convert to monetarism who worked hard over the next four years to master the theoretical groundwork for a major shift of policy, with a mild, indeed positively soporific manner which made it impossible for anyone to label him a dangerous fanatic. Mrs Thatcher found his quiet reasonableness exasperating. Even before 1979 she had started to bully him mercilessly in front of his colleagues; and she shocked a senior Treasury mandarin by asking him at a private dinner if she should replace him.[30] But Howe had a steely determination which served her well, both in opposition and later in government. Neither Joseph nor Biffen would have held so firm through the storms of 1980–1.

She promoted only five new faces to her first Shadow Cabinet. Four of them were up and coming younger figures – Norman Fowler, Nicholas Edwards, George Younger and the only other woman, Sally Oppenheim, who got the classic woman's portfolio, consumer affairs, shadowing Shirley Williams. The first three (but not Mrs Oppenheim) went on to become stalwarts of her Cabinets in the 1980s; yet not one of them could have been called a Thatcherite. In fact the only outright supporter she promoted was the fifth newcomer, the Pygmalion who had masterminded her election, Airey Neave, who was rewarded with the only front bench job he wanted, Northern Ireland. He combined this with acting as Mrs Thatcher's chief of staff, nominally running her private office – though in practice he had little time for this – and advising her on the security services and on appointments and sensitive political matters generally. Despite his background, Neave was no right-winger either, but a traditional One Nation Conservative who spent most of the next four years striving to counter the influence of her more radical advisers.[31] He was a shrewd operator, however, whose knowledge of the political underworld was invaluable to a leader as naive in worldly matters as Margaret Thatcher. She deferred to him with a mixture of gratitude and genuine respect for his heroic war record, while leaving him rather too free a hand to pursue a Unionist agenda in Ulster. His influence, though hard to pin down, was pervasive; and his murder in 1979 was a shocking blow to her.

Though the *Sun* typically described the reshuffle as 'Maggie's Night of the Long Hatpin',[32] and there was general praise for the recall of Maudling, few commentators found much else to commend in her appointments. The *Daily Express* regretted the loss of Walker, Carr, Rippon and the 'promising' Channon and Scott,[33] while *The Times* thought the new team weaker than the old. 'If she were in football management she would expect to receive a substantial transfer fee for making that swap.'[34] But if the left was upset by the dropping of Carr and Walker, the right was equally disappointed by her failure to promote more – indeed any – right-wingers. In truth there were few of ministerial calibre to promote. The same embarrassing dearth plagued her throughout her years in Downing Street; the brightest candidates for promotion were invariably on the centre-left. Of possible right-of-centre candidates, Edward du Cann preferred to continue as chairman of the 1922 Committee (where he was certainly more useful to Mrs Thatcher); while Nicholas Ridley – with Biffen the ablest of the old Powellites – she considered too undiplomatic for a front bench role, stimulating though she found his views in private. Even in 1979 she dashed Ridley's hopes of an economic job by sending him incongruously to the Foreign Office, and he did not reach the Cabinet until 1983. There was no room initially for John Nott, Teddy Taylor or any of the other backbench critics of the Heath era, though both were promoted later. Nor, despite press speculation, did she seriously consider offering a place to Enoch Powell. As she had several times stated during the leadership election, he had put himself beyond the pale by advising the electorate to vote Labour in 1974. Powell made no complaint. 'In the first place', he declared, 'I am not a member of the Conservative party and, secondly, until the Conservative party has worked its passage back a very long way it will not be rejoining me.'[35] He continued to snipe sarcastically for the next four years. It was a long time before Powell could bring himself to acknowledge Mrs Thatcher's conversion to Powellism.

So the Shadow Cabinet remained overwhelmingly Heathite. 'You will not see what I really want to do', she is reported to have told a friend, 'until the reshuffle before the General Election. But you will have some genuine indication when I change the first lot around in just about a year.'[36] In fact she did no such thing, even when urged by the 1922 Executive that the front bench needed shaking up. Outside the Shadow Cabinet she gave their first step on the ladder to a number of stars of the next decade like Nigel Lawson, Cecil Parkinson and Leon Brittan (though not Norman Tebbit). But these were more than balanced by the likes of Ken Clarke, Douglas Hurd, Malcolm Rifkind and Lynda Chalker from the left of the party. Over the whole period in opposition she made only minor changes at the top level, most of which were forced on her. She replaced Maudling in 1976 with another Heath retread not known for his interest in foreign affairs, John Davies (prompting Maudling to reflect bitterly that 'there comes a time in every man's life when he must make way for an older man').[37] When Davies in turn retired through ill health in 1978 she replaced him with Francis Pym. She took the chance to move Heseltine from Industry to Environment to make way for Biffen (on the understanding that he would not have to take Environment in government), and she found room for Nott, Taylor and Tom King. The promotion of Taylor to shadow Scottish Secretary when Alick Buchanan-Smith resigned over her withdrawal of support for devolution was a significant tilt to the right. But in November 1978, when Stevas switched to shadow Leader of the House, she unaccountably gave Education to the very liberal Mark Carlisle, who duly took the job in government five months later (just as she herself had done in 1970). The Shadow Cabinet with which she fought the General Election was just as dominated by those she subsequently dubbed 'wets' as the one she had appointed in 1975.

Reassuring as this was to the old Heathites, Mrs Thatcher quickly learned that she could treat the Shadow Cabinet as a largely honorary body. It did not really matter who was in it. In fact, several of her most critical colleagues – including both Pym and Prior – thought that she allowed a good deal more discussion in Shadow Cabinet than Heath had ever done, partly because she was less personally dominant, but also because she enjoyed an argument. In a radio interview in January 1976 she made all the right noises about collective responsibility:

> You thrash things out in private and you agree publicly to defend the collective decision . . . If you don't . . . there's no reason for having Cabinet Government. You might just as well have a Prime Minister saying 'This is what we're going to do'.[38]

By 1979, however, when she had gained in confidence and Downing Street was beckoning, she had changed her tune. 'There are two ways of making a Cabinet,' she now told Kenneth Harris in a much-quoted interview in the *Observer* three months before the election.

> One way is to have in it people who represent all the different viewpoints within the party . . . The other way is to have in it only people who want to go in the direction in which every instinct tells me we have to go . . . As Prime Minister I couldn't waste time having any internal arguments . . . It must be a 'conviction' Cabinet.[39]

This was brave talk. The truth was that she could not afford to have internal arguments on the major issues of economic management because she was liable to lose them. While the party was in opposition this did not matter. It was more important to maintain the appearance of unity, so she did not press differences on monetarism or trade union reform to a conclusion but let the Priors and Gilmours have their say, and to a great extent their way. She compensated by stamping her authority on less contentious issues. It was in these years that she developed the technique of chairing from the front: not inviting contributions and summing up at the end, in the conventional manner, but stating her own view firmly at the beginning so that argument became a challenge to her leadership. Even in Heath's Cabinet she had tended to talk too much: now that she was leader there was no one to stop her. 'Individually or with a few people', Willie Whitelaw told Patricia Murray, she would 'listen very profoundly'. But 'in a group, where she's determined to get her way, she's inclined not to listen, but to keep hammering her point home'.[40] 'Some of Margaret's faults', one exasperated colleague complained, 'were that of a bloody woman rabbiting on. She had mind-jumps from one issue to another and a weakness for sweeping assertions.'[41] At first, one of the Central Office staff who took the minutes recalled, she was 'shrill, assertive and a bit frenetic'.[42] Airey Neave conceded this, but thought that she improved. 'At first', he told David Butler in 1978, 'she had been pitchforked into a job she did not fully understand. She was not certain of herself.'

> Now it was very different. She still was perhaps a bit too talkative and interrupted people perhaps a bit too much, but that had diminished. She was pretty democratic in her use of the Shadow Cabinet as a basic source of advice, but strategic decisions were done . . . by an elite.[43]

'The entertainment value of Shadow Cabinet meetings was, to put it mildly, limited,' John Peyton recalled, 'nor was it a body in which friendships could be said to flourish.'[44] Entertainment and friendship, however, were not what Mrs Thatcher was about. Conservatives in opposition tend to divide their energies between some gentle politics and more lucrative employment in the City, refreshing their incomes while awaiting the call back into government. As a result she was able to dominate her less strenuous colleagues by sheer energy, determination and aggression. 'Most of her shadows were rather frightened of her', Neave considered, 'because of her style of argument.'[45] 'I was rather frightened by her immense competence and knowledge,' Whitelaw admitted. 'She could easily kill me in a day with the amount she's able to do.'[46] She also drew confidence from reminding herself that she had, after all, become leader by routing all her challengers. Once, when she was working in her room at the House of Commons, Jim Prior put his head round the door to ask about something. 'Nineteen votes!' she crowed scornfully when he had gone. 'He only got nineteen votes.'[47] The Shadow Cabinet was a formality she had to live with. But so long as she still had the backbenchers behind her she had the democratic legitimacy to be able to ignore it.

The place where she could impose her will was Central Office. The Conservative party organisation is the personal instrument of the leader, who has unfettered freedom to appoint the chairman and other officers. Heath had appointed his most trusted colleagues to the chairmanship – Tony Barber, Lord Carrington, Willie Whitelaw. Mrs Thatcher had no one of this sort to call upon. She wanted a chairman, she frankly admitted, who would not see the job as a 'stepping stone' to higher things.[48] So she had the inspiration of reaching back a generation to Lord Thorneycroft. Like Hailsham, Peter Thorneycroft was one of those senior Conservatives whom she had first met when they came to speak for her at Oxford. He claimed to have been 'enormously impressed' with her at that time, and she had kept in touch.[49] He had held a succession of Cabinet jobs under Churchill, Eden, Macmillan and Home, but his principal claim to fame was his resignation from the Treasury in 1957 – egged on by his junior ministers Enoch Powell and Nigel Birch – rather than go along with Macmillan's commitment to inflationary spending. In retrospect, this made him an early hero of monetarism. Recalling Thorneycroft to the colours thus combined a reassuring continuity with the pre-Heath Tory past with a symbolic statement of monetarist intent, the next best thing to embracing Powell himself. Thorneycroft was surprised, but was persuaded by Whitelaw – his cousin – to take the job. In practice he was ill for extended periods in 1975–9, and when in harness he turned out – like Neave – to be more concerned to maintain party unity than to risk division by backing controversial policies. Nevertheless he was another reassuring mentor for an inexperienced leader: another of Mrs Thatcher's father figures.

Alongside Thorneycroft she also resurrected Angus Maude, another old associate of Powell who had been passed over by successive Tory leaders. Maude became one of two deputy chairmen, paired with another robust right-winger, William Clark; he also replaced Gilmour as chairman of the Research Department. Below these an entirely new team of vice-chairmen included the 38-year-old John Moore (in charge of youth) and Lady Young (in charge of women, replacing Heath's formidable confidante, Sara Morrison). Janet Young was an Oxford contemporary who has some claim to be Mrs Thatcher's only woman friend in politics. 'She can talk straight to Margaret, who will take it from her,' one Central Office insider told Butler and Kavanagh in 1978. 'She is very near to being one of the big beasts of the jungle.'[50] It was she who deputised when Thorneycroft was ill. She also accompanied Mrs Thatcher on her election tours in April–May 1979, and in due course became the only other woman to sit, briefly, in the Cabinet before she fell from favour.

The decisive action which really showed Mrs Thatcher's hand, however, was the sacking, at the beginning of March, of Michael Wolff – Heath's former speech-writer, adviser and general factotum, whom he had installed in Central Office as Director-General the previous year. Though he had been appointed only ten months earlier, the change of leader left him badly exposed. Mrs Thatcher was perfectly entitled to remove him. Nevertheless his abrupt dismissal was the one consequence of her election which really affronted Heath's friends. Prior, Carrington, Whitelaw, Gilmour, even Geoffrey Howe, were moved to protest; Prior expressed his outrage by refusing to vote on the Finance Bill. *The Times* bluntly called Wolff's dismissal 'the act of a damn fool' – the political equivalent of the US cavalry shooting John Wayne. Tactfully blaming Thorneycroft rather than Mrs Thatcher herself for jeopardising 'the astonishing degree of unity' achieved since her election, Rees-Mogg complained that while she had appointed 'a well-balanced though not notably talented Shadow Cabinet', Thorneycroft had done her 'the great disservice of forming a quite unbalanced and even less talented Central Office team. This is not the broad, warm-hearted Conservatism that might inspire the country.'[51] Though an enthusiastic convert to monetarism, Rees-Mogg had not yet grasped the nature of Mrs Thatcher's new Conservatism.

The new leader's purge stopped short, however, of replacing the bright young director of the Research Department, Chris Patten. It has been suggested that the party could not afford the financial compensation that would have been involved in sacking both Wolff and Patten. But Mrs Thatcher always liked Patten; she recognised his ability and thought him a good speech-writer, even though she could never understand how someone so naturally combative could be so liberal. It actually suited the ambivalence of her stance in these years to leave him in place – under Maude as chairman – with Adam Ridley his equally Heathite deputy, to preserve the moderate façade of official policy-making in a state of competitive tension with the more radical unofficial work being promoted by Joseph and Sherman. Later she did strip Patten of the job of Shadow Cabinet secretary when she felt that he was putting too much of his own gloss on the minutes; and on coming into office she effectively abolished the Research Department by merging it into Central Office.

Mrs Thatcher further affronted the old guard by appointing Alistair McAlpine, a 32-year-old scion of the building family, to be party treasurer. A freewheeling dilettante of enormous charm, McAlpine had no previous connection with the Tory party; but he was an irresistible fund-raiser who had just done a good job as treasurer of the 'Yes' campaign in the European referendum. The party elders were horrified: the retiring joint treasurers actually tried to withdraw their resignations. But McAlpine turned out to be one of Mrs Thatcher's best appointments. He stayed in the job for fifteen years, becoming one of her most devoted courtiers, and was with her in Downing Street at the very end. He was a political amateur in the best sense, without conventional ambition and rich enough to be entirely independent, who brought a dash of colour – but unlike some later treasurers, no scandal – to her entourage.

Once she had made her dispositions, Mrs Thatcher showed very little further interest in Central Office. She was never concerned with party organisation for its own sake so long as it delivered the results to get her elected. Even in 1983 Cecil Parkinson was astonished at her ignorance of how the party worked: this was one area in which she was content to delegate.[52] Though she writes in her memoirs that Thorneycroft gradually replaced Heath's appointees with staff more sympathetic to the new regime, she was under no illusion that the party establishment had any love for her. As Leader of the Opposition she placed her trust instead in a small praetorian guard of personal loyalists. At the highest level her position was buttressed by an inner core of five key figures: Whitelaw, the loyal deputy; Joseph, her personal philosopher; Thorneycroft, the party chairman; Neave, her chief of staff; and Humphrey Atkins, the Chief Whip whom she inherited from Heath but who seemed to many of Heath's friends to have switched his allegiance even before the first ballot. Between them these five guided her steps, restrained or encouraged her when necessary and advised her on all aspects of party management up to 1979. More often than not the combination of Neave, Thorneycroft and Whitelaw acted to reinforce her natural caution.

The second level of protection was her private office, nominally headed by Neave but in practice run by Richard Ryder, recruited from the *Daily Telegraph* on the recommendation of its editor Bill Deedes, with somewhat mysterious help from David Wolfson from the mail order firm Great Universal Stores, who was brought in originally to handle her vastly expanded correspondence. What exactly Mrs Thatcher saw in Wolfson was a mystery to others in her team, but he evidently filled some need since his role steadily expanded to the point where he too was often said to run her office. At one point she thought of putting him in charge of Central Office

– Wolfson in place of Wolff – but instead she made him Shadow Cabinet secretary in place of Patten; after 1979 he graduated to an even more shadowy role in Downing Street which he retained until 1985. To keep her in touch with her backbenches she had two new Parliamentary Private Secretaries, Adam Butler (son of 'Rab') and John Stanley (who replaced Fergus Montgomery in 1976). Both were rewarded with middle-ranking office in 1979. She also had a succession of keen young men, including at different times Michael Dobbs and Michael Portillo, seconded from the Research Department to help with speeches and brief her for Prime Minister's Questions.

Finally, she had a devoted team of secretaries headed by the 'wonderfully bossy' Alison Ward and the equally formidable Caroline Stephens.[53] The former, her constituency secretary since 1974, is described by Carol Thatcher as 'a miracle secretary . . . who could do twenty-one jobs at once, including organising Flood Street, chauffeuring her boss to the hairdresser's and looking after constituency matters'.[54] She became so much part of the Thatcher family that Denis called her his 'other daughter'.[55] The latter, inherited from Heath, was memorably summed up by the speech-writing playwright Ronald Millar as 'an attractive masterful girl who tears about all over London on a bicycle (if I were a bus I'd be terrified of her) . . . One doesn't argue with girls like that.'[56] Caroline Stephens subsequently married Richard Ryder, while Alison Ward married John Wakeham after the death of his first wife in the IRA's Brighton bombing. Among their other functions these formidable young women took care of the feminine side of Mrs Thatcher's life – not always without hiccup. When the Spanish dictator General Franco died in 1975, Carol records that the House of Commons corridor 'resounded with Alison Ward's anguished cry: "Oh, shit! I've sent your mother's funeral gear to Sketchley's." '[57] (This was unwise, since the General had been at the point of death for weeks.)

It was not only the feminine side which sometimes went awry. For someone who prided herself on managing her life so rigorously, Mrs Thatcher was surprisingly unmethodical. Her private office in these years, before she had the civil service to impose a pattern on her days, was thoroughly chaotic. She was too highly-strung and insecure, too anxious to retain control of every detail, to be able to delegate efficiently: colleagues found it exasperatingly difficult to find a time to see her, let alone get a decision out of her. Mrs Thatcher had the benefit of much more spacious accommodation than any of her predecessors. From 1976 the Leader of the Opposition was given use of the former Sergeant-at-Arms' quarters in the House of

Commons, comprising several offices, a conference room, space for researchers, a kitchen and bathroom – a huge improvement on the cramped and dingy space occupied by Harold Wilson and Ted Heath. But there are no rules for being Leader of the Opposition. Each incumbent, with inevitably inexperienced support, has to work out a *modus operandi* without ground rules, under tremendous pressure and conflicting demands, always having to react to events, never able to shape them. For all her Superwoman image and devoted staff, Mrs Thatcher's use of her time in opposition was astonishingly disorganised.

Beyond her private office, the next ring of her support network involved a group of fiercely protective backbenchers nicknamed by the press 'the Gang of Four'. The name, derived from the clique of hardline Chinese Communists associated with Mao Zedong's widow, was originally applied by Julia Langdon in *Labour Weekly* to the quartet of Mrs Thatcher herself, Airey Neave, George Gardiner and Norman Tebbit. But after February 1975 it became transferred to a different group composed initially of Tebbit, Gardiner, Nigel Lawson and Geoffrey Pattie, later expanded to include Nicholas Ridley and Peter Rees. This group took on themselves three interrelated functions. They helped to brief Mrs Thatcher for Prime Minister's Questions, using the technique developed by Brian Walden on television for anticipating all possible answers and openings for supplementary questions. They put down questions for the Prime Minister which would give her the opportunity to intervene with a well-rehearsed barb. They also took the lead in a concerted Tory effort to harry and heckle the Government out of its stride. Tebbit and Ridley, in their different styles, were particularly good at getting under the skin of Labour ministers with this sort of guerrilla warfare, which raised the morale of Tory backbenchers and compensated for the feebleness of much of the front bench opposition.

It was the backbenchers, not her front bench colleagues, who had made Mrs Thatcher leader; and for the first ten years of her leadership at least she never forgot it. She was determined not to repeat Heath's mistake. Ironically in view of her ultimate fate, she welcomed the new rules requiring her to be re-elected leader every year, believing that the regular renewal of her mandate made her position stronger.[58] Her official channel for communicating with her backbenchers was the 1922 Committee, via its chairman Edward du Cann who had guaranteed access to her. In these early years Du Cann found her very approachable and anxious to listen. 'She went to endless lengths to keep in touch with opinion in the Conservative party and outside,' he wrote. 'Margaret at first was all reasonableness and consideration.'[59] Like Whitelaw, however, he found that she would listen best when he saw her alone. When he took other members of the 1922 Executive with him she was inclined to lecture them.

Secondly, she spent more time in these years than at any earlier or later period of her career in and around the House of Commons, simply listening to her backbenchers' anxieties.[60] She knew where her power base lay and took time and trouble to cultivate it. She made a point of knowing all her backbenchers individually, knew their families, remembered their children's names, their illnesses, even their birthdays; she was always immensely solicitous when anyone was in any sort of trouble. This human interest was such a contrast to Heath or indeed any previous male leader that it won her a significant cushion of personal gratitude, independent of her political performance. Skilfully she used her femininity – a woman's greater capacity to express sympathy – to make it almost bad manners to criticise her. Once she was Prime Minister, of course, she had less time for this sort of social lubrication, and as she became grander and more dominant she inexorably became detached from her supporters, with ultimately fatal results.

There was great anticipation of her first duels with Wilson. 'Nothing like a bit of sex challenge to bring the best out in a man,' Barbara Castle wrote in her diary.[61] In fact their first encounter was not at Prime Minister's Questions but the Wednesday immediately following her election, when Wilson made an uncontentious statement on the Civil List. Nevertheless, Mrs Castle noted, 'Harold was on the top of his form, congratulating Margaret impishly and obviously ready to take on all comers from either side. No sign of him being constrained . . . by a woman Leader of the Opposition.'[62] Mrs Thatcher, 'naturally rather tense', thanked Wilson for his courtesies, paid fulsome tribute to the Royal Family ('our greatest asset') and humbly assured the House that she knew she must not speak too often.[63] The next day Wilson was absent on a visit to the Soviet Union; so her first opportunity did not come until the following Tuesday, when she chose not to intervene at Questions. She waited until Wilson made a statement about his Moscow trip, then made three prepared points. She welcomed increased dialogue with the Soviets 'provided it never lulls this House into a sense of false security'; asked about greater freedom of information in Russia; and wanted more detail about the trade deal Wilson had signed, which she characteristically suspected gave more benefit to Russia than to Britain. The story has been repeated from biography to biography that she also made a tart riposte when Wilson tried to patronise her. 'Some of us are rather old hands at these matters,' he told her. 'What the Prime Minister means', she is supposed to have replied, 'is that he has been around for a long time – and he looks it.'[64] *Hansard* records Wilson's boast but not her reply.[65] She actually made this joke four weeks later in a speech to the Conservative Central Council at Harrogate. She did not say it to Wilson's face.[66]

In fact she continued to be very wary of mixing it with Wilson. On 18 February she asked a question about the suspension of collective Cabinet responsibility for the duration of the EC referendum, which Wilson evaded. On 25 February she left Gardiner, Tebbit, Lawson and Norman Lamont to make the running. Two days later she joined in with a question about the Government's Industry Bill, which Wilson dodged with flattery. But then on 3 March came an opening she signally failed to exploit. First Wilson took the opportunity to tease her about monetarism, picking up on a characteristic effusion by Neil Kinnock mocking the 'economic subliterates on the Opposition benches'.[67] Mrs Thatcher stayed in her seat. Then Douglas Hurd and others began baiting Wilson about a speech by Reg Prentice (the embattled Education Secretary) about the trade unions' failure to honour their side of the so-called 'Social Contract' with the Government. 'Harold was getting away with it', Barbara Castle recorded, 'not by wit but by sheer verbosity.'

> Everybody kept glancing at Margaret to see when she would take him on. She sat with bowed head and detached primness while the row went on; hair immaculately groomed, smart dress crowned by a string of pearls. At last she rose to enormous cheers from her own side to deliver an adequate but hardly memorable intervention with studied charm. Roy [Jenkins], sitting next to me, groaned and I said, 'She's not quite real, is she?'[68]

Moving out from Westminster to the country at large, Mrs Thatcher had next to sell herself to the party in the constituencies. She began well, with a tumultuous visit to Scotland ten days after her election. She was mobbed by a crowd of 3,000 in a shopping centre in Edinburgh and had to abandon a planned walkabout on police advice. That evening she spoke at a packed rally in Glasgow with overflow meetings in two additional halls near by. Yet somehow she never created the same excitement again. A similar walkabout in Cardiff drew only minimal crowds. John Moore, who accompanied her on a number of constituency visits, remembers the first two years as 'an uphill struggle', with a lot of 'ghastly trips' north of Watford, where the party was still demoralised and doubtful; there was no supportive network, poor response to her efforts to arouse enthusiasm, and little belief that she would be leader very long.[69]

In the first few weeks and months she addressed every sort of sectional and regional conference within the Tory party: Scottish Conservatives, Welsh Conservatives, Conservative women, Conservative trade unionists, the Federation of Conservative Students and the Conservative Central Council. She gave them all ringing patriotic statements of her determination to halt Britain's decline by reawakening the virtues of freedom, enterprise, individual opportunity and self-reliance. On 28 February she told party workers in Dorset that she hoped to 'make some dreams come true'; she warned that politicians should not try to please everyone, but that she would try to 'do justice to everyone' – a rather different matter.[70] She urged the Conservative students to join her in the counter-attack – 'to fight back and go on fighting for the right to a worthwhile life in a great country'.

> Because I shall never stop fighting. I mean this country to survive, to prosper and to be free . . . I haven't fought the destructive forces of Socialism for more than twenty years in order to stop now, when the critical phase of the struggle is upon us.[71]

Speaking to the Conservative Central Council in Harrogate on 15 March – her first major public speech as leader – she nailed her colours to what she described as the specifically British virtues of 'self-reliance and personal independence', virtues which ironically were under attack 'in the very country where they were previously so strongly nourished', implicitly rejecting snobbish criticism of her supposedly narrow appeal.

> Self-reliance has been sneered at as if it were an absurd suburban pretension. Thrift has been denigrated as if it were greed. The desire of parents to choose . . . the best possible education for their children has been scorned . . .
>
> Do not believe, however, in spite of all this, that the people of this country have abandoned their faith in the qualities and characteristics that made them a great people. All that has happened is that we have temporarily lost confidence in our own strength. We have lost sight of the banners. The trumpets have given an uncertain sound.

It is our duty, our purpose, to raise those banners high, so that all can see them; to sound the trumpets clearly and boldly, so that all can hear them. Then we shall not have to convert people to our principles. They will simply rally to those that are truly their own.[72]

For all her rousing rhetoric, however, she was careful to present her policies as simple common sense: moderation contrasted with Labour's extremism. Wealth must be created before it could be distributed; the country could not consume more than it produced; taxes should be cut to increase incentives. These were the familiar axioms of Tory leaders, not the blueprint for a counter-revolution. As a result she was politely rather than rapturously received. One delighted delegate at her first Conservative trade unionists' conference gushed that having a woman leader was 'like having the Queen on your side'.[73] But after a few months the content of what she had to offer was beginning to look disappointingly thin. *The Times* complained that 'the hungry sheep look up and are not fed'.[74] In June she took a risk by breaking the convention that the major party leaders did not campaign in by-elections: she made two visits to West Woolwich and was rewarded when Peter Bottomley overturned a Labour majority of 3,500. Victory at Woolwich stilled some of the voices that were already beginning to whisper that the party had made a dreadful mistake. Her ecstatic reaction – she was visiting Bonn when the result came through – showed how badly she had needed some good news. Thereafter she made a practice of visiting winnable by-elections – Walsall, Workington, Stechford, Ashfield, Ilford North – which over the next two years gradually eroded Labour's majority. Yet such victories stubbornly failed to create a bandwagon. Alistair McAlpine recalls the whole period 1975–9 as a 'long march' through a hostile wilderness, the leader sustained by her own faith and just a handful of true believers.[75]

Mrs Thatcher faced a peculiarly awkward baptism just weeks after her election in the form of the imminent referendum on Britain's continued membership of the Common Market. Suspected of being a good deal less keen on Europe than her predecessor, she nevertheless had no choice but to campaign for a vote to confirm the one unquestioned achievement of Heath's Government – which would also help to get Wilson off the hook on which the Labour party had been impaled for the past four years. It was a no-win situation for a new leader anxious to set her own agenda. Her difficulty was somewhat relieved by Heath declining her invitation to lead the Conservative campaign, preferring to conduct his own campaign under the umbrella of the all-party organisation, Britain in Europe, chaired by Roy Jenkins. Then Wilson elected to take a back seat, placing the Government's authority officially behind the 'Yes' campaign while playing little active part himself, which lent a sort of symmetry to Mrs Thatcher doing the same. Nevertheless her low profile drew a good deal of criticism.

In her memoirs Lady Thatcher blames herself for going along too tamely with the establishment consensus in favour of continued membership, ducking the hard questions about Britain's constitutional integrity and national identity which would come back to haunt her a decade and a half later.[76] At the time, however, she was under pressure to dispel the persistent impression that she was privately cool about Europe. She did so emphatically on 8 April in the Commons debate approving the referendum with a characteristically practical but wholly positive case for staying in the Community. 'Mrs Thatcher stills anti-Europe clamour,' *The Times* reported.[77] She based her case on four arguments: security; guaranteed food supplies; access to the expanded European market; and the prospect of a wider world role. 'The Community opens windows on the world for us which since the war have been closing.' She looked forward to Britain paying a lower budget contribution, and benefiting from reform of the Common Agricultural Policy, regional grants and increased inward investment. It would be 'traumatic' to come out now. There was 'not a genuine alternative', and Britain could not in honour abrogate a treaty signed only three years earlier. With hindsight the most significant passage was her definition of 'security':

> I think that security is a matter not only of defence, but of working together in peacetime on economic issues which concern us and of working closely together on trade, work and other social matters which affect all our peoples.[78]

Douglas Hurd, who became her front bench spokesman on European affairs a few months later, cites this speech to refute Lady Thatcher's claim that she never saw the EC as anything more than a free trade area.[79] On the contrary, this passage demonstrates that in 1975 she anticipated without alarm those areas of co-operation and harmonisation which she furiously denounced in the 1990s when they were given imminent reality in the form of the 'social chapter'.

Her press officer, Derek Howe, tried to explain Mrs Thatcher's invisibility during the referendum by claiming that she had originally expected the poll to be two weeks later than the actual date of 5 June, and had booked a much-needed holiday in what turned out to be the middle of the campaign.[80] But never in her life did Margaret Thatcher let a holiday come before politics. The truth is that, as Humphrey Atkins told David Butler, 'she just thought she shouldn't be seen in any way to steal Ted Heath's thunder'.[81] 'So far from being jealous', Geoffrey Howe recalled, 'she seemed almost glad to be playing a secondary role in a cause that was not very close to her heart.'[82] She felt a genuine modesty in the face of Heath's lifelong commitment to Europe. Opening the Tory campaign at the St Ermin's Hotel on 16 April, with Heath beside her in the chair, she paid tribute to his achievement in taking Britain into the Community, and went on: 'It is naturally with some temerity that the pupil speaks before the master, because you know more about it than the rest of us.'[83] It was better to let the fallen leader have his triumph, and then claim the credit as far as possible for the party as a whole.

In fact she did her bit. She did not proselytise energetically, but she made a couple of standard pro-European speeches, gave two television interviews and a press conference at which 'she tried to make plain how fully she supported the campaign',[84] and contributed an article to the *Daily Telegraph*. She paid a brief visit to the European Assembly – where she listened to a debate for all of seventeen minutes – and was filmed in front of Churchill's statue in Parliament Square organising a photocall of ladies wearing woolly jumpers representing the flags of the nine EC countries, gushing about 'Winston's vision' of Europe coming together.[85] Behind the scenes she chivvied pro-European Tory MPs to get out and campaign; and when Edward du Cann made the extraordinary suggestion that half of Tory MPs were privately against membership she firmly slapped him down.[86] Analysis for the Nuffield study of the campaign showed that she featured in fewer than half as many television news reports as Jenkins, Heath or even Wilson, who stirred himself rather more towards the end when it became clear which side was going to win.[87] But all in all she did just enough. She was able to hail the decisive 'yes' vote as a 'really thrilling' vindication of the Tory party's long-standing vision, compared with Labour's record of unprincipled somersaults, while feeling privately relieved that the divisive issue was shelved for the foreseeable future.[88] Right up to 1979 she continued to take a conventionally positive line on Europe, repeatedly berating the Government for failing to make the most of Britain's membership by being too negative and adversarial.

But Europe was never a subject on which Mrs Thatcher was

going to be able to speak with conviction. By contrast the Cold War, and the need for strong defence in the face of the ever-present threat of Soviet expansionism, was a cause close to her heart and one which she determined very early on to make her own. It is at first sight remarkable that a leader so inexperienced in foreign affairs should have chosen to take her first controversial initiative by plunging into Cold War polemics, while she remained so cautious for so long on domestic matters. Her primary mission, after all, was to halt Britain's economic decline. She claimed to be sceptical of the value of diplomacy, held a puritanical suspicion that Prime Ministers wasted their time posturing at summits and believed, with Ernest Bevin, that a strong foreign policy was dependent on a strong economy. 'A nation in debt', she reminded the Commons in November 1975, 'has no self-respect and precious little influence.'[89]

Yet from the moment she first became interested in politics she was always more stirred by foreign and military affairs than by domestic matters. Macmillan and Heath confined her within the ghetto of social policy. But as soon as she became leader she was bound to want to stretch herself on the world stage. There was no inconsistency with her primary objective, since she regarded the core problem of the British economy as too much socialism, which was merely a weaker local variant of Communism. Her short-term purpose might be freeing the British economy, but her ultimate ambition was to eradicate not just the symptoms of socialism, but the virus itself, whose source and breeding ground was the Soviet Union. Thus the struggle for the British economy was part of the global struggle against Communism. Moreover, it was a good deal easier for an opposition leader to define the battleground rhetorically in terms of grand abstractions – Freedom against Tyranny, Truth against Lies – than by getting bogged down in petty arguments about incomes policy and trade union law.

Still deeper than the ideological content of the Cold War, however, Mrs Thatcher's strong commitment to defence was rooted in her sense of national identity and her personal history. Her formative political experience was the Second World War: the lesson of appeasement was bred in her bone. After 1945 she simplistically equated Soviet Russia with Nazi Germany as the next expansionist aggressor who must be resisted. Indeed she saw no difference between Nazism and Communism, and liked to recall Hayek's reminder that Nazism was an abbreviation of National Socialism.[90] By 1975 she was convinced that the Russians were gaining ground all round the world – from Vietnam (where the Americans had admitted defeat the previous year) and Angola (where Russian-backed Cuban 'advisers' were supporting the Communist insurgents) to Portugal (where the Communists were trying to take over the democratic revolution) and Italy (where there was a danger of Communists entering the Government), as well as within the British trade union movement and the Labour party – while the West allowed itself to be duped by soft talk of peaceful co-existence, dialogue and détente. In particular she saw the forthcoming Helsinki conference, at which Western leaders were preparing to offer Russia all sorts of aid and recognition in exchange for promises of improved human rights, as a second Munich in the making. Unquestionably Mrs Thatcher also saw a role for herself as the clear-sighted Churchill figure whose mission was to warn the West of impending disaster before it was too late.

Just before the Helsinki conference convened, therefore, she resolved to make a speech. 'I did not speak to Reggie Maudling or anyone else in the Shadow Cabinet about it,' she wrote airily in her memoirs, 'because I knew that all I would receive were obstruction and warnings.'[91] The only Tory elder she consulted was Lord Home, whose unblinking view of Soviet intentions she had long respected. Replying to his congratulations on her election, she asked him for a meeting; and after Easter they began a series of informal conversations whenever he was in London. In June she specifically asked his help with her proposed speech: 'It is time I made a comprehensive speech about "Britain's Place in the World",' she wrote. 'I wonder if you would give me some advice about it.'[92] Afterwards she thanked him 'first for providing the framework . . . and then for going through it so carefully. It gave me all the confidence I should otherwise have lacked.'[93] Home in turn congratulated her. 'One always hopes that the communists will change their spots but they have not done so yet, and until there is firm evidence of change people must be warned.'[94]

The other expert to whom she turned for help was the independent British historian, Robert Conquest, whose book *The Great Terror* is still the most comprehensive exposé of Stalin's purges. Over the next few years – though he was in America for part of the time – Conquest's role in guiding Mrs Thatcher's foreign policy was analogous to Alfred Sherman's in economics. He did not have to tell her what she already thought, but he confirmed her pre-existing· view of the nature of Soviet society with a wealth of evidence and interpretation not provided by conventional academic and Foreign Office sources – 'the Sovietology gravy train', as she scornfully called it, 'which ran on official patronage . . . and a large dose of professional complacency'.[95] Conquest was her antidote to this official line, just as Churchill had his private sources of information about Nazi Germany.

Her third inspiration was Alexander Solzhenitsyn, then at the height of his prestige in the West following his expulsion from the Soviet Union the previous year. Patrick Cosgrave suggests that Mrs Thatcher had already discovered Solzhenitsyn several years earlier when she read *The First Circle* on a long flight as Education Secretary: thereafter, he claims, she 'read steadily in modern Russian literature' and Solzhenitsyn in particular.[96] She herself says that it was only when she flew to Australia in September 1976 that she picked up the book at the airport, having first seen the author interviewed on BBC television in March.[97] In fact it was Solzhenitsyn's dramatic assertion the year before that the West had been losing the Third World War ever since 1945, and had now 'irrevocably lost it', that gripped her imagination. He postulated an extreme version of domino theory whereby Thailand and South Korea, Finland and Austria were poised to follow Vietnam and Portugal into the abyss, and the free world would completely disappear in another two or three decades.[98] Mrs Thatcher did not swallow the whole of this nightmare vision; but she was already repeating the essence of his warning before the end of 1975, and the Russian prophet quickly joined her gallery of heroes. She finally got to meet him in 1983.

She delivered her speech to a hastily arranged meeting of the Chelsea Conservative Association on 26 July, two days before Wilson left for Helsinki. It was quite short but stunningly direct. She started from the premise that 'Freedom has taken a major battering in the last few months'.

> In Portugal, the first faint flickers of democracy are being snuffed out by communist reaction . . . In South-East Asia the loss of Vietnam and Cambodia was a major setback for the free world . . . Meanwhile, the world's most formidable navy – not America's, not Britain's, but Russia's – relentlessly extends its power from the Mediterranean to the Indian Ocean.

The background to Helsinki, she asserted, was that the Soviet Union was spending 20 per cent more than the United States each year on military research and development; 25 per cent more on weapons and equipment; 60 per cent more on strategic nuclear forces; while the Soviet navy possessed more nuclear submarines than the rest of the world's navies put together. 'Can anyone truly describe this as a defensive weapon?'

Détente sounds a fine word. And to the extent that there really has been a relaxation in international tension, it is a fine thing. But the fact remains throughout this decade of détente, the armed forces of the Soviet Union have increased, are increasing and show no signs of diminishing.

She recalled the crushing of the Czechoslovak spring just seven years before, and the Soviet writers and scientists – Solzhenitsyn among them – jailed for voicing their belief in freedom. The Soviet leaders, she declared uncompromisingly, were 'in principle arrayed against everything for which we stand'.

There is a lot of fashionable nonsense talked about how we misunderstand communism, misrepresent communism, see communists under every bed. An attempt is being made, it seems, to create an atmosphere where truth and commonsense on these matters is actively discouraged. I believe the people of this country understand better the truth of the matter than those who try to mislead them.

Genuine détente, she insisted, must involve genuine progress – not just words and gestures – towards the free movement of people and ideas.

We would like them to read our books and newspapers, just as we can read theirs. We would like them to visit our countries, just as we can go to theirs. We will be alert not to miss the moment when the Soviets turn to genuine détente. But until that is achieved we must quietly determine to maintain Western military strength at a level adequate to deter any aggression.

The power of NATO was 'already at its lowest safe limit', she concluded. 'Let us accept no proposals which would tip the balance of power still further against the West.'[99]

This was a speech of extraordinary simplicity and power. Written by Conquest and approved by Home, it expressed Mrs Thatcher's own uncompromising but essentially optimistic view of the Cold War. She had no time for the static view that the best outcome to be hoped for was a managed stand-off between two equally balanced superpowers; still less did she accept any moral equivalence between the two sides. She always believed, instinctively and passionately, that the Cold War should and could be won by the unwavering assertion of Western values backed by military strength. She boldly declared her position as a newly-elected opposition leader more than five years before Ronald Reagan was elected President of the United States. She held to it unflinchingly as Prime Minister, in alliance with Reagan, throughout the 1980s, and saw it triumphantly vindicated just before she left office. She made other, more celebrated speeches over the next few years; but she never essentially departed from the position she took up at Chelsea in July 1975.

Meanwhile she continued to confine her parliamentary interventions to single questions which Wilson easily evaded or turned against her: she rarely came back for a second bite. The more she condemned unemployment and called for spending cuts to curb inflation, the more scornfully he recalled the failures of the Heath years (which she was bound to deny), or pointed up Tory divisions (which she could not admit) and wearily explained to her that spending cuts would only increase unemployment. She did better in Wilson's occasional absences, when she could easily demolish his deputy, her old sparring partner at the DES, Ted Short. But time and again she failed to lay a glove on Wilson himself. Just before the House rose for the summer recess Barbara Castle – fascinated as always by her counterpart's clothes and appearance – recorded another vivid cameo:

> Margaret . . . slipped into her place as demurely tight-lipped as ever and glossy with her best suburban grooming: fresh flowered summer frock and every wave of her hair in place. How *does* she keep her hair so unchangeably immaculate? It all adds to the feeling of unreality about her political leadership. Somehow that also is too bandbox. She never risks anything: just sits there listening to Harold with a carefully modulated look of disapproval on her face, then produces one regulation question per Question Time. When she is ready for this great act she starts to lean forward slightly and an atmosphere of 'wait for it' builds up behind her. When finally she rises our chaps cheer ironically. She ignores them and fires her shaft. It never completely misses but is never (or very, very rarely) deadly. The lads behind her cheer lustily. Once again their tame bird has laid her egg.[100]

She fared little better in debate, though in fact her first two efforts were reasonably successful. On 11 March she made a good speech condemning the Government's recourse to a referendum on continued membership of the EEC as a cynical device to cover Labour's unbridgeable division on the subject. This was the sort of

forensic indictment she could always do well – marshalling the
constitutional case against referenda in principle and this one in
particular. She quoted with approval Clement Attlee's description of
referenda as 'a splendid weapon for demagogues and dictators',
which had no place in a parliamentary democracy.[101] Quite soon – as
a result of reading up Dicey and other constitutional experts – she
began to change her mind. By the time she came to write her
memoirs she had come to believe that a referendum should be
required before any major constitutional change such as the
Maastricht Treaty of 1992. Even in 1975 she conceded that a
referendum might be justified on those grounds. The difference was
that she did not at that time see membership of the EEC as involving
major constitutional change. Instead she made a straight party speech
attacking the Government. 'It was the sort of speech she could shine
at,' wrote the *Guardian*'s political editor Norman Shrapnel, 'well-
organised, emphatic and direct, though still with that hectoring air
many find oppressive . . . The Tories cheered and cheered . . . They
really liked it.'[102]

Her second speech was her familiar but wholly positive restatement of the well-worn case for staying in the Community, which
did what was required of her, if nothing more. Much more difficult
was the economy. On 22 May she had to open a debate condemning
the Government's failure to reduce inflation. She did not want to do
it and let it be known that she was too busy.[103] Airey Neave told her
firmly that she had to do it. The problem, she explained in her
memoirs, was that she had not yet had time to define her own
policy: she was in no position to repudiate Heath's approach, to
which most of her senior colleagues were still wedded, neither was
she ready to stick her neck out for the monetarist alternative.[104] So
she tried to ride both horses at once. She blamed accelerating
inflation partly on excessive Government expenditure 'beyond what
the taxpayers can bear', but also on unwarranted pay claims by
'groups of people who try to get more out of the economy than it
produces'. 'The real causes of inflation', she declared, in defiance of
what Sherman and Joseph had been teaching her for the past year,
'are not economic. They are social and they are political.'[105] The
result, as the *Sunday Times* reported, was 'a disappointing flop'. The
speech 'lacked fizz and originality and her voice had its usual garden
party quality'.[106] Denis Healey jeered at her 'monotonous recitation
of disconnected little homilies on each of the major economic
abstractions . . . charged with all the moral passion and intellectual
distinction of a railway timetable',[107] while Wilson teased her both
about her own high-spending record at the DES and her curious

silence on monetarism, noting shrewdly that 'the right hon. Lady's Rasputin' – Keith Joseph – 'has been kennelled up for this debate'.[108]

She did no better two months later when the Government was driven to impose a flat limit on pay increases of just £6 a week. With fifty-six left-wingers rebelling, the Government could in theory have been defeated; but the Tories could not be seen to vote against Labour's efforts to fight inflation by the only method the great majority of both front benches, and most of Fleet Street, understood. There was no political mileage in opposing incomes policy; so the Opposition ingloriously abstained. Indeed Mrs Thatcher actually blamed the Government for being slow to act. Recalling that Heath had imposed statutory pay restraint in 1972 when inflation was only 7.6 per cent, she demanded to know why Labour had waited until it was 26 per cent. At the same time she insisted that pay policy was only part of the answer, calling as usual for lower public spending and a halt to further nationalisation; and this time she did mention the money supply.[109] But she was plainly unconvinced by her own fudge. 'Her performance', Norman Shrapnel wrote, 'was not so much a falling-off as non-existent.'[110] At one point she had to be prompted by the Liberal leader, Jeremy Thorpe. Recording the general view that Mrs Thatcher had 'flopped' again, Barbara Castle noted that Heath, speaking later in the same debate in vigorous support of incomes policy, had 'made Margaret look like a tinny amateur and speculation began to circulate as to whether she could survive'.[111]

Mrs Thatcher was distressed by her repeated failure to shine in the House of Commons; but the fact was that the sort of simple certainties that went down well with party audiences cut no ice at Westminster. As a result she spoke less and less frequently in the House. Apart from certain fixed occasions in the parliamentary calendar which she could not avoid – the debate on the Queen's Speech every November, the Leader of the Opposition's instant response to the Budget, replies to statements by the Prime Minister following international summits – she made no more than seven major speeches in the next two years and only one in 1977–8, often leaving it to Howe, Joseph or even Prior to lead for the Opposition. She spoke slightly more over the winter of 1978–9 as the Labour Government began to crumble, but still much less frequently than Heath when he was Leader of the Opposition. Her neglect of Parliament continued even after she became Prime Minister, when she had all the information and authority needed to command the House but still spoke as rarely as she could and never memorably. The decline in the vigour and centrality of Parliament in the 1980s and 1990s has many causes, reflecting a lessening of public interest in politics and the increasing trivialisation of the media; but one factor was surely Mrs Thatcher's response to her difficult experience as Leader of the Opposition.

If her voice was carrying little weight at home, she was nevertheless determined that it should be heard in the wider world. Against the advice of the wise heads around her, she insisted on going to America at the earliest opportunity to announce herself as a robust new partner in the Western alliance. British opposition leaders have often been humiliated by the lack of attention paid to them in Washington. Not so Margaret Thatcher. Her public relations wizard, Gordon Reece, went ahead of her to stir up media interest. By the time Mrs Thatcher flew into New York in the middle of September – she made a point of flying by Freddie Laker's free enterprise airline – the novelty of her sex and the unusual clarity of her message did the rest.

Her first speech, for the most part a perfectly standard lecture to the Institute of Socio-Economic Studies in New York on the evils of excessive taxation, was beefed up at the last minute by Adam Ridley in breach of the convention that opposition leaders do not criticise their own country when speaking abroad. Mrs Thatcher did not scruple to paint a grim picture of the British economy groaning under socialism, graphically endorsing the common American perception that Britain was going down the tube. Attacking the 'progressive consensus' which she believed was stifling enterprise in pursuit of equality, she positively defended inequality in a defiant phrase perfectly geared to the American dream: 'I say "Let our children grow tall – and some taller than others if they have it in them to do so".'[112] Two years later the phrase 'Let Our Children Grow Tall' – shorn of its more provocative rider – was used as the title of her first book of collected speeches.

Rebuked by Callaghan for running Britain down, she retorted that she was 'not knocking Britain: I'm knocking socialism'.[113] 'In fact', she maintained in her memoirs, 'the message I was bringing to America about Britain was essentially one of hope, namely that the nation's potential was great enough to withstand even the effects of socialism.'[114] She deflected criticism by claiming that she had made the same speech about equality when she first entered politics 'nearly thirty years ago'.[115] Next day, still in New York, she sounded an even more apocalyptic note. Democracy in Britain was on trial, she warned: the eleventh hour had struck. 'If Britain were to break, a well-nigh mortal blow would be struck against the whole Western ideal.' Turning to the global struggle, she repeated the warning of her Chelsea speech against giving too much away at Helsinki. 'I am all for *détente*,' she affirmed. 'Who is not? But I am also for *attente*, for wanting to see results; for not letting down our guard; for keeping our powder dry.'[116]

By the time she moved on to Washington, she had captured the media's attention. She met President Ford, who had just succeeded to the White House following the disgrace of Richard Nixon, had breakfast with Secretary of State Henry Kissinger (whom she had already met in London) and had talks with both Treasury and Defense Secretaries. Her next speech, to the National Press Club, was broadcast live on CBS television. She took the opportunity to repeat the same two messages. First she gave her own gloss to Solzhenitsyn's warning that the West was losing the ideological struggle by default.

> No, we did not lose the Cold War. But we are losing the Thaw in a subtle and disturbing way. We are losing confidence in ourselves and in our case. We are losing the Thaw politically.

Second, she answered the critics of her earlier speech by emphasising her faith in Britain's potential to surmount its problems, stressing the huge windfall of North Sea oil and her favourite measure of British genius, the proud tally of seventy-two scientific Nobel Prize winners. She claimed to see a new willingness to reject the easy options.

> Slowly we are finding our way . . . A change is coming over us . . . I see some signs that our people are ready to make the tough choice, to follow the harder road. We are still the same people who have fought for freedom, and won . . . We may suffer from a British sickness now, but our constitution is sound and we have the heart and will to win through.[117]

This combination of Churchill and Mrs Miniver went down a storm. Hard-nosed bankers were heard to declare that Britain's alternative Prime Minister was 'quite a dame'.[118] The influential CBS commentator Eric Severeid gave his opinion that 'Britons were looking for a break and she could be it', while her warnings about the Soviet Union stirred perennial American anxieties. It was soon being said that she would easily beat both Ford and Ronald Reagan for the Republican presidential nomination if she were eligible to run.[119] The only sour note came with allegations that officials in the

British Embassy – where she stayed as the guest of the Ambassador, Sir Peter Ramsbotham – had been briefing the press against her. If so it had little effect. This first American trip marked the beginning of a love affair between Margaret Thatcher and the American press and public which lasted with ever-increasing enthusiasm for the next twenty years. It also greatly boosted her self-confidence. To journalists on the flight home she boasted: 'The very thing I was said to be weak in – international affairs – I've succeeded in.'[120] She felt she had now proved herself on the international stage.

The one domestic forum where Mrs Thatcher could unfailingly project her faith and rouse a large audience to enthusiasm was the Tory party's annual conference in October. Unlike any other Tory leader – from A. J. Balfour, who famously remarked that he would no more take political advice from the conference than from his valet, to Macmillan and Heath, who viewed their annual exposure to the massed activists as an ordeal to be got through as painlessly as possible – Mrs Thatcher had always loved the Tories' annual seaside jamboree, ever since she first attended it in 1946. Somehow more than at the smaller sectional conferences, which were full of Scots or trade unionists, she was in her element among the small shopkeepers and disciplinarian matrons who typified the representatives, for she was unashamedly, indeed proudly, one of them. She spoke their language and shared their concerns; and they loved her in return. At the most difficult moments of her fifteen-year leadership she could always appeal over the heads of the party establishment to the rank and file, and they would back her.

From 1978, the conference arrangements were choreographed by Harvey Thomas, who staged rallies for the American evangelist Billy Graham and volunteered his services to do the same for Mrs Thatcher, bringing the same sort of revivalist fervour to her message of born-again Conservatism. The annual conference speech henceforth became the high point of her year, a shameless festival of orchestrated leader-worship for which she prepared with meticulous, even obsessive care. The latent actress in her responded instinctively to the cameras and the razmatazz, the flagwaving and Elgar, and her speech was almost always intensely patriotic, associating Labour relentlessly with national decline and looking forward to the recovery of 'greatness' under the Conservatives. The one year her speech fell slightly flat was 1976, when the conference took place in the middle of the sterling crisis, and she felt patriotically obliged to hold back on partisan condemnation of the Government.

Her first conference speech as leader was a critical test. Over the summer she had made two poorly received economic speeches in the House of Commons, and one controversial outburst on defence. Her capacity and her judgement were alike in question. Blackpool in October was her first major opportunity to tell the party and, via television, the whole country what she was about. She was determined that she did not want to make 'just an economic speech . . . The economic crisis was a crisis of the spirit of the nation.'

> But when I discussed the kind of draft I wanted with Chris Patten and others from the Research Department I felt they were just not getting the message I wanted to despatch. So I sat down at home over the weekend and wrote out sixty pages of my large handwriting. I found no difficulty: it just flowed and flowed.[121]

At that moment Woodrow Wyatt rang up, so she got him to recast it with a journalist's eye. Patten and Adam Ridley added material worked up in the Research Department, and Angus Maude reshaped it again. Then on the Wednesday of conference week Caroline Stephens summoned Ronald Millar to Blackpool for the final rewrite.

Millar was a successful West End playwright – the author of historical romances such as *Robert and Elizabeth* and dramatisations of the novels of C. P. Snow – who had written occasional material for Ted Heath. Lady Thatcher's memoirs imply that the 1975 conference was the first time she made use of him; but in fact she had called him to the House of Commons just a few days after her election as leader to help with her first party broadcast. Millar responded reluctantly – his latest play was in rehearsal at the Haymarket and he claims he had never meant to get involved in politics at all. Yet he was instantly captivated. 'There was a kind of senior girl scout freshness about her, as though she had stepped straight out of *The Sound of Music*.' He read her some material which he had hastily prepared, ending with some lines of Abraham Lincoln which he had once learned for an audition:

You cannot strengthen the weak by weakening the strong.
You cannot bring about prosperity by discouraging thrift.
You cannot help the wage-earner by pulling down the wage-payer . . .

When he had finished she said nothing, but produced from her handbag a piece of yellowing newsprint containing the same lines. 'It goes wherever I go,' she told him.[122] From that moment they clicked. Mrs Thatcher recognised in Millar a writer whose mind was stocked from exactly the same store of homely proverbs and improving doggerel as her own. Patten, Maude, Wyatt and the rest were good writers, but they were all sophisticated politicians with ideas of their own. Millar's unique value to Mrs Thatcher was that he was not a political animal, but a professional writer with a playwright's ability to write in her voice, not his own: to give her the lines with which to create her own character. For the next fifteen years no major speech of hers was complete until it had been 'Ronnified'.

What precisely this process involved is difficult to pin down. One or two famous soundbites – most obviously the theatrical 'The Lady's Not for Turning' in 1980 – clearly bear Millar's fingerprints. He also incorporated at least one laboured joke into every speech. In her first conference speech, for instance, Mrs Thatcher – who had scarcely been into a pub since she pulled pints for the cameras in Dartford – was made to say that the Labour party reminded her of a pub which was running out of mild beer. 'Soon all that is left will be bitter, and all that is bitter will be Left.'[123] In 1977, after the Lib-Lab pact, she complained that 'Instead of having a Government with steel in its backbone we have one with Steel [the Liberal leader] in its pocket'.[124] Millar's jokes were invariably the least convincing part of her speeches, because she never sounded as if she understood them. More important, Millar himself described his 'self-appointed task of putting each syllable under the microscope'.[125] More than anyone, he was responsible for developing the characteristic Thatcher style of short staccato sentences, hammered out in a characteristic driving rhythm. No doubt other writers learned to imitate the style, but once she had come to rely on Millar she never felt happy with a speech unless he had given it the final polish.

In his entertaining memoir, *A View From the Wings*, Millar vividly describes the annual agony of producing the conference speech, which never varied from that first experience when he was summoned to Blackpool at short notice and closeted in a hotel room with Patten and Ridley, writing and rewriting until dawn. Mrs Thatcher came in around midnight, after her last engagement, and immediately took the whole process back to square one, laying out the pages on a large table – or sometimes the floor – ordering and reordering them obsessively, until Denis told her firmly to come to bed at ten past five. She rejected a peroration of which Millar and Patten were rather proud, telling them, 'It's just not me, dear' – a phrase which, Millar wrote, 'was to be a marker buoy for the next sixteen years'.[126] Another time – after she became Prime Minister –

he recalled her going through a draft and cutting out every occurrence of the word 'perhaps', telling him, 'I'm a conviction politician. I'm not in the perhaps business.'[127] As another of her writers put it with feeling, no one wrote speeches *for* Mrs Thatcher: they wrote speeches *with* her.[128] She fretted and worried over every word up to the very last minute, sometimes neglecting her host or neighbour at formal dinners while she kept on correcting her text until the moment she stood up. Paradoxically therefore, though she could use a small army of writers – or 'wordsmiths' as she called them – on a single speech, every word she spoke was in a real sense her own, or had become so by the time she uttered it.

With his experience of the theatre, Millar also coached her in how to deliver her lines, writing in the pauses and emphases she should observe. 'I'm not a performer, dear,' she told him once;[129] but she was, and much of his success with her was due to the fact that he handled her like a highly-strung actress. Before the 1975 speech she was intensely nervous. 'I wish it was over,' she told him. 'She was three days short of fifty, but she looked young and vulnerable and pretty and scared. I felt suddenly protective.'[130] As she delivered the speech, Millar stood with Patten in the wings, feeling like Henry Higgins watching Eliza Doolittle at Ascot. But the speech was a triumph.

She began with nicely judged humility, recalling her first conference in the same hall in 1946, when Churchill was leader and she never dreamed that she might one day speak from the same platform, paying tribute in turn to Eden, Macmillan, Home and Heath ('who successfully led the party to victory in 1970 and brilliantly led the nation into Europe in 1973'). Getting into her stride, however, she repeated her defence of her speeches in America – 'It was not Britain I was criticising, it was socialism, and I will go on attacking socialism and opposing socialism because it is bad for Britain' – and went on to define a 'moral challenge' for the party and the country which went deeper than the economic challenge. She damned the Labour government not just for high unemployment, high taxation, low productivity and record borrowing but, more fundamentally, for threatening the British way of life itself.

> We are witnessing a deliberate attack on our values, a deliberate attack on those who wish to promote merit and excellence, a deliberate attack on our heritage and our great past . . .

She celebrated the British genius by reference to both industry – 'We are the people that in the past made Great Britain the workshop of the world' – and science, citing a long list of British inventions from the computer and the refrigerator to the jet engine, the hovercraft, 'oh, and the best half of Concorde'. She begged 'the best and the brightest' who might be thinking of emigrating not to do so but to 'stay and help us to defeat socialism, so that the Britain you have known may be the Britain your children will know'.

'Let me give you my vision', she went on – with characteristic disregard for feminism:

A man's right to work as he will, to spend what he earns, to own property, to have the State as servant and not as master – these are the British inheritance. They are the essence of a free country and on that freedom all our other freedoms depend.

'We want a free economy,' she conceded, 'not only because it guarantees our liberties but also because it is the best way of creating wealth.' There followed a fairly standard recital of the need to stimulate private enterprise, cut the share of the economy taken by public spending and rebuild profits and incentives. The purpose of increasing prosperity, she proclaimed, was 'not merely to give people more of their own money to spend as they choose but to have more money to help the old and the sick and the handicapped'. Yet she ended with another explicit endorsement of inequality: 'We are all unequal,' she declared boldly.

No one, thank heavens, is quite like anyone else, however much the Socialists may like to pretend otherwise. We believe that everyone has the right to be unequal. But to us, every human being is equally important ... Everyone must be allowed to develop the abilities he knows he has within him – and she knows she has within her – in the way he chooses.

Finally, after a direct promise to reverse 'Mrs Castle's stupid and spiteful attack on hospital pay beds' and a warning to the trade unions not to try to obstruct another elected Conservative government; a strong assertion of the primacy of law and order; and a pledge to uphold the Union with Northern Ireland, she returned to her intensely patriotic personal faith.

I have tried to tell you something of my personal vision and my belief in the standards on which this country was greatly built, on which it greatly thrived and from which in recent years it has greatly fallen away. I believe we are coming to yet another turning point in our long history. We can go on as we have been going and continue down, or we can stop and with a decisive act of will say 'Enough'.[131]

The representatives in the hall loved it. The press loved it. 'Now I *am* Leader,' she told her entourage, accepting that she had been on probation up to that moment.[132] But almost immediately she suffered a reaction. When Millar caught up with her a couple of hours later, the confident star of the platform had been replaced by 'a nervous schoolgirl awaiting her examination results . . . She looked wan and flat and not even pretty. The adrenalin was way, way down.' When told that she had been wonderful she started worrying about how she could repeat the effect the next year. 'Brighton could be the most dreadful anticlimax.'

> This was too much for Denis. 'My God, woman, you've just had a bloody great triumph and here you are worrying yourself sick about next year! I'll get the others, shall I? Then you can settle down for another all-night session. I mean, obviously there's no time to be lost . . .' I slipped away. So long as she had this man around she was going to be all right.[133]

Back at Westminster for the autumn session, Wilson continued effortlessly to dominate her at Prime Minister's Questions every Tuesday and Thursday, alternately taunting her with her shared responsibility for 1970–4 and chiding her if she disowned it. He patronised her inexperience: 'It is a pity she never served on the Public Accounts Committee or she would have known these things.'[134] He mocked her reluctance to intervene more often, and once caught her out quoting newspaper reports of a White Paper instead of the paper itself.[135] All her intensive briefing and rehearsal with the Gang of Four rarely seemed to enable her to land a punch. When she launched an elaborate set-piece question alleging that 'record inflation, record unemployment, record borrowing and record taxation' were being met with 'record complacency and record incompetence', he easily punctured her synthetic indignation by retorting drily: 'It must have taken most of the morning to think of that.'[136] On another occasion Barbara Castle thought Mrs Thatcher missed an opening when Wilson was questioned about South African involvement in smearing the Liberal leader, Jeremy Thorpe.

She was not prepared for anything like this, with one of her carefully worked out and stylised interventions and she wasn't politician enough to react instinctively. If she could only have improvised she could have driven Harold into a corner.[137]

Mrs Thatcher maintained her attack on the Helsinki process with several more speeches during 1976. It was the first, delivered at Kensington Town Hall in January, which succeeded in striking a most satisfactory response from the Soviets. Written for her, in Conquest's absence, by Robert Moss of the right-wing Institute for the Study of Conflict, this was substantially longer, more wide-ranging and even more provocative than its Chelsea predecessor. Russia, she bluntly asserted, was 'ruled by a dictatorship of patient, far-sighted men who are rapidly making their country the foremost naval and military power in the world'. They were not doing this for self-defence: 'A huge, largely landlocked country like Russia does not need to build the most powerful navy in the world just to guard its own frontiers' –

No. The Russians are bent on world dominance, and they are rapidly acquiring the means to become the most powerful imperial nation the world has seen.

The men in the Soviet Politburo do not have to worry about the ebb and flow of public opinion. They put guns before butter, while we put just about everything before guns. They know that they are a superpower in only one sense – the military sense. They are a failure in human and economic terms.

This was breathtakingly undiplomatic. She went on to assert that her warnings the previous summer had been fully vindicated. The West had got 'nothing of substance' in return for endorsing the status quo in Eastern Europe. On the contrary, the Communists had made 'an open grab for power' in Portugal, while the Russians, through their Cuban surrogate, were now 'pouring money, arms and front-line troops into Angola'.

We must remember that there are no Queensberry rules in the contest that is now going on. And the Russians are playing to win. They have one great advantage over us – the battles are being fought on our territory, not theirs.

Again she recalled Solzhenitsyn's warning that the West had been fighting and losing 'a kind of Third World War' steadily since 1945;

she then repeated her complaint that the West put 'just about everything' before defence. 'The socialists seem to regard defence as almost infinitely cuttable.' But Soviet military power would not go away. The public had been 'sedated' by those in and out of government who assured them that Britain faced no external threat, and that 'a squadron of fighter planes or a company of Marine commandos [was] less important than a new subsidy for a loss-making plant'. She concluded with a Churchillian warning:

> There are moments in our history when we have to make a fundamental choice. This is one such moment – a moment when our choice will determine the life or death of our kind of society, and the future of our children. Let us ensure that our children have cause to rejoice that we did not forsake their freedom.[138]

She was immediately attacked for warmongering. This was simply not the language of serious statesmanship. 'Despite our differences in ideology and philosophy', Jim Callaghan, then Foreign Secretary, wrote in his memoirs, 'I have always believed that we should hold a steady course in dealing with the Soviet Union . . . We should take every opportunity to state our views plainly, without using offensive or provocative rhetoric, but at the same time seek to gain Soviet co-operation in areas in which East and West share a common concern.'[139] This was the accepted diplomatic wisdom. Old hands like Callaghan and Wilson prided themselves on their ability to do business with the enduring Soviet Foreign Minister, Andrei Gromyko, and his colleagues. Calling the Soviet leaders dictators bent on world domination was in this view merely childish and counterproductive. It certainly annoyed them. A few days after the Kensington speech the Soviet army newspaper *Red Star* denounced the Conservative leader, calling her – in what was meant to be an insult – 'the Iron Lady'. As she later noted, 'They never did me a greater favour.'[140] She immediately seized on the sobriquet and made sure it stuck. If ever there was a doubt that a woman could be Prime Minister, this Soviet epithet did more than anything else to dispel it. A few days later, in Finchley, she played up to it delightedly, exploiting her femininity and her toughness simultaneously:

> Ladies and Gentlemen, I stand before you tonight in my green chiffon evening gown, my face softly made up, my fair hair gently waved . . . The Iron Lady of the Western World. Me? A cold war warrior? . . .

Well, yes, if that is how they wish to interpret my defence of values and freedoms fundamental to our way of life.[141]

The next month her personal rating shot up by seven points. Realising that she was on to a winner, she kept up the attack. Speaking to the West German Christian Democrats in Hanover – where she met for the first time their new leader, a large but underrated provincial politician named Helmut Kohl – she embraced the Tories' sister party as allies in the fight for freedom in Europe, likening the recent advances made by the deceptively democratic 'Eurocommunist' parties in Italy, Portugal and France to the wolf dressing up as Red Riding Hood's grandmother, the better to swallow her up.[142] In July, at Dorking, she once again questioned Soviet intentions of honouring the undertakings given at Helsinki and warned the West not to cut its defences. Though *The Times* considered this speech 'more thoughtful and better balanced than its forerunner in January',[143] it was finally too much for Maudling, who had loyally defended her Kensington speech but now protested at her 'violent and sustained attack on the Soviet Government'. Mrs Thatcher had no business, he complained, committing the party to 'immediate and massive rearmament' without proper discussion in the Shadow Cabinet.[144] He was dismissed a few weeks later. She replaced him with John Davies; but she consulted Davies no more than she had Maudling. As she grew in confidence, she had no intention of committing herself to any potential Foreign Secretary.

Instead she undertook an extensive programme of globetrotting over the next three years – partly to spread her message and polish her credentials as a world leader in waiting, partly to educate herself and meet the other leaders with whom she hoped to deal once she had attained office. In all she visited twenty-three countries, including all Britain's major European partners at least once, and one or two outside the EC like Switzerland and Finland. She visited the two Iron Curtain countries least controlled by the Soviet Union – Ceauşescu's Romania and Tito's Yugoslavia; but was – unsurprisingly – not invited to Moscow. Her strong anti-Soviet stance did, however, earn her an invitation to China in April 1977. She visited Egypt, Syria and Israel in early 1976, and later the same year made an extended tour of India, Pakistan and Singapore, going on to Australia and New Zealand. She did not set foot, however, in sub-Saharan Africa, South America or the Gulf. For the most part she did not lecture her hosts about free markets – where she tried it, in Australia, it went down badly. But she did project herself successfully as a staunch defender of Freedom with a capital F, capitalising skilfully on the curiosity which attended a forceful woman politician. She dealt warily with Ceauşescu and Tito, fenced diplomatically with Chairman Hua Guofeng, but got on well with Lee Kuan Yew and Indira Gandhi – both of whom she admired though she could not fully endorse their authoritarian regimes. (Mrs Gandhi had recently introduced a draconian State of Emergency.) In Israel she visited a kibbutz and predictably did not like it. She then infuriated the Israelis by inspecting a Palestinian refugee camp in Syria; but she was even-handed in her condemnation of terrorism and refused to recognise the PLO.

It was noticeable that she rarely travelled with her shadow Foreign Secretary or other relevant senior colleagues, but preferred her own sources of expert advice. In China she was accompanied by Douglas Hurd, who had served in the Peking Embassy (as well as by her daughter Carol, on her way to work as a journalist in Australia); in Yugoslavia by Tito's wartime comrade-in-arms, the distinguished author and former Tory MP, Sir Fitzroy Maclean. Given her inexperience and forthright views she made remarkably few faux pas. If she was rude to the Russians it was at a distance, and because she meant to be. Having been impressed by the Shah when she visited Iran in April 1978 she unwisely committed herself to giving him asylum in Britain when he was overthrown a few months later, and had to send a former ambassador incognito to the Bahamas to withdraw the offer.[145] More seriously she was influenced by another of her private gurus, the mystical Afrikaner Laurens van der Post, to commit herself to supporting Ian Smith's attempt to settle the Rhodesian imbroglio by an internal settlement with Bishop Muzorewa, excluding the Patriotic Front forces of Joshua Nkomo and Robert Mugabe. This was an understanding from which Lord Carrington had to disembarrass her after the election.[146]

On her main battleground of Helsinki and the Cold War, however, she made an undoubted impact, at least while the Republican administration of Ford and Kissinger was still in the White House. Jimmy Carter, elected in November 1976, was a different kind of President, genuinely but naively determined to work for disarmament and human rights. Mrs Thatcher met him on her second visit to the States in September 1977 – a mark of some respect in itself, since Carter did not normally receive opposition leaders. She could not help liking him and was impressed by a mastery of detail equal to her own; but she was dismayed by his determination to pursue a nuclear test ban treaty and did not let him get a word in for forty-five minutes while she told him so. Even Carter, however, was constrained by the evidence that the Soviets were flouting the assurances they had given at Helsinki. Several prominent dissidents, including the founder of the Helsinki monitoring group, Yuri Orlov, were sentenced to long spells in labour camps. Despite her enthusiastic reception in 1975 Mrs Thatcher's influence in Washington should not be exaggerated. Patrick Cosgrave's claim in 1978 that the first three pages of her Dorking speech 'are now President Carter's foreign policy' was pushing it: she was only a British opposition leader, and Carter had very good relations with Jim Callaghan.[147] Yet by pointing out loudly and repeatedly the nature of the Soviet regime she certainly contributed to a general stiffening of Western resolve, evidenced in NATO's decision to increase defence spending by 3 per cent a year from 1977 and the agreement of West Germany and other European countries to accept American nuclear missiles on their soil to counter the Soviet deployment of SS-20s. These were both decisions which Mrs Thatcher strongly supported in opposition and implemented when she came to power.

Another sign of hardening American opinion was the emergence of Ronald Reagan as a presidential challenger. Mrs Thatcher first met Reagan soon after her election as leader, when he happened to be visiting London and called on her at the House of Commons. Their meeting was scheduled to last forty-five minutes, but actually lasted twice as long. 'We found', Reagan told Geoffrey Smith, 'that we were really akin with regard to our views of government and economics and government's place in people's lives and all that sort of thing.'[148] In fact Mrs Thatcher already knew of Reagan's reputation as a successful Governor of California who had got rid of a lot of controls and cut expenditure: Denis had heard him speak to the Institute of Directors back in 1969. 'In a way', she recalled, 'he had the advantage of me because he was able to say: "This is what I believe! This is what I have done!"'[149] Yet in 1975 few took the former film star seriously as a potential President. They met a second time when Reagan next came to London three years later, and again got on exceptionally well. This time their conversation ranged across international as well as domestic politics, defence as well as economics: on both their views instinctively tallied. It was not until five years later that Reagan, two years into his Presidency, called the Soviet Union 'the evil empire'. But those two words precisely encapsulated what Mrs Thatcher had been saying in her speeches ever since Chelsea.

In March 1976 the nature of Mrs Thatcher's domestic task suddenly changed when Harold Wilson unexpectedly resigned. Just a few days earlier the Government had been heavily defeated at the end of a two-day public expenditure debate – the Tories this time having no scruple about taking advantage of another left-wing revolt against Government economies. Like any Leader of the Opposition in the same situation, Mrs Thatcher immediately called on Wilson to resign. 'He must go, and go now.'[150] Unlike more cynical leaders, however, she was 'unfeignedly furious' when he merely called a confidence vote two days later to reverse the embarrassment. She had to be warned by her staff not to make too much of this constitutional outrage – as she considered it – since she might one day find herself in the same position. 'If I did', she retorted, 'I would resign.' 'It says much for her character', Patrick Cosgrave wrote, 'that nobody in the room doubted her for a moment.'[151] Four days later Wilson caught the entire political world off guard by resigning indeed. When told the news, Mrs Thatcher thought for a moment that the whole Government had resigned. Again she went through the motions of demanding an immediate election: 'Three weeks on Thursday. We shall be ready.'[152] Instead she had to pay gracious tribute to Wilson and adjust to the challenge of a new antagonist in Number Ten.

She immediately tipped Jim Callaghan to win the succession and predicted that he would be the hardest of the contenders to beat.[153] She was right on both counts. Four years older than Wilson and thirteen years older than Mrs Thatcher, Callaghan was the first Prime Minister ever to have held all three of the senior offices of state before finally reaching the premiership. Mrs Thatcher found him just as patronising as Wilson and even harder to come to grips with. As Barbara Castle – no admirer of Callaghan – wrote in her memoirs: he 'ran rings round an uncertain Margaret Thatcher, metaphorically patting her on the head like a kindly uncle'.[154] 'When the right hon. Lady has been Leader of the Opposition longer', he told her in one of their first encounters, '– and she will be that for a very long time –' she would appreciate that there was more to freedom than her narrow concern with the union closed shop.[155] When she pressed him about the terms of IMF assistance, he brushed her off with the bland assurance that 'one day the right hon. Lady will understand these things a little better'.[156] Another time, when she objected to his 'avuncular flannel', he amiably assured her that he thought of her in many ways, but never as his niece.[157]

There was a period at the nadir of the Government's fortunes when she did succeed in ruffling Callaghan's composure. In

November 1976 – just after the Workington and Walsall by-elections had reduced the Government's majority to a single vote – there was an angry exchange when he demanded that she withdraw the 'Goebbelistic' allegation that every Labour Government had left behind it a financial crisis. 'Not to a Prime Minister who has done what he has done to the British pound,' she retorted.[158] More than once he accused her of 'naked ambition'[159] – as if that were a crime in a Leader of the Opposition – and of moving a confidence motion 'to satisfy an impatient and imperious vanity'.[160] 'Her slip is showing,' he warned in March 1977. 'Her preoccupation with office comes out in nearly every question she asks.'[161] Once he had secured his position by means of the Lib-Lab pact, however, Callaghan recovered his equanimity and developed a disarming line in benign insouciance, suggesting that he could not be expected to have all the answers but was doing his best in difficult circumstances. When Mrs Thatcher asked a detailed question about the terms of a Polish shipping deal, for example, Callaghan replied blithely that he did not 'carry this complicated calculation in my head'. She was genuinely shocked that 'on one of the main issues of the day neither he nor his office took the trouble to ensure that he was properly briefed to answer questions in this House'.[162] Another time he brushed off her insistent questioning about growth targets: 'I really do not see why the Leader of the Opposition should expect me to come here charged with every figure in my head that the gang of four has sedulously fed her for Prime Minister's Questions.'

When she lectured him on what he ought to know, he thanked her ironically for the information but told her that it was not possessing information which mattered, but what one did with it.[163] By now she was much less shy of intervening, since Callaghan was not so skilful as Wilson at turning her questions against her. On the contrary, Labour MPs increasingly complained that she was monopolising Question Time by always taking her permitted three bites at the cherry. She scored one palpable hit when Callaghan called her a 'one-man band'. 'Is that not one more man than the Government have got?' she retorted.[164] But she rarely succeeded in disturbing Callaghan's masterly impersonation of a wise old statesman calmly in control of events, while she fussed about details like a terrier yapping at an elephant.

From April 1978 their twice-weekly duels were broadcast live on radio – which did Mrs Thatcher no favours at all. She had opposed the innovation – as she later opposed the televising of Parliament – realising that the increased noise level would make it even harder for her to command the House without shouting. The first broadcast was on Budget day. Making her usual instant response to the Chancellor's measures, she was clearly conscious of the microphones and even made a point of reminding radio listeners that she was having to speak 'off the cuff'. 'Off the cuff?' Labour members queried when she launched into her customary barrage of statistics. 'Of course I armed myself,' she replied. 'Some cuff!' they chortled. 'It is a very good cuff,' she retorted. 'Honourable Members should try having one themselves.'

Andrew Faulds – the bearded ex-actor who was Labour's chief heckler before Denis Skinner – asked the Deputy Speaker whether it was in order for Mrs Thatcher to refer to the proceedings of the House as 'this broadcast'. He ruled that broadcasting was now a fact of life.[165] Unquestionably from a narrow party perspective she was right to be apprehensive: the contrast between Callaghan's easy mastery and her shrill nagging, carried for the first time into people's homes and cars, was certainly a factor in the recovery of the Government's popularity that summer. Mrs Thatcher's public relations guru, Gordon Reece, who had been working to soften her image by teaching her to lower her voice, believed that his efforts were set back two years by the broadcasting of Parliament.[166]

The 1976 sterling crisis gave Labour a bad nine months, as further rounds of spending cuts and raising the minimum lending rate to 15 per cent failed to stop the pound sliding to a low point of $1.56 in late October. After rapidly exhausting two previous standby credits from the IMF, Healey could only secure a third on stringent conditions. In the short term this apparent humiliation – as Mrs Thatcher strenuously portrayed it – actually served Callaghan well, enabling him to make a stand against the left and taking much of the wind out of Mrs Thatcher's sails. In her speech at the Tory conference she was inhibited from making her usual slashing condemnation of the Government by the need not to appear to be talking down the pound. By contrast Callaghan had boldly told his conference the previous week that Keynesianism was dead: the Government could no longer spend its way out of recession. The crucial section of Callaghan's speech was written by his son-in-law Peter Jay; but it could as well have been written by Alfred Sherman.

For the next two years, under IMF tutelage, Healey enforced a regime of strict financial discipline which Mrs Thatcher could only – through gritted teeth – applaud. She was obliged to welcome the Chancellor's conversion to the importance of controlling the money supply – 'the only final way in which inflation can be held and reduced. He knows it and we know it.'[167]* She doubted whether the Labour party as a whole had yet learned the lesson; but Callaghan could equally point to divisions on the Tory side. He brazenly contrasted Labour's new-found discipline with the Tories' inflationary record in 1970–4, which she still could not disown since she and Keith Joseph had been the biggest spenders. 'We have been attempting to live within our means', he boasted modestly in May 1977, 'after the profligate extravagance of the Conservative Government.'[169] From Mrs Thatcher's point of view the one advantage of the Government's enforced conversion to monetary virtue was that, as she wrote in her memoirs, 'it outflanked on the right those members of my own Shadow Cabinet who were still clinging to the outdated nostrums of Keynesian demand management'.[170]

By putting an end to any possibility of further nationalisation, the sterling crisis made it more difficult for Mrs Thatcher to portray the Labour Government as wildly socialist. Callaghan's preference for a statesmanlike centrism was further consolidated in March 1977 by the Lib-Lab pact which sustained him in office when his majority finally disappeared. The moment of truth had come on 17 March when the Government was obliged to duck out of a vote it knew it could not win. Labour MPs humiliatingly abstained, leaving the Tories to register a hollow victory by 293 votes to nil. Mrs Thatcher immediately tabled another confidence motion, and in a speech at Torquay put her party on the alert for an early election. Callaghan actually pencilled in a date in early May. A Gallup poll gave the Tories a lead of 49 percentage points to 33. In the course of a frantic few days, however, Callaghan managed to stitch up a parliamentary deal with the Liberals, whose thirteen MPs no more wished to face the electorate at that moment than did Labour. Thwarted of an election she had seemed certain to win, Mrs Thatcher made – on her own admission – one of the poorest speeches she had ever delivered. Her contempt for the Liberals was redoubled. 'I was astonished that they had signed up to such a bad deal,' she wrote; 'but I had left out the crucial element of vanity.'[171]

She never considered for a moment the possibility that she herself might do a deal with David Steel's bunch of 'irresponsible eccentrics', whom she despised for shoring up the socialist government in the name of liberalism.[172] Following the two indecisive

---

* In her speech to the party conference that year Mrs Thatcher urged Callaghan ironically to 'keep taking the tablets'. This was another Ronald Millar joke, playing on the fact that Peter Jay had recently likened his father-in-law to Moses. But Mrs Thatcher did not get it, and had to be laboriously dissuaded from changing the line to 'keep taking the pill', which she thought was funnier.[168]

elections of 1974, politics appeared to many observers to be becoming dangerously fragmented; academics worried that the country might soon become ungovernable. Opinion polls and polls of business leaders found consistent yearning for some form of grand coalition, or government of national unity, such as Heath had unconvincingly proposed in October 1974. *The Times* campaigned for it; and in October 1976 the aged Harold Macmillan broke his thirteen years' silence to back the idea. From the moment she became leader Mrs Thatcher was repeatedly asked if she would be willing to join a coalition. She consistently answered that she could see no basis for a coalition where there was no fundamental agreement between the parties. This remained her view, even in the much-canvassed hypothesis that she in her turn might fail to win an overall majority. Frank Giles, the deputy editor of the *Sunday Times*, was present at a country house weekend when someone asked if she would form a coalition with the Liberals. Her eyes, Giles wrote, 'burned with passion': 'Her deepest emotions had obviously been stirred. Never, but never, she said, would she consider a coalition, from which could only come irresolute and debilitating government.'[173]

It was the same with proportional representation. Much of the Tory party, including probably more than half the Shadow Cabinet, was in favour of at least exploring the option of changing the electoral system, in the belief that proportional representation would preclude the nightmare of an extreme socialist government gaining power on a minority vote. Alarmed by the abuses of even the Wilson–Callaghan government, Lord Hailsham solemnly warned that the first-past-the-post system resulted in 'elective dictatorship' – a worry he mysteriously forgot once the Tories were returned to power.[174] Mrs Thatcher herself frequently denied Labour's legitimacy to govern with only 38 per cent of the national vote, and asserted that the country was being governed by 'a minority of a minority'.[175] Yet she believed passionately that proportional representation, far from excluding the hard left as its advocates argued, would actually give disproportionate influence to small minorities. As a result of her 'ridiculous intransigence', one senior shadow minister despaired, proportional representation remained 'a taboo subject' in the Shadow Cabinet, like devaluation under Wilson.[176] She was not prepared to barter her way into Downing Street by offering to share power with the Liberals or anyone else, but always insisted that the Tories must and would win a governing majority alone.

Although it enraged her at the time, the Lib-Lab pact and the whole twilight period of the Labour Government's deathbed monetarism worked to Mrs Thatcher's advantage in the long run. Had she come to power in 1977 she personally would have been less experienced, less confident and less prepared for office than she was in 1979, while the tide of intellectual and public opinion which eventually carried her into Downing Street and made possible – just – the uncompromising economic policies which she and Geoffrey Howe pursued in 1980–1, would not have been so strong. When the Tories did return to power, it was immensely helpful that Healey and Callaghan had already been keeping a tight grip on monetary policy for the past two years. It is a recurring pattern in politics that when one party reluctantly adopts the other's policies, the electorate tends to go for the party which actually believes in them. Thus in 1951 Labour had started dismantling wartime controls but Churchill was voted back to 'set the people free', while in 1964 Wilson seemed a more credible champion of modernisation and regional planning than Macmillan and Douglas-Home. 'If you want a Conservative government', she told listeners to Jimmy Young's morning radio programme in 1978, 'you'd better have a Conservative government and not a half-hearted Labour government practising Conservative policies.'[177]

By May 1979 Callaghan and Healey had already made much of Mrs Thatcher's case for her, even before the public sector unions – by wrecking Labour's central claim that it alone could control inflation without industrial confrontation – completed the job. Labour's apparent recovery in 1977–8 was temporarily alarming for Mrs Thatcher; but all the time – as Callaghan privately realised, and as she had always confidently maintained – the Tories were winning the underlying argument. The Lib-Lab pact did neither the Liberals nor Labour much good; for Mrs Thatcher it turned out to be a blessing in disguise which contributed greatly to her ultimate victory.

12

Thatcherism under Wraps

THE years of opposition were a peculiarly difficult and ambiguous time for Margaret Thatcher. She was a woman of strong convictions and a powerful sense of mission whose instinct, once she unexpectedly found herself leader, was to lead from the front. Yet at the same time, she was very conscious of the weakness of her political position, a little frightened of her own inexperience and the heavy responsibility which had suddenly been thrown upon her, and well aware of the formidable combination of habit, convention and vested interest that was ranged against her. She did not have the authority to impose a thoroughgoing free-market agenda on the Tory party, let alone project it unambiguously to the country. Moreover even if she had been in a position to proclaim her long-term vision, there was a huge gap between knowing what was right in theory and translating that knowledge into practical policies that could be compressed into a manifesto.

Even after she achieved power, and a political dominance she could never have imagined in 1975, it still took her the best part of two terms, with the full resources of the civil service at her command, to begin to frame an explicitly 'Thatcherite' programme. So long as she was in opposition her overriding priority was to make sure she did not lose the General Election, whenever it came. She could not risk getting too far ahead of her party, so had to disclaim objectives which might alarm the voters or allow her opponents to label her 'extreme'. She had to be prepared to fight on a vague prospectus that gave only the broadest hint of her true ambition. As a result, for the whole of this period in opposition, she was obliged to speak with two voices – one clear, didactic and evangelical, the other cautious, moderate and conventional – displaying a confusing mixture of confidence and caution. Right up to May 1979 no colleague or commentator could be sure which was the real Margaret Thatcher.

It is not even certain that she knew herself. Looking back from the perspective of the 1990s, Lady Thatcher in her memoirs naturally subscribes to the heroic legend of a leader who knew very clearly from the outset what she wanted to achieve and was only constrained to dissemble her intentions by her dependence on colleagues less clear-sighted and resolute than herself. And of course there is plenty of evidence to support this view. '*This* is what we believe,' she famously told a seminar at the Centre for Policy Studies, producing from her handbag a well-worn copy of Hayek's *The Constitution of Liberty* and banging it down on the table.[1] More than once she announced that her purpose was nothing less than to eliminate what she called socialism permanently from British public life. 'Our aim is not just to remove a uniquely incompetent Government from office,' she declared in May 1976. 'It is to destroy the whole fallacy of socialism that the Labour party exists to spread.'[2] At least some of the time she believed that she could do it. 'All over the world', she told John Cole, deputy editor of the *Observer*, with what he called 'the hammer beat of a doctrinaire non-doubter', 'the long night of collectivism was receding'. 'You had only to talk to her in the couple of years before the election to savour her self-confidence.'[3] Another time she gave a private audience of 'selected bankers and industrialists' what turned out to be an astonishingly accurate foretaste of the revolution she actually accomplished in the next decade.

> Mrs Thatcher made a particular effort to convince her audience not only that she was committed to wealth creation, a free market and lower taxation, but that she would abolish exchange controls, foster denationalisation, cut down local authorities and not give in to any union, even to the mineworkers.[4]

This was 'a bravura triumph', the CBI historian Keith Middlemas comments, but it is not surprising that 'it left many sceptics', since it was in such contrast to the caution of her public statements. Rarely if ever did Mrs Thatcher speak in public of abolishing exchange controls or serious denationalisation, still less of curbing local authorities or renewing the Tories' battle with the miners. In an ideal world all may have been among her long-term aspirations, but it is doubtful if she ever imagined that any of them would become practical politics. In the short term she thought more in terms of stopping things than of pursuing a radical agenda of her own. Her repeated refrain to colleagues and advisers from the think-tanks who told her what she should do in office was 'Don't tell me *what*. I know what. Tell me *how*.'[5]

Over lunch at the Institute of Economic Affairs the godfather of monetarist economics, Professor Milton Friedman, urged her that the first thing she must do was to scrap exchange controls. Mrs Thatcher listened intently, then wrote to Ralph Harris the next day expressing her agreement. 'But how can I carry my party?'[6] 'Despite her deep emotional and intellectual sympathy with the monetarist and libertarian thesis,' Cosgrave wrote in 1978, 'she realises that a remarkable and perhaps unprecedented degree of consistent and powerful public support would be necessary to give it a trial in policy.'[7] It was by no means certain that the necessary public support would ever be attainable, even if she won the election. As Prime Minister, it is clear from the memoirs of Nigel Lawson, Geoffrey Howe and others that Mrs Thatcher was often the last to be persuaded that key 'Thatcherite' policies, from the scrapping of exchange controls to the reform of the National Health Service – however desirable in principle – were in fact practicable or politically prudent. She was still more hesitant in opposition.

There were certainly times in these years when her confidence slipped. 'There were moments in those early months', Cosgrave recalled, 'when she appeared frail and tired beyond belief. If hearts did not fail, not a few fluttered.'[8] One young research assistant whom she inherited from Heath remembers the first time he went to the Leader of the Opposition's room to brief her for Prime Minister's Questions. He found her watering the plants with which she had tried to brighten up the dingy room and looking utterly exhausted. Her first words were, 'I don't know how Ted Heath did this for ten years.'[9] A couple of years later the young Michael Portillo had the job of taking the leader through her press coverage, not all of it by that time complimentary. 'You are battering me,' she told him. 'Every day you are battering me. Just because I'm Leader of the Opposition doesn't mean I don't need a bit of encouragement.'[10]

Some time around 1977 the novelist Kingsley Amis – another of that band of former Labour supporters who had fallen under Mrs Thatcher's spell – was invited to dinner in Flood Street. In his memoirs he wrote a vivid account of his evening. The house he described as 'one of those neat little joints between the King's Road and the Chelsea Embankment, comfortable but ungrand and decorated in a boldly unadventurous style'. The food likewise was 'properly unimaginative' but 'as regards drink, ample enough'. Mrs Thatcher herself he considered 'one of the best looking women I have ever met for her age'. He also noted Denis's 'deference towards his wife . . . at once respectful and ready to argue'; and was irritated by Mark's 'over-attentive conduct of his lighter'. But the real interest of the evening was Mrs Thatcher anticipating the possibility of losing the coming election:

> People have always said that the next election will be crucial. But this one really will be, and if it doesn't go the way Denis and I want then we'll stay, because we'll always stay. But we'll work very hard with the children to set them up with careers in Canada.

This bizarre idea, reminiscent of Churchill sending his children to America at the beginning of the war, crystallised for Amis the impression of 'a truly tough-minded person'.[11] On the contrary, one might feel that it reveals the very readiness to give up on Britain that she condemned in others and an extraordinary protectiveness towards her now 24-year-old children. The belief that it was up to Denis and herself to set them up in careers sits oddly with the gospel of enterprise and self-reliance; but it certainly confirms her apocalyptic view of the coming election.

'A complex compound of faith and caution' was Peter Thorneycroft's summing-up of Mrs Thatcher after four years of observing her at close quarters.

> She believed passionately that abominable things had been going on in the country and was depressed at how the country had become unproductive, undisciplined and defenceless. In private she spoke out quite freely about this. Yet on a public platform the woman's innate caution tempered her conclusions.[12]

The truth is that caution was just as integral a component of Margaret Thatcher's character as faith. She was pretty sure she would only get one chance, and as an ambitious politician she did not intend to blow it. Nor was it simply that she dare not risk commitments that might split the party. She always had a superstitious fear of giving hostages to fortune, counting chickens or crossing bridges before she came to them. The lesson of how Hugh Gaitskell – 'the best leader Labour ever had' – was reckoned to have lost the 1959 election by promising not to raise income tax was 'deeply etched on her mind';[13] and she thought that Ted Heath in opposition before 1970 had lost sight of the wood for the trees, leaving him with no sense of direction when he came in to office. 'I sometimes think we got our policies too detailed in 1969–70,' she wrote to Alec

Home soon after she took over, 'so much so that we didn't realise the nature of some of the problems had already changed.'[14] She hated the detailed pledges Heath had forced her to make on rates and mortgages in October 1974. Back in 1968 she had argued in her lecture to the Conservative Political Centre that elections should not be turned into competitive auctions. Now she seized on an essay by the political scientist S. E. Finer which lent academic authority to her distrust of the modern doctrine of the mandate, and quoted it triumphantly to her aides.[15] She believed that politics should be a contest between opposed philosophies, not catchpenny bribes. Her purpose was to win the battle of ideas.

Thus it was because she had faith that she could afford to be cautious. She was confident that the correct policies would become clear in time so long as she got the direction right. In the meantime she could compromise, bide her time and go along with policies in which, in her heart, she fundamentally disbelieved – as she had been doing, after all, for most of her career – with no fear that she would thereby lose sight of her objective or be blown off course. She felt no contradiction, for example, in telling David Butler and Dennis Kavanagh that she was utterly opposed in principle to the trade union closed shop, but recognised that for the moment she had to live with it. She explained that politics was all about timing. You could kill a good idea by floating it five years ahead of its time, she told them; but two years ahead it could take off. Judging the right moment was the test of 'real political leadership'.[16]

It was one of her harshest critics, Enoch Powell – finally converted to grudging admiration – who perhaps most shrewdly analysed Mrs Thatcher's unusual ability to compartmentalise her mind, distinguishing the tactical from the strategic and pursuing both simultaneously on different time scales. Characteristically he saw it as a specifically feminine quality:

> The consonance between thoughts and words is something in which she is basically not interested. This – as well as being a woman – enables her year after year to live with something, with a cross on a paper at the back of her mind saying 'I don't agree with that, I don't like it . . . but I can't do anything about it at the moment'. It's not exactly the mood of a person who says, 'I'm trapped'; it's more the mood of a person who says, 'I don't like that. When I can settle accounts with that, I will settle accounts with it.'[17]

In this way she contrived to fight the 1979 General Election on a manifesto that was simultaneously radical and vague, winning what was effectively a blank cheque for policies that were never spelled out. This was not dishonest or cynical on her part, since she made her fundamental values and her vision of the sort of Britain she would like to see perfectly clear to anyone who read between the lines of her speeches – or rather to anyone who believed that she actually meant what she said. It was rather that she possessed – instinctively – an exceptionally clear grasp of the art of the possible. R. A. Butler's famous definition of politics is usually interpreted as a minimalist excuse for doing only what you can. Mrs Thatcher's purpose, by contrast, was always to do as much as she could, when she could. She could not know in 1975, or in 1979, how much would become possible in the years ahead. After 1979, and particularly after 1983, opposition fell away and the horizon opened up before her to an extent that she could not have imagined in 1975. Yet she always had in her head the map which told her the road she should be following if and when it turned out to be passable. Even then she still proceeded cautiously. Mrs Thatcher liked to call herself a 'conviction politician'; a less heroic way of saying the same thing would be to call her a principled opportunist.

To win the battle of ideas Mrs Thatcher recognised that she had first to educate herself. Having come to the leadership so unexpectedly she knew she had an immense amount to learn, not merely to master the whole field of politics and government – where previously she had only had to cover one department at a time – but to equip herself intellectually to seize the opportunity which confronted her. In the twelve months since February 1974 she had sat at the feet of Keith Joseph, Alfred Sherman and Alan Walters and begun to appreciate the scale of the counter-revolution against collectivism that had suddenly taken off. She had responded instinctively to its objectives; but now in February 1975 she had to lead it. With characteristic application, but remarkable humility, she set about learning what she needed to understand about the theory and practice of the free market and its place in Tory philosophy.

Her attitude to intellectuals was ambivalent. In theory she believed in education and had inherited from her father a deep reverence for learning. In practice, however, her experience as Education Secretary had left her with a dim view of the universities and minimal respect for the majority of tenured academics – particularly those in the arts and social sciences – whom she regarded stereotypically as lazy, state-subsidised parasites, cynically abusing the privileged freedom which they enjoyed. Moreover, as the critic and travel writer Jonathan Raban pointed out in 1989, she was temperamentally anti-intellectual. She believed in convictions, not ideas. 'An idea is debatable by definition. A conviction ("a settled persuasion", *OED*) is not.'[18] Of course she enjoyed a good argument, but she had no time for what the most intellectual of all her predecessors, A. J. Balfour, once called 'philosophic doubt'. She lacked not only a sense of humour, but an intellectual's sense of irony and paradox. She regarded the enjoyment of ideas for their own sake as either a frivolous self-indulgence or, worse, a substitute for action. ('The native hue of resolution', she might have echoed Hamlet, 'is sicklied o'er with the pale cast of thought.') Paying tribute to Clement Attlee, who died in December 1976, Mrs Thatcher praised him for possessing 'an exceptionally clear mind – and in politics that is every bit as important as a highly intellectual mind and sometimes more so'.[19] No one who heard her can have doubted that she was thinking of herself. She prided herself on being above all a practical politician. 'She thought that certain things were obvious and was reluctant to call them ideas,' John Ranelagh wrote in his book *Thatcher's People*. 'If asked, she would say that they were the conclusions of a practical person.'[20] In a radio interview in 1990 marking the bicentenary of Adam Smith she insisted: 'A market economy is not a theory . . . A market place is a community.'[21] She always took it for granted that what she believed was not theory, but common sense.

On the other hand she was rare among politicians in recognising the importance of ideas. Seeing politics as a battleground of opposed philosophies, she valued, even revered, the small minority of maverick intellectuals – many of them, like Sherman and Robert Conquest, defiantly independent of the universities – who rejected the progressive consensus and could help her articulate her contempt for it. She knew that she needed the technical analysis and philosophic framework which such people could give her. Yet she never confused their role with hers. She learned from them, but never tried to ape them or pretended to be an intellectual herself. She always remained the practical politician, who developed an exceptional ability to translate complex abstractions into her own down-to-earth political language; she never fell into the trap – as Keith Joseph often did – of sounding like an academic manqué or, worse, a schoolgirl parroting ideas she did not fully understand. Though an immense amount of diligent reading and listening went into the preparation of her speeches, it was very rarely visible. She assimilated her homework seamlessly into her own corner-shop wisdom. She dealt not in ideas, but in values.

Thus Mrs Thatcher did not lead the counter-revolution which came to bear her name. Like Churchill voicing the bulldog's roar, she was lucky enough to come to power at just the moment when it was gathering strength and so was called upon to embody and express it, which she did with force and clarity. Nor did she swallow all the far-out notions floated over the next few years; she never forgot that her first task was to win the coming election. But more than any other Leader of the Opposition in history she encouraged unorthodox thinking – directly by her patronage of the plethora of think-tanks and ginger groups which were suddenly springing up all round the right-wing fringes of the Tory party, and also indirectly by the sense of challenge to the failed Keynesian collectivist ideology which her election represented. At a time of deep national demoralisation, her rhetoric of radical regeneration struck a note of urgency and passionate determination which gave the thinkers and dreamers of the New Right the belief that she – unlike Heath, Wilson or any previous leader since the sense of national decline had taken hold – could actually make a difference. 'In the beginning was the mood', Sherman recalled, 'and the mood became Thatcher.'[22] She made it politically possible to 'think the unthinkable'.

The central institutions in this market place of ideas remained the Institute of Economic Affairs and the Centre for Policy Studies. The former, still presided over by Arthur Seldon and Ralph Harris, was quasi-academic and officially non-party; the latter, directed by Alfred Sherman under Joseph's chairmanship, more overtly political; but there was substantial overlap between the work done in both and the people who frequented them. The still relatively small group of politicians excited by the new economics included Nigel Lawson, Nicholas Ridley, David Howell and Jock Bruce-Gardyne, plus of course Geoffrey Howe, the Shadow Chancellor, taking the same sort of crash course in monetarism as Mrs Thatcher. Among the professional economists who instructed them – most of them from provincial universities – were Alan Walters (until he went to America in 1976), Patrick Minford, Alan Peacock, Terry Burns and Brian Griffiths, all of whom became key advisers in government after 1979. John Hoskyns, an energetic former army officer turned systems analyst, and Norman Strauss, a prickly corporate planner with Unilever, contributed an iconoclastic brand of business expertise. Brought together by Sherman to write a paper for Mrs Thatcher, they formed a stimulating double act which carried over into her first Policy Unit in Number Ten.

Perhaps equally important – not so much for their input as for their access to public opinion – were the journalists: William Rees-Mogg, Ronald Butt, Frank Johnson and Bernard Levin from *The Times*; Samuel Brittan of the *Financial Times*; Andrew Alexander of the *Daily Mail*; John O'Sullivan, T. E. Utley and Peregrine Worsthorne from the *Telegraph*, among others. As a former Communist who had traversed the whole political spectrum from far left to far right, Sherman was particularly good at drawing in other disillusioned socialist intellectuals such as Brian Crozier, John Vaizey, Hugh Thomas and Max Beloff. Sherman described the CPS at its zenith in the late 1970s as an 'intellectual bazaar' where unexpected people met informally for freelance discussion, less academic than a university high table but less bound by electoral considerations than official party bodies had to be.[23] 'People worked at the CPS', Strauss recalled, 'because they wanted to help create a new order.'[24] There was a heady whiff of revolution in the air.

Mrs Thatcher regularly attended lunches and seminars at both the CPS and IEA where papers were read and discussed, pamphlets drafted and material for speeches tried out. In this company, she mainly listened, absorbing the arguments and asking the occasional sharp question, then took away a lot of material to read. 'She was a very good listener,' Sherman recalled. Though he later became disillusioned with her, Strauss could not but concur: 'Where she knew she had to learn she was a very good pupil.'[25]

Even as leader, she was not embarrassed to play the pupil. Ralph Harris remembers an occasion when Milton Friedman came to the IEA, some time around 1978. Mrs Thatcher hung on his words like a schoolgirl, carefully writing down everything he said and asking intelligent but elementary questions, as though it was all quite new to her.[26] William Rees-Mogg has an identical memory of her on a similar occasion 'listening to Friedrich von Hayek like a schoolgirl, her face glowing with attention'.[27] She always showed extraordinary deference towards the high priests of her faith. Even in the maturity of her memoirs Lady Thatcher describes meeting the former German Chancellor Ludwig Erhard – the architect of Germany's postwar economic miracle – on her first visit to West Germany as leader in 1975. 'He asked me a number of searching questions about my economic approach, at the end of which he seemed satisfied. I felt I had performed well in an important tutorial.'[28]

Once she had learned something Mrs Thatcher never forgot it, but stored it away with almost photographic recall for future use. 'Unlike most politicians,' one member of her staff told Ranelagh, 'she has no desire to be trendy, no desire to have new ideas . . . She just puts her head down and ploughs through, going on with the same themes repeatedly and identically.'[29] Ideas, to her severely practical mind, were expected to earn their keep. Accordingly she had much less time for the more speculative expressions of Tory soul-searching in these years, such as the Conservative Philosophy Group, set up by the academic philosophers Roger Scruton and John Casey in collaboration with Hugh Fraser and the self-proclaimed 'young meteor' Jonathan Aitken. Many of the same cast of anti-socialist and anti-corporatist journalists and politicians – including on occasion Enoch Powell – met, usually in Aitken's house in Lord North Street, to hear a paper on some aspect of Tory thinking: by contrast with the IEA and the CPS, the emphasis was on the need to balance the economic liberalism of the New Right by stressing older Tory values of hierarchy, continuity and social cohesion. Mrs Thatcher attended two or three times, but when she did so, in Scruton's recollection, 'she was more concerned to talk than to listen'. She was inevitably the centre of attention and the nature of the discussion changed.[30] It was the same when she dined at Peterhouse, Cambridge, another hotbed of self-consciously reactionary High Toryism later reputed to have been one of the nurseries of Thatcherism. The story is told that on one occasion someone remarked after dinner that the place looked like a night club. 'If it is a night club', she said, throwing off her jacket, 'you'd better have my cabaret', and proceeded to amaze her overwhelmingly male audience by answering questions, brilliantly, for two hours.[31]

She did find one guru at Peterhouse, the ecclesiastical historian Edward Norman, whose book *Church and Society in Modern England*, published in 1976, developed the idea of a natural congruence between Christianity and Conservatism, based on the moral superiority of the free market, which left the individual the responsibility of choice, over state provision which rendered him a 'moral cripple'. But this was something Mrs Thatcher had learned in childhood – it was the basis of her father's teaching back in Finkin Street. She was glad to have high-powered theological support. 'Dr Norman,' she exclaimed gratefully, 'you are a prophet.'[32] At a time when conscience and morality in politics were widely assumed to be a monopoly of the left, Norman reinforced her conviction that Conservatives should stop apologising for capitalism and claim the moral high ground for the right. But essentially all that Mrs Thatcher drew from her academic admirers was gratifying confirmation of what she already believed. In 1984 the Master of Peterhouse, the historian Maurice Cowling, wrote to *The Times* to deny the exaggerated claims being made for the influence of the 'Peterhouse mafia': 'I do not believe that the "intellectuals" most usually mentioned in this connection – Dr Casey, Dr Scruton, Dr Norman and the Conservative Philosophy and Salisbury Groups – have ever had the slightest influence on Mrs Thatcher's policies.'[33]

Roger Scruton agrees that the Conservative Philosophy Group had 'no input whatsoever into her formation' before 1979.[34] It was only many years later – after she left office – that Lady Thatcher began to take a belated interest in the warnings of the Salisbury Group – published quarterly in Scruton's *Salisbury Review* – that an excessive emphasis on the free market had dissolved the traditional bonds of family, church and civic order which she also valued. Thatcherism drew its strength from a potent mix of economic liberalism with social conservatism: but the former was always the more active ingredient. Hayek, Friedman and Sherman influenced Mrs Thatcher far more powerfully than the likes of Edward Norman and Roger Scruton.

The main theme of all her speeches in these years was simple. One day very soon – 'and it will be a day just like any other Thursday' – the British electorate would face a simple choice between opposed governing philosophies: on the one hand what she loosely labelled socialism, and others would call social democracy, corporatism, Keynesianism or the mixed economy; on the other 'what socialists call capitalism and I prefer to call the free economy'.[35] When a Labour MP interrupted her in the Commons to ask her what she meant by socialism she was at a loss to reply.[36] What in fact she meant was Government support for inefficient industries, punitive taxation, regulation of the labour market, price controls – everything that interfered with the functioning of the free economy. She accepted that many of these evils were in practice unavoidable. Even so, there were in principle, as she put it in her speech to the West German Christian Democrats, 'only two political philosophies, only two ways of governing a country', however many party labels might be invented to obscure the fact: the Marxist-socialist way, which put the interest of the state first, and the way of freedom, which put people first.[37]

Moderate Western forms of democratic socialism as practised by the German Social Democrats or the British Labour party she regarded contemptuously as merely watered down versions of Marxism without the courage of Moscow's convictions. It fitted her political model perfectly that the Labour party – under the influence of its increasingly dominant left wing – was becoming ever more openly Marxist. True to Hayek, she believed that socialism was a slippery slope – literally the road to serfdom – which would lead inexorably to Communism if the slide was not halted and reversed. 'The Labour party is now committed to a programme which is frankly and unashamedly Marxist,' she told the 1976 conference. 'Let us not mince words. The dividing line between the Labour party programme and Communism is becoming harder and harder to detect.'[38] Hence she did not, like other Tory leaders in the past, attribute the failures of the Labour Government merely to incompetence or inefficiency, but to fundamental error, which in her more generous moments she could recognise as well-intentioned. Labour Governments, she believed – and Tory ones when they fell into socialist fallacies – inevitably caused inflation, unemployment and stagnation because socialism was by its very nature simply wrong. It was wrong in practice, since self-evidently it did not work: and the reason it did not work was because it was morally wrong. It was essentially immoral and contrary to everything that she believed was best in human nature.

There was nothing original in this analysis, but like her description of the Soviet Union as a brutal dictatorship bent on world domination, her expression of it was extraordinarily blunt and unvarnished. No Conservative leader had spoken in such uncompromising terms for years. No leading Tory except Enoch Powell had dared to use the dirty word capitalism so unapologetically. Powell once said that he went down on his knees every morning to thank God for the gift of capitalism: but the only time Heath ever used the word was to condemn 'Tiny' Rowland's Anglo-African trading company Lonrho as the 'unacceptable face of capitalism', with the implication that capitalism itself was pretty unsavoury.[39] At a time when the ruling cultural ethos was still overwhelmingly if vaguely leftish, with a widespread assumption that progress was inevitably towards greater equality enforced by enlightened government action, Mrs Thatcher's defiant assertion of the practical and ethical superiority of capitalism, her ringing defence of the morality of seeking to make a profit, and her evangelical presentation of politics as a clear choice between black and white, not messy, pragmatic shades of grey, was shocking, refreshing or naive, according to choice. 'We must fight socialism wherever we find it,' she proclaimed in May 1976. 'Our aim . . . is to destroy . . . the whole fallacy of socialism.'[40] The very idea that socialism could be refuted, let alone destroyed, was breathtaking.

Her fullest exposition of the inherent superiority of capitalism was delivered, not in Britain but to the Zurich Economic Society. Patrick Cosgrave may exaggerate when he calls this 'the most prestigious platform available to a European politician';[41] but there was certainly piquancy in Britain's alternative Prime Minister expounding her capitalist vision in May 1977 to an audience largely composed of those very financiers – Wilson's famous 'gnomes of Zurich' – to whom the British Government had just gone cap-in-hand for credit. The Zurich text was written for her by Alfred Sherman; but the same arguments and some of the same phrases recur in many of her other speeches to domestic audiences. First she argued that the essential *material* failure of socialism was that 'the public sector can only live on private enterprise, on whose surplus it relies'.

> More and more of the taxpayer's money has been pumped into companies that no prudent banker could go on supporting for long, because instead of creating wealth they use up wealth created by others.

As well as punitive levels of taxation, the Government had to borrow vast sums to finance the public sector; and when this was not enough it turned to printing money, leading to the threat of hyperinflation, which undermined the very basis of society.

> And when the economic foundations are undermined, those who suffer most are the ordinary working people, the very people in whose name the socialists claim to be acting.

By contrast, she maintained, it was 'our system, the free enterprise system, which delivers the goods to the great mass of the people'. She gloried in pointing out that the Soviet Union had to import grain and technology from the West. When countries like Britain got into trouble it was to the capitalist economies of the IMF, not the socialist East, that they turned for help. Above all she stressed that capitalism did not, as the socialists claimed, benefit only the rich. On the contrary, she insisted, quoting the economist Josef Schumpeter, this was to misconceive 'the very essence of the capitalist achievement'.

> The capitalist engine is first and last an engine of mass production
> . . . It is the cheap cloth, the cheap fabric, boots, motor cars and so on that are the typical achievements of capitalist production.

'In brief', she insisted, 'the material superiority of the free society gives its main benefits to the very people the socialists claim to cherish.'[42]

More important than the material failure of socialism, however, was its *political* bankruptcy. Socialism by its controlling nature, she argued at Zurich and elsewhere, concentrated power in the state, leading to creeping centralisation, the denial of democracy, the loss of a host of individual freedoms, the corruption inherent in arbitrary powers and consequent disrespect for the rule of law. As examples she pointed to the Labour Government's pardoning of the Clay Cross councillors who had defied the Tories' Housing Finance Act;[43] the growing practice of companies rewarding their employees with perks (company cars and Christmas hampers) to get round pay controls;[44] and the Labour Attorney-General's weaselly defence of 'lawful intimidation' by trade union bullies in industrial disputes.[45] She regularly cited the figure widely quoted by economists that essential freedoms became endangered when more than 60 per cent of GNP was taken by the state; and warned that Labour, in exceeding that figure, was taking the country by 'rapid strides towards the Iron Curtain state'.[46] Capitalism by contrast, by leaving economic decisions to the choice of millions of individuals spending their own money in the market place, dispersed power from politicians to ordinary people, thus safeguarding freedom and democracy. Most provocatively, she – or Sherman – pointed to the growth of pension funds, life insurance, unit trusts and other manifestations of what she called 'the people's capitalism' to predict the blurring of the old Marxist divide between capitalists and workers, shareholders and employees. Already by these means, she claimed, '85 per cent of the population has an indirect, if not direct, share in British industry . . . We may soon be witnessing the withering away of the class struggle.' She always enjoyed turning her opponent's phrases to her own use.

Finally, she developed a powerful argument to prove the *moral* superiority of capitalism which over the next decade she made distinctively her own. 'The economic success of the Western world', she argued, 'is a product of its moral philosophy and practice. The economic results are better because the moral philosophy is superior. It is superior because it starts with the individual, with his uniqueness, his responsibility, and his capacity to choose.'

> Choice is the essence of ethics: if there were no choice, there would be no ethics, no good, no evil; good and evil have meaning only insofar as man is free to choose . . . The sense of being self-reliant, of playing a role within the family, of owning one's own property, of paying one's way, are all part of the spiritual ballast

which maintains responsible citizenship . . . That is what we mean by a moral society; not a society where the state is responsible for everything, and no one is responsible for the state.[47]

From this basic perception she went on in a number of other speeches to expound an individualist view of society which prized charity, philanthropy and voluntary service higher than collective state provision. In December 1976 she was booked to give a rare speech on social policy to a Social Services conference in Liverpool. She horrified her social services spokesman, Patrick Jenkin, by departing from the speech that had been written for her in order to stress instead her personal belief in the central importance of the family and the value of encouraging voluntary work in the community, providing services like meals on wheels. She barely mentioned the professional local authority social services at all. 'In some ways', she suggested, 'industry and trade are the basic social service because they provide a large number of jobs.'[48] Her audience of social workers had no idea what she was talking about.[49] She related this message explicitly to her Christian faith when she was invited to give an address from the pulpit of St Lawrence Jewry, in the City of London in March 1978. She praised 'the immense sacrifices which people will make for the care of their own near and dear – for elderly relatives, disabled children and so on – and the immense part which voluntary effort . . . has played in these fields.'

> Once you give people the idea that this can be done by the state . . . then you will begin to deprive human beings of one of the essential ingredients of humanity – personal moral responsibility. You will in effect dry up in them the milk of human kindness.

'So do not be tempted to identify virtue with collectivism,' she concluded. 'I wonder whether the state services would have done as much for the man who fell among thieves as the Good Samaritan did for him?'[50]

In a lecture in memory of Iain Macleod in July 1977, she placed this elevation of voluntary giving at the centre of her definition of Conservatism. The universal provision of welfare by the state, she argued, would eventually turn man into 'a moral cripple, in the same way as we should lose the faculty of walking, reading, seeing, if we were prevented from using them'. There followed a glowing tribute to the great age of philanthropy which had accompanied the burgeoning of free enterprise in the nineteenth century. Dr Barnardo's children's homes, the National Society for the Prevention of Cruelty to Children, the St John Ambulance Brigade and the Royal National Lifeboat Institution, all were founded and maintained by voluntary subscriptions. 'The Victorian age has been very badly treated in socialist propaganda', she maintained, but 'we who are largely living off the Victorians' moral and physical capital can hardly afford to denigrate them.'[51] This rosy picture of Victorian society was one to which she returned, with increasingly didactic intent, as Prime Minister.[*]

In other speeches she defended the individual's right to buy private education and health care, the right to home-ownership and the right to pass on wealth to children. These, she insisted, were *not* middle-class privileges which only benefited the few, but fundamental human rights, essential safeguards of every citizen's freedom from dependence on the state. In one of her favourite phrases she condemned the 'pocket money society' in which the state took all important decisions out of the individual's hands. 'We shall not have social responsibility', she told the House of Commons, 'unless, first, we have responsible individuals.'[53] In another Commons speech she explicitly asserted the right to inequality – 'If the only opportunity is to be equal, it is not opportunity' – and denied that there was any conflict between liberty and equality. A society which put equality before liberty, she argued, ended up with neither liberty nor equality; but the society which put liberty before equality would enjoy both.[54]

This was tendentious, simple-minded stuff which paid no regard to the complexity of modern society or the extremes of poverty, exploitation and inequality – inherited from the Victorians – which the twentieth-century welfare state had been created to relieve. While unquestionably the promotion of equality involves some sacrifice of liberty, the pursuit of liberty equally inevitably tends to promote inequality. The business of politics is about striking a balance – not denying that a balance must be struck. The idea that the refusal of government to regulate the free market conduces to equality in any but the purely legal sense is a flimsy cover for untrammelled greed, cruelly exposed in the 1980s in both Britain and America by the failure of the notion that the increased wealth of

---

[*] She was not always so keen on the nineteenth century. On *Any Questions?* in 1966 she had shuddered at the idea of going back a hundred years. '1866 wasn't a particularly attractive age in any way. The architecture was appalling. Albert had cast his influence over everything ... and families ... even the wealthiest of them, didn't enjoy the facilities and comforts that even comparatively moderate families enjoy today.'[52]

the rich and middle classes would somehow 'trickle down' to the poorest. To those who took it seriously, Mrs Thatcher's essentially nostalgic vision of Victorian philanthropy gave warning that she would seek to abandon – or at least reduce – the obligation to try to ameliorate poverty and social deprivation accepted by every previous Conservative Government since 1951. Yet there was little enough reason to take it seriously. While she lost no opportunity to hymn the benefits of liberty in the abstract, she was in practice very cautious about suggesting how her high moral sentiments might be embodied in policy.

Alongside all her talk about the iniquity and inefficiency of the public sector, for instance, Mrs Thatcher regularly cast herself as the defender of the mixed economy. She blamed Labour for unbalancing the mix by threatening to take more and more industries into public ownership, but never suggested that she intended to do anything more than rebalance it by selling back – if it were possible – the most recently nationalised industries, shipbuilding and aircraft manufacture. In a major speech to the Institute of Directors' annual convention at the Albert Hall in November 1976, she called for a definitive demarcation of the boundary between the public and private sectors. 'There is now an imperative need to stop the growth of government and to re-establish urgently just what the functions of government are.' But her practical prescription was merely that the Government should aim to 'balance its budget by matching expenditure with taxation and keeping borrowing to a strictly limited and manageable proportion'.

> I have no doubt that the role I have defined for government would permit some reduction in the burden of our taxation, although it would be wrong to promise that this could be done immediately.

She went on to talk about incentives, the restoration of differentials and freedom for the private sector to get on with the creation of wealth without political interference. What she did not suggest, even as a long-term goal, was any major redrawing of the boundary between private and public: she only appeared to want to get back to the position as it was when the Conservatives had left office in 1974.

> There is nothing in my description of the mixed economy which would offend the great majority of social democrats in the Western world. It could become part of the common currency of

British politics if our own social democrats would stand their ground.[55]

Ironically a truce in the sterile 'frontier war' between the private and public sectors was one of the principal planks in the platform of the SDP in the early 1980s. But by then Mrs Thatcher had moved on.

Likewise in this and other major speeches she always appeared to accept – if sometimes a little grudgingly – the obligations of welfare; what she called 'a long British tradition of community provision for education and welfare'.[56] In her Iain Macleod lecture she was at pains to align herself with the 'One Nation' tradition of Conservatism. She denied that the Tories were exclusively a free-market party. 'Free enterprise has a place – an honoured place – in our scheme of things, but as one of many dimensions.' She rejected 'the Marxist view which gives pride of place to economics': Conservatives recognised that man was 'a social creature, born into family, clan, community, nation brought up in mutual dependence. The founders of our religion made this a cornerstone of morality.' She claimed to share the same social concerns in 1977 that inspired Macleod's generation after the war.

> Because the postwar Keynesian recipe of endless growth and full employment through high demand levels went sour, this does not mean we turn our backs on the aspirations which underlay the 1944 White Paper on Employment Policy.

She spoke of 'new challenges' and the need to find 'a better balance . . . between the hardship we see and are moved to mitigate through the welfare system and the reaction we create when taxes fall too heavily on the taxpayer'.[57] Between the lines, it could be deduced that her preferred balance would be rather different from that struck after the war; but she managed simultaneously to invoke continuity and change, without suggesting a radical break with the postwar welfare settlement.

Thus in her speech to the Liverpool Social Services conference she suggested that personal social services might have expanded rather too fast in 1970–5 – the minister responsible was of course Keith Joseph – raising expectations that were not sustainable in the current state of the economy; but she never suggested cutting the present provision. She talked of simplifying and targeting the social security system on those in greatest need; but that had been a declared objective of Tory policy ever since 1950. She always implied – and often explicitly stated – that one of the chief purposes of getting the economy right and increasing the national wealth was to be able to afford better social services. 'The Government have failed', she charged in the confidence debate which finally precipitated the General Election in 1979, 'and the social services of other nations consequently have overtaken ours.'[58] She was no different from any other opposition leader in wanting to give the impression that there would be more of everything when she got in.

She constantly accused Labour of extremism and socialist dogma, while insisting on her own moderation, balance and above all 'common sense'. 'I am extremely careful never to be extreme,' she told the party conference – with perhaps an element of self-parody – in 1977. Even as she declared war on socialism, she wanted to be seen to be making a classless – even non-party – appeal to 'millions who are Conservatives and millions who are not'.[59] Her speech to the 1976 conference ended with an appeal to classless inclusivity. 'Today', she declared, 'we are all working people. Today it is the Conservatives and not the Socialists who represent the true interests and hopes and aspirations of the working people.'

> I call the Conservative Party now to a crusade. Not only the Conservative Party. I appeal to all those men and women of goodwill who do not want a Marxist future for themselves or their children or their children's children. This is not just a fight about national solvency. It is a crusade not merely to put a temporary brake on Socialism, but to stop its onward march once and for all.

Pitching her appeal beyond the conference hall to 'all our people, Conservative and non-Conservative, trade unionists and non-trade unionists, those who have always been with us and those who have never been with us but are prepared to support us now because they put country before party', she concluded:

> Let no one be excluded from our crusade and let no one exclude himself. We are one nation. We may not know it with our brains but we know it with our roots ... Let nothing narrow or vindictive or self-righteous be any part of our crusade. Rather let us say with humility: 'We offer you hope and a new beginning. Together we shall meet the crisis of our country – and tomorrow the day will be ours.'[60]

Her use of the phrase 'One Nation' – the coded banner of the Heathite Tories – was another instance of Mrs Thatcher's brazen ability to steal her opponents' cherished symbols and give them a meaning of her own. In this case she gave 'One Nation' a patriotic twist quite different from the sense of social cohesion it normally carried. She did it again the following year, and the year after. In 1977, condemning Labour's ritual singing of 'The Red Flag', she boasted that 'the Conservative party, now and always, flies the flag of one nation – and that flag is the Union Jack' ('So much', she added, 'for my so-called extremism').[61] And in 1978 she hit on another variation which she would use again in various forms over the years: 'We must be one nation, or we shall be no nation.'[62]

She was shameless in beating the patriotic drum, not only at the seaside. 'We in the Conservative party believe that Britain is still great,' she proclaimed in her Kensington Town Hall speech and on numerous other occasions.[63] In her Macleod lecture she defined the Tories first and foremost as 'an essentially British party'.[64] She spoke proudly of Britain's unique democratic traditions and 'unparalleled contribution to the history of the human race';[65] and condemned Callaghan's devaluation of 'the British pound'.[66] Tony Benn noted that this was a language which the Tories had 'dropped when they became Europeans'.[67] The cosmopolitan Denis Healey complacently thought Mrs Thatcher's right-wing tub-thumping too 'repugnant' to pose a danger to Labour; but Peter Shore, a defiant Little Englander himself, recognised the appeal she made to working-class voters: 'Mrs Thatcher is beginning to reflect a genuine English nationalist feeling, a deep feeling about the English and how they see themselves in terms of their own history.'[68]

Even as she talked up the unique virtues of the British genius, however, Mrs Thatcher in these years frequently insisted that there was nothing peculiarly British about the common sense economic policies she was proposing. By contrast with a decade later, when she and her followers claimed to have pioneered the free-market counter-revolution and to have exported Thatcherism all round the world, she continually stressed at this time that she was merely urging Britain to follow the best practice of other, more successful countries, like Germany, which had much lower inflation, or Australia and New Zealand, which had already shown the way by rejecting socialism.[69] Particularly after the Government had been forced to go to the IMF for help, she felt that a degree of modesty was in order on Britain's part. 'Least of all do we feel qualified to offer advice to more successful nations, on whose bounty this Government's spendthrift measures have made us dependent.'[70] She constantly anticipated the global defeat of socialism, but saw Britain as just one country among the Western nations. At Zurich in 1977 she confidently predicted that 'the crisis of socialism' was at hand.

> I have reason to believe that the tide is beginning to turn against collectivism, socialism, statism, dirigism, whatever you call it . . . It is becoming increasingly obvious to many people who were intellectual socialists that socialism has failed to fulfil its promises, both in its more extreme form in the communist world, and in its compromise versions.

This was her faith, and she certainly hoped to play a part in giving the historical process a helping hand.

> History is made by people: its movement depends on small currents as well as great tides, on ideas, perceptions, will and courage, the ability to sense a trend, the will to act on intuition and understanding. It is up to us to give intellectual content and political direction to these new dissatisfactions with socialism in practice, with its material and moral failures; to convert disillusion into understanding.

If Britain caught the tide, she concluded, 'the last quarter of our century can initiate a new renaissance matching anything in our island's long and outstanding history'.[71] But she never claimed to be in the vanguard. 'Across the Western world the tide is turning', she asserted in her speech in the confidence debate which finally brought down the Callaghan Government, 'and soon the same thing will happen here.'[72]

Meanwhile, despite Mrs Thatcher's determination not to saddle herself with specific commitments, the Opposition had to have some policies. The process of developing them was conducted simultaneously on two fronts in a skilfully balanced state of rivalry reflecting the two wings of the party. In keeping with the strategy of presenting a moderate face to the electorate, and the necessity of keeping the party outwardly united, Mrs Thatcher was content to leave the official process of policy-making in the hands of the Conservative Research Department, directed by Chris Patten and Adam Ridley, fed by a network of backbench committees. Some were more active than others, and the process was nothing like so thorough as Heath's comprehensive policy exercise in 1965–70; but Mrs Thatcher was happy to encourage it as a harmless way of keeping her MPs out of mischief.

The CRD prepared briefs for members of the Shadow Cabinet and other front bench spokesmen, co-ordinated and published formal policy statements and was eventually responsible for drafting the manifesto. So long as they controlled this official process of policy formulation the party elders remained quietly confident that the flow of crazy ideas emanating from Joseph and Sherman would never come to anything and could be safely disregarded. 'Keith was always dashing off into the woods and coming back with a new stick between his teeth,' a 'well-placed moderate' (who sounds very like Patten) told Phillip Whitehead, 'but I don't think he had any practical effect on what went into documents or became party policy, except that he kept pushing back the shrubbery.'[73] If he did not invent it, Patten certainly popularised *Private Eye*'s nickname for Joseph – 'the Mad Monk' – which cruelly encapsulated the derision with which his intellectual agonies were regarded in the sensible centre of the party. Patten remembers the mixture of horror and incomprehension in the Research Department the first time Mrs Thatcher called herself a 'radical'.[74] Yet he never found her very radical in practice. 'In fact', he told Butler and Kavanagh, 'she was so cautious and sympathetic to the tolerant left-wing approach that there was a possible problem of party management keeping the right-wing happy at so moderate a position.'[75] The practical politicians of the CRD, as they saw themselves, felt simultaneously contemptuous and complacent about the new thinking coming out of the CPS.

For their part Sherman's 'Wilfred Street irregulars' were equally scornful of the CRD, who embodied exactly the sort of woolly and discredited corporatism they were bent on replacing. Sherman thought that Patten and Adam Ridley – usually supported by Thorneycroft and Neave – were always trying to stop Mrs Thatcher following her instincts – 'trying to stop her being Thatcherite'.[76] Frustrated as they were by her caution, however, they too were reassured by the belief that her heart was really with them: she would come out in her true colours once she had safely negotiated her way into office. She thus achieved an extraordinarily successful balancing act, keeping both wings of the party reasonably happy in the confidence that she would come down on their side when power eventually forced her to choose between her heart and her head.

Somewhere between the official remit of the Research Department and the guerrilla skirmishing of the CPS there was a good deal of important policy work being done on a freelance basis by shadow ministers, particularly Geoffrey Howe and his shadow Treasury team. Some of this Mrs Thatcher followed keenly; other options appear to have been worked up without her direct knowledge. In between there was a lot of thinking, planning and discussion which she was more or less aware of; but very little of this work found its way into her public pronouncements. Though she was evidently persuaded, for instance, by her private advisers from Milton Friedman to Professor Douglas Hague, that exchange controls should be abolished as soon as possible after winning office, the option never appeared in any policy document.* Howe, with Nigel Lawson, Adam Ridley and others, was of course working on the practicalities of abolition long before the election, but Mrs Thatcher made no commitment, in public or in private. The battle for her approval had to be undertaken from square one the day after she entered Number Ten.

Likewise Howe and Lawson were working on the theory and practice of measuring and controlling the money supply, laying the foundations of what became the Medium Term Financial Strategy, introduced in 1980; and Lord Cockfield, the Tory party's long-standing taxation expert, was working with Howe on possible tax reforms, above all the proposed switch of emphasis from direct to indirect taxation. (This *was* foreshadowed in the manifesto, though not to the extent that Howe – overcoming Mrs Thatcher's doubts – actually delivered in his first Budget.) As shadow Social Services Secretary, Patrick Jenkin – an old friend of Geoffrey Howe – did a lot of work exploring alternative ways of paying for the social services: taxing benefits, encouraging private health insurance, cutting the automatic link between pensions and earnings. Some of this agenda – notably the cutting of the earnings link – was quickly implemented after 1979, while other items only emerged as practical options as late as 1987. But none of it appeared on the party's banner in May 1979.

In retrospect the biggest dog that scarcely barked before 1979 was privatisation – or as it was then known 'denationalisation'. In his memoirs Nigel Lawson insists that he and others – Joseph, Howe, John Nott and David Howell – all saw privatisation as 'an essential plank of our policy right from the start'; but he admits that 'little detailed work [was] done on the subject in Opposition', on account of 'Margaret's understandable fear of frightening the floating voter'.[78] In fact Joseph asked Nicholas Ridley to look again at the report on the subject which he had written for Heath in 1969, which had then been firmly suppressed. 'It will be different this time,' Joseph assured him. 'I'm not sure I believed him,' Ridley wrote, 'but I set about it

---

* Douglas Hague, deputy director of Manchester Business School, was her personal adviser on matters of public finance. His work with Mrs Thatcher was kept secret because he was simultaneously a member of the Price Commission.[77]

with relish.'[79] He was right to be sceptical. When his updated report was leaked to *The Economist* in May 1978 – and duly denounced by Labour ministers as revealing the Tories' hidden agenda – it was once again hurriedly disowned. Moreover by comparison with the way privatisation actually took off after 1982, Ridley's anticipation of what might be feasible was strikingly cautious. The emphasis of his new report was mainly on ways of enforcing tighter financial discipline on the nationalised industries, with the possibility that this might eventually lead on to denationalisation; even then he envisaged breaking up monopolies by hiving off profitable subsidiary operations which could be sold as separate businesses to the workers who worked in them, rather than selling whole industries to the public as actually transpired. Ridley raised the possibility of nationalising the electricity grid, splitting the telephone network from the Post Office and ending the telephone monopoly; but he did not think it would ever be practical to privatise gas, electricity or water supply.[80]

Mrs Thatcher's nervousness of the subject was demonstrated in March 1978 when Howe floated the suggestion that a Tory Government might sell some of the Government holding in BP. She firmly denied any such intention.[81] Soon afterwards, ironically, the Labour Government started selling BP shares as a way of raising money for the Treasury. In 1979 the Tory manifesto promised to 'offer to sell back to private ownership the recently nationalised aerospace and shipbuilding concerns, giving their employees the opportunity to purchase shares'; to try to sell shares in the National Freight Corporation; and to open up bus services to private operators. Beyond that it promised only that a Tory Government would 'interfere less' with the management of the nationalised industries and set them 'a clearer financial discipline in which to work'.[82] For all Mrs Thatcher's brave talk of reversing socialism, the thrust of Howe and Lawson's preparatory work in opposition – as it remained for the first three years in government – was on ways of controlling the cost of the public sector, not on fantasies of eliminating it.

Mrs Thatcher actually allowed only one general statement of Conservative policy to be officially published by the party between February 1975 and the 1979 manifesto. This was *The Right Approach*, a studiously bland document whose sole purpose was to paper over the evident differences in approach between the two wings of the party before the 1976 conference. With hindsight it is just possible to read *The Right Approach* as a prospectus of radical Thatcherism foreshadowing, as one writer has claimed, 'the end of consensus politics'.[83] But that was not how it was read at the time. On the contrary it was widely welcomed as an elegant restatement – unusually well written by Maude and Patten – of long-standing and generally uncontentious Conservative objectives: lower public spending, reduced borrowing, lower taxes, less state interference, all leading to a thriving mixed economy. But these goals were no different from Heath's in 1970: insufficient detail was offered to explain why Mrs Thatcher might be any more successful in achieving them than he had been. 'Again and again', *The Times* noted, 'the word commonsense is used' – as though common sense were a policy in itself.[84] For instance, the document's concluding section summed up the party's purpose in the blandest terms: 'In our economy today, and in every area of policy and public administration, we want to re-establish balance and common sense: this may seem a prosaic objective, but in Britain today it is essential.'[85] To detect any radical intent in such banalities required a keen ear for what Mrs Thatcher, once in office, might mean by balance and common sense. While expounding a conventionally anti-collectivist philosophy from which no Conservative could possibly dissent, *The Right Approach* specifically repudiated no element of the party's record in government before 1974 and emphasised continuity, rather than any fundamental break with Heath's approach. To ensure that they did not rock the boat, both Heath and Peter Walker were invited to approve the text before it was published.

Above all *The Right Approach* left open the critical question of incomes policy. There was simply no way a Shadow Cabinet containing Reggie Maudling, Jim Prior and Ian Gilmour, to say nothing of Willie Whitelaw and Peter Thorneycroft, would agree to abandon the blunt but trusted weapon of pay restraint in favour of Keith Joseph's new-fangled enthusiasm for controlling inflation by monetary means alone. They remembered how rashly Iain Macleod, as Heath's Shadow Chancellor, had insisted on categorically ruling out a return to incomes policy in 1970, and were determined that the party should not make the same mistake again. Nor was Mrs Thatcher so clear on the subject as she later became. Her first few Commons speeches were still confused about the causes of inflation; and Nigel Lawson remembers her as having been 'somewhat ambivalent' on the subject. He points – with some relish – to a conversation recorded by the then Irish Foreign Minister, Garret Fitzgerald, who met Mrs Thatcher for the first time at a conference in Turkey in April 1975 and found her very conscious of 'the inadequacy of the money supply approach'. She told him that 'if inflation were very high an incomes policy was necessary, but there should be a statutory policy for only a very short time'.[86] Throughout the next four years the overwhelming consensus of the business leaders she met when she spoke to the CBI or lunched in City boardrooms reinforced the message that the Tories would be mad to abandon the option of incomes policy. Accordingly *The Right Approach*, while stressing the importance of controlling the money supply and admitting the failures of past pay policies, frankly hedged its bets:

> Restraint in pay bargaining does not necessarily imply the adoption of a fully-fledged 'prices and incomes policy'. Experience does not suggest that this is the best way of finding a long-term solution to the problem. That same experience demonstrates the unwisdom of flatly and permanently denying the idea.[87]

In her memoirs Lady Thatcher calls this formula 'a fudge – but temporarily palatable'.[88] As time passed, however, she became increasingly impatient with it. More than once she tried to repudiate it, but she was always pulled back into line. Speaking in North Wales in November 1976, for instance, she declared boldly that she would 'never have any kind of incomes policy'. Challenged in the House two days later by Healey and Eric Varley she had to correct herself: 'I do not believe in a statutory incomes policy, but I believe in a voluntary incomes policy.'[89] Of course this could mean anything or nothing; what mattered was that she was obliged to maintain the agreed position. In 1977 the formula was restated in a second document entitled *The Right Approach to the Economy*, another all-things-to-all-men compromise edited by Angus Maude and published over the signatures of Howe, Joseph, Prior and David Howell.

> In framing its monetary and other policies the Government must come to *some* conclusions about the likely scope for pay increases, if excess public expenditure or large scale unemployment is to be avoided; and this estimate cannot be concealed from representatives of employers and unions whom it is consulting.[90]

Mrs Thatcher was less happy with this than with *The Right Approach*: she was particularly suspicious of Howe's persistent interest in a German-style tripartite economic forum, bringing together Government, employers and unions in some form of beefed-up NEDC, reminiscent of Heathite corporatism. 'We should recognise', she witheringly told her Shadow Chancellor, 'that the German talking shop works because it consists of Germans.'[91] She refused to allow *The Right Approach to the Economy* to be published as an official party paper.

As she grew in confidence, Mrs Thatcher's opposition to incomes policy hardened – on political as much as strictly economic grounds. On the one hand she believed that incomes policies conceded too much power to unelected trade union leaders; on the other that the paraphernalia of controls invited employers and unions to find ways around them, which brought the law into contempt. She believed that the preoccupation with incomes policy fed the illusion that people could expect annual pay increases whether they had earned them or not: 'West German pay plus British productivity equals inflation . . . Only when we stop being obsessed with pay and start to be obsessed with productivity are we going to prosper.'[92]

By the end of 1978, however, she had got herself into the position of suggesting that statutory policy might actually be preferable to the culture of nods and winks and backhanders that flourished under a voluntary policy.[93] 'Looking back on it', Jim Prior wrote, 'it is quite obvious that Margaret had in mind that she was not going to have any truck with any form of income policy at all.'[94] Yet she was still constrained by the imperative of party unity. When Ted Heath – backed by opinion polls which showed strong public support for continuing pay restraint – accused her at the 1978 party conference of reneging on the compromise reached in *The Right Approach*, Thorneycroft had once again to pull her back into line. She continued unapologetically to voice her personal scepticism; but the compromise remained in place to the election.

Launching *The Right Approach* at Brighton, Mrs Thatcher stated that the party's first task would be to 'put our finances in order. We must live within our means.' But she was at pains not to make this prescription sound draconian or harsh. 'The only common sense answer is to reduce Government spending . . . deliberately, carefully and humanely over the period of a full Parliament.' She denied that this would cause higher unemployment; on the contrary, it was Labour policies that had doubled unemployment. She insisted that incentives, not restraint, would create prosperity; and she looked forward to 'prudent financial management' leading to 'soundly based expansion'. Above all she went out of her way to promise consultation, not confrontation, with the trade unions.[95]

With memories of the three-day week still vivid, it was imperative that the Tories should be seen to be able to 'get on' with the unions. Heath had already promised in October 1974 that he would not try to reintroduce the ill-starred Industrial Relations Act which had caused his Government so much grief. His successor could not afford to be suspected of seeking another confrontation by proposing a renewed attempt to curb trade union power. Whatever the Government's difficulties, Labour's trump card was always the allegation that electing another Tory Government would bring a return to power cuts and industrial chaos. For three and a half years Jim Prior worked strenuously in his bluff way to repair relations between the Tories and the unions, assiduously playing down any right-wing threats which might be portrayed as 'union-bashing'. Mrs Thatcher had no option but to echo Prior's approach. Each year she devoted a long section of her Conference speech – plainly directed beyond her audience in the hall – to the question of relations with the unions, treading a delicate line between a determination not to be bullied and an equal concern not to appear 'provocative'. At Blackpool in 1975 she faced robustly the slippery argument that Labour was 'the natural party of government because it is the only one that the trade unions will accept'.

> If we are told that a Conservative Government could not govern because certain extreme leaders would not let it, then general elections are a mockery, we have arrived at the one-party state and parliamentary democracy in this country will have perished.

But her response was that when another Tory Government was elected it would be by the votes of millions of trade unionists who voted Conservative at every election in far greater numbers than the rigid fiction of union democracy recognised. Rather than legislation, she looked to Conservative trade unionists to defeat the militants from within.

> I want to say this to them and to all our supporters in industry: go out and join in the work of your unions; go to their meetings, and stay to the end, and learn the union rules as well as the far Left knows them. Remember that if parliamentary democracy dies, free trade unions die with it.[96]

The next year she condemned Labour's 'Social Contract' on the ground that it gave a handful of union leaders the right to dictate the level of public spending, the tax system and other central parts of the Government's economic policy. 'I am bound to say to them: "With great respect, that is not your job. It is Parliament's."' But she went on: 'Let me make it absolutely clear that the next Conservative

Government will look forward to discussion and consultation with the trade union movement about the policies that are needed to save our country.'[97]

There was no subject on which Mrs Thatcher's words were at greater variance with her real views. In private conversation and off-the-record interviews she made no secret that she regarded the trade union leaders as full-time Labour politicians who would never have any interest – however Prior might delude himself – in co-operating with a Tory Government. She left no doubt of her wish to see the overmighty unions confronted; and if she could not in the short term confront them herself, she gave covert support to a variety of ginger groups on the fringe of the Tory party who were not so inhibited. She took a close interest, for instance, in the work of the Institute for the Study of Conflict, founded in 1970 by Brian Crozier and Robert Moss to expose Trotskyist subversion in industry and the Communist links of left-wing Labour MPs; Crozier became her special adviser on security and intelligence, while Moss helped write her 'Iron Lady' speech at Kensington Town Hall. Likewise she gave private encouragement to the National Association for Freedom (later renamed the Freedom Association) founded by Norris McWhirter in 1975.

The McWhirter twins, Ross and Norris – best known as the editors of the *Guinness Book of Records* – were an energetic pair of freelance vigilantes with a long record of legal challenges to the arrogance of powerful institutions, from trade union bullies to the EEC. In November 1975 Ross McWhirter was murdered on his doorstep in North London a few days after offering a cash reward for information about recent IRA attacks: the first of a string of people close to Margaret Thatcher to be killed by the IRA or INLA over the next fifteen years. Only the day before, Harold Wilson had been teasing her in the Commons about her alleged links with 'right-wing militants'.[98] The next day she paid an exceptionally warm tribute to McWhirter, calling him 'one of the finest people of his generation' and 'an activist for liberty'.[99] A few days later, Norris went ahead undeterred with the formation of NAFF, under the chairmanship of the former Tory minister and war hero Viscount De L'Isle. Over the next few years NAFF fought several highly publicised cases against the abuse of trade union power: it supported railwaymen who lost their jobs for refusing to join the NUR, and challenged the attempt by the Post Office workers' union to impose a boycott on deliveries to and from South Africa. Mrs Thatcher attended NAFF's inaugural dinner in January 1977, where she spoke about the indivisibility of freedom, and secretly sent messages praising its work. In her memoirs she says that she gave NAFF 'as much support as I could', despite the disapproval of Jim Prior, who regarded NAFF as unhelpful to his attempts to gain the unions' trust.[100]

NAFF achieved its greatest prominence during the Grunwick strike in 1977. This was a long-running and bitter dispute over union recognition at a small North London photographic processing laboratory – not far from Finchley – which became the symbolic flashpoint of trade union activity in the later 1970s. NAFF organised volunteers to beat the union pickets by smuggling 80,000 items of post out of Grunwick. Mrs Thatcher thought this coup 'the best thing since Entebbe' (when Israeli commandos had daringly rescued more than a hundred hostages from a hijacked plane).[101] Publicly, however, she bit her lip and toed the Prior line, even when Keith Joseph spoke out in support of Grunwick's right to carry on its business and Norman Tebbit stirred the pot by comparing the appeasement of the unions with 'the morality of Laval and Pétain'.[102] At a press conference in Washington (where she had been meeting President Carter) she insisted that there was no division in the party over the closed shop.

> We do not think it is right. We are against it . . . It is against the freedom of the individual . . . But because we do not like it . . . does not necessarily mean I can pass legislation about it . . . We shall deal with it by small steps. I am afraid we cannot bring legislation against the closed shop as such.[103]

The next day she added, 'I have not the smallest intention of failing to learn from experience.'[104]

Four weeks later at Blackpool she returned to 'the key question' which she said she was always being asked: 'Will the trade unions allow a Conservative Government to govern?' People who asked that question, she warned, were 'already half way into Labour's trap'. Were the trade union leaders seriously saying that they would use their industrial muscle to get rid of an elected government which they could not control, to replace it with one they could control? 'I do not believe it. But people are asking: if it were so, what would happen?' The answer she gave was that in that context, 'and in that context only', she would consider holding a referendum: 'In those circumstances – in those special circumstances – I say "Let the people speak". But I hope, and believe, the situation will never arise.'

In case that should be seen as provocative, she then repeated first that 'a strong and responsible trade union movement is essential to this country, and its rights must be respected'; and second that 'we in

the Conservative party look forward to a long and fruitful association
with the unions, because a Conservative Britain will be as much in
the interest of union members as of the rest of the community'.[105] As
always, it is possible with hindsight to detect the steel fist behind the
olive branch; yet the lengths to which Mrs Thatcher felt she had to
go each year – until 1979 – to assure the country that she did not
want to quarrel with the unions is an eloquent reminder of the deep
scars the 1974 miners' strike had left on the Tory party.

Towards the end of 1977 Sherman and Joseph made a fresh effort
to persuade her that she must adopt a tougher strategy. At Joseph's
instigation, Hoskyns and Strauss wrote a paper entitled *Stepping
Stones* which argued that everything an incoming Tory Government
hoped to do depended on facing down trade union opposition. The
problem of trade union power was the key issue of modern British
politics. The unions had broken Wilson in 1969 and Heath in 1974,
and now had the Callaghan Government in their pocket. The Tories
too would win office without power unless they grasped the nettle in
advance and won from the electorate an explicit mandate to cut the
unions down to size. Instead of playing Labour's game by appeasing
the unions from misplaced fear of confrontation, they must trump
Labour's ace by turning the issue on its head, presenting the
Government's umbilical links with the unions as a liability, not an
asset.

Hoskyns and Strauss presented *Stepping Stones* to Mrs Thatcher at a
small dinner also attended by Joseph and Angus Maude; Willie
Whitelaw looked in later. She was instinctively sympathetic, but still
apprehensive of precipitating a showdown she might not win.* In
the Shadow Cabinet Joseph and Howe were the only hawks: a
powerful combination led by Prior, Pym, Thorneycroft, Gilmour,
Davies and Biffen successfully shelved it in favour of a more
conciliatory paper prepared by Chris Patten. Their alarm was
reflected in a leaked memo by Peter Carrington which looked back
to the Heath Government's humiliation at the hands of the
mineworkers and concluded that no Government could defeat the
miners without the use of troops.[107] 'Effectively they wanted to kill
Stepping Stones', Lady Thatcher wrote in her memoirs, 'but that I

---

* She betrayed her apprehension in a revealing exchange with a questioner on a
radio phone-in in December 1976 who told her that if she stood up to the unions
'two-thirds of the electorate would absolutely cheer to heaven'.

Mrs Thatcher: I wonder, Mrs Wingrave-Pain, if they would.
Mrs Wingrave-Pain: I think they would, Mrs Thatcher.
Mrs Thatcher: You have for that to have a really absolutely first-class case.[106]

would not allow.'[108] As so often, she exaggerates her own resolution. When Geoffrey Howe broke ranks in January 1978 with a speech arguing the case for legislation to curb the abuse of union power he was told that statements on trade union policy should be left to Prior.[109] Right up to the end of 1978, when the Winter of Discontent changed everything, the only piece of legislation she was prepared to sanction was the introduction of postal ballots for internal elections. She reluctantly ruled out legislation on the closed shop, strike ballots or even intimidatory picketing, let alone trade union legal immunities or the political levy. Had Callaghan gone to the country in October 1978 no trace of *Stepping Stones* would have found its way into the Tory manifesto. It was only the industrial anarchy of the Labour Government's last winter which shifted the debate in favour of the Tory hawks and persuaded Mrs Thatcher that it was safe to come off the fence.

In no respect did Mrs Thatcher conduct herself more like a conventional Leader of the Opposition than in her ritual condemnation of Labour's responsibility for unemployment. From the moment she became leader, the ever-rising rate of unemployment offered the easiest stick with which to beat first Wilson and then Callaghan at Prime Minister's Questions. From 600,000 in February 1974 the numbers had more than doubled to 1.5 million by 1978. Perhaps no Leader of the Opposition could be expected to resist a sitting target; but there was the most blatant opportunism in the way Mrs Thatcher repeatedly tried to tag Labour 'the natural party of unemployment'[110] and Callaghan 'the Prime Minister of unemployment'.[111] 'Our policies did not produce unemployment', she had the nerve to tell the House of Commons in January 1978, 'whereas his policies have.'[112] She contrasted Callaghan's denial of blame with Heath's acceptance of responsibility when unemployment touched a million in 1972 – the intolerable figure which more than anything else impelled him to his notorious U-turn.[113] When Callaghan and Healey retorted that her monetarist prescription would increase unemployment – as Joseph on occasion candidly admitted – she vehemently denied it. 'No,' she insisted on television in October 1976. 'This is nonsense and we must recognise it as nonsense ... A very, very small increase would be incurred, nothing like what this government has and is planning to have on present policies.'[114] 'We would have been drummed out of office if we had had this level of unemployment,' she asserted in a party broadcast the following year.[115]

As the General Election approached the Tory campaign focused more sharply on jobs than on any other issue, starting with the Saatchis' devastatingly effective poster in the summer of 1978 featuring a winding dole queue with the caption 'Labour Isn't Working'. If not quite a promise, the poster unmistakably suggested that Tory policies would quickly bring the figure down. After two or three years of Conservative government, however, when the numbers out of work had doubled again to a hitherto unimaginable figure of more than three million, Mrs Thatcher's glib exploitation of the problem in opposition had begun to look more than a little cynical. The best excuse that can be offered is that she, Joseph and Howe genuinely did not anticipate that their monetarist experiment would coincide with the onset of a world recession. Arguably the pain of an economic shake-out had to be gone through: eventually – after seven years – the figure did begin to fall. But given that the starting point of Joseph's analysis, back in his Preston speech in 1974, had been that cutting the dole queues should cease to be the central priority of economic management, a scrupulous Leader of the Opposition would not have made quite so much political capital of the headline jobless figure.

In a moment of euphoria just a few months after winning the leadership, Mrs Thatcher boasted: 'I have changed everything.'[116] Yet the fact is that she actually reversed only one major policy inherited from Ted Heath: his commitment to Scottish devolution. Heath himself had only embraced devolution somewhat abruptly in 1968, under the impact of the Scottish Nationalists' victory in the Hamilton by-election, and had done nothing about delivering it while in office. Nevertheless the Scottish Conservative establishment – from Alec Home downwards – had become heavily committed to giving Scotland an elected assembly, and Mrs Thatcher – in this as in so many other things – had no choice but to take on the obligation. On her first tumultuous visit to Edinburgh ten days after her election she assured her audience that the Scottish party – and by implication she herself – was 'absolutely in tune with the theme of devolution'.[117] In fact she was absolutely out of tune with it. She was an instinctive Unionist, with little understanding of the component nationalisms which co-exist within British patriotism. 'It was apparent from the very beginning to those who knew her best', Patrick Cosgrave wrote, 'that she was set on scuppering the whole notion of devolution. But it was necessary to move cautiously.'[118] She was fortunate that devolution was a rare issue on which Willie Whitelaw agreed with her rather than with Heath. An Anglicised Scot with an English border constituency, he had been upset by Heath's sudden lunge into devolution without what he considered proper consultation. Had Whitelaw shared the general Scottish consensus there is probably no way that Mrs Thatcher could have got out of honouring it. As it was, his skilful combination of bluff and bonhomie provided the cover which allowed her to kick it into touch.

Mrs Thatcher never understood Scotland, though she liked to think she did. She fancied she had a special affinity with the Scots, whom she imagined as thrifty, enterprising and inventive, a mixture of Adam Smith, George Stephenson and David Livingstone, hardy pioneers who had made the industrial revolution and built the British Empire. The reality was a persistent disappointment to her. Most Scots turned out to be either unreconstructed working-class socialists with an egalitarian culture of public housing and an inbred hostility to Thatcherism; or tartan Tories, patrician, feudal, paternalistic and equally disdainful of her sort of southern stridency. The upwardly mobile, home-owning middle class which formed her core support in England was a much smaller section of the population north of the border. There was a dissident faction of the Scottish Tory party, however, led by the abrasively non-patrician Member for Glasgow Cathcart, Teddy Taylor, and the tweedy but formidable Betty Harvie Anderson, which was determinedly opposed to devolution. While outwardly deferring to her shadow Scottish Secretary, Alick Buchanan-Smith, Mrs Thatcher quietly encouraged this group and bided her time.

At the Scottish Tory Conference in May 1975 and again in May 1976, she dutifully repeated her support for Scottish and Welsh assemblies, but hedged it with reservations and conditions. In the Commons in November 1975 she warned of the risk of breaking up the Union and explained that the point of devolution should be *less* government, not more.

> Devolution should move hand in hand with a conscious and deliberate attempt to scale down the size of government. The object is not more government of the people but more decisions by the people over their own lives.[119]

By the time Wilson introduced Labour's proposals in January 1976 Mrs Thatcher's scepticism had hardened. Portraying the Government's White Paper as a recipe for increased bureaucracy, constitutional anomalies and conflict between rival assemblies, she committed the Tories to support nothing more than a subordinate assembly, with no executive. *The Right Approach* that autumn still promised that limited degree of devolution. But in December, when the Government's Bill finally came before the House, she persuaded the Shadow Cabinet, after a marathon meeting, to vote against the Second Reading. This was the one issue on which – with Whitelaw's critical support – she chose to assert her will against a significant section of her party. She could get away with it because few English MPs cared deeply about devolution and in a British context the dissidents were expendable. Buchanan-Smith and his junior front-bench spokesman, Malcolm Rifkind, resigned; George Younger acquiesced in the new policy as the price of keeping his job. As her new shadow Scottish Secretary she appointed Teddy Taylor, with a particular brief to carry the fight to the Scottish Nationalists. He succeeded so well in reducing the SNP vote, however, that he lost his own constituency to Labour. He thus missed out on the Scottish Office in May 1979. Though he quickly came back for an English seat in 1980 he never won preferment again while Mrs Thatcher was leader.

Meanwhile she trod a delicate line between her own opposition and the party's continued support for devolution in principle by vigorously denouncing the Government's scheme as 'a thoroughly bad Bill' – which it was. She made one of her more successful parliamentary speeches – 'exactly the sort of forensic operation that I enjoyed'[120] – pointing up all the contradictions and anomalies which would make the Bill unworkable.[121] For the rest of the Parliament Francis Pym, who had succeeded Whitelaw as devolution spokesman, mounted a skilful parliamentary opposition, maximising the Government's difficulties with its anti–devolutionist rebels like Tam Dalyell in Scotland and Neil Kinnock in Wales. It was the obduracy of this awkward squad which precipitated the crisis from which the Government had to be rescued by the Lib-Lab pact. As devolution became ever more of a millstone round the Government's neck, the political rewards for the Tories of sharpening their opposition became irresistible. By the time she spoke to the Scottish party conference in 1977 Mrs Thatcher was able quietly to jettison the commitment to devolution without fuss. The 1979 manifesto merely promised further 'discussions about the future government of Scotland'.[122]

Devolution was one issue on which Mrs Thatcher patiently executed a gradual but successful U-turn. Sometimes, however, she tried to bounce her colleagues by speaking off the cuff. 'For someone who had the reputation for thinking things through and being over-keen on detail', Jim Prior wrote, 'she tended to make policy very much by shooting from the hip.'

> The reason was that she did not find it easy to get her own way round the Shadow Cabinet table, so she tended to make policy – usually of the more extreme kind – on television, or at Prime Minister's Questions in the Commons. She was afraid of being pushed off what she wanted to do if there was much consultation with her colleagues beforehand, so she reckoned it was better to make the policy and argue about it afterwards.[123]

She denied it, of course, claiming that if her colleagues were sometimes surprised it was because they did not read the papers from all the policy committees as thoroughly as she did.[124] But it was a technique she developed to a fine art in government. 'Never underestimate the effectiveness of simply just announcing something,' she told Kenneth Baker in 1986.[125] In opposition it was rather less effective, as she found with her attempts to repudiate incomes policy. But she knew exactly what she was doing when she went on television in January 1978 to speak her mind on the sensitive subject of immigration.

Ever since the furore stirred up by Enoch Powell's 'River Tiber' speech in 1968 immigration had been a taboo subject, carefully avoided by the respectable politicians of all parties. Mrs Thatcher had hitherto observed this polite convention; but as an ardent nationalist with a scarcely less mystical view of British identity than Powell himself she shared his concern about the impact of the growing immigrant population: she used to sound off about the 'two Granthams' worth' of coloured immigrants she believed were still arriving in Britain each year.[126] She believed that continued immigration was something ordinary voters worried about, and that politicians therefore had the right, even a duty, to articulate their worry. But she also had a baser motivation. With the economy picking up in the latter part of 1977, the Tories' private polls indicated that their most profitable issues were rising crime and other social problems. So it was not a gaffe, but quite deliberate, that when Mrs Thatcher was interviewed on Granada's *World in Action* two days after a racial incident in Wolverhampton she chose to speak sympathetically of people's fear of being 'swamped by people of a different culture'. Some of her staff tried to dissuade her; but she had determined what she was going to say – without consulting her shadow Home Secretary, Willie Whitelaw – and refused to moderate the emotive word 'swamped'. 'We are not in politics to ignore people's worries,' she declared, 'we are in politics to deal with them . . . If you want good race relations, you have got to allay people's fears on numbers', by holding out 'the prospect of a clear end to immigration'.[127]

Her words sparked an immediate outcry. In the Commons Labour MPs accused her of stirring up racial prejudice. Callaghan hoped she was not trying to appeal to 'certain elements in the electorate', and asked her to explain how she proposed to end immigration, given that all but 750 of the 28,000 admitted in 1977 – actually about one Grantham's worth – were dependants of those already here.[128] Six months later he charged that by speaking as she did she had 'knowingly aroused the fears of thousands of coloured people living in this country and it will take them a long time to recover their composure'.[129] But she hit her intended target. Like Powell in 1968, she received a huge postbag, some 10,000 letters thanking her for speaking out. Powell was delighted, hailing with characteristic hyperbole the 'great surge of hope and relief which a single word . . . by the Conservative leader evoked from one end of the country to the other'.[130] The Tories gained an immediate boost in the polls (from neck and neck with Labour at 43–43 to a clear lead of 48–39); and four weeks later won a by-election at Ilford North at which the National Front had been making the running. Polls showed that immigration was the key issue in swinging votes.

Yet Tory policy did not change. Whitelaw was furious, and briefly considered resignation. But short of assisted repatriation there was no way the policy could change. The party was already committed to a register of dependants; Mrs Thatcher could hardly reverse Whitelaw's promise not to break up families. Powell was disappointed that she never referred to the subject again, claiming that 'a chloroformed gag was immediately clapped over the leader's mouth' by Whitelaw, Carrington and Gilmour.[131] But as he reflected in a later interview: 'If you're trying to convey what you feel to the electorate, perhaps you only have to do it once.'[132] In one respect Powell was wrong. She did return to the subject, quite unapologetically, in her *Observer* interview with Kenneth Harris just before the election, when she denied that she had modified her original statement and defiantly repeated it:

I *never* modified it! I stood by it one hundred per cent. Some people have felt swamped by immigrants. They've seen the whole character of their neighbourhood change . . . Of course people can feel they are being swamped. They feel their whole way of life has been changed.[133]

But in another sense Powell was right. Her words did not have to change Tory policy in order to achieve their purpose of signalling her real views to supporters in the country who wanted to believe that she was on their side. It was a trick she often used, even as Prime Minister, to suggest that she was not responsible for the lamentable timidity of her colleagues. She did the same thing over capital punishment, losing no opportunity in the run-up to the election to remind radio and television audiences of her long-standing support for hanging murderers. Most of the time she was obliged to keep her true feelings to herself. Her immigration broadcast was one of those vivid moments that helped bring Mrs Thatcher's carefully blurred appeal into sharp focus, revealing, both to those who shared her views and those who loathed her, exactly what her fundamental instincts were.

This episode is a good example of the way Mrs Thatcher learned to project herself to the public independently of the party she led, not through specific policies or even in big ideas expressed in major speeches, but by constructing an image of the type of person she was, with attitudes, sympathies and instincts which could be guessed at when they could not prudently be spelled out. There was nothing new in projecting an image. From Baldwin's pipe-smoking country-man leaning over a gate to poke a pig to Macmillan's equally bogus pose of Edwardian unflappability, politicians have always worked hard to present a factitious version of themselves to the media of the day. Harold Wilson, with his pipe and his Gannex raincoat, one minute aping President Kennedy, the next inviting the Beatles to Downing Street, raised preoccupation with image to a new level. In his early days Wilson manipulated his presentation in the media with a professionalism which made Macmillan look like a beginner. Even Ted Heath, in opposition, was persuaded to lend himself to the efforts of various television people to humanise his chilly manner, only to turn his back – fatally – on any such gimmickry in government. From the moment she won the leadership, Mrs Thatcher realised the importance of projecting her message though her personality, selling the public a wide repertoire of carefully contrived images which made Wilson in turn look as amateurish as Macmillan. It is ironic that Mrs Thatcher, who actually had an unusually clear ideological programme to put across, was the first leader to be packaged to this extent, beginning a process which, taken ever further by her successors, has practically drained politics of ideological content altogether. It was another measure of her political weakness, however, that she was obliged to hint at attitudes whose implications she could not fully expound; and a measure of her political skill that she was able to do so successfully.

Through a combination of instinct and professionalism she understood clearly how a modern electorate needed to be wooed, and was prepared to mould herself to the necessary techniques. From her earliest campaigning days in Dartford she had shown a flair for contriving photo-opportunities to get her picture in the local paper, and she grasped earlier than most politicians of her generation the importance of coming over well on television. But she hated television – she rarely had time to watch it herself – and knew that she was not naturally good at it. 'Winston was never on television,' she complained, 'certainly never interviewed on it.'[134] The BBC reporter Michael Cockerell said that she 'reacted to television like an African tribesman faced with a tourist's camera; she almost seemed to believe it would take her soul away'.[135] But she was determined to master it. As always she needed a guru; for this practical aspect of her education the man she turned to was the former television producer, now working for EMI, Gordon Reece.

Like Ronald Millar, Reece was a non-politician whose expertise in his own field she respected. She had first met him when recording her aborted election broadcast in 1970; but following that humiliation she kept in touch and used him to coach her for her occasional television appearances as Education Secretary. A flamboyant character with a whiff of showbiz glamour, he had the knack – like Millar – of relaxing her by treating her as a woman. 'Perhaps because she is so serious and sober', Tim Bell's biographer Mark Hollingsworth has written, 'she has a weakness for extrovert gregarious men from her own class background who look her in the eye, make her laugh and gently flirt with her. Reece fitted that bill and developed an almost unassailable place in her affections.'[136] She recruited him on secondment from EMI, initially for a year, as her personal public relations adviser, and then installed him in Central Office as Director of Publicity. To the consternation of Peter Thorneycroft and Janet Young, he appeared to live on nothing but champagne; but Mrs Thatcher indulged this extravagance as a measure of his professional success, and a price worth paying for his services. She was always tolerant of the foibles of her favourites.

Reece is often credited with transforming Mrs Thatcher's image after 1975, and to an extent he did. He taught her to wear simpler and bolder clothes, to give up hats and soften her hairstyle, avoid chunky jewellery and keep her hands out of sight. Most famously he taught her to lower and soften her voice to make her sound less shrill and strident. 'The elocution lessons she had had in her youth . . . gave her a contrived, exaggerated, upper class accent that grated on the ear,' Hollingsworth has written. 'In the privacy of a closed circuit studio Reece spent many hours with her overseeing what were, effectively, reverse elocution lessons to make her speech more ordinary.'[137] He hired a voice coach from the National Theatre to teach her to breathe properly and to speak more slowly; she even had 'a rather unproductive two-hour session' with Laurence Olivier, who had famously lowered his voice a few years earlier to play Othello.[138]

Unquestionably all this greatly improved her performance and her self-projection. But Reece's role can be exaggerated. There was nothing magical in what he did for her. He simply gave her good professional advice. The credit belongs to Mrs Thatcher herself for having had the sense and the humility to seek and then to follow it. She was probably able to do this more easily because she was a woman. No male politician in 1975 would have consented to be moulded in this way – certainly not Harold Wilson with his crumpled, baggy suits, or Ted Heath with his garish casual clothes. But Mrs Thatcher was used to being judged on her appearance – most critically by other women – and took it for granted that her clothes, her hair and her voice were important weapons in her political armoury which could be deployed to help project her message – or could equally detract from it if they were unappealing. Mrs Thatcher liked clothes, but she knew that her own taste was conservative. The actress in her enjoyed dressing up, and was happy to be dressed by a skilled image-handler whom she trusted to work with the grain of her personality, not try to make her be what she was not. In television interviews and in her memoirs she gave due credit to what Reece had taught her. But she also insisted that he had not changed or misrepresented her: 'No one can give you an image you don't possess.'[139]

She probably did not need Reece to tell her to give up wearing hats. She always maintained that she only wore them to functions like fêtes and ladies' luncheons where it would have been considered rude not to look her best. It irritated her that cartoonists – specifically Jon in the *Daily Mail* – always drew her wearing the same blue and white striped one which she had worn only a few times in 1970, notably at the party conference. It was 'a bit like a radar bowl with a great big stripe on it', she told Miriam Stoppard in 1985. 'It would have done for an actress, but it was not quite right for a politician . . . I have never worn one like it since.'[140] She still felt that she should wear a hat on ceremonial occasions such as the State Opening of Parliament or at the Cenotaph. Generally, however, she unquestionably looked younger, less matronly and more stylish as a result of Reece's make-over: she obviously spent much more on buying new clothes, so that she was less often seen wearing the same outfit several times. Even so, pictures of her before 1979 show that she still had some way to go. It was only after she became Prime Minister – indeed not until her second term – that she adopted the power-dressing, the big hair and the regal costumes which fixed her image at the height of her power. As Leader of the Opposition, when she was still insecure and lacking the authority of office, she still often looked like a harassed housewife.

Nor could all the voice lessons in the world make her a natural speaker. Reece taught her to speak slowly on television, not to argue with the interviewer but to talk directly to the audience. This checked her propensity to hector, but at the cost of sounding wearyingly insistent, as though she were talking to a class of backward six-year-olds. Even such an admirer as Kingsley Amis complained that after all her efforts to soften it, her voice still sounded monotonous – 'in the literal sense of staying on one tone or note' – giving 'a sort of ring of petulance or superiority' which it did not have in private.[141] Peter Jenkins of the *Guardian* thought she sounded like the Queen – her manner 'a little too Sandringham-like, the new voice a little too huskily moderated'.[142] She never really found a style of speaking which did not put listeners' teeth on edge.

Mrs Thatcher's willingness to reinvent herself drew a good deal of satirical comment. The *Guardian* was typical (picking up one of a number of mocking nicknames for the leader coined by Norman St John Stevas):

> There was once a warrior Leaderene who frightened her followers almost as much as the enemy. Her tongue was a lash, her eyes chips of ice, her hair as stiff as an aardvark's bristle. Then one day she met a humble TV producer and a miracle occurred.[143]

During the election campaign Callaghan complained that Mrs Thatcher was being sold like a brand of soap powder. But she made no apology for availing herself of the best techniques of modern marketing. 'If you have a good thing to sell', she told Angela Rippon on a BBC programme called *The Image Makers*, broadcast in 1980, 'use every single capacity you can to sell it. It is no earthly use having a good thing and no one hearing about it.'[144] Convinced that she had a good thing to sell, however, she made it very clear that she wanted to use her personality to project the product, not herself. When Reece hired the advertising agency Saatchi and Saatchi in 1978 to handle the Tories' publicity, she told them firmly at their first interview with her what she wanted. 'If you have the skills to dupe the people, please do not use them on my behalf. If they don't want me I don't want to be elected, because if they don't want me it won't work.'[145] 'If you paint a picture of me that isn't true,' she told Tim Bell, who was handling the Conservative account, 'then I won't be able to do what I want because people will expect me to do something else.'[146] The point, she told Angela Rippon, was to put over 'the message and policy of my party and not self at all'.[147] Yet by projecting her personality she conveyed a truer image of what she was about than could be learned from her party's official policy.

In fact Reece's key insight was not so much how to project her, but where to project her. In defiance of the conventional wisdom of Central Office, he deliberately shifted the emphasis of Tory propaganda downmarket from the highbrow minority media to the more popular middlebrow and tabloid newspapers, women's magazines and mass audience television and radio programmes. He severely rationed her appearances on heavyweight political programmes like the BBC's *Panorama* where she was likely to be asked probing questions about policy, in favour of the early evening *Nationwide* or an invitation to appear with Jimmy Savile and an audience of children on *Jim'll Fix It*. 'I simply encourage her to appear everywhere she can to the best advantage,' he told Michael Cockerell, dismissing the elitist view that it was demeaning for the Leader of the Opposition to go on popular television.[148] She was not good in interviews because she bridled aggressively in the face of what she felt was hostile questioning, and tended to argue. She much preferred making speeches to a live audience from which a good soundbite could be extracted to make an effective clip on the *Nine O'Clock News* or *News at Ten*. Reece was one of the first media advisers to realise that a minute on the news was worth an hour on *Panorama*.

Of course she could not entirely avoid the major current affairs programmes; but Reece controlled the conditions under which she would agree to appear, vetoed interviewers she did not like and checked the studio beforehand, making sure that the background, the colour scheme, the type of chairs and the distance between them and the camera angles all showed her to best advantage. Her favourite vehicle, from 1977, was London Weekend Television's hour-long Sunday lunchtime interview programme, *Weekend World*, whose presenter, Brian Walden – yet another ex-Labour MP who had moved to the right – could be guaranteed to give her a tough but broadly sympathetic ride. Moreover while the programme attracted only a small, largely specialist audience, it was a good way to start a story in Monday's papers.

Reece also projected Mrs Thatcher on mass-audience radio programmes, above all *The Jimmy Young Programme* on BBC Radio 2, which she did about once a year. Here she was in her element talking directly to housewives between records, mixing glimpses of autobiography, fashion tips and recipes with flashes of her political mission and populist views on social questions where she did not have to toe the party line. It was on *The Jimmy Young Programme*, for instance, just before the election, that she took the chance to reiterate her support for capital punishment, as well as her sympathy with those worried by immigration. In the same way she gave cosy interviews to women's magazines like *Woman's Realm*, *Woman's Own*, *Vogue* and the women's pages of the national newspapers. 'The Margaret Thatcher Look' was the title of a typical piece in *Woman's Own*,[149] 'My Face, My Figure, My Diet' the headline of another in the *Sun*.[150] These overtly non-political features were in fact shrewdly directed at a section of the electorate the Tories had deliberately set out to target.

Another part of Reece's game plan was the determined cultivation of the more popular end of Fleet Street – as it then still was – rather than the self-important but low-circulation broadsheets. At the top end of the spectrum the *Daily Telegraph* did not need much cultivation: already the first paper to give regular space to the prophets of the New Right, it was now edited ('providentially', as Lady Thatcher admits in her memoirs) by Denis's old golfing chum Bill Deedes.[151] In the middle the *Daily Mail*, edited by David English, had jumped on Mrs Thatcher's bandwagon just before the second leadership ballot and now regarded itself as her pre-eminent supporter, the voice of Middle England with a particularly strong readership among women. The biggest prize was the support of the downmarket tabloid *Sun*, whose ambitious Australian proprietor, Rupert Murdoch, notoriously likes to back winners. Though a natural Conservative, Murdoch was initially doubtful about Mrs Thatcher. Reece set about wooing the new editor, Larry Lamb, arranging opportunities for him to meet her. Lamb found the Tory leader flatteringly keen to tap his knowledge of what *Sun* readers wanted; he was also impressed by her insistent theme that she – not the union-dominated Labour party – nowadays represented the true interests of working people. Himself a traditional Labour voter who planned to vote Tory for the first time in his life, Lamb was the embodiment of the sort of swing voter she was targeting, while the *Sun* – rapidly overhauling the Labour-supporting *Daily Mirror* in the tabloid circulation war – was the perfect vehicle for her campaign.[152] This was a crucial change. The Tories had always enjoyed the support of the middle-market *Mail* and *Express*, but not since the demise of the *Daily Sketch* – which sold less than a million copies a day anyway – had they had a mass-circulation daily on their side. The *Sun's* enthusiastic adoption of Mrs Thatcher – now renamed 'Maggie' – as the gutsy heroine of the patriotic and acquisitive working class helped to create a political personality very different from the strait-laced schoolmarm who had been Education Secretary just a few years earlier.

The original spin doctor, Reece had a weekly meeting with Deedes, English and Lamb to steer their coverage of Mrs Thatcher and co-ordinate her speeches with their concerns. But he did not neglect other influential journalists who could be won over. He arranged a lunch very early on for her to meet John Junor, the veteran editor of the *Sunday Express*, who was not favourably disposed to her but was quickly converted. It was also Reece who fixed up a meeting with Woodrow Wyatt, who immediately became an adoring admirer; and set up a usefully supportive interview in the *Daily Mirror* with Marjorie Proops, whom she had known in the sixties as a fellow-panellist on the BBC's all-female radio talk show, *The Petticoat Line*. Reece in effect acted as her impresario, or agent, in Fleet Street and she relied on his judgement. 'When Gordon said that we must have lunch with such-and-such an editor', she wrote in her memoirs, 'that was the priority.'[153]

From time to time she visited a newspaper office to expose the whole senior staff to the force of her personality. The impact of these visits was mixed. She made a great hit, predictably, at the *Daily Telegraph* where, knowing she was among friends, she arrived dressed to kill and charmed them with her femininity.[154] It was rather different at the *Sunday Times*, where she had to overcome initial prejudice. 'I think that few people on the *Sunday Times* were by disposition or condition pro-her. We all thought she was a rather bossy, handbaggy lady,' the deputy editor, Frank Giles, recalled.[155] 'In her bluntness and freedom from a discernible sense of humour, she was comparable to Heath.'[156]

But by the end of lunch she had argued so well, was so much in control of her facts, never lost her cool and never let anyone get away with anything without pinning it down, and carried it off so well, that everyone around the table in their different ways was impressed . . . After lunch we would stand around and have a quick post-mortem, and I remember very well everyone saying 'Ouf! She's quite something.'[157]

When she did not think she was among friends, however, she scarcely made the effort to convert anyone. Most Leaders of the Opposition take great pains to woo the BBC: not so Mrs Thatcher. In her demonology, the BBC was the very heart of the defeatist pinko-liberal conspiracy which was dragging Britain down, and she did not care who knew it. The Director-General, Ian Trethowan – a good friend of Ted Heath – insists that the broadcasters were not ill-disposed towards her. But she certainly believed she was venturing into hostile territory: 'The lady arrived with all guns firing, she showed scant interest in, let alone tolerance of, the editors' problems and berated them on their failings over a wide area, particularly their coverage of Northern Ireland.'[158] Mrs Thatcher came into office in May 1979 already determined to bring the BBC to heel.

The result of this emphasis on promoting her personality rather than her policies was to enable Mrs Thatcher to overcome the perceived handicaps of her class and her sex. In place of the Home Counties Tory lady in a stripy hat, married to a rich husband, whose children had attended the most expensive private schools, she forced the media to redefine her as a battling meritocrat who had raised herself by hard work from a humble provincial background – an inspiration to others, whatever their start in life, who had the ambition, ability and guts to do the same. 'People from my sort of background', she took a great delight in telling the 1977 party conference, 'needed grammar schools to compete with children from privileged homes like Shirley Williams and Anthony Wedgwood Benn.'[159] The transformation did not convince everyone. Despite all Reece's efforts, the waspish *Observer* columnist Katharine Whitehorn still considered her in 1977 'the archetypal Tory lady . . . God's own bazaar-opener'.[160] But long before 1979 she had shown that she could appeal much more widely than her critics had thought possible in 1974. She was not popular, but she was no longer patronised. On the contrary she had immensely widened the range of available stereotypes for a woman politician, and in doing so transformed her sex from a liability into an asset.

First of all she did not try to escape the traditional female stereotype of the housewife, but positively embraced it and turned it to her advantage. Her willingness to act up to the role of ordinary wife and home-maker infuriated feminists, who thought she thereby devalued the whole project of a woman storming the seats of male power. But Mrs Thatcher knew what she was doing. By boasting that she still cooked Denis's breakfast for him every morning, still did her own shopping – which Barbara Castle for one did not believe – and even used to 'pop up to the launderette' regularly, she encouraged millions of women to identify with her as they had never been able to identify with any previous politician, male or female. Rich though she was, she sounded as if she understood the problems of daily living in a way that Heath and Callaghan never could. 'They will turn to me', she told John Cole, 'because they believe a woman *knows* about prices.'[161] At the same time she used to boast that women, because they were used to juggling the competing demands of running a home, bringing up children and sustaining a career, as she had done, were naturally better managers than one-dimensional men. Where male politicians talked of controlling the money supply or the public sector borrowing requirement, Mrs Thatcher's homely lectures on 'housewife economics', expressed in the language of domestic budgeting, made monetarism sound like common sense. Finally there was powerful metaphorical resonance in the imagery of spring cleaning: the voters were subconsciously persuaded that what the country needed was a new broom and a vigorous Mrs Mopp to wield it.

But Mrs Thatcher was also able to tap into another range of female types: established role models of women in positions of authority whom men were used to obeying. Thus she was the Teacher, patiently but with absolute certainty explaining the answers to the nation's problems: and the Headmistress exhorting the electorate to pull its socks up. She was Doctor Thatcher, or sometimes Nurse Thatcher, prescribing nasty medicine or a strict diet which the voters knew in their hearts would be good for them. Or she was the nation's Nanny, with overtones of discipline, fresh air and regular bowel movements to get the country going. As Leo Abse noted, not entirely fancifully, there is a streak of masochism in the British male which responds to the idea of a woman in authority.[162] Up to 1979 Mrs Thatcher was only auditioning for these roles, which she would develop to the full over the next eleven years. Yet already she was striking a greater variety of chords in the electorate than either Barbara Castle or Shirley Williams could begin to touch.

Finally she was Britannia, the feminine embodiment of patriotism, wrapping herself unselfconsciously in the Union Jack. No politician since Churchill had appealed so emotionally to British nationalism. Unquestionably it was her sex that enabled Mrs Thatcher to get away with it without inviting the sort of ridicule that was heaped on Harold Wilson when he tried to invoke the Dunkirk spirit. She was not yet the full-blown Warrior Queen, the combination of Britannia, Boadicea and Elizabeth I that she became after the Falklands War. But already, thanks to the Russians, she was the 'Iron Lady' – recognised as a strong leader ready to stand up to foreign dictators, calling on the nation to look to its defences. While visiting British forces in Germany she was even able to be photographed in a tank without looking silly. No previous woman politician could have done that.

By contrast she was never shown relaxing. When she was photographed off duty she was invariably decorating or gardening or engaged in some other purposeful pursuit. More often she was curled on a sofa surrounded by papers. The impression was given – perfectly accurately – that she was always working. There were no equivalents to those pictures of Wilson loafing scruffily on a beach in the Scilly Isles or playing obviously very bad golf. Ted Heath's image makers made the most of his more strenuous and highbrow leisure pursuits – ocean racing, playing the piano and conducting; but he also allowed himself to be pictured swimming or simply sitting in the sun in undignified states of undress. Mrs Thatcher understood very well the value of good photographs, and equally the damage that could be done by bad ones. Driving a tank was one thing; but visiting Egypt in 1976 she firmly refused to be photographed riding a camel.[163] She never let herself be depicted as anything less than Superwoman. In this way any doubts about her competence to do the job of Prime Minister were disposed of long before 1979. Some – both friends and opponents – feared her extremism or her naivety. More – both supporters and commentators – underestimated her determination. Few anticipated how thoroughly she was going to change the country. But when *The Economist* announced at the beginning of the 1979 election campaign that 'The issue is Thatcher', it meant her personality and her politics, not her sex.[164] That was already a huge achievement.

13

Into Downing Street

THE summer of 1978 was the lowest point of Mrs Thatcher's leadership, when it suddenly began to look possible that she might lose the coming election. Though unemployment was still around 1.5 million, inflation was down to single figures and the pound was riding high. The economic outlook was unquestionably improving, and in his April Budget Denis Healey was able to make some modest tax cuts. The Tories' leap in the polls following Mrs Thatcher's immigration broadcast in January proved to be short-lived. By May the parties were neck and neck again, and in August Labour took a four-point lead. Callaghan's personal approval rating was consistently above 50 per cent, Mrs Thatcher's often below 40 per cent. Her efforts to portray Labour as wildly left-wing were becoming increasingly implausible; on the contrary Callaghan was widely recognised as 'the best Conservative Prime Minister we have',[1] while it was she who came over as scarily extreme. In May Peregrine Worsthorne (of all people) wrote in the *Sunday Telegraph* that she was too inflexible, too intolerant and too right-wing to win the centre ground where the election would be won and lost.[2]

In particular she seemed to be going out on a limb by promising ever more specifically that a Tory Government would restore free collective bargaining in place of any form of incomes policy. She always insisted that collective bargaining should be 'responsible' and 'realistic'.[3] But that was not under her control. In the Commons Callaghan warned her that there would be 'a serious return to inflation' if the Government abandoned pay restraint;[4] and it was evident that most of her own party agreed with him. The only other groups in the political spectrum who wanted to return to free collective bargaining were the left-wing Tribune Group and the leaders of the big unions, which only confirmed the common

411

assumption that the reality would be 'free collective chaos'. By the end of July there was a widespread expectation that Callaghan would seek to exploit the Tories' disarray by going to the country in the autumn. There was an unmistakable whiff of electioneering in the chamber when the Prime Minister opened what was expected to be the last major debate of the dying Parliament by launching an uncharacteristically scathing attack on Mrs Thatcher's fitness to govern.

'We are told that the right hon. Lady has a distaste for making policy in the Shadow Cabinet,' he began shrewdly. 'Looking at her colleagues I can understand that and sympathise with her.' But the consequence was that she made 'ill-prepared and . . . frequently contradictory' remarks on her own initiative. 'The truth is that the Opposition . . . is all over the shop on the issue of pay. There is no Opposition policy worthy of the name . . .' After three years of her leadership, people did not know what the Conservative party stood for. 'They do not know, because she does not know.' Her 'one-sentence solutions to deep-seated problems' were 'an insult to . . . the intelligence of the British people'. Her every speech was 'a rallying cry to prejudice', her party 'reluctant and sullen' at having to listen 'to the language of division the whole time'. That call to division, Callaghan confidently concluded, would fall on deaf ears. 'The British people have come to know that they achieve most when they work together . . . in unison, in social justice and in fair play.'[5]

Mrs Thatcher's reply was also framed in electioneering mode, but a good deal less bullish. Her delivery was 'nervous and faltering' and what she said only exposed the divisions in her party.[6] First, she went further than ever in rejecting even voluntary pay restraint by condemning the Government's 5 per cent 'guideline', backed by Government blacklisting of firms which broke it, as actually worse than a statutory policy.

> The truth is that we now have two kinds of law. First, there is legislation properly passed through Parliament and impartially administered. Then we have White Paper law or diktat which is arbitrary, secret and Socialist.

Then in comparing the 'long drab period' of the Labour Government which she now saw drawing to an end with the superior record of successive Tory Governments, she pointedly drew all her favourable statistics from 1951–64 rather than 1970–4. She ended with her usual assertion that the coming election would be a straight choice between 'liberty and collectivism'.[7] The speech was poorly received by her own party. Denis Healey, winding up the debate, gleefully suggested that the House had witnessed 'a historical occasion': Mrs Thatcher's last speech as Tory leader. After three years, he claimed, the Conservatives were 'a party in the last stages of decay' and 'riding to certain defeat . . . The axes and knives are already being sharpened.'[8] Rarely has political bravado been more spectacularly disproved by events; but Healey's anticipation was widely shared. Mrs Thatcher, however, was defiant. 'How are you – not depressed? Good. We'll beat the bastards yet,' she told Norman Tebbit. 'She swore so rarely that I was taken aback, but there was certainly an air of defeatism at that time.'[9]

It was specifically to try to forestall an early election that Saatchi and Saatchi came up with the famous poster, 'Labour Isn't Working'. Gordon Reece had only recently persuaded Thorneycroft to place the Conservative advertising account in the hands of this small but innovative agency. Tim Bell and Maurice Saatchi made their first presentation of possible ideas in June. The dole queue design broke the conventions of political advertising, first because it mentioned the other party by name, and second because unemployment was traditionally a 'Labour' issue on which the Tories could never hope to win. 'Why is the biggest thing on this poster the name of the opposition?' Mrs Thatcher objected. 'We're promoting the opposition.' 'No,' Bell and Saatchi replied together. 'We're demolishing Labour.'[10] She quickly saw the point. 'Labour Isn't Working', she wrote in her memoirs, was 'a simple negative message . . . designed to undermine confidence in our political opponents.'[11] No matter that it said nothing of the Tory alternative. Peter Thorneycroft did not like it; moreover the party had not budgeted for a poster campaign before the election proper. But Alistair McAlpine persuaded Saatchis to accept deferred payment, and Mrs Thatcher gave her approval for the campaign to go ahead at the beginning of August.

In fact only twenty posters ever went up, but their effect was hugely amplified by Labour howls of protest, which meant that the image was reproduced – often several times – in every newspaper and on television. Bell calculated that the Tories got £5 million of free publicity for an outlay of just £50,000.[12] The revelation that the supposed dole queue was actually made up of Young Conservatives made no difference to the message. The public was reminded that unemployment – still the most sensitive issue in British politics – was still intolerably high. The impact of 'Labour Isn't Working' had exactly the desired effect of making Callaghan think twice about an early election.

Two days after teasing the Trades Union Congress with hints of an imminent dissolution he went on television on 7 September to announce that there would be no autumn poll. Mrs Thatcher was already touring marginal constituencies in the West Midlands, giving every sign of impatience to get on with it. 'I don't suppose he's making a ministerial broadcast to say he's *not* going to hold an election,' she told reporters.[13] But that was just what Callaghan did. Not wishing to risk his job before he had to, he gambled that the economy would keep on improving over the winter. He knew that the unions were restless at the Government's tight pay policy, but he believed they would accept it from fear of letting in the dreaded Thatcher. Downing Street telephoned Mrs Thatcher in Birmingham with advance notice of the Prime Minister's announcement, which she then had to keep to herself for the rest of the day. With the press and both party machines geared up for the starting gun, she admits she shared 'the general sense of anti-climax'.[14] Of course she jeered at Callaghan's cowardice in clinging to office, but she was not unhappy. 'At the back of my mind', she told a press conference, 'I have a feeling that we shall win even better next year.'[15]

In her memoirs she recognises that Callaghan's postponement – like the Lib-Lab pact – actually served her well. From Ted Heath's refusal to step down in 1974 to Arthur Scargill's crass leadership of the 1984–5 miners' strike, Mrs Thatcher's career was repeatedly boosted by extraordinary strokes of fortune, as successive opponents played into her hands; but this was one of the biggest. Had she lost an election held in October 1978 the experiment of her leadership would almost certainly have been finished. Even had she won – as she might narrowly have done – it could well have proved a pyrrhic victory. She would immediately have faced the same explosion of pent-up pay demands which destroyed Callaghan; and she would have faced it with a divided Cabinet, the great majority of whom would not have been willing to let wages rip at the cost of increased unemployment. Sooner rather than later she would have been forced to impose some form of incomes limit, at least in the public sector, which would only have provoked further strikes, thus confirming all the predictions of the past four years that another Tory Government would lead the country straight back to confrontation. Instead it was Labour which was broken by the winter pay disputes. Not only was Callaghan's credibility destroyed, but public anger at the unions' indiscipline silenced the objections of her Tory critics and gave Mrs Thatcher's incoming Government the mandate to tackle the abuse of union power which she had lacked the previous autumn. It was Callaghan's fateful postponement which made possible the sort of government Mrs Thatcher wanted to lead.

There was a warning of trouble ahead at the Labour Party Conference, which heavily rejected the Government's 5 per cent pay norm. But in the short term the postponement of the election tore the sticking plaster from the Tories' divisions. At Brighton Ted Heath rebuked Mrs Thatcher for claiming on television that the Government's guidelines had broken down already. If that were so, he warned, there was 'nothing for gloating, nothing for joy. We should grieve for our country.'[16] 'Free collective bargaining', he spelled out on television the same evening, 'produces massive inflation . . . We cannot have another free-for-all.'[17] Jim Prior more tactfully repeated that it would be folly to rule out incomes policy altogether. In the conference hall Geoffrey Howe won a standing ovation for a skilfully ambiguous speech which appeared to repudiate both incomes policy and a free-for-all in favour of his own round-table approach to pay determination.[18] In her closing speech, however, Mrs Thatcher repeated her clear commitment to 'realistic responsible collective bargaining, free from government interference', warning the unions that they would price their members out of jobs if they pitched their demands too high.[19] Here was the starkest dispute in four years between the Tories' past and present leaders. Reporting of the conference was dominated by the Heath–Thatcher split. Worryingly for Mrs Thatcher, NOP found that more voters (71 per cent) supported Heath's approach than hers (56 per cent) – though a good many seem to have wanted both at once.[20]

The impression of disunity was blamed for the Tories' failure to win a by-election at Berwick and East Lothian on 26 October. Both leaders canvassed there, Mrs Thatcher insisting that the difference between them was 'minute' while Heath quoted from *The Right Approach to the Economy* to show that he was following the party line: it was she who was departing from it.[21] Labour's retention of the seat with the first pro-Government swing at any by-election since 1966 prompted Peter Thorneycroft to knock some heads together. At Shadow Cabinet on the eve of the new parliamentary session he insisted that all factions – and that meant Mrs Thatcher – should observe the compromise formula agreed in *The Right Approach*.[22] Next day, in her speech on the Address, she duly toed the line. Indeed she was extraordinarily conciliatory. While still arguing that rigid norms always broke down sooner or later, so that there was no choice in the end but to trust to responsible collective bargaining, she was ready to accept that the Government should aim to achieve an *average* figure for pay rises and offered the surprising assurance that she and Callaghan both wanted the same thing and were not in practice very far apart.[23]

Once again she had had to trim her convictions for the sake of unity. Her willingness to do so convinced colleagues on both sides of the argument that her policy in government would be little different from Callaghan's;[24] while Enoch Powell once again concluded that Mrs Thatcher was no different from Heath. 'If the Conservatives get in again', he predicted scornfully, 'they would be off once more on a policy of price and income control before you can say Jack Robinson.'[25] If that was so, it seemed that the public preferred the man who believed in it. A poll in early November discovered that a narrow Tory lead of 3 per cent over Labour leapt to 14 per cent if Heath were to be restored as Tory leader. When asked which would make the better Prime Minister, 55 per cent said Heath, only 33 per cent Mrs Thatcher.[26] Gallup's measure of her personal approval rating was also down to 33 per cent.[27] There was no possibility of a challenge to her leadership so close to an election; but her position had never been so weak.

At the beginning of December 1978 Callaghan came back from a European Council meeting in Brussels and announced that Britain, in common with Ireland and Italy, would not be joining the European Monetary System – the latest venture in European integration originally foreshadowed by Heath, Georges Pompidou and Willi Brandt in 1972 and now brought to fruition by Giscard d'Estaing, Helmut Schmidt and the first British President of the Commission, Roy Jenkins. Mrs Thatcher immediately condemned the Government's decision. 'This is a sad day for Europe,' she declared in the Commons.

> It is also a sad reflection on the performance of this Government that after four and a half years the Prime Minister is content to have Britain openly classified among the poorest and least influential members of the Community.[28]

In the light of her own adamant determination to stay out of the EMS over the next ten years her enthusiam for joining in 1978 is remarkable. Yet it followed naturally from her consistently positive attitude towards Europe since becoming leader. While on the stage of East–West relations the Iron Lady was already rehearsing the role she would play in government, Mrs Thatcher gave no hint in opposition of hostility towards Europe. If this was largely because she felt bound by the Tory party's long-standing commitment to Britain's place in Europe, so recently endorsed in the referendum, it also reflected political opportunism: she could not resist the easy points to be scored by criticising the Government's failure to make the most of Britain's membership. In December 1975, for instance, she told Harold Wilson that he would have better defended British interests at the EEC Council in Rome 'through co-operation instead of antagonistic tactics'. Wilson retorted that, on the contrary, he had stood up for Britain, where she would simply have surrendered.[29] Three years later she berated Callaghan for being insufficiently *communautaire* at the Paris summit in March 1979:

> It would be more to Britain's advantage if he and his colleagues dropped their abrasive and critical attitude towards our Common Market partners and behaved genuinely as partners, in which case we might get some of our problems solved.[30]

Did she ever recall her own advice when she found herself embattled with Schmidt and Giscard at Dublin just six months later? The most piquant hostage to history was offered the next day by Neil Kinnock – then a fiercely anti-European Labour backbencher – deriding Mrs Thatcher as 'the last pro-Marketeer in Britain'. He added, more accurately, that 'for the right hon. Lady to protest a dislike of abrasiveness is rather like Count Dracula professing a distaste for blood'.[31]

Still keen to promote the Tories as the party that wanted to make a success of Britain's membership of the Community, Mrs Thatcher backed the introduction of direct elections to the European Parliament in 1977, despite her own dim view of the institution and a significant backbench rebellion by several of her closest supporters, including Norman Tebbit. As they filed through the lobby she told Norman Lamont that 'she had been advised that it was necessary'.[32] In public, however, she boasted that far more Tories (229 out of 280) than Labour Members (only 132 out of 308) had supported direct elections. 'That shows the whole difference in attitude towards Europe.'[33]

Yet her own attitude to Europe was always firmly Gaullist. She wanted Britain to *lead* in Europe, not because she had a vision of European integration but because her vision of Britain demanded nothing less. In this at least she was at one with Heath. 'If we always go to the Community as a supplicant,' she told Callaghan in December 1976, 'either for subsidies or for loans, that prevents us

carrying out the wider creative role which was very much expected
of us when we joined the Community.'[34] She hated seeing Britain
stay out of the EMS, not because she believed in the system for itself
but because exclusion cast Britain 'in the second division economically of European countries, and since Britain was the victor in
Europe, this comes very hard to the British people'.[35] Her view of
Britain's proper relationship to the continent continued to be shaped
by the memory of the war.

Thus she never really grasped the idea of a European *community* as
understood by the other members, but always saw it primarily as a
defence organisation, an arm of NATO. When she visited Brussels
in December 1977 Roy Jenkins showed her round the Commission
and explained the workings of his empire. She was 'anxious to be
pleasant' and 'seemed interested', Jenkins recorded in his diary. But
she made a poor impression over lunch with the Commissioners, and
afterwards mishandled her press conference. First, 'she sounded
confused as to whether she had been visiting NATO or the
Commission, and kept on making what were essentially strategic
points'. Then, though she tried to be positive, her instinctive
scepticism kept getting in the way:

> Insofar as she let anything emerge it was that while she intended to
> be more pro-European than Callaghan, she couldn't think of any
> particular ways in which she was going to be so, and indeed chose
> – or allowed herself to be driven into – subjects of discussion on
> which she is just as uncooperative as the present British
> Government.[36]

With the benefit of hindsight, a note of reservation can usually be
read into Mrs Thatcher's statements on the future of Europe. In her
'Iron Lady' speech at Kensington Town Hall, for instance, she stated
ambiguously that 'any steps towards closer European union must be
carefully considered';[37] while in her Iain Macleod Memorial Lecture
in 1977 she identified one of the challenges facing Britain as 'how to
further our European partnership while protecting legitimate British
interests'.[38] Up to the last minute it was by no means certain that she
would come down in favour of the EMS. In September 1978 Jenkins
found Peter Carrington – by then hoping to be Foreign Secretary –
'as always . . . gloomy and critical about Mrs Thatcher', 'rather
hopeless about his ability to deal with [her]' and 'very depressed
about the prospects, saying quite firmly that he thought she would
be against the EMS and that there would not be enough pro-
European strength in a Tory Cabinet to carry her along'.[39] By

contrast the Tory anti-Marketeer Neil Marten also felt that Mrs Thatcher was 'really anti-Europe' at heart, but was 'surrounded by a hostile, pro-European Shadow Cabinet'. Marten told Tony Benn that he and Powell were working with the Labour anti-Marketeers Douglas Jay and Bryan Gould to try to stop Mrs Thatcher backing Callaghan in signing up for the EMS.[40] In fact, had Callaghan decided to join, it is more likely that she would have condemned that decision as opportunistically as she condemned his decision to stay out.

In her memoirs she pleads that it would have been 'less than human' for an Opposition to refrain from condemning the Government's failure to join the EMS, but claims that this was only a tactical position which reserved judgement on whether a Tory Government would join.[41] In the event she did not join either – but for the opposite reason. Whereas Callaghan feared joining at too high a rate which would have prevented him dealing with unemployment, she feared joining at too low a rate, which would have hindered her dealing with inflation. Jenkins maintains that they were both wrong, and that staying outside the EMS gave Britain both higher inflation and higher unemployment in the early 1980s than the countries which were inside.[42] By 1985 both Geoffrey Howe and Nigel Lawson came to agree. By then, however, Mrs Thatcher was prepared to stake her whole authority, and ultimately destroy her Government, in her absolute refusal to take the plunge which in 1978 she had castigated Callaghan for refusing.

The winter of industrial action against the Government's 5 per cent pay limit began in the private sector with a short but successful strike at the Ford Motor Company, which was doing well and preferred to pay increases of 15–17 per cent rather than suffer a long strike. The Government announced that Ford would be punished for breaching the pay policy by the withdrawal of public contracts. In the Commons Mrs Thatcher denounced this arbitrary blacklisting of a profitable company as 'a blatant injustice' which illustrated what happened when the Government interfered with free collective bargaining. Callaghan responded that the Government could not contain excessive pay rises without penalising those who broke the limit; they could not punish the tiddlers and let the big fish get away.[43] But penalising a major exporter like Ford was obviously self-defeating; and two weeks before Christmas the Government – now lacking a majority since the ending of the Lib-Lab pact – was defeated by six votes on the penal clauses, leaving the pay policy toothless before the major challenges in the New Year.

On 3 January the road haulage drivers went on strike, demanding 25 per cent, followed by the oil tanker drivers, stopping deliveries to industry, power stations, hospitals and schools. Action quickly spread to local authority and National Health Service manual workers – porters, cleaners, janitors, refuse collectors and the like – demanding a £60 minimum wage. There followed two or three weeks of near anarchy, displaying the ugliest face of militant trade unionism. The transport of goods by road practically dried up. Employees were laid off as businesses were crippled by lack of deliveries, enforced by intimidatory and often violent picketing of docks and factories. Piles of rubbish lay uncollected in the streets. Roads were not gritted (in very cold weather), schools were closed and hospitals admitted only emergency cases, while shop stewards took it on themselves to determine what was an emergency. Most famously, in Liverpool, the dead went unburied. On 22 January 1.5 million workers joined in a national Day of Action, the biggest stoppage since the General Strike in 1926. All this left the Government looking helpless and irrelevant – an impression damagingly reinforced by Callaghan's ill-judged attempt to play down the seriousness of the crisis on his return from a sunny G7 summit in Guadeloupe. He never actually used the words 'Crisis? What crisis?' But the *Sun*'s headline accurately paraphrased the impression he conveyed.[44] The whole shambles could not have been better scripted to achieve precisely what Strauss and Hoskyns had urged in *Stepping Stones*, turning Labour's hitherto biggest asset, the party's close relations with the unions, into its greatest liability and delivering the Conservatives an irresistible mandate for tougher action against the unions than Mrs Thatcher had previously dared contemplate.

Yet she was initially hesitant in gathering this electoral windfall. Interviewed by Brian Walden on *Weekend World* on 7 January she struck a more aggressive note. 'We've been afraid to talk about trade union power for four years,' she admitted; but 'public opinion has changed tremendously since 1971, it is ready for things which it was not ready for.' Yet she was still cautious in suggesting specific measures. She repeated the one commitment she had already made, to provide public funding for union elections and strike ballots if the unions wished to accept it, but would still not make them compulsory; and she floated (in lengthy technical detail) the possibility of denying social security benefits to strikers if there had not been a ballot. When Walden dismissed these proposals as 'peripheral' she suggested in addition removing the right to strike from workers in key utilities and revived the idea she had canvassed with Walden two years earlier of appealing to the public by means of a referendum. But that was all.[45] In her memoirs Lady Thatcher claims that just by mentioning compulsory ballots, in contradiction of Prior, she had moved them up the agenda. 'I had broken ranks. People could see that I was going to fight.'[46] In truth she was only putting a toe in the water.

She was a good deal more forthright three days later in a speech to the British Chambers of Commerce at the Savoy. In the short run she accused the Government of failing in its 'overriding responsibility to keep essential services and supplies going'.

In the longer run we must consider the fundamental problems arising from the industrial situation, including the whole problem of Trade Union power and the way it is used . . .

She raised again the question of strikers' benefits:

To many people it seems that we are subsidising strikers on the grounds of hardship to their families, to enable them to inflict far more serious and widespread hardship on others.

'It is time we got to grips with the causes of this recurring situation', she declared, 'and, taking public opinion with us, tackled them at their roots.'[47]

Public opinion was the key. Mrs Thatcher was still determined not to commit herself to any confrontation with the unions without first making sure that the public would be on her side. She was convinced that the great majority of decent trade unionists wanted only to be allowed to work for a fair wage without being bullied by politically motivated militants. But to win their support she must not seem to be spoiling for a fight. The critical test was the speech she was due to make when Parliament reassembled on 16 January, followed by a party political broadcast on television the next day. Her first intention was to make a conventional opposition speech, lambasting the Government for the collapse of its policy. Over the weekend of 14–15 January, however, she was persuaded by those closest to her – Peter Thorneycroft, Tim Bell and the writers working on the speech, Peter Utley, Ronnie Millar and Chris Patten – to take a rather different line and offer to support the Government, in a spirit of national co-operation, if it would take the necessary measures to disarm the militants.

Her instinctive reaction was hostile: she had spent the previous four years dismissing talk of governments of national unity. 'You don't join hands with a government you're trying to overthrow', she objected, 'except in wartime . . . You're asking me to let Callaghan off the hook.' 'No,' Thorneycroft told her. 'We're asking you to put country before party.' This argument touched a nerve, and she reluctantly agreed.[48] In the Commons she duly offered the Government Tory support for three specific measures: a ban on secondary picketing, funding of strike ballots and no-strike agreements in essential services. There was never any likelihood that Callaghan would accept – he brushed her off with his usual weary assurance that it was all much more difficult than she imagined – but the offer gained her the patriotic high ground, particularly when she repeated it on television.

'Yes,' she began as the caption faded, 'technically this is a Party Political Broadcast on behalf of the Conservative Party. But tonight I don't propose to use the time to make party political points. I do not think you would want me to do so.'

> The crisis that our country faces is too serious for that. And it is our country, the whole nation, that faces this crisis, not just one party or even one government. This is no time to put party before country. I start from there.

Successive governments over the past fifteen years, she recalled, had tried to strike a fair balance with trade union power and been defeated. No government had been able to achieve it alone.

> The case is now surely overwhelming, there will be no solution to our difficulties which does not include some restriction on the power of the unions. And if that case is overwhelming, then in the national interest surely government and opposition should make common cause on this one issue.

She repeated the three proposals which she pretended to hope the Labour Government might accept, and concluded by appealing to the 'vast majority' – including, she believed, 'the vast majority of trade unionists' – who yearned for the country to stop tearing itself apart. She ended with her favourite maxim: 'We have to learn again to be one nation, or one day we shall be no nation.'[49]

This broadcast was a huge success. 'Although she remained unconvinced by our strategy', Millar recalled, 'she did the broadcast like the professional she had become . . . For the first time she sounded like a national leader . . . It did more to swing the country

behind her than any subsequent speech.'[50] Tim Bell believes quite
simply that 'this broadcast won her the election'.[51] Certainly
Callaghan was wrong-footed. Bound to reject her poisoned offer, he
could only wring his hands at the excesses of secondary picketing
and plead with his union friends to operate a flimsy code of practice,
while insisting that existing laws already gave the police all the
powers they needed to stop picket-line violence. Meanwhile his
rejection of co-operation freed Mrs Thatcher to step up her attack
on the Government's impotence. In the Commons she called on the
Home Secretary, Merlyn Rees, to issue stronger guidance to Chief
Constables and demanded the declaration of a state of emergency,[52]
while in a speech in Glasgow she condemned the 'wreckers in our
midst' and declared more boldly than ever before that the nation had
to 'fight and win the conflicts within'.[53]

The Government's refusal of her offer – which she had taken the
precaution of clearing with the Shadow Cabinet – also wrong-footed
her own doves. Jim Prior continued to talk down the role of
legislation, but since Callaghan had declined what she now called –
in a speech to Young Conservatives – 'a bit of decent, generous,
patriotic collaboration across party lines',[54] Mrs Thatcher was
increasingly free to assert that it was now up to the Tories to
shoulder alone the responsibility of bringing the unions 'back within
the law'. 'That's the task which this government will not do, it'll run
away from it,' she mocked. 'I don't shirk any of it. I shall do it.'[55]
Appearing again on the Jimmy Young radio programme on 31
January she no longer shrank from the word 'confrontation' but
positively embraced it, insisting that it was not she who was doing
the confronting.

> Some of the unions are confronting the British people, they
> are confronting the sick, they are confronting the old, they are
> confronting the children. I am prepared to take on anyone who is
> confronting those and who is confronting the law of the land . . .
> If someone is confronting our essential liberties, if someone is
> inflicting injury, harm and damage on the sick, my God, I will
> confront them.[56]

She was still cautious in her actual proposals. When she spoke of
bringing the unions within the law, for instance, she explained that
she only meant reversing the additional privileges extended to them
by Labour since 1974, not removing the unions' legal immunity
from actions for tort which many Tories had considered the root of
the problem ever since it was conceded by Campbell-Bannerman's

Liberal Government in 1906.[57] She never suggested ending the unions' political levy, which Baldwin had temporarily curtailed after the General Strike; and she still only spoke of mitigating the effect of the closed shop, not abolishing it. In practice Prior's softly-softly approach was still in place; but at the level of rhetoric it was swept aside. For the first time Mrs Thatcher had a clearly understood cause to which the long-suffering public now emphatically responded. The polls which at the beginning of the year had still shown the Tories neck and neck with Labour, or even a few points behind, now gave them a twenty-point lead, while Mrs Thatcher's personal rating had leapt to 48 per cent.[58] The various disputes were eventually settled, on terms mostly around 9 per cent, and life returned to something like normal. But the legacy of bitterness remained. It seemed that nothing could now stop the Tories winning the election, whenever it was held.

Even though the Liberals had ended the formal arrangement of the Lib-Lab pact, Callaghan could still have tried to hang on until the autumn, cobbling together *ad hoc* alliances with the minor parties to see him through each division in the hope that the memory of the winter's humiliation would gradually fade. But his heart was not in it. The issue which finally precipitated the Government's demise was devolution. On 1 March the Welsh and Scottish people were finally given the chance to vote on Labour's proposals for assemblies in Cardiff and Edinburgh. On turnouts which suggested a profound lack of interest, the Welsh overwhelmingly rejected their proposed talking-shop (by a margin of 8–1), while the Scots voted in favour of an Edinburgh parliament by a margin too small to meet the condition written into the Bill by dissident Labour backbenchers. The Scottish result left the Scottish National Party with no reason to continue to support the Government (except that, had they considered the alternative, they were even less likely to get a Scottish parliament from Mrs Thatcher). For the first time the parliamentary arithmetic gave the Tories a real chance of bringing the Government down. On 28 March, therefore, Mrs Thatcher tabled yet another vote of confidence.

There was still no certainty that it would succeed, even when the SNP, the Liberals and most of the Ulster Unionists declared their intention to vote against the Government. There were in that Parliament an exceptionally large number of small parties and maverick individuals: Labour still held a majority of 24 over the Conservatives, but the two main parties together accounted for only

592 MPs out of the total of 635. In the days before the vote the corridors and tearooms of the Palace of Westminster saw a frenzy of arm-twisting and bribery, bluff and double bluff. The three Plaid Cymru Members were persuaded to support the Government with a promise of industrial injuries compensation for North Wales slate miners. Two 'Scottish Labour' Members announced that they would back the Government. Roy Hattersley secured two of the Ulster Unionists. The rest could still have been bought by the promise of a gas pipeline connecting Northern Ireland to the mainland: to maintain his bargaining power Enoch Powell would have grasped almost any excuse to keep the minority government in office. But by this time Callaghan saw no point in bartering his soul for a few more precarious weeks in office. He had already pencilled in 3 May for an election, whether he lost or won the crucial vote.[59]

For her part Mrs Thatcher made it clear that she would do no deals with anyone. 'I don't wheel and deal with the minor parties,' she announced. 'I don't play duck and drakes with the constitution. I am in politics because I believe certain things and I expect them to be in their particular parties because they believe certain things.'[60] Yet right up to the last moment the outcome was too close to call. The Irish nationalists Gerry Fitt and Frank Maguire were random factors, enjoying their moment of pivotal importance. Two of the Scottish Nationalists were rumoured to be reconsidering their position. One Labour Member was seriously ill but could perhaps be 'nodded through' the lobby, while the Liberal Clement Freud might be persuaded to abstain in return for Government time for his Freedom of Information Bill. When Mrs Thatcher left Flood Street that morning, telling reporters, 'We are hopeful. I think it's an even chance . . . I only know that I shall get my people out in strength', [61] the parliamentary stage was set for a rare cliffhanger. 'In my heart of hearts', she confesses in her memoirs, she thought the Government would probably survive.[62]

She made – as usual on these big occasions – a predictable and pedestrian speech indicting the Government on four familiar charges. 'First, far too little attention has been given to wealth creation and far too much to wealth distribution'; the answer to that was tax cuts, incentives and the encouragement of profits. Second, 'the Government have concentrated far too much power in the hands of the centralised state and left too little with the individual citizen', leading to – her favourite phrase – 'a sort of pocket money society'. Third, 'the balance between power and responsibility in the trade union movement needs to be restored'. A Labour Government would never make the necessary changes. 'Changes will have to be made by another Government, and I believe they will have the overwhelming support of the people, including the majority of trade union members.' Fourth, she alleged, the Government had substituted 'the rule of the mob' for the rule of law. It was not merely this Labour Government, she asserted, but socialism itself which had reached the end of the road.

> There has been a failure not only of policies but of the whole philosophy on which they are based – the philosophy which elevates the State, dwarfs the individual and enlarges the bureaucracy. Across the western world the tide is turning against that, and soon the same thing will happen here.

'The only way to renew the authority of parliamentary government', she concluded, 'is to seek a fresh mandate from the people and to seek it quickly. We challenge the Government to do so before this day is through.'[63]

It reads well enough, but it was heard 'in complete silence'. When Callaghan rose to reply the left-wing MP Eric Heffer called out 'Be kind, Jim.'[64] Callaghan made a good debating speech twitting Mrs Thatcher for putting down her confidence motion only when she knew the Liberals and Scottish Nationalists were going to vote against the Government. 'She had the courage of their convictions.'[65] At the end of the debate Michael Foot wound up with a brilliant barnstorming performance; and then came the vote. As Tory MPs filed through the lobby, the word spread that they had lost by one vote. Humphrey Atkins was heard apologising to Mrs Thatcher for having failed to muster his full strength: the House catering facilities were on strike and two or three Tories failed to get back from dinner at their clubs. Kenneth Baker best describes the scene:

> We returned to the Chamber looking rather crestfallen while the Labour benches looked very cheerful. Adam Butler, one of Margaret's PPSs, came into the Chamber and told us the vote was tied, but a Labour Whip who followed him looked very confident. Margaret was looking very dejected when suddenly Tony Berry, who had been counting in the Labour Lobby, appeared from behind the Speaker's chair and held up his thumb. We couldn't believe it. Spencer le Marchant holding the teller's slip stepped up to the table and read out 'Ayes 311 – Noes 310' . . .[66]

This was the first time a Government had lost a confidence

motion on the floor of the House since the defeat of Ramsay MacDonald's first Labour Government in 1924. Callaghan immediately announced that he would ask the Queen for a dissolution. Mrs Thatcher demanded that the election be held as soon as possible, preferably on 26 April. But that would have been difficult with Easter on 15 April. The next day Callaghan announced that it would be held on the same day as the local government elections on 3 May, giving time for Healey to produce an uncontentious caretaker Budget on 3 April before Parliament was dissolved.

Labour made no secret that they hoped a long campaign would work to their advantage. 'Maggie's Nerve Is The Target', reported the *Observer*.[67] They hoped either that Mrs Thatcher would crack under the strain, or that her moderate mask would slip, exposing divisions in the Tory leadership. With the polls showing the Tories 9 to 13 per cent ahead – a record lead at the beginning of a campaign – their only hope was to personalise the contest as much as possible, contrasting Callaghan's experience and reassuring conservatism with Mrs Thatcher's inexperience and alarming radicalism. 'If this was a Presidential election', noted the *Financial Times*, 'there would be no doubt about the outcome.'[68]

Contrary to the received wisdom that television confrontations usually benefit the challenger, therefore, Labour was keen to accept a proposal from Thames TV to bring the two leaders together for a head-to-head debate. For her part Mrs Thatcher wanted to agree: after three years of Prime Ministers' Questions she reckoned she could handle Callaghan. But both Peter Thorneycroft and Willie Whitelaw, and perhaps more importantly Gordon Reece, were firmly against the idea. Their strategy was to keep the campaign as low-key as possible, avoiding any risks which might jeopardise their commanding lead. All Reece's efforts over the previous four years to give her a softer image could have been ruined in five minutes by the sight of Mrs Thatcher laying into Uncle Jim. 'She might have won', Thorneycroft told David Butler, 'but then many men would have resented it. They would have said "There's my wife" and it wouldn't have been a good thing.'[69] The argument that probably persuaded Mrs Thatcher was that the Liberal leader David Steel would either have had to be included in a three-way debate or else compensated with a long interview to himself. The one outcome she feared was the Liberals coming through the middle preaching moderation between the two extremes, as Thorpe had done in February 1974.

So she wrote back to Thames formally declining the invitation: 'We are not electing a President, we are choosing a Government.'[70]

Generally speaking she was pretty confident, though she never liked to count her chickens: she had a superstitious nightmare that she might win the national election but lose her own seat in Finchley.[71] Unlike many politicians Mrs Thatcher thoroughly enjoyed electioneering, and after four years of frustration she threw herself into the contest – her ninth – with relish, knowing that it would either make or break her. The only thing she hated was having to wait two weeks to get started. Central Office decided that she should not start campaigning in earnest before Easter. In the meantime she was driving her staff to distraction, so to try to take her mind off politics Ronnie Millar took her three times to the theatre. She found the humour of the Two Ronnies live on stage a lot bluer than on television, and was not amused, even when Millar explained that blue was a good Conservative colour. The sentimental American musical *Annie* was more her cup of tea, but she insisted on going backstage to see Sheila Hancock – a lifelong socialist – who had pointedly withdrawn to her dressing room to avoid having to meet her. Finally Millar took her to *Evita*, Andrew Lloyd Webber's musical about the Argentine political adventuress Eva Peron. Here was a heroine she could identify with, up to a point, yet one who challenged her simple sense of right and wrong. 'I was thinking', she wrote to Millar the next day, 'if a woman like that can get to the top without any morals, how high could someone get who has one or two?'[72]

Though she could take nothing for granted and firmly deflected all questions about the composition of her Cabinet, she was nevertheless making some dispositions. For instance she had already chosen her chief press officer. Her first choice was Tony Shrimsley, the assistant editor of the *Sun*; but he turned her down. In complete contrast she alighted next on Henry James, the former head of the Central Office of Information, who had retired from the civil service in October to take up a job with Vickers. James was reluctant to go back into Whitehall, but she insisted and persuaded Vickers to release him for six months, starting the day after the election. The appointment was kept secret until then, but it was not in the least hypothetical. Mrs Thatcher appeared to James absolutely confident that she would soon be Prime Minister. [73] At the same time Richard Ryder was making the necessary arrangements for the handover of power with Callaghan's principal private secretary, Kenneth Stowe. This is standard civil service procedure during General Elections; but it went exceptionally smoothly on this occasion. Mrs Thatcher had met Stowe several times in the normal course of Government–Opposition co-operation over the past three years and – after some initial suspicion – had come to trust him. He too had the impression that she was confident of winning.[74]

The electoral strategy set by Reece and Thorneycroft had three strands – neutral, negative and positive. The first priority was to protect the Tory lead by keeping the campaign as dull as possible and allowing Mrs Thatcher to say nothing that might frighten the voters. The negative strand was to keep the heat on Labour, reminding the electors in simple language of the Government's record since 1974: inflation ('prices'), unemployment ('jobs'), cuts in public services (schools, homes and hospitals) and above all the strikes and picket-line violence of the winter. Building on the success of 'Labour Isn't Working', Saatchis produced another series of posters on the same theme: 'Labour Still Isn't Working' (this time showing a queue of patients trying to get into hospital), 'Educashun isn't Working', 'Britain Isn't Getting Any Better'. From this the positive appeal followed naturally – the simplest electoral cry of all, 'Time for a change' (or as another poster put it: 'Cheer Up! Labour Can't Hang On For Ever'). For a party wishing to present itself as the wind of change without being specific about the precise nature of that change, Mrs Thatcher's gender was a godsend. The possibility of electing the first woman Prime Minister gave the Tory campaign a radical *frisson*, independent of anything she might say. If the country needed a new broom, who better to wield it than a brisk, no-nonsense woman? 'Maggie' – as she was now universally known – symbolised a fresh start before she even opened her mouth.

When the question of her sex was raised, as it always was, on phone-ins and television question-and-answer programmes, Mrs Thatcher sometimes tried to insist that it made no difference at all. 'I just hope that they will take me as I am, for what I can do. Not as a man or a woman, but as a personality who has an absolute passion for getting things right for Britain.'[75] More often, though, she made the most of being different. She liked to point out that Britain had done pretty well under female rulers – particularly Elizabeth I – in the past. Sometimes she mentioned Golda Meir (but never Indira Gandhi) as a contemporary role model.[76] Alternatively she claimed that any woman who had brought up a family had more experience of management than most men, and brushed off doubts about her strength or stamina: 'Any woman who has had to get up in the night to her children and still cope can stand this. By comparison, all this is a doddle.'[77]

Above all she shamelessly played up to her conviction that 'they will turn to me because they believe a woman knows about prices'.[78] Right at the beginning of the campaign Reece encouraged her to go shopping for the benefit of the cameras in the King's Road, near Flood Street. She bought four and a half pounds of mince, in three bags for the freezer, and two days later explained to George Gale in the *Daily Express* that she would take one out to make a shepherd's pie that night. Mince was so versatile, she added: you could make hamburgers, bolognese sauce, all sorts of things with it.[79] Later in the campaign she visited a supermarket in Halifax, bought four jars of instant coffee and a lump of cheese (with a five pound note!) and discoursed knowledgeably about the prices of butter and tea, holding up two shopping bags, red and blue, to illustrate how much prices had risen under Labour.[80] She repeatedly insisted that managing public expenditure was no different from running a household budget: the country, like every ordinary household, must live within its means. In Bristol, she was presented with a big broom with which to sweep the country clean of socialism.[81]

The *Daily Mirror* tried to turn her femininity against her by portraying the Tory leader as a witch. ('What would YOUR life be like under Mrs Thatcher's broomstick?')[82] But on balance her housewife image, skilfully exploited, was an asset. It made her appear homely, practical and unthreatening, helping to counteract the more alarming aspects of her personality and message. 'A Woman's Place Is In No. 10', the *Sun* proclaimed on 21 April.[83] She undoubtedly attracted support from some surprising quarters because she was a woman: Harold Wilson disclosed that his wife Mary was thinking of voting for her, and his former political secretary Marcia Falkender offered covert assistance.[84] There is little evidence that the Tories suffered any equivalent defection from men who disapproved of a female Prime Minister. On the contrary, male supremacists – what one might call the Alf Garnett vote – were precisely those who responded most strongly to her views on immigration, hanging, strikers and defence.

The Conservative manifesto – published five days after Labour's on 11 April – was unusually short and deliberately vague: it did not even have a title. Drafted by Chris Patten and Adam Ridley and edited by Angus Maude, it concentrated on the broad themes which Mrs Thatcher had been plugging for the past four years – tax cuts, spending cuts, incentives, reducing the share of the national income taken by the state, control of the money supply, freedom under the law, strong defence – but made extraordinarily few specific commitments. Even on taxation, it promised only to cut the top rate of income tax 'to the European average', giving no figure, and to switch 'to some extent' from taxes on earnings to taxes on spending, concealing the scale of the switch Geoffrey Howe actually had in mind. The only suggested targets for spending cuts were the National Enterprise Board, whose activities would be scaled down, and that oldest standby of Oppositions, 'waste, bureaucracy and over-government'.

The one part of the manifesto which had been beefed up since October was the section on trade union law, where Mrs Thatcher's three proposed reforms – to limit secondary picketing, introduce compensation for workers dismissed as a result of a closed shop and provide postal ballots for union elections – were spelled out, together with a new promise to ensure that unions should 'bear their fair share of the cost of supporting those of their members who are on strike'. Her determination to restore 'responsible collective bargaining' in the private sector was reiterated, with the warning that 'at the end of the day no one should or can protect [companies and workers] from the results of the agreements they make'. Public sector pay would be subject to cash limits. The recently nationalised aircraft and shipbuilding industries would be denationalised, 'giving their employees the opportunity to purchase shares', and shares in the National Freight Corporation would also be sold to raise investment. Private bus operators would be encouraged. Meanwhile other nationalised industries like railways would be expected to improve their productivity. There was no suggestion of privatising them.

There was a strong section on law and order, promising to increase police pay, introduce longer sentences and tougher detention centres for young offenders, plus a new Nationality Act and stricter controls on immigration. There were promises to sell council houses and encourage private renting; to stem (as Mrs Thatcher had failed to do in 1970–4) the continuing march of comprehensive schools, introduce a Parents' Charter and assisted places to make up for Labour's abolition of Direct Grant schools, and set 'national standards in reading, writing and arithmetic'. A slightly guarded promise was given that 'it is not our intention to reduce spending on the National Health Service', together with an unspecific pledge to 'end Labour's vendetta against the private health sector'. The usual Conservative promise was given to simplify and target social security on those in greatest need, with a specific pledge to honour Labour's increase in pensions.[85]

Finding clear policies in this manifesto, Denis Healey mocked, was 'like looking for a black cat in a dark coal cellar'[86] – which is not to say that the cat was not there. The day after her shopping trip to Halifax, the *Daily Telegraph* cartoonist, Nicholas Garland, drew Mrs

Thatcher holding up two shopping bags – one representing Labour's record bulging with strikes, unemployment and increased crime, the other almost empty labelled 'We'll let you know after we win'.[87] This was very near the mark, as two little-noticed sentences in the Introduction hinted. 'Those who look in these pages for lavish promises or detailed commitments on every subject will look in vain,' it acknowledged. '*We may be able to do more in the next five years than we indicate here. We believe we can.*' All the manifesto aimed to do, Mrs Thatcher stated in her brief Foreword, was to set out 'a broad framework for the recovery of our country, based not on dogma, but on reason, on common sense, above all on the liberty of the people under the law'.[88]

All elections are about winning votes; but the first priority of the major British parties has usually been to get their own supporters out, and then hope to win some of the 'floating' voters in the middle, rather than trying to convert the opposition. The Tory campaign in 1979, by contrast, was determinedly aimed at winning over voters who had never voted Conservative before and still did not think of themselves as Tories – specifically the patriotic, acquisitive, upwardly mobile, *Sun*-reading upper working class, those defined by the advertisers as C2s: skilled workers who were fed up with trade union bullying and restrictive practices which prevented them working longer hours for higher pay; lower middle class men and women living in council estates who wanted to own their own homes. They also targeted first-time voters (18 to 22-year-olds) and those who had voted Liberal in 1974; but it was the explicit appeal to disillusioned Labour voters which was novel. Reece and Tim Bell studied their target audience, co-ordinated their presentation with Larry Lamb and deliberately set out to project values and emotions, rather than policies.[89] The *Sun* ran a series of articles by former Labour ministers – Reg Prentice, Richard Marsh, Lord George-Brown, Lord Robens and Lord Chalfont – explaining why they had switched their allegiance. Mrs Thatcher appealed to others to follow their example in her first big speech of the election on 16 April. With typical chutzpah she launched her campaign on Callaghan's home territory, Cardiff, and set out to pluck the heart strings of old Labour voters everywhere.

'There used to be, in this country, a Socialism which valued people,' she recalled without a trace of irony. 'It had dignity and it had warmth.' But that old socialism was a world away from 'the officious, jargon-filled intolerant Socialism practised by Labour these last few years', the Socialism of flying pickets, kangaroo courts 'and all the other ugly apparatus that has been strapped like a harness on our people'.

> I think that many traditional Labour supporters want the same things that we want, believe the same things that we believe, but they're somehow held back by old loyalties and prejudices. To them I would say this . . . We understand the deep-seated loyalties and affections that make you hesitate to cross the Rubicon. We know that it's not easy to forsake the habits of a lifetime, but the modern Labour party is no longer the party of Clement Attlee, of Hugh Gaitskell and of Roy Jenkins . . .

Recalling Burke's aphorism that all that is necessary for the triumph of evil is for the good people to do nothing, she went on:

> All that is necessary for the triumph of Marxist Socialism in this country is that a majority of you, who normally vote Labour, should believe that the Labour party of today and tomorrow is the same as the Labour party of yesterday. It isn't. If you care deeply for our country, and you do not care for the way your present day Labour party is going, come with us. We offer you a political home where you can honourably realise the ideals which took you into the Labour party in the first place.[90]

It is impossible to say how many Labour voters, genuinely troubled by the abuse of union power and the growing militant takeover of local Labour parties, fell for this soft sell. Academic analysis of the 1979 result suggests that the Tories did do exceptionally well among their target groups, gaining an 11 per cent swing among the skilled working class (the C2s) and 9 per cent among the unskilled.[91] Many of these converts continued to vote Conservative throughout the 1980s. But there is also plentiful anecdotal evidence of lifelong Labour voters who were persuaded to vote Conservative for the first time, and spent the next ten years bitterly regretting it.

One who recorded his reasons at the time was the Director of the strike-ravaged National Theatre, Peter Hall. 'We are a society of greed and anarchy,' he wrote in his diary at the height of the winter chaos in terms which Mrs Thatcher herself could not have bettered. 'No honour, no responsibility, no pride. I sound like an old reactionary, which I'm not, but what we have now isn't socialism, it's fascism with those who have the power injuring those who do not.'[92] Three months later he shocked himself by deciding to vote

Tory, having come to the conclusion that Labour was no longer the party of social justice. 'It's now the party of sectional interest; the party that protects pressure groups and bully boys.'[93] 'It wasn't at all difficult this morning to vote Tory,' he wrote on 3 May. 'In fact it positively felt good . . . we have to have change.'[94] Hall wanted Mrs Thatcher to 'sort out' the unions. Fourteen years later he could not deny her the credit for having done so, though he loathed practically everything else she did, particularly the commercialisation of the arts. 'I can understand even now why I voted Tory,' he reflected in 1993. 'I very much wish I hadn't had to.'[95]

Mrs Thatcher dominated the Conservative campaign. Ironically the next most prominent figure was Ted Heath, who threw himself into the election with a belated display of loyalty transparently intended to make it impossible for her to exclude him from her Government. He kept off the sensitive subject of incomes policy but spoke mainly about foreign affairs – practically the only candidate in the election to do so – and clearly had his eye on the Foreign Office. Pressed in every interview to say if she would include him, however, Mrs Thatcher firmly declined to name her Cabinet in advance. The most visible members of the Shadow Cabinet were Willie Whitelaw, Jim Prior and Geoffrey Howe – all reassuring figures. Keith Joseph was kept out of sight – like Tony Benn and Michael Foot on the other side. Mrs Thatcher herself chaired eleven of the party's sixteen morning press conferences, flanked more often than not by Howe, sometimes by Prior, with a variety of other colleagues from St John Stevas to Rhodes Boyson appearing once each. At the opening press conference to launch the manifesto, with nearly all the party's heavyweights present, she made a big effort to show off her team:

> 'Keith, would you like to say a word about that?' she asked with motherly firmness. 'Francis, would you like to add anything?' And 'Perhaps someone will remember that Willie Whitelaw is here.'[96]

Another time, when Geoffrey Howe modestly declined to add anything to her economic answers, she told him firmly: 'Geoffrey, you've got to speak *sometime*.' 'It was the first time her headmistress tendencies had appeared in public,' John Cole recalled. 'She was on a nervous high, obviously enjoying herself, feeling already like a Prime Minister.'[97]

After the morning press conference she made flying sorties into the country, sometimes by air from Gatwick, sometimes in a specially equipped campaign 'battlebus', but almost always returning to London the same evening. She was normally accompanied by a large entourage comprising Janet Young, David Wolfson, Ronnie Millar and several more speech-writers, researchers and secretaries; Derek Howe, her chief press officer; usually one of her two PPSs; and a number of Central Office staff to keep the show on the road. The usual pattern was a factory visit or a walkabout in two or three key constituencies, an interview for regional television or local radio, followed by a big speech to a ticket-only rally of local Conservatives in the evening. Security was necessarily tight, following the murder of Airey Neave, blown up by an Irish car bomb two days after the election was declared, but the ticket-only rule – copied by Reece from his experience of Republican campaigning in the United States – reflected the Tories' strategy of shielding Mrs Thatcher from the possibility of encountering hostile audiences or demonstrations: as far as possible she should be shown only in controlled situations, speaking to rapturous congregations of the faithful.

In fact she was warmly received wherever she went and enjoyed meeting real people when she could get to them through the mass of journalists and film crews. In Ipswich – against the advice of her handlers – she 'braved a frightening crush of supporters to walk among the enthusiastic crowds' and made 'a short, confident, impromptu electioneering speech to a crowd of shoppers and passers-by . . . from the steps of the Town Hall'. ' "It was like being on the hustings thirty years ago," enthused one of her entourage.'[98] Michael White of the *Guardian*, covering her visit to a hospital in Swansea, was impressed by her 'capacity to work hard at her personal contact with the voters'.

> It is as if she knows she must compensate for her television image. She waxed knowledgeable about anaemia, double vision and false kneecaps, creating, as she can, little havens of intimacy despite the encircling wall of cameras.[99]

But of course it was all for the benefit of the cameras. Mrs Thatcher, normally with Denis in tow, lent herself patiently to every sort of charade in order to get a good picture in the local paper or clip on the television news. In a Leicester clothing factory she took over a sewing machine and stitched the pocket on a blue overall. In Cadbury's factory at Bourneville she operated a machine wrapping and packing chocolates. 'She picked up the job very well,' the foreman commented. 'I'd certainly employ her if she loses.' ('It was marvellous,' Mrs Thatcher gushed, perhaps a little tactlessly, 'a real break.')[100] In Milton Keynes she and Denis had their heartbeats and blood pressure tested. '"Steady as a rock," she declared triumphantly as the figures ... flashed on the screen. "They can't find anything wrong with me. They never can."' When someone said that her heart and lungs would last till polling day, she shot back confidently, 'Yes, and for the next twenty years in Downing Street.' She took the chance to remind the press that she would be not only the first woman Prime Minister, but the first with a science degree, and 'proceeded to deliver a brisk lecture on the system to monitor the temperature in containers at Tilbury', talking about computers 'with the same ease with which she had been discussing prices with shoppers'. Then she suddenly flashed a winning smile and said, 'There – didn't I learn my briefing well?'[101]

Most famously, visiting a farm in Norfolk, she cradled a new born calf in her arms. She held it for thirteen minutes, while the cameramen covered all the angles, until Denis warned that if she held it much longer they would have a dead calf on their hands. 'It's not for me – it's for the photographers,' she announced. 'They are the really important people in this election.'[102] 'Would you like another take?' she would ask them until they were happy.[103] Callaghan was contemptuous of these vacuous photo-opportunities. 'The voters don't want to see you cuddling a calf,' he told her. 'They want to be sure you're not selling them a pig in a poke.'[104] Some journalists began to realise that they were being manipulated. Adam Raphael wrote an article in the *Observer*, 'The Selling of Maggie', criticising the way the Tory leader was being packaged in a series of cosy images, devoid of political content.[105] But Reece knew exactly what he was doing. The press were offered seats on the Thatcher battlebus for £600 per head, and took them gratefully. In future elections they would grow more cynical. In 1979 they were still happy to print what they were fed.

The only serious interrogation she faced was on television and radio. Even Reece could not deny the heavyweight media their chance entirely. But Mrs Thatcher accepted only one major television interview and two audience question-and-answer sessions during the campaign, as well as two radio interviews and a phone-in. She initially refused to appear on Thames Television's *TV Eye* because she disapproved of the programme's regular interviewer, Llew Gardner, who had given her a tough going-over the only previous time he had interviewed her in 1976. To secure her co-operation, Gardner was replaced by Denis Tuohy; but as Butler and Kavanagh wrote, 'When an interviewer is publicly blackballed, the substitute is forced to show his mettle.'[106] Tuohy pressed her hard on her two clearest commitments, tax cuts and trade union reform: her refusal to put a figure on the scope for tax cuts until she had 'seen the books' left her looking uncharacteristically evasive, while she allowed herself to get angry with his line of questioning on the unions, accusing him of wanting to abolish democracy.[107] All Reece's training about speaking slowly, keeping her voice soft and making her point to the audience, not arguing with the interviewer, went out of the window on this occasion.

Her only other extended interviews were both on radio, with Jimmy Young on Radio 2 and Laurie Mayer on Radio 1. Jimmy Young did press her on how she was going to be able to cut taxes in view of all the extra spending she had promised on defence, police pay and pensions, but he was always a relaxed and sympathetic interviewer – he called her Margaret, she called him Jimmy – and questions from listeners gave her good opportunities to voice her views on the unions, capital punishment and Europe.* On Radio 4's *Election Call*, chaired by Robin Day, she firmly stood her ground on immigration, defending her use of the word 'swamped' and giving no hope to an Indian lady who wanted her adult son to be allowed to come to Britain.[109] Her other two major television appearances also brought her up against real voters. The BBC *Nationwide* programme gave a panel of eight members of the public the chance to question her; and Granada's *Granada 500* faced all three party leaders – separately but on the same evening – with an audience of five hundred voters in the marginal constituency of Bolton East. On neither did Mrs Thatcher say anything new, but the Bolton audience responded warmly to her populist line on hanging and immigration, and she was judged to have performed better than Callaghan.[110]

Contrary to Labour hopes that she would crack under the strain of a long campaign she made no serious blunders. The worst gaffe was committed on her behalf by one of her correspondence secretaries, Matthew Parris, who wrote back to a lady who complained of the Tories' hostility to council tenants that she should count herself lucky to enjoy accommodation 'that the rest of us are paying for out of taxes'.[111] Mrs Thatcher quickly apologised and denied that this represented her attitude – although of course it did – and the embarrassment passed. In her memoirs she claims that she refused to be gagged by Thorneycroft and others at Central Office who were always pressing her to tone down her strongly held convictions.[112] It

---

* This was one of the very few times she mentioned Europe in the campaign, and it was one of her strongest early statements of the limits she placed on European integration. 'I see no possibility of a federal Europe at all,' she told Jimmy Young.[108]

is true that she opened her campaign in Cardiff with a ringing declaration of her contempt for compromise:

> If you've got a message, preach it! The Old Testament prophets didn't go out on to the highways saying 'Brothers, I want consensus.' They said 'This is my faith and my vision! This is what I passionately believe.' And they preached it. We have a message. Go out, preach it, practise it, fight for it – and the day will be ours.[113]

Yet as the campaign went on she increasingly found it prudent to trim her sails. She regularly tempered her radical rhetoric with assurances that of course she would not 'suddenly change the whole economy' or 'tear everything up by the roots', as Callaghan alleged. 'We are the party of roots, of tradition,' she insisted in her first election broadcast. 'Paying your way isn't tearing things up by the roots. Paying your way is good husbandry.'[114] Asked about continued support for British Leyland, she admitted that 'You cannot suddenly chop off any industrial subsidy'.[115] Another time she promised to maintain 'a strong regional policy' and denied that this was not mentioned in the manifesto,[116] while at her last press conference she strenuously repudiated any plans to sell more BP shares.[117] As she explained to Jimmy Young:

> You know, you don't do anything at a stroke . . . It's really like driving a car . . . you don't just slam on the brakes . . . You stop gently, reverse, turn round and go steadily and continuously in a different direction. That's what we'll do, so there won't be any dislocation.[118]

She came under considerable pressure to promise to keep the value of old age pensions in step not just with prices, but with earnings. This she could not honestly do, since she must have known that Howe was planning to break the earnings link in his first Budget; but several times she said disingenuously that she *hoped* to be able to increase pensions in line with earnings.[119] Likewise she had to be careful what she said about increasing VAT; she denied that the Tories would double it, as Labour alleged, but every time the question was raised she emphasised how many essential items of expenditure were exempt.[120] She denied any intention of raising the price of school meals, or immediate plans to raise prescription charges.

Above all, she was obliged to make two commitments during the campaign which subsequently tied her hands. Firstly she had to promise to honour any pay awards that might be made by the Comparability Commission, chaired by Professor Hugh Clegg, set up by Labour in January as part of the settlement of the public sector strikes. This ran contrary to everything she had said about setting cash limits in the public sector and doing away with all the bureaucratic paraphernalia of incomes policy. But she was persuaded by Prior, Thorneycroft, Teddy Taylor (who was under pressure from the Scottish teachers) and 'a host of others' that it was electorally unavoidable.[121] Geoffrey Howe wrote in his memoirs he could 'think of no other democratic leader who would have resisted for so long as she did'.[122] But in the end she submitted. It proved an expensive commitment.

Secondly Patrick Jenkin, as shadow Health Secretary, significantly hardened the manifesto's tentative undertaking not to cut health spending. He asked his old friend Howe to authorise him to promise in a television interview that Labour's planned increases in spending on the Health Service would be honoured. Very likely Mrs Thatcher would have agreed to this, too: she was always nervous of touching the NHS. In fact Howe gave Jenkin the go-ahead off his own bat. As a result the NHS was the one part of the welfare state which was protected from public spending cuts for most of her first term.[123]

As the three-week campaign progressed the Tory lead in the polls was steadily cut back, from an average of around 11 per cent down to around 3 per cent, while Callaghan's personal lead over Mrs Thatcher widened. The Liberals, as usual during elections, picked up support, leading to renewed speculation about a hung Parliament (or what David Steel liked to call a 'People's Parliament'). Mrs Thatcher naturally insisted that she wanted and expected to win an overall Conservative majority, and vowed that she would do no deals with the Liberals or anyone else if she fell short. But from about the middle of the second week she began to sound more defensive, and sometimes a bit rattled.

At her press conference on 25 April – the day after her prickly interview on *TV Eye* – she was wrong-footed by Callaghan offering to show her 'the books', and did not seem to know how to reply.[124] Then she flew to Scotland for two days. She was unwinding in a hotel near Glasgow airport after a particularly successful speech in Edinburgh when Janet Young was called to the phone and came back with a message that Thorneycroft wanted to invite Ted Heath to join her at her final press conference. Ronnie Millar witnessed her reaction: 'Margaret exploded in a mixture of fury and supreme contempt. "Scared rabbits! They're running scared, that's what's the matter with them! The very idea! How *dare* they?" '[125]

Thorneycroft's suggestion, she wrote in her memoirs, was 'about as clear a demonstration of lack of confidence in me as could be imagined'.

> If Peter Thorneycroft and Central Office had not yet understood that what we were fighting for was a reversal not just of the Wilson–Callaghan approach but of the Heath Government's approach they had understood nothing. I told Janet Young that if she and Peter thought that then I might as well pack up.

'This', she adds, 'was the closest I came in the campaign to being really upset.'[126] Millar's account puts it rather higher than that. Denis told him the next morning that Margaret had not slept a wink all night. He had 'never seen her in such a state'. When she got back to Flood Street that evening after a day spent touring farms and fisheries around Aberdeen and Elgin, she made it clear that she absolutely refused to share a platform with Heath. 'After all the flak she had taken from him since she replaced him as Leader, she wasn't going to have him come in at the last minute, kiss and make up and claim he's won the election for her.'[127]

Tory election campaigns always seem to suffer an attack of panic about a week before polling day. What triggered this one was advance word of a NOP poll – not actually published until 1 May – which gave Labour for the first time a narrow lead (43.1 per cent to 42.4 per cent). It turned out to be a rogue poll, but at the time it was consistent with other evidence that Labour was closing the gap. As party chairman, Thorneycroft's first concern had always been for unity: from that perspective getting Heath on side was an obvious priority. When David Wolfson showed Mrs Thatcher the NOP data in Flood Street that evening, however, 'she considered it for about a minute in total silence. At length she said with impressive certainty, "I don't think I believe this", and got on with preparing the evening meal as though nothing had happened.'[128]

At her press conference the next morning, however, she was still visibly edgy. She jumped on a perfectly sensible question from the veteran labour correspondent, Geoffrey Goodman, and shouted at him, as if trying to refute suggestions that her voice was giving out.[129] That afternoon she had a row with a BBC political editor and cancelled a planned visit to Fulham. Angus Maude asked Millar to try to calm her down. 'It's urgent,' Maude told him. 'If she blows up at this stage it could blow the election.' Ever resourceful, Millar came up with the slogan 'Cool, calm – and elected' and persuaded Mrs Thatcher to adopt it, telling her that of course she was perfectly calm, but it was important that she help to keep those around her calm. She fell for it.[130]

After a quiet Saturday on home ground in Finchley and Enfield, publicly shrugging off the narrowing polls, her campaign moved into top gear over the last three days. First Harvey Thomas staged a spectacular rally of Conservative trade unionists at the Wembley Conference Centre on Sunday afternoon. This was her highlight of the whole campaign – 'an inspiring sight', she told Patricia Murray, 'and one which I will never forget'.[131] The disc jockey Pete Murray compered: Lulu and Vince Hill sang, and Mrs Thatcher entered the hall to the strains of *Hello Dolly*, rewritten by Millar and recorded by Vince Hill:

> Hello, Maggie,
> Well, hello, Maggie,
> Now you're really on the road to Number Ten . . .*

With this event, wrote the *Daily Mail*, 'the barn-storming, star-studded traditions of American politics arrived in Britain'. The result was 'a noisy excited cross between a Rod Stewart pop concert and a Cup Final'.[134] Mrs Thatcher's speech reiterated her by now standard appeal to patriotic trade unionists to join her and bury once and for all the myth that the members of trade unions were all 'Marxists and militants'.[135]

She spent the rest of that day at Saatchi and Saatchi's headquarters in Tottenham Court Road working with Reece, Bell and Millar (but no political colleagues) on her final TV broadcast which went out on Monday evening. She spoke solemnly for ten minutes direct to camera, stressing the need for a change of direction and her own deep sense of responsibility, promising – in a phrase she had already tried out several times during the campaign – that 'Somewhere ahead lies greatness for our country again'.

---

* The song included the line 'Give 'em the old one-two, Maggie', but Mrs Thatcher did not know what it meant. 'Daughter Carol let out her usual affectionate but exasperated "Oh, Mum,"' Millar wrote, 'and I explained that it was a boxing term for a knock-out. Strange, I thought, she who knows what most people don't doesn't know what everyone does.'[132] Millar was frequently amazed by Mrs Thatcher's unworldliness. Another time, discussing Richard Nixon's famous televised debate with Jack Kennedy, she had to be told what 'five o'clock shadow' was.[133]

Look at Britain today and you may think that an impossible dream. But there is another Britain of thoughtful people, tantalisingly slow to act, yet marvellously determined when they do.

The essential conservatism of her appeal was embodied in her mawkish final words:

> Let us make this a country safe to work in.
> Let us make this a country safe to walk in.
> Let us make it a country safe to grow up in.
> Let us make it a country safe to grow old in . . .
> May this land of ours, which we love so much, find dignity
>   and greatness and peace again.[136]

Safety first. It might almost have been Stanley Baldwin speaking.

She had one final rally on Tuesday evening, in Bolton, a town which boasted two of the most marginal seats in the country, constituencies which traditionally voted the same way as the nation as a whole. Heath had won both in 1970, and lost them again in 1974. 'Wave,' Mrs Thatcher instructed Wolfson and Millar as the battlebus drove to the Town Hall. 'It's a marginal!'[137] In fact Labour retained both seats. This closing rally was another showbiz event, with the comedian Ken Dodd warming the audience up with a blue feather duster for half an hour before Mrs Thatcher made her appearance. When she finally got to speak she was once again careful to stress that she was not extreme, but in touch with the people. Tax cuts? Home-ownership? Secret ballots? The rule of law? 'If all these things are extreme', she declared, 'then the great majority of the British people are extreme.' She laid greater stress than hitherto on social issues – jobs, education and pensions – which was also the thrust of the Saatchis' last-minute advertising blitz – and betrayed a niggling alarm at signs of a Liberal bandwagon by offering a little warning rhyme:

> Voting for anyone else to win
> Could mean letting Labour in.
> Remember it has happened before,
> And twice in 1974.

But she finished with a strong declaration of her confidence that history was on her side:

There's a world-wide revolt against big government, excessive taxation and bureaucracy . . . An era is drawing to a close . . . At first . . . people said 'Ooh, you've moved away from the centre.' But then opinion began to move too, as the heresies of one period became, as they always do, the orthodoxies of the next.

Throughout the campaign, she claimed, she had heard no one seriously question the Conservative case. 'Not even the Prime Minister. He's trying to get on the bandwagon.'

It's said that there is one thing stronger than armies, and that is an idea whose time has come . . . Tonight its time has come, and I believe that on Thursday our great nation will say the same.[138]

She was more right than she could have known. It was at just about this time, in the last days of the campaign, that Jim Callaghan told his senior policy adviser, Bernard Donoughue, that every thirty years or so there occurred 'a sea change in politics'.

It then does not matter what you say or do. There is a shift in what the public wants and what it approves. I suspect there is now such a sea-change – and it is for Mrs Thatcher.[139]

Callaghan was right. In the view of most commentators, Labour fought the better campaign in 1979.[140] Mrs Thatcher's message was muffled and in retrospect surprisingly timid. But the force was with her.

On Sunday night, after recording her final broadcast, she shyly asked Ronnie Millar if he had, by any chance, thought of a few words that she might say on the steps of Downing Street if it should turn out that she needed them. It was he who would not tell her at that stage what he had in mind.[141] Three days later, at her last press conference, a journalist asked her about the G7 summit conference coming up in June. 'I have got it in my diary,' she replied crisply.[142] There is no doubt that she was genuinely confident. 'She looks more powerful', Jean Rook noted in the *Daily Express*, 'and her soaring ambition and huge mental span are beginning to show.'[143] The final opinion polls all showed the Tories clearly ahead – the margins ranging from 2 per cent (Gallup) to 8 per cent (the very latest sampling by MORI in the London *Evening Standard*), with the Liberals up to 13 or even 15 per cent.

The polling day headlines hailed her expected victory. 'The Woman Who Can Save Britain', trumpeted the *Daily Mail*; 'Give

The Girl A Chance', urged the *Daily Express*; while the *Sun*, urging Labour supporters to 'Vote Tory This Time – It's The Only Way To Stop The Rot', looked forward to 'The First Day of the Rest of Our Lives'.[144] Yet up to the last minute she was still nervous that it might all be snatched away. 'We never count chickens before they are hatched,' she told a reporter as she was driven 150 yards down the King's Road to cast her vote for Nicholas Scott, 'and we don't count Number Ten before it is thatched.'[145] Another Millar joke? More seriously she talked anxiously during the day of Thomas Dewey, the American presidential candidate who had appeared to have the 1948 election for the White House sewn up before Harry Truman unexpectedly pipped him at the last.[146] Jim Callaghan – a solid incumbent who had never expected to become Prime Minister but had turned out surprisingly popular – was not unlike Harry Truman. At least three of her closest entourage – Gordon Reece, Tim Bell and Alistair McAlpine – were privately pessimistic.[147]

By the time Mrs Thatcher and Denis arrived at Barnet Town Hall for her own count just before midnight it was clear that she would be Prime Minister, with an adequate if not overwhelming majority, though she still made a point of not claiming victory until she had 318 seats. In the end the Conservatives won 339 seats to Labour's 269, with the Liberals holding eleven, the Scottish and Welsh nationalists reduced to two each and the various Ulster parties twelve, giving an overall majority of 43. They gained 51 seats from Labour, mainly in the South-East and Midlands, plus seven from the Scottish Nationalists and three from the Liberals; but lost four of their by-election gains and Teddy Taylor's Cathcart seat to Labour. The overall swing to the Tories (5.1 per cent) was the biggest since the war; but it was significantly greater in the South and Midlands (7.7 per cent) than in the North and Scotland (4.2 per cent). To that extent those who had maintained that Mrs Thatcher could never win in the North were vindicated. She did unprecedentedly well among the traditionally Labour-supporting C2 voters whom Central Office had particularly targeted, and actually achieved a higher swing among men than among women (though more women always vote Conservative to start with). Yet at just under 44 per cent her share of the total vote was the lowest winning share – apart from the two inconclusive elections of 1974 – since the war. (Heath in 1970 had won 46.4 per cent.)[148] Her fear that she might lose her own constituency was of course groundless. When her result was declared at 2.25 a.m. she had doubled her majority to nearly 8,000:

Margaret Thatcher (Conservative)	20,918
Richard May (Labour)	13,040
Anthony Paterson (Liberal)	5,254
William Verity (National Front)	534
Elizabeth Lloyd (Independent Democrat)	86
Conservative majority	7,878

She arrived in triumph at Central Office around 4.00 a.m. still only admitting that she had moved from 'cautiously optimistic' to 'optimistic'. She was 'aware of the very great responsibility'. It was 'very exciting', but 'somehow one is very calm about it, because you have to be'.[149] She was punctilious in thanking all the party workers who had helped in the campaign. Eventually she beckoned Millar into a corridor. 'I think it's going to be all right,' she said cautiously. Now would he tell her what she should say on the steps of Number Ten? Millar offered her the supposed prayer of St Francis of Assisi, beginning 'Where there is discord, may we bring harmony . . .'

The lady rarely showed deep feelings but this . . . proved too much. Her eyes swam. She blew her nose. 'I'll need to learn it,' she said at length. 'Let's find Alison and get her to type it.'[150]

She returned to Flood Street around 5.15 a.m. for a few hours' sleep but was back at Central Office by 11.30 a.m. to hear the final results and await the call to the Palace. By now she was having second thoughts about St Francis's prayer. Reece and Bell thought it was a hostage to fortune. Millar told her the lines expressed an aspiration, not a promise. 'She brightened visibly . . . She obviously wanted to say them but needed maximum reassurance.' 'What shall I tell the boys?' she asked. 'Tell them it's too soon to get cold feet before you've kissed hands.'[151] She then sat nervously in the Leader's office for two or three hours with Denis, Mark and Carol and an uncertain number of her political family. Millar describes the scene as if he alone, together with Caroline Stephens, stayed with the Thatchers, eating cold lamb in the almost deserted building as the clock ticked. But Gordon Reece and Alistair McAlpine were also around; and Lady Thatcher herself writes that 'There were many friends with me . . . during those long hours in Conservative Central Office'. Even so she felt 'an odd sense of loneliness and anticipation' as she waited. Instead of thinking about the job to come she worried about trivial questions of protocol and procedure.[152] When the telephone rang it was not Buckingham Palace but Ted Heath, ringing to offer his congratulations. Mrs Thatcher did not go to the phone, but quietly asked Caroline to thank him.[153] Eventually, soon after three o'clock, the call came. After an audience with the Queen lasting forty-five minutes she arrived in Downing Street around four o'clock as Prime Minister.

The prayer of St Francis that Ronnie Millar gave her to intone on the steps of Number Ten has come to be seen, in the words of Jim Prior, as 'the most awful humbug: it was so totally at odds with Margaret's belief in conviction politics and the need to abandon the consensus style of politics'.[154] It is true that, the way she delivered it, shyly against the uproar of reporters and cameras, it sounded uncharacteristically humble, consensual and conciliatory:

> Where there is discord, may we bring harmony;
> Where there is error, may we bring truth;
> Where there is doubt, may we bring faith;
> And where there is despair may we bring hope.

But that impression is deceptive. The words – particularly the second and third lines – bear a much more didactic interpretation than was generally put on them at the time. Margaret Thatcher had no time for doubt or error: she was in the business of truth and faith. Where there was discord she intended to bring harmony on her own terms – around the acceptance of her own ideas, not on the basis of a corporatist consensus. To those who shared her capitalist vision she undoubtedly brought hope, though to others less fortunate or less motivated she equally certainly brought despair. For a woman with a reputation for plain speaking she had a remarkable gift of clothing harsh ideas in warm-sounding words.

St Francis's apocryphal prayer – it was actually a nineteenth-century invention – was not the only piety she uttered on the steps of Downing Street. Before she went inside to set about forming her Cabinet someone asked if she had any thoughts, at this moment, about Mrs Pankhurst and her father: an incongruous pair. She had no thought for Mrs Pankhurst but seized the chance to pay tribute to Alfred Roberts.

> Well, of course, I just owe almost everything to my own father. I really do. He brought me up to believe all the things I do believe and they're just the values on which I've fought the Election. And it's passionately interesting to me that the things that I learned in a

small town, in a very modest home, are just the things that I
believe have won the Election.

Gentlemen, you're very kind. May I just go . . .[155]

And so the grocer's daughter entered Number Ten.

Notes and References

1 Dutiful Daughter

1 *The Times*, 1 February 1975.
2 Remarks on the steps of Downing Street, 4 May 1979.
3 Private information.
4 *Grantham Journal*, 6 February 1981.
5 Ibid., January 1917.
6 Alan Clark, *Diaries* (Weidenfeld & Nicolson, 1993; Phoenix paperback edition), p. 69n.
7 TV interview with Sir Laurens van der Post, 29 March 1983.
8 John Julius Norwich to the author, 11 June 1999.
9 Office of Population and Surveys.
10 Margaret Thatcher, *The Path to Power* (HarperCollins, 1995), p. 9.
11 George Gardiner, *Margaret Thatcher: From Childhood to Leadership* (William Kimber, 1975), p. 14.
12 Thatcher, p. 16.
13 *Grantham Guardian*, 21 December 1945; Thatcher, p. 4.
14 *Palmer's Almanack*, 1925, 1926, 1927.
15 Thatcher, p. 5.
16 Private information.
17 *Sunday Express*, 20 July 1975.
18 *Palmer's Almanack*, 1925.
19 Thatcher, p. 5.
20 Gardiner, p. 16.
21 Thatcher, p. 4.
22 G. K. Chesterton, *The Napoleon of Notting Hill* (Bodley Head, 1904; WDL paperback edition), p. 89.
23 Nicholas Wapshott and George Brock, *Thatcher* (Macdonald, 1983; Futura paperback edition), p. 26.

24 *Daily Mail*, 12 February 1975.

25 *Grantham Journal*, 8 February 1936.

26 Ibid., 4 May 1945.

27 Ibid., 9 October 1937.

28 Ibid., 16 November 1945.

29 *Grantham Guardian*, 20 September 1946.

30 Ibid., 15 February 1946.

31 *Grantham Journal*, 23 May 1952.

32 Ibid.

33 Oliver Anderson, *Rotten Borough* (Fourth Estate, 1989), pp. 141–2. The book originally appeared in 1937 under the name of Julian Pine, published by Ivor Nicholson and Watson. It was rediscovered by Richard Boston in the *Guardian*, 9 July 1988.

34 Private information.

35 See Rupert Davies, *Methodism* (Penguin 1964), p. 187.

36 Peter Jenkins, *Mrs Thatcher's Revolution: The Ending of the Socialist Era* (Jonathan Cape, 1987), p. 83.

37 *Sunday Express*, 20 July 1975.

38 Gardiner, p. 18.

39 Patricia Murray, *Margaret Thatcher* (W. H. Allen, 1980), p. 13.

40 Kenneth Harris, *Thatcher* (Weidenfeld & Nicolson, 1988), p. 46.

41 Thatcher, p. 13.

42 *Who's Who, 1960* (A. & C. Black, 1960).

43 Carol Thatcher, *Below the Parapet: The Biography of Denis Thatcher* (Harper-Collins, 1996), p. 57.

44 Murray, p. 27.

45 *Daily Express*, 17 April 1961.

46 Miriam Stoppard interview, *Woman to Woman*, Yorkshire Television, 19 November 1985.

47 Thatcher, *The Path to Power*, p. 12.

48 Leo Abse, *Margaret, Daughter of Beatrice* (Jonathan Cape, 1989), pp. 25–40.

49 Murray, p. 10.

50 Thatcher, p. 5.

51 Ibid., p. 16.

52 Unpublished Brian Walden interview, 28 January 1981. (Thatcher archive.)

53 *Daily Telegraph*, 13 February 1975.

54 Private information.

55 Ibid.

56 *Time*, 16 February 1981, quoted in Macdonald Daly and Alexander George (eds.), *Margaret Thatcher in her own Words* (Penguin. 1987), p. 118.

57 *Sunday Telegraph*, 14 February 1982.

58 Murray, p. 21.

59 Thatcher, p. 8.

60 BBC Radio 2, *The Late Show*, 7 February 1982.

61 Harris, p. 46.

62 Ronald Millar, *A View from the Wings* (Weidenfeld & Nicolson, 1993), p. 333.

63 Thatcher, p. 6.

64 Gardiner, p. 19.

65 Thatcher, p. 13.

66 Murray, p. 22.

67 Thatcher, p. 8.

68 Miriam Stoppard interview, 19 November 1985.

69 Ibid.

70 Murray, p. 22.

71 Ibid., pp. 15–16.

72 Ernle Money, *Margaret Thatcher, First Lady of the House* (Leslie Frewin, 1975), p. 38.

73 Murray, p. 21.

74 Thatcher, p. 10.

75 Ibid., pp. 14–15.

76 Murray, p. 14.

77 Carol Thatcher, p. 86.

78 Kenneth Baker, *The Turbulent Years: My Life in Politics* (Faber, 1993), p. 88.

79 Thatcher, *The Path to Power*, p. 15.

80 Interview, Judy Campbell.

81 Thatcher, p. 14.

82 Murray, p. 19.

83 Miriam Stoppard interview, 19 November 1985.

84 *KGGS Magazine*, 1938–44.

85 Russell Lewis, *Margaret Thatcher* (Routledge & Kegan Paul, 1975), p. 10.

86 Thatcher, p. 28.

87 Ibid., p. 19.

88 Ibid., p. 6.

89 Gardiner, p. 20.

90 *Sunday Telegraph*, 14 February 1982.

91 Remarks on the steps of Downing Street, 4 May 1979.

92 London Weekend TV, *Weekend World*, 16 January 1983.

93 Murray, p. 50.

94 BBC TV, *In the Limelight*, 11 August 1980.

95 Unpublished Brian Walden interview, 28 January 1981.

96 BBC Radio 4, *Any Questions?*, 3 November 1967.

97 *Sunday Express*, 20 July 1975.

98 Carol Thatcher, p. 64.

99 Wapshott and Brock, p. 63.

100 Unpublished Brian Walden interview, 28 January 1981.

101 Private information.

2 Serious Schoolgirl

1 Russell Lewis, *Margaret Thatcher* (Routledge & Kegan Paul, 1975), p. 11.
2 I am grateful to Hugo Young for letting me see copies of Margaret Roberts' school reports, which are no longer in the possession of KGGS.
3 Margaret Thatcher, *The Path to Power* (HarperCollins, 1995), p. 18.
4 Interview, Madeline Hellaby (née Edwards); Patricia Murray, *Margaret Thatcher* (W. H. Allen, 1980), p. 17.
5 George Gardiner, *Margaret Thatcher: From Childhood to Leadership* (William Kimber, 1975), p. 25.
6 Murray, p. 17.
7 Interviews: Dorothy Cooke (née Deakin), Margaret Wickstead (née Goodrich).
8 Private information.
9 Thatcher, p. 10.
10 Nicholas Wapshott and George Brock, *Thatcher* (Macdonald, 1983), p. 39.
11 Interview, Margaret Wickstead.
12 Marjorie Sansbury to the author, 2 February 1996.
13 BBC TV, *A Chance to Meet . . .*, 21 March 1971.
14 Thatcher, p. 13.
15 *Grantham Journal*, 6 February 1937.
16 *KGGS magazine*, 1936–44.
17 *The History of Kesteven and Grantham Girls' School, 1910–1987*, p. 14.
18 *Grantham Journal*, 18 May 1945; Malcolm Knapp, *Grantham: The War Years 1939–45* (Lincolnshire Books, 1995); Walter Lee, *Grantham Day by Day* (Imperial War Museum and Grantham Library).
19 *Sunday Times*, 28 May 1995. Following the publication of Lady Thatcher's memoirs the journalist Tim Rayment traced Edith Nokelby (née Muhlbauer) in Brazil. He tried to set up a reunion in London the same year; both ladies expressed polite enthusiasm, but it never took place.
20 Thatcher, pp. 24, 26.
21 BBC Radio 4, *Talking Politics*, 25 July 1974.
22 *Grantham Journal*, 1934.
23 Speech to the Czechoslovak Federal Assembly, Prague, 18 September 1990.
24 *Grantham Journal*, 28 January 1939.
25 Ibid., 16 November 1945.
26 See Lisa Budreau, *An Analysis of the Anglo-American Alliance during the Second World War in Grantham* (Grantham Museum, 1993).
27 TV interview with Sir Laurens van der Post, 29 March 1983.
28 School reports (see note 2).

29 *The History of KGGS*, p. 18.
30 Interviews: Madeline Hellaby (née Edwards), Margaret Wickstead (née Goodrich), Christine Rathbone (née Goodison).
31 Interview, Madeline Hellaby.
32 Jim Allen, *The Grantham Connection* (Grantham Book Centre, 1986), p. 18.
33 Thatcher, p. 36.
34 School reports (see note 2). Only the last two reports were written by Miss Gillies.
35 Interview, Christine Rathbone (née Goodison).

3 Oxford Tory

1 Patrick Cosgrave, *Margaret Thatcher: A Tory and her Party* (Hutchinson, 1978), p. 138.
2 Margaret Thatcher, *The Path to Power* (HarperCollins, 1995), p. 35.
3 Ibid., p. 37.
4 Interview, Margaret Wickstead.
5 Patricia Murray, *Margaret Thatcher* (W. H. Allen, 1980), p. 37.
6 Interview, Margaret Wickstead.
7 George Gardiner, *Margaret Thatcher: From Childhood to Leadership* (William Kimber, 1975), p. 37.
8 Hugo Young and Anne Sloman, *The Thatcher Phenomenon* (BBC, 1986), p. 17.
9 Ibid.
10 Nicholas Wapshott and George Brock, *Thatcher* (Macdonald, 1983), p. 49.
11 Margaret Roberts to Donald Southgate, July 1946.
12 Thatcher, p. 39.
13 Interview, Mrs Jean Darmon (née Southerst).
14 Ibid.
15 Interview, Rev. Nigel Jilson.
16 Nina Bawden, *In My Own Time* (Virago, 1994), pp. 76–7.
17 Ann Dally, *A Doctor's Story* (Macmillan, 1990), pp. 8–10.
18 Wapshott and Brock, p. 46.
19 Cosgrave, p. 135.
20 Murray, p. 38.
21 Kenneth Harris, *Thatcher* (Weidenfeld & Nicolson, 1988), p. 48.
22 Murray, p. 38.
23 *Daily Express*, 17 April 1961.
24 BBC Radio 4, *Woman's Hour*, 25 November 1968.
25 Thatcher, pp. 59–60.
26 Interview, Margaret Wickstead.
27 Interview, Sheila Browne.

28 *Grantham Journal*, June 1945.

29 *Sleaford Gazette*, 29 June 1945.

30 Thatcher, p. 46.

31 *Grantham Journal*, June 1945.

32 Thatcher, p. 38.

33 Nicholas Henderson, *Mandarin: The Diary of an Ambassador* (Weidenfeld & Nicolson, 1994), p. 388.

34 Dr Donald Southgate to the author, 16 May 1997.

35 Penny Junor, *Margaret Thatcher: Wife, Mother, Politician* (Sidgwick & Jackson, 1983), p. 20.

36 Dr Donald Southgate to the author, 16 May 1997.

37 Ibid.

38 Young and Sloman, p. 18.

39 Dr Donald Southgate to the author, 16 May 1997.

40 Harris, pp. 48–9.

41 Ibid.

42 Maurice Chandler, in Young and Sloman, p. 17.

43 Bodleian Library, Oxford (22 775 e28/1). The third author was Patrick O'Donovan, later an *Observer* journalist.

44 Wapshott and Brock, p. 49.

45 Harris, pp. 49–50.

46 Wapshott and Brock, p. 49.

47 I am grateful to Michael Kinchin-Smith for lending me a copy of this paper.

48 Hugo Young, *One of Us: A Biography of Margaret Thatcher* (Macmillan, 1989), p. 22.

49 Thatcher, p. 48.

50 House of Commons, 23 October 1984 (cited in Jon Sopel, *Tony Blair: The Moderniser* (Michael Joseph, 1995), pp. 79–80.

51 *Evening Standard*, 28 March 1946.

52 Thatcher, p. 47.

53 Brendan Bracken to Lord Beaverbrook, 7 October 1946, in Richard Cockett (ed.), *My Dear Max: The Letters of Brendan Bracken to Lord Beaverbrook, 1925–1958* (Historians' Press, 1990), p. 58.

54 Thatcher, p. 48.

55 Margaret Roberts to Donald Southgate, 26 July 1946.

56 Ibid., early July 1946, and 26 July 1946.

57 I am grateful to Dr Donald Southgate for lending me a copy of the OUCA programme for the Michaelmas term, 1946.

58 David Blair, *The History of the Oxford University Conservative Association* (OUCA, 1995), p. 15.

59 *Daily Telegraph*, 17 July 1970.

60 Thatcher, p. 42.

61 Dr Donald Southgate to the author, 16 May 1997.

62 Thatcher, p. 42.
63 Ludovic Kennedy, *On My Way to the Club* (Collins, 1989), pp. 174–9.
64 Thatcher, p. 49.
65 Ibid.
66 Ibid., p. 37.
67 Ibid., p. 58.
68 Margaret Wickstead to the author, 20 January 1997.

4 Young Conservative

1 Penny Junor, *Margaret Thatcher: Wife, Mother, Politician* (Sidgwick & Jackson, 1983), pp. 26–7.
2 Margaret Thatcher, *The Path to Power* (HarperCollins, 1995), p. 62.
3 Nicholas Wapshott and George Brock, *Thatcher* (Macdonald, 1983), p. 51.
4 Interview, Peter Marrian.
5 Ernle Money, *Margaret Thatcher: First Lady of the House* (Leslie Frewin, 1975), p. 45.
6 Wapshott and Brock, pp. 51–2.
7 *East Anglian Daily Times*, 18 April 1996.
8 Mrs Clare Woodage (Stanley Booth's secretary) to the author, 15 January 1996.
9 Colchester *Evening Gazette*, 30 January 1978.
10 Wapshott and Brock, p. 51.
11 Interview, Mary Pratt.
12 Conservative party archive (CCO 1/7/360).
13 Interview, Philip Fell.
14 Interview, Mary Fairland.
15 Thatcher, p. 62.
16 Interview, Philip Fell.
17 Philip Fell to the author, 12 February 1996.
18 Ibid.
19 Thatcher, pp. 49–50.
20 Interviews: Marie Joliffe, Sheila Diss and others.
21 Conservative party archive (CCO 1/8/397).
22 Ibid. (CCO 1/7/397).
23 Carol Thatcher, *Below the Parapet: The Biography of Denis Thatcher* (HarperCollins, 1996), pp. 57–8.
24 E. J. Tranter to J. P. L. Thomas, 14 January 1949 (CCO 1/7/397).
25 Sir Waldron Smithers to J. P. L. Thomas, 5 February 1949 (loc. cit.).
26 J. P. L. Thomas to Sir Waldron Smithers, 9 February 1949 (loc. cit.).
27 E. J. Tranter to J. P. L. Thomas, 2 March 1949 (loc. cit.).
28 *Erith Observer & Kentish Times*, 4 March 1949.

29 Thatcher, *The Path to Power*, p. 67.

30 *Erith Observer*, 17 June 1949.

31 Patricia Murray, *Margaret Thatcher* (W. H. Allen, 1980), p. 41.

32 *Sunday Express*, 20 July 1975.

33 E. J. Tranter to Conservative Central Office (CCO 1/7/397).

34 *Erith Observer*, 18 November 1949.

35 Conservative party archive (CCO 1/7//397, 1/8/397).

36 E. J. Tranter to Conservative Central Office, 12 August 1949 (CCO 1/7/397).

37 *Erith Observer*, 2 December 1949, 7 October 1949, 29 April 1949.

38 *Daily Mail*, 28 June 1949.

39 *Erith Observer*, 19 August 1949.

40 Ibid., 8 April 1949.

41 Russell Lewis, *Margaret Thatcher* (Routledge & Kegan Paul, 1975), p. 18.

42 *Erith Observer*, 2 December 1949.

43 Ibid., 8 April 1949.

44 *Kentish Independent*, 23 September 1949.

45 Beryl Cook to Conservative Central Office, 5 February 1950 (CCO 500/24/53).

46 Beryl Cook to Conservative Central Office, 14 February 1950 (CCO 1/7/397).

47 Wapshott and Brock, p. 55; see also *Heute*, February 1950.

48 *People*, 12 February 1950; *Erith Observer*, 17 February 1950.

49 *Erith Observer*, 10 February 1950.

50 Ibid.

51 Ibid., 17 February 1950.

52 Ibid.

53 Thatcher, p. 70.

54 *Gravesend Reporter*, 28 January 1950.

55 Margaret Roberts' election address, Dartford 1950 (Conservative party archive).

56 Beryl Cook to Conservative Central Office, 14 February 1950 (CCO 1/7/397).

57 Murray, p 43.

58 *Erith Observer*, 3 March 1950.

59 *Dartford Chronicle*, 31 March 1950.

60 Conservative party archive (CCO 500/24/53).

61 Thatcher, p. 68.

62 Interview, Sir Clive Bossom.

63 *Erith Observer*, 27 January 1950.

64 Ibid., 30 December 1949.

65 Ibid., 29 December 1950.

66 Beryl Cook to Conservative Central Office, 10 July 1951 (CCO 1/8/397).
67 Wapshott and Brock, p. 54.
68 Thatcher, p. 66.
69 Ibid.
70 *Sunday Dispatch*, 7 February 1960.
71 Carol Thatcher, p. 66.
72 Thatcher, *The Path to Power*, p. 67.
73 Ibid., p. 66.
74 Carol Thatcher, p. 63.
75 Thatcher, *The Path to Power*, p. 67.
76 Edward du Cann, *Two Lives: The Political and Business Careers of Edward du Cann* (Images, Upton-upon-Severn, 1995), p. 206.
77 Thatcher, p. 75.
78 *Erith Observer*, 6 July 1951.
79 Ibid., 12 October 1951; *Gravesend Reporter*, 13 October 1951.
80 *Erith Observer*, 19 October 1951.
81 *Daily Graphic*, 10 October 1951.
82 *Erith Observer*, 14 December 1951.
83 Thatcher, p. 76.
84 Junor, p. 33.
85 Carol Thatcher, p. 64.
86 Miriam Stoppard interview, *Woman to Woman*, Yorkshire TV, 19 November 1985.

5 Superwoman

1 Margaret Thatcher, *The Path to Power* (HarperCollins 1995), p. 77.
2 Ibid.
3 Ibid., p. 78.
4 Carol Thatcher, *Below the Parapet: The Biography of Denis Thatcher* (Harper-Collins, 1996), p. 73.
5 *Sunday Graphic*, 17 February 1952.
6 Thatcher, *The Path to Power*, p. 79.
7 John Hare memorandum, 19 June 1952 (CCO 1/9/17).
8 Margaret Thatcher to R. H. M. Marriott, 2 September 1952 (CCO 1/9/17).
9 Michael Cockerell, *Live from Number Ten: The Inside Story of Prime Ministers and Television* (Faber, 1988), p. 10.
10 Ann Dally, *A Doctor's Story* (Macmillan, 1990), pp. 9–10.
11 Ibid., p. 10.
12 Thatcher, p. 80.
13 Carol Thatcher, p. 69.

14 Nicholas Wapshott and George Brock, *Thatcher* (Macdonald, 1983), p. 60.

15 Thatcher, *The Path to Power*, p 83.

16 BBC Radio 4, *Woman's Hour*, 11 December 1986.

17 George Gardiner, *Margaret Thatcher: From Childhood to Leadership* (William Kimber, 1975), p. 53.

18 Thatcher, p. 85.

19 Ibid., p. 87.

20 CCO 4/7/91, cited by Richard Cockett, 'The Party, Publicity and the Media' in Anthony Seldon and Stuart Bell (eds.), *The Conservative Century* (Oxford, 1994), p. 566.

21 *Evening News*, 5 October 1959.

22 *Observer*, 7 February 1971.

23 *Daily Mail*, 17 April 1979.

24 Patricia Murray, *Margaret Thatcher* (W. H. Allen, 1980), p. 48.

25 Election press conference, Glasgow airport, 26 April 1979.

26 *Evening News*, 25 February 1960.

27 Thatcher, p. 103.

28 Miriam Stoppard interview, Yorkshire TV, 19 November 1985.

29 BBC Radio 2, *The Late Show*, 5 March 1982.

30 Thatcher, p. 82.

31 Election press conference, Glasgow airport, 26 April 1979.

32 *Today*, 23 February 1988.

33 *Sunday Dispatch*, 7 February 1960.

34 *Daily Express*, 17 April 1961.

35 Gardiner, p. 51.

36 Carol Thatcher, p. 71.

37 Murray, p. 50.

38 Carol Thatcher, p. 71.

39 Gardiner, p. 54.

40 Cited by Simon Hoggart in *Punch*, 14 March 1984.

41 Gardiner, p. 54.

42 Murray, p. 50.

43 Carol Thatcher, p. 72.

44 Ibid., p. 89.

45 Interview, Margaret Wickstead.

46 Carol Thatcher, p. 88.

47 Ibid.

48 *Daily Express*, 17 April 1961.

49 Interview, Lord Jenkin.

50 Ibid.

51 Miriam Stoppard interview, Yorkshire TV, 19 November 1985.

52 See, for example, her speech to the 1966 party conference, 12 October 1966.

53 Conservative party archive (CCO 1/12).

54 Ibid. (CCO 1/12/322).

55 Ibid. (CCO 1/12/411).

56 Ibid.

57 Ibid. (CCO 1/12/375).

58 Ibid.

59 Dennis Walters, *Not Always with the Pack* (Constable, 1989), pp. 103–4.

60 Conservative party archive (CCO 1/12/375).

61 *Finchley Press*, 18 July 1958.

62 Ibid.

63 *Evening Standard*, 15 July 1958.

64 Conservative party archive (CCO 1/12/375).

65 *Finchley Press*, 8 August 1958.

66 Ibid., 13 February 1959.

67 Bernard Donoughue, 'Finchley' in David Butler and Anthony King, *The British General Election of 1964* (Macmillan, 1965), p. 241.

68 Margaret Thatcher to Miss Burgess, 17 September 1958 (CCO 1/12/375).

69 CCO 1/12/375.

70 *Finchley Press*, 20 February 1959.

71 Ibid., 27 February 1959.

72 Thatcher, *The Path to Power*, p. 92.

73 *Finchley Press*, 25 September 1959.

74 Ibid., 20 March 1959.

75 Ibid., 23 January 1959.

76 Ibid.

77 Ibid., 25 September 1959.

78 Ibid.

79 Ibid., 20 March 1959.

80 *Daily Mirror*, 23 September 1959.

81 Interview, Eric Deakins.

82 Margaret Thatcher's election address in Finchley, 1959 (Conservative party archive).

83 *Finchley Press*, 9 October 1959.

84 Ibid., 23 January 1959.

85 Thatcher, pp. 87–91.

86 *Finchley Press*, 9 October 1959.

87 Ibid., 16 October 1959.

6 Backbencher

1 Margaret Thatcher, *The Path to Power* (HarperCollins, 1995), p. 107.

2 James Prior, *A Balance of Power* (Hamish Hamilton, 1986), p. 21.

3 Peter Rawlinson, *A Price Too High* (Weidenfeld & Nicolson, 1989), pp. 246–7.

4 Interview, Sir Edward du Cann.

5 Julian Critchley, *Palace of Varieties: An Insider's View of Westminster* (John Murray, 1989), p. 122.

6 *People*, 25 October 1959.

7 Patricia Murray, *Margaret Thatcher* (W. H. Allen, 1980), p. 92.

8 Thatcher, p. 108.

9 Denis Healey, *The Time of My Life* (Michael Joseph, 1989), p. 487.

10 Interview, Margaret Wickstead.

11 *Evening News*, 9 October 1959.

12 *Finchley Press*, 8 January 1960.

13 BBC Light Programme, *Any Questions?*, 8 January 1960; Woodrow Wyatt, *Confessions of an Optimist* (Collins, 1985), p. 343.

14 *Evening News*, 25 February 1960.

15 Carol Thatcher, *Below the Parapet: The Biography of Denis Thatcher* (Harper-Collins, 1996), p. 85.

16 *Evening News*, 29 February 1960.

17 *Finchley Press*, 25 March 1960.

18 Carol Thatcher, p. 83.

19 *Finchley Press*, 29 July 1960.

20 Thatcher, *The Path to Power*, p. 109.

21 *Daily Telegraph*, 11 November 1959; Ernle Money, *Margaret Thatcher: First Lady of the House* (Leslie Frewin, 1975), p. 57.

22 Thatcher, p. 110.

23 *Grantham Journal*, 16 October 1937.

24 See Henry Brooke in the House of Commons, 5 February 1960 [Vol. 616, col. 1436].

25 George Gardiner, *Margaret Thatcher: From Childhood to Leadership* (William Kimber, 1975), p. 67.

26 Thatcher, p. 111.

27 Ibid.

28 *Independent*, 23 November 1994.

29 *The Times*, 29 January 1960.

30 *Independent*, 23 November 1994.

31 *The Times*, 4 February 1960.

32 *Finchley Press*, 12 February 1960.

33 House of Commons, 5 February 1960 [Vol. 616, cols. 1350–8].

34 Ibid. [col. 1358].

35 Ibid. [col. 1413].

36 Ibid. [col. 1390].

37 Ibid. [col. 1422].

38 Ibid. [col. 1398].

39 Ibid. [col. 1430].

40 Ibid. [col. 1436].

41 House of Commons, 16 March 1960 [Standing Committee C, col. 31].

42 Ibid. [col. 45].

43 *The Times*, 14 April 1960.

44 House of Commons, 13 April 1960 [Standing Committee C, col. 272].

45 House of Commons, 13 May 1960 [Vol. 623, col. 836].

46 *The Times*, 31 December 1962.

47 *Finchley Press*, 23 July 1966, 16 August 1968.

48 *Independent*, 23 November 1994.

49 Ibid.

50 *Daily Telegraph*, 6 February 1960.

51 *Sunday Dispatch*, 7 February 1960.

52 R. A. Butler, *The Art of the Possible* (Hamish Hamilton, 1971), p. 200.

53 House of Commons, 14 February 1961 [Standing Committee B, cols. 551–7].

54 *Sunday Pictorial*, 23 April 1961.

55 BBC Light Programme, *Any Questions?*, 4 November 1960.

56 House of Commons, 19 April 1961 [Vol. 638, cols. 1226–32].

57 Thatcher, p. 116.

58 House of Commons, 19 April 1961 [Vol. 638, cols. 1226–32].

59 *Yorkshire Post*, 7 October 1960.

60 Jean Mann, *Woman in Parliament* (Odhams, 1962), p. 31.

61 Thatcher, p. 127.

62 *Finchley Press*, 18 August 1961.

63 House of Commons, 19 April 1961 [Vol. 638, cols. 1226–32].

64 *Finchley Press*, 13 October 1961.

7   Junior Minister

1 George Gardiner, *Margaret Thatcher: From Childhood to Leadership* (William Kimber, 1975), p. 68.

2 Margaret Thatcher, *The Path to Power* (HarperCollins, 1995), pp. 117–18.

3 *The Times*, 11 October 1961.

4 *Guardian*, 11 October 1961.

5 *Daily Mail*, 9 October 1961.

6 Interview, Sir Michael Partridge.

7 Margaret Thatcher, *The Downing Street Years* (HarperCollins, 1993), p. 423.

8 Thatcher, *The Path to Power*, p. 123.

9 Interview, Margaret Wickstead.

10 TV interview with Sir Laurens van der Post, 29 March 1983.

11 John Boyd-Carpenter, *Way of Life* (Sidgwick & Jackson, 1980), p. 133.

12 Interview, Sir Michael Partridge.

13 Interview, Sir Clive Bossom.

14 Interview, Sir Kenneth Stowe.

15 Thatcher, p. 123.

16 Ibid.

17 Interview, Lord Holderness.

18 Interview, Sir Michael Partridge.

19 Interview, Lord Holderness.

20 Interview, Sir Michael Partridge.

21 House of Commons, 6 February 1963 [Vol. 671, col. 614].

22 Ibid., 13 December 1961 [Vol. 651, col. 508].

23 Ibid., 13 March 1962 [Vol. 655, col. 1176].

24 Thatcher, p. 125.

25 Interview, Sir Michael Partridge.

26 House of Commons, 22 January 1964 [Vol. 687, col. 1184].

27 Ibid., 13 March 1962 [Vol. 655, col. 1206].

28 Ibid., 13 December 1961 [Vol. 651, col. 508].

29 Ibid., 6 February 1963 [Vol. 671, col. 604].

30 Ibid., 13 July 1962 [Vol. 662, col. 1766].

31 Ernle Money, *Margaret Thatcher: First Lady of the House* (Leslie Frewin, 1975) p. 61.

32 House of Commons, 5 February 1963 [Vol. 671, cols. 273–4].

33 Ibid., 6 February 1963 [Vol. 671, cols. 604, 614].

34 See, for example, ibid., 13 December 1961 [Vol. 651, col. 508].

35 Ibid., 17 June 1963 [Vol. 679, col. 6].

36 Ibid., 17 February 1964 [Vol. 689, col. 818].

37 Ibid., 6 February 1963 [Vol. 671, col. 614]; 26 November 1962 [Vol. 668, col. 18].

38 Ibid., 6 February 1963 [Vol. 671, cols. 558–9].

39 Ibid., 6 February 1963 [Vol. 671, col. 557].

40 *Liverpool Daily Post*, 14 March 1962.

41 House of Commons, 13 March 1962 [Vol. 655, cols. 1156–70].

42 Ibid. [Vol. 655, col. 1218].

43 Russell Lewis, *Margaret Thatcher* (Routledge & Kegan Paul, 1975), p. 32.

44 House of Commons, 16 July 1962 [Vol. 633, cols. 3–5].

45 Norman Shrapnel, *The Performers: Politics as Theatre* (Constable, 1978), p. 128.

46 Thatcher, p. 118.

47 *Finchley Press*, 23 March 1962.

48 Conservative party archive (CCO 1/14/35).

49 *Finchley Press*, 7 August 1962.

50 Private information.

51 Alistair Horne, *Macmillan, 1957–86* (Macmillan, 1989), p. 532.

52 Speech to women unionists' lunch, Edinburgh, 28 June 1963 (*Scotsman*, 1 July 1963).

53 Thatcher, pp. 128–9.

54 *Finchley Press*, 25 October 1963.
55 Thatcher, p. 130.
56 Interview, Lord Holderness.
57 *Finchley Press*, 30 March 1962, 18 May 1962.
58 Ibid., 26 October 1962.
59 Conservative party archive (CCO 1/14/35).
60 *Finchley Press*, 17 April 1964, 15 May 1964.
61 Labour election address, Finchley 1964, in the Conservative party archive.
62 *Finchley Press*, 18 September 1964.
63 David Butler and Anthony King, *The British General Election of 1964* (Macmillan, 1965), p. 244.
64 *Finchley Press*, 2 October 1964.
65 John Pardoe to the author, 22 May 1995.
66 Butler and King, p. 250.
67 *Finchley Press*, 9 October 1964.
68 Ibid., 23 October 1964.
69 Gardiner, p. 72.
70 Carol Thatcher, *Below the Parapet: The Biography of Denis Thatcher* (Harper-Collins, 1996), p. 93.
71 Ibid., pp. 91–2.
72 Ibid., p. 94.

8 Opposition

1 House of Commons, 31 October 1969 [Vol. 790, col. 590].
2 Interview, Lord Holderness.
3 House of Commons, 25 November 1964 [Vol. 702, col. 1312].
4 Ibid., 3 December 1964 [Vol. 703, cols. 856–63].
5 Ibid.
6 Carol Thatcher, *Below the Parapet: The Biography of Denis Thatcher* (Harper-Collins, 1996), p. 93.
7 *Finchley Press*, 29 January 1965.
8 Conservative party archive (LCC(65)12).
9 R. A. Butler papers. (Thanks to Dr Rodney Lowe.)
10 Conservative party archive (ACP(65)15, PG/13/65/51). I am grateful to Dr Rodney Lowe for drawing my attention to these reports.
11 House of Commons, 19 May 1965 [Vol. 712, cols. 1630–4].
12 Ibid., 6 July 1965 [Vol. 715, cols. 1505–22].
13 Margaret Thatcher, *The Path to Power* (HarperCollins, 1995), p. 133.
14 Ibid., p. 134.
15 Ibid.
16 Ibid., p. 136.

17 *Finchley Press*, 13 August 1965.

18 Ibid., 12 March 1965.

19 Conservative Party Conference, 14 October 1965.

20 House of Commons, 6 December 1965 [Vol. 722, col. 155].

21 Ibid., 11 November 1965 [Vol. 720, cols. 479–88].

22 Richard Crossman, *The Diaries of a Cabinet Minister: Volume One: Minister of Housing, 1964–66* (Hamish Hamilton & Jonathan Cape, 1975), p. 560 (4 July 1966).

23 *Daily Express*, 25 January 1967.

24 Thatcher, p. 137.

25 *Finchley Press*, 12 March 1965, 13 August 1965.

26 Ibid., 18 March 1965.

27 Ibid., 25 March 1965.

28 Margaret Thatcher's Election Address, Finchley 1966 (Conservative party archive).

29 *Finchley Press*, 25 March 1966.

30 Ibid.

31 Margaret Thatcher's Election Address, Finchley 1966.

32 *Finchley Press*, 25 March 1966.

33 Margaret Thatcher's Election Address, Finchley 1966.

34 James Prior, *A Balance of Power* (Hamish Hamilton, 1986), p. 42.

35 Nicholas Wapshott and George Brock, *Thatcher* (Macdonald, 1983), p. 85.

36 Nigel Fisher, *Iain Macleod* (André Deutsch, 1973), p. 288.

37 Robert Shepherd, *Iain Macleod* (Hutchinson, 1994), p. 429.

38 Interview with Geoffrey Parkhouse, cited in John Ranelagh, *Thatcher's People: An Insider's Account of the Politics, the Power and the Personalities* (HarperCollins, 1991), p. 93.

39 Shepherd, p. 430.

40 *The Times*, 6 May 1966.

41 House of Commons, 5 May 1966 [Vol. 727, cols. 1890–1907].

42 *The Times*, 6 May 1966.

43 House of Commons, 5 May 1966 [Vol. 727, col. 1992].

44 Angus Maude interviewed on BBC TV, *Panorama*, 14 May 1979, cited in Shepherd, p. 429.

45 *Daily Mail*, 10 May 1966.

46 House of Commons, 27 June 1966 [Vol. 730, col. 1352].

47 Ibid., 28 July 1966 [Vol. 732, cols. 1913–16].

48 *Finchley Press*, 2 September 1966.

49 Ibid., 13 August 1965.

50 Thatcher, p. 139.

51 *Daily Telegraph*, 13 October 1966.

52 *Daily Mail*, 18 October 1966.

53 *Sun*, 13 October 1966. -

54 *Daily Mail*, 14 October 1966.

55 *Conservative Party Conference Report, 1966*, pp. 24–6.

56 Interview, Patrick Jenkin.

57 House of Commons, 25 October 1966 [Vol. 734, cols. 944–56].

58 Richard Crossman, *The Diaries of a Cabinet Minister: Volume Two: Lord President of the Council and Leader of the House of Commons, 1966–68* (Hamish Hamilton & Jonathan Cape, 1976), p. 92.

59 House of Commons, 17 April 1967 [Vol. 745, col. 128].

60 Ibid., 6 June 1967 [Vol. 747, cols. 952–6].

61 Thatcher, pp. 153–4.

62 *Sunday Times*, 5 March 1967.

63 *Finchley Press*, 25 April 1969.

64 Interview, Paul Channon.

65 Interview, Chris Patten.

66 Peter Rawlinson, *A Price Too High* (Weidenfeld & Nicolson, 1989), p. 247.

67 *Sunday Express*, 30 June 1968.

68 *Sunday Mirror*, 28 December 1969.

69 Private information.

70 Thatcher, p. 144.

71 Conservative party archive (CCO 500/56/1).

72 *Sunday Telegraph*, 15 October 1967.

73 Ibid.

74 Conservative Party Conference, 2 October 1967.

75 Thatcher, p. 143.

76 Interview, Lord Holderness.

77 House of Commons, 26 October 1967 [Vol. 751, cols. 1988–99].

78 Conservative Party Conference, 20 October 1967.

79 House of Commons, 1 November 1967 [Vol. 753, cols. 282–93].

80 Ibid. 28 November 1967 [Vol. 755, cols. 261–76].

81 Ibid. 22 January 1968 [Vol. 757, col. 148].

82 Ibid. 5 December 1967 [Vol. 755, cols. 1271–6].

83 John Ramsden, *The Winds of Change: Macmillan to Heath, 1957–1975* (Longman, 1996), p. 280.

84 Ibid.

85 Arthur Seldon to Geoffrey Howe, 24 October 1969, cited in Richard Cockett, *Thinking the Unthinkable: Think-Tanks and the Economic Counter-Revolution, 1931–1983* (HarperCollins, 1994), p. 171.

86 Howe to Seldon, 28 October 1969, loc. cit.

87 Thatcher, p. 143.

88 Margaret Thatcher to Sir Edward Boyle, 17 January 1968 [Boyle papers, 660/23799].

89 Shepherd, p. 476, citing Conservative party archive, EPG/66/70 (8 February 1968).

90 *The Times*, 13 September 1968.

91 *Daily Mirror*, 10 October 1968.

92 *Guardian*, 11 October 1968.

93 Thatcher, pp. 146–7.

94 *The Times*, 13 September 1968.

95 Ibid.

96 For Mrs Thatcher's debt to Powell, see Wapshott and Brock, pp. 89–90.

97 Margaret Thatcher, *What's Wrong With Politics?* (CPC, 1968).

98 Margaret Thatcher, 'Consensus – or choice?' in *Daily Telegraph*, 17 March 1969.

99 Margaret Thatcher, 'Participation – in what?' in *Daily Telegraph*, 26 April 1969.

100 Thatcher, 'Consensus – or choice?', loc. cit.

101 Barbara Castle, *The Castle Diaries, 1964–70* (Weidenfeld & Nicolson, 1984), p. 435 (1 May 1968).

102 *Daily Telegraph*, 2 May 1968.

103 Ibid., 3 May 1968.

104 *Daily Telegraph*, 15 November 1968.

105 House of Commons, 29 November 1968 [Vol. 774, col. 946].

106 *Daily Telegraph*, 15 November 1968.

107 Thatcher, *The Path to Power*, p. 143.

108 *Daily Telegraph*, 20 November 1968.

109 House of Commons, 29 November 1968 [Vol. 774, cols. 946–56].

110 Ibid., 17 December 1968 [Vol. 775, cols. 1254–65].

111 Ibid., 19 May 1969 [Vol. 784, col. 177].

112 Interview, Paul Channon.

113 Thatcher, pp. 154–6.

114 *Finchley Press*, 17 October 1969.

115 Ibid., 2 January 1970.

116 Thatcher, p. 150.

117 House of Commons, 19 December 1966 (homosexuality); 22 July 1966 (abortion); 9 February 1968, 17 December 1968, 12–13 June 1969 (divorce). She voted for the Second Reading of the Sexual Offences Bill and the Medical Termination of Pregnancy Bill, but in both cases abstained or was absent from the Third Reading. She voted against the Divorce Bill not only on Second Reading (twice, since it fell and had to be reintroduced) but also several times at the Report Stage – though she was not one of the hard core of about forty, predominantly Roman Catholic, Members led by Sir John Biggs-Davison, who stayed up all night voting against it.

118 Ranelagh, p. 186.

119 *Finchley Press*, 22 November 1968.

120 *Daily Telegraph*, 12 February 1969.

121 Edward Boyle to John Vaizey, 11 September 1975 [Boyle papers, 660/10081].

122 Margaret Thatcher to Edward Boyle, 15 October 1969 [Boyle papers, 660/7845].

123 Edward Boyle to John Vaizey, 11 September 1975 [Boyle papers, 660/10081].

124 *Daily Express*, 22 October 1969.

125 *Financial Times*, 22 October 1969.

126 *Daily Telegraph*, 22 October 1969.

127 *Sunday Telegraph*, 26 October 1969.

128 *Observer*, 26 October 1969.

129 *Finchley Press*, 25 March 1966.

130 Ibid., 16 May 1969.

131 Nicholas Timmins, *The Five Giants: A Biography of the Welfare State* (HarperCollins, 1995; Fontana edition), p. 243.

132 Edward Boyle to Alderman Fred Hutty, 29 September 1969 (Conservative party archive, CCO 505/3/9).

133 *Daily Mail*, 22 October 1969.

134 *Finchley Press*, 24 October 1969.

135 *Daily Express*, 23 October 1969.

136 Conservative Party Conference, 10 October 1969.

137 *Guardian*, 23 October 1969.

138 BBC Radio 1 and 2, *Any Questions?*, 24 October 1969.

139 House of Commons, 31 October 1969 [Vol. 790, col. 539].

140 Ibid. [cols. 578–85].

141 Ibid. [cols. 590–601].

142 *The Times*, 7 November 1969.

143 Thatcher, p. 159.

144 Peter Bagueley (Research Officer) to nine LEAs, 13 November 1969 (Conservative party archive, CCO/505/3/44).

145 *The Times*, 7 November 1969.

146 Interview, Brian MacArthur.

147 House of Commons, 2 February 1970 [Vol. 795, col. 1535].

148 Ibid. [cols. 1473–88].

149 Ibid. [cols. 1549–50].

150 Ibid. [cols. 1574–84].

151 Chris Patten interviewed by David Butler, 11 December 1969.

152 *The Times*, 29 November 1969.

153 House of Commons, 18 February 1970 [Vol. 796, col. 415].

154 Russell Lewis, *Margaret Thatcher* (Routledge & Kegan Paul, 1975), p. 65. Lady Thatcher subtitles the relevant section of her memoirs 'Selsdon Woman' (Thatcher, p. 156).

155 Conservative party archive (CCO 500/56/1).

156 *Finchley Press*, 6 February 1970.

157 Ibid., 6 March 1970.

158 Ibid., 20 March 1970.

159 Thatcher, p. 161.

160 Michael Cockerell, *Live from Number Ten: The Inside Story of Prime Ministers and Television* (Faber, 1988), p. 213; see also Ronald Millar, *A View From the Wings* (Weidenfeld & Nicolson, 1989), p. 214.

161 Cockerell, loc. cit.

162 *Sun*, 10 April 1970.

163 *Finchley Press*, 5 June 1970.

164 Ibid., 12 June 1970; see also *Any Questions?*, 4 October 1968, and *Woman's Hour*, 9 April 1970.

165 Margaret Thatcher's Election Address, Finchley 1970 (Conservative party archive).

166 *Finchley Press*, 29 May 1970.

167 *The Times*, 27 May 1970.

168 *Finchley Press*, 5 June 1970.

169 Thatcher, pp. 162–3.

170 Carol Thatcher, p. 97.

171 *Finchley Press*, 26 June 1970.

172 Ibid.

9   Education Secretary

1 Kenneth Baker, *The Turbulent Years: My Life in Politics* (Faber, 1993), p. 161.

2 *Guardian*, 22 July 1970.

3 Private information. (The Minister was Fred Mulley.)

4 Private information. (The Permanent Secretary was Sir Herbert Andrew.)

5 Margaret Thatcher, *The Path to Power* (HarperCollins, 1995), p. 166.

6 *Sunday Times*, 28 July 1970.

7 Interviews, various DES officials.

8 Melanie Phillips, *The Divided House* (Sidgwick & Jackson, 1980), p. 33.

9 Interview, Sir Toby Weaver.

10 *Spectator*, 22 July 1972.

11 Margaret Thatcher, *What's Wrong with Politics?* (CPC, 1968).

12 *Spectator*, 15 July 1972.

13 George Gardiner, *Margaret Thatcher: From Childhood to Leadership* (William Kimber, 1975), p. 33.

14 Interview, Sheila Browne.

15 Thatcher, *The Path to Power*, p. 38.

16 Interviews, Sir William Pile, Philip Halsey, David Tanner.

17 Nicholas Timmins, *The Five Giants: A Biography of the Welfare State* (HarperCollins, 1995; Fontana edition), pp. 373–4.
18 Peter Hennessy, *Whitehall* (Secker & Warburg, 1989), p. 626.
19 Interview, John Hudson.
20 Interview, Sir William Pile.
21 Interview, Philip Halsey.
22 Interview, Sir William Pile.
23 Interview, Sheila Browne.
24 BBC TV, *Panorama*, 1979.
25 Phillips, p. 20.
26 Ibid.
27 Interview, Sir Kenneth Berrill.
28 Norman St John Stevas, *The Two Cities* (Faber, 1984), p. 16.
29 Thatcher, p. 165.
30 Interviews, various DES officials.
31 Stevas, p. 16.
32 Interviews, Sir Toby Weaver and others.
33 Interviews, Philip Halsey, Sir Toby Weaver and others.
34 Thatcher, p. 165.
35 Conservative Party Conference, 7 October 1970.
36 *Spectator*, 18 July 1970.
37 Brian Cox, *The Great Betrayal* (Chapman, 1992), p. 212.
38 House of Commons, 8 July 1970 [Vol. 803, cols. 667–76].
39 *People*, 12 July 1970.
40 *Daily Mirror*, 3 July 1970.
41 *The Times*, 3 August 1970.
42 Confidential source interviewed by David Butler, June 1970.
43 *The Times*, 12 November 1970.
44 House of Commons, 8 July 1970 [Vol. 803, cols. 676–88].
45 *Observer*, 5 July 1970.
46 *Guardian*, 8 October 1970.
47 *Sun*, 6 July 1970.
48 Interview, Sheila Browne.
49 House of Commons, 5 November 1971 [Vol. 825, cols. 510–27].
50 *Finchley Press*, 26 June 1970.
51 Ibid., 9 October 1970.
52 Ibid., 8 January 1971.
53 *The Times*, 13 July 1971.
54 *Finchley Press*, 31 March 1972.
55 House of Commons, 18 November 1971 [Vol. 826, cols. 637–54].
56 Cecil King, *The Cecil King Diary, 1970–74* (Jonathan Cape, 1975), pp. 166–7 (31 January 1972).
57 Conservative Party Conference, 12 October 1972.

58 House of Commons, 1 February 1973 [Vol. 849, cols. 1639–54].

59 *Times Higher Education Supplement*, n.d.

60 Interview, Sir William Pile.

61 Conservative Party Conference, 14 October 1971.

62 Ibid., 7 October 1970.

63 Ibid., 12 October 1972.

64 House of Commons, 5 November 1971 [Vol. 825, col. 510].

65 Conservative Party Conference, 7 October 1970.

66 BBC TV, *A Chance to Meet . . .*, 21 March 1971; *Finchley Press*, 26 March 1971.

67 *Finchley Press*, 28 January 1972.

68 Ibid., 7 August 1970.

69 *The Times*, 6 August 1973.

70 Timmins, p. 299.

71 *The Times*, 12 November 1970.

72 BBC Radio 4, *Today*, 30 July 1970.

73 *The Times*, 26 June 1971.

74 Conservative Party Conference, 14 October 1971.

75 Thatcher, p. 179.

76 *The Times*, 12 November 1970.

77 *Spectator*, 12 September 1970.

78 Interviews, Sir William Pile, Sir Toby Weaver, Bill Elliott, Philip Halsey.

79 Confidential source interviewed by David Butler, June 1970.

80 Interview, Lord Jenkin.

81 Interview, Lord Harris of High Cross.

82 Conservative Party Conference, 7 October 1970.

83 *Daily Telegraph*, 23 April 1971.

84 *The Times*, 1 July 1971.

85 King, p. 167 (13 January 1972).

86 Conservative party archive (LCC 74/13, 13 May 1974).

87 House of Commons, 14 June 1971 [Vol. 819, cols. 42–56].

88 BBC Radio 4, *Analysis*, 31 January 1973.

89 House of Commons, 14 June 1971 [Vol. 819, col. 56].

90 Ibid., 5 November 1971 [Vol. 825, col. 563].

91 Ibid., 18 November 1971 [Vol. 826, col. 605].

92 Ibid., [col. 617].

93 *Sun*, 9 July 1971.

94 Ibid., 25 November 1971.

95 *Evening Standard*, 13 January 1972.

96 BBC TV, *Panorama*, 26 April 1971; *Daily Telegraph*, 27 April 1971.

97 Interview, Bill Elliott.

98 BBC TV, *Panorama*, 27 July 1970.

99 *Daily Sketch*, 15 April 1971.

100 Thatcher, p. 182.

101 Interviews, Sir Toby Weaver, Sir William Pile.

102 *Guardian*, 2 November 1971.

103 *Daily Mail*, 15 December 1971.

104 *Daily Express*, 20 February 1974.

105 Carol Thatcher, *Below the Parapet: The Biography of Denis Thatcher* (Harper-Collins, 1996), p. 98.

106 Ronald Millar, *A View from the Wings* (Weidenfeld & Nicolson, 1989), p. 219.

107 *The Times*, 18 March 1971.

108 Interviews, Philip Halsey, Sir Toby Weaver.

109 *Daily Mail*, 31 January 1972.

110 Miriam Stoppard interview, Yorkshire TV, 19 November 1985.

111 BBC Radio 4, *Any Questions?*, 5 July 1974.

112 Thatcher, *The Path to Power*, p. 185.

113 King, p. 166 (13 January 1972).

114 Ibid., p. 154 (11 December 1971).

115 *Daily Mail*, 31 January 1972.

116 House of Commons, 3 February 1972 [Vol. 830, cols. 673–5].

117 Thatcher, p. 189.

118 *The Times*, 18 January 1972.

119 *Sun*, 5 April 1972.

120 *Daily Express*, 5 April 1972.

121 *Sunday Telegraph*, 9 April 1972.

122 *The Times*, 20 June 1972.

123 *Education: A Framework for Expansion* [Cmnd 5774] (HMSO, 1972); House of Commons, 19 February 1973 [Vol. 851, cols. 41–57].

124 Interviews, Sir William Pile, Sir Toby Weaver, Philip Halsey.

125 Thatcher, pp. 190–1.

126 Ibid., p. 191.

127 Gardiner, p. 111.

128 *The Times*, 3 January 1973.

129 Ibid., 30 December 1972.

130 *Finchley Press*, 18 December 1970.

131 *The Times*, 3 January 1973.

132 Interviews, Philip Halsey, Stuart McClure.

133 Speech to the League of Jewish Women, *Finchley Press*, 18 December 1970.

134 *The Times*, 29 September 1972.

135 House of Commons, 20 November 1973 [Vol. 864, cols. 1218–30].

136 Stevas, p. 67.

137 Ibid., p. 69.

138 Interview, Lord Jenkin.

139 House of Commons, 28 January 1974 [Vol. 868, cols. 39–49].

140 James Prior, *A Balance of Power* (Hamish Hamilton, 1986), p. 117.

141 John Ranelagh, *Thatcher's People: An Insider's Account of the Politics, the Power and the Personalities* (HarperCollins, 1991), p. 136.

142 King, p. 22 (14 July 1970).

143 Interview, Lord Carlisle.

144 Interview, Sir William Pile.

145 Thatcher, p. 202.

146 Ibid., p. 206; Carol Thatcher, p. 99.

147 Thatcher, *The Path to Power*, p. 215.

148 *The Times*, 17 May 1972.

149 Conservative Party Conference, 12 October 1972.

150 Thatcher, p. 221.

151 Ibid., p. 196.

152 For example, *Finchley Press*, 12 March 1971.

153 Nicholas Ridley, '*My Style of Government': The Thatcher Years* (Hutchinson, 1991), p. 6.

154 Ranelagh, p. 111.

155 Peter Walker, *Staying Power* (Bloomsbury, 1991), pp. 123–4.

156 Thatcher, p. 196.

157 *Finchley Press*, 16 February 1973.

158 Ibid., 2 February 1973.

159 Ibid., 9 March 1973.

160 Thatcher, pp. 208, 210.

161 *Finchley Press*, 13 August 1971, 20 August 1971.

162 David Shields to the author, 8 November 1994.

163 *Observer*, 2 December 1973.

164 Walker, p. 92.

165 Thatcher, p. 225.

166 *Daily Mirror*, 21 November 1973.

167 *Observer*, 23 January 1973.

168 *Finchley Press*, 23 November 1973.

169 Ibid., 1 February 1974.

170 Prior, pp. 89–90.

171 *Finchley Press*, 23 November 1973.

172 Ibid., 11 January 1974.

173 Thatcher, p. 233.

174 *Finchley Press*, 1 February 1974.

175 Ibid., 15 February 1974.

176 Mrs Thatcher's Election Address, Finchley, February 1974 (Conservative party archive).

177 *Finchley Press*, 22 February 1974.

178 Ibid., 19 October 1973.

179 *Times Higher Education Supplement*, 22 February 1974.

180 David Butler and Dennis Kavanagh, *The British General Election of February 1974* (Macmillan, 1974).

181 *THES*, 22 February 1974.

182 *Finchley Press*, 15 February 1974, 22 February 1974.

183 Ibid, 1 March 1974.

184 *Sunday Telegraph*, 24 February 1974.

185 Thatcher, p. 237.

186 Ibid., p. 239.

187 John Ramsden, *The Winds of Change: Macmillan to Heath, 1957–1975* (Longman, 1996), p. 359, citing interviews with Robert Carr and Geoffrey Howe.

188 Margaret Thatcher to Peter Carpenter, 14 March 1974.

189 *The Times*, 14 March 1974.

190 *Guardian*, 14 January 1974.

191 *The Times*, 14 March 1974.

192 Rodney Lowe, 'The Social Policy of the Heath Government' in Stuart Ball and Anthony Seldon (eds.), *The Heath Government* (Longman, 1996), pp. 210–13.

193 Thatcher, p. 195.

194 Ibid., p. 239.

10 The Peasants' Revolt

1 Phillip Whitehead, *The Writing on the Wall: Britain in the Seventies* (Channel 4/Michael Joseph, 1985), p. 330.

2 Geoffrey Howe to Arthur Seldon, 7 February 1972, quoted in Richard Cockett, *Thinking the Unthinkable: Think-Tanks and the Economic Counter-Revolution, 1931–83* (HarperCollins, 1994), pp. 206–7.

3 Interview, Lord Joseph.

4 Keith Joseph, *Reversing the Trend* (Barry Rose, 1975), p. 4; see also 'Escaping the Chrysalis of Statism', Sir Keith Joseph interviewed by Anthony Seldon in *Contemporary Record*, Vol. 1, no. 1, Spring 1987.

5 BBC Radio 4, 16 May 1990, quoted in John Ranelagh, *Thatcher's People: An Insider's Account of the Politics, the Power and the Personalities* (HarperCollins, 1991), p. 192.

6 Margaret Thatcher, *The Path to Power* (HarperCollins, 1995), p. 242.

7 Lord Joseph, interviewed for Brook Associates, *The Thatcher Factor*.

8 John Junor, *Listening for a Midnight Tram* (Chapman, 1990; Pan edition), p. 227.

9 Conservative party archive (LCC 74/9).

10 Keith Middlemas, 'The Party, Industry and the City' in Anthony Seldon and

Stuart Ball (eds.), *The Conservative Century: The Conservative Party since 1990* (Oxford, 1994), p. 484.

11 Thatcher, p. 252.

12 Conservative party archive (LCC 74/9).

13 Peter Walker, *Staying Power* (Bloomsbury, 1991), p. 126.

14 Ranelagh, p. 127.

15 John Ramsden, *The Winds of Change: Macmillan to Heath, 1957–1975* (Longman, 1996), p. 416.

16 Joseph, pp. 5–6.

17 Ibid., p. 21.

18 James Prior, *A Balance of Power* (Hamish Hamilton, 1986), p. 97.

19 Thatcher, pp. 254–5.

20 Cecil Parkinson, *Right at the Centre* (Weidenfeld & Nicolson, 1992), p. 125.

21 Nicholas Ridley, *'My Style of Government': The Thatcher Years* (Hutchinson, 1991), p. 20.

22 Interview, Sheila Browne.

23 TV interview with Sir Laurens van der Post, 29 March 1983.

24 House of Commons, 29 April 1974 [Vol. 872, cols. 798–814].

25 Ibid.

26 Ibid., 24 June 1974 [Vol. 875, cols. 1014–24].

27 Conservative Party archive (LCC 74).

28 Interviews, Chris Patten, Stephen Sherbourne.

29 Thatcher, p. 243.

30 Ibid., p. 247.

31 *The Times*, 28 September 1974.

32 Simon Jenkins, *Accountable to None* (Hamish Hamilton, 1995), p. 175.

33 Thatcher, p. 246.

34 *The Times*, 24 June 1974.

35 Thatcher, p. 246.

36 Conservative party archive (LCC 74).

37 House of Commons, 27 July 1974 [Vol. 875, cols. 1750–62].

38 Thatcher, p. 249.

39 *The Times*, 29 August 1974.

40 Ibid., 4 October 1974.

41 Ibid., 29 September 1974.

42 Ibid., 4 October 1974.

43 David Butler and Dennis Kavanagh, *The British General Election of October 1974* (Macmillan, 1975), pp. 237, 264.

44 Thatcher, p. 260.

45 BBC Radio 4, *Any Questions?*, 4 October 1974.

46 *The Times*, 10 October 1974.

47 Michael Cockerell, *Live from Number Ten: The Inside Story of Prime Ministers and Television* (Faber, 1988), pp. 213–14.

48 Butler and Kavanagh, p. 121.
49 London Weekend TV, *Weekend World*, 29 September 1974.
50 Alan Watkins, *A Conservative Coup: The Fall of Margaret Thatcher* (Duckworth, 1991), p. 52.
51 *Weekend World*, 29 September 1974.
52 *Finchley Press*, 30 September 1974.
53 Butler and Kavanagh, p. 122.
54 Interview, Stephen Sherbourne.
55 *Finchley Press*, 4 October 1974.
56 Ibid., 20 September 1974.
57 Ibid., 4 October 1974.
58 Ibid., 18 October 1974.
59 Edward Heath, *The Course of My Life* (Hodder & Stoughton, 1998), p. 528.
60 *Daily Express*, 9 April 1974.
61 *The Times*, 11 September 1974.
62 *Sunday Times*, 20 October 1974.
63 Ibid., 13 October 1974.
64 *The Times*, 16 October 1974.
65 *Financial Times*, 30 September 1974.
66 BBC Radio 4, *Any Questions?*, 4 October 1974.
67 Patrick Cosgrave, *Margaret Thatcher: A Tory and her Party* (Hutchinson, 1978), p. 41.
68 *Evening News*, 11 October 1974.
69 Thatcher, p. 261.
70 Ibid., p. 266.
71 BBC TV, *A Chance to Meet . . .*, 21 March 1971; *Finchley Press*, 26 March 1971.
72 BBC TV, *Val Meets the VIPs*, 5 March 1973.
73 *Evening News*, 23 September 1974.
74 *Sunday Express*, 20 October 1974.
75 Norman Fowler, *Ministers Decide* (Chapman, 1991), p. 13.
76 Thatcher, p. 266.
77 Carol Thatcher, *Below the Parapet: The Biography of Denis Thatcher* (Harper-Collins, 1996), p. 3.
78 Alistair McAlpine, *Once a Jolly Bagman* (Weidenfeld & Nicolson, 1997), p. 191.
79 Melanie Phillips, *The Divided House* (Sidgwick & Jackson, 1980), p. 17.
80 Ibid., p. 18.
81 Thatcher, *The Path to Power*, p. 267.
82 *The Times*, 30 December 1974.
83 *The Economist*, 30 November 1974.
84 Whitehead, p. 327.
85 Thatcher, p. 267.

86 Ibid.

87 *Daily Mail*, 25 November 1974.

88 *Finchley Press*, 29 November 1974.

89 *Spectator*, 28 December 1974.

90 *Daily Mirror*, 28 September 1970.

91 Junor, p. 226.

92 Frank Giles, *Sundry Times* (John Murray, 1986), p. 164.

93 Norman Tebbit interviewed for Brook Associates, *The Thatcher Factor*.

94 Gardiner, p. 175.

95 *Sunday Mirror*, 9 February 1975.

96 *Financial Times*, 31 January 1975.

97 *The Times*, 31 January 1975.

98 *Daily Mail*, 1 February 1975.

99 *The Times*, 28 November 1974.

100 *Finchley Press*, 6 December 1974.

101 *The Times*, 28 November 1974.

102 Cosgrave, p. 18.

103 *Spectator*, 7 December 1974.

104 Cosgrave, p. 20.

105 *Evening News*, 23 September 1974.

106 BBC Radio 4, *Any Questions?*, 30 January 1970.

107 Walker, p. 127.

108 Heath, p. 529.

109 House of Commons, 17 December 1974 [Vol. 883, col. 1414].

110 Ibid. [cols. 1383–98].

111 Ibid. [col. 1398].

112 Ibid. [cols. 1412–13].

113 *The Times*, 18 December 1974.

114 Edward du Cann interviewed for Brook Associates, *The Thatcher Factor*.

115 Edward du Cann, *Two Lives: The Political and Business Careers of Edward du Cann* (Images, Upton-upon-Severn, 1995), pp. 206–7.

116 Heath, p. 531.

117 House of Commons, 21 January 1975 [Vol. 884, cols. 1383–9].

118 Ibid., 22 January 1975 [Vol. 884, cols. 1552–4].

119 Ridley, p. 9.

120 Francis Pym, *The Politics of Consent* (Hamish Hamilton, 1984), p. 5.

121 *The Times*, 23 January 1975.

122 *Daily Telegraph*, 30 January 1975.

123 *The Times*, 1 February 1975.

124 David Wood in *The Times*, 25 November 1974.

125 *Daily Mirror*, 3 February 1975.

126 *Daily Mail*, 24 January 1975.

127 *Daily Mirror*, 3 February 1975.

128 Wendy Webster, *Not a Man to Match Her: The Marketing of the Prime Minister* (Women's Press, 1990), p. 56.

129 *Daily Mail*, 24 January 1975.

130 Granada TV, *World in Action*, 31 January 1975; Cockerell, p. 217.

131 *The Times*, 4 February 1975.

132 BBC TV, *Midweek*, 30 January 1970.

133 Norman Tebbit, *Upwardly Mobile* (Weidenfeld, 1988), p. 139.

134 Fowler, p. 3.

135 Interview, Lord Carlisle.

136 Interview, Lord Jenkin.

137 *The Times*, 3 February 1975.

138 *Sunday Times*, 26 January 1975.

139 Barbara Castle, *The Castle Diaries, 1974–76* (Weidenfeld & Nicolson, 1980), p. 291 (22 January 1975).

140 *Daily Mail*, 1 February 1975.

141 *Daily Telegraph*, 4 February 1975.

142 *The Times*, 1 February 1975.

143 Ibid., 1 February 1975.

144 Norman St John Stevas, *The Two Cities* (Faber, 1984), p. 17.

145 *The Times*, 3 February 1975.

146 Interview, Chris Patten.

147 *Daily Express*, 3 February 1975.

148 Philip Cowley and Matthew Bailey, 'Peasants' Uprising or Religious War?: Re-examining the 1975 Conservative Leadership Contest' in *British Journal of Political Science*, September 1999.

149 Tam Dalyell, *Misrule* (Hamish Hamilton, 1987), p. xx.

150 Nigel Fisher, *The Tory Leaders: Their Struggle for Power*, (Weidenfeld & Nicolson, 1977), p. 169.

151 Cowley and Bailey, p. 4.

152 Michael Crick, *Michael Heseltine* (Hamish Hamilton, 1997; Penguin edition), p. 180.

153 Nicholas Wapshott and George Brock, *Thatcher* (Macdonald, 1983), p. 131.

154 *Daily Mail*, 5 February 1975.

155 Cosgrave, p. 72.

156 *Daily Telegraph*, 6 February 1975.

157 Geoffrey Howe, *Conflict of Loyalty* (Macmillan, 1994), pp. 92–3.

158 *Sun*, 5 February 1975.

159 *Finchley Press*, 7 February 1975.

160 *Daily Express*, 5 February 1975.

161 Ibid.

162 Castle, p. 303 (5 February 1975).

163 *Sunday Telegraph*, 9 February 1975; *Financial Times*, 11 February 1975.

164 *Daily Express*, 5 February 1975.

165 *Sun*, 5 February 1975.

166 *Sunday Times*, 9 February 1975.

167 *Daily Mail*, 1 February 1975.

168 Cowley and Bailey, pp. 17–19.

169 Kenneth Baker, *The Turbulent Years: My Life in Politics* (Faber, 1993), p. 395.

170 Thatcher, p. 278.

171 *The Times*, 10 February 1975.

172 *Daily Telegraph*, 7 February 1975.

173 *Daily Mail*, 10 February 1975.

174 *Sunday Telegraph*, 9 February 1975.

175 Ibid.

176 Cockerell, p. 219.

177 William Deedes in *Crossbow*, April 1975, quoted in Ramsden, p. 453.

178 Norman Shrapnel, *The Performers* (Constable, 1978), p. 132.

179 *Daily Express*, 8 February 1975.

180 Carol Thatcher, pp. 3–8.

181 Cockerell, p. 219.

182 *Sun*, 12 February 1975.

183 Ramsden, p. 456.

184 Thatcher, *The Path to Power*, p. 280.

185 Carol Thatcher, p. 10.

186 House of Commons, Standing Committee A, 11 February 1975 [cols. 1244–5].

187 Carol Thatcher, pp. 11–12.

188 *Daily Mail*, 12 February 1975.

189 *Daily Express*, 12 February 1975, 13 February 1975.

190 Marcia Falkender, *Downing Street in Perspective* (Weidenfeld & Nicolson, 1983), p. 233.

191 Tony Benn, *Against the Tide: Diaries, 1973–76* (Hutchinson, 1989), p. 311 (4 February 1975).

192 Castle, p. 309 (11 February 1975).

193 Benn, loc. cit.

194 Castle, loc. cit.

195 Peter Jenkins, *Mrs Thatcher's Revolution: The Ending of the Socialist Era* (Jonathan Cape, 1987), p. 64.

196 Interview, Paul Channon.

197 Malcolm Balen, *Kenneth Clarke* (Fourth Estate, 1994), p. 97.

198 Ibid., p. 98.

199 Harold Macmillan to Sir John Wheeler-Bennett, 27 February 1975, in Alistair Horne, *Macmillan 1957–86* (Macmillan, 1989), p. 616.

200 Norman Tebbit interviewed for Brook Associates, *The Thatcher Factor*.

201 Tebbit, p. 142.

202 *Sun*, 12 February 1975.

203 *Daily Mail*, 12 February 1975.
204 *Daily Telegraph*, 12 February 1975.

11 Leader of the Opposition

1 *Finchley Press*, 14 February 1975.
2 Barbara Castle, *The Castle Diaries, 1974–76* (Weidenfeld & Nicolson, 1980), p. 330 (4 March 1975).
3 Norman Tebbit, *Upwardly Mobile* (Weidenfeld & Nicolson, 1988), p. 147.
4 Noel Annan, *Our Age* (Weidenfeld & Nicolson, 1990), p. 433.
5 Roy Jenkins, *European Diary, 1977–1981* (Collins, 1989), p. 215 (2 February 1978).
6 Ernle Money, *Margaret Thatcher: First Lady of the House* (Leslie Frewin, 1975), p. 95.
7 Paul Johnson, 'Farewell to the Labour Party', *New Statesman*, 9 September 1977.
8 Woodrow Wyatt, *Confessions of an Optimist* (Collins, 1985), p. 345.
9 Phillip Whitehead, *The Writing on the Wall: Britain in the Seventies* (Channel 4/ Michael Joseph, 1985), p. 216.
10 Reference mislaid.
11 James Prior, *A Balance of Power* (Hamish Hamilton, 1986), p. 107.
12 *The Times*, 10 October 1977.
13 David Butler and Dennis Kavanagh, *The British General Election of 1979* (Macmillan, 1980), p. 68.
14 Hugo Young, *One of Us: A Biography of Margaret Thatcher* (Macmillan, 1989), p. 119.
15 Nicholas Wapshott and George Brock, *Thatcher* (Macdonald, 1983), p. 141.
16 Margaret Thatcher, *The Path to Power* (HarperCollins, 1995), p. 284.
17 Ibid., p. 290.
18 *The Times*, 19 February 1975.
19 Peter Walker to Edward Boyle, 27 February 1975 [Boyle papers, 660/9959].
20 Thatcher, pp. 287, 319–20.
21 Airey Neave interviewed by David Butler and Dennis Kavanagh, 22 August 1978.
22 BBC Radio 2, *The Jimmy Young Programme*, 19 February 1975.
23 Julian Critchley, *Palace of Varieties: An Insider's View of Westminster* (John Murray, 1989), p. 130.
24 Prior, p. 108.
25 Thatcher, p. 319.
26 Beryl Maudling reported in London *Evening Standard*, 27 June 1995, quoted in Tam Dalyell, *Misrule: How Mrs Thatcher Has Misled Parliament from the Sinking of the Belgrano to the Wright Affair* (Hamish Hamilton, 1987), p. xxiii.

27 *The Jimmy Young Programme*, 19 February 1975.
28 Patrick Cosgrave, *Margaret Thatcher: A Tory and her Party* (Hutchinson, 1978), p. 179; Tony Benn, *Conflicts of Interest: Diaries 1977–80* (Hutchinson, 1990), p. 39 (16 February 1977).
29 Thatcher, p. 287.
30 Private information.
31 Airey Neave interviewed by Butler and Kavanagh, 22 August 1978.
32 *Sun*, 19 February 1975.
33 *Daily Express*, 19 February 1975.
34 *The Times*, 19 February 1975.
35 Simon Heffer, *Like the Roman: The Life of Enoch Powell* (Weidenfeld & Nicolson, 1998), p. 747.
36 Cosgrave, p. 178.
37 Author's recollection.
38 BBC Radio 4, *The World This Weekend*, 2 January 1976.
39 *Observer*, 25 February 1979.
40 Patricia Murray, *Margaret Thatcher* (W. H. Allen, 1980), p. 118.
41 Confidential source, interviewed by Butler and Kavanagh, 1978.
42 Private information.
43 Airey Neave interviewed by Butler and Kavanagh, 22 August 1978.
44 John Peyton, *Without Benefit of Laundry* (Bloomsbury, 1997), p. 168.
45 Airey Neave interviewed by Butler and Kavanagh, 22 August 1978.
46 Murray, p. 120.
47 Private information.
48 Margaret Thatcher interviewed by David Butler and Dennis Kavanagh, 9 August 1978.
49 Lord Thorneycroft interviewed by David Butler and Dennis Kavanagh, 18 July 1978.
50 Chris Patten interviewed by David Butler and Dennis Kavanagh, 13 April 1978.
51 *The Times*, 7 March 1975.
52 Cecil Parkinson, *Right at the Centre* (Weidenfeld & Nicolson, 1992), p. 144.
53 Private information.
54 Carol Thatcher, *Below the Parapet: The Biography of Denis Thatcher* (Harper-Collins, 1996), pp. 100–1.
55 Rodney Tyler, *Campaign: The Selling of the Prime Minister* (Grafton Books, 1987), p. 16.
56 Ronald Millar, *A View from the Wings* (Weidenfeld & Nicolson, 1989), p. 232.
57 Carol Thatcher, p. 111.
58 Margaret Thatcher interviewed by David Butler and Dennis Kavanagh, 9 August 1978.

59 Edward du Cann, *Two Lives: The Political and Business Careers of Edward du Cann* (Images, Upton-upon-Severn, 1995), p. 212.

60 Parkinson, pp. 143–4.

61 Castle, p. 309 (11 February 1975).

62 Ibid., p. 310 (12 February 1975).

63 House of Commons, 12 February 1975 [Vol. 886, cols. 376–7].

64 See for example, Cosgrave, p. 201; Michael Cockerell, *Live from Number Ten: The Inside Story of Prime Ministers and Television* (Faber, 1988), p. 220.

65 House of Commons, 18 February 1975 [Vol. 886, cols. 1115–16].

66 Speech to Conservative Central Council, Harrogate, 15 March 1975.

67 House of Commons, 3 March 1975 [Vol. 887, col. 1262].

68 Castle, p. 328 (4 March 1975).

69 Interview, Lord Moore of Lower Marsh.

70 Speech in Beaminster, Dorset, 28 February 1975.

71 Speech to Federation of Conservative Students, Sheffield, 24 March 1975.

72 Speech to Conservative Central Council, Harrogate, 15 March 1975.

73 *The Times*, 3 March 1975.

74 Ibid., 15 March 1975.

75 Interview, Lord McAlpine.

76 Thatcher, *The Path to Power*, p.334.

77 *The Times*, 9 April 1975.

78 House of Commons, 8 April 1975 [Vol. 889, cols. 1021–33].

79 Mark Stuart, *Douglas Hurd: The Public Servant* (Mainstream, 1998), p. 93.

80 Derek Howe interviewed by David Butler and Dennis Kavanagh.

81 Humphrey Atkins interviewed by David Butler and Dennis Kavanagh, 1975.

82 Geoffrey Howe, *Conflict of Loyalty* (Macmillan, 1994), p. 95.

83 Speech to the Conservative Group for Europe, 16 April 1975.

84 David Butler and Uwe Kitzinger, *The 1975 Referendum* (Macmillan, 1976), p. 174.

85 *Daily Express*, 5 June 1975; BBC TV, *The Poisoned Chalice*, 16 May 1996.

86 Press conference, 3 June 1975; *The Times*, 4 June 1975.

87 Butler and Kitzinger, p. 194.

88 *The Times*, 7 June 1975.

89 House of Commons, 19 November 1975 [Vol. 901, cols. 19–28].

90 Cosgrave, p. 140.

91 Thatcher, p. 351.

92 Margaret Thatcher to Lord Home, 23 June 1975, in D. R. Thorpe, *Alec Douglas-Home* (Sinclair-Stevenson, 1996), pp. 450–1.

93 Margaret Thatcher to Lord Home, July 1975, loc. cit.

94 Lord Home to Margaret Thatcher, 13 August 1975, loc. cit.

95 Thatcher, p. 351.

96 Cosgrave, p. 200.

97 Thatcher, pp. 363, 387.

98 *The Times*, 31 May 1975.

99 Speech to Chelsea Conservative Association, 26 July 1975; Margaret Thatcher, *The Collected Speeches*, ed. Robin Harris (HarperCollins, 1997), pp. 23–8.

100 Castle, p. 487 (5 August 1975).

101 House of Commons, 11 March 1975 [Vol. 888, cols. 304–17].

102 Norman Shrapnel, *The Performers: Politics as Theatre* (Constable, 1978), p. 133.

103 Cosgrave, p. 196; *The Times*, 16 May 1975.

104 Thatcher, *The Path to Power*, p. 297.

105 House of Commons, 22 May 1975 [Vol. 892, cols. 1637–54].

106 *Sunday Times*, 25 May 1975.

107 House of Commons, 22 May 1975 [Vol. 892, cols. 1754–62].

108 Ibid. [Vol. 892, cols. 1654–78].

109 Ibid. [Vol. 896, cols. 76–89].

110 Shrapnel, p. 134.

111 Castle, p. 473 (22 July 1975).

112 Speech to the Institute of Socio-Economic Studies, New York, 15 September 1975; Margaret Thatcher, *Let Our Children Grow Tall: Selected Speeches, 1975–77* (Centre for Policy Studies, 1977), pp. 51–8.

113 Cosgrave, p. 190.

114 Thatcher, *The Path to Power*, p. 359.

115 ITN, 26 September 1975; *The Times*, 27 September 1975.

116 Speech to the Pilgrims of the United States, New York, 16 September 1975.

117 Speech to the National Press Club, Washington DC, 19 September 1975.

118 *The Times*, 18 September 1995.

119 Ibid., 22 September 1975.

120 Henry Miller, *Daily Telegraph*, 25 September 1975; Fred Emery, *The Times*, 26 September 1975.

121 Thatcher, pp. 305–6.

122 Millar, pp. 225–7.

123 Speech to Conservative Party Conference, Blackpool, 10 October 1975; *Collected Speeches*, pp. 29–38.

124 Speech to Conservative Party Conference, Blackpool, 14 October 1977.

125 Millar, p. 235.

126 Ibid.

127 Ibid., p. 257.

128 Private information.

129 Millar, p. 275.

130 Ibid. p. 238.

131 Speech to Conservative Party Conference, Blackpool, 10 October 1975.

132 Cosgrave, p. 195.

133 Millar, p. 240.

134 House of Commons, 16 October 1975 [Vol. 897, col. 1587].

135 Ibid., 6 November 1975 [Vol. 899, cols. 605–6].

136 Ibid., 28 October 1975 [Vol. 898, cols. 1286–7].

137 Castle, p. 678 (9 March 1976).

138 Speech at Kensington Town Hall, 19 January 1976; *Collected Speeches*, pp. 39–47.

139 James Callaghan, *Time and Chance* (Collins, 1987), p. 366.

140 Thatcher, p. 362.

141 Speech in Finchley, 31 January 1976.

142 Speech to CDU Conference, Hanover, 25 May 1976; *Let Our Children Grow Tall*, pp. 61–6.

143 Speech at Dorking, 31 July 1976; *The Times*, 2 August 1976.

144 Whitehead, p. 336.

145 David Owen, *Time to Declare* (Michael Joseph, 1991; Penguin edition), pp. 401–2.

146 Ibid., p. 370.

147 Cosgrave, p. 25.

148 Geoffrey Smith, *Reagan and Thatcher* (Bodley Head, 1990), p. 1.

149 Ibid., p. 2.

150 Speech at the Cambridge Union, 12 March 1976.

151 Cosgrave, p. 196.

152 House of Commons, 16 March 1976 [Vol. 907, cols. 1123–4].

153 Cosgrave, p. 212.

154 Barbara Castle, *Fighting All The Way* (Macmillan, 1993), p. 513.

155 House of Commons, 8 April 1976 [Vol. 909, col. 631].

156 Ibid., 8 June 1976 [Vol. 912, cols. 1192–3].

157 Ibid., 29 June 1976 [Vol. 914. cols. 190–1].

158 Ibid., 9 November 1976 [Vol. 919, cols. 209–10].

159 Ibid., 1 March 1977 [Vol. 927, cols. 184–5].

160 Ibid., 9 June 1976 [Vol. 902, cols. 1472].

161 Ibid., 3 March 1977 [Vol. 927, cols. 606–7].

162 Ibid., 8 December 1977 [Vol. 940, cols. 1640–1].

163 Ibid., 7 March 1978 [Vol. 945, cols. 1221–2].

164 Ibid., 9 May 1978 [Vol. 949, cols. 971–2].

165 Ibid., 11 April 1978 [Vol. 947, cols. 1209–15].

166 Cockerell, p. 239.

167 House of Commons, 1 November 1978 [Vol. 957, cols. 21–35].

168 Wapshott and Brock, p. 161.

169 House of Commons, 26 May 1977 [Vol. 932, cols. 1541].

170 Thatcher, p. 320.

171 Ibid., pp. 327–8.

172 Ibid.

173 Frank Giles, *Sundry Times* (John Murray, 1986), p. 226.

174 Lord Hailsham, *The Dilemma of Democracy* (Collins, 1978).

175 House of Commons, 23 March 1977 [Vol. 928, cols. 1285–94].
176 Confidential source interviewed by David Butler and Dennis Kavanagh, 1978.
177 BBC Radio 2, *The Jimmy Young Programme*, 31 January 1978.

12   Thatcherism Under Wraps

1 Richard Cockett, *Thinking the Unthinkable: Think-Tanks and the Economic Counter-Revolution, 1931–83* (HarperCollins, 1994), p. 174.
2 Speech to the Junior Carlton Club, 4 May 1976 (*Let Our Children Grow Tall: Selected Speeches, 1975–77* [Centre for Policy Studies, 1977], pp. 51–8).
3 John Cole, *As It Seemed To Me* (Weidenfeld & Nicolson, 1995), p. 187.
4 Keith Middlemas, 'The Party, Industry and the City' in Anthony Seldon and Stuart Ball (eds.), *The Conservative Century: The Conservative Party since 1900* (Oxford, 1994), p. 486.
5 David Butler and Dennis Kavanagh, *The British General Election of 1979* (Macmillan, 1980), p. 65.
6 Interview, Lord Harris of High Cross.
7 Patrick Cosgrave, *Margaret Thatcher: A Tory and her Party* (Hutchinson, 1978), p. 126.
8 Ibid., p. 183.
9 Private information.
10 *Independent*, 22 February 1999.
11 Kingsley Amis, *Memoirs* (Hutchinson, 1991), pp. 315–16.
12 Lord Thorneycroft interviewed by David Butler and Dennis Kavanagh, 18 July 1978.
13 Margaret Thatcher interviewed by Butler and Kavanagh, 9 August 1978.
14 Margaret Thatcher to Lord Home, 2 April 1975, in D. R. Thorpe, *Alec Douglas-Home* (Sinclair-Stevenson, 1996), p. 450.
15 Cosgrave, pp. 167–8.
16 Margaret Thatcher interviewed by Butler and Kavanagh, 9 August 1978.
17 John Ranelagh, *Thatcher's People: An Insider's Account of the Politics, the Power and the Personalities* (HarperCollins, 1991), p. 28.
18 Jonathan Raban, *God, Man and Mrs Thatcher* (Chatto, 1989), p. 49.
19 House of Commons, 20 December 1976 [Vol. 923, col. 36].
20 Ranelagh, p. 3.
21 BBC Radio 4, *Mrs Thatcher's Enlightenment: Two Hundred Years of Adam Smith*, 16 May 1990.
22 Ranelagh, p. 180.
23 Brian Harrison, 'Mrs Thatcher and the Intellectuals' in *Twentieth Century British History*, Vol. 5, No. 2 (1994).
24 Ranelagh, p. 40.

25 Cockett, p. 265.

26 Interview, Lord Harris of High Cross.

27 *The Times*, 13 April 1995.

28 Margaret Thatcher, *The Path to Power* (HarperCollins, 1995), p. 344.

29 Ranelagh, pp. 30–1.

30 Interview, Professor Roger Scruton.

31 Cosgrave, p. 16.

32 Julian Critchley, *Some of Us: People Who Did Well Under Thatcher* (John Murray, 1992), p. 126.

33 *The Times*, 4 February 1984.

34 Interview, Professor Roger Scruton.

35 Iain Macleod Memorial Lecture, Caxton Hall, London, 4 July 1977 (Margaret Thatcher, *The Collected Speeches*, ed. Robin Harris [HarperCollins, 1997], pp. 58–69).

36 House of Commons, 25 July 1978 [Vol. 954, col. 1405].

37 Speech to CDU Conference, Hanover, 25 May 1976.

38 Speech to Conservative Party Conference, Brighton, 8 October 1976.

39 John Campbell, *Edward Heath* (Jonathan Cape, 1993), p. 528.

40 Speech to the Junior Carlton Club, 4 May 1976.

41 Cosgrave, p. 218.

42 Speech to the Zurich Economic Society, 14 March 1977 (*Collected Speeches*, pp. 48–57).

43 See, for example, speech to Conservative Local Government Conference, Southport, 21 March 1975; speech to Scottish Conservative Conference, Dundee, 25 May 1975; speech to Conservative Party Conference, Blackpool, 10 October 1975.

44 See, for example, speech to the Institute of Directors, Albert Hall, London, 11 November 1976 (*Let Our Children Grow Tall*, pp. 73–8).

45 See, for example, House of Commons, 30 January 1979 [Vol. 961, col. 1236]; *Observer*, 25 February 1979; House of Commons, 28 March 1979 [Vol. 965, col. 468].

46 House of Commons, 9 June 1976 [Vol. 912, cols. 1446–57].

47 Speech to the Zurich Economic Society, 14 March 1977.

48 Speech to Social Services Conference, Liverpool, 2 December 1976 (*Let Our Children Grow Tall*, pp. 81–6).

49 Nicholas Timmins, *The Five Giants: A Biography of the Welfare State* (HarperCollins, 1995), p. 359.

50 Address at St Lawrence Jewry, 30 March 1978 (*Collected Speeches*, pp. 70–7).

51 Iain Macleod Memorial Lecture, 4 July 1977.

52 BBC Radio 4, *Any Questions?*, 18 November 1966.

53 House of Commons, 28 March 1979 [Vol. 965, col. 467].

54 Ibid., 24 November 1976 [Vol. 921, cols. 16–22].

55 Speech to the Institute of Directors, 11 November 1976.

56 Ibid.

57 Iain Macleod Memorial Lecture, 4 July 1977.

58 House of Commons, 28 March 1979 [Vol. 965, cols. 461–70].

59 Speech to Conservative Party Conference, 14 October 1977.

60 Ibid., 8 October 1976.

61 Ibid., 14 October 1977.

62 Ibid., 13 October 1978.

63 Speech at Kensington Town Hall, 19 January 1976.

64 Iain Macleod Memorial Lecture, 4 July 1977.

65 House of Commons, 13 January 1976 [Vol. 903, cols. 229–41].

66 Ibid., 9 November 1976 [Vol. 919, cols. 209–10].

67 Tony Benn, *Against the Tide: Diaries, 1973–76* (Hutchinson, 1989), p. 625. (8 August 1978).

68 Tony Benn, *Conflicts of Interest: Diaries, 1977–80* (Hutchinson, 1990), p. 282 (19 February 1978).

69 See, for example, House of Commons, 19 November 1975 [Vol. 901, col. 26]; Kensington Town Hall, 19 January 1976; speech to Scottish Conservative Party Conference, 15 May 1976; House of Commons, 11 October 1976 [Vol. 917, cols. 147–56].

70 Iain Macleod Memorial Lecture, 4 July 1977.

71 Speech to Zurich Economic Society, 14 March 1977.

72 House of Commons, 28 March 1979 [Vol. 965, col. 470].

73 Phillip Whitehead, *The Writing on the Wall: Britain in the Seventies* (Channel 4 / Michael Joseph 1985), p. 332.

74 Chris Patten interviewed for Brook Associates, *The Thatcher Factor.*

75 Chris Patten interviewed by Butler and Kavanagh, 24 October 1978.

76 Ranelagh, p. 218.

77 Interview, Professor Sir Douglas Hague.

78 Nigel Lawson, *The View From No. 11: Memoirs of a Tory Radical* (Bantam, 1992; Corgi edition), p. 199.

79 Nicholas Ridley, *'My Style of Government': The Thatcher Years* (Hutchinson, 1991), p. 15.

80 *The Economist*, 27 May 1978; *The Times*, 29 May 1978; Ridley, p. 16.

81 House of Commons, 21 March 1978 [Vol. 946, cols. 1326–8].

82 *The Conservative Manifesto, 1979*, p. 15.

83 Rodney Tyler, *Campaign: The Selling of the Prime Minister* (Grafton Books, 1987), p. 9.

84 *The Times*, 4 October 1976.

85 *The Right Approach* (Conservative Central Office, 1976), p. 71.

86 Lawson, p. 47; Garret Fitzgerald, *All In a Life* (Macmillan, 1991), pp. 161–2.

87 *The Right Approach*, p. 37.

88 Thatcher, p. 317.

89 House of Commons, 29 November 1976. [Vol. 921, col. 610].

90 *The Right Approach to the Economy* (Conservative Central Office, 1977), p. 16.
91 Thatcher, p. 404.
92 Speech to Conservative Local Government Conference, London, 2 March 1979.
93 House of Commons, 25 July 1978 [Vol. 954, col. 1396].
94 James Prior interviewed for Brook Associates, *The Thatcher Factor*.
95 Speech to Conservative Party Conference, 8 October 1976.
96 Ibid., 10 October 1975.
97 Ibid., 8 October 1976.
98 House of Commons, 27 November 1975 [Vol. 901, col. 1040].
99 Ibid., 28 November 1975 [Vol. 901, cols. 1193–4].
100 Thatcher, p. 399.
101 Interview, Norris McWhirter.
102 *The Times*, 13 September 1977.
103 Press Conference, Washington DC, 13 September 1977.
104 *The Times*, 15 September 1977.
105 Speech to Conservative Party Conference, 14 October 1977.
106 BBC Radio 4, *It's Your Line*, 15 December 1976.
107 *The Times*, 18 April 1978.
108 Thatcher, p. 422.
109 Geoffrey Howe, *Conflict of Loyalty* (Macmillan, 1994), p. 106.
110 House of Commons, 20 January 1976 [Vol. 903, cols. 1129–30].
111 Ibid., 24 January 1978 [Vol. 942, cols. 1174–5].
112 Ibid.
113 Ibid., 3 March 1977 [Vol. 927, cols. 606–7].
114 ITN, 4 October 1976.
115 Party Political Broadcast, 4 May 1977.
116 Cosgrave, p. 197.
117 *The Times*, 22 February 1975.
118 Patrick Cosgrave, *The Lives of Enoch Powell* (Bodley Head, 1989), p. 405.
119 House of Commons, 19 November 1975 [Vol. 901, col. 23].
120 Thatcher, p. 325.
121 House of Commons, 13 December 1976 [Vol. 922, cols. 993–1007].
122 *The Conservative Manifesto*, 1979, p. 21.
123 James Prior, *A Balance of Power* (Hamish Hamilton, 1986), p. 107.
124 *Observer*, 25 February 1979.
125 *Times Education Supplement*, 31 May 1976.
126 Cole, p. 189.
127 Granada TV, *World in Action*, 27 January 1978.
128 House of Commons, 31 January 1978 [Vol. 943, cols. 241–5].
129 Ibid., 25 July 1978 [Vol. 954, col. 1392].
130 Cosgrave, *Enoch Powell*, p. 444.
131 Ibid.

132 Enoch Powell interviewed for Brook Associates, *The Seventies.*

133 *Observer*, 25 February 1979.

134 Michael Cockerell, *Live from Number Ten: The Inside Story of Prime Ministers and Television* (Faber, 1988), p. 220.

135 Ibid.

136 Mark Hollingsworth, *The Ultimate Spin Doctor: The Life and Fast Times of Tim Bell* (Hodder & Stoughton, 1997), p. 51.

137 Ibid., p. 53.

138 Richard Cockett in Seldon and Ball, p. 573.

139 Cockerell, p. 263.

140 Miriam Stoppard interview, Yorkshire TV, 19 November 1985.

141 Amis, p. 316.

142 *Guardian*, 19 January 1979.

143 Cockerell, p. 263.

144 Ibid.

145 Ranelagh, p. 214.

146 Hollingsworth, p. 61.

147 Cockerell, p. 263.

148 Ibid., p. 235.

149 *Woman's Own*, 31 January 1976.

150 *Sun*, 16 March 1979.

151 Thatcher, p. 293.

152 Sir Larry Lamb interviewed for Brook Associates, *The Thatcher Factor.*

153 Thatcher, p. 294.

154 Interview, Lord Deedes.

155 Frank Giles interviewed for Brook Associates, *The Thatcher Factor.*

156 Frank Giles, *Sundry Times* (John Murray, 1986), p. 226.

157 Frank Giles interviewed for Brook Associates, *The Thatcher Factor.*

158 Ian Trethowan, *Split Screen* (Hamish Hamilton, 1984), p. 181.

159 Speech to Conservative Party Conference, 14 October 1977.

160 *Observer*, 4 September 1977.

161 Cole, p. 187.

162 Leo Abse, *Margaret, Daughter of Beatrice: A Politician's Psycho-Biography of Margaret Thatcher* (Jonathan Cape, 1989), pp. 131–50.

163 Thatcher, p. 375.

164 *The Economist*, 31 March 1979.

13   Into Downing Street

1 David Butler and Dennis Kavanagh, *The British General Election of 1979* (Macmillan, 1980), p. 151.

2 *Sunday Telegraph*, 14 May 1978.

3 See, for example, House of Commons, 25 July 1978 [Vol. 954, cols. 1393–4]; BBC TV, 10 October 1978.

4 House of Commons, 15 June 1978 [Vol. 951, cols. 1174–5].

5 Ibid., 25 July 1978 [Vol. 954, cols. 1379–93].

6 *Financial Times*, 26 July 1978.

7 House of Commons, 25 July 1978 [Vol. 954, cols. 1393–1406].

8 Ibid., [Vol. 954, col. 1506].

9 Norman Tebbit, *Upwardly Mobile* (Weidenfeld & Nicolson, 1988), p. 157.

10 Mark Hollingsworth, *The Ultimate Spin Doctor: The Life and Fast Times of Tim Bell* (Hodder & Stoughton, 1987), p. 65, citing *Evening Standard*, 12 October 1994.

11 Margaret Thatcher, *The Path to Power* (HarperCollins, 1995), p. 411.

12 Ivan Fallon, *The Brothers: The Rise and Rise of Saatchi and Saatchi* (Hutchinson, 1988), p. 159.

13 Central TV, 7 September 1978.

14 Thatcher, p. 412.

15 *Guardian*, 8 September 1978.

16 Speech to Conservative Party Conference, Brighton, 11 October 1978.

17 *The Times*, 12 October 1978.

18 Geoffrey Howe, *Conflict of Loyalty* (Macmillan, 1994), p. 103.

19 Speech to Conservative Party Conference, 13 October 1978 (Margaret Thatcher, *The Collected Speeches*, ed. Robin Harris [HarperCollins, 1997], pp. 78–90).

20 *Daily Mail*, 18 October 1978.

21 *The Times*, 13 October 1978.

22 Butler and Kavanagh, p. 84.

23 House of Commons, 11 November 1978 [Vol. 957, cols. 21–35].

24 Confidential sources interviewed by Butler and Kavanagh, 1978–9.

25 Simon Heffer, *Like the Roman: The Life of Enoch Powell* (Weidenfeld & Nicolson, 1998), p. 813.

26 *The Times*, 10 October 1978.

27 David Butler and Gareth Butler, *British Political Facts, 1900–1994* (Macmillan, 1994), p. 255.

28 House of Commons, 6 December 1978 [Vol. 959, cols. 1424–5].

29 Ibid., 4 December 1975 [Vol. 901, cols. 1935–6].

30 Ibid., 13 March 1979 [Vol. 964, cols. 455–6].

31 Ibid., 15 March 1979 [Vol. 964, col. 693].

32 Norman Lamont, *In Office* (Little, Brown, 1999), p. 450.

33 House of Commons, 7 December 1977 [Vol. 940, cols. 1389–90].

34 Ibid., 1 December 1976 [Vol. 921, cols. 920–1].

35 Ibid., 10 July 1978 [Vol. 953, cols. 1027–8].

36 Roy Jenkins, *European Diary, 1977–81* (Collins, 1989), pp. 179–80 (2 December 1977).

37 Speech at Kensington Town Hall, 19 January 1976.

38 Iain Macleod Memorial Lecture, 4 July 1977.

39 Jenkins, pp. 307, 309 (4 September 1978, 11 September 1978).

40 Tony Benn, *Conflicts of Interest: Diaries, 1977–80* (Hutchinson, 1990), p. 363 (10 October 1978).

41 Thatcher, p. 339.

42 Roy Jenkins, *A Life at the Centre* (Macmillan, 1991), pp. 483–4.

43 House of Commons, 28 November 1978 [Vol. 959, cols. 210–11].

44 *Sun*, 11 January 1979.

45 London Weekend TV, *Weekend World*, 7 January 1979.

46 Thatcher, pp. 424–5.

47 Speech to British Chambers of Commerce, 10 January 1979.

48 Ronald Millar, *A View from the Wings* (Weidenfeld & Nicolson, 1989), pp. 247–8.

49 Party Political Broadcast, 17 January 1979.

50 Millar, p. 249.

51 Hollingsworth, p. 68.

52 House of Commons, 18 January 1979 [Vol. 960, cols. 1958–9].

53 Speech in Glasgow, 19 January 1979.

54 Speech to Young Conservative Conference, Bournemouth, 10 February 1979.

55 BBC TV, 14 February 1979.

56 BBC Radio 2, *The Jimmy Young Programme*, 31 January 1979.

57 Ibid.

58 Butler and Butler, p. 255.

59 James Callaghan, *Time and Chance* (Collins, 1987), p. 561; Kenneth O. Morgan, *Callaghan* (Oxford, 1997), p. 682.

60 BBC TV, 3 March 1979.

61 *Evening News*, 28 March 1979.

62 Thatcher, p. 432.

63 House of Commons, 28 March 1979 [Vol. 965, cols. 461–70].

64 Kenneth Baker, *The Turbulent Years: My Life in Politics* (Faber, 1993), p. 51.

65 House of Commons, 28 March 1979 [Vol. 965, cols. 470–9].

66 Baker, pp. 511–12.

67 *Observer*, 1 April 1979.

68 Butler and Kavanagh, p. 169.

69 Lord Thorneycroft interviewed by Butler and Kavanagh, 31 May 1979.

70 Butler and Kavanagh, p. 169.

71 Cecil Parkinson, *Right at the Centre* (Weidenfeld & Nicolson, 1992), pp. 26–7.

72 Millar, pp. 252–5.

73 Interview, Henry James.

74 Interview, Sir Kenneth Stowe.

75 BBC TV, *Campaign '79*, 27 April 1979.

76 BBC Radio 1, *Newsbeat*, 25 April 1979; LBC, 28 April 1979.

77 *Leicester Mercury*, 19 April 1979.

78 John Cole, *As It Seemed To Me* (Weidenfeld & Nicolson, 1995), p. 187.

79 *Daily Express*, 10 April 1979.

80 *Daily Telegraph*, 25 April 1979.

81 *Evening News*, 17 April 1979.

82 *Daily Mirror*, 2 May 1979.

83 *Sun*, 21 April 1979.

84 Butler and Kavanagh, p. 177; Alistair McAlpine, *Once a Jolly Bagman* (Weidenfeld & Nicolson, 1997), p. 219.

85 *Conservative Manifesto, 1979*, pp. 9, 11, 12, 15, 25 and 26.

86 Butler and Kavanagh, p. 188.

87 *Daily Telegraph*, 26 April 1979.

88 *Conservative Manifesto, 1979*, pp. 7 and 5.

89 Hollingsworth, p. 71.

90 Speech in Cardiff, 16 April 1979.

91 Butler and Kavanagh, p. 343.

92 *Peter Hall's Diaries: The Story of a Dramatic Battle* (Hamish Hamilton, 1983), p. 407 (13 January 1979).

93 Ibid., p. 429 (9 April 1979).

94 Ibid., p. 434 (3 May 1979).

95 Peter Hall, *Making an Exhibition of Myself* (Sinclair-Stevenson, 1993), pp. 297–8.

96 *Guardian*, 12 April 1979.

97 Cole, p. 194.

98 *Spectator* 28 April 1979.

99 *Guardian*, 17 April 1979.

100 *Birmingham Post*, 20 April 1979.

101 *Sunday Telegraph*, 22 April 1979; BBC Radio News, 21 April 1979.

102 *Daily Mail*, 19 April 1979.

103 Private information.

104 Butler and Kavanagh, p. 172.

105 *Observer*, 22 April 1979.

106 Butler and Kavanagh, p. 216.

107 Thames TV, *TV Eye*, 24 April 1979.

108 BBC Radio 2, *The Jimmy Young Programme*, 25 April 1979.

109 BBC Radio 4, *Election Call*, 17 April 1979.

110 BBC TV, *Nationwide: On the Spot*, 20 April 1979; Granada TV, *Granada 500*, 30 April 1979.

111 Butler and Kavanagh, pp. 190–1.

112 Thatcher, p. 440.

113 Speech in Cardiff, 16 April 1979.

114 Party election broadcast, 2 April 1979.

115 Election press conference, 11 April 1979.

116 ITN, 2 May 1979.

117 Election press conference, 2 May 1979.

118 BBC Radio 2, *The Jimmy Young Programme*, 25 April 1979.

119 See, for example, speech in Bolton, 1 May 1979.

120 See, for example, *The Jimmy Young Programme*, 25 April 1979; BBC TV, 2 May 1979.

121 Thatcher, p. 439.

122 Howe, p. 115.

123 Nicholas Timmins, *The Five Giants: A Biography of the Welfare State* (HarperCollins, 1995), pp. 374–5.

124 Election press conference, 25 April 1979.

125 Millar, p. 262.

126 Thatcher, p. 456.

127 Millar, p. 262.

128 Ibid.

129 Election press conference, 27 April 1979.

130 Millar, pp. 259–60.

131 Patricia Murray, *Margaret Thatcher* (W. H. Allen, 1980), p. 198.

132 Millar, p. 261.

133 Ibid, p. 258.

134 *Daily Mail*, 30 April 1979.

135 Speech to Conservative Trade Unionist rally, Wembley Conference Centre, 29 April 1979.

136 Party election broadcast, 30 April 1979.

137 Millar, p. 262.

138 Speech at Bolton, 1 May 1979.

139 Bernard Donoughue, *Prime Minister: The Conduct of Policy under Harold Wilson and James Callaghan* (Jonathan Cape, 1987), p. 191.

140 Butler and Kavanagh, p. 323.

141 Millar, pp. 263–4.

142 Election press conference, 2 May 1979.

143 *Daily Express*, 30 April 1979.

144 *Daily Mail, Daily Express, Sun*, 3 May 1979.

145 *Evening News*, 3 May 1979.

146 Interview, Lord McAlpine.

147 Ibid.

148 Butler and Kavanagh, pp. 197–9, 343, 393–5.

149 BBC Radio News, 4 May 1979.

150 Millar, p. 266.

151 Ibid., p. 267.

152 Margaret Thatcher, *The Downing Street Years* (HarperCollins, 1993), p. 17.

153 Millar, p. 268.

154 James Prior, *A Balance of Power* (Hamish Hamilton, 1986), p. 113.

155 Remarks on the steps of Downing Street, 4 May 1979.

Sources and Bibliography

Primary Sources

Margaret Thatcher, *Complete Public Statements, 1945–1990 on CD-ROM* (Oxford University Press, 1999).

The Conservative Manifesto, 1979 (Conservative Central Office, 1979).

Conservative Party Archive (Bodleian Library, Oxford).

Edward Boyle Papers (Brotherton Library, Leeds University).

David Butler/Dennis Kavanagh interviews (Nuffield College, Oxford).

Indictment of Margaret Thatcher, Secretary of State for Education 1970–73, in Defence of the Education Act 1944 (PSW Publications, Leicester 1973).

Interviews for Brook Productions' TV series *The Seventies* and *The Thatcher Factor* (London School of Economics).

Dartford Chronicle; Erith Observer; Finchley Press; Grantham Guardian; Grantham Journal; Kentish Independent; The Times

Parliamentary Debates, House of Commons, Fifth Series, 1959–1979.

Conservative Party Conference reports (Conservative Central Office).

Annual Register.

KGGS Magazine, 1938–44.

Palmer's Almanack (Grantham).

The Right of Approach (Conservative Central Office 1976).

The Right of Approach to the Economy (Conservative Central Office 1977).

Who's Who (A. & C. Black).

Secondary sources

Leo Abse, *Margaret, Daughter of Beatrice: A Politician's Psycho-Biography of Margaret Thatcher* (Jonathan Cape 1989).

Jim Allen, *The Grantham Connection* (Grantham Book Centre 1986).

Kingsley Amis, *Memoirs* (Hutchinson 1991).

Oliver Anderson, *Rotten Borough* (Ivor Nicholson & Watson 1937; reissued Fourth Estate 1989).

Noel Annan, *Our Age: Portrait of a Generation* (Weidenfeld & Nicolson 1990).

Kenneth Baker, *The Turbulent Years: My Life in Politics* (Faber 1993).

Malcolm Balen, *Kenneth Clarke* (Fourth Estate 1994).

Stuart Ball and Anthony Seldon eds., *The Heath Government, 1970–74* (Longman 1996).

Nina Bawden, *In My Own Time* (Virago 1994).

Robert Behrens, *The Conservative Party from Heath to Thatcher* (Saxon House 1980).

Tony Benn, *Against the Tide: Diaries, 1973–76* (Hutchinson 1989).

—, *Conflicts of Interest: Diaries, 1977–80* (Hutchinson 1990).

David Blair: *The History of the Oxford University Conservative Association* (OUCA 1995).

Robert Blake, *The Conservative Party from Peel to Thatcher* (Faber 1985).

Robert Blake and John Patten, ed., *The Conservative Opportunity* (Macmillan 1976).

John-Boyd-Carpenter, *Way of Life* (Sidgwick & Jackson 1980).

Lisa Budreau, *An Analysis of the Anglo-American Alliance During the Second World War in Grantham* (Grantham Museum 1993).

David Butler, *The British General Election of 1951* (Macmillan 1952).

David Butler and Gareth Butler, *British Political Facts, 1900–1994* (Macmillan 1994).

David Butler and Richard Rose, *The British General Election of 1959* (Macmillan 1960).

David Butler and Anthony King, *The British General Election of 1964* (Macmillan 1965).

—, *The British General Election of 1966* (Macmillan 1967).

David Butler and Michael Pinto-Duchinsky, *The British General Election of 1970* (Macmillan 1971).

David Butler and Dennis Kavanagh, *The British General Election of February 1974* (Macmillan 1974).

—, *The British General Election of October 1974* (Macmillan 1975).

—, *The British General Election of 1979* (Macmillan 1980).

David Butler and Uwe Kitzinger, *The 1975 Referendum* (Macmillan 1976).

R. A. Butler, *The Art of the Possible* (Hamish Hamilton 1971).

James Callaghan, *Time and Chance* (Collins, 1987).

Beatrix Campbell, *The Iron Ladies: Why do Women Vote Tory?* (Virago 1987).

John Campbell, *Edward Heath* (Jonathan Cape 1993).

Barbara Castle, *The Castle Diaries, 1964–70* (Weidenfeld & Nicolson 1984).

—, *The Castle Diaries, 1974–76* (Weidenfeld & Nicolson 1980).

—, *Fighting All The Way* (Macmillan 1993).

Alan Clark, *Diaries* (Weidenfeld & Nicolson 1993).

Peter Clarke, *A Question of Leadership: Gladstone to Thatcher* (Hamish Hamilton 1991).

Michael Cockerell, *Live From Number Ten: The Inside Story of Prime Ministers and Television* (Faber 1988).

Richard Cockett, *Thinking the Unthinkable: Think-Tanks and the Economic Counter-Revolution, 1931–83* (HarperCollins 1994).

Richard Cockett, ed., *My Dear Max: The Letters of Brendan Bracken to Lord Beaverbrook, 1925–1958* (Historians' Press 1990).

John Cole, *As It Seemed To Me* (Weidenfeld & Nicolson 1995).

Patrick Cormack ed., *Right Turn: Eight Men Who Changed Their Mind* (Leo Cooper 1978).

Patrick Cosgrave, *Margaret Thatcher: A Tory and her Party* (Hutchinson 1978).

—, *The Lives of Enoch Powell* (Bodley Head 1989).

Philip Cowley and Matthew Bailey, 'Peasants' Uprising or Religious War?: Re-examining the 1975 Conservative Leadership Contest' in *British Journal of Political Science*, September 1999.

Maurice Cowling ed., *Conservative Essays* (Cassell 1978).

Brian Cox, *The Great Betrayal* (Chapman 1992).

Michael Crick, *Michael Heseltine* (Hamish Hamilton 1997).

Julian Critchley, *Palace of Varieties: An Insider's View of Westminster* (John Murray 1989).

—, *Some of Us: People Who Did Well Under Thatcher* (John Murray 1992).

Richard Crossman, *The Diaries of a Cabinet Minister* (Hamish Hamilton & Jonathan Cape 1975, 1976, 1977).

Iain Dale ed., *As I Said to Denis: The Margaret Thatcher Book of Quotations* (Robson Books 1997).

Macdonald Daly and Alexander George, *Margaret Thatcher in her Own Words* (Penguin 1987).

Ann Dally, *A Doctor's Story* (Macmillan 1990).

Tam Dalyell, *Misrule: How Mrs Thatcher has Misled Parliament from the Sinking of the Belgrano to the Wright Affair* (Hamish Hamilton 1987).

Rupert E. Davies, *Methodism* (Penguin 1963).

Robin Day, *Grand Inquisitor* (Weidenfeld & Nicolson 1989).

Bernard Donoughue, *Prime Minister: The Conduct of Policy Under Harold Wilson and James Callaghan* (Jonathan Cape 1987).

Edward du Cann, *Two Lives: The Political and Business Careers of Edward du Cann* (Images, Upton-upon-Severn, 1995).

Marcia Falkender, *Downing Street in Perspective* (Weidenfeld & Nicolson 1983).

Ivan Fallon, *The Brothers: The Rise and Rise of Saatchi and Saatchi* (Hutchinson 1988).

Nigel Fisher, *Iain Macleod* (Andre Deutsch 1973).

—, *The Tory Leaders: Their Struggle for Power* (Hamish Hamilton 1977).

Garret Fitzgerald, *All in a Life* (Macmillaan 1991).

Andrew Gamble, *The Conservative Nation* (Routledge & Kegan Paul 1974).

Norman Fowler, *Ministers Decide* (Chapman 1991).

George Gardiner, *Margaret Thatcher: From Childhood to Leadership* (William Kimber 1975).

Frank Giles, *Sundry Times* (John Murray 1986).

Ian Gilmour, *Inside Right: A Study of Conservatism* (Hutchinson 1977).

Philip Goodhart, *The 1922: The Story of the Conservative Backbenchers' Parliamentary Committee* (Macmillan 1973).

Lord Hailsham, *The Dilemma of Democracy* (Collins 1978).

Morrison Halcrow, *Keith Joseph: A Single Mind* (Macmillan 1989).

Peter Hall, *Peter Hall's Diaries: The Story of a Dramatic Battle* (Hamish Hamilton 1983).

—, *Making an Exhibition of Myself* (Sinclair-Stevenson 1993).

Paul Halloran and Mark Hollingsworth, *Thatcher's Gold: The Life and Times of Mark Thatcher* (Simon & Schuster 1995).

Kenneth Harris, *Thatcher* (Weidenfeld & Nicolson 1988).

Ralph Harris and Brendon Sewill, *British Economic Policy, 1970–74: Two Views* (Institute of Economic Affairs, 1975).

Brian Harrison, 'Mrs Thatcher and the Intellectuals' in *Twentieth Century British History*, 1994.

Denis Healey, *The Time of My Life* (Michaeal Joseph 1989).

Edward Heath, *The Course of My Life* (Hodder & Stoughton 1998).

Simon Heffer, *Like the Roman: The Life of Enoch Powell* (Weidenfeld & Nicolson 1998).

Nicholas Henderson, *Mandarin: The Diary of an Ambassador* (Weidenfeld & Nicolson 1994).

Peter Hennessy, *Whitehall* (Secker & Warburg 1989).

Judy Hillman and Peter Clarke, *Geoffrey Howe: The Quiet Revolutionary* (Weidenfeld & Nicolson 1988).

Mark Hollingsworth, *The Ultimate Spin Doctor: The Life and Fast Times of Tim Bell* (Hodder & Stoughton 1997).

Martin Holmes, *Political Pressure and Economic Policy: British Government, 1970–74* (Butterworth 1982).

Michael Honeybone, *The Book of Grantham* (Barracuda Books, Buckingham, 1980).

Alistair Horne, *Macmillan, 1957–86* (Macmillan 1989).

Geoffrey Howe, *Conflict of Loyalty* (Macmillan 1994).

Peter Jenkins, *Mrs Thatcher's Revolution: The Ending of the Socialist Era* (Jonathan Cape 1987).

Roy Jenkins, *European Diary, 1977–1981* (Collins 1989).

—, *A Life at the Centre* (Macmillan 1991).

Simon Jenkins, *Accountable to None: The Tory Nationalisation of Britain* (Hamish Hamilton 1995).

Keith Joseph, *Reversing the Trend: A Critical Reappraisal of Conservative Economic and Social Policies* (Barry Rose 1975).

—, *Monetarism Is Not Enough* (Conservative Political Centre 1976).

—, *Stranded on the Middle Ground* (Conservative Political Centre 1976)

—, 'Escaping the Chrysalis of Statism', Keith Joseph interviewed by Anthony Seldon in *Contemporary Record*, Vol. 1, no. 1, Spring 1987.

John Junor, *Listening for a Midnight Train* (Chapman 1990).

Penny Junor, *Margaret Thatcher: Wife, Mother, Politician* (Sidgwick & Jackson 1983).

Dennis Kavanagh, *Thatcherism and British Politics: The End of Consensus?* (Oxford 1987).

Ludovic Kennedy, *On My Way to the Club* (Collins 1989).

Cecil King, *The Cecil King Diary, 1970–74* (Jonathan Cape 1975).

Malcolm Knapp, *Grantham, The War Years 1939–45* (Lincolnshire Books 1995).

—, *Grantham* (Sutton Publishing, Stroud, 1996).

Norman Lamont, *In Office* (Little, Brown 1999).

Nigel Lawson, *The View from Number 11: Memoirs of a Tory Radical* (Bantam 1992).

Zig Layton-Henry ed., *Conservative Party Politics* (Macmillan 1980).

Russell Lewis, *Margaret Thatcher* (Routledge & Kegan Paul 1975).

Jean Mann, *Woman in Parliament* (Odhams 1962).

Reginald Maudling, *Memoirs* (Sidgwick & Jackson 1978).

Alistair McAlpine, *Once a Jolly Bagman* (Weidenfeld & Nicolson 1997).

Keith Middlemas, *Power, Competition and the State*, Vol. 3: *The End of the Post-War Era: Britain Since 1974* (Macmillan 1991).

Ronald Millar, *A View From The Wings* (Weidenfeld & Nicolson 1989).

Ernle Money, *Margaret Thatcher, First Lady of the House* (Leslie Frewin 1975).

Kenneth O. Morgan, *The People's Peace: British History, 1945–1989* (Oxford 1990).

—, *Callaghan* (Oxford 1997).

Patricia Murray, *Margaret Thatcher* (W. H. Allen 1980).

H. G. Nicholas, *The British General Election of 1950* (Macmilllan 1950).

Philip Norton, *Conservative Dissidents: Dissent within the Parliamentary Conservative Party, 1970–74* (Temple Smith 1978).

—, *Dissension in the House of Commons, 1974–1979* (Oxford 1980).

Amy C. Old, *The History of Kesteven and Grantham Girls' School, 1910–1987* (Privately printed).

David Owen, *Time to Declare* (Michael Joseph 1991).

Cecil Parkinson, *Right at the Centre* (Weidenfeld & Nicolson 1992).

John Peyton, *Without Benefit of Laundry* (Bloomsbury 1997).

Melanie Phillips, *The Divided House* (Sidgwick & Jackson 1980).

James Prior, *A Balance of Power* (Hamish Hamilton 1986).

Francis Pym, *The Politics of Consent* (Hamish Hamilton 1984).

Jonathan Raban, *God, Man and Mrs Thatcher* (Chatto 1989).

John Ramsden, *The Making of Conservative Party Policy: The Conservative Research Department since* 1929 (Longman 1980).

—, *The Winds of Change: Macmillan to Heath, 1957–1975* (Longman 1996).

—, *An Appetite for Power: A History of the Conservative Party since 1830* (HarperCollins 1998).

John Ranelagh, *Thatcher's People: An Insider's Account of the Politics, the Power and the Personalities* (HarperCollins 1991).

Peter Rawlinson, *A Price Too High* (Weidenfeld & Nicolson 1989).

Nicholas Ridley, *'My Style of Government': The Thatcher Years* (Hutchinson 1991).

Andrew Roth, *Heath and the Heathmen* (Routledge & Kegan Paul 1972).

Anthony Seldon and Stuart Bell eds., *The Conservative Century: The Conservative Party Since 1900* (Oxford 1994).

Robert Shepherd, *The Power Brokers: The Tory Party and its Leaders* (Hutchinson 1991).

—, *Iain Macleod* (Hutchinson 1994).

—, *Enoch Powell* (Hutchinson 1996).

Norman Shrapnel, *The Performers: Politics as Theatre* (Constable 1978).

—, *The Seventies: Britain's Inward March* (Constable 1980).

Alan Sked and Chris Cook, *Post-War Britain: A Political History, 1945–1992* (Penguin 1993).

Geoffrey Smith, *Reagan and Thatcher* (Bodley Head 1990).

Tom Stacey and Roland St Oswald, *Here Come the Tories* (Tom Stacey 1970).

David Steel, *Against Goliath: David Steel's Story* (Weidenfeld & Nicolson 1989).

Norman St John Stevas, *The Two Cities* (Faber 1984).

Mark Stuart, *Douglas Hurd: The Public Servant* (Mainstream 1998).

Robert Taylor, *The Trade Union Question in British Politics: Government and Unions since 1945* (Blackwell 1993).

Norman Tebbit, *Upwardly Mobile* (Weidenfeld & Nicolson 1988).

Carol Thatcher, *Below the Parapet: The Biography of Denis Thatcher* (HarperCollins 1996).

Margaret Thatcher, *What's Wrong With Politics?* (Conservative Political Centre 1968).

—, *Let Our Children Grow Tall: Selected Speeches, 1975–77* (Centre for Policy Studies 1977).

—, *In Defence of Freedom: Speeches on Britain's Relations with the World, 1976–1986* (Prometheus Books 1987).

—, *The Downing Street Years* (HarperCollins 1993).

—, *The Path to Power* (HarperCollins 1995).

—, *The Collected Speeches*, edited by Robin Harris (HarperCollins 1997).

George Thomas, *Mr Speaker* (Century 1986).

D. R. Thorpe, *Alec Douglas-Home* (Sinclair-Stevenson 1996).

Nicholas Timmins, *The Five Giants: A Biography of the Welfare State* (HarperCollins 1995).

Ian Trethowan, *Split Screen* (Hamish Hamilton 1984).

Rodney Tyler, *Campaign: The Selling of the Prime Minister* (Grafton Books 1987).

Peter Walker, *Staying Power* (Bloomsbury 1991).

Dennis Walters, *Not Always With The Pack* (Constable 1989).

Nicholas Wapshott and George Brock, *Thatcher* (Macdonald 1983).

Alan Watkins, *A Conservative Coup: The Fall of Margaret Thatcher* (Duckworth 1991).

Wendy Webster, *Not a Man to Match Her: The Marketing of the Prime Minister* (Women's Press 1990).

Phillip Whitehead, *The Writing on the Wall: Britain in the Seventies* (Channel 4/ Michael Joseph 1985).

William Whitelaw, *The Whitelaw Memoirs* (Aurum 1989).

Woodrow Wyatt, *Confessions of an Optimist* (Collins 1985).

Hugo Young, *One of Us: A Biography of Margaret Thatcher* (Macmillan 1989, revised 1991).

Hugo Young and Anne Sloman, *The Thatcher Phenomenon* (BBC 1986).

Index